Workshop Manual JAGUAR MK 7, 8, 9 XK120, 140, 150 1948-1961

A Floyd CLYMER Publication by:
www.VelocePress.com
Copyright 2018 Veloce Enterprises

INTRODUCTION

Welcome to the world of digital publishing ~ the book you now hold in your hand, was printed using the latest state of the art digital technology. The advent of print-on-demand has forever changed the publishing process, never has information been so accessible and it is our hope that this book serves your informational needs for years to come. If this is your first exposure to digital publishing, we hope that you are pleased with the results. Many more titles of interest to the classic automobile and motorcycle enthusiast, collector and restorer are available via our website at www.VelocePress.com. We hope that you find this title as interesting as we do.

NOTE FROM THE PUBLISHER

The information presented is true and complete to the best of our knowledge. All recommendations are made without any guarantees on the part of the author or the publisher, who also disclaim all liability incurred with the use of this information.

TRADEMARKS

We recognize that some words, model names and designations, for example, mentioned herein are the property of the trademark holder. We use them for identification purposes only. This is not an official publication.

INFORMATION ON THE USE OF THIS PUBLICATION

This manual is an invaluable resource for those interested in performing their own maintenance. However, in today's information age we are constantly subject to changes in common practice, new technology, availability of improved materials and increased awareness of chemical toxicity. As such, it is advised that the user consult with an experienced professional prior to undertaking any procedure described herein. While every care has been taken to ensure correctness of information, it is obviously not possible to guarantee complete freedom from errors or omissions or to accept liability arising from such errors or omissions. Therefore, any individual that uses the information contained within, or elects to perform or participate in do-it-yourself repairs or modifications acknowledges that there is a risk factor involved and that the publisher or its associates cannot be held responsible for personal injury or property damage resulting from the use of the information or the outcome of such procedures.

WARNING!

One final word of advice, this publication is intended to be used as a reference guide, and when in doubt the reader should consult with a qualified technician.

CONTENTS

PAGE

Page	Chapter	Title
2	CHAPTER 1	ENGINE
28	CHAPTER 2	CARBURETTERS & FUEL SYSTEM
42	CHAPTER 3	IGNITION SYSTEM
54	CHAPTER 4	COOLING SYSTEM
62	CHAPTER 5	CLUTCH
74	CHAPTER 6	MANUAL GEARBOX
93		OVERDRIVE
104		AUTOMATIC TRANSMISSION (Early Cars)
156		AUTOMATIC TRANSMISSION (Later Cars)
182	CHAPTER 7	REAR SUSPENSION, REAR AXLE & PROPELLER SHAFT
194	CHAPTER 8	FRONT SUSPENSION
202	CHAPTER 9	STEERING
203		Recirculating Ball Type
214		Power Assisted Steering
218		Rack & Pinion Type
224	CHAPTER 10	BRAKES
226		Drum
237		Disc
246	CHAPTER 11	ELECTRICAL SYSTEM
256	CHAPTER 12	BODYWORK
264	CHAPTER 13	APPENDIX
265		General Data
266		Technical Specifications
278		Tuning Data
283		Lubrication
286		Wiring Diagrams

INDEX – ENGINE

SECTION	PAGE	
000	3	Basic Diagnostic Testing & Troubleshooting
001	8	Description
002	9	Overhauling
003	9	Engine Removal
004	11	Cylinder Head Removal
005	16	Cylinder Head Servicing
006	19	Timing Gear
007	20	Oil Pump & Sump
008	21	Oil Filter & Pump Relief Valve
009	22	Connecting Rods & Pistons
010	23	Clutch & Flywheel Removal
011	24	Crankshaft
012	25	Engine Reassembly
013	26	Modifications by Engine Number and Model
014	26	Fault Diagnosis Chart

ENGINE
Basic Diagnostic Testing & Troubleshooting

Two very important gauges are needed to locate mechanical engine defects: a vacuum and a compression gauge. The vacuum gauge measures the amount of vacuum in the intake manifold and is an excellent indicator of the over-all efficiency of the engine. Many engine mechanical defects can be identified with a vacuum gauge. The compression gauge is used to identify the exact cylinder in which a compression defect exists.

1 Using a vacuum gauge

The vacuum gauge is connected to the intake manifold. The engine should be run until it is at operating temperature and then idled to obtain a reading.

CORRECTIONS. A vacuum gauge indicates the difference between the pressure inside the intake manifold and the atmospheric pressure outside. It is calibrated in inches of mercury (Hg). Consequently, the reading will be affected by any variation in atmospheric pressure, such as altitude and weather conditions; therefore, the most important thing about a vacuum gauge is the action of the needle rather than a theoretical numerical reading. Generally speaking, the vacuum gauge reading will be 1" lower for each 1000' of elevation.

NORMAL ENGINE. A normal engine will show a gauge reading of 18"–22" Hg with the pointer steady. Eight-cylinder engines will read toward the high side whereas 6- and 4-cylinder engines will read closer to the low side. On many later model cars, with overlapping valve timing, the gauge needle will fluctuate widely. To overcome this, many gauges have a constrictor valve which can be adjusted until the fluctuations are reduced to the width of the pointer tip. On gauges without this valve, the hose can be pinched until the undesirable fluctuations cease.

LEAKING VALVE. If a valve is leaking, the pointer will drop from 1"–7" at regular intervals whenever the defective valve attempts to close during idle.

STICKING VALVE. A sticking valve is indicated by a rapid, intermittent drop each time the valve is supposed to close when the engine is idling. A sticky valve condition can be pinpointed by applying a small amount of penetrating oil or lacquer thinner to each guide in turn. When the sticky valve is reached, the situation will be remedied temporarily.

WEAK OR BROKEN VALVE SPRING. If the pointer fluctuates rapidly between 10"–22" Hg at 2,000 rpm, and the fluctuations increase as engine speed is increased, weak valve springs are indicated. If a valve spring is broken, the pointer will fluctuate rapidly every time the valve attempts to close at idle.

WORN VALVE GUIDES. Worn valve guides admit air which upsets carburetion. The vacuum gauge reading will be lower than normal with fluctuations of about 3" Hg on each side of normal when the engine is idling.

PISTON RING DEFECTS. Open the throttle and allow the engine to pick up speed to about 2,000 rpm, and then close the throttle quickly. The pointer should jump from about 2"–5" Hg or more above the normal reading if the rings are in good condition. A lower gain should be investigated by making a compression test to localize trouble.

BLOWN CYLINDER HEAD GASKET. The pointer will drop sharply 10" Hg from a normal reading and return each time the defective cylinders reach firing position with the engine idling.

INCORRECT IDLE AIR-FUEL MIXTURE. When the needle drifts slowly back and forth on idle, the fuel mixture is too rich. A lean mixture will cause an irregular drop of the needle.

INTAKE MANIFOLD AIR LEAKS. If there are any air leaks in the induction system, the needle will drop from 3"–9" Hg below normal with the engine idling, but will remain quite steady.

RESTRICTED EXHAUST SYSTEM. Open the throttle until about 2,000 rpm is reached. Close the throttle quickly. If there is no excessive back pressure, the pointer will drop to not less than 2", increase to 25" Hg, and then return to normal quickly. If the gauge does not register 5" Hg or more above the normal reading, and the needle seems to stop momentarily in its return, the exhaust system is partially restricted.

LATE IGNITION TIMING. A low steady reading on idle indicates late ignition timing or a uniformly close setting of the tappet adjustments. The timing must never be set with a vacuum gauge; use a timing light for accuracy.

LATE VALVE TIMING. A steady but very low reading is generally caused by late ignition timing or late valve timing. If advancing the ignition timing does not increase the gauge reading to normal, then the valve timing is out of adjustment.

2 Using a compression gauge

Another very important engine testing gauge is the compression tester. It measures the pressure within the cylinder in pounds per square inch (psi). As with the vacuum gauge, the theoretical numerical reading is not so important as the variation between cylinders. The cylinder pressures should not vary over 15 psi; otherwise, the engine cannot be tuned properly. Variations cause uneven idling and loss of power.

To use the gauge, remove all the spark plugs and insert the rubber tip into each spark plug hole in turn. With the throttle held wide open, crank the engine to obtain about 6 power impulses on the gauge; record the reading. Do this at each cylinder and compare the results. Generally, modern high-compression engines have a reading close to 175 psi. If one cylinder is low, insert a tablespoonful of heavy oil on top of the piston. Turn the engine over several times to work the oil around the piston rings, and then repeat the test. If the pressure shows a decided increase, there is a compression loss past the piston and rings. If the pressure does not increase, the valves are seating improperly. A defective cylinder head gasket will show a loss of compression in two adjacent cylinders.

A compression gauge is important for checking the valve and ring condition. In practice, an equal number of pulses are recorded.

Low compression fault diagnosis chart

TROUBLES & CAUSES

1. **Valves**
    1a. Insufficient tappet clearance
    1b. Sticking valves
    1c. Warped heads or bent stems
    1d. Burned, pitted, or distorted valve faces and seats
    1e. Weak or broken valve springs
    1f. Distortion of cylinder head and/or block caused by uneven tightening of the bolts
    1g. Incorrect valve timing
2. **Pistons and rings**
    2a. Excessive clearance between pistons and cylinder walls
    2b. Eccentric or tapered cylinder bores
    2c. Scored cylinder walls
    2d. Scored pistons
    2e. Broken pistons
    2f. Scuffed rings
    2g. Insufficient piston ring end gaps
    2h. Stuck piston rings
    2i. Binding of rings due to "set" caused by mechanic overstretching during installation
    2j. Insufficient piston ring-to-wall tension due to weak expanders
    2k. Ring lands worn unevenly
    2l. Ring grooves too deep for the expanders used
    2m. Standard rings installed in oversize bores
    2n. Top rings running dry because oil control rings are too severe
    2o. Top rings running dry because of gasoline dilution caused by stuck manifold heat control
    2p. Abrasive dust left in cylinder bores from honing or grinding valves
3. **Gaskets**
    3a. Warped head and/or block
    3b. Blown-out cylinder head gasket
    3c. Cylinder head bolts tightened unevenly
    3d. Incorrect type of gasket

3 Excessive oil consumption troubleshooting

Oil can be consumed in the combustion chamber or lost through leaks. If the engine is actually burning oil, a blue-gray smoke will emerge from the exhaust pipe whenever the engine is accelerated, especially after it has idled for a short period of time. Fouled spark plugs are a good indication that oil is being burned in the combustion chambers.

Oil can pass into the combustion areas in only 3 ways: it can go past the piston rings, past the valve guides, or it can pass through a defective crankcase ventilation system. Leaks can be caused by defective or improperly installed gaskets, by excessive crankcase pressures caused by blow-by, or by plugging of the crankcase ventilating system. Unless the vents are clean, blow-by pressures can force enough oil vapors from the crankcase to cause a noticeable increase in oil consumption.

Oil leaks

Fresh oil on any engine housing usually washes the dirt from that part and is an excellent indication that oil is leaking from that area.

It is somewhat surprising just how much oil can be lost through a small leak. One drop of oil every hundred feet causes an oil loss of a quart per thousand miles. Note how the center of each driving lane is covered with oil from external leaks, and you will realize the need for checking this loss. Note that these drippings are much heavier on an upgrade due to blow-by pressures forcing the oil through defective gaskets and bearings.

Crankcase ventilator

Where a positive-type crankcase ventilating system is used, clogging of the metering valve, located in the line between the crankcase and the intake manifold, will cause crankcase pressure to increase, which will force the oil out from around the pan gaskets and oil seals. If the valve sticks open, large quantities of oil vapors will be drawn into the combustion areas under high-vacuum operating conditions with resulting high oil consumption.

Since oil can be lost in any combination of the above ways, it is necessary to examine the engine carefully before it is disassembled.

Excessive oil consumption fault diagnosis chart

TROUBLES & CAUSES
1. **Piston and ring defects**
   1a. Piston improperly fitted or finished
   1b. Snaky piston ring grooves
   1c. Ring grooves worn overwidth or flared
   1d. Insufficient number of drain holes in oil ring grooves
   1e. Drain holes in oil ring grooves too small
   1f. Piston and connecting rod assembly out of alignment
   1g. Excessive clearance between piston and cylinder bore
   1h. Badly worn or collapsed pistons
   1i. Scuffed rings
   1j. Improper seating of rings in grooves
   1k. Insufficient clearance at ring gap
   1l. Insufficient ring tension
   1m. Out-of-round rings from improper installation
   1n. Warped or twisted rings from improper installation
   1o. Not enough side clearance between rings and grooves
   1p. Compression rings installed upside down
   1q. Wrong size rings
   1r. Insufficient ventilation in oil rings
   1s. Slots in oil rings clogged
2. **Bearing defects**
   2a. Scored rod bearings
   2b. Spurt holes in rods with worn bearings adding to excessive bearing throw-off
   2c. Worn crankshaft throws
   2d. Worn main bearing oil seals
   2e. Excessive clearance
3. **Valve guide defects**
   3a. Worn valve guides
   3b. Intake valve guides installed upside down
   3c. Valve stem oil seals incorrectly installed or worn
4. **Cylinder bore defects**
   4a. Excessively worn, tapered, or out-of-round cylinder bores
   4b. Wavy cylinder bores caused by heat distortion or uneven tightening of head bolts
   4c. Ring ledge at top or bottom of cylinder bore
   4d. Scored cylinder bores
   4e. Rough finish on cylinder walls causing rapid ring wear
   4f. Cylinder block out of alignment with crankshaft
5. **Crankcase defects**
   5a. Main bearing oil return pipe clogged
   5b. Oil level too high
   5c. Broken pipe in oil line spraying oil into cylinder bores
   5d. Clogged breather pipe
   5e. Stuck valve in positive-type crankcase ventilating system
   5f. Excessive crankcase pressures caused by blow-by
   5g. Improper reading of dip stick (not pushed in fully)

4 Engine noise troubleshooting

One of the more difficult problems facing the mechanic is the locating of foreign noises. Engine noises vary in intensity and frequency, depending on their source. It is difficult to describe engine noises with mere words. Experience will have to be built up using the descriptions which follow as a guide.

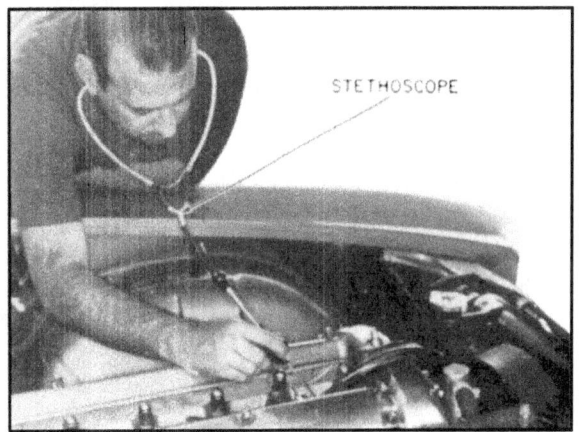

A stethoscope or a listening rod is handy to locate the source of engine noises.

Crankshaft knocks

Noises classified as crankshaft knocks are usually dull, heavy metallic knocks which increase in frequency as the speed and load on the engine are increased. Or they may become more noticeable at extremely low speed when the engine is idling unevenly.

The most common crankshaft knock, due to excessive clearance, is usually apparent as an audible "bump" under the following conditions: when the engine is pulling hard, when an engine is started, during acceleration, or at speeds above 35 mph (56 km./h.). If excessive clearance exists at only one or two of the crankshaft journals, the "bump" will be less frequent and less pronounced. Usually, alternate short circuiting of each spark plug will determine the approximate location of a loose bearing.

Excessive crankshaft end-play causes a sharp rap to occur at irregular intervals, usually at idling speeds, and, in bad cases, can be detected by the alternate release and engagement of the clutch. To detect a loose flywheel, advance the engine idle to a road speed equivalent to 15 mph (24 km./h.). Turn off the ignition switch and, when the engine has almost stopped, turn the switch on again. If this operation is repeated several times and if, of course, the flywheel is loose, one distinct knock will be noted each time the switch is turned on.

Connecting rod bearing noises

Connecting rod bearing noises are usually a light rap or clatter of much less intensity than main bearing knocks. The noise is most audible when the engine is "floating" or running with a light load at approximately 25 mph (40 km./h.). The noise becomes louder as engine speed is increased. Connecting rod bearing knocks can be located best by grounding out each of the spark plugs, one at a time. Generally, the noise cannot be eliminated entirely by a short circuit, but ordinarily will be reduced considerably in intensity.

Piston noises

The commonest piston noise is a slap due to the rocking of the piston from side to side in the cylinder. Although, in some engines, piston slap causes a clicking noise, usually it is a hollow, muffled, bell-like sound. Slight piston noises that occur when the engine is cold, and disappear after the engine is warm, do not ordinarily warrant correction. Piston ring noises generally cause a click, a snap, or a sharp rattle on acceleration.

Short circuit each spark plug in turn to locate piston and ring noises. As this test will affect other engine noises, sometimes the result is confusing. To detect piston slap more accurately, drive the car at low speeds under a load. The noise generally increases in intensity as the throttle is opened and additional load applied. On some engines, with very loose pistons, a piston rattle is encountered at speeds between 30-50 mph (48-80 km./h.) when the engine is not being accelerated.

To eliminate piston and ring noises momentarily, put 1-2 oz. (25-50 gr.) of very heavy engine oil into each cylinder through the spark plug hole. Crank the engine for several revolutions with the ignition switch turned off until the oil works itself down past the piston rings. Then install the spark plugs, start the engine, and determine whether or not the noise still exists.

Piston (gudgeon) pin noises

The commonest piston pin noise is the result of excessive piston pin clearance. This causes a sharp, metallic, double-knock, generally audible with the engine idling. On some engines, however, the noise is more noticeable at car speeds of 25-35 mph (40-56 km./h.). Interference between the upper end of the connecting rod and the pin boss (bossing) is difficult to diagnose and can be mistaken for a valve lifter noise.

To test for piston pin noises, allow the engine to run at idle speed. In most cases, a sharp metallic double-knock will become more evident when the spark plug, in the cylinder with the loose piston pin, is shorted out. Retarding the spark will generally reduce the intensity of the knock. If the pins in all pistons are loose, a metallic rattle, which is impossible to short out in any one cylinder, will be heard.

Valve mechanism noises

Noisy valve mechanism has a characteristic clicking sound occurring at regular intervals. Inasmuch as the valves are operating at half crankshaft speed, the frequency of valve action noise is generally lower than that of other engine noises.

To determine whether the noise is due to excessive valve clearance, insert a feeler gauge between the camshaft (note rotation direction) and the tappet. If the noise stops, the clearance is probably excessive and the tappet adjusting pad should be replaced. Never reduce the clearance to below factory specification or the valve will burn.

A sticky valve will cause a clicking sound similar to a loose tappet adjustment which comes and goes according to driving conditions. A sticky valve can be detected by driving the car hard until the engine is well heated. Then quickly allow the engine to idle. If there is a sticky valve, the clicking will become quite pronounced but will lessen gradually and sometimes disappear as the engine returns to normal operating temperature. The noise is accompanied by a rhythmic jerk due to the misfiring cylinder. As the noise disappears, so does the jerk, and the engine will finally smooth out as the valve seats.

A loose timing gear generally can be detected by a sharp clatter at low engine speeds with an uneven idle. When testing for this condition, short circuit one or two spark plugs to produce the necessary rough idle.

Spark knock (pre-ignition)

Preignition, or spark knock, causes a metallic ringing sound, often described as a "ping." Usually, it is encountered when the engine is laboring, being accelerated rapidly, or is overheated. Preignition is caused by an incandescent particle of carbon or metal in the combustion chamber igniting the mixture prematurely while the piston is coming up on the compression stroke. This results in very heavy pressure being applied to the piston at the wrong time, causing the piston, the connecting rod, and the bearing to vibrate, and resulting in the sound known as "spark knock."

Detonation is caused most frequently by a fuel of too low an octane rating. It burns too rapidly, resulting in sudden and abnormal pressure against the piston.

Accessory noises

Noises in the generator or water pump can be checked by removing the drive belt for a short operating period. If the noise remains, it is not in the generator or the water pump.

Engine noise fault diagnosis chart

TROUBLES & CAUSES

1. **Crankshaft knocks**
   1a. Excessive bearing clearance
   1b. Excessive end-play
   1c. Eccentric or out-of-round journals
   1d. Sprung crankshaft
   1e. Bearing misalignment
   1f. Insufficient oil supply
   1g. Restricted oil supply to one main bearing
   1h. Low oil pressure
   1i. Badly diluted oil
   1j. Loose flywheel
   1k. Loose crankshaft damper
   1l. Broken crankshaft web
2. **Connecting rod bearing knocks**
   2a. Excessive bearing clearance
   2b. Out-of-round crankpin journals
   2c. Misaligned connecting rods
   2d. Insufficient oil supply
   2e. Low oil pressure
   2f. Badly diluted oil
3. **Piston noises**
   3a. Collapsed piston skirt
   3b. Excessive piston-to-cylinder bore clearance
   3c. Eccentric or tapered cylinder bores
   3d. Piston pin too tight
   3e. Connecting rod misalignment
   3f. Piston or rings hitting ridge at top of cylinder bore
   3g. Piston striking carbon accumulation at top of cylinder bore
   3h. Piston striking cylinder head gasket
   3i. Broken piston ring
   3j. Excessive side clearance between a ring and its groove
   3k. Piston pin hole out of square with the piston
   3l. Ring lands not properly relieved
4. **Piston pin noises**
   4a. Excessive piston pin clearance
   4b. Tight pin causing piston to slap
   4c. Piston pin rubbing against cylinder wall
   4d. Worn piston pin bushing
5. **Valve mechanism noises**
   5a. Excessive clearance between valve stem and tappet
   5b. Sticky valve
   5c. Weak or broken valve spring
   5d. Inverted valve spring
   5e. Warped valve head
   5f. Valve seat not concentric with guide
   5g. Excessive stem-to-guide clearance
   5h. End of valve stem not faced square
   5i. Loose timing gear
6. **Spark knock**
   6a. Low octane fuel
   6b. Excessive carbon deposits
   6c. Ignition timed too early
   6d. Excessively lean air-fuel mixture
   6e. Weak automatic advance weight springs
   6f. Spark plugs too hot
   6g. Burned spark plug porcelain
   6h. Sharp metallic edges in combustion chamber
   6i. Cylinder head gasket projecting into combustion chamber
   6j. Overheated valves
   6k. Excessive engine coolant temperatures
   6l. Loose fan belt
7. **Accessory noises**
   7a. Defective generator bearings
   7b. Loose generator drive pulley
   7c. Brushes not seating
   7d. Loose drive belt
   7e. Defective water pump bearings
   7f. Loose water pump drive pulley
   7g. Bent and out-of-balance fan

NOTES

ENGINE - SERVICE

The engines for all models covered in this manual are virtually identical, the basic unit being a 6 cylinder, 3.4 litre, Jaguar XK type engine which was developed from the highly successful Jaguar racing engine. The main differences in the various models are obtained by variations in cylinder head design and the number and types of carburetters.

The XK150 3.8, XK150 3.8S and the Mk IX are of a larger capacity than the others being 3.8 litres, this is achieved by a small increase in the standard cylinder bore diameter.

A brief comparison of data for the various models is given in the table below. Complete detailed data for each model may be found in the appendix of this manual.

Comparative engine data

	XK 120 MK VII, VIII		XK 140, 150, 150S			XK 150 3.8 XK150 3.8S MK IX
Cubic capacity (cc)	3442		3442			3781
Bore (inch)	3.2677		3.2677			3.425
Stroke (inch)	4.1732		4.1732			4.1732
Compression ratio	7 to 1	8 to 1	7 to 1	8 to 1	9 to 1	8 to 1
B.H.P. output	150	160	190	210	250	220

1 Description

The Jaguar XK engine is an in-line 6 cylinder, twin overhead camshaft unit a cutaway drawing of which is shown in **FIG 1**. The chromium/iron cylinder block and crankcase form an integral unit down to the crankshaft centre line (see **FIG 2**). These house the tin plated pistons, the connecting rods, crankshaft and the timing gear. The detachable aluminium alloy cylinder head (see **FIG 3**) has machined hemispherical combustion chambers with the inlet and exhaust valves set in line on either side of the head. The valves are operated by the twin overhead camshafts, one for inlet and the other for exhaust valves, located in the cylinder head each being supported in four steel backed whitemetal bearings. These camshafts are operated from the forged steel crankshaft via the timing gear (see **FIG 4**) which

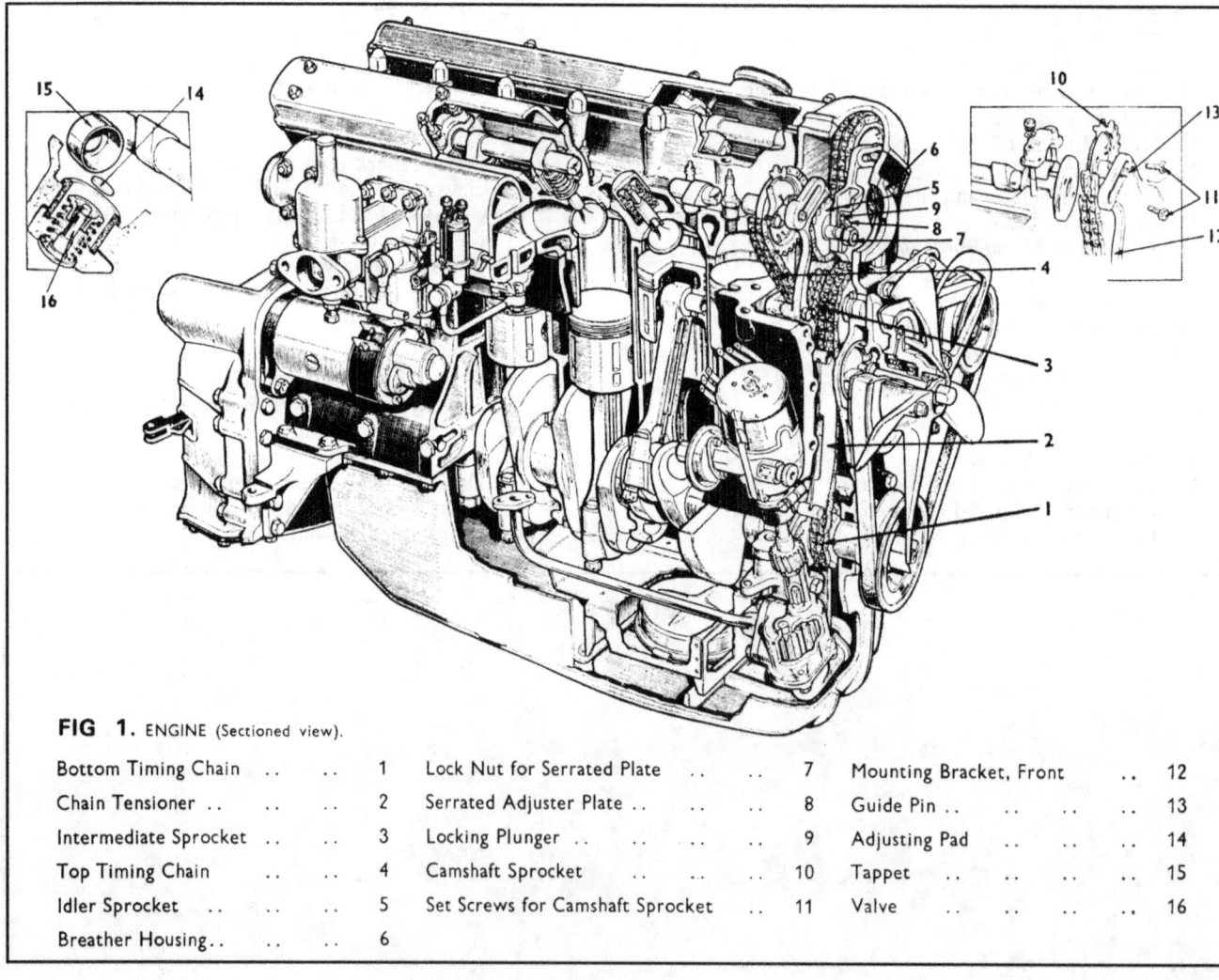

FIG 1. ENGINE (Sectioned view).

Bottom Timing Chain	1	Lock Nut for Serrated Plate	7	Mounting Bracket, Front	12
Chain Tensioner	2	Serrated Adjuster Plate	8	Guide Pin	13
Intermediate Sprocket	3	Locking Plunger	9	Adjusting Pad	14
Top Timing Chain	4	Camshaft Sprocket	10	Tappet	15
Idler Sprocket	5	Set Screws for Camshaft Sprocket	11	Valve	16
Breather Housing	6				

consists of upper and lower duplex chain drives, the upper being adjusted by an eccentric, the lower having an automatic tensioner.

The crankshaft which is supported in seven steel backed whitemetal bearings (see **FIG 2**) also provides a common drive for the distributor and oil pump. The gear type oil pump mounted within the pressed steel sump draws oil through a floating suction filter and passes it through a fullflow pressure filter, externally mounted, to the main oil line in the cylinder block which feeds the main, connecting rod and gudgeon pin bearings and the timing gear. A separate feed is taken to the cylinder head to supply the camshafts, tappets and valve gear.

Light aluminium alloy tin plated pistons are used with fully floating gudgeon pins, they house three piston rings, two are compression and the other one an oil scraper. The upper compression ring is hard chrome plated. The connecting rods have a steel backed phosphor/bronze bush for the small-end bearing and easily removeable steel backed whitemetal shell bearings at the big-end.

2 Overhauling

The information which follows concerning dismantling, overhaul and replacement procedure will apply regardless of the object of such work, which may range from simple decarbonizing to complete renovation.

Normal dismantling, maintenance and adjustment may be carried out without removing the engine from the car so long as a pit or ramp is available for working underneath. In addition to decarbonizing, attention to valve gear and camshafts, the sequences which can be carried out with the engine in position include, splitting the connecting rod big-ends, to remove the bearings or to remove the pistons upwards out of the cylinder bore when the head and sump have been removed. The crankshaft, damper and pulley, the timing gear and the water pump (see **Chapter 4**) may be removed and serviced on removal of the radiator. The carburetters may also be dismantled and overhauled as recommended in **Chapter 2**.

3 Removing engine from car

The engine and gearbox are best removed as one assembly by lowering the rear of the unit and lifting it forwards and upwards.

1 Raise the bonnet and support whilst unscrewing the four setscrews from the rear hinges which should be marked to indicate their exact location on the bonnet. Lift bonnet clear and disconnect the battery leads. If the battery is to be left in the car it should be covered to prevent damage or the ingress of dirt, it is however preferable to remove the battery so that it can be kept clean and recharged. The battery will need to be recharged if the engine is removed for any length of time.

2 Drain the radiator and cylinder block by means of the two drain taps provided and collect in clean containers if antifreeze has been added.

3 (a) On the Mk VII model remove the radiator grille by unscrewing the two setscrews holding it to the tie panel at the top and the two setscrews to the radiator frame at the bottom. Remove the setscrews holding the tie panel (see **FIG 5**) and remove the supporting channel to each wing valance. Slacken the top and bottom hose connections and pull off hoses. Remove the four radiator mounting bolts.

(b) On the XK120 model disconnect the thermostat housing from the radiator header tank, slacken both top and bottom hoses and pull clear. Detach the righthand felt covered support plate at the forward side of the radiator by removing the three setscrews securing it to the wing valance. Remove the metal plate adjacent to the radiator drain tap by unscrewing the three drive screws. Detach the radiator tie rods (see **FIG 6**) from their brackets on the header tank by removing the two nuts and bolts. Disconnect and remove the radiator securing rods from the brackets on the sides of the radiator block.

4 Withdraw the radiator block upwards turning the fan blades to avoid fouling the stub pipe at the radiator base. This procedure should be carried out carefully as the radiator fins are easily damaged and difficult to repair.

5 Remove the electrical connections to the generator and remove the adjuster bolt situated at the top of the generator. Slacken the two mounting bolts below the generator and push the generator towards the engine to release the fan belt tension. Remove the two mounting bolts and nuts and lift out the generator at the same time disengaging the fan belt.

6 Remove the screws holding the air silencer to the carburetter flanges, and on the Mk VII model remove the silencer support bracket. Remove the air silencer. Disconnect the throttle linkage by releasing the rear flexible joint or by releasing the throttle rod on the XK120 model. Remove fuel supply connections to the carburetters at the pipe union and release the electrical connections to the starter carburetter. Disconnect the electrical lead to the starter motor and remove the earth strap. Remove the thermometer bulb from the thermostat housing on the Mk VII model and the water manifold on the XK120 model taking care not to twist the capilliary tube. Disconnect and remove the heater hoses, oil pressure pipes and breather pipe. Disconnect the revolution counter cable and the speedometer cable. Remove the vacuum pipe from the inlet manifold and disconnect the ignition wiring. Disconnect the exhaust down pipes by unscrewing the eight setscrews at each manifold flange.

7 Remove the gearbox and bell housing cover and the gearlever, release the speedometer cable at the gearbox. Mark the propeller shaft and gearbox (or overdrive if fitted) flanges in relation to one another then disconnect.

8 Disconnect the clutch linkage, in the case of the hydraulic type this consists of removing the flexible pipe from the clutch operating cylinder taking care not to strain it, the end should then be plugged to prevent loss of fluid; in the models fitted with mechanical linkage it is necessary to remove the splitpin and clevis pin securing the adjusting rod to the clutch pedal shaft lever, remove the pinch bolt securing the clutch pedal to the shaft and remove the clutch pedal shaft through the chassis frame.

9 Place the slings around the engine and gearbox unit and take up the weight before trying to release the

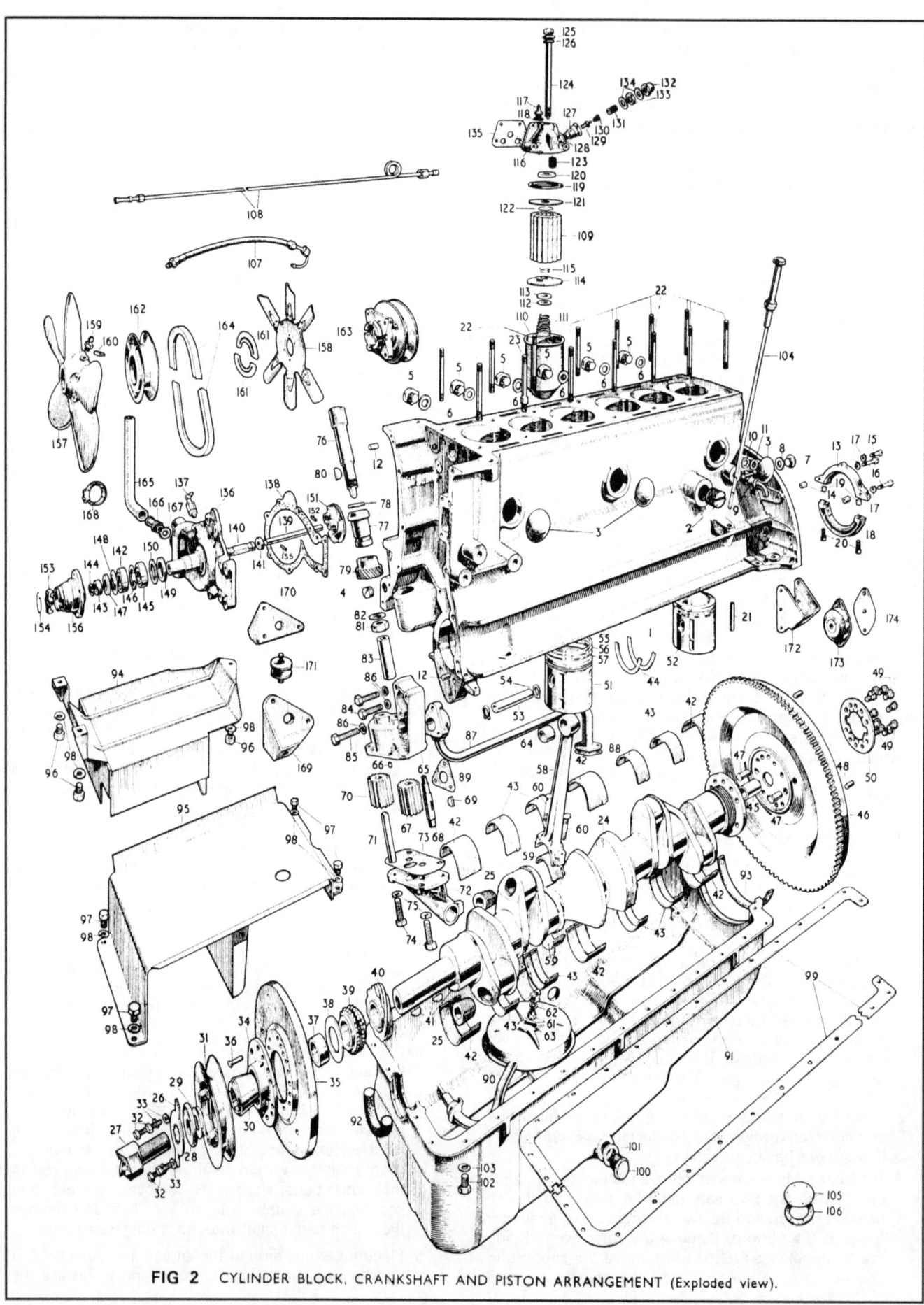

FIG 2 CYLINDER BLOCK, CRANKSHAFT AND PISTON ARRANGEMENT (Exploded view).

FIG 2 CYLINDER BLOCK, CRANKSHAFT AND PISTON ARRANGEMENT (Exploded view).

Description	No.	Description	No.	Description	No.
Cylinder Block	1	Connecting Rod	58	Screw, Union, at top of Filter Head	117
Plug, on left hand side of Block, sealing aperture for Heater Element	2	Bearing, Big End	59	Washer (Fibre) under Union Screw	118
Plug, Core, on left hand and right hand sides of Block	3	Bolt, securing Caps to Connecting Rods	60	Seal (Rubber) on Filter Head	119
Plug, in front end of Oil Gallery (⅞" A.N.F.)	4	Nut on Bolt	61	Washer (Felt) under top Pressure Plate	120
Plug, in side of Oil Gallery (⅜" A.N.F.)	5	Washer under Nuts	62	Plate, Pressure, on Filter Head	121
Washer, Copper, on Oil Gallery Plugs	6	Pin, Split, locking Nuts	63	Circlip, securing top Pressure Plate	122
Plug in rear end of Oil Gallery (⅜" A.N.F.)	7	Bearing, Small End	64	Valve, Balance, Assy., in Filter Head	123
Washer, Copper, on rear Plug	8	Body only	65	Bolt, through Filter Head and Canister	124
Tap, Water Drain, in left hand side of Block	9	Dowel in Pump Body	66	Washer (Steel) under Head of Bolt	125
Washer (Copper) on Water Drain Tap	10	Gear, Driving	67	Washer (Rubber) on Bolt	126
Washer (Fibre) on Water Drain Tap	11	Spindle for Driving Gear	68	Body for Relief Valve	127
Dowel on front face of Block	12	Key, locking Driving Gear on Spindle	69	Washer (Copper) between Body and Filter Head	128
Cover on rear face of Cylinder Block	13	Gear, Driven	70	Valve, Relief	129
Dowel, Ring, between Rear Cover and Block	14	Spindle for Driven Gear	71	Spring, for Relief Valve	130
Bolt, Centre, securing Rear Cover to Block	15	Cover at bottom of Pump Body	72	Housing, for Relief Valve Spring	131
Bolt, Outer, securing Rear Cover to Block	16	Gasket between Cover and Pump Body	73	Nut, Dome, on Housing	132
Washer, Spring, on Bolts	17	Bolt securing Cover to Pump Body	74	Nut, Lock	133
Ring, Sealing, on Rear Cover	18	Washer, Shakeproof, on Bolts	75	Washer (Copper) at each side of Locknut	134
Dowel, Ring, between Sealing Ring and Rear Cover	19	Shaft, Drive, between Distributor and Coupling Shaft	76	Gasket, between Oil Cleaner and Cylinder Block	135
Screw, Cap, securing Sealing Ring to Rear Cover	20	Bush on Drive Shaft	77	Body only	136
Tube, Drain, in Rear Bearing Cap	21	Washer on Drive Shaft (Top of Bush)	78	Greaser, Hydraulic, on Pump Body	137
Stud, securing Cylinder Head	22	Gear, Helical, driving Oil Pump and Distributor	79	Gasket, between Pump and Cylinder Block	138
Stud, Dowel, securing Cylinder Head	23	Key (Woodruff No. 50) locking Helical Gear on Drive Shaft	80	Spindle	139
Crankshaft	24	Nut on bottom of Drive Shaft	81	Bush for Spindle	140
Plug, Screwed, for Crankshaft Journals	25	Washer, Special, Locking Nut	82	Seal for Spindle	141
Washer, locking Starter Jaw	26	Shaft, coupling Driving Gear and Drive Shaft	83	Bearing, Ball, Front (Hoffman S.9)	142
Jaw, Starter	27	Bolt, securing Oil Pump to Bearing Cap	84	Collar for Front Bearing	143
Washer, behind Starter Jaw	28	Bolt, securing Oil Pump to Bearing Cap	85	Circlip, on Pump Body, retaining Front Bearing	144
Shim, Packing, behind Washer	29	Washer, Shakeproof, on Bolts	86	Bearing, Ball, Rear (Hoffman S.10)	145
Cone, Split, between Damper Centre and Crankshaft	30	Oil Delivery Pipe from Pump	87	Circlip, in Fan Hub, retaining Rear Bearing	146
Pulley, Fan	31	Gasket, under Flange of Oil Pipe	88	Washer (Felt) Front	147
Bolt, securing Fan Pulley to Damper Centre	32	Gasket, between Elbow and Oil Pump	89	Disc for Front Washer	148
Washer, Shakeproof, on Bolts	33	Oil Sump	90	Washer (Felt) Rear	149
Centre for Damper	34	Seal (Asbestos) at front end of Sump	91	Disc for Rear Washer	150
Damper	35	Seal (Cork Rubber) at rear end of Sump	92	Impellor	151
Rivet, securing Damper to Centre	36	Tray for Oil Sump, Front	93	Pin (Mills) securing Impellor to Spindle	152
Piece, Distance	37	Tray for Oil Sump, Rear	94	Dog, Driving	153
Thrower, Oil	38	Screw, Set, securing Front Tray to Bearing Caps	95	Circlip, around Fan Hub, securing Driving Dog	154
Gear, Timing	39	Screw, Set, securing Rear Tray to Sump	96	Pin (Mills) securing Driving Dog to Spindle	155
Gear for Oil Pump Drive	40	Washer, Shakeproof, on Setscrews	97	Hub, Fan	156
Key (Woodruff 90)	41	Gasket, between Oil Sump and Cylinder Block	98	Fan for Water Pump	157
Bearing, Main, Front, Centre and Rear	42	Plug, Drain, at bottom of Oil Sump	99	Fan for Water Pump	158
Bearing, Main, Intermediate	43	Washer on Drain Plug	100	Nipple, Grease, on Fan	159
Washer, Thrust, bottom of Centre Bearing Cap	44	Screw, Set, securing Oil Sump to Cylinder Block	101	Washer, Tab, under Grease Nipple	160
Bush, in rear end of Crankshaft, for Constant Pinion Shaft	45	Washer, Spring, on Setscrews	102	Balance-Piece for Fan	161
Flywheel	46	Dipstick Assembly for Oil Sump	103	Pulley for Fan	162
Dowel in centre of Flywheel	47	Blanking Plate on side of Oil Sump	104	Pulley for Fan (complete with Hub)	163
Dowel on outer face of Flywheel	48	Gasket for Blanking Plate	105	Belt for Fan Pulley	164
Screw, Set, securing Flywheel to Crankshaft	49	Flexible Oil Pipe	106	By-Pass Water Hose	165
Plate, locking Setscrews	50	Oil Pipe to Gauge	107	Adapter, in Water Pump and Outlet Elbow for By-Pass Hose	166
Piston, complete	51	Element	108	Washer (Copper) for Adapter	167
Piston, complete	52	Canister	109	Clip (Cheney 'O') securing By-Pass Hose	168
Pin, Gudgeon	53	Spring at bottom of Canister, for bottom Pressure Plate	110	Bracket, Left Hand, for Front Engine Mounting	169
Circlip	54	Washer on top of Spring	111	Bracket, Right Hand, for Front Engine Mounting	170
Ring, Pressure, Upper	55	Washer (Felt) under bottom Pressure Plate	112	Front Engine Mountings	171
Ring, Pressure, Lower	56	Plate, Pressure, at bottom of Canister	113	Bracket, Left Hand, for Rear Engine Mounting	172
Ring, Scraper	57	Circlip, securing bottom Pressure Plate	114	Rear Engine Mountings	173
		Filter Head	115	Plate, Packing, under Rear Engine Mountings	174
			116		

engine mountings. Remove the front mountings by unscrewing the nuts and releasing the rubbers. On the Mk VII model disconnect the rear mounting rubbers attached to the chassis plates leaving behind the rubbers attached to the bell housing brackets. The XK120 rear mounting brackets are connected to a platform under the gearbox extension and the mountings are released by unscrewing the four bolts and nuts.

10 **Before lifting the combined unit out of the car check carefully that all connections between engine and chassis or bodywork have been removed.** Lift engine out by pulling forward to clear the gearbox from its mounting then raise slowly, tilting the front end upwards.

4 Removing the cylinder head

Removal of the cylinder head may be carried out with the engine in the car and for this reason the following description assumes the engine has not been removed. If the engine has been removed the operation is simplified as many components will have already been removed.

1 Disconnect the battery leads and drain cooling system by means of the radiator and cylinder block drain taps. The cooling water should be conserved in a clean vessel if antifreeze has been added. Remove air

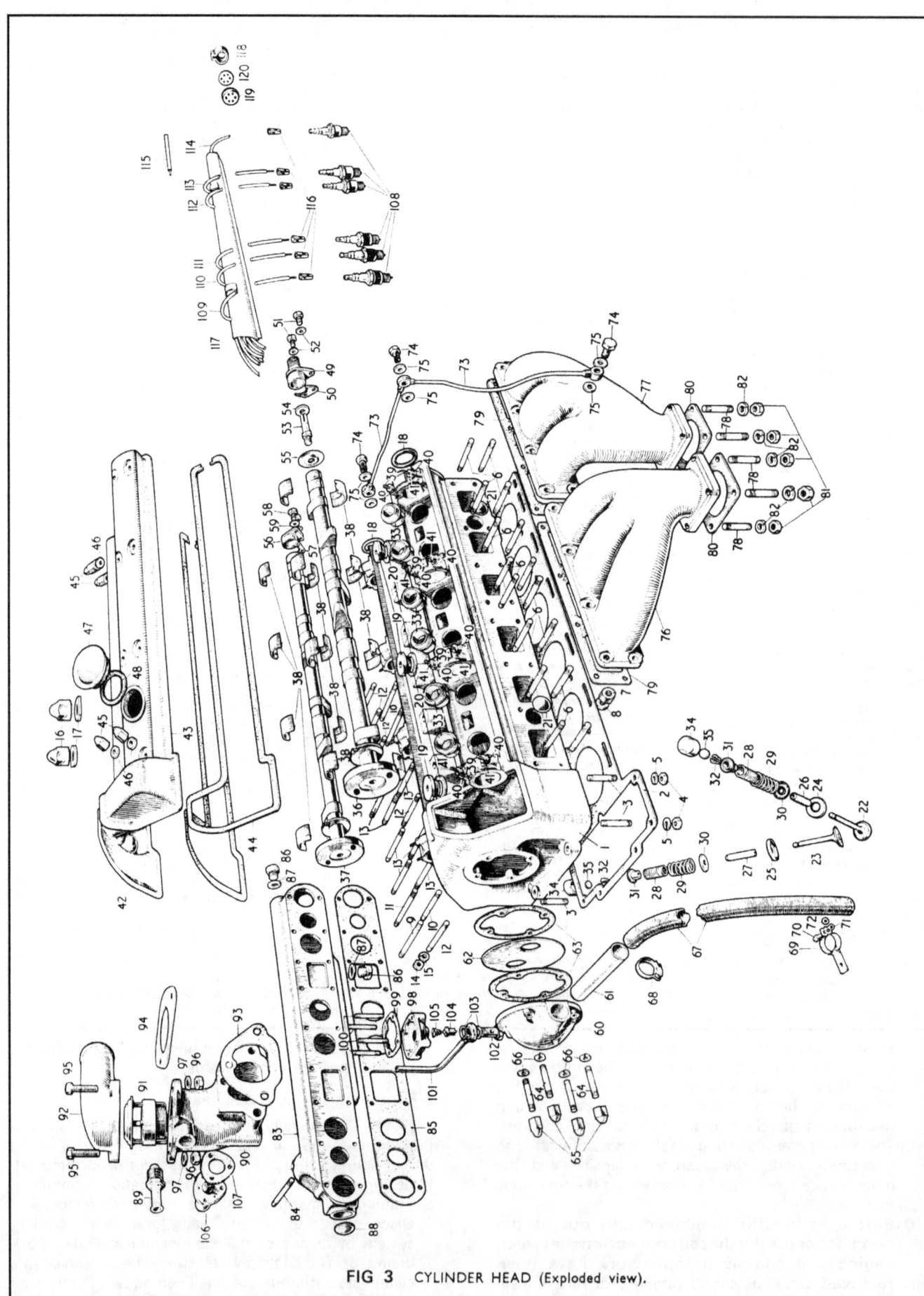

FIG 3   CYLINDER HEAD (Exploded view).

FIG 3 CYLINDER HEAD (Exploded view).

1	Cylinder Head
2	Gasket, between Head and Block
3	Stud, on underside front end of Head
4	Nut, on Studs
5	Washer, Spring, under Nuts
6	Stud, on Head, for Exhaust Manifolds
7	Nut, on Studs
8	Washer, Spring, under Nuts
9	Stud, for Inlet Manifold (Water Housing attachment)
10	Stud, for Inlet Manifold and Heater Pipe attachment
11	Stud, Long, for Inlet Manifold
12	Stud, Short, for Inlet Manifold
13	Stud, Medium, for Inlet Manifold
14	Nut, for Inlet Manifold Studs
15	Washer, Spring, under Nuts
16	Nut, Dome, securing Cylinder Head to Block
17	Washer 'D' under Cylinder Head Dome Nuts
18	Ring, Seal, rear end, between Head and Cam Covers
19	Plug, Core (Headed) on top of Cylinder Head
20	Washer (Copper) under Headed Core Plug
21	Plug, Core, for Exhaust face of Cylinder Head
22	Valve, Inlet
23	Valve, Exhaust
24	Insert for Inlet Valves
25	Insert for Exhaust Valves
26	Guide for Inlet Valves
27	Guide for Exhaust Valves
28	Spring, Inner
29	Spring, Outer
30	Seat for Springs
31	Collar at top of Valve Stems
32	Cotter
33	Guide for Tappets
34	Tappet
35	Pad, Adjusting
36	Camshaft, Exhaust
37	Camshaft, Inlet
38	Bearing for Camshafts
39	Stud, in Head, securing Camshaft Bearing Caps and Covers
40	Washer 'D' top of Bearing Caps
41	Nut, securing Bearing Caps
42	Cover for Camshaft, Right Hand
43	Cover for Camshaft, Left Hand
44	Gasket, between Covers and Head
45	Nut, Dome, securing Covers
46	Washer (Copper) under Dome Nuts
47	Cap, Filler, on Left Hand Camshaft Cover
48	Washer, Jointing, on Filler Cap
49	Rev. Counter Adapter
50	Gasket for Rev. Counter Adapter
51	Screw, Set, securing Adapter
52	Washer (Copper) on Setscrews
53	Shaft, Oil, for Rev. Counter Adapter
54	Seal, Oil, on Shaft
55	Thrower, Oil, on Shaft
56	Flanged Sealing Plug
57	Gasket for Sealing Plug
58	Screw, Set, securing Sealing Plug
59	Washer (Copper) on Setscrews
60	Front Cover and Breather Housing
61	Pipe for Breather
62	Baffle, behind Front Cover
63	Gasket, front and rear of Baffle
64	Stud, in Cylinder Head, for Front Cover
65	Nut, Dome, securing Front Cover
66	Washer, Spring, under Dome Nuts
67	Flexible Breather Pipe for Front Cover
68	Clip (Griptite No. 25) securing Flexible Pipe to Tube in Front Cover
69	Clip, securing Flexible Pipe to Wing
70	Screw, Set, securing Clips to Flexible Pipe
71	Nut on Setscrews
72	Washer, Shakeproof, under Nuts
73	Oil Pipe from Cylinder Block to Head
74	Bolt, Union, securing Oil Pipe to Head and Block
75	Washer (Copper) on Union Screws
76	Exhaust Manifold, Front
77	Exhaust Manifold, Rear
78	Stud, in Manifold Flanges, for attachment of Exhaust Pipes
79	Gasket for Exhaust Manifolds
80	Gasket for Outlet Flanges
81	Nut, securing Exhaust Pipes to Manifolds
82	Washer, Spring, under Nuts
83	Inlet Manifold
84	Stud, in Manifold, for attachment of Water Outlet Housing
85	Gasket, for Inlet Manifold
86	Plug, in Inlet Manifold
87	Washer (Copper) on Plugs
88	Plug, Core, in Inlet Manifold
89	Nozzle, on Inlet Manifold, for Brake Servo Connection
90	Water Outlet and Thermostat Housing
91	Thermostat in Housing
92	Elbow at top of Housing
93	Gasket, between Housing and Inlet Manifold
94	Gasket, between Elbow and Housing
95	Bolt, securing Elbow to Housing
96	Nut on Bolts
97	Washer, Shakeproof, under Nuts
98	Flange for Starting Pipe
99	Gasket, for Starting Pipe Flange
100	Stud, for Starting Pipe Flange
101	Starting Pipe
102	Bolt, Banjo, securing Pipe to Flange
103	Washer (Copper) at each side of Banjo Bolt
104	Anti-Blow-Back Valve in Banjo Bolt
105	Spring on Anti-Blow-Back Valve
106	Thermostat for Carburetter on Water Outlet Housing
107	Gasket for Thermostat
108	Sparking Plug
109	Lead, H.T. No. 1
110	Lead, H.T. No. 2
111	Lead, H.T. No. 3
112	Lead, H.T. No. 4
113	Lead, H.T. No. 5
114	Lead, H.T. No. 6
115	Lead, H.T. to Coil
116	Terminal for Sparking Plug Leads
117	Conduit for H.T. Leads
118	Clip for H.T. Leads around Spacer
119	Fibre Spacer for H.T. Leads (Thick)
120	Fibre Spacer for H.T. Leads (Thin)

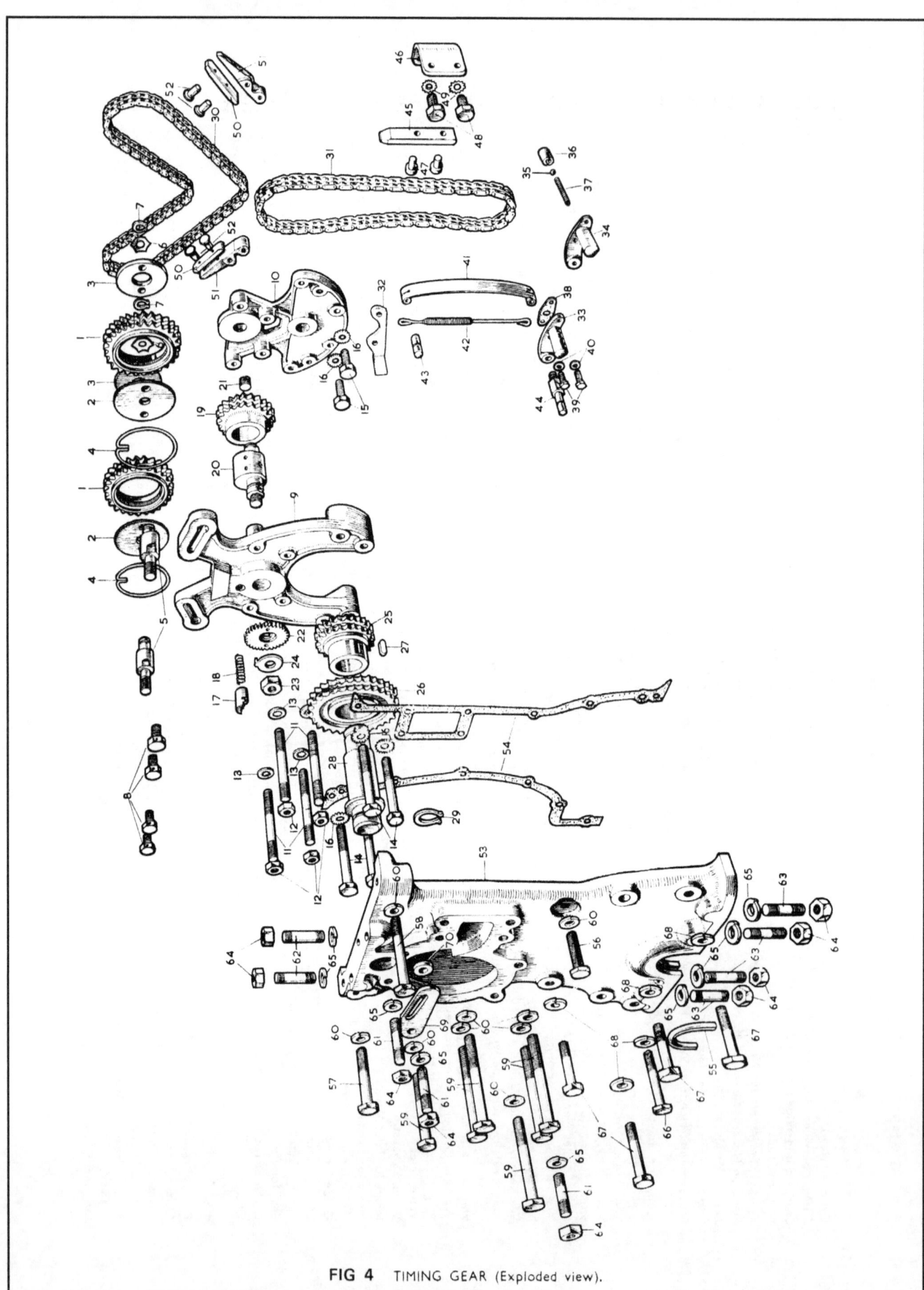

FIG 4 TIMING GEAR (Exploded view).

FIG 4 TIMING GEAR (Exploded view).

1	Sprocket for Camshaft
2	Plate, Adjusting, in Cam Sprockets
3	Plate, Clamping, in Cam Sprockets
4	Circlip, retaining Clamping Plates
5	Pin, Guide, through Clamping Plates
6	Washer, Star, on Guide Pin
7	Circlip, securing Guide Pin
8	Screw, Set, securing Sprocket Assembly to Camshafts
9	Mounting Bracket, Front
10	Mounting Bracket, Rear
11	Stud, in Rear Bracket
12	Nut, on Studs
13	Washer, Shakeproof, under Nuts
14	Bolt (Long) securing Brackets to Cylinder Block
15	Bolt (Short) securing Brackets to Cylinder Block
16	Washer, Shakeproof, on Bolts
17	Pin, Plunger, in Front Bracket, locking Adjusting Plate
18	Spring in Plunger
19	Idler Sprocket (21 Teeth)
20	Eccentric Shaft through Idler Sprocket
21	Plug (Screwed) in end of Eccentric Shaft
22	Adjusting Plate on Eccentric Shaft
23	Nut, securing Adjusting Plate
24	Washer, locking Nut
25	Intermediate Sprocket (20 Teeth)
26	Intermediate Sprocket (28 Teeth)
27	Key, locking Intermediate Sprocket
28	Shaft, holding Intermediate Sprockets
29	Circlip, securing Shaft
30	Timing Chain, Top
31	Timing Chain, Bottom
32	Guide Bracket for Chain Tensioner
33	Oil Spray Bracket (early type)
34	Oil Spray Bracket (later type)
35	Ball for Oil Spray Valve
36	Seat for Ball
37	Spring behind Ball
38	Gasket, between Oil Spray Bracket and Cylinder Block
39	Screw, Set, securing Oil Spray Bracket to Block
40	Washer, Shakeproof, on Setscrews
41	Timing Chain Tensioner
42	Spring for Chain Tensioner
43	Pin, securing Spring Tensioner
44	Pin, securing Spring and Tensioner to Oil Spray Bracket
45	Vibration Damper for Timing Chain
46	Bracket Mounting Vibration Damper
47	Rivet, securing Vibration Damper to Bracket
48	Screw, Set, securing Mounting Bracket
49	Washer, Shakeproof, on Setscrews
50	Damper for Upper Timing Chain
51	Carrier for Upper Dampers
52	Rivet, securing Dampers to Carriers
53	Front Timing Cover
54	Gasket, between Timing Cover and Cylinder Block
55	Seal, Oil, between Timing Cover and Oil Sump
56	Bolt, securing Timing Cover to Block
57	Bolt, securing Timing Cover to Block
58	Bolt, securing Dynamo Adjusting Link and Timing Cover to Block
59	Bolt, securing Water Pump and Timing Cover to Block
60	Washer, Spring, on Bolts
61	Stud, in Front Cover, for attachment of Water Pump
62	Stud, Front Cover to Cylinder Block
63	Stud, Front Cover to Oil Sump
64	Nut on Studs
65	Washer, Spring, under Nuts
66	Bolt, securing Front Cover to Cylinder Block
67	Bolt, securing Front Cover to Cylinder Block
68	Washer, Spring, on Bolts
69	Link, Adjusting Dynamo
70	Piece, Distance, behind Adjusting Link

silencer and disconnect the throttle linkage. Remove the vacuum feed pipe from the front carburetter and the electrical connections from the starting carburetter. Disconnect the petrol feed pipes at the carburetter float chamber unions taking care not to damage the cone filter. Remove the revolution counter drive from the rear of the lefthand camshaft and disconnect the oil supply pipes also at the rear of the camshaft housing. Loosen the clip holding the top hose connection and pull hose clear of cylinder head, repeat the procedure on the heater hoses if fitted.

2 Disconnect the high-tension leads from the sparking plugs and remove the sparking plugs discarding the copper washers. Disconnect the engine breather pipe 67 (see **FIG 3**) from the breather housing 60 at the front end of the cylinder head. Unscrew the eight dome nuts 45 holding the camshaft covers and lift off the covers 42, 43 and gaskets 44, discard gaskets.

3 Remove the four nuts securing the breather housing 60 observing the position of the baffle plate 62 which has the two holes located vertically. Slacken the top timing chain by loosening the nut on the eccentric idler sprocket shaft (see **FIG 7**), depressing the spring-loaded stop peg and rotating the serrated adjuster plate clockwise (viewed from front of engine). Break the locking wire on the two setscrews securing the camshaft sprockets to their respective camshafts. Mark the sprocket and shaft to indicate their relative positions then remove the setscrews and withdraw sprockets with chain. Retiming will be necessary if the circlip between the sprocket and adjuster is removed so that care should be taken not to disturb it if it is not intended to dismantle the timing gear. Slide the two camshaft sprockets up the support brackets and hold in position by screwing nuts on the guide pins, the exhaust manifold nuts are of a suitable size. Remove each exhaust down-pipe from its manifold connection. Care should be taken not to turn the engine whilst the camshafts are disconnected as the valves may be in a position to damage the piston crowns.

Remove the fourteen cylinder head nuts 16 (see **FIG 3**), and the six nuts 4 securing the cylinder head to the cylinder block in the order shown in **FIG 8** half a turn at a time to prevent cylinder head distortion. Release the spring clips on the distributor and remove distributor cap from body. The high-tension leads and lead carrier, with the distributor cap may be lifted clear after disconnecting the high-tension lead to the coil.

4 **Check that all connections between the cylinder head and body or cylinder block have been removed** then lift cylinder head off complete with exhaust manifolds, inlet manifold and carburetters. If difficulty is encountered in lifting the cylinder head, tap it lightly on a block of wood with a hammer to break the cylinder head joint.

5 Having removed the cylinder head place it carefully on the bench as the inlet valves may project below the cylinder head joint face.

5 Servicing cylinder head

Remove the cylinder head as described in the previous section, with the head on the bench remove the inlet manifold 83 (see **FIG 3**) complete with carburetters and both exhaust manifolds 76 and 77. Remove the four bearing caps from each camshaft noting the mating marks, lift out the camshafts and bearings in order so that they may be replaced in their correct positions. Lift out the twelve floating tappets 15 (see **FIG 1**) and adjusting pads 14 situated between tappets and valve stems 16. Lay out tappets and pads in order again to ensure that they can be replaced in their original guides.

The carbon deposits may now be removed from the cylinder head combustion chambers, with the valves in position to avoid damage to the valve seats. Extreme care should be taken in removing the carbon as the cylinder head being an aluminium alloy will be easily damaged. The best materials to use are worn emerycloth and paraffin, scraping tools should be avoided. Place the cylinder head on the bench with the joint face downwards and with a mallet and small drift give each valve collar a tap to free the split cotters. With a suitable valve spring compressor compress the valve springs and remove the split cotters. Release the spring compressor and lift out the valve collars, valve springs and spring seats. Remove the valves which are numbered in sequence from Number 1 cylinder which is at the flywheel end of the engine. Valves must be refitted on assembly to their original positions.

The cylinder head should now be cleaned thoroughly to remove carbon deposits from the inlet and exhaust ports, and scale deposits from the water passages. With a straight edge or a reliable flat surface such as plate glass check the cylinder head for distortion. If there is slight distortion it may be removed by lapping the surface on the plate glass with pumice powder. However if the distortion is marked, this usually being indicated by a leaking cylinder head gasket between cylinders it will have to be machined flat.

Remove all traces of carbon from the valves and examine them for wear on the stems and damage to the seats. If the stem is badly scored or the seat burnt (usually exhaust valves) renew the valve(s). Light pitting on the valve seat on the valve or its mate in the cylinder head may be removed by careful grinding. However large pits or burn marks on the cylinder head seat will require the seat to be recut or a new seat insert to be fitted, both of these jobs should preferably be carried out by a garage due to the accurate concentricity required.

To grind valve seats which are only lightly pitted, place the valve in its correct guide with a light spring between the cylinder head and the valve head, lightly smear the valve seat with grinding paste, then with a suction cup tool grind with a light semi-rotary action allowing the valve to rise off the seat occasionally. The grade of grinding paste will depend on the depth of pitting but it is best to use the finest grade that will do the job. When both surfaces of the seat are a smooth grey matt finish clean off all traces of grinding paste with paraffin.

Place a good valve in the valve guide and feel the play between valve and guide if this is greater than .002 to .004 inch or there is evidence of wear on the guide it should be renewed. The old valve guide may be pressed or drifted out with a piloted drift downwards through the combustion chamber. To fit a new valve guide the guide hole in the cylinder head must first be reamed to a diameter of .505 + .005 or — .002 inch. Then heat the cylinder head in boiling water for 30 minutes, coat the new guide with graphite grease and drive into position with a piloted drift from the combustion chamber end, until the guide protrudes $\frac{5}{16}$ inch above the valve spring seat face. Renewal of a valve guide will require that the valve seat is re-cut to ensure concentricity of the valve.

Examine the valve tappets for wear or indentation and renew if necessary. Similarly examine the tappet guides for play between tappet and guide, if this is excessive a new guide is necessary. The removal and renewal of a tappet guide requires careful machining and for this reason is best carried out by a competent garage. Clean the valve springs and compare them for length with the figures given in the data at the end of this manual, if they are shorter than the figures given replace the springs. Sometimes the spring may pass this test but not be suitable because it is weak, to check this place a new spring on top of the old one and compress in a clamp. Then measure both with a ruler, again if the original spring is shorter than the new renew it.

Examine the camshafts and their bearings for wear, it is unlikely that wear will occur until extremely high mileages have been achieved, if wear is found the only solution is to renew both camshaft and bearings since undersized bearings are not obtainable. The bearing shells should not be hand scraped nor the bearing caps filed. Replace the valves, valve springs, collars, split cotters, adjusting pads and tappets in their respective positions in the cylinder head. The camshafts are then refitted taking care with the inlet camshaft as these valves may protrude below the cylinder head face. With a feeler gauge measure and record the clearance between the back of each cam and the valve tappet. The correct clearances for all models are inlet valves .004 inch, exhaust valves .006 inch with the exception of the XK120 model where the clearances are .006 inch and .008 inch respectively. If the XK150S model is intended to be used for racing or motoring for long distances at high speeds it is recommended that the valve clearances should be increased to .006 and .010 inch respectively.

If any of the valve clearances require correction, remove the appropriate camshaft, tappet and adjuster pad, examine and record the etched letter which appears on the pad. The letter designates the thickness of the pad which varies from .085 to .103 inch, with variations in lettering from A to S, each change in letter being equivalent to a change in thickness of .001 inch. Say for example an inlet valve clearance was measured and found to be .009 inch with an adjuster pad lettered F, then to obtain the correct clearance of .004 inch a pad .005 inch thicker is required, i.e. F+5=K. Refit camshafts and tighten the bearing caps to a torque of 15 lb ft.

Before attempting to clean the cylinder block joint face, place non-fluffy rag in the waterways and smear the top edge of the cylinder bores with grease. The rag is to prevent the ingress of dirt to the cooling system and the grease will catch any loose carbon going into the bores. Clean off all traces of carbon from the cylinder block, paying particular attention to the base of cylinder head studs, with a soft scraper such as a piece of sheet brass. To remove carbon from the piston crowns, turn the engine over to bring the piston to the top of the bore and place an old piston ring on the piston crown, with a soft scraper ease off the carbon deposits within the ring. The object of the old piston ring is to preserve a small annulus of

FIG 5   Radiator mounting, Mk VII

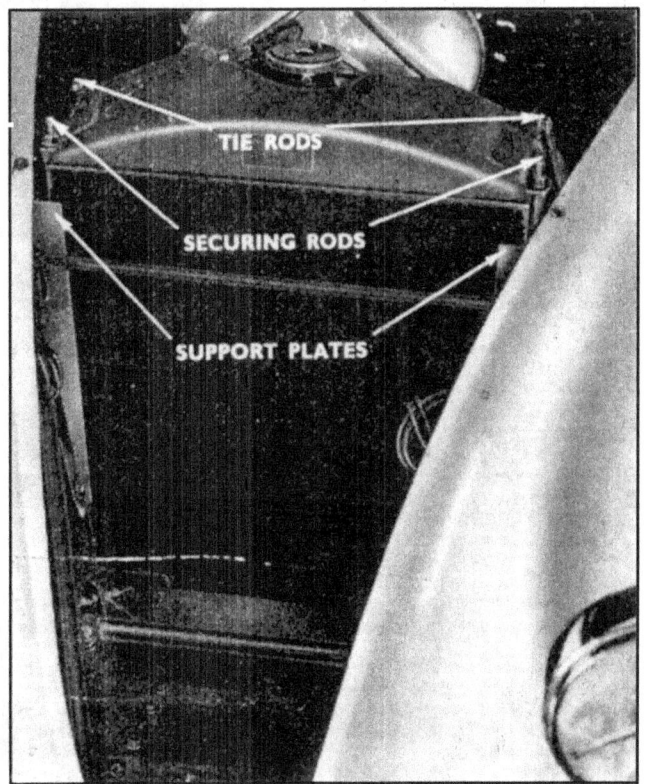

FIG 6   Radiator mounting, XK 120

FIG 7 Upper timing chain adjuster

FIG 8 Cylinder head nut sequence

FIG 9 Valve timing gauge

carbon which, with that left at the top of the cylinder bore, provides an efficient oil seal. Remove all loose carbon after cleaning the piston crowns, clean off the grease at the top of the cylinder bore and remove the rag plugging the cylinder waterways.

Refit to the cylinder head the exhaust manifold and the inlet manifold complete with carburetters, but do not replace the cylinder head until the following operation has been carried out, as unless the camshafts are in the correct position the inlet valves may foul the piston crowns.

Turn the camshafts one at a time until the keyways cut in the front flange of the camshafts are vertical in relation to the camshaft cover face, accurately position using the valve timing gauge (see **FIG 9**). Rotate the engine until number six piston (front) is at TDC, accurately position by aligning the timing marks on the flywheel and crankcase (see **FIG 10**), and check that the distributor rotor arm is pointing to number six cylinder segment in the distributor cap. Place a new cylinder gasket on the cylinder with the side marked top uppermost, the gasket may be lightly smeared with grease or jointing compound to form a good seal. Carefully replace the cylinder head on the cylinder block, refit the distributor cap and the HT leads with their carrier. Ensure that the carrier for the HT leads has its clips located on the correct cylinder head studs. Replace the fourteen dome cylinder head nuts by hand and then tighten half a turn at a time in the sequence shown in **FIG 8** to a torque of 54 lb ft.

Through the breather aperture at the front of the cylinder head check that the locknut securing the serrated plate is free (see **FIG 7**). Release the camshaft sprockets from their support brackets and replace them on their respective shafts. If the timing gear has not been disturbed the marks made on the shafts and sprockets on removal should line up. However if the timing has been disturbed the valves may be retimed in the following manner:

With the camshaft sprockets on their flanges, tension the upper timing chain, by depressing the locking plunger inwards and rotating the serrated adjuster plate, by means of the two holes in it, in an anticlockwise direction. The chain is correctly tensioned when there is only slight flexibility on both sides of the camshaft sprockets, check tension after rocking the engine in either direction. The valve timing cannot be accurately carried out until the top chain is correctly tensioned.

Accurately position the camshafts with the valve timing tool (see **FIG 9**) tapping the sprockets off the shafts if necessary, ensure that the valve timing tool is seated correctly as indicated in **FIG 9**. Check that the engine is still in the correct position, i.e. with number six piston at TDC.

Replace the camshaft sprockets on the shafts and check that the setscrew holes in the adjuster plate are exactly aligned with the tapped holes in the camshaft flanges. If they are in alignment replace the setscrews, if not remove the circlip retaining the adjuster plate (see **FIG 4**) with a pair of pliers, pull the adjuster plate forward by the guide pin until the serrations disengage, rotate the plate through 180 deg. and replace, replace the circlip, screw up the setscrews and lock in position with wire.

Replace the camshaft covers complete with new gaskets and tighten the dome retaining nuts. Refit exterior components in the reverse order to that observed in the cylinder head removal, replacing gaskets as necessary especially those at the exhaust down pipe manifolds. Before replacing the sparking plugs, clean them thoroughly and check that the gaps are correct, always refit with new copper gaskets. Top up the cooling system and **check that all connections between the engine and chassis, bodywork have been made.** Start up the engine and allow to run up to normal temperature, checking for water or oil leaks. The cylinder head nuts should be checked when the engine has reached its operating temperature. They should also be checked when the engine has been run for some time as changes in the head occur due to thermal expansion and the bedding down of the new cylinder head gasket.

Refit bonnet taking care to line up to the marks made on removal, as a small variation of positioning of the hinge is exaggerated at the front end of the bonnet.

6 Timing gear

To remove the complete timing gear the cylinder head must be removed, if however only the lower timing chain and tensioner need to be removed, the timing cover may be removed without disturbing the cylinder head. It will be necessary to remove the four studs securing the timing cover to the cylinder head and care should be taken on removal or reassembly not to damage that portion of the cylinder head gasket exposed.

Timing gear removal

Remove the radiator as described in **Section 3**, disconnect the generator lead and remove generator by releasing the adjuster and mounting bolts. Where a five bladed fan is fitted (see **FIG 11**) unscrew the five setscrews and lift off fan and pulley. In the case of six bladed fans (see **FIG 12**) remove the four setscrews securing the fan and pulley, after marking the position of the semicircular balance pieces. These are marked on initial assembly with a small hole through the balance weights, fan and pulley. Lift off fan, balance weights and pulley. Detach the hose connections from the water pump, unscrew the six setscrews and three nuts holding the water pump, remove pump and discard pump gasket.

Remove the cylinder head as described in **Section 4**. knock back the tab washer on the crankshaft, locking the starter dog and remove the setscrew, unscrew starter dog and remove. Pull off the crankshaft damper and pulley unit by giving the split cone which secures them a sharp tap on the end. Unscrew the drain plug on the sump and drain out engine oil, unscrew the setscrews holding the coverplate at the front end of the clutch and remove. On the Mk VII model remove the anti-roll bar by detaching it from the chassis brackets. Unscrew the setscrews holding the sump and lower sump clear of car. The XK120 model has the front engine bearer attached to the timing cover so that it is essential to support the front end of the engine before removing the bearer.

Unscrew the setscrews holding the timing cover 53 (see **FIG 4**) to the cylinder block and lift timing cover off noting the distance piece 70 behind the generator link 69, remove the gasket 54 and discard. On Mks VII, IX, XK120 and early XK140 models, remove the chain

FIG 10 Timing marks (numbers 1 and 6 cylinders TDC)

tensioner blade 41 and spring 42 from the guide pins 43/44. Unscrew the setscrews 39 and remove the timing chain tensioner bracket 33/34. Later XK140 models from engine numbers G.4411 to G.4420 and G.4431 onwards with all Mk VIII and XK150 models are fitted with a Reynolds hydraulic chain tensioner. To remove the hydraulic type tensioner, knock back the tab and remove the small hexagon headed screw from the tensioner body, insert an Allen key into the tapped hole to engage with the spring retainer, turn the Allen key clockwise until the rubber slipper is free of spring pressure, unscrew the two setscrews retaining the tensioner and lift off complete with guide plate and shim. Unscrew the short setscrews 15 and the long setscrews 14 holding the sprocket mounting brackets and remove the complete timing gear assembly.

Dismantling

Unscrew and remove the nut 23 and washer 24 from the front end of the idler shaft 20, withdraw the plunger 17 and spring 18. Remove the four nuts holding the front mounting bracket 9 to the rear bracket 10 and the two nuts holding the camshaft sprocket guide pins, withdraw front bracket forward. Lift the lower timing chain off the intermediate sprocket 26, remove the camshaft sprockets and lift the upper timing chain off its intermediate sprocket 25. Remove the circlip 29 on the end of the intermediate shaft and press the shaft out of the mounting bracket. The two intermediate sprockets can be slid off the shaft and separated, note the key in the shaft which holds them. The crankshaft sprocket may be removed in the same manner.

Examine the chains and sprockets for wear. On the sprockets, wear is indicated by broad flat spots. The chain rollers will have ridges in if the chain is worn. The chain may however be stretched, this fault is usually very obvious if the chain is wrapped round one of the sprockets, **the rollers drop in the sprocket at the start of the chain but come out of alignment further round the sprocket.**

If it is necessary to replace the timing chains it is essential that the crankshaft and camshaft sprockets are renewed as well. This is because a new chain on old

FIG 11 Five bladed fan

FIG 12 Six bladed fan

sprockets, under stress causes a very rapid rate of wear on both the sprockets and the chain. Where a chain tensioner blade and spring are fitted it is advisable to fit new ones with a new chain. A hydraulic tensioner will only need replacing if the pad or spring are worn or damaged.

Replacement of the timing gear is the reverse of the removal procedure, special care being taken to clean sprocket shafts and the joint faces between items. When replacing the timing gear keep the sprocket in line as much as possible to prevent any undue side stress being put on the chain. Renew the timing cover gasket, smearing the joint faces of the crankcase and timing cover lightly with jointing compound. Before refitting the sump carefully renew the two halves of the crankshaft oil seals 55 (**FIG 4**) and 92 (**FIG 2**) making sure that the ends are cut off flush with the sump face. Replacement of the hydraulic chain tensioner should be carried out in the following manner, press the spring and retainer into the bore of the tensioner, engaging the groove in the retainer with the pin in the bore, and rotate clockwise at the same time. The spring and retainer are now held in position in the bore of the tensioner. The shim guide plate and tensioner body should be fitted to the body in this order and secured in place by the two setscrews. Remove the small hexagon-headed screw from the tensioner body, insert an Allen key and turn clockwise until the spring is released. Check that the plunger operates freely then refit the hexagon-headed screw and lock in position with the tab washer.

Having replaced the timing gear, chain tensioner, sump and cover, refit the cylinder head. The upper timing chain should be adjusted to give the correct tension and the valve timing checked. If the valve timing is found to be incorrect it should be adjusted as described in **Section 5**.

7 Oil pump and sump

Drain the engine oil from the sump drain plug into a container, this is carried out quickest when the engine is hot as the oil will flow more readily. Examine the oil, if it is dirty or has been diluted discard it. Unscrew the setscrews holding the cover plate at the front end of the clutch and remove screws and plate. It is also necessary on the Mk VII model to remove the anti-roll bar by detaching it from its chassis brackets. The pressed steel sump is held in position by twenty-six setscrews and four nuts, these should be unscrewed evenly all round to prevent distortion on removal. When all nuts and screws have been removed, lower the sump and withdraw it, peel off the cork gasket and discard it.

The sump should be cleaned thoroughly by scrubbing with a stiff brush and paraffin then allow to dry. With the sump removed the floating oil filter for the pump is exposed this is removed by withdrawing the splitpin holding it to the pump body. The suction filter is best cleaned in the same manner as that described for the sump, rags, especially fluffy ones should never be used as they may well block the filter and thus reduce the oil flow to the engine bearings.

Remove the oil tray, by unscrewing the setscrews holding it to the front and centre main bearing caps, and clean it by washing down in paraffin. Disconnect the oil delivery pipe from the pump body with its gasket after removing the three setscrews. Remove the setscrews holding the pump body to the front main bearing cap, noting that the top two are dowels (see **FIG 13**), the oil pump and coupling shaft can then be removed by withdrawing downwards.

Remove the coupling shaft from the pump and clean it in paraffin. Turn the pump shaft by hand and feel if there is any binding or play in the gears. Dismantle the pump by removing the four setscrews holding the bottom cover and associated gasket, withdraw the driving and driven gears. Clean the pump components in paraffin and allow to dry. Examine the gears for wear and look for scoring or wear on the gear shafts, wear will have been indicated when turning the pump by hand if the gears do

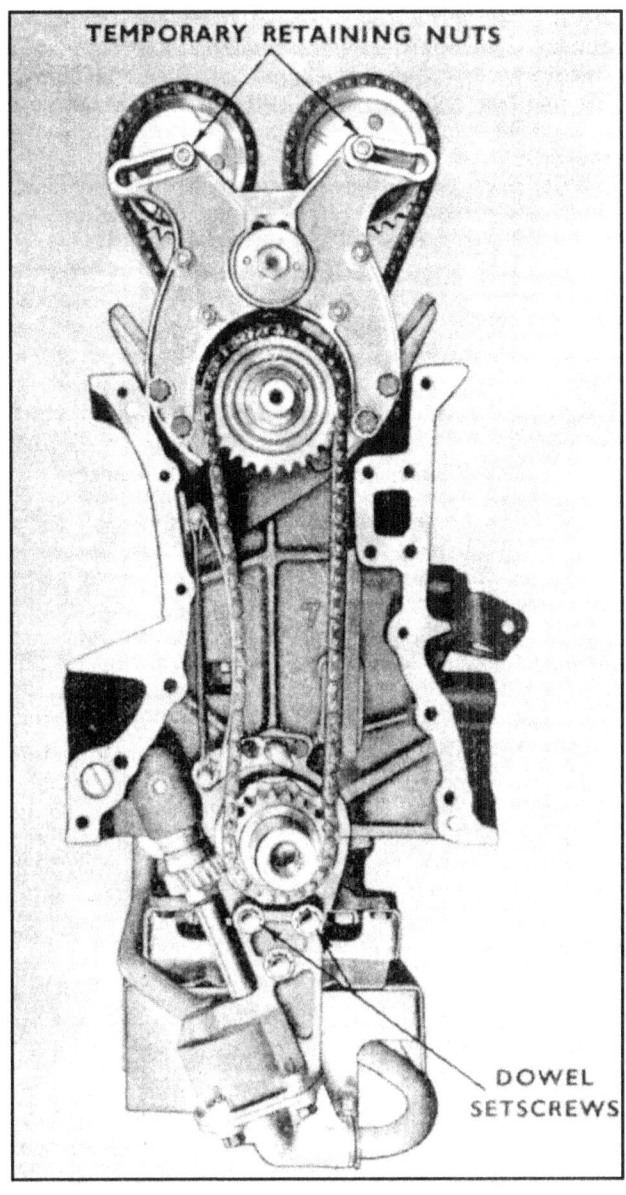

FIG 13 Oil pump and timing gear

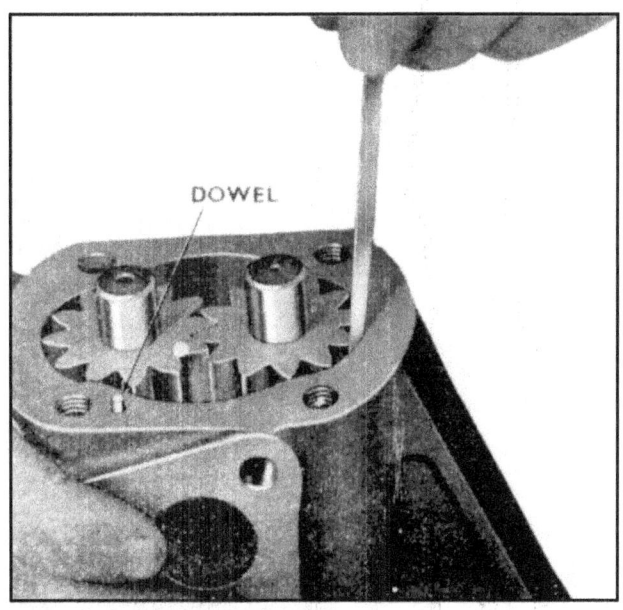

FIG 14 Oil pump side clearance

FIG 15 Oil pump end clearance

not move smoothly. If wear is found the gears may be renewed or better still an exchange pump unit should be fitted. Reassemble the pump gears after lightly oiling and check the clearances between the gears and the pump body with a feeler gauge (see **FIGS 14** and **15**). The clearance between the sides of the gears and the pump body should be .0045 to .007 inch if this is exceeded then the gears need replacing (see **FIG 14**). The clearance between the gears and the bottom face of the pump body should be .0015 to .0035 inch (see **FIG 15**). If this is too high it may be reduced by removing the gears and lapping the pump body face on a smooth flat surface such as a piece of plate glass.

Reassembly of the pump is the reverse of the removal sequence, ensure however that new gaskets are fitted and note the locating dowel between the pump body and the cover (see **FIG 14**).

8 Oil filter and pump relief valve

The oil filter assembly is shown in the exploded diagram (see **FIG 2**) and the complete unit is shown in **FIG 16**. To remove the complete assembly, clean off the outside with a rag soaked in paraffin, disconnect the oil pressure gauge pipe union from the top of the filter body, support the assembly whilst removing the four setscrews securing it to the cylinder block, lift assembly clear complete with gasket. Both the filter element and the pump relief valve may be removed independently from the assembly without detaching it from the cylinder block, it is however far more convenient to carry out either by adopting the above procedure.

The filter element is removed by unscrewing the central bolt securing the filter canister 124 (see **FIG 2**) and withdrawing the canister complete with the element. Due to the tendency of some oils to form sludge the filter element should be rinsed in petrol every 2500 miles and

FIG 16 Oil filter assembly

renewed every 5000 miles, after rinsing in petrol the element should be allowed to dry off completely before attempting to replace it. If this is not done the oil may well be diluted by the petrol held in the element. The canister can be cleaned out with a non-fluffy rag or preferably rinsed in petrol and dried out. Examine the rubber sealing ring 119 (see **FIG 2**) for damage or distortion and renew if necessary. Replace the rubber seal in its groove which should be checked for cleanliness, offer up the canister complete with the filter element and tighten up the central bolt 124.

The oil pressure relief valve is removed as a complete unit from the filter assembly by means of the hexagon head 127. To dismantle the unit, hold the hexagon head of the unit, unscrew the dome nut 132 and release the locknut 133, unscrew the adjuster 131 and withdraw adjuster, spring and valve. Clean the components in petrol and allow to dry then examine the spring and valve seat for signs of wear or damage and renew as necessary. Replacement is the reverse of the removal procedure taking care to replace the copper gaskets between the pressure relief valve and body, and either side of the locknut.

Replace the complete filter assembly on the cylinder block with a new gasket and screw home the four setscrews. Reconnect the pressure gauge pipe.

To adjust the oil relief valve, remove the dome nut and washer, this exposes the adjusting screw. Start the engine and allow to run until it reaches the normal working temperature then set the throttle to maintain an engine speed of about 2000 rev/min. Loosen the locknut on the adjusting screw and turn the screw to give an oil pressure reading of between 40 and 45. Clockwise rotation of the adjuster screw increases the pressure and anticlockwise movement reduces it. When the correct pressure has been achieved tighten the locknut and replace the washer and dome nut, reset the throttle adjustment.

The above relief valve adjustment is intended to be carried out when the oil filter element has been either cleaned or renewed. **Adjustment of the relief valve should never be carried out without first checking that the oil filter is clean,** since a dirty or blocked oil filter may cause a drop in oil pressure of between 5 and 10 lb/sq in.

9 Connecting rods and pistons

Removal of the connecting rods may be effected with the engine in the car providing there is sufficient access under the car. If the car is to be held jacked up, ensure that the jacks are positioned correctly and put blocks under the rear wheels to prevent any movement of the car.

Remove the cylinder head, sump, suction filter and oil pump as described in the earlier sections. From under the car remove the splitpins from the connecting rod bolt nuts and unscrew nuts. Tap the bolts upwards and remove the lower bearing shell with the bearing cap. Each cap is marked with the cylinder number and mates up with the same number on the connecting rod. Remove the connecting rod bolts and lay them out in order. Before attempting to push the pistons out of the bores the ring of carbon at the top of the cylinder bore should be scraped off. Check that there is no ridge around the top of the bore with the carbon removed. This ridge arises in worn bores as the piston rings do not reach the top of the bore and hence there is no wear in this region. If there is a ridge it must be removed by hand scraping or the pistons and rings will be damaged on trying to remove them. Having ensured that the cylinder bores are smooth push the connecting rod from below and ease the pistons upwards out of the bores. Lift the pistons and connecting rods clear of the engine and temporarily replace the bearings, caps, nuts and bolts to their respective connecting rods. It is essential that when replacing these components that they are fitted to their original positions.

If it is more convenient to remove the piston rings and clean the pistons with the connecting rods attached, by holding the connecting rods lightly in a soft jawed vice. There are three piston rings the two upper ones being compression rings and the other an oil control ring. To remove the piston rings start with the upper compression ring, gently ease one end of the ring out of its groove, insert an old fairly sturdy feeler gauge (say .02 inch) between the ring and the piston, then by easing the end of the ring upwards and at the same time sliding the feeler gauge progressively round the piston from the free end lift the ring up over the piston crown. Repeat the procedure with the other two rings. Always remove or replace the piston rings over the piston crown never over the piston skirt.

Having removed the piston rings clean out the ring grooves with an old ring, making sure there are no sharp edges on it which may score the piston. When cleaning the grooves check that all the oil holes through the piston are also cleared as these will make a noticeable difference in oil consumption as well as engine wear. Clean the rest of the piston and the rings to remove all the carbon deposits.

To remove the piston from the connecting rod remove the circlip at either end of the gudgeon pin with a pair of circlip pliers. If ordinary pliers are used place a rag over the circlip and pliers to prevent loss of the circlip when it springs free. Immerse the piston in warm oil then press the gudgeon pin through the connecting rod until the connecting rod may be removed.

Examine the side clearance of each ring in its groove this should be .001 to .003 inch if the clearance is more than this renew the piston rings. With new rings recheck the side clearance if it is still excessive new pistons are required. The correct thicknesses of piston rings and the specification of piston sizes is given in the appendix of this manual under the piston section in **Technical Data**. Examine the pistons for scoring or burning of the skirts and replace if necessary.

Check the cylinder bores for obvious signs of wear such as scoring or a pronounced ridge at the top of the bore. If either is apparent then the cylinders should be rebored and the required oversized pistons fitted. Pistons are available in the following oversizes +.005 inch, +.010, +.015, +.020 and +.030 inch, the size is stamped on the piston crown. Note that if the cylinder bore is in such a bad condition, or has already been bored previously, such that it cannot be cleared with a standard oversize then it is possible to bore the cylinder larger still and fit a liner in the cylinder block. The fitting of liners to the engine has to be carried out very accurately and is best carried out by a specialist in this field. If a liner is fitted the finished bore size will be the standard, or initial factory produced bore dimension.

New piston rings must be tested in an unworn part of the bore before refitting to the pistons. To do this, place the ring to be tested about an inch down the cylinder bore on top of a piston, to keep it square within the bore. Measure the gap between the two ends of the ring with a feeler gauge and check this measurement with the correct values given in the Technical Data. If the gap is found to be too small the ends of the ring may be ground carefully to obtain the correct gap.

The connecting rods should be examined for distortion, this is usually indicated by heavy scoring of the pistons or by the need to apply side pressure to locate the big-end on the crankpin. The connecting rod should be replaced if distortion is found or if the big-end bearing has run, as this may well have caused fatigue in the rod. Check the small end bush for wear by inserting the gudgeon pin and feeling for play. The gudgeon pin should be a good sliding fit in the bush and any play indicates that bush renewal is required. Check the gudgeon pin for wear or scoring and renew if necessary, this is most unlikely since the gudgeon pin which is hardened steel wears far less quickly than the small-end bush. To renew the small-end bush, the old can be pressed out with the new one taking care that the oil hole in the new bush lines up with that in the connecting rod. Having renewed the bush it should be reamed out to suit the gudgeon pin which should be a tight push fit.

Examine the big-end shell bearings which are of either the whitemetal or indium type, both are easily replaceable and do not need bedding in. Although both types are fitted they should not be mixed in individual engines and neither type should be scraped. Replace the connecting rod on its crankshaft journal with the bearings, bearing cap, nuts and bolts and check for free movement. These should be between .001 and .002 inch vertical movement and between .006 and .009 inch end float. If the movement (as specified) is found to be greater than this remove the connecting rod and examine the crankshaft journal for ovality or scoring. The crankshaft ovality is measured using a micrometer and taking readings of the crankpin around its diameter, the difference between the highest and lowest readings will indicate the ovality. The ovality measured in this manner may be up to .003 inch before regrinding of the crankshaft is required, providing excessive scoring is not found when the crankshaft should be reground anyway. After examination of the big-end bearing it is decided that the crankshaft needs regrinding, the crankshaft will require removing from the engine, this being covered in **Section 11**. If the bearings are to be renewed only, check the size of the old bearings before buying replacements since the crankshaft may have already been reground. Never file the bearing caps to take up play in the big-end bearing as due to the ovality caused excess pressures are exerted upon it and also the cap will become a non-standard item which cannot be used for exchange purposes.

When overhauling the connecting rods and big-ends it is good practice to renew the connecting rod nuts and bolts which take a considerable amount of stress.

To reassemble the connecting rods and pistons, place both in warm oil and press the gudgeon pin through the connecting rod, ensuring that it is located centrally in the piston. Refit the cirlips in the piston these prevent excessive side movement in the gudgeon pin which otherwise might score the cylinder bores. Refit the piston rings carefully in a similar manner to which they were removed, and arrange the gaps in the rings to be at 90 deg. to one another to give a good gas seal. Slide the bearing shells into the connecting rod and bearing cap and lightly oil the bearing surface. After removing the cylinder bore glaze, place the connecting rod with its piston in the bore with the piston skirt or connecting rod stamped number, facing the exhaust side of the engine. Then with a suitable ring compressor, compress the piston rings to the bore diameter and push the piston down into the bore until the connecting rod big-end is located on the crankshaft journal. From under the car refit the connecting rod bolts, offer up the bearing cap and secure with the nuts. The nuts should be tightened to a torque of 37.5 lb ft after checking that the number stamped on the bearing cap and connecting rod line up on the exhaust side of the engine and are in the correct cylinder. Lock the nuts in position by fitting new splitpins.

10 Removing the clutch and flywheel

With the engine and gearbox removed as a unit, support the gearbox and remove the pressed steel plate from the bottom of the clutch housing. Unscrew the setscrews and bolts holding the clutch housing to the engine, withdraw the gearbox and bell housing from the engine very carefully to avoid straining the clutch drive plate and the gearbox constant pinion shaft.

Fit three ¼ inch distance pieces (see **FIG 2, Chapter 5**) one between each of the three release levers and the clutch cover to reduce the thrust spring pressure and assist the clutch removal. Unscrew the setscrews securing the clutch body to the flywheel a turn at a time in a diagonal sequence to prevent distortion of the cover. Remove the clutch assembly from the flywheel, slide off the driven plate assembly and withdraw bearing. Release the tab washers and unscrew the ten flywheel mounting bolts, remove the bolts and the locking plate. On removal of the bolts and the locking plate the two mushroom headed dowels locating the flywheels to the crankshaft are exposed. Lever the flywheel off the crankshaft carefully, to avoid damage to the crankshaft boss and the flywheel. To prevent the flywheel dropping off the end of the shaft insert a length of $\frac{7}{16}$ inch dia. rod through the flywheel during the latter stage of removal.

Examine the clutch and flywheel for wear, the clutch examination is covered in detail in **Chapter 5**. Wear on the flywheel will be only on the starter gear teeth and will be evident as broad flat spots on the teeth. If the teeth are badly worn the flywheel will require renewing as the gear teeth are an integral part of the flywheel. Fitting a new flywheel will necessitate balancing of the clutch and flywheel assembly which is carried out in the following manner.

Reassemble the clutch and flywheel assembly carefully centring the clutch and aligning the balance marks 'B' on both components. Place the complete assembly on a mandrel and support this mandrel on two parallel knife edges. If the assembly is found to be out of balance, this being indicated by the assembly after rotation, stopping with the same portion of the assembly at the bottom it will be necessary to part the assembly and drill $\frac{3}{8}$ inch dia. holes $\frac{1}{2}$ inch deep (on the heavy side) of the flywheel at the same radius as the clutch cover dowels until balance is obtained.

Before refitting the assembly examine the bronze bush fitted to the crankshaft spigot for wear and renew as necessary. The bush is a press fit in the spigot. Refit the flywheel to the crankshaft when all burred edges have been removed and the engine has been turned until No. 1 and 6 pistons are at TDC. The flywheel should be fitted with the balance mark 'B' at the bottom, when fitted tap home the two dowels and replace the locking plate and bolts. Tighten the bolts to a torque of 67.5 lb ft and lock in position with the tabs on the locking plate. Replacement of the clutch requires careful attention in order to ensure that it is centralized. This work is described in detail in the clutch section (see **Chapter 5**).

11 Crankshaft
to be carried out carefully to

The details of the crankshaft assembly can be seen in the lower portion of **FIG 2**. The forged steel crankshaft is supported in the crankcase by seven main bearings. Both the big-end bearings of the connecting rod and the main bearing shells are of the steel-backed type and require no bedding in.

To remove the crankshaft the engine must be removed from the car and the following components removed from the assembly, cylinder head, sump, oil pump, crankshaft pulley and damper, timing gear, clutch and flywheel, the procedures for which are described in the foregoing sections. Having removed these components, slacken the distributor clamp plate bolt and lift out the distributor, remove the setscrews and lift off the clamping plate, discard the cork gasket. From under the crankcase remove the distributor and oil pump drive gear by knocking back the tab washer, remove the nut and washer by tapping the square end of the distributor shaft through the gear. Remove the drive shaft and key, slide gear out and remove.

Knock back the tab washers on the main bearings and remove the splitpins on the big-end bearings. Remove the bearing cap nuts and lift out lower halves of bearings with the bearing caps. In the case of the centre main bearings also remove the thrust washers fitted in recesses. Split the oil return thread at the flywheel end of the crankshaft by releasing the two Allen screws and tapping lightly, the two halves being located by dowels. The crankshaft can now be lifted out together with the upper halves of the main and big-end bearing shells and the thrust washers. When removing the bearing components lay them out in their correct order to ensure that they are refitted to their original locations.

Examine the crankshaft journals for signs of wear or scoring and with a micrometer measure each journal diameter in several positions to check for ovality. Up to .003 inch ovality may be tolerated before the crankshaft requires regrinding. Check the main and big-end bearings for scoring or breaking up and discard any which have these faults. There are as mentioned two types of bearing shell material, whitemetal and lead/indium, the **Technical Data** in the appendix indicates on which models these are fitted. **No attempt should be made to mix these types of bearings** they may however be replaced in complete sets. The filing of bearing caps, as mentioned previously, is not to be attempted since these components will be rendered useless when bearings are eventually replaced.

The crankshaft may be reground or exchanged for a factory reground one. The crankshaft may be ground in the following sizes since bearings are manufactured to suit these sizes, .020, .030 and .040 inch. Regrinding below .040 inch is not recommended and thus if the journals are still oval after grinding to this dimension a new crankshaft will be required.

Clean out the oilways in the crankshaft thoroughly with paraffin preferably under pressure, especially if any of the bearings have run. It is also necessary to clean all the other oilways in the engine if a bearing has run and essential to replace the oil filter element. The cylinder block oilways may be cleaned by removing the blanking plugs 4 and 5 (see **FIG 2**).

Before refitting the crankshaft check the distributor and pump drive bush for wear and renew if necessary. The bush is a press fit and the oil hole in it must be lined up with that in the crankcase.

Replace the upper halves of big-end and main bearing shells with the thrust washers. Refit the crankshaft onto the bearing surfaces after lightly oiling all bearing journals, replace the lower halves of the bearings and thrust washers and secure with nuts. The main bearings should be tightened to a torque of 85 lb ft and the big-end bearings to a torque of 37.5 lb ft. Check the end float of the crankshaft with a feeler gauge this should be between .006 and .008 inch. The end float may be increased or decreased by the insertion of the two sizes of thrust-washer which are given in the appendix under the heading of **Technical Data**.

12 Reassembly of stripped engine

This process is mainly a reversal of the removal and dismantling procedure but there are several general operations it is advisable to carry out. These are:
1. Clean all joint faces of components, carefully removing any traces of dirt, carbon or jointing compound. This is especially important around the base of protruding studs or dowel pins.
2. Clean out all oilways thoroughly with paraffin preferably under pressure and then flush through with engine oil.
3. Check all threads on components and run a tap or die down suspect ones then lightly oil.
4. Examine the bottoms of tapped or dowel holes to ensure all are clear of compressed dirt or jointing compound.
5. When applying jointing compound to joint faces use a fine point brush and put only a fine layer on. Excess compound may find its way into the oilways and block them.

The reassembly starts with the refitting of the crankshaft. Lay this on the upper bearing shells in the crankcase and refit the main bearing caps with the lower bearing shell. Tighten the numbered bearing caps to the correct torque, check the end float and fit oversize thrust washers as necessary.

Place the piston and connecting rod assemblies less the big-end bearing caps into their respective bores and with a suitable ring compressor ease them fully down the bore until the big-end bearing is located on the crankpin. Replace the big-end bearing caps, tighten to the correct torque and lock the nuts in position with new splitpins.

Replace the crankshaft oil spray bracket and gasket, and secure to the front face of the cylinder block. Fit the Woodruff key on the crankshaft, remove all burrs and drive on the crankshaft gear with the widest portion of the boss to the rear. Fit the other Woodruff key on the crankshaft and drive on the crankshaft sprocket, refit oil thrower washer and distance piece.

The distributor and oil pump drive gear should be replaced next ensuring it meshes correctly with the crankshaft gear. Lock in position with the tab washer and nut after ensuring the offset slot in the top of the distributor drive is parallel with the cylinder block centre line with number 6 piston at TDC.

Replace the oil pump and delivery pipe noting that there are gaskets at both ends of the pipe. Refit the oil tray to the main bearing caps, place the end of the floating suction filter pipe into the pump extension and line up the annular groove in the pipe with the hole in the extension, replace splitpin.

Refit the timing gear and cover, taking care to renew the semicircular oil seal in the base of the cover and checking that, the generator adjusting link and spacer are fitted to the correct bolts.

Replace the oil sump with new oil seals front and rear and a new cork gasket, tighten the sump setscrews a turn at a time to prevent distortion. **It is worthwhile to note here that all screws and nuts should be checked for tightness on completion of each stage of the assembly procedure** as it is extremely easy to miss one out especially on the sump which has so many.

Refit the clutch and flywheel on the crankshaft ensuring that the balance marks on both are lined up. Replacement of the clutch requires a dummy mandrel to be fitted to ensure that the assembly is centralized before the securing setscrews are tightened. If the clutch is not centralized extreme difficulty will be experienced in trying to refit the gearbox.

Replace and secure the cylinder head complete with exhaust, inlet manifolds and carburetters, taking great care that the camshafts and pistons are in their correct respective positions or the pistons may well be damaged by the inlet valves.

Reset the valve timing, as previously described, after making sure that the upper timing chain is correctly tensioned. Refit the oil feed pipes to the cylinder head with the banjo bolts and replace the oil filter assembly. **Early engines were fitted with grooved banjo bolts and plain banjo's, on later engines this was reversed, i.e. plain bolts and grooved banjo's. It is therefore essential that the correct bolts are fitted or the oil supply to the cylinder head will be cut off.**

Refit the crankshaft damper and pulley on the split cone and lock in position with the chamfered washer and starter dog. Replace the water pump and fan, in the case of models with the five-bladed fan do not assemble the fan and pulley until the pump has been fitted to the timing cover.

Fir a new cork seal in the recess at the top of the distributor shaft housing and replace and secure the distributor clamping plate. Turn the engine over to place No. 6 piston (front) at TDC by lining up the timing marks on the flywheel and crankcase and check that it is on the firing stroke by the position of the valves. Lower the distributor into position and check that the rotor arm points to the No. 6 segment in the distributor cap. If it does not then the distributor drive has been replaced incorrectly and will require removing and refitting correctly.

Replace the sparking plugs with new copper washers and attach the HT leads. Fit the camshaft covers on the cylinder head with new gaskets and tighten the nuts finger tight. Fit the revolution counter adaptor and flanged plug to the rear of the camshaft covers with the rubber sealing rings seated in the recesses provided, fit new half gaskets to the adaptor on sealing plug and secure with the setscrews. Tighten the camshaft cover nuts fully.

On the XK120 model fit the front bearer plate to the four studs in the timing cover and secure with nuts and washers.

Fit the gearbox and clutch housing to the engine, taking care not to put any strain on the clutch or gearbox shaft. Refit the starter motor to the clutch housing ensuring the earth bonding strap is fitted to the top bolt with a good clean mating contact.

The engine may now be replaced in the car by lowering carefully in position. When in position reconnect all components in the reverse order to that in which they were removed. When replacing the generator adjust the fan belt tension to give approximately $\frac{1}{2}$ inch deflection in line with the pulleys. Tighten the adjusting and mounting bolts and check that the tension has not been altered. If the belt is adjusted too lightly it will cause undue strain on the water pump and generator bearings.

The rubber hoses are fitted more easily if the inside of the hose is smeared lightly with jointing compound as it acts as a lubricant when pushing the hose onto its stub as well as providing a better joint.

Fill the cooling system with water, the gearbox and engine with the correct grades of oil, making sure drain plugs and cocks are fitted correctly.

In the case of models fitted with hydraulically operated clutches bleed the system as detailed in **Chapter 5** and top up the reservoir.

Reset the ignition timing as recommended in **Chapter 3. Before starting the engine check that all connections to the engine have been made, especially the electrical ones.**

Start the engine and allow to run up to the normal operating temperature. Check the engine for signs of leaks and rectify any that occur.

13 Modifications

Commencing at engine number G.1908 the gear type pump was replaced by a Hobourn Eaton eccentric rotor pump on the XK140 models. Servicing of this pump is basically the same as that described for the gear type, but the pressure relief valve is situated on the oil filter head. Also on the XK140 models fitted with a type 'C' cylinder head the exhaust valve and guide were modified by reducing the guide length and reducing the valve diameter under its head. This modification commenced at engine number G.6678S.

The Mk VIII and XK150 models have several modifications which are common. These are, the change of connecting rod big-end bearing shells from whitemetal to lead/indium at engine numbers NA.3386 and V.6709 respectively, an increase in length of the inlet valves from $1\frac{1}{2}$ to $1\frac{13}{16}$ inches at engine numbers N.8478 and V.1281, the cylinder block rear cover and sealing ring were modified to allow the Allen screws to be inserted from the top at engine numbers N.9062 and V.1631, the insertion of an oil filter in the hydraulic chain tensioner at engine numbers N.8252 and V.1191.

The lead/indium bearings may be fitted to earlier models but must be done so in complete sets. The oil filter may be fitted to all models having a hydraulic chain tensioner. However, care must be taken in fitting the filter to ensure that the conical filter is placed in the cylinder block pointed end first.

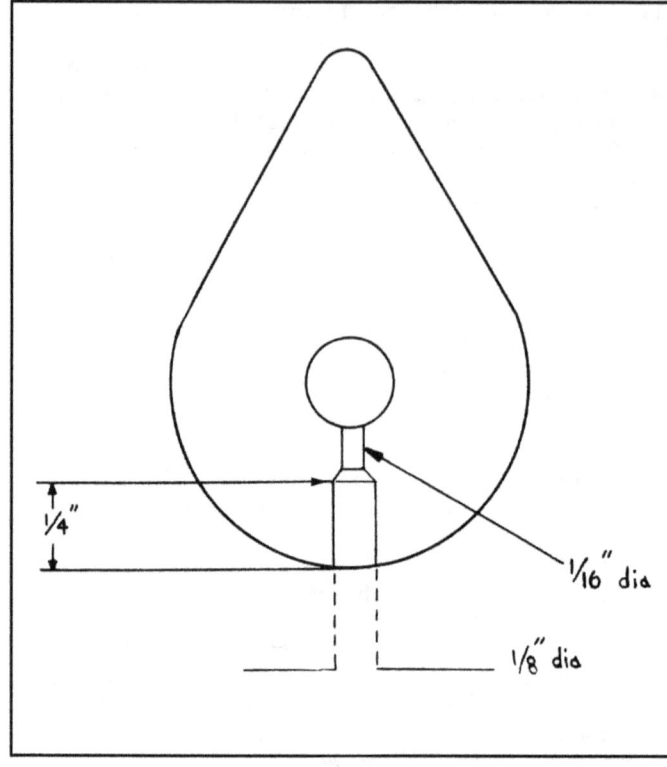

FIG 17   Modified camshaft Mk VIII

The camshaft on the Mk VIII model was modified to reduce tappet noise when the engine is cold this commenced at engine number N.6662. The modification consists of providing oilways through the base of each cam. This modification may be carried out in earlier models if tappet noise is found to be excessive when the engine is cold. To do this remove the camshafts and clamp in position on vee blocks, then drill the back of each cam with high-speed $\frac{1}{8}$ and $\frac{1}{16}$ inch drills as indicated in **FIG 17**. Ensure that all burrs are removed and the oilways are thoroughly cleaned before replacing.

14 Fault Diagnosis

(a) Engine will not start

1 Defective coil
2 Faulty distributor capacitor
3 Dirty, pitted, or incorrectly set contact breaker points
4 Ignition wires loose or insulation faulty
5 Water on sparking plug leads
6 Corrosion of battery terminals or discharged condition
7 Faulty or jammed starter
8 Sparking plug leads wrongly connected
9 Vapour lock in fuel lines
10 Defective fuel pump
11 Faulty starter carburetter setting or defective solenoid
12 Blocked petrol filter or float chamber needles
13 Leaking valves
14 Sticking valves
15 Valve timing incorrect
16 Ignition timing incorrect

(b) Engine stalls

Check 1, 2, 3, 4, 10, 11, 12, 13, 14 in (a)
1 Sparking plugs defective or gap incorrect
2 Retarded ignition
3 Mixture too weak
4 Water in fuel system
5 Petrol tank breather choked
6 Incorrect valve clearance

(c) Engine idles badly

Check 1 and 6 in (b)
1 Air leak at manifolds
2 Slow running screws out of adjustment
3 Air leak in carburetters
4 Over-rich mixture
5 Worn piston rings
6 Worn valve stems or guides
7 Weak exhaust valve springs
8 Carburetters not synchronized

(d) Engine misfires

Check 1, 2, 3, 4, 5, 8, 10, 12, 13, 14, 15, 16 in (a);
1, 2, 3, 6 in (b) and 8 in (c)
1 Weak or broken valve springs

(e) Engine overheats (see Chapter 4)

(f) Compression low

Check 13 and 14 in (a); 5 and 6 in (c) and 1 in (d)
1 Worn piston ring grooves
2 Broken piston rings
3 Scored or worn cylinder bores

(g) Engine lacks power

Check 3, 10, 11, 12, 13, 14, 15, 16 in (a); 1, 2, 3, 6 in (b);
5, 6, 8 in (c); 1 in (a); (e) and (f)
1 Leaking joint washers
2 Fouled sparking plugs
3 Automatic advance not operating
4 Carburetter piston damper—lack of oil or incorrect grade of oil
5 Carbon build up in combustion chambers or on piston crowns

(h) Burnt valve or seats

Check 13 and 14 in (a); 6 in (b); 1 in (d) and (e)
1 Excessive carbon around valve seat and head

(j) Sticking valves

Check 1 in (d)
1 Bent valve stem
2 Scored valve stem or guide
3 Incorrect valve clearance

(k) Excessive cylinder wear

Check 11 in (a) and see Chapter 2
1 Lack of oil
2 Dirty or diluted oil
3 Piston rings gummed up or broken
4 Badly fitting piston rings
5 Connecting rods bent

(l) Excessive oil consumption

Check 5 and 6 in (c) and check (k)
1 Ring gaps too wide
2 Oil return holes in piston blocked
3 Scored cylinders
4 Oil level too high
5 External oil leaks

(m) Crankshaft and connecting rod bearing failure

Check 1 in (k)
1 Blocked oilways
2 Worn journals or crankpins
3 Loose bearing caps
4 Bent connecting rod

(n) Low oil pressure

Check 1, 2, 3 in (m)
1 Oil filter blocked
2 Diluted oil
3 Leakage around pump body
4 Incorrect gear clearance in pump body

(o) Poor circulation (see Chapter 4)

(p) Internal water leakage (see Chapter 4)

(q) High fuel consumption (see Chapter 2)

(r) Engine vibration

1 Loose generator bolts
2 Fan blade out of balance
3 Mounting rubbers defective
4 Exhaust pipe mounting too tight
5 Crankshaft damper defective

NOTES

INDEX – FUEL SYSTEM & CARBURETTERS

SECTION	PAGE	
000	29	Basic Diagnostic Testing & Troubleshooting
001	31	Fuel System Description

THE FUEL PUMP

002	31	Description & Operation
003	32	Routine Maintenance
004	32	Removal & Disassembly
005	34	Examination & Reassembly
006	34	Testing

THE CARBURETTERS

007	36	Description & Operation
008	36	Routine Maintenance
009	36	Removal & Disassembly
010	37	Servicing & Reassembly
011	37	Centering the Jet
012	38	Float Level
013	38	Tuning & Synchronizing
014	39	HD Type Throttle Linkage Setting
015	40	Air Cleaners

THE AUXILIARY CARBURETTER

016	40	Description & Operation
017	40	Adjustment
018	40	Thermostatic Switch Removal & Reassembly
019	40	Modifications by Engine Number & Model
020	41	Fault Diagnosis Chart

FUEL SYSTEM & CARBURETTERS
Basic Diagnostic Testing & Troubleshooting

The fuel system furnishes a combustible air-fuel mixture to each cylinder. Failure of the fuel system to function properly can result in various complaints: hard starting, poor performance, and excessive fuel consumption.

1 Hard starting

An engine may not start because of either too much or not enough fuel in the combustion chamber. Too much fuel can be caused by percolation or overchoking. Insufficient fuel may be the result of a defective fuel pump, a restricted line, a porous flexible line, a plugged gas tank vent, or an empty gas tank.

2 Poor performance

Loss of power, resulting from defects in the fuel system, is due to an air-fuel mixture that is either too lean or too rich.

Lean Mixture. The most commonly experienced fuel system trouble is a pause or "flat spot" on acceleration. A lean condition can also produce a feeling of "mushiness" as the throttle is opened gradually; the engine doesn't seem to respond. In severe cases, the engine may backfire through the carburetor.

A lean condition can also result from a weak fuel pump or a restricted gas line. Generally, the engine seems to run out of fuel at a certain road speed when there are defects in the supply line.

Rich Mixture. A rich mixture will also cause a loss of power. Excessive quantities of fuel will not vaporize and burn completely. Liquid fuels wash the lubricant from the cylinder walls, allowing the rings to make metal-to-metal contact. Scuffed rings and excessive oil and fuel consumption result.

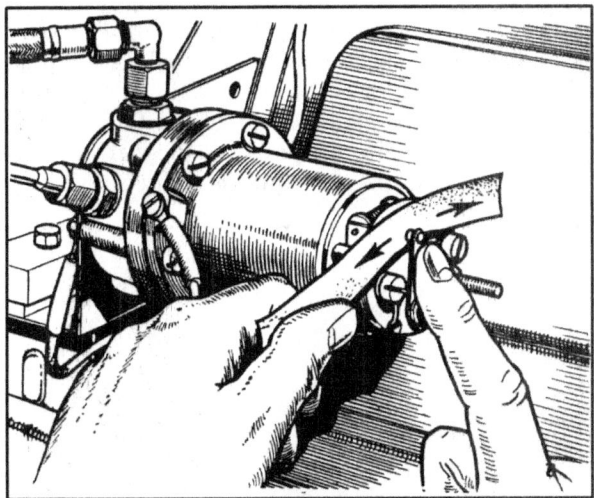

Cleaning the contact points of the electric fuel pump with sandpaper.

A rich mixture may result from high fuel pump pressure which forces the carburetor needle valve off its seat, causing flooding. It also can result from defects in the automatic choke.

3 Fuel pump troubleshooting

A pump in good condition will pump 1 pint (0.57 litre) per minute. If the pump is weak or does not work at all, it can be checked out as follows: (1) Test the battery supply by turning on the ignition switch and checking for current with the wire disconnected from the pump terminal. (2) If there is current at the wire, but the pump does not work, remove the bakelite cover and touch the hot wire to both contact points in turn. If the pump operates with current supplied to the bottom point, but not when it is supplied to the top, then the contact points are dirty. They can be cleaned by passing a sheet of sandpaper through the points while holding them closed. Finish with a piece of cardboard to remove all traces of sand which could hold the points apart. (3) Check to see that the points open and close when the output line from the carburetor to the pump is disconnected. This releases pressure on the output line so that the pump should operate. (4) If the pump operates noisily and rapidly, it is an indication that there is an air leak in the line from the tank. (5) If the pump operates without delivering fuel, one of the valves is not seating. (6) If the pump operates, but works hard and overheats, it is probable that the filter is clogged.

Fuel pump fault diagnosis chart

CAUTION: When bench testing the fuel pump, extinguish all flames in the vicinity and do not allow the cables to spark when making connections.

1. **Not enough fuel**
   1a. Check the level of the fuel in the tank.
   1b. Check the fuse.
   1c. If replacement fuse blows, check for a short circuit in the feed cable or the pump unit.
   1d. If fuse has not blown, locate the cable connectors located in the spare wheel compartment and check the voltage and current available at the terminal ends with the ignition switched ON. The voltage should be 12 volts and the current should not exceed 1.8 amperes.
   1e. If no voltage appears, check for an intermittent connection in the switch, feed, or ground.
   1f. If no current or an excessive current measurement is shown, the pump is defective.
2. **Too much fuel**
   2a. Defective carburetor needle valve.
   2b. Check the output pressure at the carburetor which should be between 2–2.5 psi (0.14–0.17 kg/cm^2).

4 S.U. Carburettor troubleshooting

Each S.U. carburettor has a piston-lifting pin (*arrow*) for checking the fuel-air ratio. To check the mixture, lift the piston about 1/32" with the lifting pin, or with a screwdriver inserted in the air intake port. The engine should speed up momentarily slightly if the mixture is correctly adjusted. If the engine speed increases and continues to run faster, the mixture is too rich. If the engine speed decreases, the mixture is too lean.

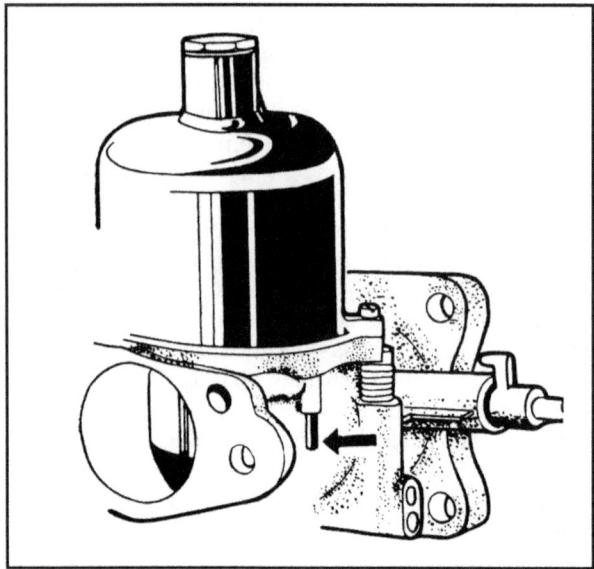

The pin (arrow) lifts the piston for checking the mixture.

S.U. Carburettor fault diagnosis chart

1. **Lean fuel mixture**
   1a. Main jet adjusted too lean
   1b. Wrong air valve spring
   1c. Dirt in main jet
   1d. Too little oil in damper reservoir
   1e. Fuel pump pressure too low
   1f. Needle valve sticking
2. **Flooding**
   2a. Dirt in needle valve and seat
   2b. Defective needle valve and seat
   2c. Heavy float
3. **Sticking piston**
   4a. Dry piston rod
   4b. Dirt between the piston and rod

Troubleshooting hints

PISTON STICKING

The piston rod slides in a bearing in the center of the suction chamber which may gum up and affect carburettor performance. It can be checked by removing the dashpot piston damper, inserting your finger into the air intake, and lifting up the piston. When released, the piston should fall freely onto its seat. If sticking does occur, remove the assembly, clean it, and lubricate the piston rod. *CAUTION: No oil must be used on any other part of the piston assembly.*

WATER OR DIRT

Should a particle of dirt stick between the jet and needle, it can be flushed out by pushing on the float-depressing plunger and flooding the carburettor. If the dirt cannot be flushed out, start the engine, open the throttle wide, and hold your hand over the air intake. If this does not remove the dirt, the carburettor must be disassembled and cleaned.

FLOAT CHAMBER FLOODING

If gasoline flows from the air intake, the needle valve is not seating. Generally, this is due to particles of dirt between the needle and seat. Press on the float-depressing plunger to flood the carburetor which will generally flush out the dirt. Should leaking continue, the needle and seat assembly should be replaced.

FLOAT NEEDLE STICKING

Sometimes the needle will stick to the seat because of gum formation. If the engine stops from lack of fuel, and the fuel pump output is satisfactory with the inlet pipe to the carburettor disconnected, the probable cause is sticking of the needle. Remove the float chamber lid to clean the gum. Be sure to clean the rest of the system to remove all gum or it will occur again.

MIXTURE CONTROL FAILING TO LOCK

On some later models a mixture control, having a radial movement of 90°, is fitted. To ensure proper functioning of the device, it is important that the cable be given an initial twist of one-half turn in a clockwise direction, looking at the end of the cable, before the clamp is tightened.

NOTES

FUEL SYSTEM & CARBURETTERS - SERVICE

1 Description

All models covered by this manual are fitted with SU electric pumps and SU carburetters. Only one type of fuel pump, the LCS model, is used throughout, although on some models such as the Mk VII two pumps are installed with a split fuel tank to provide separate fuel supplies. The Mk VII and XK120 models are fitted with twin H6 type carburetters these being very similar to the twin HD6 type fitted to the Mks VIII, IX and XK140 models and the triple HD8 type fitted to the XK150 models.

Variations are made in the carburetters of each model in the type of needle fitted, this is to take into account the various types of cylinder head and compression ratios which are available for these models. A comprehensive guide to the needles fitted to each model may be found in the **Technical Data** section of the Appendix of this manual.

All of the models are fitted with an auxiliary starting carburetter, on the Mk VII and XK120 models it is an integral part of the rear carburetter float chamber, and on the other models it is a separate unit attached to the front carburetter float chamber. Both types contain the same internal components and they operate in an exactly similar manner.

2 Description and operation of the fuel pump

The electric fuel pump SU type PP31/LCS which consists of three main assemblies, the body, the magnet and the contact breaker is shown in sectional view in **FIG 1**.

The cast aluminium body A houses the inlet and outlet disc valves and the filter. Access to these components is obtained by removing the body lids B and C. The diaphragm J is clamped between the body A and the magnet and coil housing K. This diaphragm J is connected to the armature M and to the contact breaker points via a bronze rod L. This bronze rod passes through the magnet core to the inner and outer rockers T and U. The function of the rockers is to give a 'throw over' movement which opens and closes the contact breaker points very rapidly. The armature M has located between it and the housing K a series of spherical ended rollers R to hold it central and provide free lateral movement of the armature. The magnet consists of the cast iron housing K in which the magnet core is fitted with a surrounding insulated copper wire coil.

The contact breaker assembly consists of a small bakelite moulding S carrying the two rockers T and U. The outer rocker is fitted with a tungsten point on a spring blade V which is electrically connected to one end of the magnet coil. The other end of magnet coil is connected to the terminal W. A short length of wire joins the outer rocker to earth via the bakelite housing screw.

The fuel pump operates in the following manner. With the contact breaker points touching current passes through the magnet coil and thus attracts the magnet core. The movement of the core causes the diaphragm to be pulled back sucking petrol through the inlet valve. Towards the end of the diaphragm stroke the 'throw over' rocker mechanism operates and opens the contact points thus breaking the current flow. Due to the break in current the magnetic attraction of the core stops and the core is returned to its original position under the action of the spring. The diaphragm which is connected to the core thus forces the petrol out through the outlet valve at the

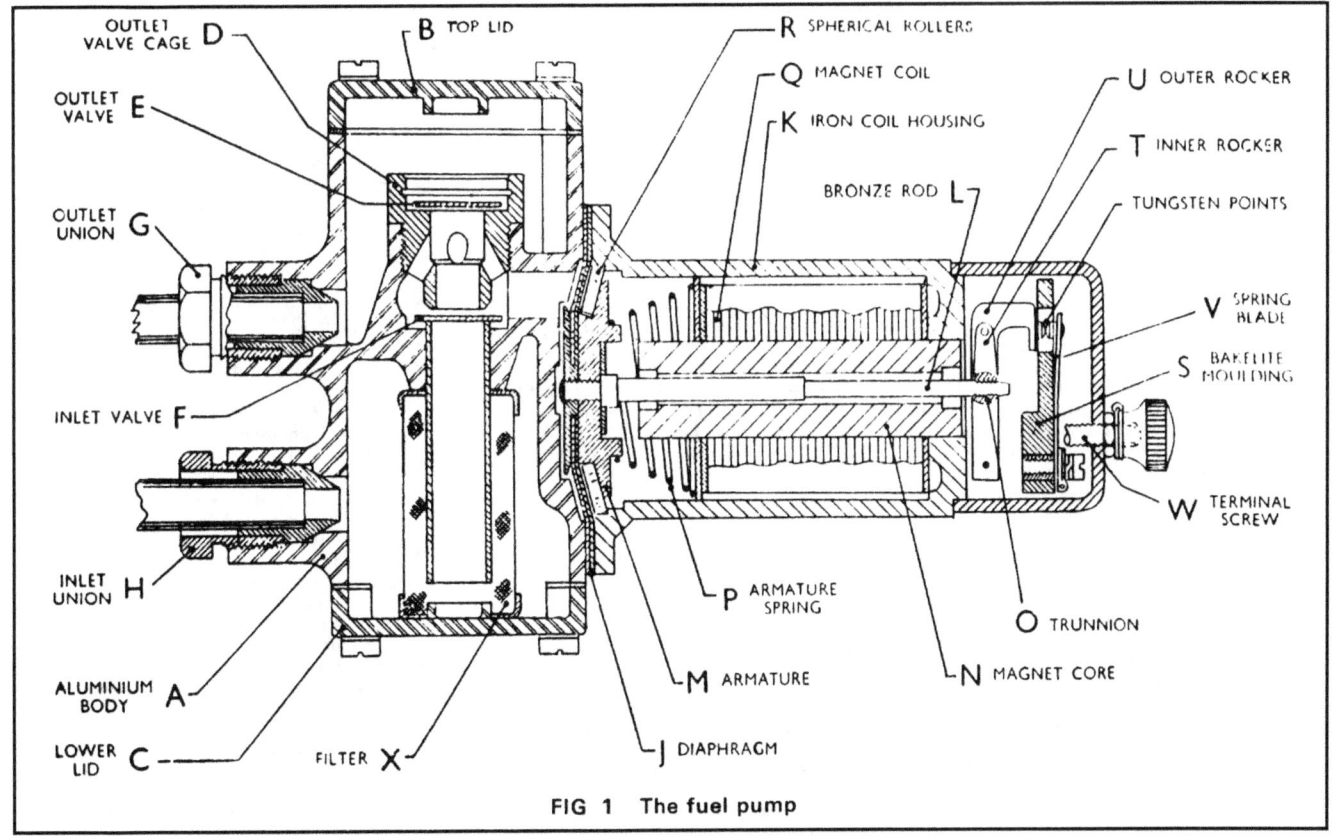

FIG 1 The fuel pump

same time shutting off the inlet valve. The 'throw over' mechanism again operates towards the end of this return stroke to close the contact points and the whole operating cycle begins again.

3 Routine maintenance

The normal maintenance of the SU LCS type pump consists of cleaning the pump filter and checking that the contact breaker points are clean and correctly adjusted.

Before attempting to remove the filter the inlet union to the pump should be disconnected and connected to a length of rubber hose the other end of which should be held at a higher level than the petrol tank. This procedure is necessary to prevent draining the petrol tank which is at a higher level than that of the pump. With the inlet pipe thus removed, remove the 2 BA screws securing the lower lid C (see **FIG 1**) to the pump body and remove the lid and filter. The filter should be washed thoroughly in petrol and blown through to ensure that all the sediment has been removed. **Rag should never be used on this filter.** Clean the lower lid C and remove all traces of sediment. Replace the filter and lid C ensuring that a new gasket is fitted between the lid and pump body. Reconnect the inlet pipe at the pipe union.

The contact breaker points may be cleaned after removing the bakelite cover by placing a thin piece of card or clean paper between the contacts and pulling it backwards and forwards.

To check the contact breaker gap the spring blade V should be held in contact with the moulding S and a feeler gauge placed between the white fibre rollers on the outer rocker and the pump body. The clearance should be .030 inch. To adjust the contact breaker assembly the outer rocker should be pressed to coil housing in this position the contact blade V should just rest on the small ledge projecting from the main face of the bakelite pedestal. If it does not slacken the attachment screw of the spring blade, swing the blade clear of the pedestal and then bend it down slightly so that when repositioned it rests lightly on the ledge. Check that the original clearance of .030 inch between the outer rocker rollers and the pump body is maintained. If this clearance has not been achieved repeat the procedure until it does.

4 Removal and dismantling

Removal:

Since the petrol pump is below the petrol tank level the following procedure should be carried out to prevent drainage of the tank. Disconnect the delivery pipe union and attach it to a length of rubber hose as soon as it is detached from the pump body. The other end of the rubber hose should be held at a higher level than that of the petrol tank.

Disconnect the upper or delivery pipe at the pump union, disconnect the electrical connections at the terminal and the bakelite housing, disconnect the earth wire. Remove the two securing nuts and withdraw the pump.

Dismantling:

Unscrew the screws securing the lower lid C (see **FIG 1**) and remove the lid, gasket and filter. Loosen the outlet valve cage D and remove, remove the inlet valve disc by pushing up from below. The outlet valve disc is removed from the cage D by carefully extracting the circlip retaining it.

Unscrew the six screws holding the two main pump components together and separate them carefully to avoid damaging the diaphragm. Over the bench ease the edge of the diaphragm away from the coil housing and unscrew it. The armature spring P will push the diaphragm from the body and as this occurs the eleven brass rollers R will be released. Care should be taken to ensure that none of the rollers are mislaid. Remove the diaphragm and spindle, the rollers and the armature spring.

Remove the terminal connection W and lift off the contact breaker cover. Unscrew the spring blade securing screw and remove with the spring blade and coil connection. Unscrew the lower nut of the terminal screw and cut away the flattened lead washer below it and remove the coil connection. Unscrew the two screws securing the bakelite pedestal S and disconnect the earth lead to the outer rocker. Push out the steel pin and remove the rocker assembly complete. **Do not attempt to dismantle the rocker assembly further.**

FIG 2 The H6 type carburetter

1—Carburetter—front complete.
2—Carburetter—rear complete.
3—Needle—jet.
4—Screw—locking jet needle.
5—Disc (butterfly).
6—Spindle—throttle, for front carburetter.
7—Spindle—throttle, for rear carburetter.
8—Stop on throttle spindles.
9—Screw—adjusting throttle stops.
10—Spring—locking adjusting screws.
11—Lever on throttle spindles.
12—Body—front carburetter.
13—Body—rear carburetter.
14—Vacuum pipe union—ignition.
15—Float chamber—front carburetter.
16—Float chamber—rear carburetter.
17—Float chamber cover.
18—Cover gasket.
19—Capnut for 17.
20—Washer (plain) for 19.
21—Washer (serrated) for 19.
22—Banjo bolt—fuel pipe.
23—Fibre washer for 22.
24—Float.
25—Needle and seat.
26—Float lever.
27—Pin for 26.
28—Fuel filter gauze.
29—Suction chamber (with piston).
30—Piston return spring.
31—Thrust washer for 30.
32—Screw (long) securing suction chamber.
33—Screw (short) securing suction chamber.
34—Piston damper (complete).
35—Fibre washer for 34.
36—Jet and head unit.
37—Adjusting screw for jet and head unit.
38—Jet sealing ring (brass).
39—Jet sealing ring (cork).
40—Jet gland washer (plastic).
41—Jet gland washer (brass).
42—Jet gland spring.
43—Jet bearing (top half).
44—Jet bearing (bottom half).
45—Washer (copper) for 43.
46—Washer (copper) for 44.
47—Nut securing jet assembly.
48—Cap nut on bottom bearing 44.
49—Bolt securing float chamber to body.
50—Washer (aluminium) for 49.
51—Washer (fibre) for 49.
52—Carburetter solenoid (complete).
53—Plunger and valve.
54—Return spring for 53.
55—Circlip (half-round).
56—Circlip (wire) securing solenoid to carburetter.
57—Carburetter thermostat jet.
58—Washer (fibre) on 57.
59—Auxiliary starting needle (with bridge piece and compression spring).
60—Compression spring.
61—Screws securing needle.
62—Spring washers for 61.
63—Spring finger locating adjusting screw.
64—Shaft coupling front and rear carburetters.
65—Adaptor for 64.
66—Flexible coupling on rear carburetter.
67—Connecting shaft—flexible coupling to scuttle bracket.
68—Lever on 67.
69—Ball-pin in 68.
70—Gasket—carburetter flange to cylinder head.
71—Front carburetter overflow pipe.
72—Rear carburetter overflow pipe.
73—Feed pipe—carburetter to flexible pipe.
74—Flexible pipe assembly.
75—Starting pipe.

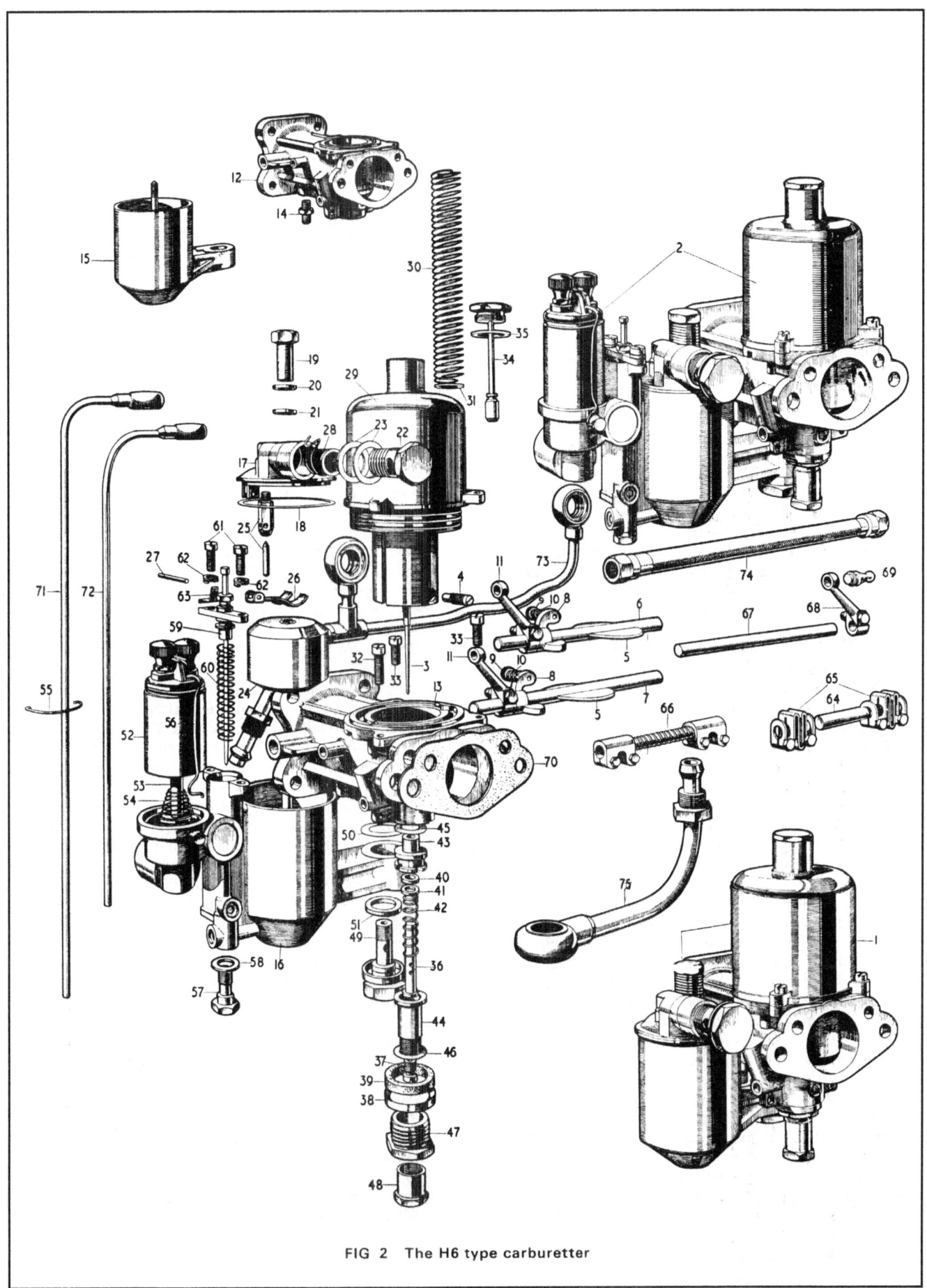

FIG 2 The H6 type carburetter

5 Examination and reassembly

Examination:

Clean all of the pump components by washing in petrol to remove all traces of sediment. Inspect for cracks, damaged joint faces and threads. Examine the valve seats and disc valves for signs of pitting and renew if necessary. If the valve seats are pitted the pump body will require renewal as they are an integral part of it.

Inspect the contact breaker points for burning or pitting any severe signs of either of these faults will mean the replacement of the complete rocker assembly and blade.

Carefully examine the diaphragm for cracking and undue stiffness. Deterioration is usually shown up by external leakage of petrol or a tendency for the pump to operate very rapidly. If the diaphragm is found to be defective it must be renewed as a unit with the spindle L (see **FIG 1**).

Reassembly:

Reassembly is largely a reversal of dismantling but some care should be taken with the following assemblies.

When refitting the disc valves ensure that the smooth side is placed downwards onto the valve seat or leakage is liable to occur. Care should be taken when fitting the outlet valve disc retaining circlip not to damage or distort it as it may prevent the correct clearance being available to the valve.

Reassembly of the rocker mechanism entails the refitting of the steel hinge pin if this is worn replace it with the correct component as it is case-hardened, a piece of wire of the same diameter is no good as a substitute.

To reassemble or renew the diaphragm with its associated spindle proceed as below.

Swing to one side the spring blade V (see **FIG 1**). Fit the armature spring with its larger diameter towards the coil and the smaller towards the armature taking care not to stretch the spring. Feed the armature spindle into the magnet housing K and as it meets the threaded centre of the rocker assembly, screw it clockwise. Hold the pump with the rocker end downwards and refit the eleven rollers in their recess. This operation is facilitated by peeling back the diaphragm edge. Turn the assembly into the horizontal plane and continue screwing clockwise until the rocker will not throw over, but do not jam the armature. Push the diaphragm firmly in without jerking it and unscrew the diaphragm and spindle a little at a time between pushing and releasing until the rocker can just throw over. The diaphragm should then be unscrewed a further two-thirds of a turn and then aligned with the holes in the housing flange. Note that when a new diaphragm is fitted considerable pressure will probably be required to push the armature right home. Replace the spring blade over the contact point. The pump chamber body may then be placed in position aligned to the magnet body, check that the rollers are still in their correct position, then screw the six flange screws into position and tighten them finger tight. Do not use jointing compound on the diaphragm. The screws should only be tightened with the diaphragm in the stretched condition. This condition is obtained by lightly holding the contact breaker points together so that they do not separate and connecting a lead from the bakelite pedestal terminal to a battery. Touch another lead from the battery to the pump body to complete the circuit and magnetize the coil. This will extend the diaphragm to the full suction position and when held thus, the six flange screws should be tightened evenly. It is best to have assistance to carry out this procedure as current should not pass through the coil for too long. However it is possible to carry out the work single handed as the points may be held in the closed position by inserting a matchstick under a fibre roller on the outer rocker. Alternatively the diaphragm may be stretched with the aid of a wedged tool inserted under the rocker trunnion, this method does not require the coil to be energized.

6 Testing the pump

The pump can be tested on the bench by running it from a battery and connecting flexible tubing to the inlet and outlet unions, the tubes leading out of a good-sized jar and back into it.

The pump should prime without any trouble, any air bubbles in the fuel should cease after a few strokes. It should operate steadily with full long delivery strokes, the stroke should be as long as possible with the 'throw over' action occuring. The pump should hold its charge of petrol for several seconds if it does not the valves are probably not seating correctly.

If the pump is noisy and operates too rapidly a worn diaphragm or an air leak is probable. An air leak will be indicated by a continuous stream of air bubbles in the jar.

If the pump is to be tested in the car check that all pipe unions are tightened correctly and that there are no leaks. It is also a wise precaution to disconnect the pipes at the pump end and at the carburetter float chamber union. Then by connecting a foot pump to the lines blow them through to remove any blockage or sediment in the pipes.

In the event of any trouble, firstly disconnect the petrol delivery pipe at the carburetters, if the pump then operates the most likely fault is a sticking float chamber needle. This should be removed and cleaned as described in **Section 8**. Should the pump not operate disconnect the lead from the terminal and strike it against the pump body, if it sparks current is available. If there is no spark check the electrical circuit. With current available remove the bakelite cover and strike the terminal with the lead, if there is no sparking and the contacts are touching they may require cleaning. If the contacts are open check that the 'throw over' mechanism is operating correctly.

With the pump running in the car, if it is found to be noisy a similar test for air leaks may be carried out as that done on the bench. Connect a flexible hose to the delivery side of the pump and place the other end in a glass jar. Run the pump and observe the jar to see if air bubbles are produced, if they are, rectify the leak which will probably be on the suction side.

If the pump operates but does not supply petrol it is possible that one of the valves is being held open. In this case remove the valve lids, clean the disc valves and replace them smooth side downwards to their seats.

A blocked filter in the pump or an obstruction on the suction side will cause the pump to overheat and will eventually leads to pump failure.

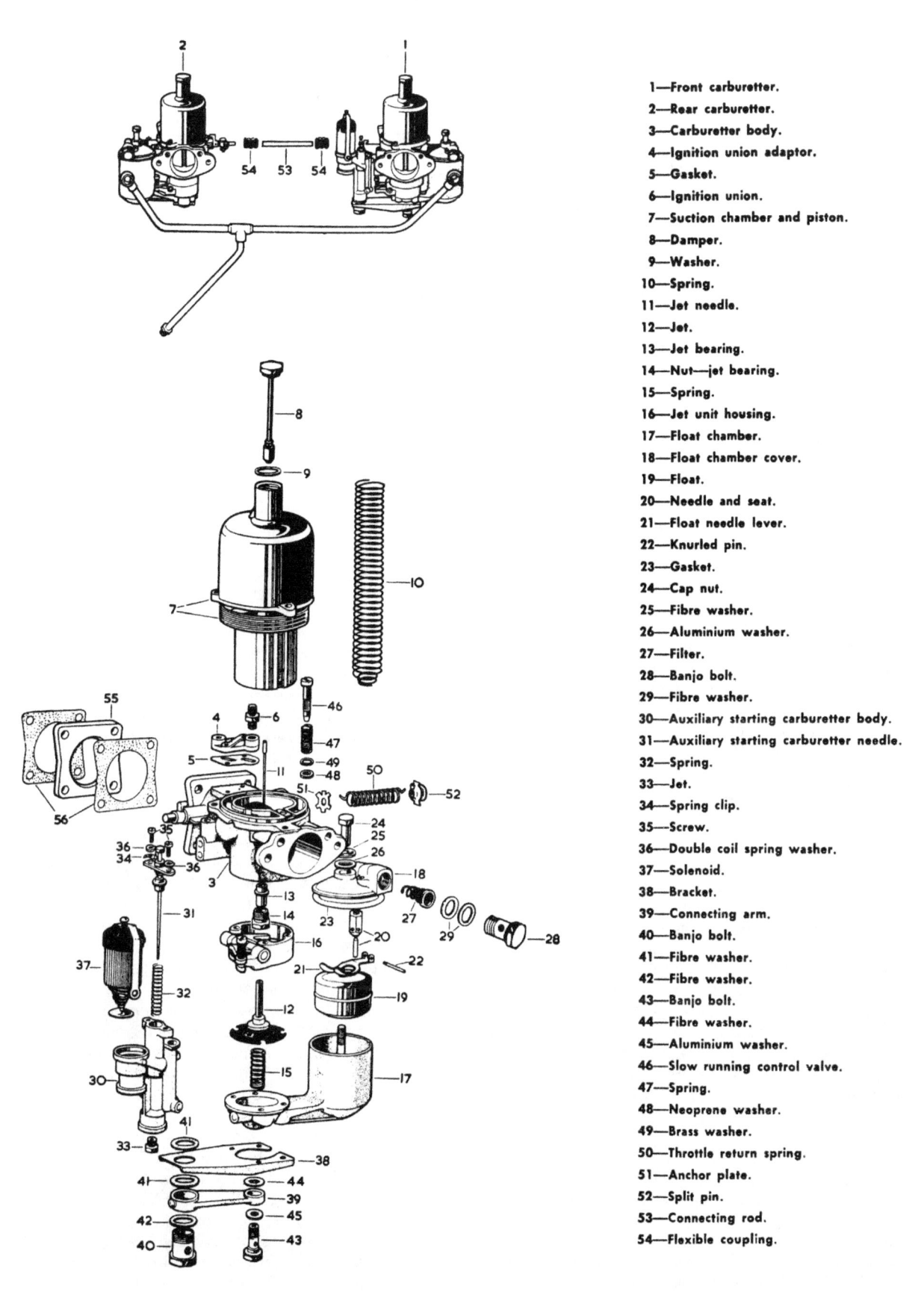

FIG 3 The HD6 type carburetter

THE CARBURETTERS

7 Description and operation

There are three types of carburetters fitted to the models covered by this manual the H6, HD6 and HD8 all are of SU manufacture. The H6 type as fitted to the XK120 and Mk VII models is an earlier type than the HD6 and 8 which are fitted to the remaining models. The HD6 and HD8 models differ basically only in their bore diameters.

The main differences between the H6 and the HD6 types are as follows. The jet glands on the H6 model are replaced by a flexible diaphragm connected to the jet on the HD6 model. The idling mixture is controlled by the throttle disc on the H6 model whereas the HD6 has a separate passage way with a metering screw.

The type of carburetter with the corresponding needle sizes is given in detail in the **Technical Data** section of the Appendix to this manual.

The operation of all three types of carburetters are identical and their action is as follows.

The area of the air intake and the orifice of the fuel jet are automatically varied by means of a sliding piston to which is attached a tapered jet needle. The piston is raised and lowered by variations governed by engine speed and throttle butterfly opening. This depression operates on the piston through a drilling passing from the atmosphere side of the throttle butterfly through the body of the carburetter and dashpot to the top of the piston. When the piston is raised, a larger area is available for the entry of air, and also, since the tapered needle rises with the piston, more fuel is allowed to pass through the jet. The piston and tapered needle in conjunction with the jet are proportioned to provide the correct mixture at all speeds and loads. To prevent too rapid movement in the piston and to smooth out rapid fluctuations in depression a damper is fitted in the top of the piston.

An exploded drawing of the H6 carburetter is shown in **FIG 2** and that of the HD6 is shown in **FIG 3**.

8 Routine maintenance

Routine maintenance is confined to cleaning the petrol filters, checking that the auxiliary starting carburetter electrical connections are clean and tight, and that the piston dampers are topped up with the correct grade of oil.

The petrol filters on all models except the XK150 types are located in the float chamber covers and are withdrawn on removal of the banjo bolts. They should be cleaned with petrol to remove all sediment but under no circumstances should rag be used. The XK150 models have a glass bowl type filter with a flat gauze filter inside. The filter is located between the centre and rear carburetters. With this type of filter the gauze element should be cleaned every 5000 miles or more frequently if the bowl shows signs of becoming full of sediment. To do this slacken the locking nut, swing the retaining clip to one side and remove the bowl, sealing washer and filter gauze. Clean the gauze and bowl by washing in petrol. Examine the sealing washer and renew if necessary.

To top up the hydraulic dampers unscrew the caps on top of the dash-pots and top up with SAE30 oil until the hollow piston spindle is filled. Replace caps. The correct grade of oil must be used or difficulties will arise when sudden changes in throttle control are required. If the oil is too thin or there is a lack of it, the piston will not be damped sufficiently this will cause weakness of the mixture on snap throttle openings. Too thick an oil will over-damp the piston and give a slow response to throttle changes.

Occasionally the carburetters should be removed and dismantled for thorough cleaning. In view of the fine tolerances to which the working parts are machined, metal polish or other abrasives must under no circumstances be used to clean these working parts.

9 Removal and dismantling

Removal:

Remove the air silencer. On the Mk VII model remove the two bolts holding the air silencer manifold to the carburetter flanges and remove the manifold. On the XK120 model (super sports) withdraw the four bolts securing the air cleaners to the carburetter flanges and remove the air cleaners. On the remaining models remove the air intake pipe by unscrewing the setscrews to the carburetter flanges. Remove the banjo bolts securing the petrol supply pipes to the float chamber covers. On all models except the XK150 types remove the inlet gauze filters and retaining springs. Disconnect the throttle linkage at the rear flexible connection and remove the throttle return spring (if fitted).

Disconnect the distributor vacuum pipe from the front carburetter. Remove the cover on the auxiliary carburetter and disconnect both electrical leads. Unscrew the auxiliary carburetter feed pipe union from the inlet manifold. Remove the clip attaching the overflow pipes from the float chambers to the oil filter mounting setscrews. Unscrew the eight carburetter flange nuts and remove them with their spring washers. Withdraw the carburetters and disconnect the butterfly valve interconnections to separate the carburetters.

Refitting is the reverse of the removal procedure care being taken, to renew carburetter manifold and flange gaskets, and to replace the filters in the float chamber covers.

Dismantling H6 type:

Unscrew the dampers 34 (see **FIG 2**) on top of the dashpots. Withdraw the three screws 32, 33 securing the dashpot 29 to the carburetter body 12 and lift out dashpot and piston carefully to avoid damaging the needle 3. Remove the screw at the base of the piston and remove the needle. Unscrew the hexagon nut 49 under the carburetter body retaining the float chamber 16 and remove nut and float chamber.

Remove the overflow pipe 71 and withdraw the float chamber cover 17 with its gasket 18. Dismantle the float chamber needle assembly situated in the cover 17 by removing the pin 27 and withdrawing the float lever 26. The needle and seat 25 may now be unscrewed from the float chamber cover. Lift out the float 24 from the chamber.

To dismantle the jet assembly remove the bottom cap nut 48 followed by the jet screw 37 and jet securing nut 47. The jet 36 may now be removed together with the top and bottom bearings 43 and 44. Note the relationship of the plastic 40, cork 39, copper 45, 46 and brass 38, 41 washers and the jet spring 42. See **FIG 9** (auxiliary carburetter) and release the auxiliary carburetter solenoid clips and remove the solenoid 5 with its core plunger 4, valve 3 and spring. Unscrew the two setscrews and withdraw the auxiliary carburetter jet needle assembly and spring 10.

Dismantling HD6, HD8 types:

Refer to **FIG 3**.

Unscrew the cap 8 on top of the dashpot 7, withdraw the three securing screws holding the dashpot to the carburetter body 3 and lift out dashpot, piston and spring 10. This should be carried out carefully to avoid damaging the needle 11. Remove the screw at the base of the piston and remove the needle.

On the front carburetter remove the banjo bolts, 40 and 43, securing the connecting arm 39 between the auxiliary carburetter and the main carburetter. Remove the auxiliary carburetter. Remove the two setscrews 35 and lift out the auxiliary carburetter needle assembly and spring. Withdraw the cap nut 24 in the float chamber cover and remove the overflow pipes, cover 18 and gasket 23. The needle valve 20 may be removed from the float chamber cover after removing the knurled pin 22 to release the float lever 21.

Remove the four setscrews securing the float chamber to the carburetter body, separate carefully the float chamber 17, pump body 3 and jet housing 16. Remove the jet 12 and its spring 15. The jet bearing is removed after releasing the locknut 14.

10 Servicing and reassembly

Wash all components thoroughly in petrol and remove all traces of sediment in the float chamber bowls. In the case of the HD type carburetters also ensure that all sediment is cleaned from the bowl at the bottom of the carburetters attached to the float chambers.

Examine the jet springs and ensure that they are in good order, renew if in any doubt.

Inspect the needles and jets for any signs of scoring and renew if necessary, the needle size is stamped on the side or top face of the parallel portion of the needle.

It is worthwhile mentioning at this stage that as twin (or triple) carburetters are fitted that a great deal of trouble in synchronizing of the carburetters may be avoided by observing the following. If it is found necessary to replace a working component such as a jet or jet needle in one carburetter renew this item in both (or all three) carburetters as renewing only the one may cause serious unbalance between the carburetters.

Check the fit of the piston in the dashpot in the following manner. Hold the piston upside down in the right hand with a finger covering the small air hole (see **FIG 4**). With the left hand push the dashpot onto the piston as far as it will go. When the left hand is removed the dashpot will fall until clear of the piston; the time taken for this fall should be between four and five seconds.

Reassembly is the reverse of the dismantling procedure except for the centring of the jet which is covered in the following section. When assembling it is essential to fit new gaskets to prevent any air or petrol leakage which will seriously effect the carburetter performance. On refitting the jet needle ensure that the shoulder on the needle is positioned flush with the lower face of the piston.

11 Centring the jet

This operation is always necessary if the jet bearing screw or locknut is loosened or removed, or if a new needle is fitted. It is also the possible cure for a sticking piston. If the damper is removed and the piston lifted with a pencil it should fall freely and hit the jet bridge smartly. If it does not, and cleaning of the piston and dashpot does not cure the trouble, then centring the jet will almost certainly succeed.

H6 type carburetter

Centring the jet on this type of carburetter as fitted to the Mk VII and XK120 models may be carried out with the carburetters fitted in the car after removal of the air cleaners.

Remove the cap nuts at the base of the jet and rotate the jet adjusting screw upwards as far as it will go to position the jet at its highest point. Ensure that the jet parts are assembled in the correct position and release the jet securing nut.

Unscrew the cap and remove the hydraulic piston damper. Raise and lower the piston to centralize the jet with the jet needle and finally tighten the securing nut. It may be necessary to slacken the jet securing nut several times before the piston is found to fall freely. When the jet has been centred correctly bring the jet adjusting screw back to its original position and fit the cap nut.

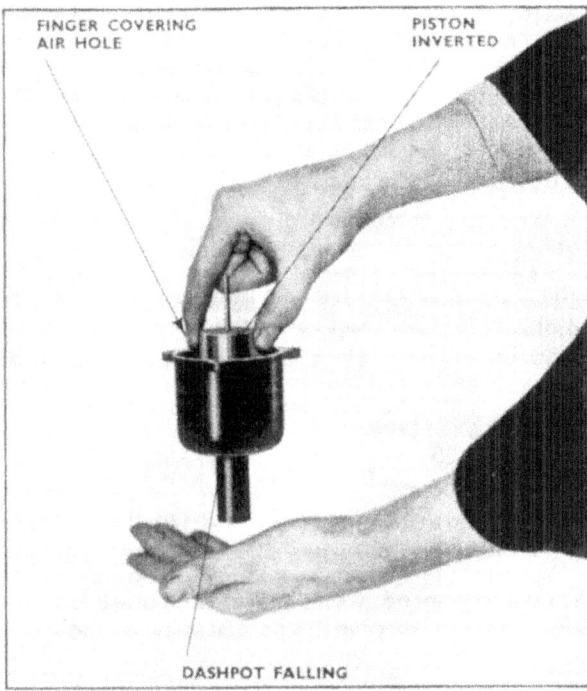

FIG 4 Checking the piston fit

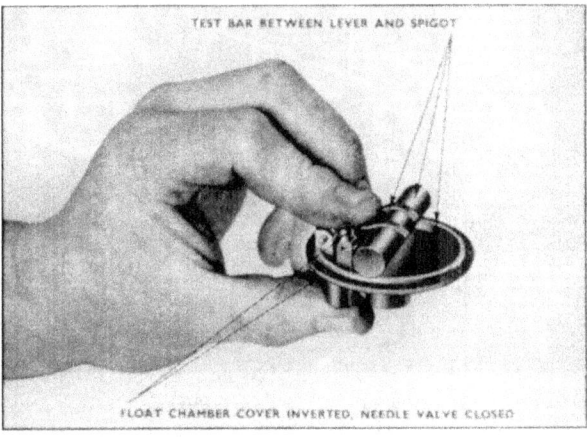

FIG 5 Checking the petrol level

HD type carburetters

Remove the carburetter from the engine as discribed earlier in this chapter.

Remove the four setscrews securing the float chamber to the carburetter body. Remove the float chamber, jet housing and jet. Unscrew and withdraw the hydraulic damper. With a ring spanner slacken the jet locking nut approximately half a flat then replace the jet and diaphragm assembly.

To centre the jet push the jet and diaphragm assembly as high as possible with the hand and with a pencil gently press the piston down on to the jet bridge. Centralization will be facilitated if the side of the carburetter body is tapped lightly. Tighten the jet locking nut.

The centring must be carried out with the setscrew holes in the jet diaphragm and carburetter in alignment. After tightening the jet locking nut the jet diaphragm must be kept in the same position relative to the carburetter body. The simplest way to ensure this is to mark one of corresponding holes in the diaphragm and carburetter body with a soft pencil.

Check that the centralization is correct by noting if there is any difference in the sound of the piston hitting the jet bridge with the piston being released from its highest and lowest positions. If there is a difference in sound then the foregoing procedure will need to be repeated.

If difficulty is encountered in centring the jet, the needle may be lowered in the piston to make centralizing easier. However the needle must be restored to its correct position when checking the centring.

12 Float level

The level of fuel in the float chamber and, therefore the level in the jet is controlled by the angle to which the forked float lever is set.

To check and reset the float level remove the float chamber cover and holding this inverted press the forked float lever downwards with the finger above the hinged end, thus ensuring that the needle valve is in the closed position. If the petrol level is correct a round test bar will just slide between the lever and the spigot on the cover (see **FIG 5**). The test bar should be $\frac{1}{2}$ inch dia. for the H6 type of carburetter and $\frac{7}{16}$ inch for the HD types.

If the float lever fails to conform to this value, it must be carefully bent at the start of the fork section in the correct direction. Take care to keep both prongs of the fork level with each other and maintain the straight portion of the lever dead flat.

It is not advisable to alter the fuel level unless there is trouble with flooding which cannot be traced to any other fault such as a stuck needle valve or punctured float.

13 Tuning and synchronizing

It is useless to attempt carburetter tuning until the cylinder compressions, valve clearances, spark plug gaps and contact breaker point gaps have been tested, checked and adjusted if necessary. The distributor centrifugal advance mechanism and vacuum advance operation should be checked and the ignition timing set to the correct figure.

Only two adjustments are provided at the carburetters see **FIGS 6** and **7**. (1) the slow running or throttle adjusting screw A, which governs the idling speed and (2) the jet adjusting screw B (**FIGS 6** and **7**), which is used to adjust the mixture strength. Correct setting of the mixture strength at idling speed ensures that the carburetters are correctly adjusted throughout their entire range.

Ensure that the needles are correctly located in the pistons, that is with the shoulder of the needles flush with the lower face of the pistons. Check that the pistons are free in the dashpots, the petrol filters are clean and that the hydraulic dampers are topped up with the correct grade of oil. Lubricate the throttle linkage and check for free operation and full travel.

Before carrying out the instructions which follow, it is desirable to ensure that the mixture strength of both carburetters is correct. To do this on the HD types screw out both mixture screws B until the tops of the jets are flush with the jet bridge in each carburetter body; this can be observed through the piston chamber after removing the piston and dashpot. Then screw in the mixture screws until the jets start to move and then rotate the screws a further $3\frac{1}{2}$ turns.

To ensure that the mixture strength on the H6 carburetters is approximately correct, screw the jet adjusting screws clockwise as far as they will go and then unscrew then $2\frac{1}{2}$ turns, ensuring that the jets are not sticking and are following the movement of the adjusting screws.

On the HD types of carburetter slacken one clamp bolt on the coupling between the throttle spindles and check that both butterfly valves are fully closed by rotating both throttle spindles clockwise when viewed from the front.

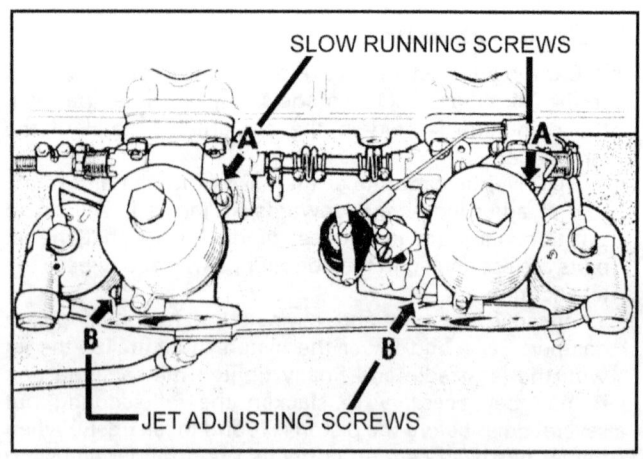

FIG 6   Carburetter adjustment HD type

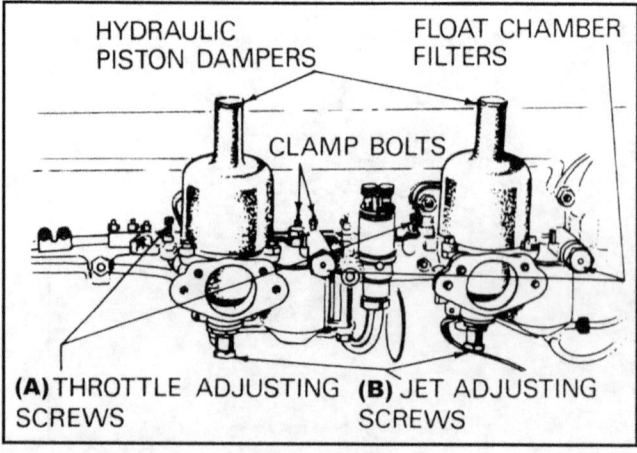

FIG 7   Carburetter adjustment H6 type

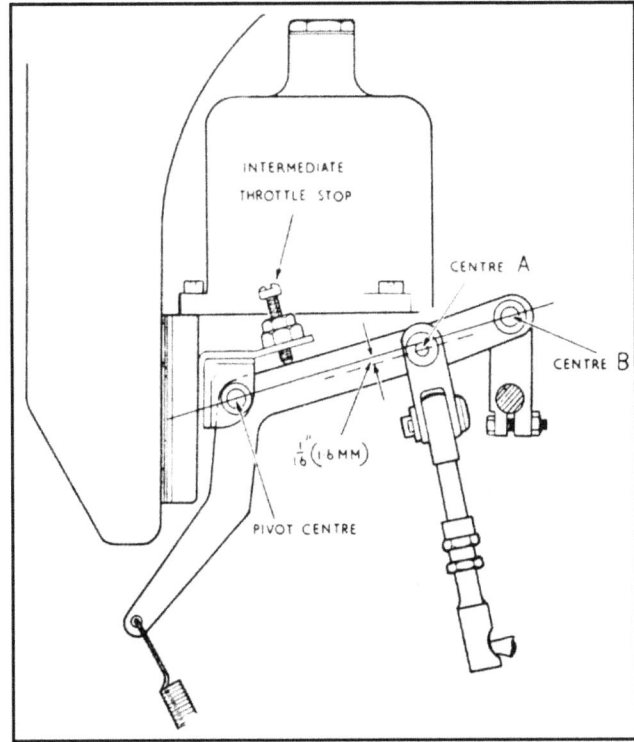

FIG 8 Throttle linkage setting

Screw in the slow running volume screws A (see **FIG 6**) until they are down fully on their seatings then unscrew them 2½ turns.

Start the engine and run until the normal operating temperature is reached.

Then by placing a piece of rubber tube in the intake of the carburetter with the other end in the ear check that each carburetter is sucking the same amount of air as the other. This can be judged by the relative levels of the hissing of the intake air. If they are not the same adjust the slow-running screws (after slackening the clamp bolt on the throttle spindles H6 type) to give the same air intake at about 500 rev/min engine speed. Tighten the clamp bolt on the throttle spindles H6 type.

The mixture strength may be checked with the engine running and by lifting the piston pin of the front carburetter the piston, $\frac{1}{32}$ inch HD type, $\frac{1}{4}$ inch H6 type when if:
1. The engine speed increases and the engine continues to run at increased speed, this indicates that the mixture strength of the front carburetter is too rich.
2. The engine speed decreases. This indicates that the front carburetter mixture strength is too weak.
3. The engine speed increases momentarily then returns to its original speed the mixture is correct on the front carburetter.

Repeat the above operation on the rear carburetter to test its mixture strength and after adjustment recheck the front carburetter since the two carburetters are interdependent.

To enrich the mixture on the HD type carburetters screw the adjusting screw in clockwise, to weaken screw the screw anticlockwise.

On the H6 carburetters the mixture is enriched by removing the dome nut covering the jet and screwing the jet adjusting screw in an anticlockwise manner. To

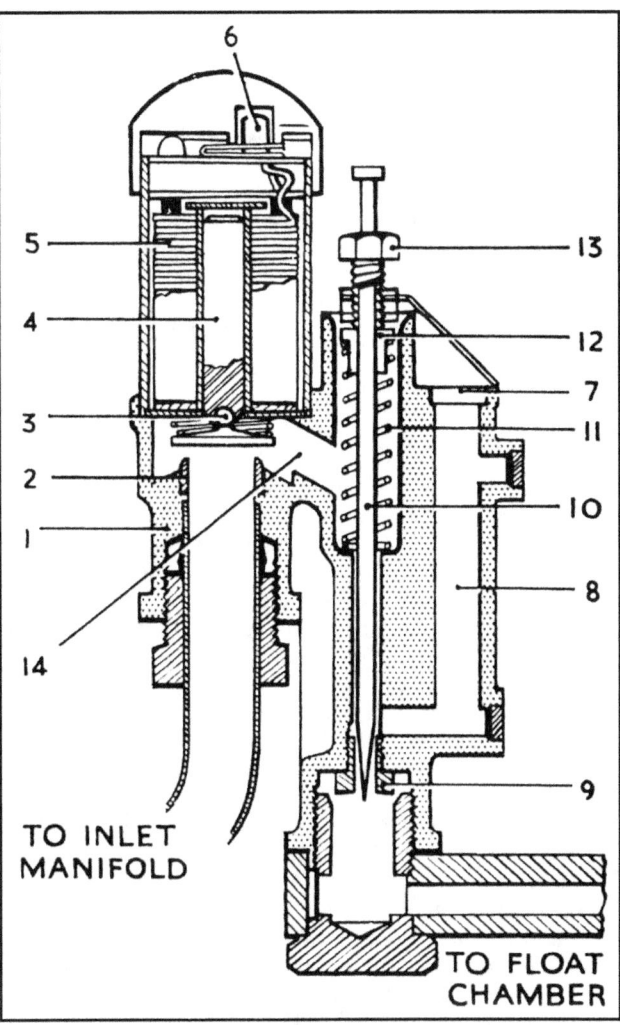

FIG 9 Auxiliary carburetter

Key to Fig 9
1 Main body casting
2 Valve seating
3 Valve
4 Solenoid core plunger
5 Solenoid
6 Solenoid terminal
7 Air intake
8 Air passage
9 Needle jet
10 Needle
11 Compression ring
12 Needle disc
13 Adjusting stop
14 Induction passage

weaken the mixture turn the jet adjusting screw clockwise. Always replace the dome nut after any adjustment.

Some slight adjustment of the slow running to maintain the engine at 500 rev/min may now be necessary following alteration of the mixture strength, in which case ensure that the two slow running screws are each rotated by exactly the same amount or the adjustments previously made will be upset.

It is essential to road test the engine and make final adjustments with the air cleaners fitted.

14 Throttle linkage setting HD types

If the carburetter has been removed or the throttle control linkage has been disturbed, particular attention must be paid to the setting adjustment of the control linkage.

To adjust proceed as follows. Disconnect the front carburetter coupling and rear carburetter throttle lever by releasing the clamp bolts. Check that both butterflies are fully closed and that the rear carburetter coupling bolt is clearing the manifold nut. With both carburetters fully closed, tighten the front coupling.

Unscrew the intermediate throttle stop and push down the bell crank lever until centre A (see **FIG 8**) is $\frac{1}{16}$ inch below a line from centre B to the pivot centre. When in this position screw down the stop onto the intermediate throttle lever and lock in position. Lock the lever to carburetter spindle.

Ensure that when the throttle is closed the intermediate lever does not foul the petrol connection pipe. Open the throttle fully and check that both butterflies are in the fully open position.

15 Air cleaners

There are three types of air cleaner fitted to the various models covered by this manual they are; the paper element, the gauze element and the oil bath air cleaner.
1 The paper element type should be cleaned by holding in the vertical position and tapping the fins after every 5000 miles. This type of element should be renewed every 15000 miles.
2 The wire gauze element type should be removed after every 5000 miles and washed thoroughly in paraffin and allowed to dry. When dry the gauze should be wetted with clean engine oil and replaced. Renewal is only necessary if the element is damaged.
3 The oil bath air cleaner is generally fitted to export or overseas models. This type should be cleaned every 2500 miles or more frequently if the car is used in a very dusty environment. Cleaning is carried out by lifting the filter gauze from the assembly and washing it thoroughly in paraffin. The oil held in the bowl should be poured out and the bowl cleaned before filling with clean oil to the indicated level. Replace the gauze element checking that the gaskets are clean and in good condition.

THE AUXILIARY CARBURETTER

16 Description and operation

On early cars the auxiliary starting carburetter is integral with the float chamber of the rear carburetter. On later models the starter carburetter (see **FIG 9**) is a separate unit attached to the front carburetter but the internal parts and operations are the same.

The main body houses two assemblies, the solenoid and the needle. The solenoid assembly consists of a solenoid coil 5 (see **FIG 9**) with an internal core plunger which is attached by a flexible joint to the valve. The valve is held down on its seat 2 by a spring.

The needle assembly consists of the needle 10 which is able to slide up and down within the main body its movement being controlled by a compression spring 11 which acts on a movable disc 12. The overall movement of the needle is limited by an adjusting screw 13. The tapered portion of the needle moves in and out of a removable jet 9 located in the lower portion of the auxiliary carburetter body.

The auxiliary carburetter is brought into operation by means of a thermal switch situated in the water outlet pipe from the cylinder head. This switch supplies current to the solenoid if it senses a water temperature below 86 to 95°F. With current supplied to the solenoid, the coil is energized and the plunger and valve are lifted away from the valve seat. The inlet manifold is then connected via the induction passage 14 to the needle chamber. The suction from the inlet manifold induces petrol from the float chamber via the jet, and air via the air passage 8, to the engine.

The correct air/petrol mixture is obtained by the taper of the needle 10, the jet size 9 and the suction pressure acting on the jet disc 12 which causes the needle to move up and down.

17 Adjustment

The only adjustment provided consists in setting the stop screw 13 which limits the movement of the needle 10. Screwing this down clockwise weakens, screwing it anticlockwise richens the idling mixture.

Run the engine up to normal working temperature and then bring the auxiliary carburetter into action by short-circuiting the thermostatic switch. A convenient way of doing this is to place a screwdriver in contact with the centre terminal and the body of the switch. Flick open the throttle momentarily to enable the valve 3 to clear the seat 2.

The stop screw should now be adjusted to give the richest mixture consistent with even running.

18 Thermostatic switch removal and refitting

Removal:

The thermostatic switch which controls the operation of the auxiliary starting carburetter is situated at the front end of the inlet manifold water jacket.

Remove the electrical cable from the switch by releasing the dome nut.

If the radiator filler cap is securely tightened, no appreciable amount of water will escape when the thermostatic switch is removed. Alternatively a small amount of water can be drained from the radiator. Remove the three securing setscrews and washers and withdraw the switch and cork gasket.

Refitting:

Refitting is the reverse of the removal procedure. A new cork gasket must be fitted when the switch is replaced. If any water has been drained from the radiator or has escaped during the removal of the switch the radiator should be topped up.

19 Modifications

A change in recommendation to the type of carburetter needle fitted to the XK140 models was made from engine number G.3250. The newly recommended needle W02 (part number C.7858) is fitted to all engines after this number and some individual engines prior to it.

On engines prior to that stated above, if spitting back from the carburetter occurs on full throttle at approximately 2000 rev/min check that the correct thermostat is fitted and that the W02 needle is fitted. If a SL type needle is fitted (part number C.9246) replace with the W02 type.

20 Fault diagnosis

(a) Leakage or insufficient fuel delivered
1 Fuel pipes blocked
2 Air leaks at pipe connections
3 Pump filter blocked
4 Pump gaskets damaged
5 Pump diaphragm defective
6 Pump valves sticking or seating badly
7 Fuel vapourizing in pipelines due to overheating

(b) Excessive fuel consumption
1 Carburetters out of tune
2 Fuel leakage
3 Auxiliary carburetter staying in operation
4 Dirty air cleaner
5 Excessive engine temperature
6 Brakes binding
7 Tyres under inflated
8 Idling speed too high
9 Car overloaded
10 Float chamber needles sticking

(c) Idling speed too high
1 Rich fuel mixture
2 Carburetter controls sticking
3 Slow-running screws incorrectly adjusted
4 Worn carburetter butterfly valve(s)

(d) Noisy fuel pump
1 Loose mountings
2 Air leaks on suction side and at diaphragm
3 Obstruction in fuel pipe
4 Pump filter blocked

(e) No fuel delivery
1 Float needles stuck
2 Electrical connections to pump faulty
3 Pump contact points dirty
4 Pipeline obstructed
5 Pump diaphragm stiff or damaged
6 Inlet valve in pump stuck open
7 Bad air leak on suction side of pump

NOTES

INDEX – IGNITION SYSTEM

SECTION	PAGE	
000	43	Basic Diagnostic Testing & Troubleshooting
001	47	Description
002	47	Routine Maintenance
003	48	Distributor Removal
004	48	Distributor Disassembly
005	49	Distributor Reassembly
006	50	Distributor Installation
007	50	Ignition Timing
008	50	High Tension Leads
009	50	Spark Plugs
010	51	Testing
011	52	Modifications by Engine Number & Model
012	52	Fault Diagnosis Chart

IGNITION
Basic Diagnostic Testing & Troubleshooting

The efficient operation of the ignition system probably has a great deal more to do with the smooth operation of an internal combustion engine than any other mechanical or electrical part. The importance of the ignition system can be realized from the fact that every minute 15,000 sparks are developed and delivered to the spark plugs of an 6-cylinder engine running at high speed. And, that these sparks must be distributed to each of the cylinders when they have been charged with an explosive air-fuel mixture that has been compressed to the point of maximum efficiency. Naturally, any slipup in the chain of events needed to create and time the sparks will result in poor engine performance.

The spark needed to fire the compressed air-fuel mixture is close to 20,000 volts. To step up the battery's 12 volts to the high voltage needed to jump the gaps of the spark plugs is the duty of the ignition coil. This transformer contains a primary and a secondary winding. The primary circuit, operating on the battery voltage, consists of the battery, ignition switch, ignition contact points, condenser, primary winding of the ignition coil, and ballast resistor. The secondary circuit develops the high voltage needed to fire the spark plugs, and it consists of the ignition coil, rotor, distributor cap, high tension wiring, and spark plugs.

The primary circuit contains a set of contact points which interrupts the circuit. The action of interrupting the primary circuit develops the high-tension spark in the secondary circuit. At the same time, the contact-point interruption is precisely timed so as to send the spark to the cylinder at the instant the air-fuel charge has been compressed to the point of maximum efficiency. Naturally, the contact point set must open and close once for each spark delivered, or 15,000 times per minute at top speed. It is no wonder, then, that the contact points require periodic servicing. Without it, they soon deteriorate and cause such troubles as hard starting, misfiring, poor performance, and low fuel mileage.

There is no way to test the performance of the ignition system with accuracy except with precision test equipment. Any other way is subject to error. However, a rough check can be made of the ignition system by road testing the car while placing the engine under a heavy load. Drive the car in high gear at about 6 mph (10 km./h.) on a smooth road; place your left foot lightly on the brake pedal to put a load on the engine. Open the accelerator fully with your right foot. As the engine picks up speed, apply the foot brake to keep the car speed constant at about 25 mph (40 km./h.). Ignition troubles will cause the car to jerk sharply. Defective spark plugs are especially sensitive to such a test.

Two common ignition system troubles, with regard to power losses, are late ignition timing and misfiring cylinders.

Late ignition timing causes overheating and loss of power. It can be detected by too smooth an idle, a deep-sounding exhaust, a low vacuum gauge reading, and a lack of "ping" on acceleration. Misfiring cylinders are characterized by a rough idle, a stuttering exhaust on acceleration, and a jerky vacuum gauge needle.

1 Testing the ignition system

To Test the Primary Circuit (Test 1). Loosen the distributor cap retaining bails and move the cap to one side. Remove the rotor. Turn the engine over by means of the fan belt or starting motor until the contact points close. Turn on the ignition switch. Remove the high tension wire leading to the center of the distributor cap; this is the main wire from the ignition coil which supplies the high voltage to the rotor for distribution to the spark plugs. Hold this wire about ½" (12 mm.) from any metallic part of the engine. Open and close the contact points with a screwdriver. Hold the screwdriver against the movable point only as shown. A good, regularly occurring spark from the high tension wire to ground means a good primary circuit and a good ignition coil. No spark, or a weak erratic one, from the high tension wire to ground means primary circuit trouble or a bad ignition coil.

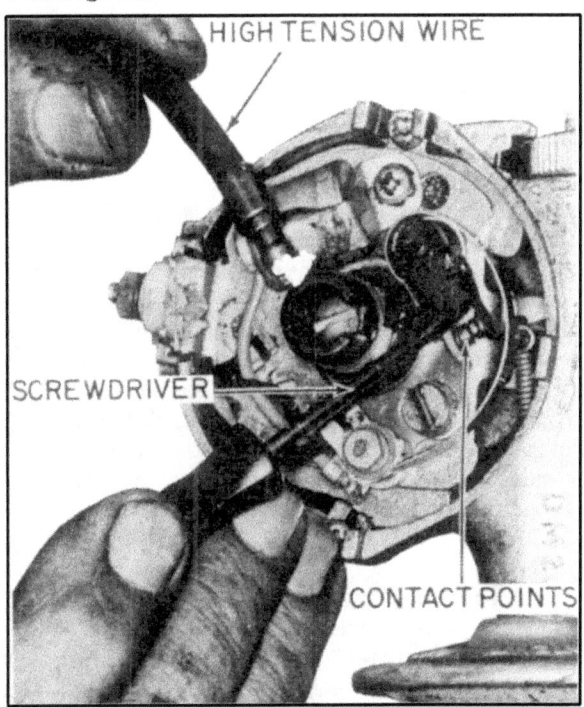

Opening and closing the ignition points with a screwdriver (Test 1), while holding the main high tension wire close to a metallic part of the engine, is a simple test of the primary circuit efficiency.

To Test the Ignition Contact Points (Test 2).
To test the condition of the ignition contact set, turn the engine over with the fan belt or starting motor until the contact points are separated. Slide

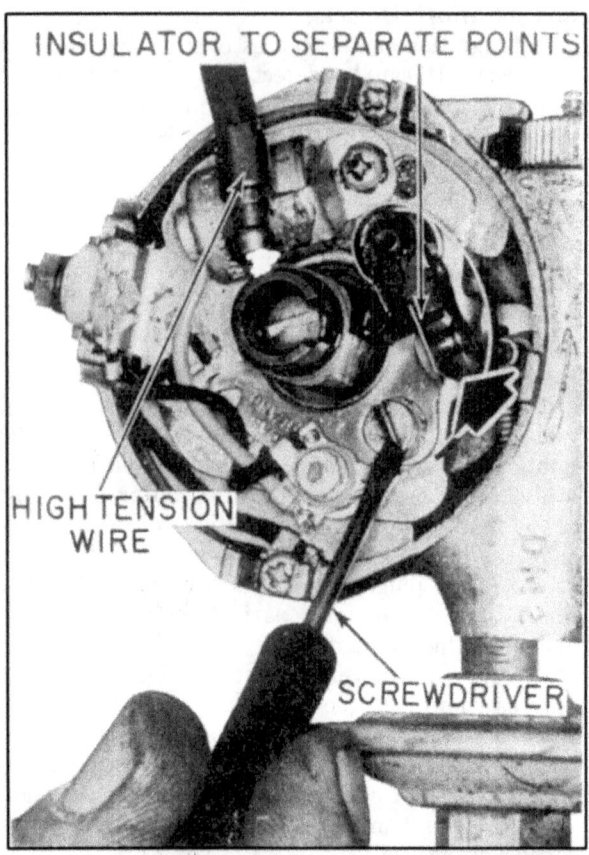

Using the screwdriver as a set of points (Test 2). Use a cleaned insulator (arrow) to keep the points apart, and then slide the screwdriver blade up and down to make intermittent contact with the point plate.

the screwdriver blade up and down, making contact between the movable point and the bottom plate of the distributor, as shown. You are now using the screwdriver tip and the bottom plate of the distributor as a set of contact points. A good spark from the high tension wire to the ground, after having had no spark in Test 1, means that you have a defective set of contact points. No spark, or a weak one, means primary circuit trouble, other than the ignition contact points, or a bad ignition coil.

To Test the Condenser (Test 3). A shorted condenser can be checked by noting, in the previous ignition contact point test (Test 2), whether or not the tip of the screwdriver blade sparked against the ground plate as it was slid up and down. No spark at the tip of the blade means either a shorted condenser or a break in the primary circuit.

This can be checked further by disconnecting the condenser case where it is screwed to the distributor (do not disconnect the condenser wire lead). Hold the condenser so that its case does not make contact with any metallic part of the distributor. Repeat the test of moving the screwdriver blade up and down while holding it against the movable point. Be sure that the contact points are open while making this test. A spark at the screwdriver tip now, which was not present with the condenser in the circuit, means that the condenser is shorted out.

No spark at the screwdriver tip with the condenser out of the circuit means that there is an open circuit somewhere in the primary. Check the small wire lead from the primary terminal to the movable contact point. This wire lead sometimes parts under the constant flexing of operation.

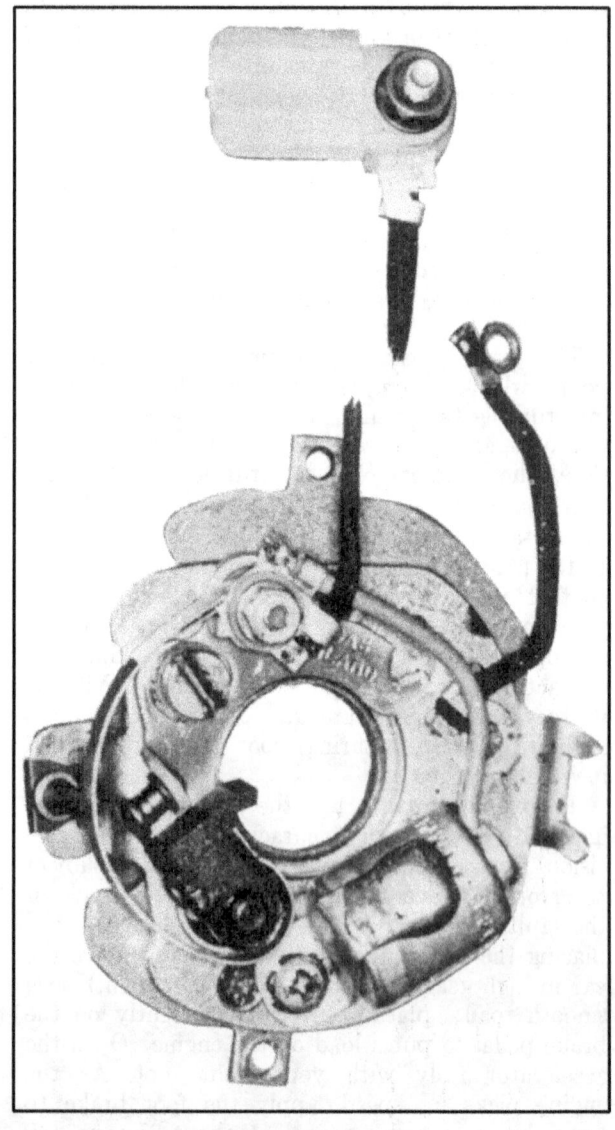

A broken primary lead may not show up until you pull on it. The insulation hides the damage.

To Test the Secondary Circuit (Test 4).
The secondary circuit cannot be tested until the primary circuit is functioning perfectly. If the primary circuit tests good, or after the necessary repairs have been made to the primary circuit, then the secondary circuit can be tested.

To test the secondary circuit, turn the engine over until the contact points close. Then turn on the ignition switch. Hold the main high tension wire (from the center terminal of the distributor cap) about ½" (12 mm.) from any metallic part of the engine. Open and close the contact points with a screwdriver blade held against the movable contact point only. No spark, or a weak one, from the wire to the block (*with a good primary circuit*), means a bad ignition coil or a defective main high tension wire from the coil to the distributor (especially where it runs through metal conduit). A good spark here (with no spark to the spark plugs) means that the trouble must be in the distributor cap, rotor, or spark plugs. It is seldom that spark plug high tension wires (unless obviously rotted) will keep an engine from starting. To check the main high tension wire, from the coil to the center of the distributor cap, replace it with a new piece of high tension wire, or remove the old wire from the metal conduit and repeat Test 4 while keeping the suspected wire away from any grounded surface.

To Test the Distributor Rotor (Test 5).
Test the distributor rotor by replacing it on the distributor shaft and holding the main high tension wire (from the coil) about ¼" (6 mm.) from the top of the rotor. With the ignition switch turned on, crank the engine with the starter. If the high tension spark jumps to the rotor, it is grounded (defective); if not, the cap must be defective. Inspect the cap for carbon tracks which indicate the passing of high voltage electricity.

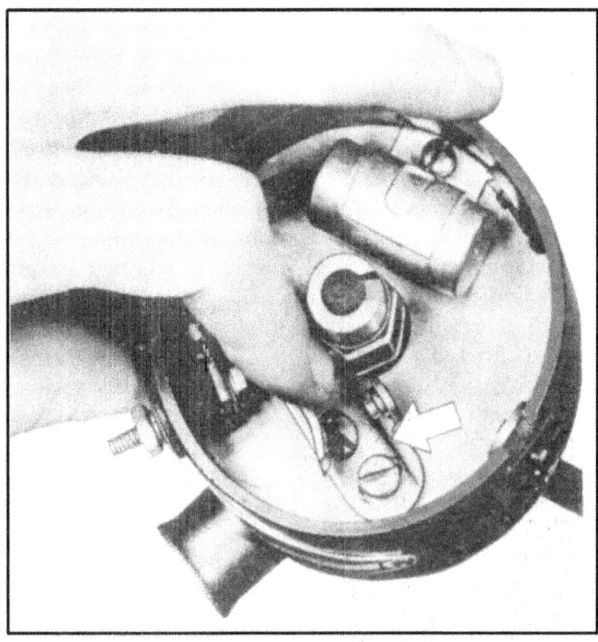

Oil on the contact point faces is a frequent offender of burned points. Its presence can often be detected by the smudge line under the contact points.

2 Checking the ignition timing

A timing light should be used to check the ignition timing. One of the test instrument leads is connected to the distributor primary terminal and the other to ground. With the ignition switch turned on, the engine should be rotated by hand until the lamp lights, which indicates the moment of point opening.

Generally, the crankshaft pulley has a notch to indicate TDC (top dead center), and it is necessary to measure along the edge of the pulley to locate the exact point that ignition must occur. In many cases, no timing or degree scale is provided. The ignition timing specification can be found in the Appendix under 'Tuning Data' according to car model.

To set the timing, turn the engine by hand until the pointer is at the exact point on the flywheel specified in the table. Loosen the distributor clamp bolt, and then turn the distributor in a direction opposite that of normal rotation until the points just separate (timing lamp lights). Lock the distributor in this position.

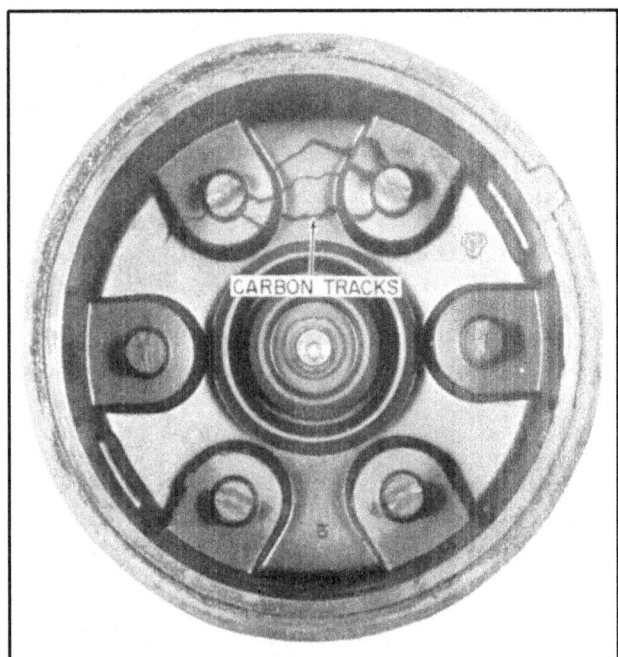

A cracked distributor cap always shows these characteristic carbon tracks. A crack between two terminals will cause misfiring, but a crack from the center terminal to the outside will prevent the engine from starting. Cracks often start from moisture on the surface of the insulating material.

3 Testing for a miss

An engine is composed of several cylinders arranged to fire successively in order to develop a smooth flow of power. If one of these cylinders does not fire, it causes the engine to jerk, lose power, and waste fuel. A misfiring cylinder can be caused by a lack of spark, fuel, or compression.

The best test for a misfiring cylinder is to short out all the cylinders with the exception of one, and thereafter have the engine operate on each cylinder in turn. Any variation in power, or a cylinder which is not firing, will show up, because the engine will not run at all when the defective cylinder has to carry the load alone.

To make this test, loosen each high tension wire from its spark plug terminal before starting the engine, but do not disconnect any until needed. With the engine running fast enough to prevent stalling, short out each cylinder, except number 1, by removing its spark plug wire and laying it on the engine block. This is done so that the spark does not reach the spark plug and the cylinder cannot fire. To minimize the chances of getting an electrical shock when handling high tension wires, keep your fingers at least an inch from the metallic tip.

After all the cylinders, except one, have been shorted out, adjust the engine speed so that the engine runs as slowly as possible without stalling. Change the wires, one at a time. In this way, you can run the engine on each cylinder in turn. If a vacuum gauge is connected during this test, a very accurate comparative measurement can be made between the relative efficiency of each cylinder.

To Find the Cause of the Miss. Remove the defective cylinder spark plug wire; hold it ¼" (6 mm.) from the spark plug terminal, then start the engine. If a steady spark jumps to the spark plug terminal, the trouble must be fuel, compression, or a defective spark plug. If no spark jumps to the spark plug terminal, the trouble is in the ignition system.

To make a compression test, use a compression gauge or hold your thumb over the spark plug hole while cranking the engine.

If the engine misses on adjacent cylinders, the trouble may be a blown cylinder head gasket or a leaky intake manifold gasket. A blown cylinder head gasket will lack compression in either of the two affected cylinders. To test for a leaking intake manifold gasket, squirt water around the suspected surfaces. A sucking noise will indicate the entrance of the water into the manifold.

Ignition system fault diagnosis chart

TROUBLES & CAUSES

1. **Primary circuit troubles causing misfiring or hard starting**
    1a. Defective contact points
    1b. Point dwell not set correctly
    1c. Defective condenser
    1d. Defective coil
    1e. Defective primary wire in distributor
    1f. Resistance contacts in ignition switch
    1g. Discharged battery
    1h. Low voltage due to resistance connections
    1i. Worn distributor shaft bushings
2. **Secondary circuit troubles causing misfiring or hard starting**
    2a. Defective spark plugs
    2b. Spark plug gaps set too wide
    2c. Defective high tension wiring
    2d. Cracked distributor cap
    2e. Defective rotor
    2f. Defective coil
    2g. Moisture on the ignition wires, cap, or spark plugs
3. **Ignition troubles causing poor acceleration**
    3a. Ignition timing incorrect
    3b. Centrifugal advance incorrect
    3c. Vacuum advance unit incorrect
    3d. Defective vacuum advance diaphragm
    3e. Preignition due to wrong heat-range spark plugs, or to overheated engine
    3f. Spark plug gaps set too wide
    3g. Defective spark plugs
    3h. Cracked distributor cap
    3i. Weak coil
4. **Ignition troubles causing erratic engine operation**
    4a. Defective contact points
    4b. Sticking point pivot bushing
    4c. Worn distributor shaft bushings
    4d. Worn advance plate bearing
    4e. Defective ignition coil
    4f. Spark plug gaps set too wide
    4g. High resistance spark plugs
    4h. Defective high tension wiring

NOTES

IGNITION SYSTEM - SERVICE

1 Description

The coil ignition equipment consists of a high tension coil and a combined distributor, contact breaker, timing control assembly which is driven at half engine speed from the crankshaft.

All the models of vehicle covered by this manual are fitted with type DVX6A distributors which incorporate both centrifugal and vacuum control timing advance mechanisms. The minor differences between the distributors on each model are given in the **Technical Data** section of the Appendix to this manual. The main difference between models is the speed at which the centrifugal advance mechanism comes into operation and the amount of advance it produces.

The centrifugal advance system consists of a pair of governor weights located below the contact breaker mechanism held in position by small springs. These weights are forced outwards by increasing speed and, being connected directly to the distributor cam, cause the cam to be rotated. This rotation of the cam relative to the camshaft produces an advance in the ignition timing.

The vacuum advance system operates by means of the low pressures maintained on the induction side of the inlet manifold to the engine. The low pressure acts upon a diaphragm via a small bore pipe connected to the inlet manifold. The movement of the diaphragm is transmitted through a linkage to the contact breaker plate which rotates in relation to the distributor cam. The contact breaker plate moves to advance the ignition timing with decreasing pressure (increasing vacuum). An exploded view of the vacuum advance system is shown in **FIG 3**. Also connected to the vacuum advance mechanism is a micrometer screw which by direct linkage to the contact breaker plate is able to move the plate. This micrometer screw is fitted to provide very fine adjustment to the ignition timing which may be required to account for changes in engine condition or the variations in engine fuel.

The vacuum advance system is designed to give a good timing advance at small throttle openings with no load and the centrifugal advance system is designed to give increasing advance with increasing engine speed. Thus the combination of centrifugal and vacuum advance gives greater flexibility and efficiency to the engine under all conditions of load and speed.

2 Routine maintenance

Lubrication

Lubrication of the distributor components should be carried out at intervals of not more than 2500 miles, care being taken to ensure that no oil or grease comes in contact with the contact breaker points.

Replenish the oil well with one or two teaspoonful of good grade engine oil to lubricate the automatic advance mechanism and the distributor shaft. Check that the automatic advance mechanism is free by twisting the cam against the retaining spring pressure.

Lightly smear the cam with Mobilgrease No. 2 or equivalent and lubricate the pivot of the contact breaker points with the slightest trace of the same grease.

Remove the rotor arm (see **FIG 3:1**) by pulling it off vertically or ease it upwards gently with a screwdriver if it is a tight fit. Insert a few drops of clean thin oil into the

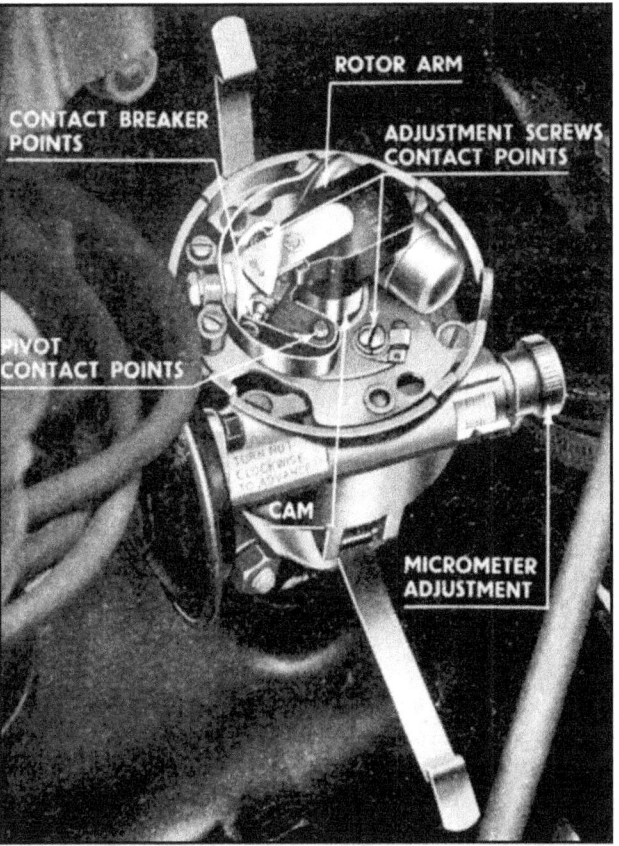

FIG 1 The distributor

top of the distributor spindle to lubricate the cam bearing. Add a few drops of light oil to the pivot on the contact breaker plate connecting it to the vacuum advance unit and check that the plate is free to move by pushing the pivot in both directions.

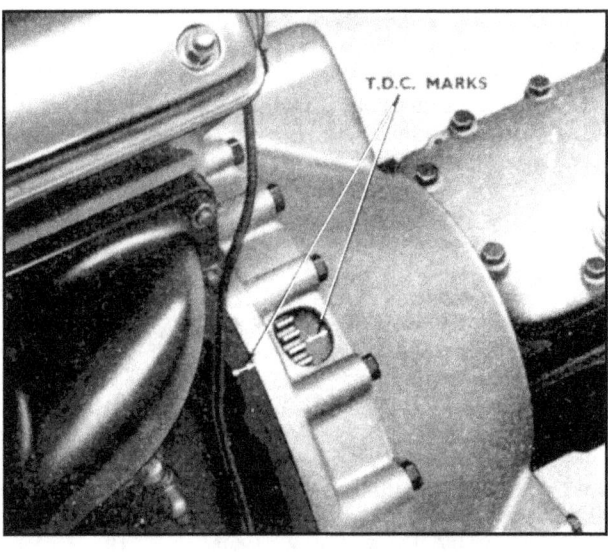

FIG 2 The timing marks

Cleaning:

The distributor components should be checked and cleaned at intervals of about 5000 miles. Having removed the distributor cap by releasing the two spring retaining clips check that the inside of the cap is clean. It may be cleaned with a soft dry cloth, particular attention being made to clean between the metal electrodes. If there are signs of tracking across the interior of the cap indicated by thin dark lines the cap will need renewal as it is not possible to remove the tracking marks without removing the glaze from the surface of the cap. Check that the small carbon brush moves freely in its holder in the centre of the cap and that the brush and metal electrodes are free from pitting. If pitting is evident it may be removed by careful scraping or with fine emerycloth and then cleaning off all traces of dust from the cap.

Lift off the rotor arm or ease it off gently with a screwdriver. Examine the rotor arm for any signs of tracking on the plastic moulding or burning or pitting on the metal portion. If there are signs of tracking renew the rotor arm. Pitting or burns on the metal portion of the rotor arm may be removed by very light rubbing with fine emerycloth and then thorough cleaning.

Examine the contact breaker. The contacts must be quite free from grease or oil. If they are pitted or burnt they may be cleaned after removal with a fine carborundum stone making sure that the two mating surfaces remain square and that all carborundum dust is removed preferably with a cloth soaked in petrol.

To remove the contact breaker contacts, slacken the nut on the moulded terminal block and lift out the end of the contact breaker spring. Lift off the contact breaker lever from its pivot. The fixed contact plate may be removed by unscrewing the two retaining screws. Check tha the moving contact moves freely on its pivot with the contact breaker plate out of the car. If it is found to be tight polish the pivot pin with fine emery cloth and after cleaning smear a very small amount of grease on the pin.

Replace the contact breaker points in the distributor in the reverse order to the removal, taking care with the plate securing screws to ensure they do not fall down the side of the contact breaker plate.

Before tightening the screws on the plate check that the contact breaker gap is correct. The gap between the contacts at their maximum opening should be .012 inch. Turn the engine until the contacts are at their widest apart (when the contact breaker lever is touching the highest points on the cam) insert a feeler gauge to measure the gap. Having set the gap tighten the contact breaker screws and turn the engine until the points open fully again, and again check the gap. Repeat this procedure until the distributor cam has turned one complete turn and the points have been opened by each of the high spots on the cam. The gaps measured in this manner should all be .012 inch.

Tighten the nut on the moulded terminal holding the contact breaker spring. Replace the rotor arm and make sure that it is pressed fully down or the distributor cap may be damaged. Replace the distributor cap.

3 Distributor removal

Before removing the distributor turn the engine to the TDC position indicated by the timing marks on the flywheel and crankcase shown in **FIG 2**. Check that the rotor arm is pointing to the terminal of No. 6 plug lead in this position, (No. 6 cylinder is that nearest the radiator). This positioning gives a datum for the distributor and will give an obvious indication if components have been assembled correctly on replacement.

Disconnect the battery positive lead and the low-tension lead from the terminal on the body of the distributor. Unscrew the union nut on the vacuum pipe at the vacuum advance unit and remove the pipe. Loosen the distributor clamp bolt located below the distributor body and lift out the distributor from the cylinder block.

4 Dismantling the distributor

When removing components as described in the following section note their location with respect to other components and mark them if in any doubt. This observation will save a great deal of time when reassembling. Use **FIGS 3** and **4** for reference.

Lift off the rotor arm from the top of the distributor spindle. Unscrew the nut on the moulded terminal holding the end of the contact breaker spring and the capacitor connecting strip. Lift out the end of the spring at the same time lifting the fibre contact breaker lever with the moving contact off the pivot pin. Remove the insulating washer from the base of the pivot pin. Unscrew and remove the two securing screws with their washers securing the fixed contact plate. Lift out the fixed contact.

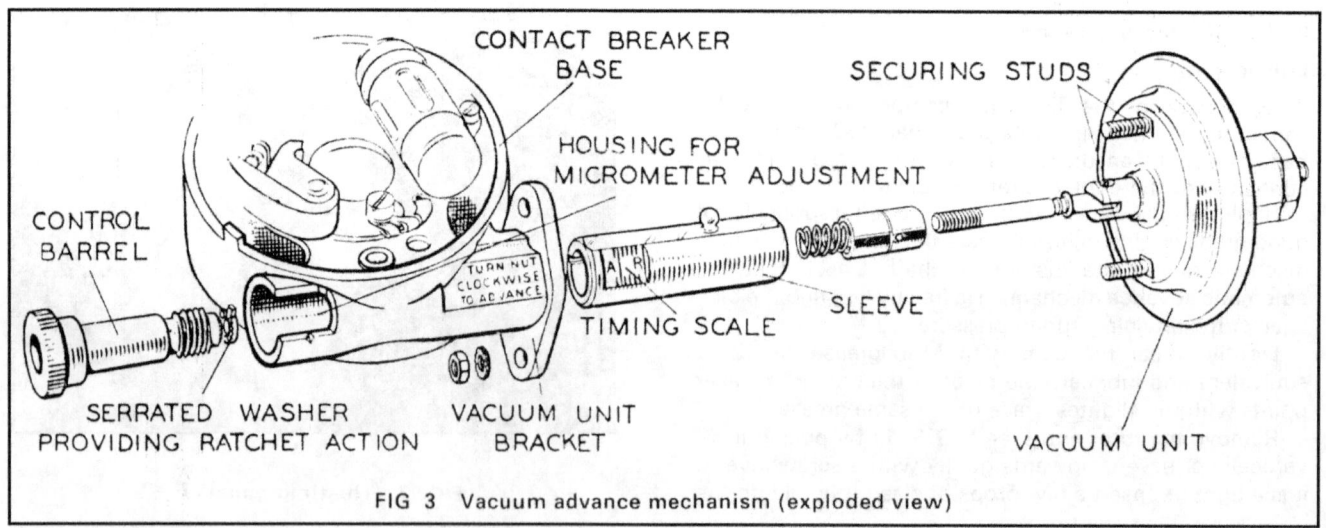

FIG 3 Vacuum advance mechanism (exploded view)

Unscrew the securing screw holding the capacitor and remove the capacitor complete with the connecting strip. Undo the three screws fitted at the edge of the contact breaker base casting and lift them out. The screws are accessible through the holes cut in the contact breaker plate. The contact breaker base can then be removed from the body of the distributor. Remove the jump ring from the underside of the contact breaker base, lift off the star-shaped spring and slide the contact breaker plate out of the base, first withdrawing the screw securing the earth connection to the base.

Unscrew and remove the two nuts holding the vacuum advance unit to the distributor. Ease the vacuum unit away from its seating until the protruding studs are clear then unscrew the unit from the control barrel. Ensure that the spring and serrated washer located at the end of the control barrel are not misplaced when unscrewing the barrel from its sleeve. Slide the sleeve which has the micrometer scale on it out of its housing.

Tap out the tapered pin securing the driving dog and remove the dog from the lower end of the distributor shaft, after noting its relative position to the slot in the top of the cam.

Remove the screw at the top of the distributor spindle and lift out the cam. Turn the distributor upside down and press out the distributor shaft complete with the centrifugal advance system from the distributor body. There are two bearings housed in the distributor body one is a ball-bearing the other a bush. Both may be removed by pressing out with a suitably shouldered mandrel. It is however not advisable to touch these bearings unless they are to be replaced due to wear.

Clean all the components carefully with clean rag and lightly oil all moving parts with the exception of the ball-bearing which should be lightly greased.

5 Reassembly

New bearings are fitted by pressing them into their housing with a suitably shouldered mandrel. A new ball-bearing should be lightly greased and a new bush should be allowed to soak in an oil bath for at least twenty-four hours before fitting. It is preferable to use a thin oil for this soaking.

Check that the centrifugal advance weights are correctly located and that they are free to move. Also examine the retaining springs to ensure they are not broken or stretched, renew as necessary.

Replace the centrifugal advance unit and distributor shaft with the thrust washer into the distributor body. Place the distributor cam onto the shaft and check that the pegs protruding from the cam foot locate correctly in the dowel holes in the centrifugal advance weights. Tighten home the securing screw in the top of the spindle.

Replace the driving dog on the lower end of the shaft checking that its location is correct relative to the slot in the top of the cam. Tap the dog securing pin into position.

Fit the sleeve of the micrometer adjustment into its housing in the contact breaker base, so that the timing scale appears in the window on the right of the body. Screw the control barrel fully home in the sleeve. With the barrel and sleeve pushed as far into the housing as they will go, screw the vacuum unit connecting rod into the barrel. Check that the serrated washer is correctly fitted. Locate the studs on the vacuum unit in their respective holes on the unit bracket, replace the spring washers and nuts to secure the unit.

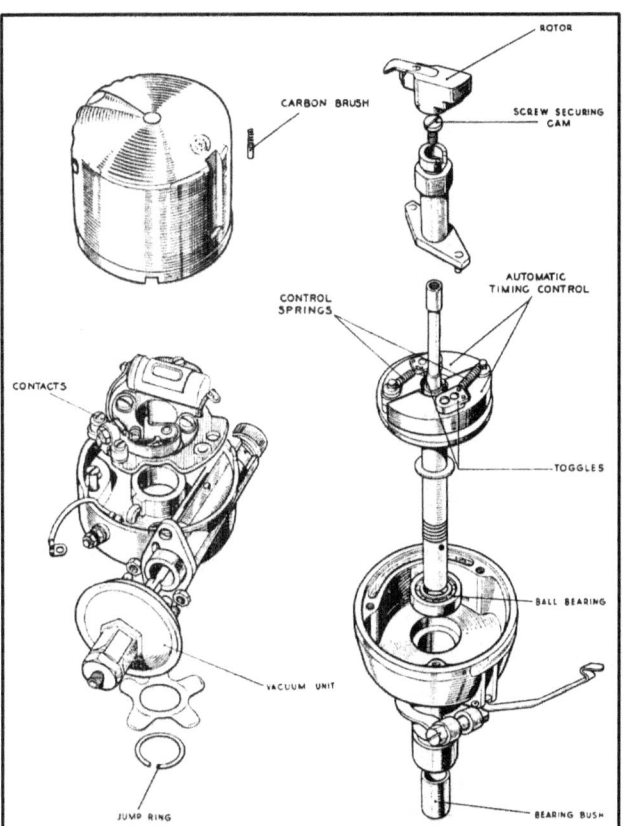

FIG 4 The distributor (exploded view)

Connect the two cables to the terminal and the earthing screw in the base casting. Position the contact breaker plate in the base casting so that the peg fitted in the control barrel locates in the hole provided in the contact breaker plate. Position the star-shaped spring over the bearing sleeve on the underside of the base casting and secure by springing the jump ring into its groove. Replace the capacitor complete with connecting strip and tighten the securing screw.

Examine the contact breaker points for burning or pitting. If they are lightly pitted or burnt they may be cleaned up with a carborundum stone taking care to keep the mating faces flat and parallel. Badly pitted or burnt contacts should be renewed. If renewal is necessary both the fixed and free contacts must be renewed as a complete set.

Check that the moving contact moves freely on the pivot pin before reassembling the contact breaker unit. Any resistance to movement should be removed by polishing the pivot pin and/or a slight trace of oil.

Position the plate carrying the fixed contact on the contact breaker base and secure it by replacing and lightly tightening the two screws with their spring and flat steel washers. The eyelet on the end of the cable connected to the earthing screw must be fitted under the head of one of these screws. Place the insulating washer on the pivot pin and then position the contact breaker lever on the pin at the same time locating the end of the spring on the moulded terminal block.

Insert the square headed bolt in the terminal block to clamp the capacitor connecting strip, the contact breaker spring and the connection to the low-tension terminal. Tighten the securing nut.

Adjust the position of the fixed contact breaker to give a maximum contact opening of .012 inch at each of the high spots on the cam.

Place the rotor arm on top of the spindle locating it correctly and pushing it full home.

6 Installation

Set the micrometer adjustment on the vacuum advance unit to the centre of the scale. Place the distributor in the cylinder block and turn the rotor arm to engage the driving dog in the distributor driving shaft. Providing assembly has been carried out correctly the rotor arm should point to No. 6 cylinder, sparking plug lead, terminal in the distributor cap.

Reconnect the vacuum pipe at the union on the vacuum advance unit. Replace the battery positive lead and the low-tension lead to the distributor body.

It will be necessary to leave the clamp bolt in the loosened state in order to set the ignition timing. The setting of the timing is necessary if at any time the clamp bolt is loosened and the distributor moved. It is dealt with in the following section.

7 Ignition timing

Remove the distributor cover by releasing the two spring clips securing it. Remove the sparking plugs. Turn the engine over and check that the contact breaker gap is correctly adjusted as described in **Section 2**.

Rotate the engine to line up the timing marks on the flywheel and the crankcase (see **FIG 2**) with the rotor arm pointing to the terminal of No. 6 cylinder sparking plug lead. Having set the flywheel to the TDC position turn the crankshaft back by means of the fan belt until the crankcase mark lines up with the correct ignition setting for the car concerned. The correct ignition setting for all models is given in the **Tuning Data** section of the Appendix of this manual.

The distributor should then be rotated by hand until the contact breaker points just part. The exact position when the contact breaker points just part is extremely difficult to judge by eye so that the best procedure is to set the distributor electrically. This method is carried out as follows.

Turn the distributor anticlockwise until the points are fully closed. Connect a 12 volt lamp between the terminal on the distributor body and a good earth. Switch on the ignition and turn the distributor in a clockwise direction until the lamp just lights up, this indicates that the points have just opened. Clamp the distributor in this position by tightening the clamp bolt. Remove the timing light, replace the sparking plugs and the distributor cap.

Stroboscopic method:

The ignition timing may be set using a stroboscopic lamp which is connected so that the lamp flashes when the contact breaker points open. The lamp should be positioned so that the timing marks on the crankcase and flywheel are illuminated. Loosen the distributor clamp bolt and disconnect the vacuum advance pipe to the distributor. Start the engine and let it run below the speed at which the centrifugal advance begins to operate. The operating speeds for the centrifugal advance weights is given in the **Technical Data**.

The distributor should then be rotated by hand so that the timing marks on the flywheel and crankcase are correctly aligned for the ignition timing of the individual model being set. Stop the engine, disconnect the timing lamp and tighten the clamp bolt on the distributor. Reconnect the vacuum pipe to the vacuum advance unit. If the speed of the engine is allowed to exceed that at which the centrifugal advance mechanism operates or the vacuum pipe is connected while the above method of ignition timing is carried out the timing will be incorrectly set.

Having set the ignition timing by one of the two methods described it is essential that a series of road tests are carried out to find the optimum setting of the ignition timing. This is achieved by driving the car up a slightly inclined slope in top gear and checking the time taken to travel a fixed distance between two points up the incline with the ignition adjusted by means of the micrometer screw to several positions. The best position is that which provides the shortest time to cover the fixed distance. During the above road tests the micrometer screw should be turned no more than six clicks in either direction.

8 High tension leads

The high tension leads from the distributor to the sparking plugs and from the coil to the distributor should be examined periodically. They should be renewed if there are any signs of deterioration such as perishing or cracking. To fit a new HT lead to the ignition coil cut a suitable length of 7mm rubber covered ignition cable using the original lead as a guide. Pass the cable through the knurled, moulded nut connector to the coil. Bare about $\frac{1}{4}$ inch of the end of the cable and thread this through the brass washer removed from the original cable. Bend back the strands of the cable so that they are in contact with the brass washer. Refit the knurled nut to the ignition coil.

To connect new leads to the distributor cap remove the cap and loosen the terminal screw from within the cap. Cut the lead to the required length and push the end firmly into the correct hole in the moulding of the cap. Tighten the terminal screws which pierce the rubber insulation to make good contact with the cable core. The connection to the centre terminal is made accessible by removing the small carbon brush. Check that the HT leads are connected to the correct sparking plugs to provide the correct firing order.

9 Sparking plugs

The sparking plugs should be cleaned and inspected at regular intervals to maintain the engine efficiency.

Remove the sparking plugs by loosening them a couple of turns and then blowing away any excess dirt with compressed air or a tyre pump before fully unscrewing. When removing the plugs always use a box or tubular spanner as the insulators are easily damaged. Store the sparking plugs in their order of removal.

Examine the plug gaskets. If they are about half their original thickness they may be used again, if not they must be renewed.

Inspect the firing end of the plug to note the type of deposit formed. These deposits should be normally powdery and range in colour from brown to greyish tan. There will also be slight wear of the electrodes and the general effect is one which comes from mixed periods of high and low speed motoring. If the deposits are white or yellowish they indicate long periods of constant speed driving or much low speed city driving. Black wet deposits are caused by oil entering the combustion chamber past worn piston rings or valve guides. Sparking plugs of a type which run hotter may help to alleviate the problem but the only real cure is an engine overhaul. Dry, black, fluffy deposits are usually the result of running with a rich mixture or incomplete combustion due to ignition faults or excessive idling. A blistered white centre electrode usually accompanied with an erroded side electrode indicates overheating of the sparking plug. This may be due to insufficient cooling, incorrect ignition timing, or sustained high speeds with heavy loads.

File the electrodes until they are clean, bright and parallel and then have them cleaned thoroughly in an abrasive blasting machine. They should then be tested under pressure in a test rig. Renew any plugs which are doubtful. It is also advisable to renew any plugs where the centre electrode is below the level of the rim of the plug.

With a feeler gauge set the electrode gap on each plug to .025 inch by bending the side electrode (never try to bend the centre electrode or the insulation will be damaged). Clean the insulator portion of the sparking plug as accumulated dust on this portion will provide a leakage path to earth and hence weaken the spark. The threads of the sparking plugs are best cleaned with a wire brush. If it is found that the plugs cannot be screwed into place by hand run a tap down the thread to remove any carbon deposits.

The threads in the head may be cleaned by means of an old sparking plug with the threads cross cut if a tap is not available. Tighten the plugs to a torque of 30 lb ft. If a torque wrench is not available tighten with a box spanner through half a turn to provide a gas tight fit.

10 Testing

Before carrying out any tests check that the battery is not discharged as this condition may produce the same symptoms as a fault in the ignition circuit.

Uneven firing:

Set the engine to run at a fast idling speed. Then short out each sparking plug in turn by placing the blade of a screwdriver in contact with the plug terminal and the cylinder head. When carrying out this procedure it is advisable to use an insulated screwdriver and to take care not to touch any exposed part of the plug lead to avoid any electrical shocks. The shorting out of a plug which is firing correctly will produce a marked change in the engine running whereas the same check on a faulty one will make little or no change.

Having thus detected the faulty cylinder, stop the engine and remove the plug lead and hold the end about $\frac{3}{16}$ inch from the cylinder head. Restart the engine and check that there is a spark between the end of the cable and the cylinder head. The spark if a good one will be a light blue in colour whereas a weak spark is yellowish. If there is a good spark the fault lies in the sparking plug and it should be removed, cleaned and adjusted or renewed. If however there is a weak irregular spark or no spark at all check the HT lead from the plug to the distributor cap and renew if perished or cracked. Remove the distributor cap and check that the interior is clean and free from tracking. Tracking is indicated by thin black lines across the surface and if found, necessitates the renewal of the distributor cap.

Ignition failure:

Remove the distributor cap and lift off the rotor arm, carefully levering with a screwdriver if necessary. Check that the contacts are clean and that the contact breaker gap is correctly set as indicated in **Section 2**.

Switch on the ignition and turn the engine by hand and observe the ammeter. The ammeter reading should rise and fall with the closing and opening of the contacts. If the reading does not fluctuate a short circuit across the points is indicated. No reading at all indicates a broken connection in the low-tension circuit.

Low tension circuit:

Turn the engine until the contact breaker points are fully open and switch on the ignition. Then check the voltage readings between the following points, in each case the correct reading should be 12 volts, no reading will indicate a broken or loose connection in the section under test:

1 **Battery to ammeter:**
   Connect the voltmeter between the ammeter terminal 3 and a good earth.
2 **Ammeter**
   Connect the voltmeter between the ammeter terminal A and earth, no reading indicates a faulty ammeter.
3 **Ammeter to control box:**
   Connect the voltmeter between the control box terminal A and earth.
4 **Control box**
   Connect the voltmeter between the control box terminal A1 and earth. No reading indicates a broken connection in the series winding in the control box.
5 **Control box to ignition switch**
   Connect the voltmeter between the ignition switch terminal which is connected to the control box via terminal A of the lighting switch and a good earth.
6 **Ignition switch:**
   Check the voltage between the other ignition switch terminal and earth. No reading indicates a faulty switch.
7 **Ignition switch to coil:**
   Remove the lead from the ignition coil SW terminal and connect the voltmeter between the end of the lead and earth. If no reading is shown check the voltage between the control box A3 terminal and earth as the switch is connected to the coil via this terminal. Reconnect the lead to the SW terminal.
8 **Ignition coil:**
   Disconnect the lead from the CB terminal of the coil and connect the voltmeter between the CB terminal and earth. No reading indicates a fault in the primary side of the coil, the coil should be checked by a dealer and renewed if necessary. Reconnect the lead to the CB terminal.
9 **Ignition coil to distributor:**
   Disengage the lead to the distributor and measure the voltage between the end of the lead and earth. Reconnect the lead to the terminal.
10 **Contact breaker and capacitor:**
   Connect the voltmeter across the contact breaker points. If there is no reading remove the capacitor and check again. If a reading is now given the capacitor is faulty and should be renewed. If it is possible for the capacitor to be faulty and pass this

test and the only other test possible is to substitute a new capacitor in its place. A faulty capacitor is usually indicated by rapid pitting of the contact breaker points.

If after carrying out these tests the fault is not located, remove the HT lead from the centre terminal of the distributor. Switch on the ignition and turn the engine until the contacts close. Flick open the contacts while the HT lead from the coil is held about $\frac{3}{16}$ inch from the cylinder block. For a healthy circuit a good spark will be obtained. If there is no spark the secondary winding of the coil is faulty and will need replacing. This fault may also be indicated by the incorrect fitting of an ignition suppressor. The suppressor should be fitted to the centre distributor terminal but if fitted to the coil will provide a $\frac{1}{4}$ inch air gap which may produce ignition failure symptoms.

11 Modifications

On the Mk VIII models from chassis numbers RH drive 760989 and LH drive 780777 the distributor type was changed to the DMB2 model which incorporates a suppressor, the normal suppressor fitted to the centre terminal of the distributor is unnecessary and should not be fitted.

On some models the coil terminal markings were revised to + (positive) and − (negative) these may be taken to be the SW and CB terminals respectively.

12 Fault diagnosis

(a) Engine will not fire
1 Battery discharged
2 Distributor contact points dirty, pitted or maladjusted
3 Distributor cap dirty, cracked or 'tracking'
4 Carbon brush in distributor cap not touching rotor
5 Faulty cable or loose connection in low-tension circuit
6 Distributor rotor arm cracked or 'tracking'
7 Faulty coil
8 Broken contact breaker spring
9 Contact points stuck open

(b) Engine misfires
Check 2, 3, 5 and 7 in (a)
1 Weak contact breaker spring
2 HT leads cracked or perished
3 Sparking plug(s) loose, gap incorrectly set or insulation cracked
4 Ignition timing too far advanced
5 Faulty capacitor
6 Broken centrifugal advance spring(s)

NOTES

NOTES

INDEX – COOLING SYSTEM

SECTION	PAGE	
000	55	Basic Diagnostic Testing & Troubleshooting
001	56	Description
002	56	Maintenance (Draining/Refilling etc)
003	57	Water Pump Servicing
004	58	Thermostat Servicing
005	59	Temperature Gauge
006	59	Cold Weather Precautions
007	59	Core Plugs Removal & Replacement
008	60	Fault Diagnosis Chart

COOLING SYSTEM
Basic Diagnostic Testing & Troubleshooting

The cooling system is thermostatically controlled in order to regulate both the engine operating temperature and provide for a short warm-up period. Engine overheating and slow warm-up are the two engine troubles most commonly attributed to the cooling system.

1 Overheating

Loss of coolant, the accumulation of rust and scale in the coolant chambers, and the passing of hot exhaust gases into the coolant through an internal leak are the main causes of overheating.

Loss of coolant can be checked visually by the red rust stains that often form around the leak area. Loss of coolant through an internal crack is often detected by noting the condition of the oil on the dip stick, where water bubbles will appear with the oil.

2 Testing for an exhaust gas leak

Start the test with a cold engine. Disconnect the fan belt so that the water pump does not operate. Disconnect the upper hose at the radiator. Drain the system until the water level is even with the top of the block. Remove the thermostat and replace the housing. Fill the radiator until the water reaches the top of the thermostat housing.

The object of this test is to place a load on the engine so that combustion chamber pressures approach maximum to force hot exhaust gases through any small leak that might exist.

To load the engine: jack up the rear wheels, start the engine, place the shift lever in high gear, open the accelerator wide with your right foot; at the same time apply the foot brakes with your left foot to hold the engine speed to about 20 mph (32 km./h.) road speed.

Gas bubbles or surging at the upper outlet indicate that exhaust gas is leaking into the cooling system. The test must be conducted quickly to prevent the coolant from boiling in the head.

Another method of testing the engine for leaks is to use a special radiator pressure pump. Drain some water until the level is about ½" (12 mm.) below the radiator neck. Attach the tester and apply 15 psi (1.0 kg./cm.^{2}) pressure. If the pressure drops, check all points for an exterior leak.

If you cannot locate an exterior leak after the gauge shows a drop in pressure, detach the tester and run the engine to normalize it. Reattach the tester and pump it to 7 psi (0.5 kg./cm.^{2}) while the engine is running. Race the engine and, if the dial fluctuates, it indicates a combustion leak. *CAUTION: Pressure builds up fast!* Never let the pressure exceed 15 psi (1.0 kg./cm.^{2}). Release excess pressure immediately!

Cooling system fault diagnosis chart

TROUBLES & CAUSES

1. **Overheating**
   1a. Insufficient coolant
   1b. Rust and scale formations in cooling system
   1c. Fan belt slipping
   1d. Defective water pump
   1e. Radiator or hoses clogged
   1f. Radiator air flow restricted
   1g. Thermostat stuck closed
2. **Engine fails to reach normal operating temperature**
   2a. Thermostat defective
   2b. Temperature sending unit defective
   2c. Temperature indicator defective
3. **Slow warm-up**
   3a. Thermostat defective
   3b. Top radiator hose temperature valve stuck open
   3c. Choke not closing properly

NOTES

COOLING SYSTEM - SERVICE

1 Description

The cooling water is circulated by an impeller-type pump which is mounted on the front of the cylinder block, together with a fan, and driven by a V-belt from the front end of the crankshaft. The cooling water is drawn by the pump from the bottom of the radiator, through the bottom hose, and discharges into the cylinder head. The water passes from the cylinder head to the block through waterways and after circulating around the combustion chamber jacketing enters the radiator header tank via the top water hose.

The heated water from the engine then passes down through finned water tubes to the bottom of the radiator. These finned tubes which have the effect of presenting a large surface area to the air, are placed in close proximity to the fan which draws air through them and so dissipates the heat.

The cooling system as described above is not required to come into full operation until the engine has reached its normal working temperature and it is desirable that this should be brought about as quickly as possible after starting the engine from cold. To accomplish this a thermostatically operated valve is incorporated in the system located in a cast body which is integral with the top water hose.

This thermostatic valve remains closed whilst the engine is cold, the water then returns to the pump through a bypass pipe which connects the thermostat housing, on the engine side of the valve to the pump. This means that the water is not allowed through the radiator to become cooled.

As the water temperature rises the valve opens and the circuit functions normally with water passing through the radiator.

2 Maintenance

Draining the system:

Draining should always be carried out on level ground to prevent any small pockets of water being trapped.

Turn the air conditioner hot/cold control on the facia panel to the hot position to allow the water in the heater to flow out into the system.

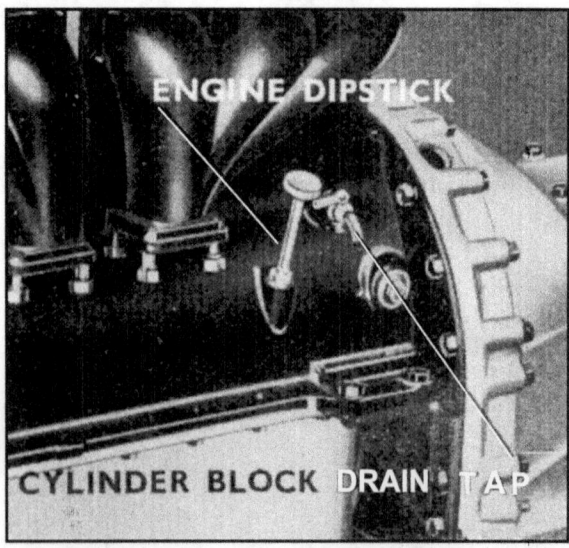

FIG 1 Engine drain tap location

Open the radiator and engine drain taps and remove the radiator cap. If antifreeze is contained in the system it may be collected in a clean container strained and used again, but remember if topping up is necessary when replacing it more antifreeze will require to be added.

If a drain tap is found to be completely blocked, the tap should be unscrewed and cleaned with hot cleansing solution and careful prodding with a suitable piece of wire. The screwed boss which receives the tap should be brushed clean taking care not to damage the threads. The location of the engine drain tap is shown in **FIG 1**. On replacing the tap apply a small amount of jointing compound to the thread to prevent leakage.

Filling the system:

Ensure that the radiator block and cylinder block drain taps are closed. Fill the system with soft water or as soft as is available. The softer the water used the better as this reduces the amount of sediment produced in the system. Open the heater control and slacken the outlet hose clip on the front face of the heater radiator. Run the engine for a few minutes to circulate the water and when water flows from the outlet hose, tighten the hose clip. Top up the radiator as necessary (the correct level is when the water just reaches the bottom of the filler neck).

On early Mk VII models a bleeder valve is fitted on the front face of the heater radiator on the scuttle. This valve should be closed when filling the system and then opened when the engine is run to circulate the water. The valve should be kept open until water flows out of it and then closed. Tighten the valve and check that the radiator is topped up to the correct level.

Cleaning:

The water should be flushed periodically to clear away sludge and deposits which tend to block the narrow passages. To do this remove the filler cap and the radiator drain tap, open the cylinder block drain tap, insert a hose in the radiator filler neck. Allow the water to flow through the system with the engine running at a fast idle, until the water flowing from the engine is observed to be clean.

When the radiator is seriously choked, it is often possible to clear the radiator tubes by reverse flushing. This is carried out by removing the radiator filler cap and the bottom hose connection. The water supply hose should be then connected to the bottom hose stub to give a reasonably water-tight joint, a standard hose adaptor is quite suitable for this purpose. A short length of hose should be similarly attached to the radiator filler tube to direct the overflowing water away from the engine. Turn on the water and allow to run until the overflowing water is clear.

If the radiator is so blocked that no water overflows but the bottom hose connection forces itself out **do not ram the adaptor home to force the obstruction out. The radiator block is not designed to withstand the high pressures obtained from a water supply and may be seriously damaged if forced to do so.** A radiator so obstructed should be removed as described in **Chapter 1, Section 3**, and turned upside-down and then flushed through.

Routine checks:

At intervals of 2500 miles grease should be applied sparingly to the water pump and fan nipples to lubricate the pump spindle and fan bearings.

Every 5000 miles the fan belt tension should be checked and adjusted and the fan belt examined for signs of deterioration. (When the belt is correctly tensioned it can be flexed approximately $\frac{1}{2}$ inch either way in the centre of its run between the fan and crankshaft pulleys). If the fan belt is incorrectly adjusted, slacken the adjusting screw and the two mounting bolts of the generator (dynamo) (see **FIG 2**) and move the generator outwards until the belt is correctly tensioned. Tighten the two mounting bolts and the adjusting screw, check that the belt tension is still correct, readjust if necessary.

The fan belt is best examined for deterioration removed from the car as it is extremely difficult to see any faults with it fitted. To remove the fan belt, slacken the generator front mounting bolt and remove the rear mounting bolt and the adjusting screw, swing the rear of the generator outwards until the fan belt can be removed from the generator pulley. Examine the inside edge of the fan belt for signs of cracking and renew if any cracks are found. Also examine the 'V' faces for signs of glazing (shiny hard patches) which are normally caused by a loose fitting belt which slips, again renew as necessary. Replacement of the fan belt is the reverse procedure of removal. The fan belt should only be stretched over the pulleys by hand as the use of any lever may well damage the fan belt. Recheck the belt tension before finally tightening the generator mounting bolts and the adjusting screw.

Antifreeze:

Before adding antifreeze solution the cooling system should be cleaned by flushing as described earlier. The cylinder head gaskets must be in good condition and the cylinder head bolts checked for tightness since if the solution leaks into the crankcase a mixture will be formed with the engine oil which is likely to cause blocking of oilways with consequent damage resulting. Check that all water hoses are tight at the joints as the antifreeze mixture is far more searching than water and will leak out where perhaps water will not. Mix up the correct mixture and antifreeze solution in a clean container and fill the radiator carefully with the solution. When topping-up is necessary it should be carried out using antifreeze solution and not water or the coolant will become diluted and the degree of frost protection reduced.

3 The water pump

Removal:

Remove the radiator as described in **Chapter 1, Section 3**. Slacken the two mounting bolts and the adjusting screw of the generator (see **FIG 2**) and push the generator towards the engine to reduce the fan belt tension. Where a five bladed fan is fitted (see **FIG 3**) remove the five setscrews and lift off the fan and pulley. In the case of a six bladed fan (see **FIG 4**) remove the four setscrews securing the fan after marking the position of the semicircular balance pieces, as these must be replaced in their original positions. Remove the fan, balance weights and the pulley.

FIG 2 Fan belt adjustment

FIG 3 Five-bladed fan

FIG 4 Six-bladed fan

Detach the hose connections to the water pump. Unscrew the six setscrews and three nuts securing the pump to the timing cover. Lift off water pump and gasket.

Dismantling:

Remove the large wire circlip securing the driving dog to the fan hub. Tap out the Mills pin holding the driving dog to the spindle and remove the driving dog.

Withdraw the impeller and spindle from the pump body. From the inside of the fan hub at the front end remove the front bearing circlip and then the bearing collar. Withdraw the fan hub complete from the spindle housing. The bearings may be removed with a suitable bearing extractor after removing the appropriate felt seals and seal discs.

Reassembly:

Refit the spindle bush. If a new bush is to be fitted the bush should be pressed into the pump body with the flat of the bush in line with the greasing hole. The end of the bush should be flush with the bottom of the spindle seal recess. The new bush will then require reaming to a diameter of .377 inch. Refit the spindle seal into its recess ensuring that the seal spring faces towards the impeller.

Fit the smaller felt seal into the fan hub after soaking the seal in oil and then fit the seal disc with the concave face towards the seal. Push the smaller bearing into the hub after greasing and retain in position with the circlip.

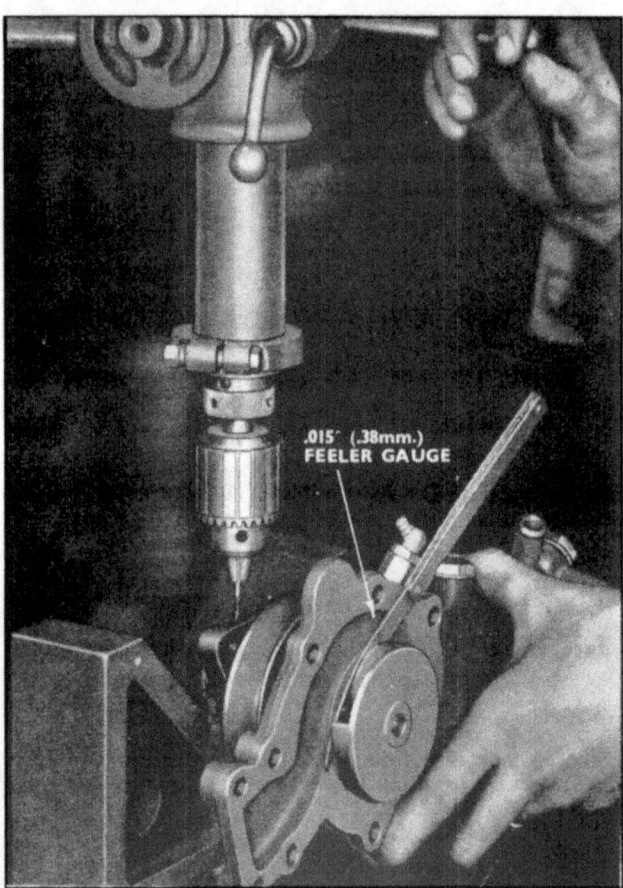

FIG 5 Water pump, new spindle

Pack the fan hub with the correct grade of grease and press the remaining bearing into the hub. Soak the oil seal in oil then press the seal disc then the seal into the hub checking that the convex side of the seal disc is facing the bearing.

Push the fan hub onto the spindle bush housing as far as it will go and then fit the front bearing collar with the chamfered side inwards into the fan hub and retain in position with the circlip.

Examine the spindle for signs of wear especially at the point of contact with the water seal and renew if necessary. If a new spindle is to be fitted it will be necessary to drill a hole for the Mills pin securing the driving dog. To do this fit the impeller to the spindle and push it through the spindle bush. Fit the driving dog and hold it in position with the wire circlip. Insert a .015 inch feeler gauge between the impeller vanes and the pump body and with the feeler gauge in position drill a $\frac{1}{8}$ inch hole through the spindle using the hole in the driving dog as a guide (see **FIG 5**). Remove the wire circlip, dog and the feeler gauge and clean off any rough edges to the holes and remove metal particles.

Fit the driving dog to the front end of the spindle and secure with a new Mills pin. Replace the wire circlip to secure the driving dog to the fan hub.

Refitting:

This is the reverse of the removal procedure, noting that the five-bladed type of fan should not be fitted to the water pump until the pump has been fitted to the timing cover.

Readjust the fan belt tension as described in **Section 2**.

4 The thermostat

Drain the radiator by removing the filler cap and opening the drain tap on the radiator. On Mk VII models with engine numbers A.2001 to A.6000 it is necessary to first remove the water temperature bulb before attempting to remove the thermostat. This is carried out in the following manner, hold the flats on the thermometer bulb and carefully unscrew the union so as not to twist the capillary tube which is easily fractured. Disconnect the wire from the starter carburetter thermostat terminal. Remove the three nuts securing the thermostat housing to the inlet manifold and withdraw the housing. Remove the two bolts and nuts holding the elbow pipe to the housing and remove the elbow. Unscrew the setscrew and remove with the copper washer on the side of the thermostat housing then lift out the thermostat from the housing.

On all the other Mk VII models it is only necessary to remove the elbow pipe to enable the thermostat to be lifted out of its housing.

On the XK120 models remove the two nuts securing the thermostat housing to the radiator, lift up the housing and withdraw the thermostat.

On all models thoroughly clean the thermostat and check that the small bypass hole in it is unobstructed.

The thermostat may then be checked for operation by placing it in a container of cold water with a thermometer. The container should then be heated and the temperature reading on the thermometer noted when the thermostat begins to open and when it is fully open.

The readings obtained in this manner should be checked against those figures given in the Technical Data section of the Appendix to this manual. If the temperatures disagree with those given in the Technical Data or the thermostat does not open fully renew it. The thermostat cannot be adjusted or repaired so that it is preferable to renew it if in any doubt. If a new one is not readily available it may be left out of the system, but in this case the engine should be allowed more time to warm up after starting prior to driving it.

Refitting the thermostat is the reverse procedure to the removal operation. A new gasket should be fitted to the thermostat housing on the XK120 models or the elbow pipe on the Mk VII models. The relative locations of the thermostats on these two models are shown in **FIGS 6 & 7**.

5 The temperature gauge

The water temperature gauge fitted to all the models is connected to a sensing bulb screwed into the water thermostat housing by a capillary tube which is an integral part of the gauge and bulb. The gauge capillary tube and bulb are serviced only as a complete assembly. If it is necessary to remove the sensing bulb it may be carried out by holding the flats on the bulb and unscrewing the union nut very carefully to avoid twisting the capillary tube.

6 Frost precautions

It is recommended that an antifreeze compound of inhibited ethylene glycol base is used in the cooling system in cold water conditions. These compounds should be added in the quantities stipulated by the manufacturers to provide the correct degree of protection. Use of an antifreeze mixture prevents the cooling system freezing under cold conditions whilst the vehicle is stationary or being driven. Those mixtures using alcohol as a base are not considered suitable as alcohol tends to evaporate.

It is essential that antifreeze compound is used when a heater is fitted as the heater unit is liable to freeze and draining of the cooling system does not drain the heater.

Systems containing antifreeze require to be topped up carefully as the mixture may affect the paintwork and therefore it is best to avoid overfilling. Do not add antifreeze to windscreen washers.

If the radiator is not protected with antifreeze compound it should be drained before it is left standing for any length of time in cold weather. It will be found advantageous if the radiator has been drained for this reason, to fill the system with warm water before starting the engine.

7 Core plugs

Core plugs are fitted to the water jackets of the cylinder block and may be removed by striking the centre of the plug using a hammer and punch. Having removed the plug carefully clean the recess for the plug and remove any burrs. A new plug is fitted with the convex face outwards this face being tapped lightly until the plug is a tight fit. If plugs are found to persistently leak when renewing, smear a small amount of jointing compound around the seat.

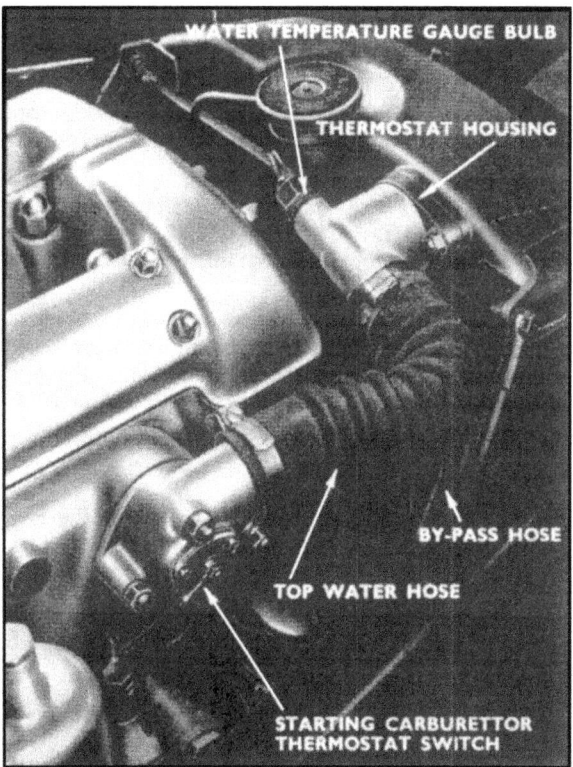

FIG 6 Thermostat, XK120 model

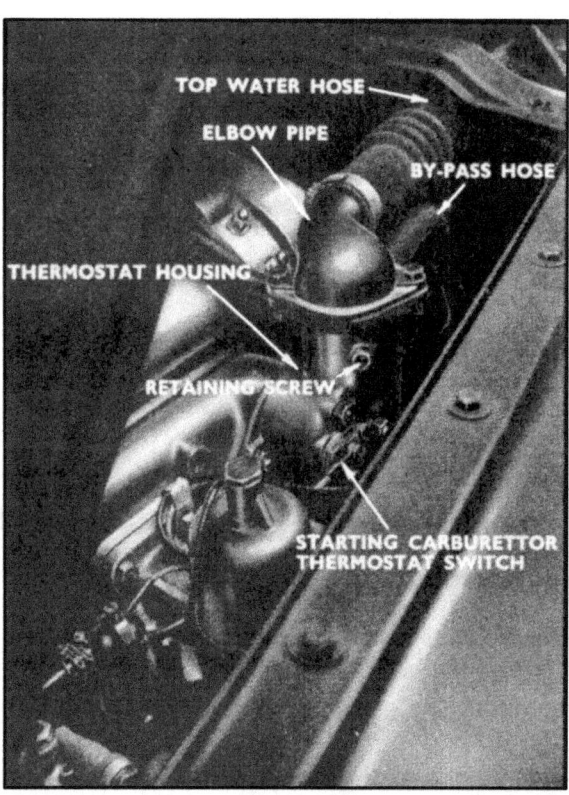

FIG 7 Thermostat, Mk VII model

8 Fault diagnosis

(a) Internal water leakage

1 Cracked cylinder wall
2 Loose cylinder head nuts
3 Cracked cylinder head
4 Faulty head gasket
5 Cracked water manifold

(b) Poor circulation

1 Radiator blocked
2 Engine water passages restricted
3 Low water level
4 Loose fan belt
5 Defective thermostat
6 External leaks
7 Faulty water pump

(c) Corrosion

1 Impurities in the water
2 Infrequent draining and/or flushing

(d) Overheating

1 Check (b)
2 Faulty ignition timing
3 Incorrect valve timing
4 Mixture too weak
5 Brakes binding
6 Slipping clutch
7 Insufficient or diluted oil
8 Choked exhaust system

NOTES

NOTES

INDEX – CLUTCH

SECTION	PAGE	
000	63	Basic Diagnostic Testing & Troubleshooting
001	63	Description & Operation
002	64	Removal & Disassembly
003	65	Reassembly & Installation
004	65	Adjustments
005	70	Master Cylinder Servicing
006	71	Slave Cylinder Servicing
007	73	Bleeding the Hydraulic System
008	73	Modifications by Engine Number & Model
009	73	Fault Diagnosis Chart

CLUTCH
Basic Diagnostic Testing & Troubleshooting

To test a clutch for slipping, set the hand brake tightly, open the throttle until the engine is running at about 30 mph (48 km./h.) road speed, depress the clutch pedal, and shift into high gear. Now, release the clutch; the engine should stall if the clutch is good. If the clutch is slipping, the engine will continue to run.

Check to see that the slipping is not due to a tight adjustment of the clutch pedal linkage. There must be free play at the pedal, before the clutch thrust bearing contacts the clutch pressure plate levers.

The only other clutch trouble is chattering when starting in first or reverse gear. Loose engine mounts and uneven adjustment of the pressure plate levers contribute to this trouble.

Clutch fault diagnosis chart

TROUBLES & CAUSES

1. **Slipping**
   1a. Worn facings
   1b. Weak pressure plate springs
   1c. Pedal linkage out of adjustment
   1d. Sticking release levers
   1e. Pressure plate binding against the drive lugs

2. **Dragging**
   2a. Pedal linkage adjustment too loose
   2b. Warped clutch disc
   2c. Splined hub sticking on clutch shaft
   2d. Torn disc facings
   2e. Release fingers adjusted unevenly
   2f. Sticking pilot bearing
   2g. Sticking release sleeve
   2h. Warped pressure plate
   2i. Misalignment of clutch housing

3. **Noise**
   3a. Clutch release bearing requires lubrication
   3b. Pilot bearing requires lubrication
   3c. Loose hub in clutch disc
   3d. Worn release bearing
   3e. Worn driving pins in pressure plate
   3f. Uneven release lever adjustment
   3g. Release levers require lubrication

4. **Chattering**
   4a. Oil or grease on clutch disc facings
   4b. Glazed linings
   4c. Warped clutch disc
   4d. Warped pressure plate
   4e. Sticking release levers
   4f. Unequal adjustment of release levers
   4g. Uneven pressure plate spring tension
   4h. Loose engine mounts
   4i. Loose splines on clutch hub
   4j. Loose universal joints or torque mountings
   4k. Misalignment of clutch housing

CLUTCH - SERVICE

1 Description and operation

The clutch used on the models covered by this manual is operated through either mechanical or hydraulic linkage and is of the single dry plate type consisting of a driven plate assembly, a cover assembly and a self-lubricating graphite release bearing. A sectional view of the clutch is shown in **FIG 1**.

The driven plate assembly is of the flexible centre-type in which the splined hub 15 located on the gearbox constant pinion shaft is indirectly attached to a disc 14 on either side of which facings 17 are riveted. Power is transmitted to the splined hub from the friction facings via a number of coil springs located around the driven plate.

The cover assembly consists of a pressed steel cover 1 and a cast iron pressure plate 2 loaded by the thrust springs 3. Mounted on the pressure plate are three release levers 8 which pivot on floating pins 9 retained by eyebolts 10. Adjusting nuts 12 are screwed on the eyebolts and secured by staking. Struts 13 are located between lugs on the pressure plate and the outer ends of the release levers 8. Anti-rattle springs 11 load the release levers and the retainer springs 7 connect the release levers to a release lever plate 4. The release bearing consists of a graphite bearing 5 shrunk into a metal cup 6, the cup being located by the operating forks and the release bearing retainer springs.

In the normal drive position the clutch is in the position indicated in the sectional view **FIG 1**, i.e. the driven plate is held between the pressure plate and the flywheel. Power is thus transmitted from the flywheel through the facing linings to the driven plate and then to the gearbox via the splined hub.

On depressing the clutch-pedal the pedal movement is transmitted either mechanically or hydraulically to the operating fork. This movement applies pressure to the release plate via the release bearing which acts on the release levers causing the pressure plate to be lifted away from the driven plate against the action of the thrust springs. Since the driven plate is no longer held in contact with the flywheel no power will be transmitted from the engine to the gearbox. Releasing the pedal causes the clutch to revert to its original position under the action of the thrust springs.

The hydraulic linkage from the pedal to the clutch where fitted consists of a master cylinder, a fluid reservoir and a slave cylinder. The slave cylinder is fitted to the clutch and acts on the clutch shaft lever via an adjustable link.

Maintenance:

The only maintenance required on the clutch system is to check that there is sufficient free pedal movement and that the hydraulic fluid level is correctly maintained.

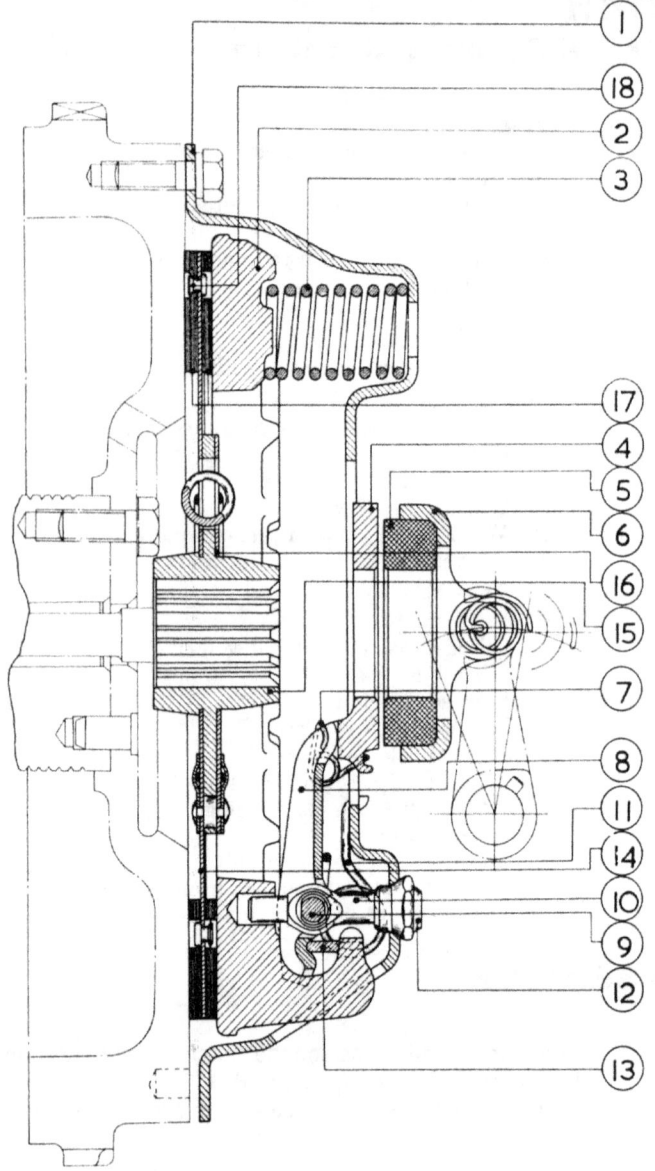

FIG 1 Clutch (sectional view)

Key to Fig 1
1 Cover
2 Pressure plate
3 Thrust springs
4 Release lever plate
5 Release bearing (graphite)
6 Release bearing cup
7 Release lever plate retaining spring
8 Release levers
9 Release lever floating pins
10 Eyebolts
11 Anti-rattle springs
12 Adjustment nuts
13 Struts
14 Clutch plate disc
15 Clutch plate splined hub
16 Clutch plate damper assembly
17 Clutch plate facing
18 Clutch plate facing rivet

The necessity for the free pedal movement (movement of the pedal before acting upon the clutch mechanism) is due to the fact that as the facing linings on the driven plate wear the free pedal movement is reduced and if it is not maintained very rapid wear of the linings will occur.

On models fitted with hydraulic linkage the required free pedal movement is 1¼ inch and it is also necessary to check that there is 1 inch clearance between the pedal and the side of the toe board to ensure that the master cylinder plunger may return fully. The correct level of fluid in the reservoir is to the base of the cap and the level should not be allowed to fall to more than ¾ inch below this.

On models with mechanical linkage the required free pedal movement is 1 inch.

On all models no attempt should be made to lubricate the clutch drive bearing as the lubricant may well be forced onto the driven plate facings and cause rapid deterioration.

2 Removal and dismantling

Removal:

Remove the engine and gearbox as one unit as described in **Chapter 1, Section 3.** Alternatively in the case of the XK120 models the engine may be left in situ and the gearbox only removed. If the gearbox only is to be removed in the following manner, it should be noted that the repositioning of the gearbox requires extreme care to align the gearbox constant pinion shaft to the driven plate of the clutch.

Remove both seats and floor carpets and place clear of the car. Remove the gearlever knob and locknut. Lift out floorboards. The propeller shaft tunnel may be removed on removal of the floorboards this is not essential but gives much better access to the propeller shaft coupling.

Disconnect the reverse light wires from the switch on the remote control. Disconnect the speedometer cable and tie in a position clear of the gearbox. Remove the four bolts from the front end of the propeller shaft at the gearbox coupling and slide the front section of the shaft rearwards as far as possible to clear the gearbox coupling flange. Remove the splitpin and clevispin securing the adjusting rod to the clutch pedal shaft lever. Remove the pinch bolt securing the pedal stem to the top of the clutch pedal and withdraw the stem. Remove the pinch bolt securing the clutch pedal to the shaft. Withdraw the clutch pedal shaft through the chassis frame until the inner end of the shaft is well clear of the bearing housing in the side of the clutch housing.

Support the rear of the engine on a jack with suitable packing to distribute the load. Remove the four bolts and nuts securing the platform under the gearbox extension to the mounting. Remove the three bolts and nuts securing the mounting to the bracket and the front crossmember. Remove the setscrew securing the torque arm

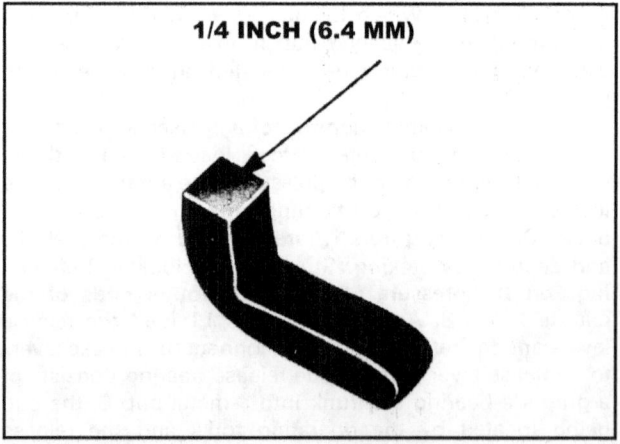

FIG 2 Release lever distance piece

to the mounting on the chassis frame. The torque arm is situated just forward of the clutch housing on the opposite side to the steering column. The gearbox will have to be raised to enable the mounting to be removed from the crossmember bracket.

Remove the six setbolts securing the coverplate to the underside of the bellhousing and remove the plate. Remove the clutch bellhousing bolts and withdraw the gearbox and bellhousing to the rear over the crossmember. The gearbox must be supported during this operation in order to avoid strain on the constant pinion shaft and distortion of the driven plate assembly.

Where the engine and gearbox have been removed as one unit the gearbox should be separated from the engine by removing the pressed steel coverplate from the bottom of the clutch housing then unscrewing the setscrews and bolts holding the clutch housing to the engine. Again care must be taken to avoid any strain on either the driven plate or the constant pinion shaft.

Fit three $\frac{1}{4}$ inch distance pieces (see **FIG 2**) one between each of the three release levers and the clutch cover to reduce the thrust spring pressure and assist the clutch removal. Unscrew the setscrews holding the clutch body to the flywheel a turn at a time in a diagonal sequence to prevent any distortion of the cover occuring.

Remove the complete clutch assembly from the flywheel, slide off the driven plate assembly and withdraw bearing. Release the tab washers and unscrew the ten flywheel mounting bolts. Place a $\frac{7}{16}$ inch dia. rod through the flywheel into the crankshaft spigot to support the flywheel during removal by levering each side of the flywheel taking care not to damage the crankshaft boss or drop the flywheel. Removal of the flywheel only becomes necessary if it is required to renew components in the clutch assembly and then only for the purposes of balancing.

After removal of the clutch cover assembly the driven plate will be completely free and should be carefully examined for the following faults.

The splines in the hub must not be worn, nor the edges of the flange which engages the springs in the plate. These springs should not be broken or weakened to such an extent that they are free to rattle. Examine the friction linings for excessive wear, loose rivets, cracks and discolouration. The polished glaze is quite normal and does not affect the transmission of power, however, the linings should be light in colour with the grain of the material quite clearly visible through the glaze. Oil deposits on the lining are indicated by dark patches which obliterate the grain these cannot be cleaned off with cleaning fluids and any attempt to do so may well damage the lining material.

It is not advisable to rivet new facing linings to an old plate as the plate may be distorted and will cause a balancing problem. If any of the defects described are found the driven plate should be renewed.

Next inspect the pressure plate assembly. If the friction surface of the plate is scored or pitted it should be renewed. Also examine the machined surface of the release plate where it comes into contact with release bearing, for signs of wear indicated by a ridge. If there is wear the plate will need renewing.

The renewal of the above parts of the cover assembly should be left to a capable, well equipped agent. If there has been trouble with slip or drag the agent can check it with special equipment. The agent can also set the release levers. The alternative to having an agent renew these parts is to obtain a factory reconditioned clutch assembly on an exchange basis and it is recommended that this service is utilised in preference to overhauling the existing unit. Exploded diagrams of the clutch are shown in **FIGS 3** and **4**.

3 Assembly and refitting

If a new clutch unit and/or flywheel is to be fitted it will be first necessary to balance the clutch and flywheel as an assembly. To balance the clutch and flywheel refit the clutch assembly to the flywheel aligning the balance marks 'B' (see **FIG 5**) and refit the setscrews to secure the cover assembly. Place the complete assembly on a mandrel and rest the mandrel on two parallel knife edges (see **FIG 6**). If the assembly is found to be out of balance it will be necessary to part the flywheel and clutch assembly and drill $\frac{3}{8}$ inch diameter holes in the flywheel not more than $\frac{1}{2}$ inch deep on the same diameter as the clutch cover dowels until balance is obtained.

Refit the flywheel after ensuring that all burrs are removed in the following way.

Turn the engine to the TDC position for number 1 and 6 cylinders. Rotate the flywheel until the balance mark 'B' is at the bottom and fit to crankshaft flange. Tap home the two dowels, fit the locking plate and screw home the flywheel setscrews to a torque of 67.5 lb ft. These should then be secured by the tab washers.

Assemble the driven plate to the flywheel taking care to place the larger chamfered spline end of the hub towards the gearbox, that is the rear of the car. Centralize the driven plate by means of a dummy shaft which fits the splined bore of the driven plate hub and the spigot bearing in the flywheel. (A constant pinion shaft may be used for this purpose). Fit the three $\frac{1}{4}$ inch distance pieces (see **FIG 2**) between the release levers and the clutch cover. Fit the cover assembly to the flywheel by means of the securing screws, tightening them a turn at a time in a diagonal sequence.

Ensure that the clutch is assembled in the balanced position by aligning the balance marks (see **FIG 5**) and the flywheel dowels to the clutch housing holes. **Do not remove the dummy shaft until all the setscrews are securely tightened.** Remove the dummy shaft. Remove the lockwire and check the tightness of the taper lock bolt retaining the release bearing operating fork to the shaft. Tighten if necessary and lock with new wire. Refit withdrawal bearing and then finally remove the $\frac{1}{4}$ inch distance pieces.

Refitting of the gearbox to the engine and refitting the engine is the reverse procedure to that of removal and is covered in **Chapter 1, Section 3**. Where the gearbox only has been removed this again is replaced in the reverse sequence to that of removal. In both cases however extreme caution should be taken to support the gearbox to prevent any strain on the constant pinion shaft and the driven plate of the clutch.

4 Adjustments

Clutch pedal hydraulic operation:

Adjustment is made at the pushrod situated between the hydraulic operating cylinder and the clutch shaft lever

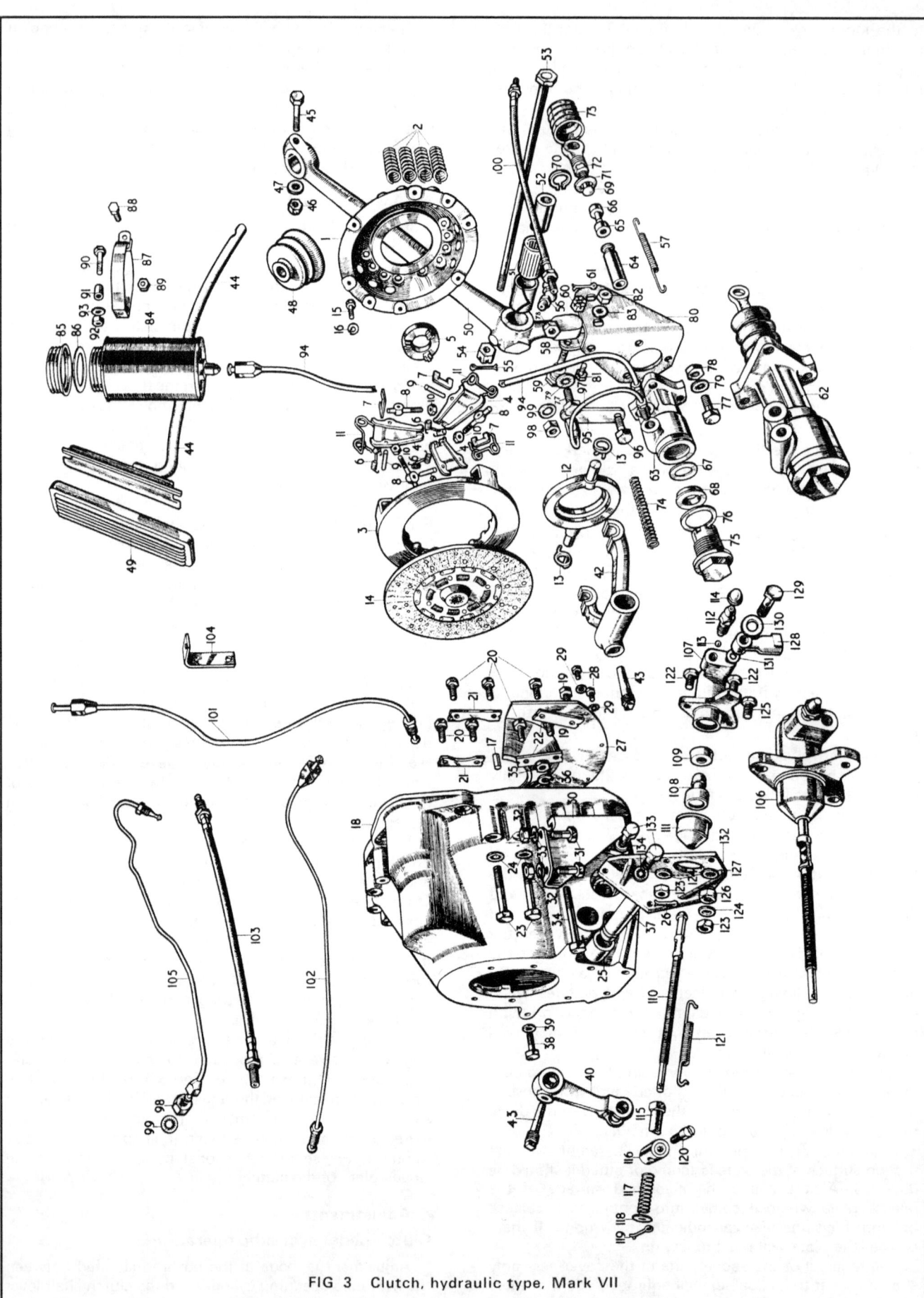

FIG 3 Clutch, hydraulic type, Mark VII

FIG 3   Clutch, hydraulic type, Mark VII

1	Cover only
2	Spring, Thrust
3	Plate, Pressure
4	Lever, Release
5	Plate, Release Lever
6	Retainer, Release Lever
7	Strut, Release Lever
8	Eyebolt, Release Lever
9	Pin through Eyebolt
10	Nut on Eyebolt
11	Spring, Anti-rattle
12	Release Bearing and Cup Assembly
13	Retainer for Release Bearing
14	Driven Plate Assembly
15	Bolt, securing Clutch Unit to Flywheel
16	Washer, Spring, on Bolt
17	Dowel
18	Clutch Housing
19	Screw, Set, securing Clutch Housing to Gearbox
20	Screw, Set, securing Clutch Housing to Gearbox
21	Plate, locking Set Screws inside Clutch Housing
22	Plate, locking Set Screws inside Clutch Housing
23	Bolt, securing Clutch Housing to Cylinder Block
24	Washer, Shakeproof, on Bolt
25	Bush in Clutch Housing for Operation Shaft
26	Pin, Split, in Drain Hole at bottom of Clutch Housing
27	Cover Plate for Clutch Housing
28	Screw, Set, securing Cover Plate
29	Washer, Shakeproof, on Set Screws
30	Support Bracket, Right-hand
31	Bolt, securing Support Bracket to Cylinder Block
32	Nut on Bolts
33	Washer, Spring, under Nuts
34	Bolt, securing Support Bracket to Cylinder Block
35	Nut on Bolts
36	Washer, Spring, under Nuts
37	Clutch Operating Shaft
38	Bolt for Clutch Shaft Location
39	Washer, Spring, on Bolt
40	Lever on Clutch Shaft
42	Clutch Operation Fork
43	Pin (Tapered), locating Lever and Fork on Clutch Shaft
44	Pedal Stem and Plate Assembly
45	Bolt, securing Stem to Clutch Pedal
46	Nut on Bolt
47	Washer, Shakeproof, under Nut
48	Draught Excluder on Pedal Stem
49	Pad (Rubber) on Stem Plate
50	Clutch Pedal
51	Bearing, Roller, in Clutch Pedal Boss
52	Cleeve on Roller Bearing
53	Shaft, supporting Clutch Pedal
54	Nut, Slotted, securing Pedal to Shaft
55	Pin, Split, retaining Nut
56	Nipple, Grease, in Pedal Boss (Tec. NA.5790)
57	Spring, Return
58	Anchor for Return Spring
59	Pin, Fulcrum, connecting Pedal to Master Cylinder
60	Nut on Fulcrum Pin
61	Pin, Split, retaining Nut
62	Master Cylinder for Clutch Operating (Girling H.4007)
63	Body only
64	Plunger
65	Seal on Plunger
66	Retainer for Seal in end of Plunger
67	Shim in Body under Recuperating Seal
68	Seal, Recuperating
69	Rod, Push
70	Circlip, retaining Push Rod in Body
71	Washer, Retaining, on Push Rod
72	Nut, Lock, on Push Rod
73	Boot (Rubber) over Push Rod and end of Body
74	Spring, Return, inside Plunger
75	Cover, End
76	Gasket for End Cover
77	Bolt, securing Master Cylinder to Mounting Bracket
78	Nut on Bolts
79	Washer, Shakeproof, under Nuts
80	Bracket, mounting Master Cylinder
81	Screw, Set, securing Mounting Bracket
82	Nut on Set Screw
83	Washer, Shakeproof, under Nut
84	Supply Tank (less Clip) (Girling 4050404)
85	Cap for Supply Tank
86	Washer, Jointing, inside Cap
87	Clip, securing Supply Tank to Scuttle (Girling H.1509)
88	Screw, Set, clamping Clip to Supply Tank
89	Bolt, securing Clip to Scuttle
90	Nut on Set Screw
91	Piece, Distance, on Bolt
92	Nut on Bolt
93	Washer, Shakeproof, under Nut
94	Low Pressure Pipe from Supply Tank to Master Cylinder
95	Bracket on Master Cylinder for High Pressure Pipe
96	Bolt, securing Bracket to Master Cylinder
97	High Pressure Pipe from Master Cylinder to Bracket
98	Nut, securing High Pressure Pipe to Bracket on Master Cylinder
99	Washer, Shakeproof, under Nut
100	High Pressure Hose from Bracket to Slave Cylinder (Girling H.3670/D)
101	Low Pressure Pipe from Supply Tank to Master Cylinder
102	High Pressure Pipe from Master Cylinder to Bracket on Chassis Frame
103	High Pressure Hose from Pipe to Bracket on Clutch Housing (Girling 497124)
104	Bracket on Clutch Housing for High Pressure Pipe
105	High Pressure Pipe from Hose to Slave Cylinder
106	Slave Cylinder at Right-hand Side of Clutch Housing (Girling 495356)
107	Body only for Slave Cylinder
108	Piston
109	Seal
110	Rod, Push
111	Boot (Rubber)
112	Screw, Bleed
113	Ball (Steel) under Bleed Screw
114	Cap, Dust, on Bleed Screw
115	Nut, Adjusting, on Push Rod
116	Trunnion on Push Rod
117	Spring, tensioning Adjusting Nut
118	Washer, Plain, retaining Washer
119	Pin, Split, retaining Washer
120	Pin in Trunnion, anchoring Return Spring
121	Spring, Return, between Trunnion and Mounting Bracket
122	Bolt, securing Slave Cylinder to Mounting Bracket
123	Nut on Bolts
124	Washer, Shakeproof, under Nuts
125	Bolt, securing Slave Cylinder to Mounting Bracket
126	Nut on Bolt
127	Washer, Shakeproof, under Nut
128	Banjo on Slave Cylinder
129	Bolt, securing Banjo to Slave Cylinder
130	Gasket on Banjo Bolt
131	Gasket on Banjo Bolt
132	Bracket, mounting Slave Cylinder
133	Screw, Set, securing Bracket to Clutch Housing
134	Washer, Shakeproof, on Set Screws

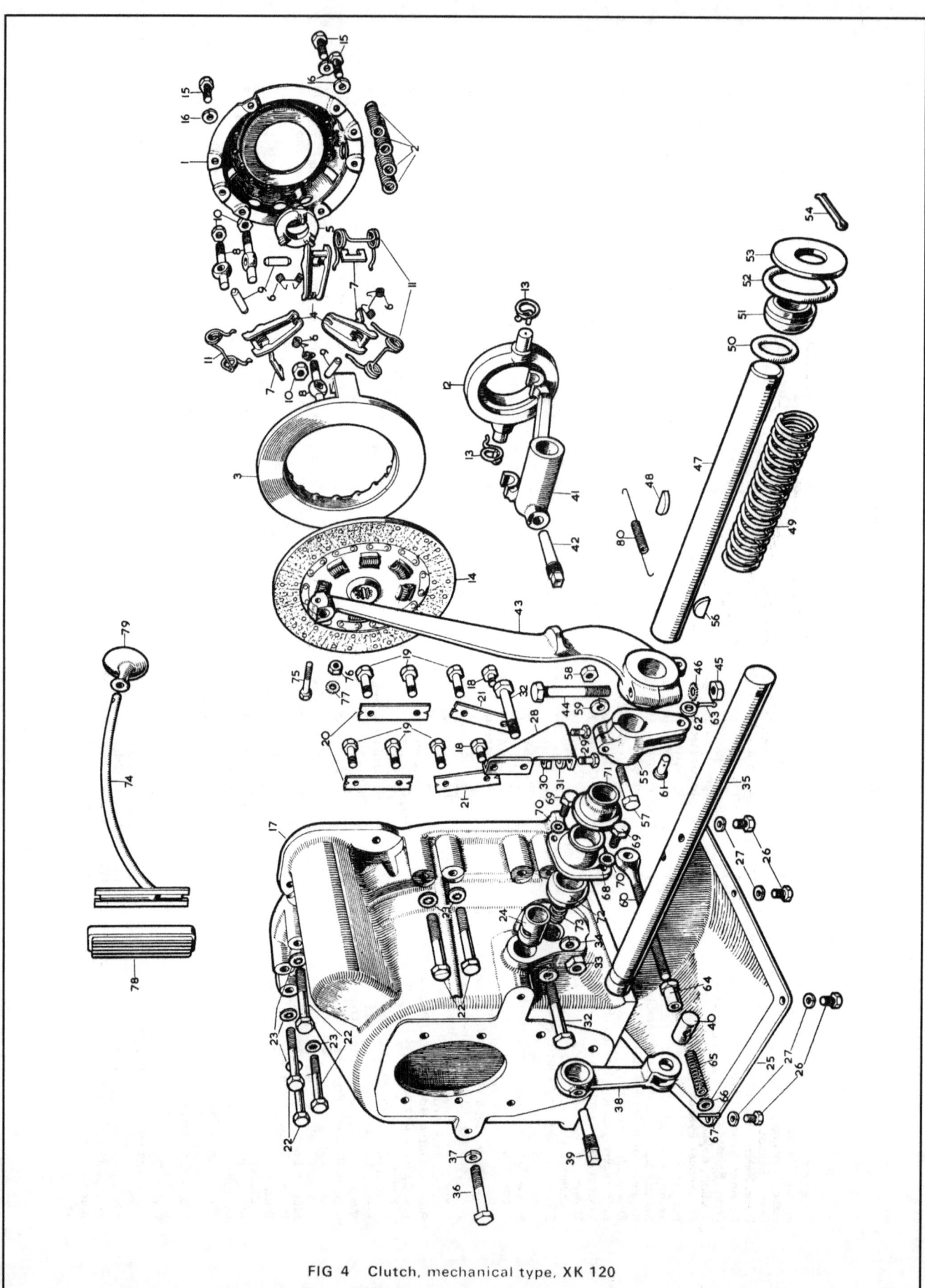

FIG 4 Clutch, mechanical type, XK 120

FIG 4   Clutch, mechanical type, XK 120

1	Cover only
2	Spring, Thrust
3	Plate, Pressure
4	Lever, Release
5	Plate, Release Lever
6	Retainer, Release Lever
7	Strut, Release Lever
8	Eyebolt, Release Lever
9	Pin, through Eyebolt
10	Nut on Eyebolt
11	Spring, Anti-rattle
12	Release Bearing and Cup Assembly
13	Retainer for Release Bearing
14	Driven Plate Assembly
15	Screw, Set, securing Clutch Unit to Flywheel
16	Washer, Spring, on Set Screws
17	Clutch Housing
18	Screw, Set, securing Clutch Housing to Gearbox
19	Screw, Set, securing Clutch Housing to Gearbox
20	Plate, locking Set Screws inside Clutch Housing
21	Plate, locking Set Screws inside Clutch Housing
22	Bolt, securing Clutch Housing to Cylinder Block
23	Washer, Shakeproof, on Bolts
24	Bush in Clutch Housing for Operating Shaft
25	Cover Plate for Clutch Housing
26	Screw, Set, securing Cover Plate
27	Washer, Spring, on Set Screws
28	Support Bracket, Right-hand
29	Bolt, securing Support Bracket to Cylinder Block
30	Nut on Bolts
31	Washer, Spring, under Nuts
32	Bolt, securing Support Bracket to Cylinder Block
33	Nut on Bolts
34	Washer, Spring, under Nuts
35	Clutch Operating Shaft
36	Blot for Clutch Shaft Location
37	Washer, Spring, on Bolt
38	Lever on Clutch Shaft
39	Pin (Tapered), locating Lever on Shaft
40	Trunnion in Fork of Lever
41	Clutch Operating Fork
42	Pin (Tapered), locating Fork on Operating Shaft
43	Clutch Pedal
44	Bolt, securing Clutch Pedal to Shaft
45	Nut on Bolt
46	Washer, Shakeproof, under Nut
47	Shaft, supporting Clutch Pedal
48	Key (Woodruff 90), locating Pedal on Shaft
49	Spring (Outer) on shaft
50	Ring, Sealing (Small), adjacent to Outer Spring
51	Bearing (Spherical) on Shaft, adjacent to Sealing Ring
52	Ring, Sealing (Large), adjacent to Spherical Bearing
53	Washer at end of Shaft
54	Pin, Split, holding Outer Spring under compression
55	Lever on Clutch Pedal Shaft
56	Key (Woodruff 90), locating Lever on Shaft
57	Bolt, securing Lever to Shaft
58	Nut on Bolt
59	Washer, Spring, under Nut
60	Adjusting Rod, between Lever on Pedal and Lever on Clutch Shaft
61	Pin, Clevis, securing Adjusting Rod to Lever on Pedal Shaft
62	Washer (Plain) on Clevis Pin
63	Pin, Split, retaining Clevis Pin in Lever
64	Nut, Barrel, on Adjusting Rod
65	Spring on Adjusting Rod
66	Washer (Plain) on Adjusting Rod at end of Spring
67	Pin, Split, retaining Spring on Adjusting Rod
68	Bearing Housing on Clutch Housing
69	Screw, Set, securing Bearing Housing
70	Washer, Shakeproof, on Set Screws
71	Gaiter on Pedal Shaft over Bearing Housing
72	Bearing (Spherical) inside Housing
73	Spring (Inner), adjacent to Spherical Bearing
74	Pedal Stem and Plate Assembly
75	Bolt, securing Stem to Pedal Shaft
76	Nut on Bolt
77	Washer, Shakeproof, under Nut
78	Pad (Rubber) on Stem Plate
79	Draught Excluder on Pedal Stem
80	Spring, Return, for Clutch Pedal

FIG 5 Clutch and flywheel balance marks

FIG 6 Clutch and flywheel balancing

(see **FIG 7**). To adjust, slacken the locknut behind the brass nut, hold the pushrod with a spanner on the flats provided and rotate the adjuster nut to give 1¼ inch free movement at the pedal pad.

Clutch pedal to master cylinder, Mk VII model:

Adjustment is made at the eccentric pin located at the base of the clutch pedal which bears against the master cylinder pushrod. To adjust, slacken back the eccentric pin to give some clearance on the master cylinder pushrod, set the clutch pedal pad in line laterally with the brake pedal and adjust the eccentric pin so that it contacts but does not depress the master cylinder pushrod. Check that there is 1 inch clearance between the clutch pedal and the engine side of the toeboard.

Clutch pedal mechanical linkage:

Adjustment is carried out at the brass nut fitted to the clutch operating rod. Clockwise rotation of the nut reduces the pedal free travel and anticlockwise rotation increases it. Rotate the adjuster nut (see **FIGS 8 and 9**) until there is 1 inch free movement at the clutch pedal pad. The nut is retained in position by the spring fitted to the operating rod.

5 The master cylinder
Removal:

Unscrew the union nuts securing the two hydraulic pipes to the top of the master cylinder. Plug the ends of the pipes to avoid loss of fluid. Remove the eccentric pin connecting the master cylinder pushrod to the bottom end of the pedal and telease the pedal return spring. Remove the three bolts and nuts securing the master cylinder to the mounting bracket and withdraw the cylinder.

Dismantling:

Prepare a clean space free from oil, grease, dirt etc upon which to work and lay the components (see **FIG 10**). Unscrew the end cap and remove with gasket. Withdraw the plunger return spring, pull back the rubber boot and remove the circlip with a pair of pliers. Withdraw the pushrod. Push the plunger out of the body from the end cap end and detach the seal retainer and end seal. Remove the seal and shim from the body.

Carefully examine all the components for signs of wear and renew as necessary. It is especially important to renew any seals which appear distorted or lack resilience.

Reassembly:

Thoroughly clean all parts with clean Girling brake fluid which should be then discarded—**under no circumstances should other cleaning fluids such as petrol, paraffin or trichlorethelene be used.** The rubber seals and plunger should be smeared with clean fluid immediately before assembly.

Insert the steel shim into the end cap end of the cylinder against the shoulder provided. Replace the seal with the back of the seal towards the shim. Fit the end seal to the plunger with the lip of the seal first so that it is facing away from the concave end of the seal retainer which is refitted next. Insert the plunger open end first into the cylinder from the pushrod end, easing the end seal

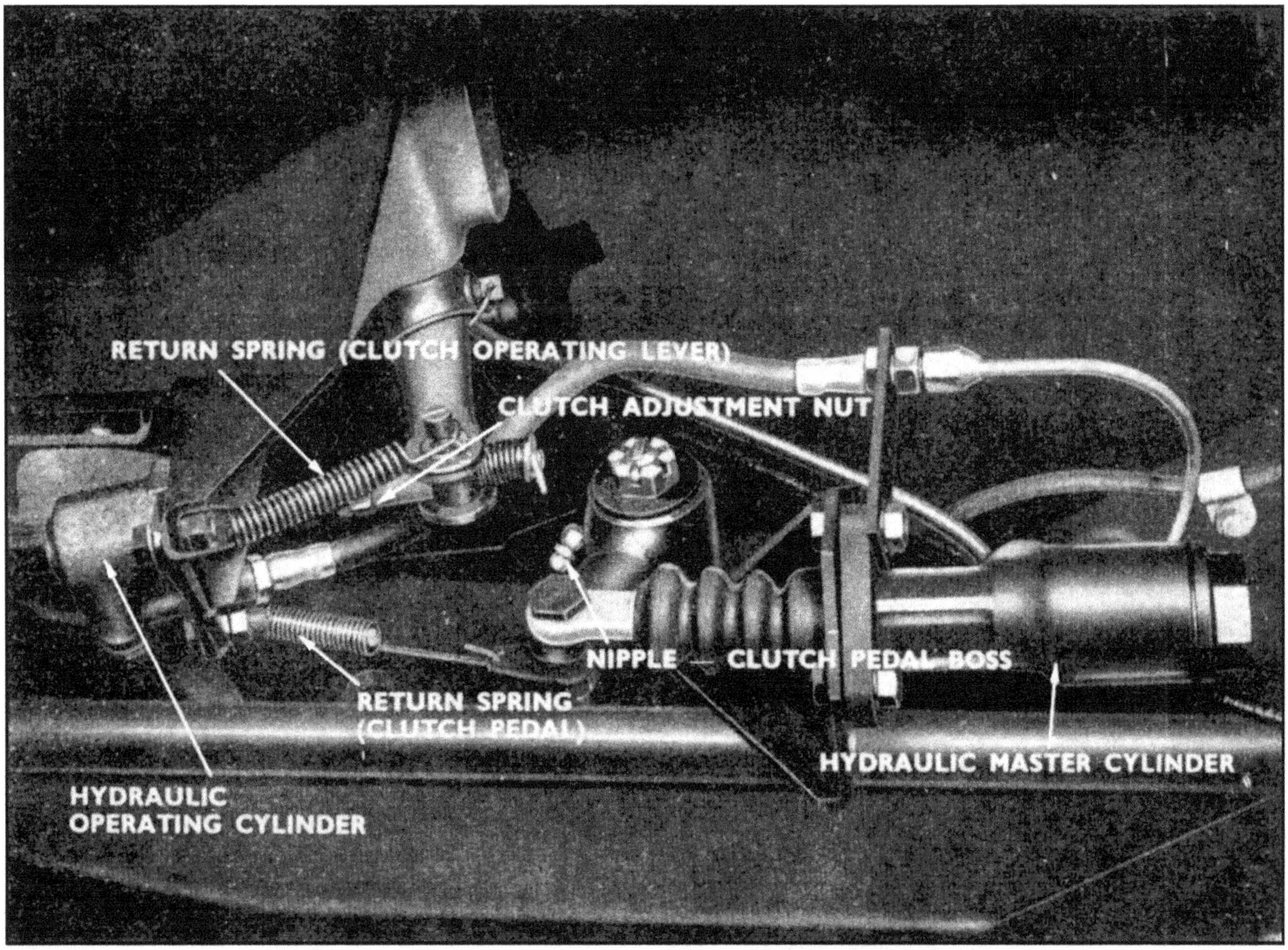

FIG 7 Clutch pedal adjustment hydraulic

carefully into the bore. The lips of both seals should then be facing towards the end cap end of the cylinder. Insert the pushrod assembly rounded end first, into the cylinder bore and replace the washer and circlip. Pack the rubber boot with Girling rubber grease Number 3 red and stretch it over the end with the smallest aperture seating in the collar. Place the plunger return spring into the other end. Refit the end cap and gasket and tighten firmly.

Refitting:

Refitting is the reverse procedure to that described under removal. When the master cylinder has been fitted it is necessary to check that the stroke of the master cylinder pushrod when operated is $1\frac{1}{2}$ inch. The stroke can be set by moving the master cylinder support bracket by means of the slotted holes and resetting the the eccentric pin as described in **Section 4.** Bleed the system to remove air.

6 Clutch operating slave cylinder
Removal:

The slave cylinder does not need to be removed to dismantle it as the components may be removed with the body in situ. To remove the complete unit unscrew the

FIG 8 Clutch pedal adjustment XK 120

FIG 9 Clutch pedal adjustment Mk VII

union and plug the end of the pipe to prevent loss of hydraulic fluid. Unscrew the three bolts securing the body to the clutch bellhousing. Disconnect the pushrod from the clutch shaft lever and withdraw the unit.

Dismantling:

If it is not required to remove the cylinder body the components may be removed after disconnecting the pushrod from the clutch shaft lever. Remove the dust-cover followed by the pushrod, the piston and then the seal as indicated in **FIG 11.** The same standard of cleanliness is required as that observed when dismantling the master cylinder. Examine the components for signs of wear and renew as necessary. Particular attention should be taken of the seal condition which must be renewed if it is distorted or lacks resilience.

Assembly:

Refit the seal with its back to the piston and located over the piston shoulder. Smear the seal and piston with

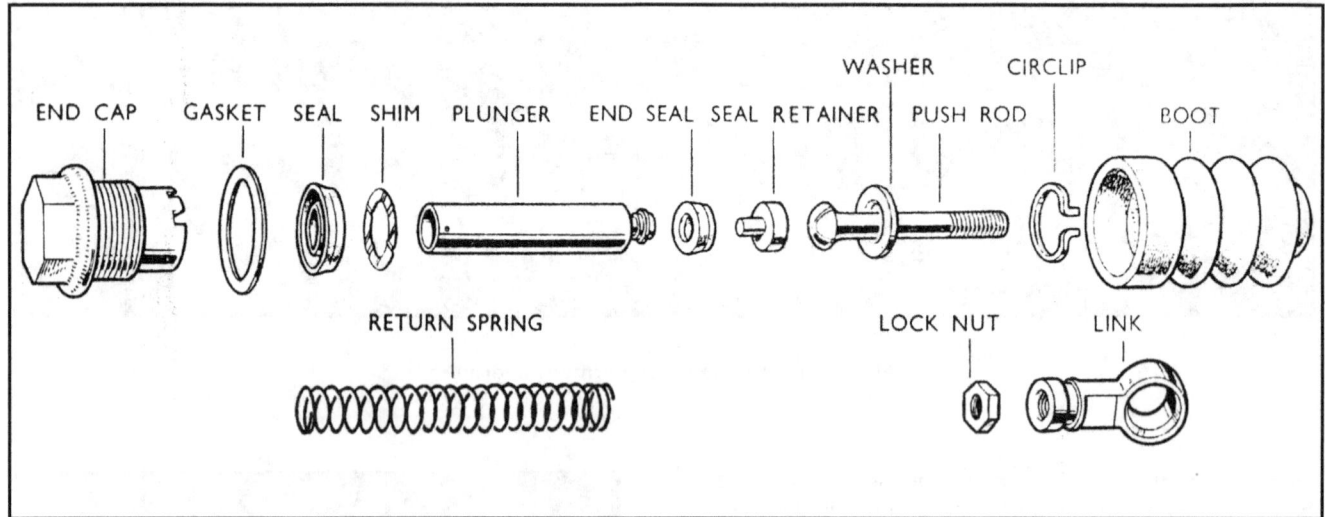

FIG 10 Master cylinder

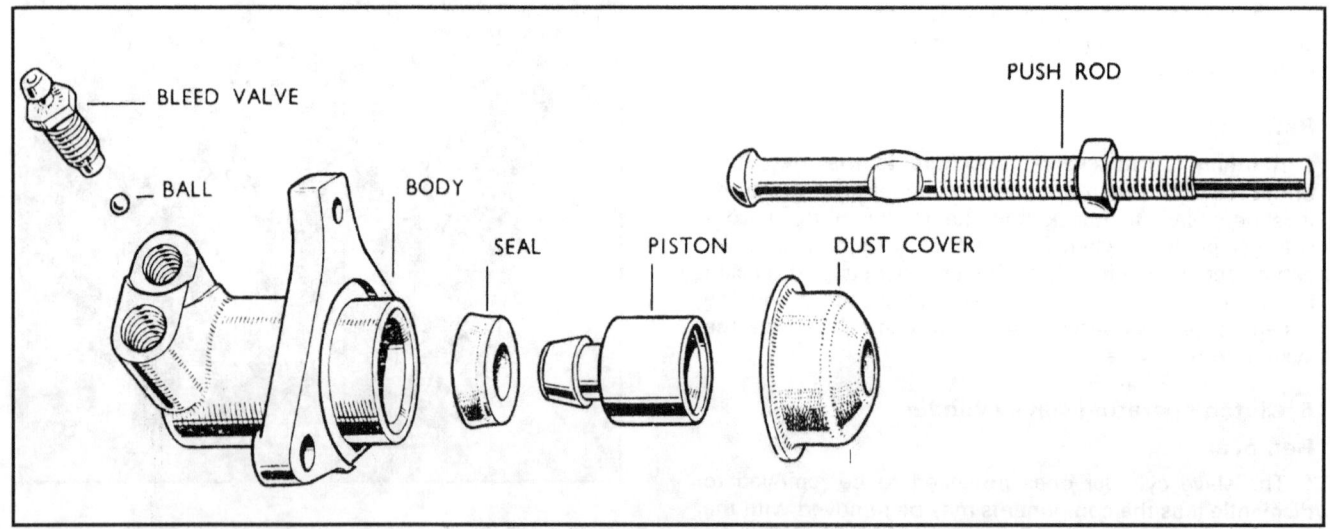

FIG 11 Slave cylinder

clean Girling crimson brake fluid and carefully insert into the cylinder seal first. Replace the rubber dust cover. Reconnect the pushrod to the clutch shaft lever if the body has not been removed from the clutch bellhousing. If the body has been removed refitting is the reverse procedure to that described for removal. Bleed the system.

7 Bleeding the system

Top up the fluid reservoir tank with Girling Crimson Brake Fluid. Remove the rubber dust cap from the bleed nipple on the slave operating cylinder situated at the righthand side of the clutch bell housing. Fit a rubber bleed tube over the bleed nipple the other end of which should be placed in a clean glass jar containing clean hydraulic fluid. This tube must be kept below the surface lever of the fluid throughout the following operation. Unscrew the bleed nipple about three-quarters of a turn and operate the clutch pedal to its full travel a few times, allowing a two or three second pause between strokes. Pumping must be continued until no further air bubbles are produced in the container. Care must be taken to keep the fluid level in the reservoir up or air will get into the system and the whole operation wasted. When there are no further traces of air hold the clutch pedal in the depressed position and tighten the bleed screw. Remove the bleed tube and replace the rubber dust excluder.

8 Modifications

The only modification made to the clutch system was the introduction of a strengthened slave cylinder support bracket on the XK150 and the Mk IX models from chassis numbers:

		Righthand drive	Lefthand drive
XK150	Open 2-seater	820043	832089
	Fixed head coupé	824903	836227
	Drop head coupé	827379	838273
Mk IX		771823	791081

If on these models prior to the chassis numbers given it is found that the clutch does not fully disengage when the normal pedal adjustment is correct, an examination should be made to ascertain if the clutch slave cylinder mounting bracket is flexing when the clutch pedal is fully depressed.

If this is found to be so, a strengthened type of bracket should be fitted.

There has also been a change in the recommended fluid to be used for the clutch hydraulic system. The recommended fluids for use in the clutch may be found in the Lubrication Data section in the Appendix of this manual.

9 Fault diagnosis

(a) Drag or spin

1 Oil or grease on driven plate facings
2 Misalignment between engine and gearbox first motion shaft
3 Leaking master cylinder, slave cylinder or pipeline
4 Driven plate hub binding on first motion shaft splines
5 Binding of first motion shaft spigot bearing
6 Distorted clutch plate
7 Warped or damaged pressure plate or clutch cover
8 Broken driven plate facing linings
9 Air in clutch hydraulic system

(b) Fierceness or snatch

1 Check 1, 2 and 3 in (a)
2 Worn clutch linings

(c) Slip

1 Check 1 and 2 in (a)
2 Check 2 in (b)
3 Weak pressure springs
4 Siezed piston in slave cylinder
5 No free pedal movement

(d) Judder

1 Check 1 and 2 in (a)
2 Pressure plate not parallel with flywheel face
3 Contact area of driven plate linings not evenly distributed
4 Bent first motion shaft
5 Buckled driven plate
6 Faulty engine or gearbox mountings
7 Worn suspension shackles
8 Weak rear springs
9 Loose propeller shaft bolts
10 Worn propeller shaft universal joints
11 Loose rear spring clips

(e) Rattle

1 Check 3 in (c)
2 Broken springs in driven plate
3 Worn release mechanism
4 Excessive backlash in transmission
5 Wear in transmission bearings
6 Release bearing loose on fork

(f) Tick or knock

1 Worn first motion shaft spigot or bearing
2 Badly worn splines in driven plate hub
3 Release plate misaligned
4 Faulty Bendix drive on starter motor
5 Loose flywheel

(g) Driven plate fracture

1 Check 2 in (a)
2 Drag and distortion due to weight of gearbox acting on driven plate hub

INDEX – MANUAL GEARBOX & OVERDRIVE

SECTION	PAGE	
		MANUAL GEARBOX
001	75	Description of SH, JH, SL, JL & JS Gearboxes
002	75	Routine Maintenance
003	75	Removal
004	75	Disassembly (General)
	84	Disassembly SH Series
	86	Disassembly JH Series
005	89	Inspection
006	91	Reassembly
007	92	Fault Diagnosis Chart
		OVERDRIVE
008	93	Description & Operation
009	93	Driving Technique
010	97	Routine Maintenance & Adjustments
011	98	Electrical Circuit (Single & Two Relay Systems)
012	100	Modifications by Engine Number & Model
013	101	Disassembly & Reassembly
014	103	Fault Diagnosis Chart

GEARBOX

This chapter is divided into four parts. The three main sections are (1) The Manual Gearbox (2) The Overdrive unit and (3) The Automatic Gearbox. Section (3) is sub-divided into two parts covering both the early and late models of Borg Warner automatic transmissions.

MANUAL GEARBOX - SERVICE

1 Description

There are five types of gearbox fitted to the range of models covered by this manual. These are the series SH, JH, SL, JL and JS gearboxes. All models are synchromesh gearboxes, the constant mesh gears, that is second, third and top having helical teeth. The constant mesh gears are brought into engagement by synchronizing dog clutches of the toothed variety. The internally toothed members slide on synchronizing sleeves which are splined to the mainshaft; these members are combined with internal cones for the synchromesh mechanism, the corresponding external cones and external dogs being formed on the gearwheels. First and reverse gears are of straight tooth form, the reverse wheel being bushed and mounted on a short shaft situated to the offside (righthand) and slightly above the countershaft. Selection of the gears is by rods and forks operated by a lever mounted on an extension of the gearbox cover. An exploded diagram of the top cover and gearbox casing of the SH and JH types is shown in **FIG 1**, and exploded diagrams of the gears for the SH and JH series are shown in **FIGS 2** and **3** respectively.

The SH and JH series gearboxes are fitted to early models and are fully interchangeable as complete units even though their internal construction differs. The difference between these two gearbox types is in the construction of the constant pinion shaft and the countershaft gears, the constant pinion shaft wheel being dogged to the shaft on the series SH and integral with the shaft on the JH. On the series JH the countershaft gears consist of 1st speed and integral splined sleeve on which are mounted second, third and constant mesh gears. On the series SH the countershaft gears, first, second, third and constant mesh are a cluster gear. These differences can be seen in **FIG 2** and **3**.

For identification purposes the gearbox number is prefixed with the designating letters SH or JH, this number is stamped on a boss situated at the nearside (lefthand) rear at the top of the gearbox case and on the rim of the core plug aperture in the top cover. The number is also given on a plate fixed to the scuttle.

On the later Jaguar models the series SL and JL gearboxes are fitted, these differ from the earlier types in that they have a shorter mainshaft and no rear extension and bearing, the rear end cover being directly attached to the rear face of the gearbox casing. On cars fitted with SL or JL gearboxes a longer propeller shaft (or front shaft) and a different length speedometer cable are fitted so that they are not interchangeable with the earlier types. It should also be noted that these later gearboxes are not interchangeable between the various models of cars.

The final type of gearbox fitted is the JS series which is fitted to the Mk VIII model this is very similar to the series JL and SL models.

The descriptions and illustrations in this section apply specifically to the SH and JH series gearbox units. The SL and JL units being very similar in construction with the exception of the rear extension and bearing.

2 Maintenance

At intervals of 2500 miles the oil level in the gearbox should be checked by means of the dipstick with the car on level ground.

The dipstick is accessible after removing the inspection plate situated just forward of the gearlever. If necessary top up the gearbox with the correct grade of oil through the dipstick aperture. If an overdrive unit is fitted the oil level in it is determined by that in the gearbox so that both will be covered by the one check.

Every 10,000 miles the gearbox should be drained of oil and then flushed out with a good flushing oil and then refilled with new oil of the correct grade. The gearbox drain plug is accessible from beneath the car and draining will be made easier and more thorough if carried out with the gearbox warm, i.e. after a good run.

3 Removal

The engine and gearbox are best removed as one unit from the car this method is described fully in **Chapter 1, Section 3**. On the XK120 model it is possible to remove the gearbox only, this method is covered fully in **Chapter 5, Section 2**.

Where the engine and gearbox have been removed as one unit the gearbox may be removed from the engine in the following manner.

Remove the two bolts and nuts securing the starter to the clutch housing and withdraw the starter motor. Remove the pressed steel coverplate from the bottom of the clutch housing. Unscrew the bolts securing the clutch housing to the engine whilst supporting the gearbox. The gearbox unit may then be separated from the engine by withdrawing it backwards in line with the engine. Care must be taken during this operation to ensure that the gearbox is adequately supported or undue strain may be placed on the clutch driven plate and the constant pinion shaft.

4 Dismantling

Drain the gearbox by removing the drain plug situated underneath. Withdraw the dipstick then remove the ten setscrews with their spring washers securing the top cover. Lift off the top cover carefully as there are locating dowels. If the joint is very firm tap the cover with a mallet to break the seal. The cover gasket should be removed and discarded.

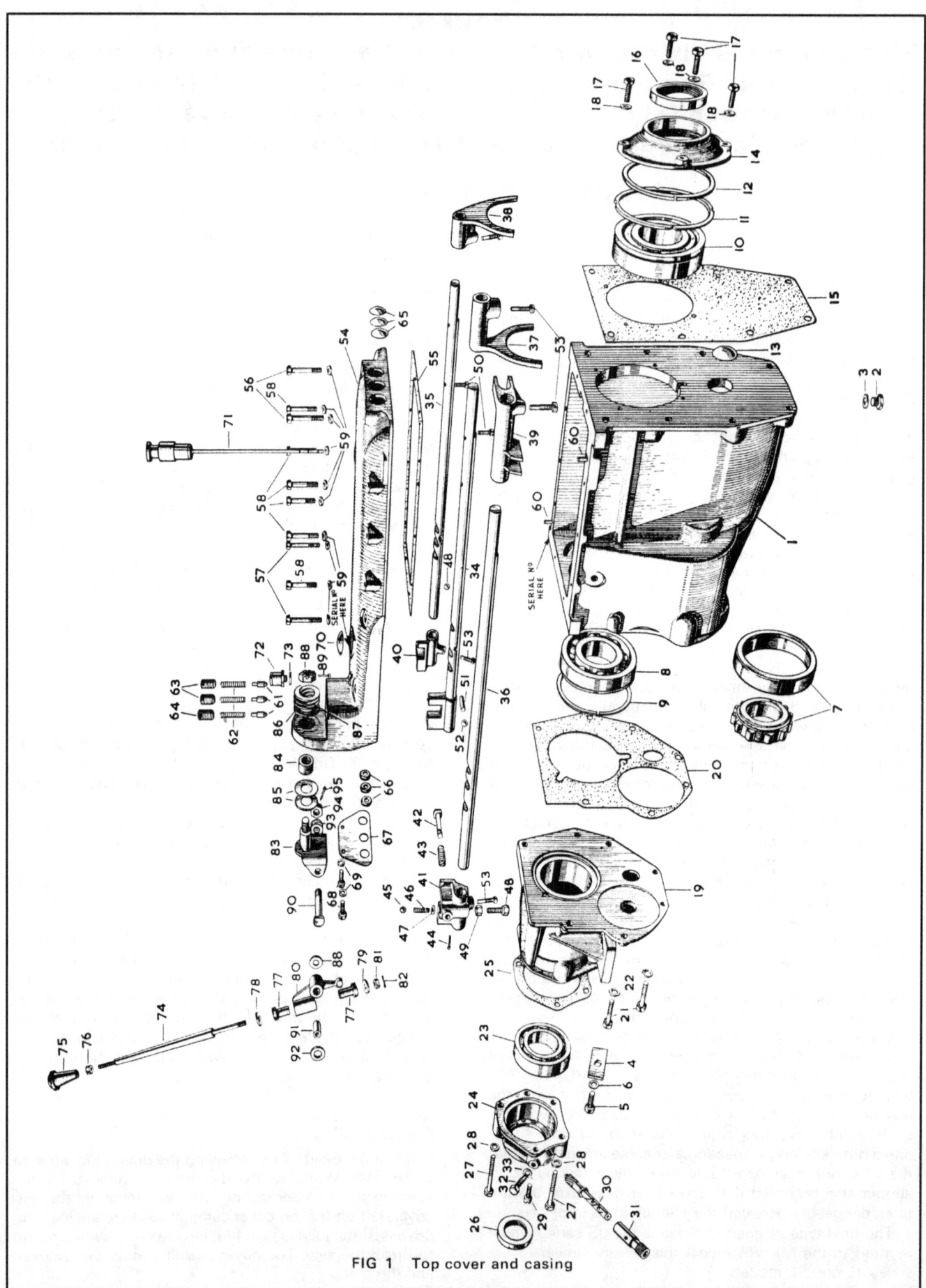

FIG 1 Top cover and casing

FIG 1   Top cover and casing

1	Gearbox Casing
2	Plug, Drain, at bottom of Casing
3	Washer (Fibre) on Drain Plug
4	Plate, locking Counter and Reverse Shafts
5	Screw, Set, securing Locking Plate
6	Washer, Spring, on Setscrews
7	Bearing, Roller, for Mainshaft
8	Bearing, Ball, for Mainshaft
9	Circlip on Mainshaft Bearing
10	Bearing, Ball, for Constant Pinion Shaft
11	Collar between Casing and Circlip
12	Circlip on Ball Bearing, behind Collar
13	Washer (Fibre) in Casing, at front end of Countershaft
14	Front End Cover
15	Washer, Jointing, between Front Cover and Casing
16	Seal, Oil
17	Screw, Set, securing Cover to Casing
18	Washer (Copper) on Setscrews
19	Gearbox Extension
20	Washer, Jointing, between Extension and Casing
21	Screw, Set, securing Extension to Casing
22	Washer, Spring, on Setscrews
23	Bearing, Ball
24	Rear End Cover
25	Washer, Jointing, between Rear End Cover and Extension
26	Seal, Oil
27	Bolt, securing Cover to Extension
28	Washer, Spring, on Bolts
29	Screw, Set, in aperture for Speedo Driven Gear, securing Cover to Extension
30	Gear, Speedometer Driven
31	Bearing for Speedometer Driven Gear
32	Screw, locking Bearing in Cover
33	Washer, Spring, on Locking Screw
34	Rod, Striking (1st/2nd Gears)
35	Rod, Striking (3rd/Top Gears)
36	Rod, Striking (Reverse Gear)
37	Fork, Change-Speed (1st/2nd Gears)
38	Fork, Change-Speed (3rd/Top Gears)
39	Fork, Change-Speed Plunger in Reverse Selector
40	Selector (3rd/Top)
41	Selector (Reverse)
42	Plunger in Reverse Selector
43	Spring on Plunger
44	Pin, Split, securing Plunger in Reverse Selector
45	Ball, locking Plunger
46	Spring, under Ball
47	Shim, under Spring
48	Screw, Set, in Reverse Selector, adjusting tension on Spring
49	Nut, locking Setscrew in position
50	Pin, Stop, on 1st/2nd and 3rd/Top Striking Rods
51	Roller for Interlock (in 1st/2nd Striking Rod)
52	Balls for Interlock (in 3rd/Top and Reverse Striking Rods)
53	Screw, Set (Taper), securing Forks and Selectors
54	Top Cover
55	Washer, Jointing, between Cover and Casing
56	Bolt, securing Cover
57	Bolt, securing Cover
58	Washer, Spring, on Bolts
59	Dowel, in Casing, positioning Top Cover
60	Plunger, engaging Striking Rods
61	Spring, top of Plungers
62	Screw, Grub, applying tension to Plungers for 1st/2nd and 3rd/Top Striking Rods
63	Screw, Grub, applying tension to Plunger for Reverse Striking Rod
64	Plug in front end of Cover
65	Washer (Felt) in rear end of Cover
66	Plate, covering Felt Washers
67	Screw, Set, securing Cover Plate
68	Washer, Spring, on Setscrews
69	Plug, Core, on top of Cover
70	Dipstick
71	Plug, Breather, on top of Cover
72	Washer (Fibre) on Breather Plug
73	Change-Speed Lever
74	Knob on Lever
75	Nut, locking Knob to Lever
76	Bearing, Flexible, housing Change-Speed Lever in Selector Lever
77	Washer at top of Flexible Bearing
78	Washer at bottom of Flexible Bearing
79	Lever, Selector, housing Change-Speed Lever
80	Nut, Slotted, securing Change-Speed Lever in Selector Lever
81	Pin, Split, securing Slotted Nut
82	Jaw, Pivot, for Pivot Jaw
83	Bush for Pivot Jaw
84	Washer, Thrust, on Pivot Jaw
85	Washer, Locking, on Pivot Jaw
86	Washer, Spring, on Pivot Jaw
87	Nut, Slotted, securing Pivot Jaw
88	Pin, Split, securing Slotted Nut
89	Pin, Pivot, mounting Selector Lever in Pivot Jaw
90	Bush, in Selector Lever, for Pivot Jaw
91	Washer, Thrust, at each side of Selector Lever
92	Washer, Spring, between Thrust Washer and Pivot Jaw
93	Nut, Slotted, securing Pivot Pin
94	Pin, Split, securing Slotted Nut

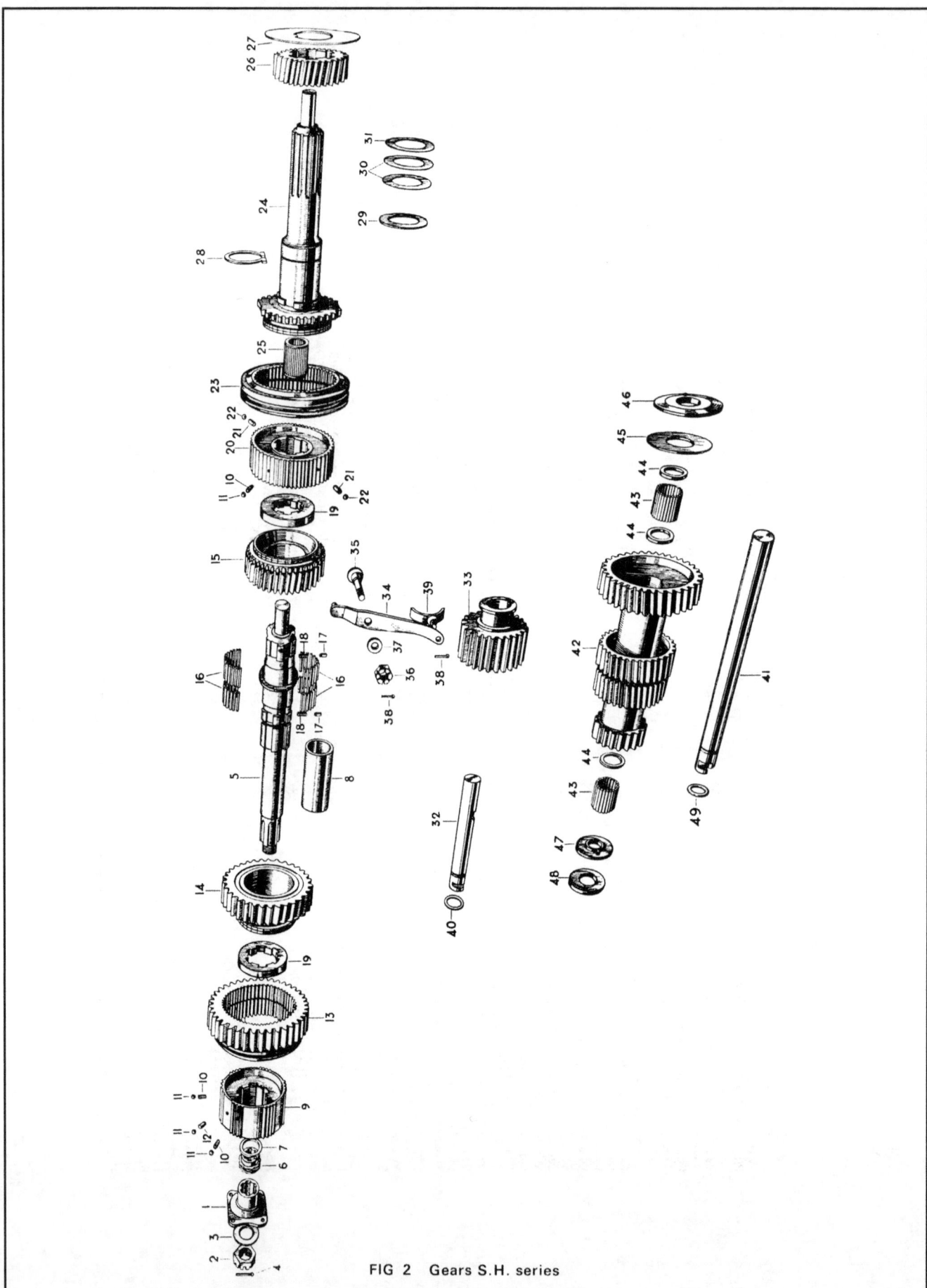

FIG 2 Gears S.H. series

FIG 2 Gears S.H. series

1	Flange on Mainshaft
2	Nut, Slotted, securing Flange
3	Washer, Plain, under Slotted Nut
4	Pin, Split, securing Slotted Nut
5	Mainshaft
6	Gear, Speedometer Driving
7	Piece, Distance, behind Speedometer Gear
8	Sleeve, Distance, on Mainshaft
9	Sleeve, Synchronising, 2nd Speed
10	Spring in 2nd and 3rd/Top Speeds Synchro Sleeves
11	Ball in 2nd and 3rd/Top Speeds Synchro Sleeves
12	Plunger in 2nd Speed Synchro Sleeve
13	Wheel, Gear, 1st Speed
14	Wheel, Gear, 2nd Speed
15	Wheel, Gear, 3rd Speed
16	Roller, Needle, in 2nd and 3rd Speed Gear Wheels
17	Plunger, in Mainshaft, locking 2nd and 3rd Speed Gear Wheels
18	Spring under Plungers
19	Washer, Thrust, front and rear of 2nd and 3rd Speed Gear Wheels
20	Sleeve, Synchronising, 3rd/Top Speeds
21	Plunger in 3rd/Top Synchro Sleeve
22	Ball for Plungers
23	Sleeve, Operating, 3rd/Top Speeds
24	Constant Pinion Shaft
25	Bearing, Roller, inside Shaft
26	Pinion, Constant
27	Thrower, Oil
28	Circlip, behind Shims on Shaft (Seeger 40 mm. Ext.)
29	Washer, Packing, between Ball Bearing and Shims
30	Shim, .003" thick, between Packing Washer and Circlip
31	Shim, .005" thick, between Packing Washer and Circlip
32	Reverse Spindle
33	Gear, Reverse (complete with Bush)
34	Lever, operating Reverse Gear
35	Pin, Fulcrum, for Operating Lever
36	Nut, Slotted, securing Fulcrum Pin
37	Washer, Plain, under Slotted Nut
38	Pin, Split, securing Fulcrum Pin and Reverse Slipper
39	Slipper, Reverse
40	Ring, Sealing (Cord), for Reverse Spindle
41	Countershaft
42	Gear Unit (Cluster)
43	Roller, Needle, inside Gear Unit
44	Ring, retaining Needle Rollers
45	Washer, Thrust, Inner, at front of Countershaft
46	Washer, Thrust, Outer, at front of Countershaft
47	Washer, Thrust, Inner, at rear of Countershaft
48	Washer, Thrust, Outer, at rear of Countershaft (.156" thick)
48	Washer, Thrust, Outer, at rear of Countershaft (.159" thick)
48	Washer, Thrust, Outer, at rear of Countershaft (.162" thick)
48	Washer, Thrust, Outer, at rear of Countershaft (.152" thick)
48	Washer, Thrust, Outer, at rear of Countershaft (.164" thick)
49	Ring, Sealing (Cord), for Countershaft

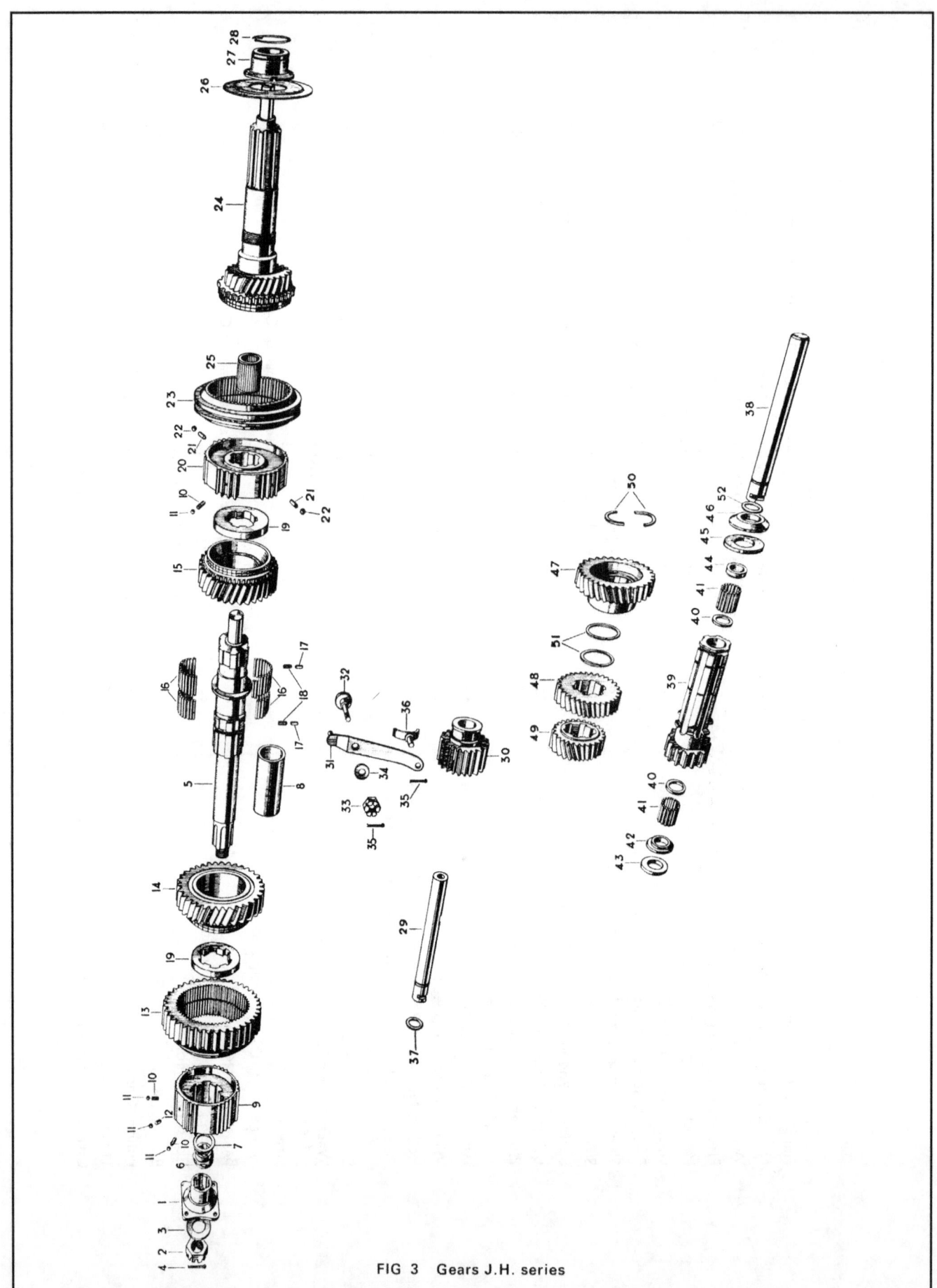

FIG 3 Gears J.H. series

FIG 3 Gears J.H. series

1	Flange on Mainshaft
2	Nut, Slotted, securing Flange
3	Washer, Plain, under Slotted Nut
4	Pin, Split, securing Slotted Nut
5	Mainshaft
6	Gear, Speedometer Driving
7	Piece, Distance, behind Speedometer Driving Gear
8	Sleeve, Distance, on Mainshaft
9	Sleeve, Synchronising, 2nd Speed
10	Spring, in 2nd and 3rd/Top Speeds Synchro Sleeves
11	Ball in 2nd and 3rd/Top Speeds Synchro Sleeves
12	Plunger in 2nd Speed Synchro Sleeve (.490" long)
12	Plunger in 2nd Speed Synchro Sleeve (.495" long)
12	Plunger in 2nd Speed Synchro Sleeve (.500" long)
13	Wheel, Gear, 1st Speed
14	Wheel, Gear, 2nd Speed
15	Wheel, Gear, 3rd Speed
16	Roller, Needle, in 2nd and 3rd Speed Gear Wheels
17	Plunger, in Mainshaft, locking 2nd and 3rd Speed Gear Wheels
18	Spring under Plungers
19	Washer, Thrust, front and rear of 2nd and 3rd Speed Gear Wheels (.471"/.472" thick)
19	Washer, Thrust, front and rear of 2nd and 3rd Speed Gear Wheels (.473"/.474" thick)
19	Washer, Thrust, front and rear of 2nd and 3rd Speed Gear Wheels (.475"/.476" thick)
20	Sleeve, Synchronising, 3rd/Top Speeds
21	Plunger in 3rd/Top Synchro Sleeve
22	Ball for Plungers
23	Sleeve, Operating, 3rd/Top Speeds
24	Constant Pinion Shaft Assembly
25	Bearing, Roller, inside Shaft
26	Thrower, Oil
27	Nut, locking Bearing to Shaft
28	Circlip, securing Locknut
29	Reverse Spindle
30	Gear, Reverse (complete with Bush)
31	Lever, operating Reverse Gear
32	Pin, Fulcrum, for operating Lever
33	Nut, Slotted, securing Fulcrum Pin
34	Washer, Plain, under Slotted Nut
35	Pin, Split, securing Fulcrum Pin and Reverse Slipper
36	Slipper, Reverse
37	Ring, Sealing (Cord) on Reverse Spindle
38	Countershaft
39	Gear, 1st Speed (on Counter)
40	Ring, Retaining, at rear of Needle Rollers
41	Roller, Needle
42	Washer, Thrust, Inner, at rear end of Counter, adjacent to Needle Rollers
43	Washer, Thrust, Outer, at rear end of Counter (.156" thick)
43	Washer, Thrust, Outer, at rear end of Counter (.159" thick)
43	Washer, Thrust, Outer, at rear end of Counter (.162" thick)
43	Washer, Thrust, Outer, at rear end of Counter (.152" thick)
43	Washer, Thrust, Outer, at rear end of Counter (.164" thick)
44	Ring, Retaining, on outer end of Front Needle Rollers
45	Washer, Thrust, Inner, at front end of Counter
46	Washer, Thrust, Outer, at front end of Counter
47	Wheel, Constant
48	Gear, 3rd Speed
49	Gear, 2nd Speed
50	Ring, Split, locating Constant Wheel
51	Circlip, positioning 3rd Speed Gear and Constant Wheel
52	Ring, Sealing (Cord) on Countershaft

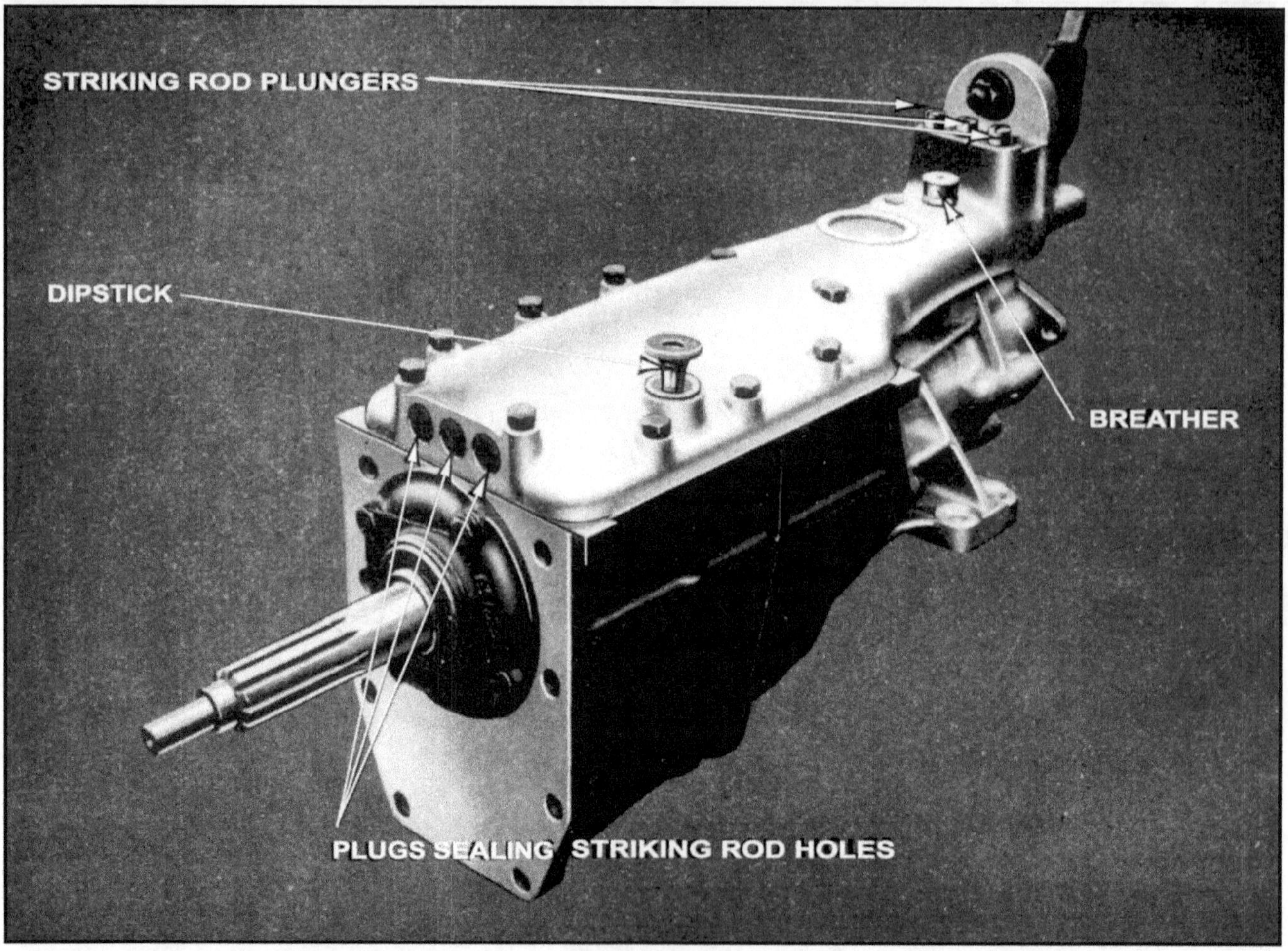

FIG 4 Top cover front view

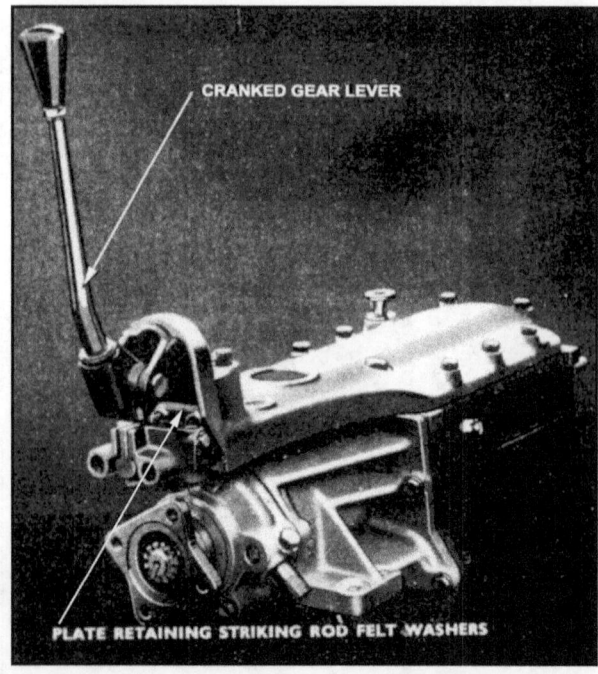

FIG 5 Top cover rear view

Top cover dismantling:

The top cover is shown externally in **FIGS 4** and **5** and an exploded view is shown in **FIG 1**.

Remove the splitpin and slotted nut with its spring washer securing the selector lever pivot pin 94 and 95 (see **FIG 1**). Withdraw the selector lever 80 complete with changespeed lever 74. Note the bush 91 with two thrust washers 92 for the selector lever. Remove the splitpin 82, and slotted nut 81, securing the changespeed lever 74, to the selector lever 80, and dismantle, noting the flexible rubber bearings in two halves 77, with thrust washers 78 and 79. Release and remove locknut 76 and lever knob 75.

Remove the split pin 89 and slotted nut 88 securing pivot jaw 83, noting the relative positions of the bush 84, thrust washers 85, 87 and the locking washer 86.

Unscrew the breather 72 and the reverse lamp switch and remove. Break the wire on the three striking rod plunger grub screws 63, 64. Remove the grubscrews, springs and plungers 61.

Break the locking wire and remove the stop pin from first/second and third/top striking rods 34 and 35. Break the locking wire and remove the lockbolts 53 securing the changespeed forks to the three striking rods. Draw the striking rods 34, 35 and 36, one at a time, to the rear out of the cover, collecting the interlock roller 51 and two interlocking balls 52, as they are released. Remove the selectors from third/top and reverse striking rods by breaking locking wire and withdrawing lockbolts. Note that the first and second selector is integral with the striking rod. Dismantle the reverse selector 41 by withdrawing split pin 44 and removing plunger 42 with spring 43 and locking ball 45 and springs 46.

The front ends of the striking rod holes in the top cover are sealed by plugs 65. Tap the centre of the plug with a hammer and punch until they are free. The rear ends of the striking rods are sealed by a plate 67, retaining felt seals 66 in recesses in each striking rod hole. Remove the two setscrews with spring washers securing plate to the cover and withdraw the plate and felt washers.

Gearbox dismantling:

Break the locking wire and remove the four setscrews with copper washers securing the front end cover 14 to the gearbox casing. Remove the front end cover. Remove the oil seal 16. Note the oil drain at the bottom of the cover which mates with a return hole in the gearbox casing with interposed felt washer 13 (see **FIG 6 & 1**).

Engage top and reverse gears to lock the gear train, remove the split pin, slotted nut and plain washer securing the propeller shaft drive flange to the mainshaft. Tap the drive flange off the shaft. Remove the four bolts

FIG 6   Front end covers

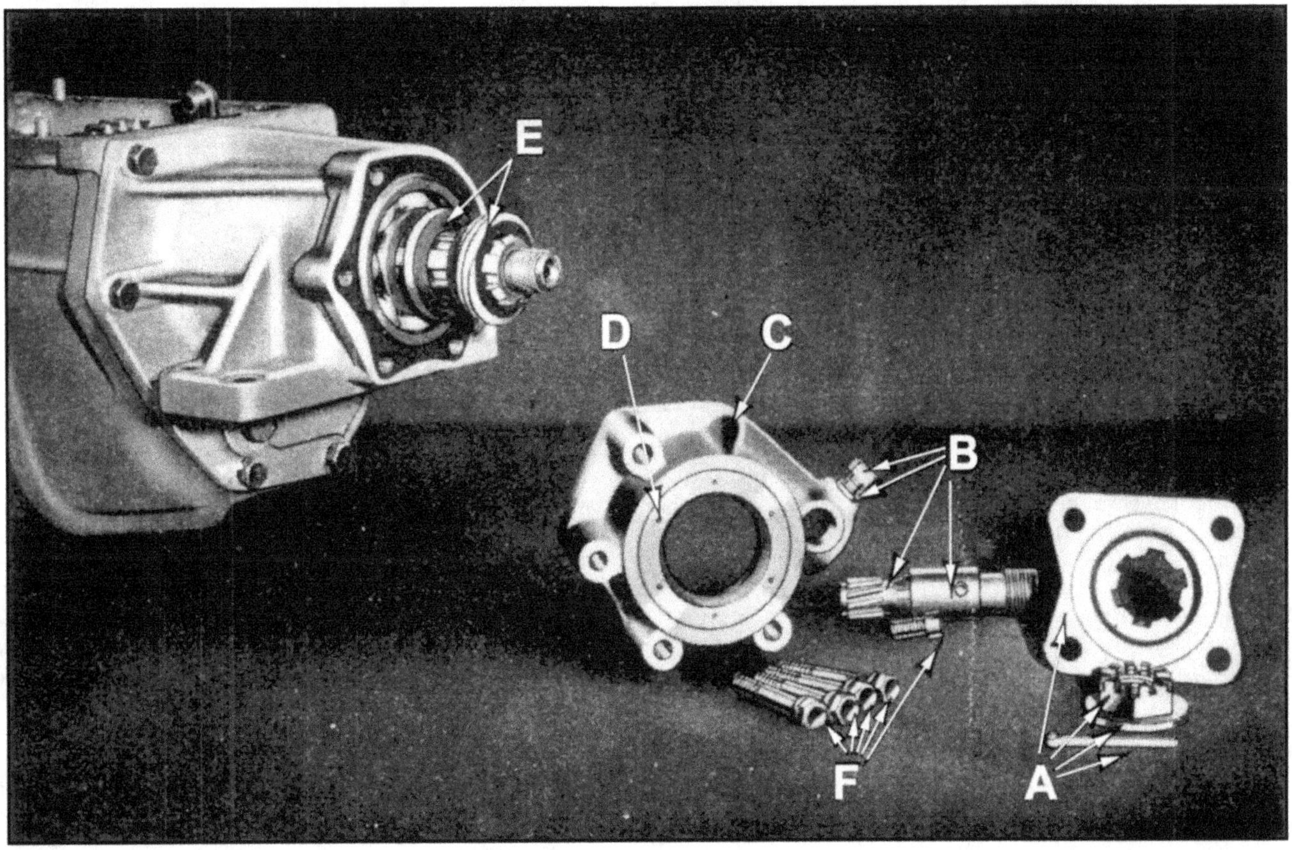

FIG 7   Rear end cover

A Propeller shaft drive flange, slotted nut, washer and splitpin
B Speedometer driven gear, bush, lockscrew and spring washer
C Rear end cover
D Oil seal
E Speedometer driving gear and distance piece
F Cover securing bolts and cheeseheaded setscrew

83

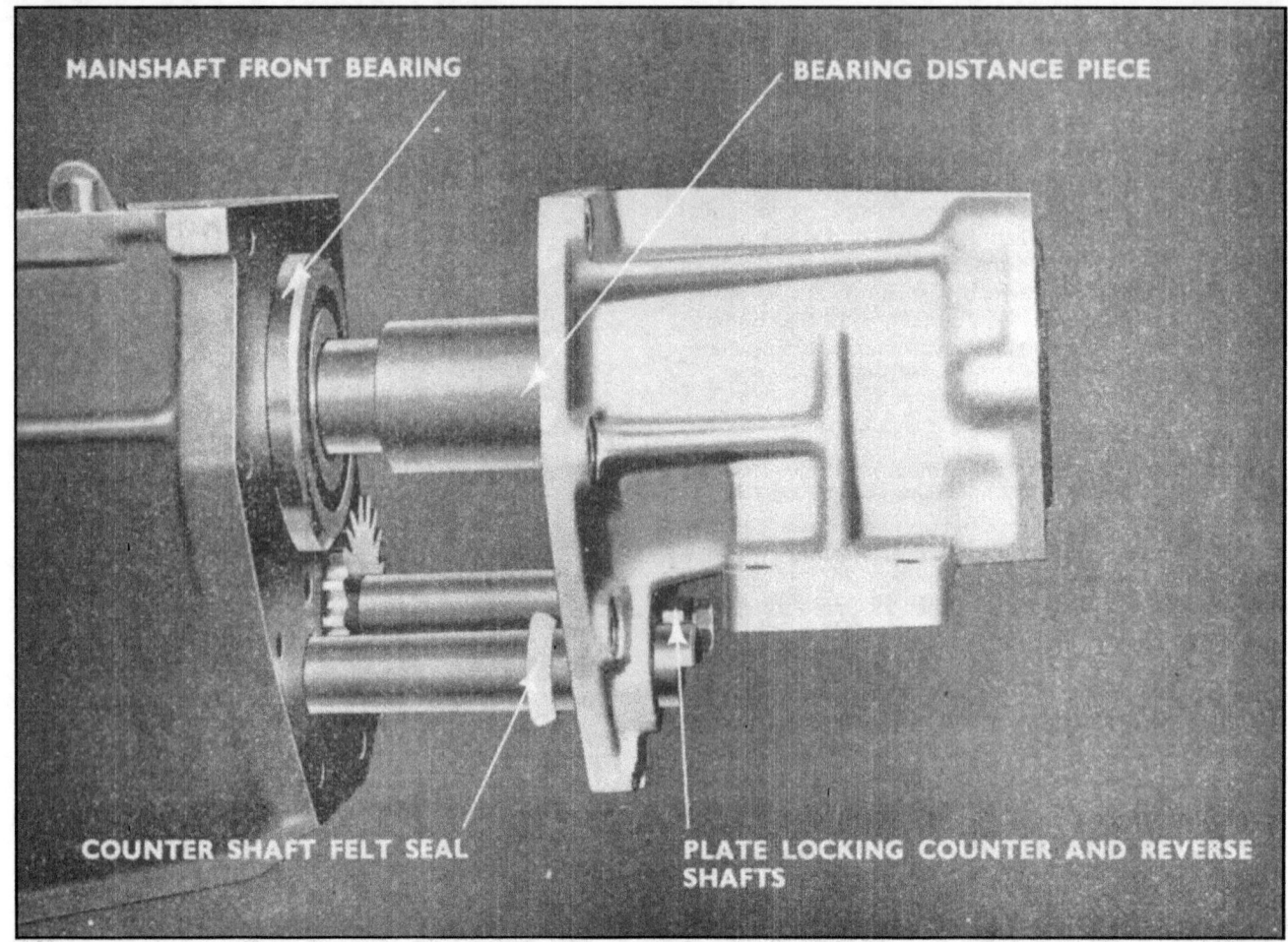

FIG 8 Extension

with spring washers securing the rear end cover 24 to the extension 19. Remove the locking screw 32 with spring washer securing the speedometer driven gear in the rear end cover. Withdraw the driven gear 30, and bearing 31. Remove the cheeseheaded setscrew now disclosed securing cover to extension. Remove the rear end cover (see **FIG 7**). Remove and scrap the oil seal from the cover and the joint washer. Withdraw the speedometer driving gear and distance piece behind gear from mainshaft (see **FIG 7**).

Disengage top and reverse gears to position the gearbox in neutral. Remove the seven setscrews with spring washers securing the extension to the case. Do not disturb the plate locking counter and reverse shafts (see **FIG 8**) since these will be withdrawn with the extension. Using a suitable puller engaging on the mainshaft and the extension draw off the extension complete with the mainshaft rear ballbearing, counter and reverse shafts. Remove the distance piece between the mainshaft front and rear bearings (see **FIG 8**). The countershaft gears will now rest at the bottom of the casing out of engagement with the mainshaft gears. Remove and scrap the felt washer fitted on the countershaft between the extension and the countershaft gears. Remove the setscrew with spring washer securing the plate locking counter and reverse shafts, remove locking plate and carefully remove any burrs on the locked ends of the shafts which might damage the shaft mounting holes in the extension when the shafts are withdrawn.

Withdraw the shafts forwards. Tap the ballbearing out of the extension. Observe the oil return hole at the bottom and the breather hole at the top of the extension mating with the oil return and breather holes in the case and the jointing washer (see **FIG 9**). Remove and discard the jointing washer.

Rotate the constant pinion shaft until the two cutaway portions of the toothed driving gear are facing the top and bottom of the casing. Tap the mainshaft to the front to knock the constant pinion shaft with ballbearing forward out of the case. Remove the constant pinion shaft and withdraw roller bearing from shaft spigot (see **FIG 10**).

The constant pinion shaft may now be dismantled in the following manner:

SH Series:

Remove the circlip (see **FIG 11**), packing washer and shims if fitted. Remove the collar and circlip from the bearing. With a suitable bearing puller draw the bearing off the shaft. Remove the oil thrower and constant pinion.

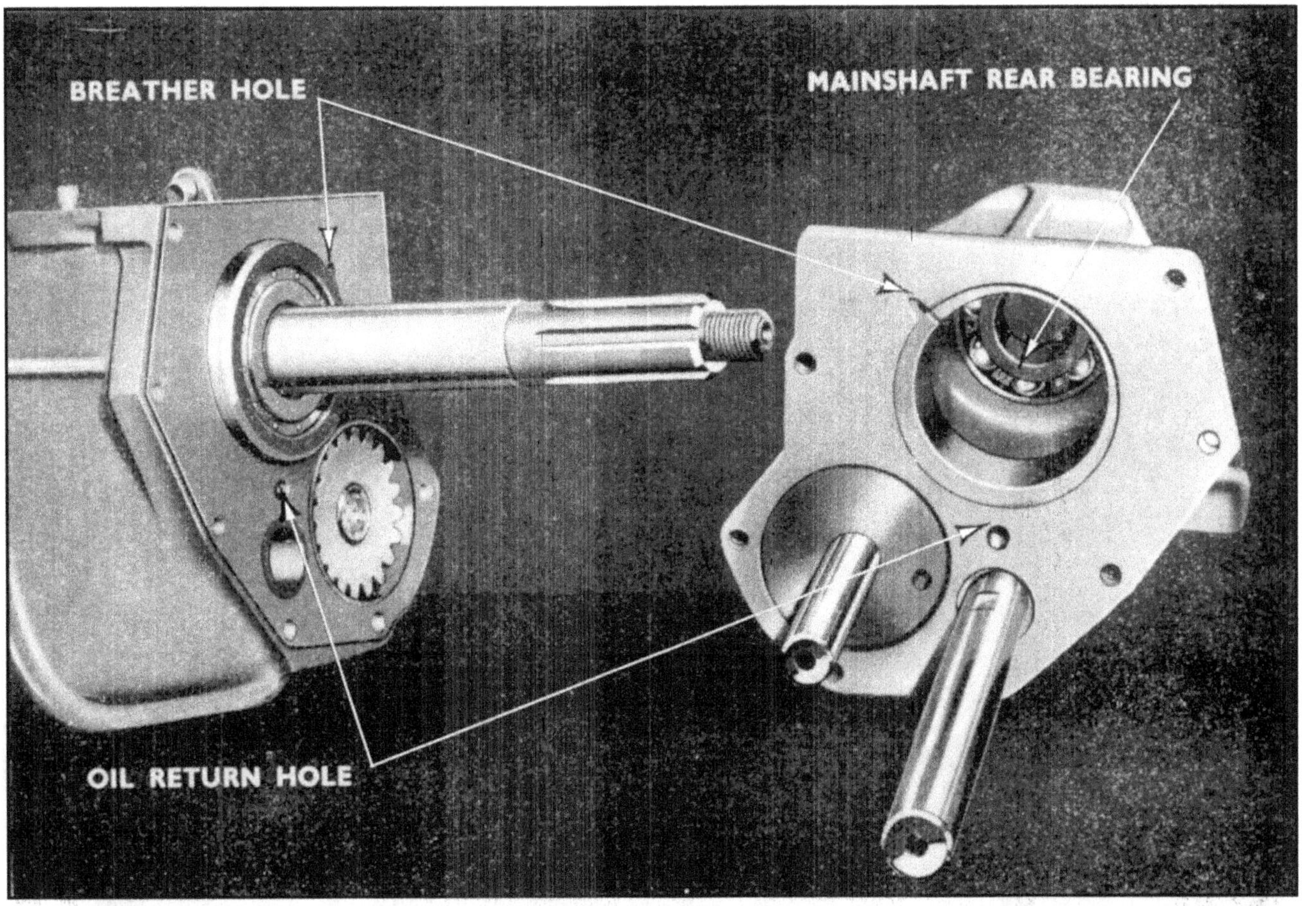

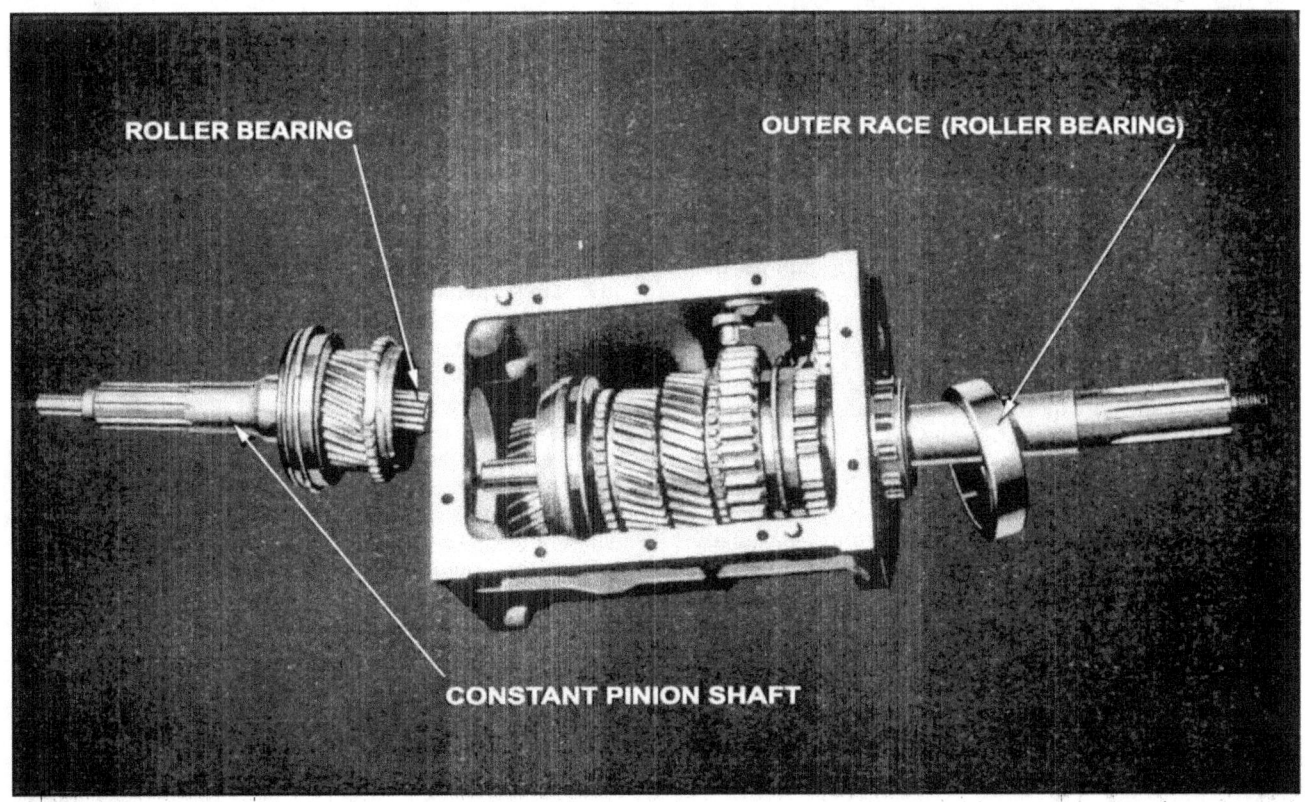

FIG 9　Extension removed

FIG 10　Removal of constant pinion shaft

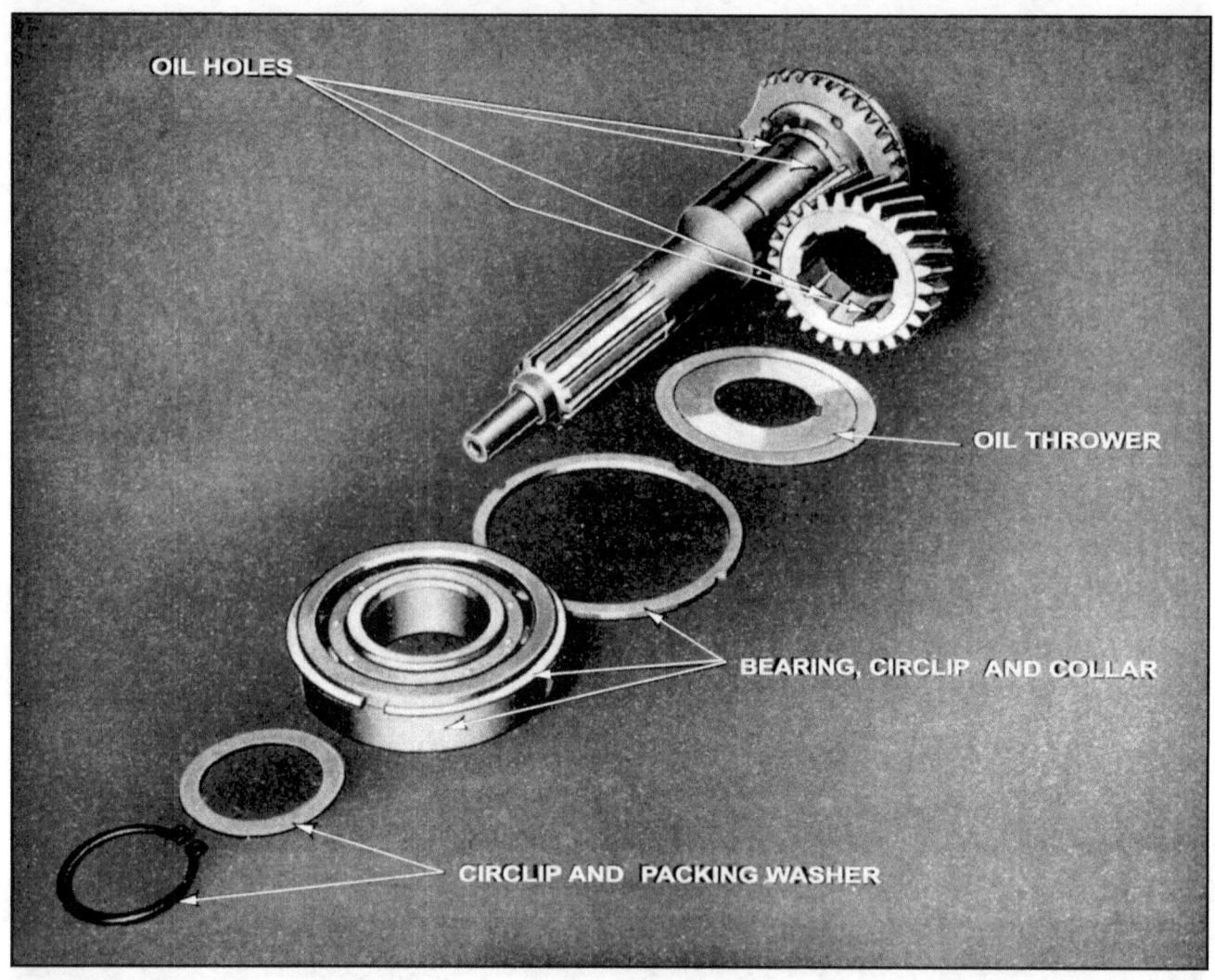

FIG 11 Constant pinion shaft assembly S.H.

JH Series:

Withdraw the circlip (see **FIG 12**), securing the locknut and rotate locknut off the shaft, this nut has a left-handed thread. Remove the collar and circlip from the bearing. With a suitable bearing puller draw the bearing off the shaft and remove the oil thrower. On later models the locknut and circlip fixing is replaced by a circlip, packing washer and shims as on the SH series gearboxes.

Mainshaft:

There are two types of bearing fitted to the mainshaft of the various gearboxes, one is a roller bearing and the other a ballbearing. If a roller bearing is fitted: tap the mainshaft to the rear until the outer race of the bearing can be withdrawn off the shaft leaving the rollers and the inner bearing on the shaft which is now free to be withdrawn as indicated in **FIG 13**.

If a ballbearing is fitted. Use a suitable drift and tap the inner race of the bearing rearwards down the shaft until the complete bearing can be removed and the shaft is free to be withdrawn.

Push reverse gear forward out of engagement to clear the mainshaft first-speed gearwheel. Lift the front end of the shaft upwards and withdraw the shaft with mainshaft gears forward out of the casing leaving the countershaft gears at the bottom of the case.

Withdraw the top and third gear operating and synchronizing sleeves forward off the shaft. Press the operating sleeve off the synchronizing sleeve and remove the six synchronizing balls and springs.

Remove the second gear synchronizing sleeve complete with the first-speed gearwheel rearwards off the shaft. Press the first-speed gear off the synchronizing sleeve and again remove the six synchronizing balls and springs. Remove the ball and plunger locking the second-speed synchronizing sleeve to the mainshaft. Press the plunger locating the second-speed gearwheel thrust washer and rotate this washer until the splines are in line then withdraw the washer plunger and spring. Remove the washer to the rear of the shaft followed by the second-speed gearwheel taking care not to loose any needles which will emerge as the wheel is removed. The mainshaft components are shown in **FIG 14, 15** and **16**.

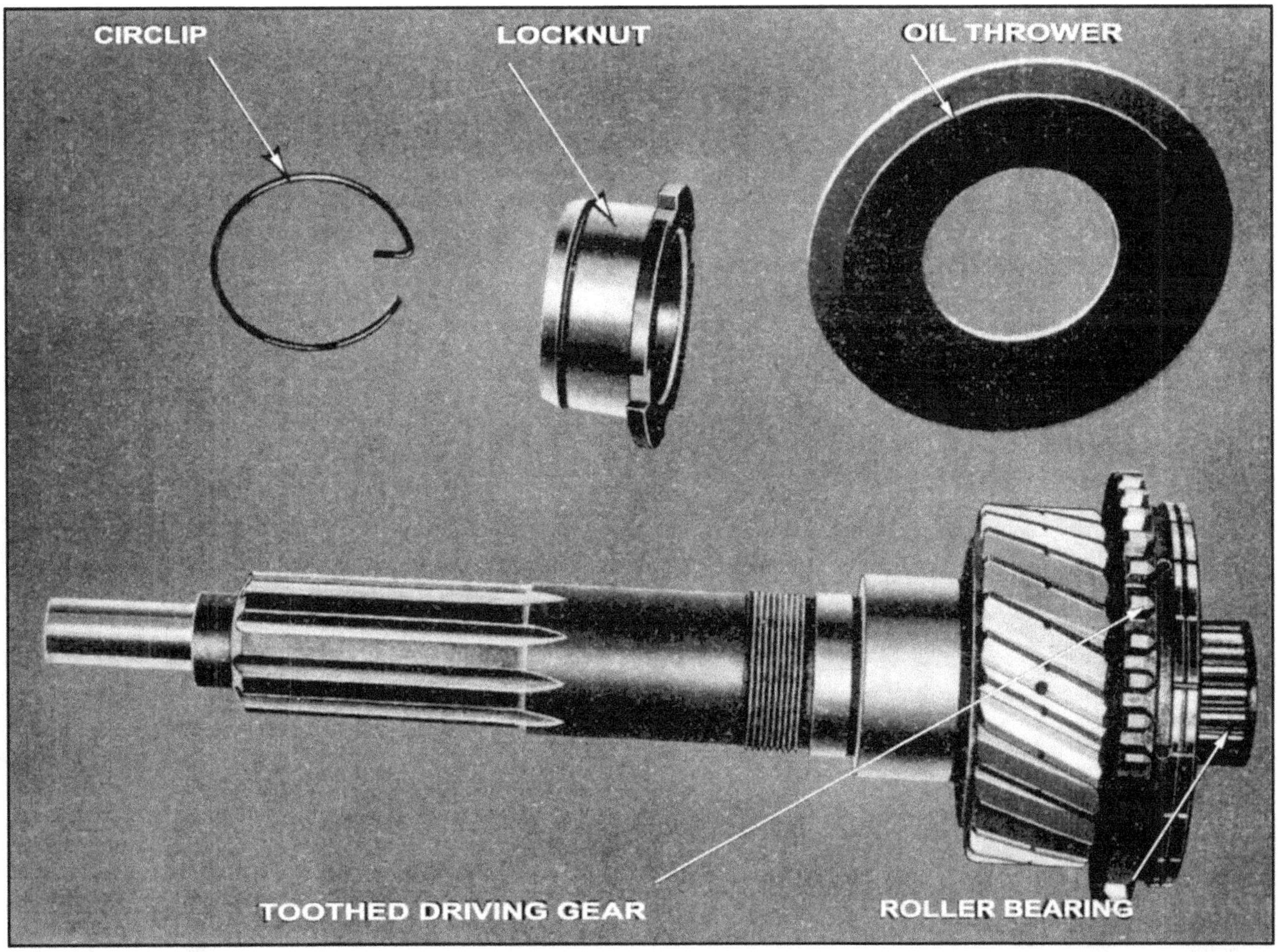

FIG 12   Constant pinion shaft assembly J.H.

FIG 13   Removal of mainshaft

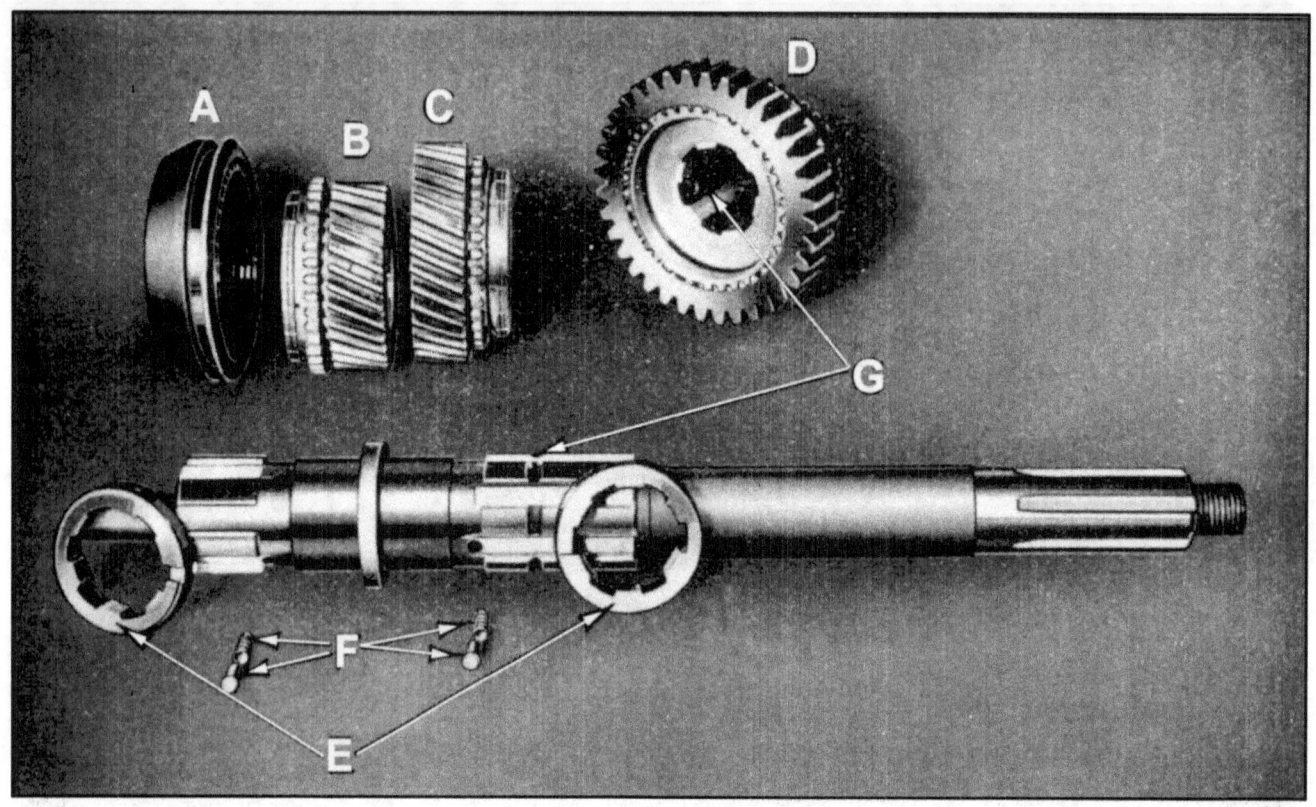

FIG 14 Mainshaft assembly

Key to Fig 14
A Third and top operating and synchronizing sleeves
B Third speed gearwheel
C Second speed gearwheel
D Second speed synchronizing sleeve with first speed wheel
E Second and third speed gearwheel thrust washers
F Thrust washer locking plungers and springs
G Second speed synchronizing sleeve locking plunger & groove on mainshaft

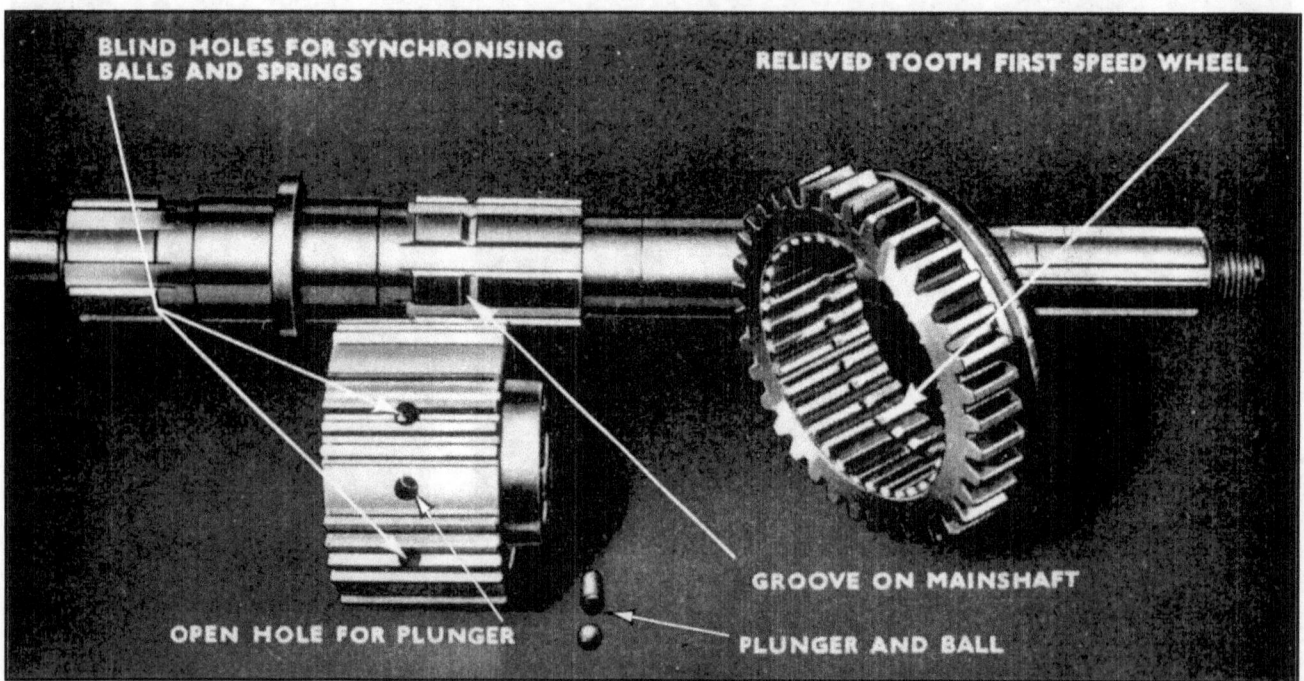

FIG 15 Second gear synchronizing sleeve and first speed wheel

88

Countershaft gears:

Draw the reverse gearwheel as far as possible rearwards to clear the first-speed gearwheel. Lift out the countershaft gears noting the inner and outer thrust washers fitted at either end. Again take special care not to misplace any of the needles which are located at either end of the gear unit. Remove the fibre washer from the hole in the casing supporting the front end of the countershaft.

On the SH series the countershaft gear is a cluster and is withdrawn as a single unit. The series JH countershaft gears are separate and may be removed in the following manner. Remove the circlip located behind top gear and push the gearwheel as far as possible up the shaft. Remove the splitring and withdraw the constant mesh wheel. Remove the circlip at the front of the second and third gears and withdraw these wheels. These components are shown clearly in the exploded diagram (see **FIG 3**). Push the reverse wheel back into the casing and withdraw from above. The reverse wheel has a bush which is a press fit in it. Remove the splitpin from the slotted nut with a plain washer securing the fulcrum lever pivot pin. Withdraw the pin, lever and reverse slipper. Remove the splitpin securing the reverse slipper to the fulcrum lever and separate these components.

5 Inspection

Top cover:

Examine the top cover for flaws or cracks and ensure that all machined faces are free from burrs. Check the bores of the striking rod holes for signs of wear or damage and ensure that the breather passage into the underside of the top cover is not obstructed.

Check the striking rods, selectors and changespeed forks for wear also check the fit of the selectors and the changespeed forks on the shaft and renew if there is appreciable play. Check the alignment of the forked portion of the changespeed forks on the first/second and third/top striking rods to ensure that they are not bent. If they are misaligned they may be straightened by careful bending.

The most likely points at which wear will be found in changespeed lever assembly will be at the tip of the selector lever and the bearings of the pivot jaw, the selector pivot pin and changespeed lever. The tip of the selector lever if worn may be built up and dressed to size or alternatively renewed. The bearings are all bushes which are easily replaced.

Gearbox:

Check the case for any flaws or cracks particularly at the reverse wheel lever fulcrum lug and at all bosses. Ensure that all machined faces are undamaged and free from burrs. It is recommended that after thorough cleaning the interior of the gearbox is painted with an oil resisting paint.

Reverse gear:

Check the fulcrum lever pivot pin and slipper for wear and renew if worn or if the pivot pin and shank of the slipper have excessive clearance in the respective operating holes in the fulcrum lever. If the reverse gearwheel is not moving sufficiently into engagement, the fulcrum lever may be set by bending to give the required travel. Check that the teeth of the gear are sound, are not pitted and that the case hardening, is not flaking. Check that the reverse slipper engages with the sleeve on the gear without excessive side play. The reverse gearwheel bush is integral with the gear and the gearwheel will require replacement if either are worn. The correct clearance for the bush on the shaft is between .0014 and .0024 inch.

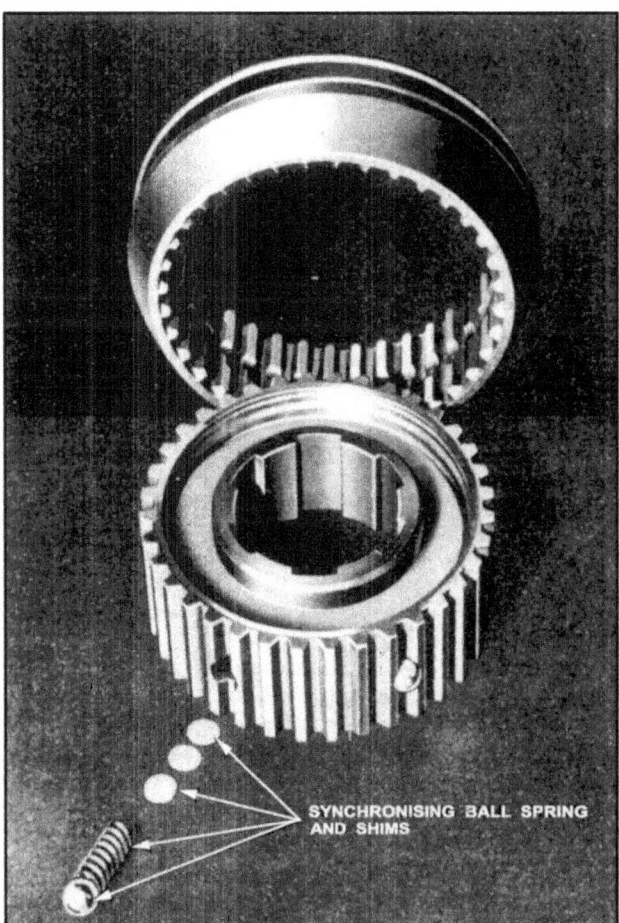

FIG 16 Top & third synchronizing & operating sleeves

Countershaft gears:

Check the gears for wear, pitting, and flaking of the case hardening. As the countershaft gears on the SH series are a cluster they are renewed as a unit. Check the needle rollers, needle retaining rings, outer and inner thrust washers for wear and renew as necessary. Assemble the countershaft gears with the inner and outer thrust washers in position. Place the gears in the casing and insert the countershaft to ensure that the bore of the gears are in alignment with the holes in the casing and extension. The countershaft end float should be between .002 to .004 inch, to obtain this the outer thrust washers are available in the following thicknesses: .152, .156, .159, .162 and .164 inch.

Mainshaft gears:

Examine all shoulders, splines and threads of the mainshaft for damage or wear and renew the shaft if necessary.

Check the internal bearing faces of the second and the third gearwheels and needle rollers for damage or wear. Again check gears for wear, pitting, and flaking of the case hardening. This check should also cover the toothed driving members and the synchromesh cones. Renew the second and third gearwheel thrust washers and ensure that the locking springs and plungers are sound. The correct end float for second and third gear on the mainshaft is between .002 to .004 inch.

Check the fit of the first-speed wheel on the second gear synchromesh sleeve and the fit of the sleeve on the mainshaft splines. If the internal teeth on the first-speed gear bottom on the second gear synchronizing sleeve or if the sleeve is not a good fit on the shaft splines renew the sleeve. Examine the first-speed gear for wear, pitting and flaking of the case hardening. Grind the second gear synchronizing cones with fine grinding paste until the two mating surfaces are bedded together and a good bite is obtained when they are in engagement. Ensure that all trace of the grinding paste is removed by thorough cleaning. Examine the synchronizing balls and springs and renew if the balls show signs of wear or the springs appear fatigued.

Assemble the six synchronizing balls and springs into the blind holes in the synchronizing sleeve. Check the tension by trying to move the operating sleeve off the the synchromesh sleeve which should require 62 to 65 lbs pressure. Fit shims under the spring to obtain the required pressure, but ensure that the springs are not closed up. As a rough check half of the ball should protrude when the ball is resting on the spring with no pressure applied.

Examine the ball and plunger locking second-speed synchronizing sleeve and renew if worn. Fit the locking plunger and ball into the hole which passes through the sleeve, rounded end of the plunger next to the shaft. Fit the first-speed gear to the second-speed synchronizing sleeve with the plain face of the gear to the cone of the sleeve. Check that the relieved internal tooth on the rear of the first-speed gear lines-up with the locking plunger on the second gear sleeve. Fit the assembly to the mainshaft and check that the plunger locks the second-speed synchronizing sleeve to the mainshaft when first gear is engaged and remains so on disengagement until the teeth of first gear are clear of the first-speed wheel on the countershaft

Check the fit of third and top operating sleeve on the synchronizing sleeve and the fit of the sleeve on the mainshaft. Examine the synchronizing balls and springs and renew as necessary. Assemble the six synchronizing balls and springs into the blind holes in the synchronizing sleeve. Check the tension by trying to slide the operating sleeve off the synchronizing sleeve, the correct pressure required is between 42 to 45 lbs. Check the teeth for signs of wear. Grind in the synchromesh cones as described for second gear. Examine the mainshaft front and rear bearings for wear and renew as necessary. The end play for the mainshaft is corrected by shims at the rear end cover and is dealt with under the heading of rear end cover in this chapter.

Constant pinion shaft:

Check the constant pinion wheel, toothed driving member and top gear synchromesh for signs of wear or pitting. On the SH series gearboxes the constant pinion wheel is serviced separately and the toothed driving gear is integral with the shaft (see **FIG 11**). The constant pinion wheel on the JH series gearboxes is integral with the shaft (see **FIG 12**).

Examine the spigot in the rear end of the shaft and the needle bearings for wear. Renew components as necessary. Check the ballbearing for wear again replace if wear is obvious. Examine the clutch plate splines on the shaft and offer up the shaft to the clutch plate to ensure that it slides easily without circumferential play on the splines. Fit a new oil thrower and circlip. The constant pinion shaft should have no end float when fitted.

Gearbox extension SH and JH series only:

Check the extension casing for cracks and ensure that all machined faces are in good condition and free from burrs. The countershaft and the reverse shaft should be a firm fit in the extension holes, it is advantageous to apply jointing compound sparingly to the holes before the shafts are fitted. Always renew the felt sealing washer on the countershaft with the rounded end of the washer fitted in the recess of the extension. When the two shafts are in position and secured by the locking plate they should be checked to ensure they are parallel.

Rear end cover:

Check the cover for signs of deterioration or damage. Check that the distance piece and speedometer driving gear, shoulder to front are fitted before fitting the cover. The speedometer gears should be greased on assembly to provide some initial lubrication.

Always fit a new oil seal to the cover with the lip of the seal pointing to the interior of the case. When fitting the cover and seal use a short length of tube to ease the seal onto the mainshaft to prevent distortion or damage occuring.

Where the mainshaft bearing is a ballbearing the end float is determined between the front and rear bearings. The correct end float is between .002 to .006 inch with the drive flange fully tightened and the mainshaft tapped forward. To increase the end float fit shims at one or other of the bearings and to decrease the end float the sleeve must be machined.

If the mainshaft front bearing is of the roller-type the end float is controlled by the rear ballbearing. It is therefore only necessary to check that the outer track of the bearing is nipped between the extension and the end cover. However if the distance piece is too short the mainshaft may jam when the drive flange slotted nut is fully tightened. If this fault occurs it may be overcome by fitting shims at one or other ends of the sleeve.

Front end cover:

Check the cover for flaws or cracks and ensure that the machined faces are clean and free from burrs. Fit a new fibre washer at the front end of the countershaft. Always fit a new joint washer and ensure that the oil return hole is cut in the joint and that the grooves in the case and cover are clear (see **FIG 6**).

Fit a new oil seal to the cover with the lip of the seal pointing towards the interior of the casing. The fitting of the seal should be carried out carefully to prevent distortion or damage occuring.

6 Reassembly

Top cover:

Assemble the reverse selector by fitting the plunger and spring, securing the plunger with a new splitpin. Fit the plunger locking ball and spring. Fit the reverse selector and the top selector to their respective striking rods and secure in position with lockbolts.

Fit a new felt washer into each recess in the striking rod holes at the rear of the cover. Thread the plate over one or other of the outside rods and slide the rod into the cover not forgetting to fit the changespeed fork, before the rod enters the front hole in the cover, until it is in the neutral position. This can be checked by looking through the grub screw hole on top of the cover and checking that the neutral groove is directly below. Fit the other outside rod in the same manner through the plate. Place an interlock ball in the groove in each rod using the centre hole to gain access to the rods which are in the correct position. Fit the interlock plunger in the hole of the centre rod and pass the rod through the plate and the changespeed fork, into position.

Fit the lockbolts to the three changespeed forks and stop pins to first/second and third/top striking rods. Both bolts and pins should be locked in position with new wire.

Fit three new plugs into the striking rod holes in the front of the cover, tapping the centre of the plug with a hammer and punch to ensure a good fit. Secure the plate with the two setscrews and spring washers.

Move all of the rods into the neutral position and then place a plunger in each of the three holes followed by the springs and grub screws. The longer grub screw is that for the reverse rod. Tighten grub screws until the correct tension is obtained and then lock in position with new wire.

Screw the reverse lamp switch and breather into their respective holes in the cover ensuring a new fibre washer is fitted to the breather.

The changespeed lever reassembly is the reverse procedure of dismantling. If a cranked gearlever is fitted check that the cranked portion faces forward to put the knob towards the front of the gearbox.

Gearbox:

Offer up the fulcrum lever with the reverse slipper pinned in position and secure to the casing with the pivot pin, plain washer, slotted nut and splitpin. Place the bushed reverse wheel in the slipper and draw the wheel rearwards as far as it will go to enable fitting of the countershaft gears.

Assemble the countershaft gears for the JH series as follows. Press second gear and third gearwheels onto the splined extension of first gear and locate with a circlip. Press on the constant-mesh wheel as far as it will go. Fit the splitring and draw the gearwheel forward onto the ring then fit the circlip behind top gearwheel.

Fit the needle retainer rings into either end of the gear unit followed by needle rollers (29 each end). Apply grease to the needle rollers to ease assembly. Fit the outer roller retaining ring at the front end then offer up the inner and outer thrust washers at either end of the gear unit and lower gears into the casing through the top. It will be necessary to insert a thin rod to locate the gears in position.

The next unit to assemble is the mainshaft which is carried out as follows. Fit the needle rollers applying a little grease behind the shoulder on the shaft and slide the second-speed gearwheels synchronizing cone to rear onto the rollers. Fit second-speed thrust washer spring and plunger into the plunger hole. Slide the thrust washer up the shaft then compress the spring and rotate the washer into the locked position. Fit the needles in front of the shoulder on the shaft and slide third gearwheel synchronizing cone to the front onto the rollers. Fit third gear thrust washer spring and plunger as outlined for second gear.

Assemble the six synchronizing balls and plungers into the blind holes in the second-speed synchronizing sleeve. Fit the locking plunger and ball into the hole passing through the sleeve, plain face of gear facing synchronizing cone end of sleeve, ensuring that the relieved tooth at the rear of first gear internal spline lines up with the locking plunger ball in the synchronizing sleeve. Slide the sleeve onto the splines of the mainshaft with the synchronizing cone facing forward. Assemble the six synchronizing balls and plungers into the blind holes in third and top synchronizing sleeves. Press on the operating sleeves, large boss facing the front then slide the synchronizing sleeve onto the mainshaft splines.

On the JS series gearbox check when assembling the third/top synchronizing sleeve to third/top operating sleeve that the large boss of the inner sleeve is on the same side as the wide chamfer of the outer synchronizing sleeve. The holes in the inner sleeve for the balls and plungers must be in-line with the two relieved teeth in the outer sleeve. When fitting the synchronizing sleeve assembly to the mainshaft on this series gearbox ensure that the end of the outer sleeve with the wide chamfer is facing forward towards the spigot end. There are two transverse grooves on the mainshaft splines, the one for the top synchronizing sleeve assembly is nearest to the spigot end. If the sleeve is fitted in-line with the other groove it will not be possible to fully engage top and third gears.

Assemble the constant pinion shaft SH series in the following manner. Press the constant pinion wheel onto the shaft, ensuring that the two oil holes in the wheel line-up with the companion holes in the shaft. Fit the oil thrower followed by the ballbearing with the circlip and collar fitted to the outer track of the bearing. Fit shims as necessary to eliminate all end float and secure with a circlip. Fit the roller race into the shaft spigot.

In the case of the JH series fit the oil thrower followed by the ballbearing onto the shaft with the circlip fitted to the outer bearing track. Screw on the locking nut which has a lefthand thread and secure in position with circlip. Fit the roller race into shaft spigot.

If the mainshaft front bearing is a roller-type press the inner race and rollers onto the shaft from the rear until the face butts against the second-speed synchronizing sleeve. If the front bearing is of the ball-type it must be fitted with the mainshaft in the gearbox casing.

Enter the mainshaft through the top of the casing and pass to the rear through the bearing hole. Offer up the constant pinion shaft at the front end of the casing with the cutaway portions of the toothed driving member facing the top and bottom of the casing. Tap the constant pinion shaft to the rear until the collar and circlip on the bearing butt up against the casing. Holding the constant pinion shaft in position tap in the outer race, internal flange outwards, of mainshaft front bearing. If it is a ball-bearing then the complete bearing is tapped in.

Assemble the extension in the following manner then apply a little jointing compound to the countershaft and reverse shaft holes in the extension. Fit the countershaft and reverse shaft into the extension and secure in position with the locking plate and setscrew. Fit a new felt washer to the countershaft, pressing the rounded surface of the washer into the extension recess. Place a new joint washer on the rear of the gearbox face ensuring that the oil return hole and breather hole openings are cut in the washer and fit the mainshaft distance sleeve. Lift the countershaft gears up into engagement with the mainshaft gears using the thin rod left in position when the countershaft gears were fitted. Pass a spare countershaft through the gears to act as a pilot, check that none of the rollers are dislodged in this process. Offer up the extension and tap into position, driving the pilot countershaft out of the casing. Secure the extension with the seven setscrews and fit a new fibre washer at the front end of the countershaft.

Fit a new oil seal into the rear end cover with the lip of the seal facing the interior of the gearbox. Fit a new joint washer to the rear face of the extension. Assemble the distance piece followed by the speedometer driving gear, shoulder to front onto the mainshaft (see **FIG 7**). Fit the rear end cover and secure with the four bolts and spring washers. Fit the cheese-headed setscrew securing the cover to the extension. Fit the speedometer driven gear into the bearing, place in the end cover and locate with the locking screw ensuring that the screw does not bottom and foul the driven gear.

Engage top and reverse gears to lock the gearbox then tap the propeller shaft drive flange onto the mainshaft splines, fit the plain washer and secure with the slotted nut and splitpin. Place the top and reverse gears in neutral.

Fit a new oil seal into the front end cover with the lip of the seal facing the interior of the gearbox. Fit a new joint washer to the front face of the casing ensuring that the oil return hole is cut in the washer. Offer up the front cover checking that the oil drain groove is at the bottom and mating with the return hole in the case (see **FIG 6**). Secure the cover with the four setscrews and plain washers and lock with new wire.

Fit a new joint washer to the top face of the gearbox casing. Offer up the top cover observing that this is located by two dowels then secure in position with the ten setscrews and spring washers. The two long setscrews are fitted to the front and the two short setscrews to the rear. Replace the oil dipstick and gearbox drain plug.

Refitting of the gearbox to the engine is the reverse procedure of that described for removal in **Chapter 1 Section 3 & Chapter 5 Section 2**. Extreme care should be taken when assembling the gearbox to the engine to ensure that the gearbox weight is not supported by the pinion shaft or the driven plate of the clutch.

7 Fault diagnosis

(a) Jumping out of gear

1 Broken spring behind locating ball for selector rod
2 Excessively worn locating groove in selector rod
3 Worn coupling dogs
4 Fork to selector rod securing screw loose

(b) Noisy gearbox

1 Insufficient oil
2 Excessive play in countershaft gear
3 Worn or damaged bearings
4 Worn or damaged gear teeth

(c) Difficulty in engaging gear

1 Incorrect clutch pedal adjustment
2 Worn synchromesh cones

(d) Oil leaks

1 Damaged joint washers
2 Worn or damaged oil seals
3 Front, rear or top covers loose or faces damaged.

NOTES

OVERDRIVE - SERVICE

The overdrive

8 Description and operation

The overdrive is an additional gear unit between the gearbox and propeller shaft. When in operation it provides a higher overall gear ratio than that given by the final drive crownwheel and pinion. The primary object of the overdrive is to provide open road cruising at an engine speed lower than that it would be in normal top gear. This reduced engine speed gives a considerable reduction in petrol consumption and engine wear. The Laycock de Normanville overdrive unit type 'A' as fitted to the Jaguar models is shown in **FIGS 19a, 19b** and **20**.

The overdrive is operated by an electric solenoid controlled by a switch which is either a manual control on the facia panel only or with an automatic control on the throttle linkage. Both types have an inhibitor switch to prevent the operation of the overdrive in any gear other than top gear.

With the manual switch the overdrive may be engaged at any speed whereas with the automatic switch it is engaged on the throttle opening.

The overdrive gears are epicyclic and consist of a central sun wheel meshing with three planet gears which in turn mesh with an internally toothed annulus. The planet carrier is attached to the input shaft and the annulus is integral with the output shaft (see **FIGS 17** and **18**). An extension of the gearbox mainshaft forms the overdrive input shaft.

In direct drive (see **FIG 17**), power is transmitted from the gearbox mainshaft 'A' to the inner member of a uni-directional clutch 'N' and then to the outer member 'C' of this clutch through rollers 'B' which are driven up inclined faces and wedged between the inner and outer members. The outer member 'C' forms part of the combined annulus and output shaft 'D'. In this position the gear train is inoperative. A cone clutch 'E' is mounted on the externally splined extension 'F' of the sun wheel and is loaded onto the annulus by a number of springs which have their reaction against the casing of the overdrive unit. The spring load is transmitted to the clutch member through a thrust ring and ballbearing. This arrangement causes the inner friction lining 'G' of the cone clutch to contact the outer cone of the annulus 'H' and rotate with the annulus, whilst the springs and thrust ring remain stationary. Since the sun wheel is splined to the clutch member the whole gear train is locked, permitting overrun and reverse torque to be transmitted.

With the overdrive engaged (see **FIG 18**). It can be seen that the cone clutch is no longer in contact with the annulus, but that it has moved forward so that its outer friction lining 'J' is in contact with a brake ring 'K' forming part of the overdrive casing. The sun wheel 'I' to which the clutch is attached is therefore held stationary. The planet carrier 'L' rotates with the input shaft 'A' and the planet wheels 'M' are caused to rotate about their own axis and drive the annulus at a faster speed than the input shaft.

Movement of the cone clutch in a forward direction is effected by means of hydraulic pressure which acts upon two pistons, when a valve is opened by the action of the operating switch. This hydraulic pressure overcomes the springs and causes the clutch to engage the brake ring to hold the sun wheel at rest.

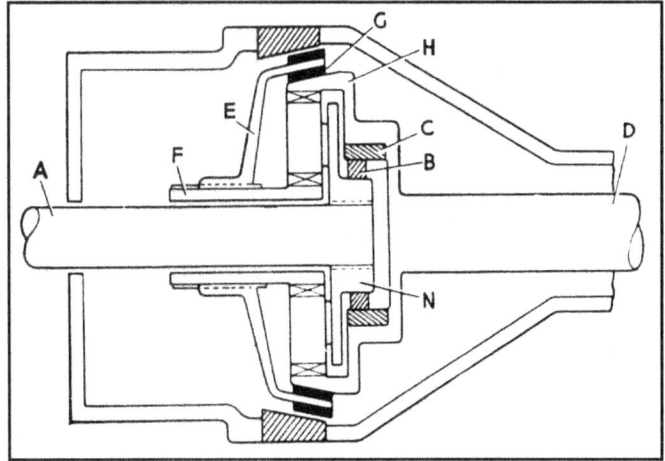

FIG 17 Overdrive unit in direct drive

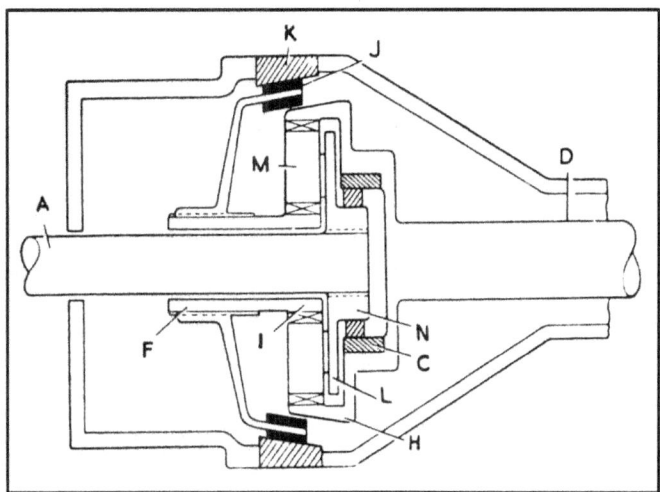

FIG 18 Overdrive unit in overdrive

When the hydraulic pressure is removed the overdrive reverts to its original position under the action of the springs.

Hydraulic pressure is developed in the system by a plunger pump, cam-operated, from the input shaft. The pump draws oil through a wire mesh strainer in which is incorporated a magnet to remove any metal particles. The oil is then delivered to the operating valve of the unit via a hydraulic accumulator which controls the working pressure. The correct working pressure for the unit is given in the Technical Data in the appendix of this manual.

9 Driving technique

The overdrive will operate in top gear only and is brought into operation by the switch mounted on the facia.

Use of the clutch pedal when changing into or out of overdrive is unneccessary as the unit is designed to operate under fully loaded conditions. To ensure maximum smoothness of operation when changing down from overdrive to top gear the accelerator pedal should be

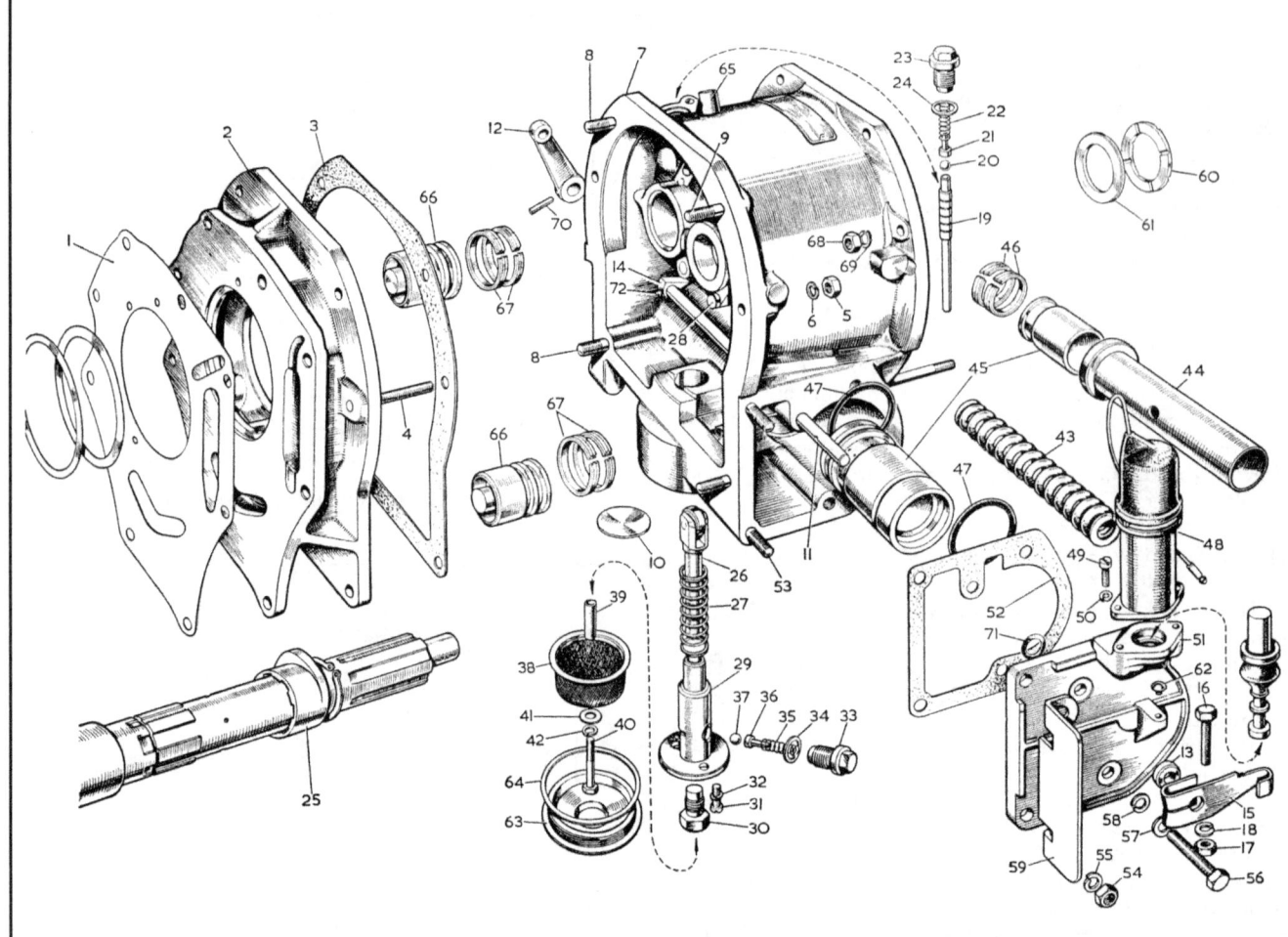

FIG 19a Overdrive front casing

1. Joint washer.
2. Adapter plate.
3. Joint washer.
4. Locating stud.
5. Nut.
6. Spring washer.
7. Main casing.
8. Stud.
9. Stud.
10. Welch plug.
11. Valve operating shaft.
12. Setting lever.
13. Collar.
14. Shaft cam.
15. Solenoid lever.
16. Adjusting screw.
17. Nut.
18. Washer.
19. Valve push rod.
20. Ball valve.
21. Ball valve plunger.
22. Valve spring.
23. Valve plug.
24. Copper washer.
25. Third motion shaft.
26. Pump plunger.
27. Plunger spring.
28. Guide peg.
29. Pump body.
30. Pump body plug.
31. Body screw.
32. Spring washer.
33. Valve plug.
34. Plug washer.
35. Valve spring.
36. Ball valve plunger.
37. Ball valve.
38. Pump filter.
39. Distance piece.
40. Filter bolt.
41. Plain washer.
42. Spring washer.
43. Accumulator spring.
44. Distance tube.
45. Piston assembly.
46. Piston rings.
47. Rubber rings.
48. Solenoid unit.
49. Unit screw.
50. Spring washer.
51. Solenoid lever housing.
52. Joint washer.
53. Stud.
54. Nut.
55. Spring washer.
56. Setpin.
57. Plain washer.
58. Spring washer.
59. Solenoid shield.
60. Thrust washer.
61. Spacing washer.
62. Rubber stop.
63. Drain plug.
64. Drain plug washer.
65. Breather.
66. Piston.
67. Piston rings.
68. Nut.
69. Spring washer.
70. Cotter pin.
71. Oil seal.
72. Peg.

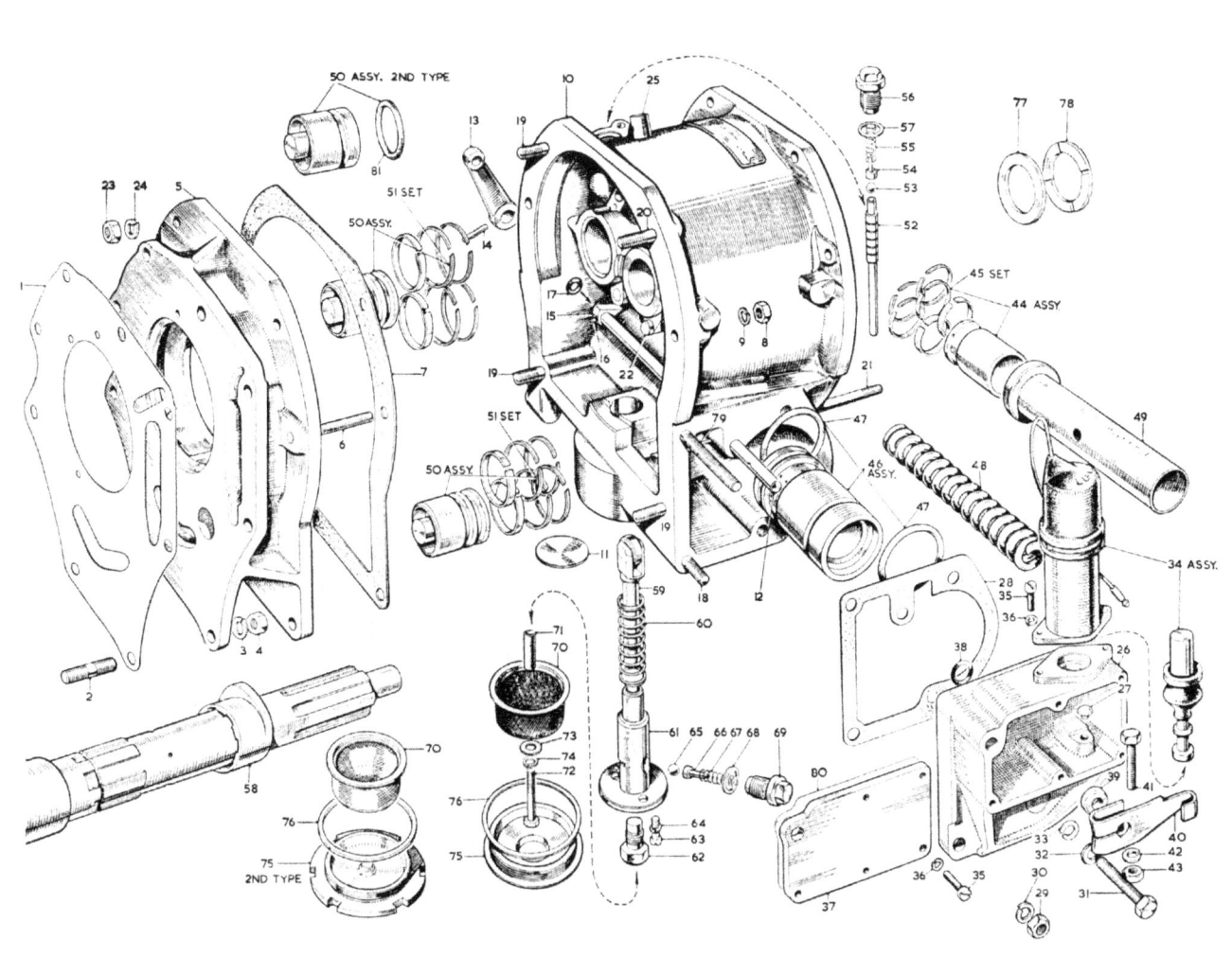

FIG 19b Overdrive front casing (Alternate piston assemblies)

No.	Description	No.	Description	No.	Description
1.	Joint—overdrive unit.	28.	Joint—bracket to case.	55.	Spring for plunger.
2.	Stud—overdrive unit.	29.	Nut—bracket to casing.	56.	Plug for valve—screwed.
3.	Washer for stud (spring).	30.	Washer for nut (spring).	57.	Washer for plug.
4.	Nut for stud.	31.	Screw—bracket to casing.	58.	Cam—oil pump.
5.	Plate—adaptor.	32.	Washer for screw.	59.	Plunger assembly—oil pump.
6.	Stud—adaptor to casing.	33.	Washer for screw (spring).	60.	Spring for plunger.
7.	Joint—adaptor to casing.	34.	Solenoid.	61.	Body—oil pump.
8.	Nut—plate stud to casing.	35.	Screw—solenoid to bracket.	62.	Plug for body—screwed.
9.	Washer for stud (spring).	36.	Washer for screw (spring).	63.	Screw—body to front casing.
10.	Casing—front.	37.	Plate—solenoid bracket cover.	64.	Washer for screw (spring).
11.	Plug.	38.	Seal, oil—valve operating shaft.	65.	Ball valve.
12.	Shaft—valve operating.	39.	Distance collar.	66.	Plunger, ball.
13.	Lever for shaft.	40.	Lever—solenoid.	67.	Spring for plunger.
14.	Pin—lever to shaft.	41.	Screw—lever to spindle.	68.	Washer for valve plug (copper).
15.	Cam—valve operating.	42.	Washer for screw (spring).	69.	Plug—valve.
16.	Pin for cam.	43.	Nut for screw.	70.	Strainer—oil pump.
17.	Seal for shaft.	44.	Piston assembly—accumulator.	71.	Distance tube for strainer.
18.	Stud for solenoid bracket.	45.	Ring—piston.	72.	Bolt for strainer.
19.	Stud for plate—long.	46.	Housing assembly—accumulator.	73.	Washer for bolt.
20.	Stud for plate—short.	47.	Ring, rubber.	74.	Washer for bolt (spring).
21.	Stud—front to rear casing.	48.	Spring—accumulator pressure.	75.	Plug—oil drain.
22.	Peg—oil pump plunger guide.	49.	Tube for spring.	76.	Washer for plug.
23.	Nut—front casing to adaptor plate.	50.	Piston—assembly—operating.	77.	Washer, steel.
24.	Washer for nut (spring).	51.	Ring, piston.	78.	Washer—phosphor bronze.
25.	Breather.	52.	Valve, operating.	79.	Stud for solenoid bracket.
26.	Bracket solenoid.	53.	Ball for valve.	80.	Joint for cover plate.
27.	Stop (rubber).	54.	Plunger, ball.	81.	Ring—piston.

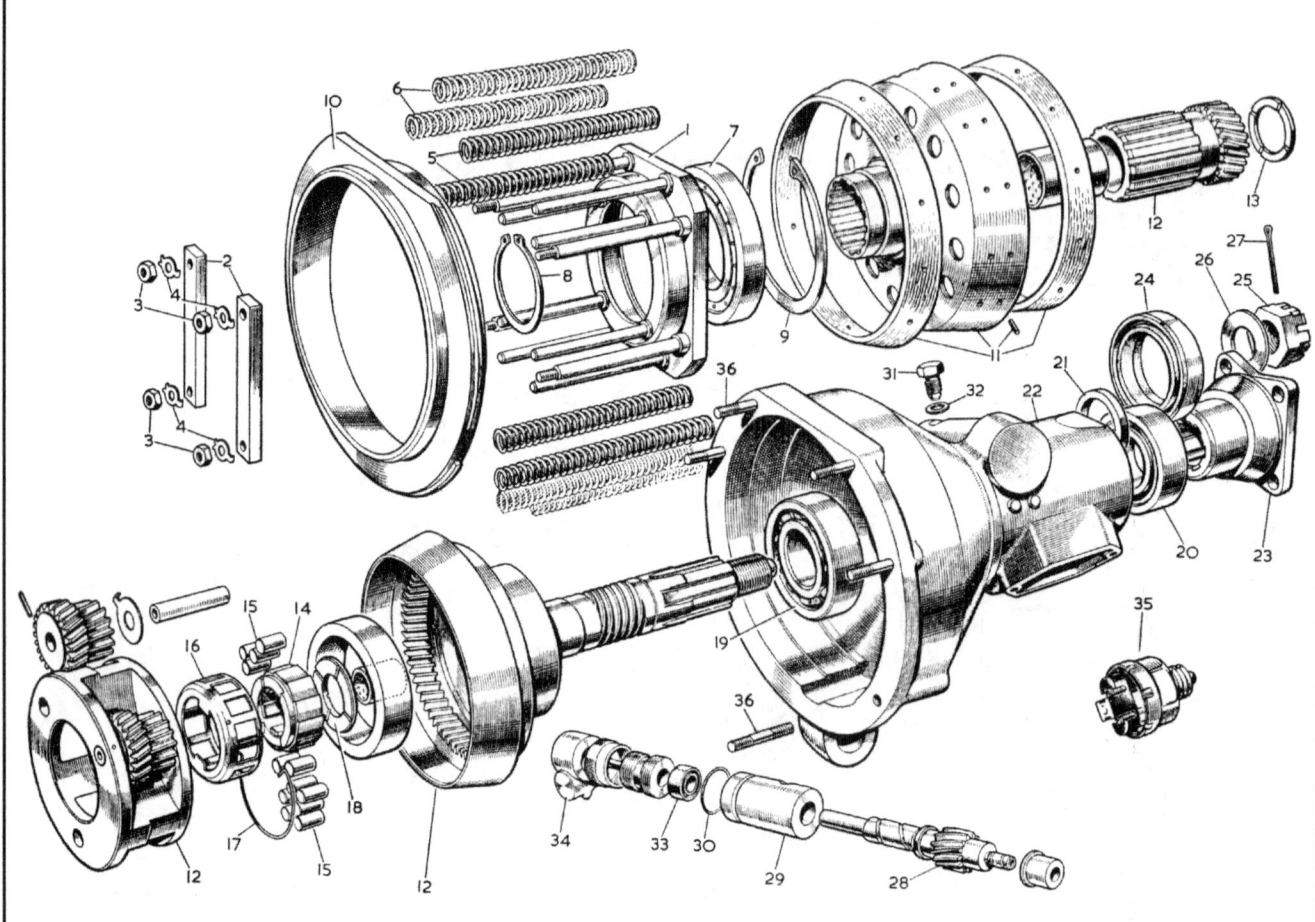

FIG 20 Overdrive rear casing

1. Clutch thrust ring.
2. Bridge pieces.
3. Nuts.
4. Locking washers.
5. Clutch spring (long).
6. Clutch spring (short).
7. Front bearing.
8. Circlip (small).
9. Circlip (large).
10. Brake ring.
11. Clutch assembly.
12. Sun wheel assembly.
13. Thrust washer.
14. Uni-directional clutch.
15. Rollers.
16. Outer casing.
17. Securing clip.
18. Thrust washer.
19. Inner bearing.
20. Outer bearing.
21. Spacing washer.
22. Rear housing.
23. Driving flange.
24. Oil seal.
25. Flange nut.
26. Washer.
27. Split pin.
28. Speedometer spindle.
29. Spindle sleeve.
30. Washer.
31. Locking peg.
32. Washer.
33. Oil seal.
34. Spindle adaptor.
35. Overdrive switch.
36. Stud.

WARNING

THE INTERNAL SPRING MECHANISM IN THE OVERDRIVE ASSEMBLY IS VERY STRONG AND GREAT CARE SHOULD BE EXERCISED WHEN DISMANTLING THESE UNITS.

slightly depressed. This operation of changing from overdrive to top gear should be avoided at very high speeds as it may cause excessive engine revolutions.

For driving in town, heavy traffic or hilly country when the maximum flexibility and low speed performance is required the switch should be in the out position so that normal top gear is in use. For normal driving in open country the overdrive should be brought into operation when the required cruising speed has been obtained.

10 Maintenance and adjustments

At intervals of 2500 miles check the oil level in the overdrive unit. This is carried out by checking the oil level in the gearbox with the dipstick as both units have a common oil supply.

At intervals of 10,000 miles the overdrive unit should be drained of oil and the gauze filter thoroughly cleaned. The filter is accessible when the drain plug is removed (see **FIG 21**). Do not use rag to clean the filter especially not fluffy rag.

It is essential that an approved lubricant be used when refilling, preferably a straight mineral oil with no EP additives. On no account should any anti-friction additives be put into the oil.

After refilling the gearbox and overdrive, recheck the oil level after the car has been run for a short distance as a certain amount of oil will be distributed round the hydraulic system. It is most important to use clean oil at all times and great care should be taken to avoid the entry of dirt whenever any part of the casing is opened. Dirt or even fluff from a rag, which finds its way into a valve will cause trouble.

The operating valve:

The operating valve plug is located on the top of the unit and access to it is through the floor of the car. Operate the solenoid several times to release the hydraulic pressure before removing the valve plug. If the valve plug is tight a sharp tap on the top will help. Remove the plunger ball and spring. The operating valve is shown in section in **FIG 22** 'A' and 'B', 'A' is the position of the valve in direct drive and 'B' the position of the valve in the overdrive position.

The operating valve can be removed by inserting a piece of stiff wire down its centre and drawing it up carefully to avoid damaging the seat at the top of the valve.

Check that the valve is not choked before replacing. If necessary the ball can be reseated by placing the ball on a block of wood and sharply tapping the valve after positioning it on the ball. Clean the valve seat in the casing and if necessary reseat the ball by tapping it gently on its seat with a copper drift. Do not tap the ball too hard or the mouth of the hole with be closed up.

Solenoid operating levers:

The operating valve is lifted by a cam on a transverse shaft. The solenoid operates a lever attached to this shaft (see **FIG 23**), and when it operates the valve must be fully opened. The transverse shaft passes right through the casing, where it protrudes there is a setting lever attached. This lever has a $\frac{3}{16}$ inch. hole in its outer end. The hole should align with a similar hole in the overdrive casing when the solenoid is energized. For the purpose of

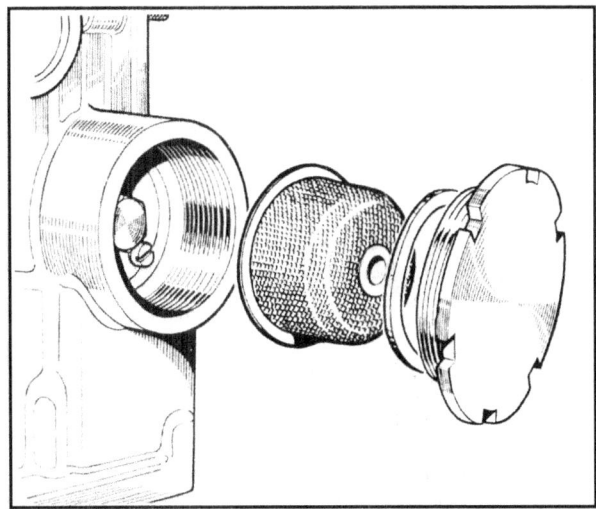

FIG 21   Filter

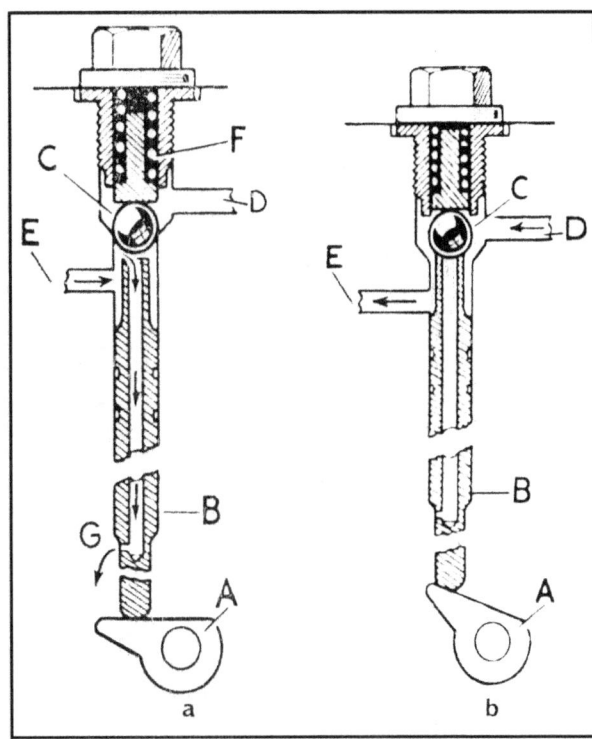

FIG 22   Operating valve

A   Cam
B   Valve
C   Ball
D   Supply
E   to operating cylinders
F   Spring
G   Restrictor

checking the setting of the solenoid lever a $\frac{3}{16}$ inch. pin, such as a drill shank, should be inserted through the hole in the lever to engage with the hole in the casing (see **FIG 24**). If the pin will not register in the casing the solenoid lever requires adjustment as follows. Remove the cover plate from the solenoid housing. Loosen the clamp bolt on the lever (see **FIG 23**), then rotate the shaft until the pin inserted in the check lever registers in the hole in the casing. Push the solenoid plunger as far as it will go and hold the lever fork lightly against the collar on the plunger. Tighten the clamp bolt and remove the check pin. Operate the solenoid and recheck the position of the check lever with the pin.

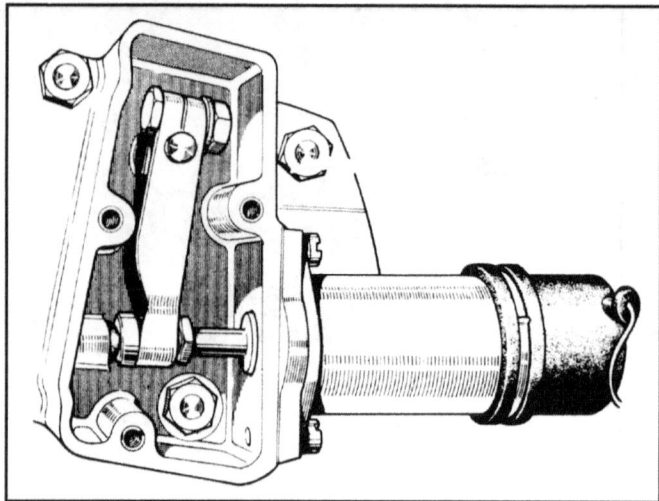

FIG 23 Solenoid and operating lever

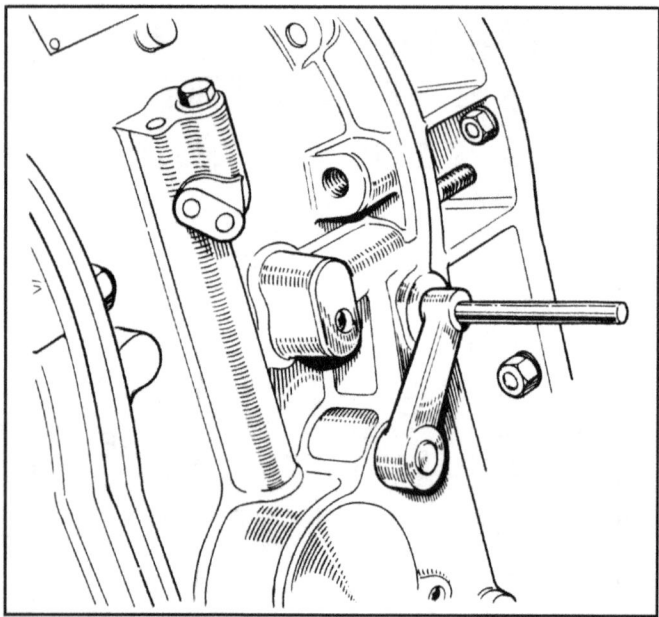

FIG 24 Operating lever check

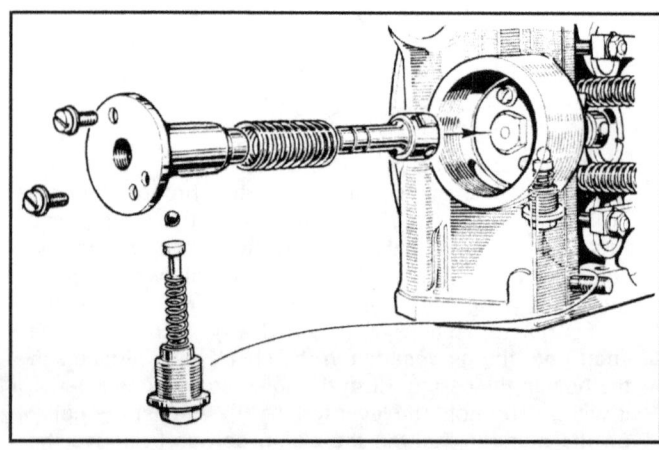

FIG 25 Pump valve

The pump valve:

If the unit fails to operate after resetting the operating valve check that the pump is working. Jack-up the rear wheels of the car securely, remove the operating valve plug and start the engine. Engage top gear with the engine running slowly and watch for oil being pumped into the valve chamber. If none appears the pump is not functioning and its non-return valve should be cleaned. A flow of oil does not necessarily mean that the hydraulic pressure is correct, this can only be established by means of a pressure gauge on a special adapter which fits into the operating valve plug recess. To clean the pump valve proceed as follows. Drain off the oil, remove the cover from the solenoid bracket and remove the solenoid. Slacken off the clamp bolt in the solenoid lever and remove the lever and solenoid plunger. Remove the distance collar under the lever. The solenoid bracket is secured by two $\frac{5}{16}$ inch. studs and two bolts remove the studs before undoing the bolts. The two bolts should be unscrewed together releasing the compression on the accumulator spring (see **FIG 25**). Remove the spring and guide tube. The pump valve plug will then be seen in the cavity. The valve consists of a spring plunger and ball. The ball should be cleaned carefully and reseated if necessary by tapping it sharply onto its seating. Reassembly is the reverse procedure to dismantling. The solenoid lever positioning will require to be reset.

11 Electrical circuit:

Single relay system

Before embarking on the full procedure for fault location it will be helpful to keep the following points in mind.

Many operational failures are due to corroded terminals and faulty wiring, so make a point of checking the wiring and connections first.

Good earth connections are essential on all earthed components especially the solenoid which takes heavy current each time it is actuated.

A schematic wiring diagram is shown in **FIG 26**.

If the overdrive fails to operate and the wiring has been checked proceed as follows:

1. Short out terminals of 'C1' and 'C2' of the relay, switch on the ignition and engage top gear. If the solenoid fails to operate suspect faulty inhibitor switch. If the solenoid operates the inhibitor switch and solenoid are in order. Proceed to test 4.
2. Connect terminal of 'C1' to 'A3'. If solenoid operates the inhibitor switch is faulty if it does not operate suspect a faulty solenoid.
3. Connect solenoid terminal to 'A3'. If the solenoid fails to operate or is sluggish, it is faulty.
4. Connect 'W1' of relay to 'A3' with the control switch closed (on models with this switch on the throttle linkage the accelerator pedal will need to be depressed). If the solenoid operates, relay and control switch are satisfactory. If the solenoid does not operate proceed to next test.
5. Link 'W2' of relay to earth. If the solenoid fails to operate the relay is faulty. If the solenoid operates the control switch is faulty.
6. Connect feed terminal of the control switch to earth with switch closed. If the solenoid operates the control switch is faulty.

Two relay system:

Overdrive and Warning Light Fail to Operate:

1. Check fuse to which overdrive circuit is connected. If fuse has blown, disconnect the overdrive supply cable at fuse terminal and fit new fuse. Operate each of the components protected by it. If the fuse again blows, the fault is in one of the external circuits and not in the overdrive circuit. If the fuse does not blow, examine carefully all wiring of the overdrive circuit for signs of short-circuits or loose connections, before reconnecting the overdrive supply cable.

2. If the fuse has not blown and the wiring is in order then, with the engine stopped and ignition switched on, check as follows (see **FIG 27**).

(a) Engage top gear and short out terminals C1-C2 of relay R1. The overdrive solenoid and warning light should operate. If no operation takes place, the top gear switch may be defective. This can be checked by linking terminal above to the fuse, using a suitable length of insulated cable. Operation of the solenoid and warning light indicates a defective top gear switch. Remove test link and fit new top gear switch.

(b) Engage top gear and short out terminals C1-C2 of relay R2. The overdrive solenoid and warning light should operate. If no operation takes place, either the coil or the contacts of relay R1 may be defective. This may be checked by shorting out terminals C1-C2 of relay R1. Operation of overdrive solenoid and warning light indicates a defective relay R1. Disengage top gear and fit new relay.

(c) Engage top gear, switch on manual switch and short out centrifugal switch terminals.

(d) The overdrive solenoid and warning light should now operate. Operation will indicate a faulty centrifugal switch.

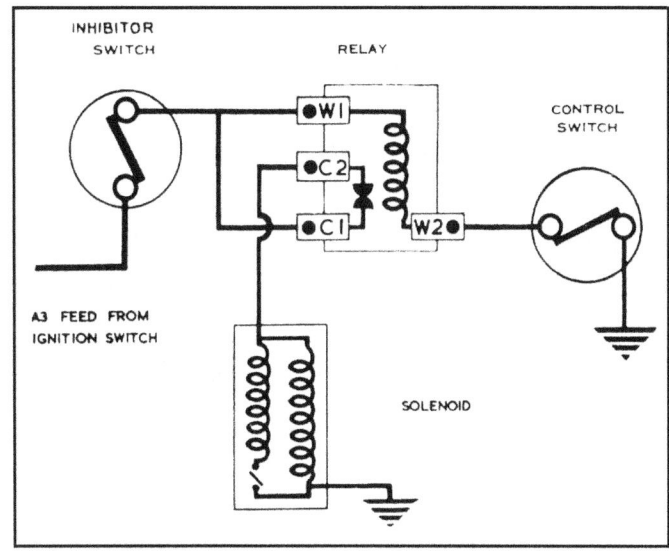

FIG 26 Wiring diagram - single relay

Warning:

Any movement of the car in a forward direction with a centrifugal switch loose or removed will result in the speedometer driven gear being displaced. Ensure that this gear is correctly fitted when replacing the centrifugal switch.

(e) Failure of solenoid and warning light to operate in above test may indicate a faulty manual switch. To check this, short out terminals C1-C2 of relay R2. Operation of the overdrive solenoid and warning light indicates a faulty manual switch.

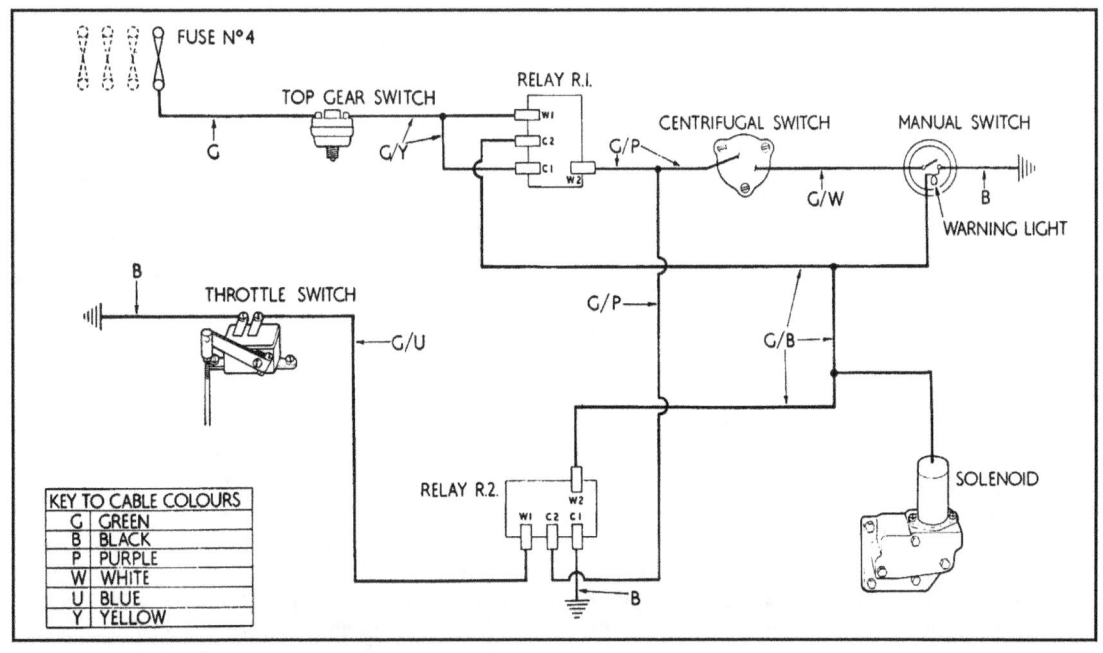

FIG 27 Wiring daigram - two relay

Throtle switch adjustment single relay:

With the engine running check that the idling speed is 500 rev/min, if not adjust the slow-running screws (volume) by equal amounts until it is. Switch off engine. Engage top gear. With a screwdriver short out the 'C1' and 'C2' terminals on the relay. The solenoid will then be heard to operate with a click. Slacken the pinch bolt securing the operating lever to the spindle of the throttle switch.

By trial and error position the operating lever in the spindle so that when the carburetter spindles are rotated, the full throttle stops on the spindles move approximately $\frac{1}{8}$ inch. before the overdrive solenoid is heard to disengage.

On the XK 150 model the throttle switch is located between the two carburetters and is adjusted as follows. Check the idling speed to give 500 rev/min. Switch off engine. Slacken the locknut and screw down the switch until the plunger in the centre of the switch is fully depressed by the lever on which it operates. Tighten the locknut.

Throtle switch adjustment two relay:

1. Ensure that the throttle adjusting screws are on their stops and that the idling speed is set at 500 r.p.m.

2. Stop the engine. Insert a ·050" feeler between the rear throttle adjusting screw and its stop.

3. Connect a wire, with a bulb in circuit, between the battery negative terminal and the throttle switch terminal to which the green and blue wire is connected.

4. Slacken the operating lever pinch bolt and with a screwdriver, turn the spindle until the bulb lights up. Turn the spindle anti-clockwise until the light is just flickering out and tighten the pinch bolt.

5. Immediately the throttle is opened further, the bulb should go out. Remove the feeler from the throttle adjusting screw stop when the bulb should light up fully.

6. Reinsert the ·050" feeler gauge and recheck the adjustment. If fine adjustment is required slacken the locknut on the throttle switch lever operating rod, and turn the rod in the desired direction.

Note: If at any time adjustment is made to the idling speed of the engine, the throttle switch adjustment must be checked, and if necessary, reset.

Operating solenoid two relay:

The solenoid is made up of a soft iron plunger, a holding coil of high resistance, a closing coil of low resistance and a pair of normally closed contacts. These contacts are connected in series with the closing coil.

When the contacts of relay R1 close, both coils in the solenoid become energised and actuate the soft iron plunger. Movement of the plunger opens the **solenoid internal switch and cuts out the low resistance closing coil, the magnetism due to the high resistance coil alone being sufficient to keep the plunger in the overdrive position.**

Electrical fault diagnosis two relay:

Warning Light Illuminated but Overdrive Fails to Operate:

Electrically, this symptom indicates a defective solenoid. If no mechanical faults are suspected, remove solenoid and fit new unit.

Warning Light Illuminated but Action of Overdrive Solenoid Weak:

Solenoid is defective and should be replaced.

Warning Light Illuminated and Overdrive Operates, but Solenoid Unit Overheats:

Solenoid is defective and should be replaced.

Note: The normal current consumption of the system should be approximately 1·0-1·5 amperes. The above fault will be accompanied by a current of approximately 18-20 amperes.

Overdrive drops out with throttle closed, accompanied by slight fluttering of warning light and noticeable braking effect:

1. Check setting of throttle switch and, if necessary, reset.

2. Check throttle switch contacts as follows: Engage top gear, close throttle, switch on ignition, and short out terminals C1-C2 of relay R1, the solenoid should now operate. If it does not, link terminal of relay R2 to earth. Operation of overdrive will indicate a faulty throttle switch.

3. Check for faulty operation of relay R2 contacts as follows:

(a) Connect a 0-20 voltmeter to terminals C1-C2 of relay R2, switch on ignition and engage top gear. A reading of approximately 12 volts should be obtained.

(b) Short out terminals C1-C2 of relay R1. If previous checks have been satisfactory, the overdrive will operate and the voltmeter reading should drop immediately to zero.

If any reading at all is obtained, replace the relay with a good unit.

Overdrive operates satisfactorily but Warning Light fails to Indicate:

Check warning light bulb for loose connection or burnt out filament and, if necessary, replace.

12 Modifications:

An overdrive throttle switch was added to the XK 140 models commencing at the following chassis numbers.

	RH drive	LH drive
Open 2 seater	800062	811866
Fixed Head Coupé	804523	815252
Drop Head Coupé	807319	818193

The incorporation of the throttle switch as on the other Jaguar models prevents a change from overdrive to top gear being made if decelerating with a closed throttle as the throttle switch overrides the manual switch until the throttle is opened for acceleration.

13 Disassembly and reassembly:

WARNING:

BEFORE COMMENCING ANY DISMANTLING OPERATIONS IT IS IMPORTANT THAT THE HYDRAULIC PRESSURE IS RELEASED FROM THE SYSTEM

As the unit is fitted with a speed responsive control it is not possible to operate the overdrive by means of the overdrive manual switch. The pressure in the system should be released by moving the valve operating lever manually (FIG 24) at least 10-12 times.

Removing the overdrive from the gearbox (FIG 28)

1. Remove the gearbox top cover and packing piece, noting the two gaskets.

2. The overdrive unit is separated from the gearbox at the joint between the gearbox rear extension and the overdrive front casing which are attached by seven studs **two of which are extra long.**

3. Remove the five nuts on the short studs before those on the longer studs are touched.

4. Slacken the two nuts on the long studs by equal amounts to release the compression of the clutch springs.

5. Remove the two nuts when the overdrive unit can be withdrawn off the mainshaft.

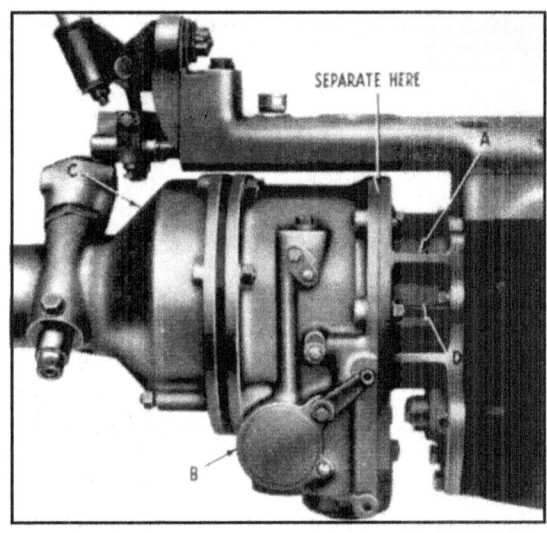

FIG 28 Separating the overdrive from the gearbox

A. Gearbox rear extension. C. Overdrive rear casing.
B. Overdrive front casing. D. Extra long stud.

Dismantling the overdrive

1. Remove the clutch springs from their pins, noting that the four inner springs are shorter than the eight outer springs.

2. The two bridge pieces against which the operating pistons bear can now be removed. Each is secured by two $\frac{1}{4}$" nuts locked by tab washers. Withdraw the two operating pistons.

3. The pump valve can be dismantled without removing the solenoid bracket from the housing and there is no need to disturb the latter unless it is necessary to remove the accumulator piston and spring.

4. Remove the nuts securing the two halves of the housing and separate them, removing the brake ring which is spigotted into the two pieces. Lift out the planet carrier assembly. Remove the clutch sliding member complete with the thrust ring and bearing, the sun-wheel and thrust washers. Take out the inner member of the uni-directional clutch, the rollers, cage, etc.

5. If it is necessary to remove the planet gears from the carrier, the three Mills pins securing the planet bearing shafts must be extracted before the latter can be knocked out.

6. To remove the annulus, first take off the coupling flange at the rear of the unit, remove the speedometer gear, centrifugal switch, etc., and drive out the annulus from the back. The front bearing will come away on the shaft leaving the rear bearing in the housing.

Inspection

Each part should be thoroughly inspected after the unit is dismantled and cleaned to ensure what parts should be replaced. It is important to appreciate the difference between parts which are worn sufficiently to affect the operation of the unit and those which are merely "worn in".

1. Inspect the front casing for cracks, damage, etc. Examine the bores of the operating cylinders and accumulator for scores and wear. Check for leaks from the plugged ends of the oil passages. Ensure that the welch washer beneath the accumulator bore is tight and not leaking. Inspect the support bushes in the centre bore for wear and damage.

2. Examine the clutch sliding member assembly. Ensure that the clutch linings are not burned or worn. Inspect the pins for clutch springs and bridge pieces and see that they are tight in the thrust ring and not distorted. Ensure that the ball bearing is in good condition and rotates freely. See that the sliding member slides easily on the splines of the sun-wheel.

3. Inspect the clutch springs for distortion or collapse. Free length $4\frac{9}{16}$" outer springs, $4\frac{13}{32}$" inner springs.

4. Inspect the teeth of the gear train for damage. If the sun-wheel or planet bushes are worn the gears will have to be replaced since it is not possible to fit new bushes in service because they have to be bored true to the pitch line of the teeth.

5. Inspect steel and bronze thrust washers.

6. Inspect the uni-directional clutch. See that the rollers are not chipped and that the inner and outer members of the clutch are free from damage. Make sure that the outer member is tight in the annulus. Ensure that the spring is free from distortion.

7. Inspect the ball bearings on the output shaft and see that there is no roughness when they are rotated slowly.

8. Inspect the mainshaft splines for nicks and burrs. See that the oil holes are open and clean.

9. Inspect the oil pump for wear on the pump plunger and roller pin. Ensure that the plunger spring is not distorted. Free length 2″. Inspect the valve seat and ball and make sure that they are free from nicks and scratches.

10. Inspect the operating valve for distortion and damage and see that it slides easily in its bore in the front casing.

Reassembling the overdrive

The unit can be reassembled after all the parts have been thoroughly cleaned and checked to ensure that none are damaged or worn.

1. Assemble the annulus into the rear casing, not forgetting the spacing washer which fits between a shoulder on the shaft and the rear ball bearing. This washer is available in different thicknesses for selective assembly and should allow no end float of the annulus (output shaft) and no preloading of the bearings.

Selective washers are furnished in the following sizes:

Jaguar Part No.	Size
C.5981	·146″ ±·0005″
C.5694	·151″ ±·0005″
C.5695	·156″ ±·0005″
C.5696	·161″ ±·0005″
C.5697	·166″ ±·0005″

2. Replace the thrust washer and uni-directional clutch inner member with its rollers and cage. A fixture is needed for retaining the rollers in position when assembling the clutch. Ensure that the spring is fitted correctly so that the cage urges the rollers up the ramps on the inner member.

3. Fit the pump cam on to gearbox mainshaft, offer up the front housing to the gearbox rear extension and secure temporarily with two nuts. In order to determine the amount of end float of the sun-wheel which should be ·008″ to ·014″, an extra thrust washer of known thickness should be assembled with the two normally used in front of the sun-wheel.

4. Fit the planet carrier, with its planet gears, over the sun-wheel with the marked teeth of the planets radially outwards as shown in **FIG 29** and with the assembly in this position offer it up to the annulus.

FIG 29 Assembly of planet gears
(Note positions of marked teeth)

5. Assemble the brake ring to the front casing, then offer up the front and rear assemblies, leaving out the clutch sliding member with its springs, etc. The gap between the flanges of the brake ring and rear casing should be measured. This gap will be less than the thickness of the extra thrust washer by the amount of end float of the sun-wheel. If this is between the limits specified the unit may be stripped down again and reassembled without the extra thrust washer. The clutch sliding member bridge pieces, etc., must then be replaced.

6. If the indicated end float is more or less than that required it must be adjusted by replacing the steel thrust washer at the front of the sun-wheel by one of less or greater thickness, as required. Washers of varying thicknesses are stocked for this purpose.

Seven sizes are available, as follows:

Jaguar Part No.	Size
C.5943	·113″—·118″
C.5944	·107″—·104″
C.5945	·101″—·102″
C.5946	·095″—·096″
C.5947	·089″—·090″
C.5948	·083″—·084″
C.5949	·077″—·078″

7. Care must be taken to ensure that the thrust washers at the front and rear of the sun-wheel are replaced in their correct positions. At the front of the sun-wheel the steel washer fits next to the head of the support bush in the housing and the bronze washer between the steel one and the sun-wheel. At the rear the steel washer is sandwiched between the two bronze washers. The latter are similar and their positions interchangeable.

It is essential when assembling the gear train to ensure that the planets are turned to their correct relative positions as shown in **FIG 29**.

Refitting the overdrive to the gearbox

1. Place the overdrive unit upside down in a vice.

2. Fit the oil pump operating cam on the gearbox mainshaft with the long plain end facing the gearbox, and with the back of the cam towards the bottom of the casing.

3. Ensure that the splines in the uni-directional clutch and planet carrier are in alignment. These splines are visible at the bottom of the bore in the overdrive unit. If alignment is necessary, turn the rearmost splines in an anti-clockwise direction by means of a long-bladed screwdriver.

4. Engage a gear, turn the gearbox up on end and enter the mainshaft into the overdrive unit. Turn the constant pinion shaft until the splines engage.

5. Ensure that clutch springs are over their respective bosses on the gearbox rear extension. Press the gearbox down to test the cushioning of springs.

6. Fit two nuts to the long studs and tighten up until there is approximately $\frac{3}{4}$″ gap between the overdrive casing and the gearbox rear extension, meanwhile **ensuring that the oil pump cam does not drop down off the splines on the mainshaft.**

7. Enter two screwdrivers into the gap between the overdrive casing and the gearbox rear extension, with one, compress the oil pump plunger, and with the other, lever the cam down into alignment with the plunger roller (**FIG 30**).

8. Tighten the two nuts on the long studs by equal amounts until the remaining five nuts can be started. Fully tighten the seven nuts by turning by equal amounts.

9. Refit the packing piece with a gasket on each side, to the top face of the gearbox. Refit the gearbox top cover.

IMPORTANT

When fitting the overdrive to the gearbox, compress the oil pump plunger and align the operating cam with the plunger roller (see FIG 30).

14 Fault diagnosis

(a) Overdrive does not engage

1 Insufficient oil in gearbox
2 Electrical system not functioning
3 Solenoid operating lever out of adjustment
4 Insufficient hydraulic pressure due to pump non-return valve incorrectly seating
5 Insufficient hydraulic pressure due to worn accumulator
6 Pump not working due to choked filter
7 Pump not working due to damaged roller or cam
8 Leaking operating valve
9 Internal damage

(b) Overdrive does not disengage

If this occurs do not reverse the car or extensive damage to the unit may occur.

1 Fault in electrical system
2 Solenoid sticking
3 Blocked restrictor jet in operating valve
4 Solenoid lever incorrectly adjusted
5 Sticking clutch
6 Internal damage

FIG 30 Fitting the overdrive to the gearbox

(c) Clutch slip in overdrive

1 Insufficient oil in gearbox
2 Solenoid lever out of adjustment
3 Non-return valve incorrectly seating
4 Worn accumulator
5 Operating valve incorrectly seated
6 Worn or glazed clutch lining

(d) Clutch slip in reverse or free wheel position

1 Solenoid operating lever out of adjustment
2 Partially blocked restrictor jet in operating valve.
3 Worn or burnt inner clutch lining

Before removing any of the valve plugs it is essential to operate the solenoid several times in order to release all hydraulic pressure from the system.

NOTES

INDEX – AUTOMATIC GEARBOX – PART 1

SECTION	PAGE	
		PART 1 - AUTOMATIC GEARBOX AS FITTED TO THE EARLY CARS
001	105	Description (General)
002	105	Description - Torque Converter Assembly
003	107	Description - Hydraulic Transmission Assembly
004-009	108-110	Operation by Gearshift Position
010	110	Description - Anti-Creep System
011	111	Description – Transmission Operation Chart
012	112	Driving Instructions
013-014	112-117	Routine Maintenance & Service Adjustments
015-020	117-120	Removal & Installation of the Transmission & Components
021-027	120-124	Testing and Checking the Operation of the Transmission
028-034	124-129	Fault Diagnosis Chart (Faults, Causes & Remedies)
035-045	129-154	Servicing the Transmission (Dismantling & Reassembly)

AUTOMATIC GEARBOX - SERVICE
PART 1

There are minor differences between the automatic gearbox fitted to the earlier MK VII and the later models that utilize the Borg Warner automatic unit. As the predominance of the service and repair procedures are similar, and in order to simplify and avoid duplication of those processes, the earlier unit is used to describe those procedures (PART 1) and the subsequent changes and modifications are dealt with in a separate section (PART 2). Where applicable, those changes are cross referenced in the text such that the information contained in both PART 1 and PART 2 (when combined) cover the relevant service and repair information for all Mark and XK series of Jaguars that were equipped with automatic gearboxes.

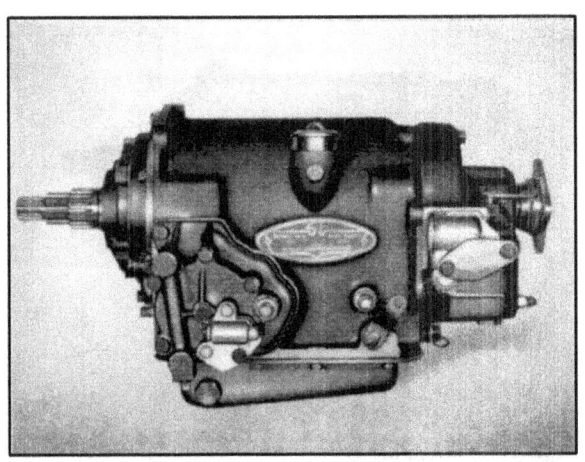

Gearbox Unit

Torque Converter

1:1 GENERAL DESCRIPTION

The transmission assembly consists of a three-element hydraulic torque converter followed by two planetary gear sets which permit the elimination of the clutch pedal and normal gear-shift lever. The planetary gear sets incorporate freewheels and are controlled by hydraulically-operated band and disc clutches.

The two major assemblies of the Automatic Transmission are:

1. A torque converter assembly which (a) provides for a smooth transfer of power through use of fluid, (b) supplies a range of torque multiplication, and (c) combined with the transmission assembly permits elimination of the clutch pedal.

2. A hydraulically controlled planetary transmission which provides three forward ratios and one reverse ratio — one of these forward ratios is a direct drive ratio which is obtained automatically through the use of a direct drive clutch enclosed in the torque converter assembly.

1:2 TORQUE CONVERTER ASSEMBLY

The torque converter in the Automatic Transmission consists of: an impeller (A, Fig 2) (driving member) connected to the engine crankshaft, a turbine (B) driven member splined to the converter output shaft, and a stator (C) connected to the transmission case through a freewheeling unit (D and E). The impeller, driven by the engine, transmits the power to the turbine which in turn transmits the power to the transmission. The stator redirects the flow of oil as it leaves the turbine so that it enters the impeller at the most efficient angle to assist the engine in driving the impeller.

The maximum torque multiplication through the torque converter is approximately 2 to 1 and occurs when the turbine is stationary and the impeller is turning at approximately 2,000 rpm. As the speeds of the impeller and turbine become substantially equal, the torque multiplication ceases and the unit acts only to transmit engine torque to a 1 to 1 ratio. When torque multiplication ceases, the stator is no longer needed to redirect oil flow and the freewheeling unit which fastens it to the transmission case permits it to rotate in the same direction as the impeller and turbine.

For compactness, the direct drive clutch is enclosed within the torque converter assembly. It consists of three units: a hydraulically-operated pressure plate (A Fig 3), a driven member (B), and a backing plate (C). Oil pressure to the pressure plate locks these three units together, allowing engine torque to be transmitted to the rear axle assembly at a 1 to 1 ratio.

The torque converter and transmission assembly employ a cooling system which is entirely independent of the engine cooling system. Screened openings allow

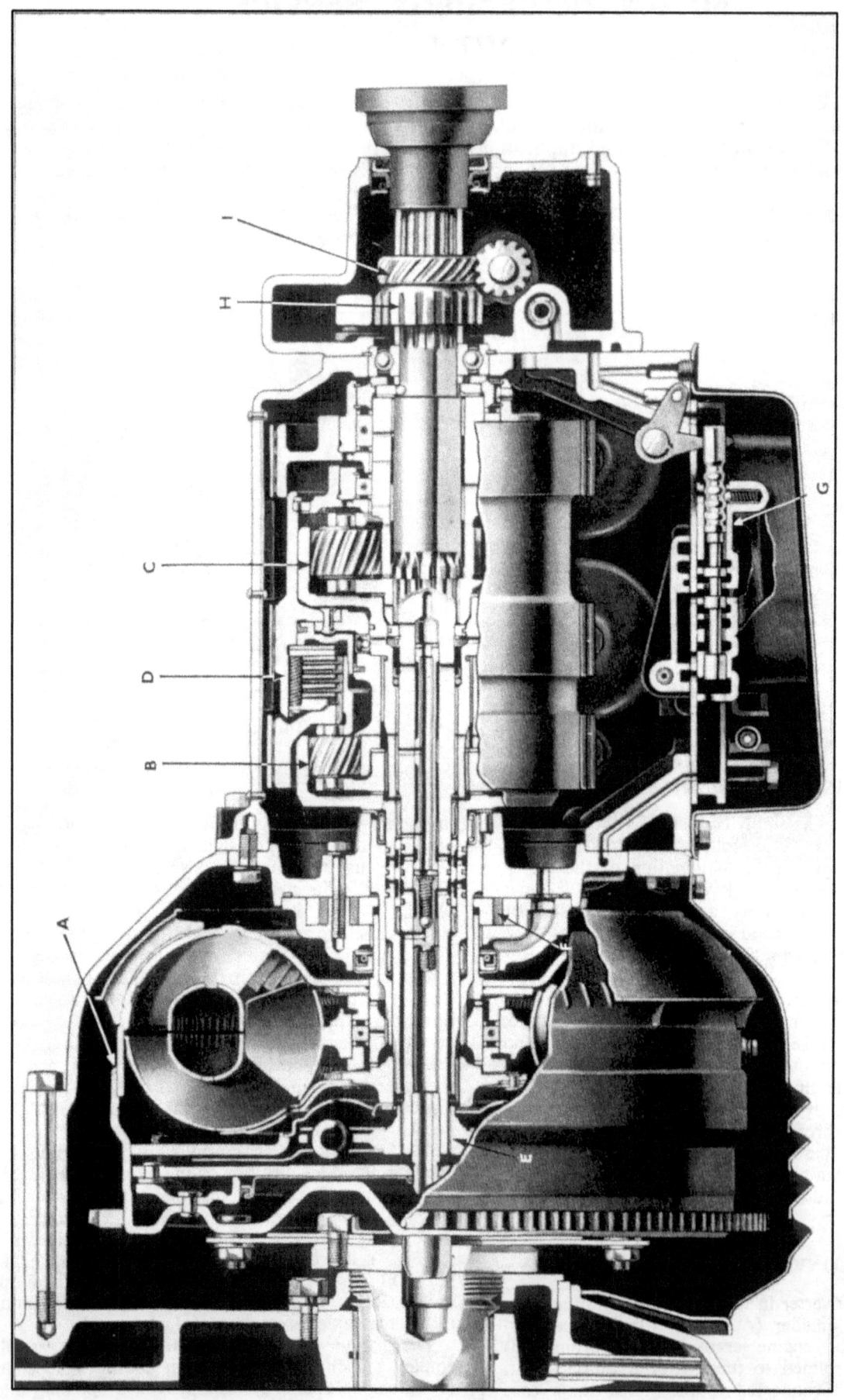

Fig 1.—The transmission assembly. Sectioned view.

A. Torque converter.
B. Front planetary gear set.
C. Rear planetary gear set.
D. Multiple disc clutch.
E. Direct drive clutch.
F. Front pump.
G. Selector valve.
H. Parking gear.
I. Governor and rear oil pump drive gear.

air to enter the housing. A blower on the torque converter spreads the air over the entire surface of the converter. It is then expelled through louvres in the converter housing cover plate.

NOTE. The internal parts of the torque converter assembly are not supplied separately; the torque converter is supplied only as an assembly.

1:3 HYDRAULIC TRANSMISSION ASSEMBLY

The hydraulically controlled transmission assembly consists of:

1. **A front pump** (see Figs 4 and 42) which is of the external-internal gear type and is driven by the converter hub. Its function is to supply the necessary oil pressure to the torque converter and the hydraulic control system, and oil for lubrication during idling, low speed, and reverse operation.

2. **A rear pump** (see Figs 5 and 41) which is of the external gear type and is driven by the mainshaft. Its function is to supply the necessary oil pressure to the torque converter and the hydraulic control system, and oil for lubrication at higher car speeds. It also supplies the necessary oil pressure to operate the transmission when pushing the car to start the engine.

3. **A low and forward servo assembly** (see Figs 6 and 77), located on the right side of the transmission, controls the operation of the low and forward brake bands.

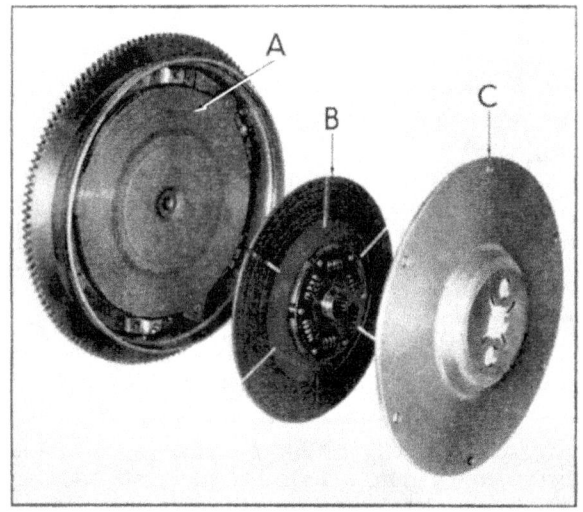

Fig 3.—The direct drive clutch.

A. Pressure plate.   B. Driven member.   C. Backing plate.

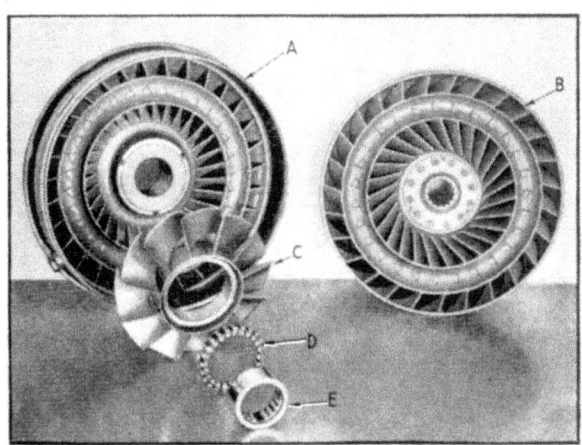

Fig 2.—Exploded view of the torque converter.

A. Impeller.   D. Free wheel unit.
B. Turbine.   E. Inner race.
C. Stator.

4. **A reverse servo unit** (see Figs 7 and 72), located on the left side of the transmission, consists primarily of two pistons which, actuated by oil pressure, control the operation of the reverse brake band.

5. **An extension case assembly** (see Fig 28), mounted on the rear of the transmission case, consists of the governor assembly, the rear oil pump assembly, parking pawl and toggle assembly, speedometer drive gear assembly and the direct drive control assembly.
NOTE: See also 2:48

6. **A governor valve,** located in the extension housing, controls the operation of the direct drive clutch.
NOTE: See also 2:48

7. **A parking interlock piston** which prevents engagement of the parking pawl when the car is moving forward.

8. **A reverse shuttle valve** which provides for smooth engagement of the reverse band.
NOTE: See also 2:48

9. **A valve block assembly,** mounted on the bottom of the transmission (see Fig 46), controls the flow of oil in the hydraulic system.

The valves included in the valve block assembly are:
(a) A selector valve which controls the oil flow from the oil pump to the servo units and through the governor valve to the multiple disc clutch and direct drive clutch.
(b) A front and rear pump relief valve assembly which regulates the pressure of the respective pumps.

Fig 4.—Front pump location.

(c) A converter valve which regulates and supplies oil to the torque converter.

(d) A reverse interlock valve which prevents application of the reverse band when the car is moving forward.

10. **A mainshaft assembly** (Fig 54), supported at the rear by a ball bearing and at the front by the front pump, consists of the mainshaft, three brake drums, multiple disc clutch (D, Fig 1), and the planetary gear sets (B and C, Fig 1).

11. **A multiple disc clutch** (see D, Fig 1) which locks the members of the front planetary set into a single unit when a straight drive through this unit is desired.

12. **Two freewheeling units** (see Figs 67 and 68) which simplify the valving required to accomplish smooth shifts from intermediate (second speed) to direct drive.

13. **Three bands** (see Fig 69), combined with their servo mechanisms, which control the operation of the planetary gear sets.

1:4 OPERATION

The Automatic Transmission is controlled by the position of the selector lever as indicated by the quadrant pointer. The selector lever has five positions:

P or Park — provides a safe, positive lock on the rear wheels when the car is stopped. Movement of the selector lever to the P position actuates a mechanical locking device in the transmission which prevents the rear wheels from turning in either direction. Consequently, should the car be pushed either from the front or rear with sufficient force the rear tyres will slide. This condition is quite similar to that encountered when a car with conventional transmission is parked in gear or with the handbrake applied firmly.

The fact that the engine may be started with the selector in P position is convenient when parked on an incline.

N or Neutral. This position permits idling the engine without possibility of setting the car in motion by depression of the accelerator and may be used when starting the engine.

D or Drive. This position provides two automatic forward drive ranges, intermediate and direct, which are sufficient for most driving conditions.

L or Low. This position provides an emergency power range for heavy pulling, rapid acceleration from a standstill, and engine braking.

R. or Reverse. This position provides a reverse driving range.

1:5 P or PARK POSITION

With the selector lever in the P or Park position and engine running, the selector valve prevents oil pressure from being applied to any of the band servo mechanisms or the clutches. The front pump and the front pump relief valve are, however, maintaining line pressure and are supplying oil pressure to the converter valve to maintain converter pressure and to provide lubrication.

In addition, should the selector lever be placed in this position while the car is moving forward above 3 to 5 mph, a hydraulically-operated parking interlock piston is provided which operates off the rear pump pressure to prevent engagement of the parking pawl.

In this position there is no power flow through the transmission. However, with the selector lever in this position and the car standing still, the parking pawl engages a mating gear splined to the transmission mainshaft, thus locking the mainshaft to the transmission case and preventing the rear wheels from turning.

Engine Starting. Operation of the instrument panel starter push button energises the starter solenoid switch only when the selector lever is in the P or N position. In the D, L or R position the starter cut-out control switch, which is operated by the selector lever, opens the starter solenoid from being energised even though the starter control switch is operated.

Fig 5.—Rear pump location.

1:6 N or NEUTRAL POSITION

With the selector lever in this position, the selector valve does not admit pressure to any of the clutches or bands, although, if the engine is running, oil pressure from the front pump is being admitted to the converter valve to maintain converter pressure and to provide lubrication.

There is no power flow through the transmission in this position. Since the parking pawl is not engaged in this position, the car can be moved as desired.

1:7 D or DRIVE POSITION

(See also 2:49)

Intermediate. With the selector lever in the D position, line pressure from the front pump relief valve is directed by the selector valve to the forward band servo mechanism and, through the governor valve to the piston of the multiple disc clutch.

Application of the multiple disc clutch locks together the planet carrier and the sun gear of the front planetary set. The front planetary set, therefore, revolves at unity since, when any two members in a single planet set are locked together, the entire set rotates as one.

Fig 6.—Low and forward servo location.

Engagement of the forward band locks the forward band drum to the case, holding the sun gear of the rear planetary set stationary through the action of the forward band drum freewheeling unit. With the sun gear stationary and the power input through the ring gear, the output of the set is through the planet carrier to the transmission mainshaft.

Power flow is from the engine to the torque converter to the ring gear of the front planetary set. Since the front planetary set revolves at unity, the power is transmitted unchanged from the front planetary carrier to the ring gear of the planetary set as these units are connected directly together. The rear planetary set, in turn, transmits the power to the transmission mainshaft at a ratio of approximately 1.4 to 1. The combination of this gear reduction and torque multiplication in the torque converter gives a maximum ratio of approximately 2.9 to 1 through the automatic transmission.

Direct. As the car speed increases above 18 mph with the selector lever in the D position, the governor and the governor valve act to allow line pressure to flow to the direct drive clutch, applying this clutch in addition to the units already engaged. If the accelerator is completely depressed, however, the transmission will not shift to direct until car speed reaches approximately 55 mph.

Also, as car speed increases, the oil pressure output of the rear pump becomes sufficient to supply the needs of the transmission hydraulic system. At this time, the rear pump relief valve acts to regulate rear pump pressure and to return the output of the front pump directly to the oil pan. The power required to drive the front pump is thereby greatly reduced, increasing the overall efficiency of operation.

Power flow with the direct drive clutch engaged is from the engine through this clutch to the transmission mainshaft. This provides a positive drive from the engine to the rear axle assembly, by-passing the torque converter and the planetary gear sets through the freewheeling units. Since the torque converter and the planetary gears are by-passed, the efficiency of the drive is greatly increased. In this range there is no torque multiplication.

Hill Holding Characteristics. When the selector lever is in Drive position, the transmission acts to prevent the car from rolling rearward when stopped on normal upgrades with the engine running. This is due to the action of the freewheeling units which prevent reverse rotation of the transmission mainshaft when the multiple disc clutch and the forward band are engaged.

1:8 L or LOW POSITION

With the selector lever in this position, the selector valve allows line pressure to flow to the servo mechanisms of the low and forward bands, applying both bands. In this position, the selector valve also cuts off pressure to the governor valve, thus cutting off line pressure to the direct drive clutch and the multiple disc clutch and preventing these units from being applied regardless of the car speed.

With the bands applied, the low band holds the sun gear of the front planetary set stationary while the forward band holds the sun gear of the rear planetary set stationary through the medium of the rear freewheeling unit. In a simple planetary set, a forward drive ratio is obtained through the planet carrier when the input is through the ring gear and sun gear is held stationary. Engine braking is provided through application of the low band.

Power flow in low is from the engine to the torque converter, to ring gear of the front planetary set. The power then goes from the planet carrier of the front planetary set to the ring gear of the rear planetary set and out the planet carrier of this set to the transmission mainshaft. The product of the ratio through the front planetary set and the rear planetary set is approximately 2.3 to 1 which, combined with the torque multiplication through the converter, gives a maximum ratio in low of approximately 4.6 to 1 through the Automatic Transmission.

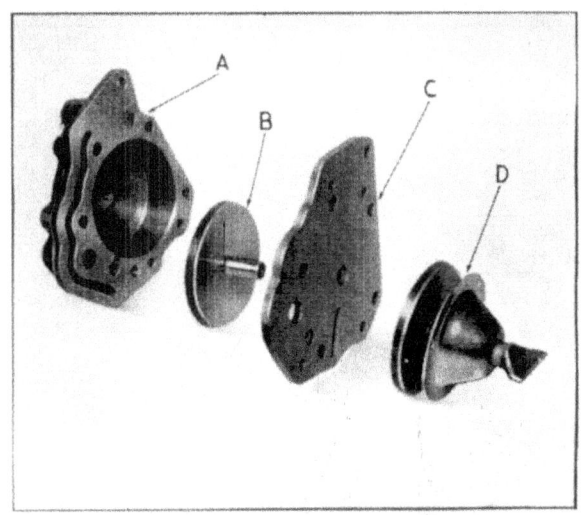

Fig 7.—Reverse servo exploded.

A. Brake cylinder and outer gasket.
B. Outer piston.
C. Cylinder plate.
D. Inner piston.

1:9 R or REVERSE POSITION

With the selector in this position, the selector valve allows the line pressure to flow to the servo mechanism of the reverse band, applying this band. Line pressure also flows to the back of the front relief valve and this pressure plus the value of the front pump relief valve spring increases line pressure from its normal value of 80 lb per sq in to 200 lb per sq in. A connecting passage also allows line pressure to flow to the back of the converter valve and this pressure plus the converter valve spring maintains converter pressure at approximately 27 lb per sq in.

It should be noted that, for smoothness of engagement, one reverse servo piston receives unrestricted oil flow while the other piston receives pressure only after the spring in the reverse shuttle valve has been compressed and the reverse band has been applied by the inner piston. When operating in reverse, all pressure for the hydraulic system is provided by the front pump as the rear pump is being operated in reverse rotation and therefore supplies no pressure.

A reverse interlock valve is also incorporated in the transmission to prevent engagement of the reverse band, should the selector lever be accidentally placed in the R position at higher forward car speeds. This valve operates off rear pump pressure and acts to prevent pressure from being built up in the reverse servo mechanism.

Application of the reverse band holds stationary the planet carrier of the front planetary set, and the ring gear of the rear planetary set. In the front planetary set (a simple planetary system), when the input is through the ring gear and the planet carrier is held stationary, the sun gear is driven in reverse. In the rear planetary set (another simple planetary system), when the ring gear is held stationary and the input is through the sun gear, the planet carrier is driven in the same direction as the sun gear.

Power flow is from the engine to the torque converter to the ring gear of the front planetary set. The front planetary set reverses the direction of rotation and transmits the power from the sun gear of this set to

Fig 8.—The anti-creep throttle switch.

A. Switch.
B. Locknut.
C. Switch plunger.
D. Operating lever.

the sun gear of the rear planetary set through the front freewheeling unit.

The planetary set supplies a gear reduction in transmitting the power to the transmission mainshaft. The product of the gear ratios supplied by the planetary sets is a reverse ratio of approximately 2 to 1. The combination of this gear reduction and the torque multiplication through the torque converter provides a maximum reverse ratio of approximately 4 to 1 through the Automatic Transmission in reverse.

1:10 ANTI-CREEP SYSTEM

The anti-creep system employed with the Automatic Transmission consists of:

A solenoid valve which holds brake pressure on the rear wheel brakes whenever the anti-creep circuit is closed.

A pressure control switch which is operated by rear pump pressure to open the anti-creep circuit when the car is moving forward and to close the circuit when the car is stationary or moving in reverse.

An anti-creep throttle switch (A, Fig 8) which opens and closes the anti-creep circuit as the accelerator is depressed or released.

These units are connected as shown in Fig 9.

With the ignition switch ON the accelerator released (anti-creep throttle switch closed) and the car stationary (pressure control switch closed) the anti-creep circuit is completed and the solenoid valve is energised. When the brakes are applied under these conditions the anti-creep solenoid valve will retain approximately 400 lb per sq in pressure at rear wheels brakes to prevent "creeping".

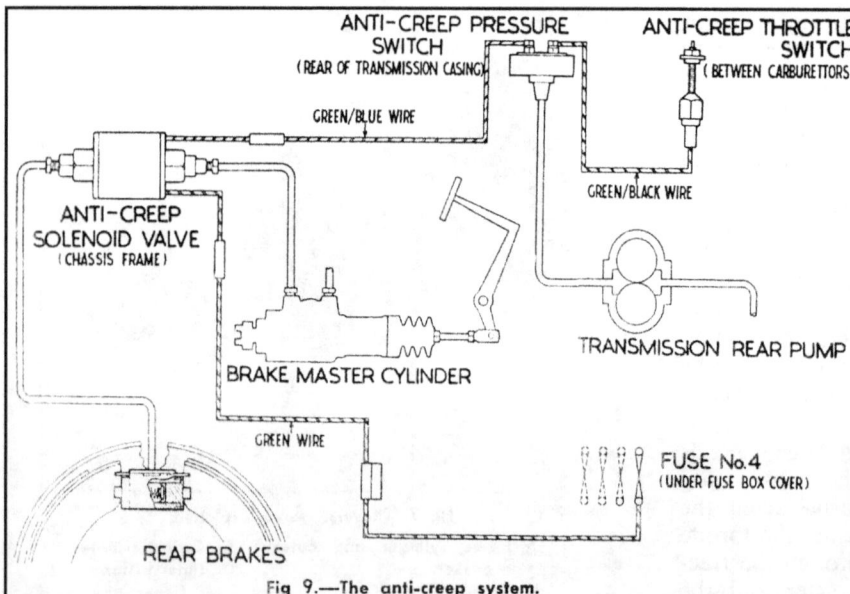

Fig 9.—The anti-creep system.

When the accelerator pedal is depressed the circuit is opened at the anti-creep throttle switch allowing the solenoid to de-energise thereby releasing the brakes instantly. When the car is moving forward, normal brake operation is not affected since the rear pump pressure holds open the anti-creep pressure control switch thus preventing the solenoid from energising.

1:11 AUTOMATIC TRANSMISSION OPERATION CHART

The operation chart is a summary of the action of the units within the Automatic Transmission and shows which units are in operation under the various driving conditions. From it, can readly be determined which units are in operation in a given driving range and also in which driving ranges any unit operates.

NOTE: See 2:47 for first speed start transmission.

Driving Units

	Park	Neutral	Drive Intermediate	Drive Direct	Low	Reverse
Forward Band Servo	—	—	Applied	Applied	Applied	—
Multiple Disc Clutch	—	—	Applied	Applied	—	—
Low Band and Servo	—	—	—	—	Applied	—
Reverse Band and Servo	—	—	—	—	—	Applied
Direct Drive Clutch	—	—	—	Applied	—	—
Forward Drum Freewheel	Free	Free	Locked	Locked	Locked	Free
Low Drum Freewheel	Free	Free	Free forward but locked against rollback	Free	Locked	Locked

Hydraulic Control Units

	Park Neutral	Drive Intermediate Drive Direct Low	Reverse
Front Pump	Supplies oil pressure to hydraulic system for lubrication and for converter operation.	Supplies oil pressure until rear pump takes over (below approximately 20 mph). Transmission oil at normal operating temperature.	Supplies oil pressure.
Front Pump Relief Valve	Regulates front pump pressure at 60-80 lb sq in.	Regulates front pump pressure at 60-80 lb sq in until rear pump takes over (below approximately 20 mph). Transmission oil at normal operating temperature.	Regulates front pump pressure at 180-200 lb sq in.
Rear Pump		Supplies oil pressure to hydraulic system above approximately 20 mph forward speed. Transmission oil at normal operating temperature.	
Rear Pump Relief Valve		Regulates rear pump pressure at 80 lb sq in and releases front pump pressure.	
Converter Valve	Regulates supply of oil to converter at 25-35 lb sq in at all times.		
Selector Valve	Directs flow of oil within transmission at all times.		
Reverse Interlock Valve		Releases reverse system at forward car speeds above approximately 10 mph.	
Park Interlock Plunger		Prevents engagement of parking pawl above approximately 5 mph.	
Reverse Shuttle Valve			Controls oil flow to outer reverse brake cylinder.
Governor Valve		Directs oil to multiple disc clutch and direct drive clutch.	
Parking Pawl	Engaged		

1:12 DRIVING INSTRUCTIONS

Note: See also 2:50

The operation of the Automatic Transmission is controlled by the position of the selector lever which is indicated by the quadrant pointer. The quadrant is marked P, N, D, L and R. The lever must be raised when selecting P, L or R and when moving from P to any other position.

To start the engine the selector lever must be in the P or N positions.

P (Park) provides a safe, positive lock on the rear wheels when the car is stopped. Movement of the selector lever to the P position actuates a mechanical locking device in the transmission which prevents the rear wheels from turning in either direction. This condition is quite similar to that encountered when a car with conventional transmission is parked in gear or with the handbrake applied firmly. The fact that the engine may be started with the selector in P position is convenient when parked on an incline.

When the car has been parked on a grade, releasing the selector from P position will usually require a sharp movement of the level rather than a steady pull. This is necessary to overcome the added pressure against the parking pawl imposed by the weight of the car on the incline.

N (Neutral) position permits idling the engine without possibility of setting the car into motion by pressure on the accelerator and may be used when starting the engine.

D (Drive) provides the normal forward driving range and includes automatic shifting between intermediate and direct drive ranges. Virtually all forward driving, accelerating, and stopping can be done with the lever in D position. Once the engine is started and the lever is moved to D, it can be left in this position for all normal driving. When accelerating in D, the transmission shifts automatically from intermediate to direct drive between 18 and 55 mph, depending upon position of the accelerator pedal. On deceleration, it will shift automatically from direct drive to intermediate at approximately 12 mph.

L (Low) is an emergency engine power range for use on unusually long and steep grades or for braking on descents, for extra heavy pulling, and for rocking the car out of mud, sand or snow.

R (Reverse) position of the selector lever provides reverse driving range.

Additional Power and Acceleration for hill climbing or passing while in D range (below 60 mph) is available by depressing the accelerator pedal all the way to the floorboard. The transmission will then shift into intermediate and will continue in this range until either the accelerator pedal is momentarily released or until the car speed reaches approximately 68 mph.

Hard Pulling, such as encountered in deep snow, mud or other adverse driving conditions, is best accomplished in the L range.

Extra-Fast Getaway from a standstill can be obtained with the selector lever in the L range. If the L position is selected for this purpose, move the selector lever to the D position before reaching a car speed of 40 mph and without releasing the accelerator.

Rocking Out of Mud, Sand or Snow is accomplished with the accelerator pedal slightly depressed and held steady while making quick alternate selections of L and R ranges.

Anti-creep is a special braking feature which prevents the car from creeping forward when stopped on level ground or slight grades, as long as the ignition switch is turned ON. Apply the foot brake to stop the car and then remove the foot from the brake pedal. The car will not creep forward or backward. Any movement of the accelerator pedal, or turning off the ignition switch releases the anti-creep action.

Push Starting may sometimes be necessary, as in case of a flat battery. Turn ignition key ON, place selector lever in the N position. The car may now be pushed and when it has reached 15 to 20 mph move the selector lever to D or L position. **Do not tow the car to start the engine — it may overtake the tow car.**

Engine Braking, for descending long mountainous grades, is easily secured by bringing the car speed below 40 mph and momentarily depressing the accelerator while placing the selector lever in the L position.

Prolonged Idling is sometimes unavoidable. In such cases, as a safety precaution, move the selector lever to the P or N position.

Roll-back, when stopped on normal upgrades with the selector lever in D position, is prevented by another design feature of the Automatic Transmission. On normal upgrades, whenever forward motion stops, the car will not roll back as long as the engine is running and the selector lever remains in the D position. It is not necessary to keep the brake pedal depressed on a normal upgrade for a change in the traffic lights.

NOTE: See also 2:50

Towing should be done with the selector lever in the **N position.** Car should not be towed in excess of 30 mph.

1:13 MAINTENANCE

Every 1,250 miles, check Transmission Fluid level as follows:

Remove the cover plate from underneath the floor carpet to expose the dipstick. Clean the area around the dipstick hole.

With the car on a level floor, set the hand brake firmly. Set the selector lever in the P position and start engine. Move the selector lever to L and, with the foot brake applied, raise the transmission fluid temperature by running the engine at 800 rpm until the normal operating temperature is attained.

Remove the dipstick and wipe it dry. With the engine idling at its normal speed, check the fluid level. Add sufficient fluid to bring the level up to the "Full" mark on the dipstick. DO NOT OVERFILL. The space between the "Full" and "Low" marks on the dipstick represents approximately one pint.

Every 15,000 miles, drain and refill Transmission as follows:

With the car on a level floor set the hand brake firmly. Set selector lever in the P position and start engine. Move selector lever to L and raise transmission fluid temperature by idling engine to the normal engine operating temperature.

Stop the engine and remove the cover plate from underneath the floor carpet to expose the dipstick. Clean the area around the dipstick hole and remove the dipstick.

Remove the transmission oil pan drain plug.

Remove the converter housing cover plate and rotate the converter until drain plug is in position for draining. Remove the converter drain plug.

To facilitate draining, remove the square-headed converter pressure take-off plug from the bottom of the housing attached to the left-hand side of the transmission casing.

After fluid has drained, refit and tighten the drain plugs in the transmission oil pan and converter. Refit the converter housing cover plate. Refit and tighten the converter pressure take-off plug.

Pour 10 Imperial pints of the recommended grade of fluid into the transmission through dipstick hole.

Start the engine and idle for approximately one minute with the selector lever set in the L position to transfer the fluid to the converter from the transmission case.

With the engine still idling and the selector lever in the L position add additional fluid, approximately 5 Imperial pints, to bring the level to the FULL mark on the dipstick. DO NOT OVERFILL. Finally, recheck the level of the oil as described in "Check Transmission Fluid Level".

1:14 SERVICE ADJUSTMENTS

Manual Selector Linkage Adjustment

Place the manual selector lever in the D position.

Disconnect the control rod from the selector valve lever at the left-hand side of the transmission casing.

Set the selector valve lever in the D position, that is the centre of the five positions that can be obtained (see Fig 10).

Adjust the length of the vertical control rod at the adjustable point (A, Fig 11) until the ball pin of the selector valve control rod will slip easily into the hole in the selector valve lever.

Connect the control rod to the selector valve lever and check operation of transmission in the five positions of the manual selector lever quadrant.

Accelerator To Transmission Fulcrum Levers

It is important that the forward arms of the fulcrum levers at each end of the adjustable rod (C, Fig 11) are parallel to each other.

These levers are set parallel at the factory and should not require resetting unless the adjustment of the rod has been altered or unless new fulcrum levers have been fitted.

The positions of the levers are adjusted as follows:

Disconnect the control rod from the governor control lever (see Fig 11).

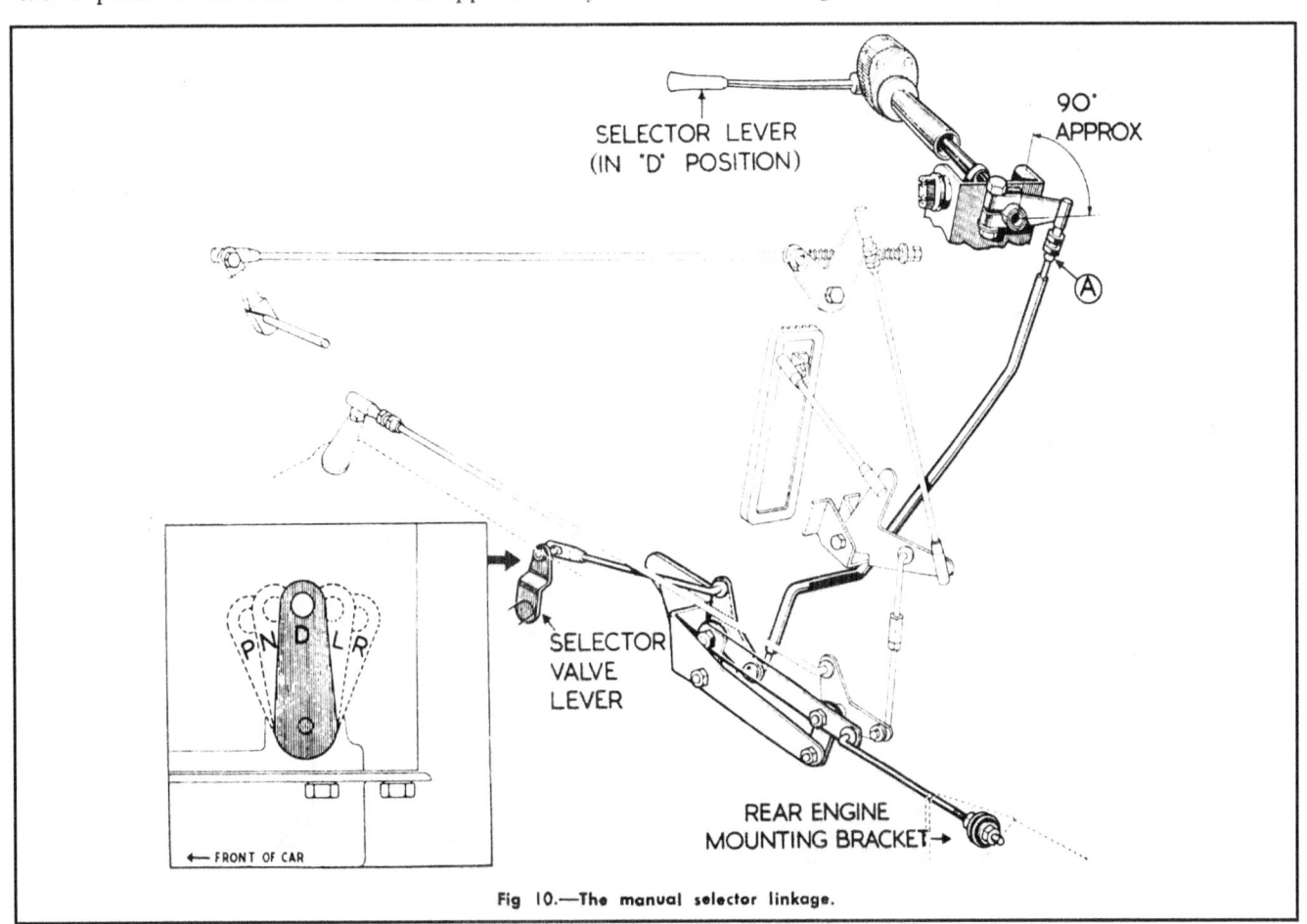

Fig 10.—The manual selector linkage.

Check that the carburettor throttle adjusting screws are on their stops and that the idling speed of the engine is approximately 500 rpm.

Disconnect the adjustable rod from the lower fulcrum lever.

Slacken locknut and adjust rod to the required length to bring forward arms of fulcrum levers parallel.

Re-instal the rod in the lower fulcrum lever and tighten locknut.

Adjust the accelerator to governor lever control rod as described in the following paragraphs.

Accelerator To Governor Lever Adjustment

Before making any adjustment to the accelerator pedal to governor lever linkage (see Fig 11) the points enumerated under the sub-headings "Carburettor Idling Speed" and "Kickdown Overtravel Spring" should be checked and, if necessary, adjusted.

Disconnect the control rod from the governor control lever (note that the control rod ball pin is installed in the inner of the two holes).

Slacken the locknut retaining the anti-creep throttle switch (B, Fig 8) and screw switch downwards out of operation.

Adjust the idling speed of the engine to 500 rpm by rotating the two throttle adjusting screws by exactly equal amounts.

Reset anti-creep throttle switch as described on the following page.

Check that the operating lever at the rear of throttle rod is at approximately 30° to the vertical when the throttle adjusting screws are on their stops (idling speed).

The term "kickdown" applies to the extra travel of the accelerator pedal beyond the full throttle position, which enables a change from direct drive to intermediate gear to be made at the will of the driver.

The "kickdown" overtravel spring (A, Fig 11) is situated at the left-hand end of the transverse carburettor control rod to the rear of the left-hand camshaft cover.

On cars fitted with a full throttle stop (E, Fig 11) adjust the position of stop in its bracket to just contact end of transverse carburettor control rod when rod is in the full throttle position.

NOTE: Obtain the full throttle position by depressing the accelerator pedal; do NOT operate the linkage by hand to obtain full throttle.

Adjust loading of "kickdown" overtravel spring by means of the nuts at end of transverse carburettor control rod to overcome tension of throttle return spring and to compress **only** after the full throttle position has been reached.

NOTE: Obtain the full throttle position by depressing the accelerator pedal; do NOT operate the linkage by hand to obtain full throttle.

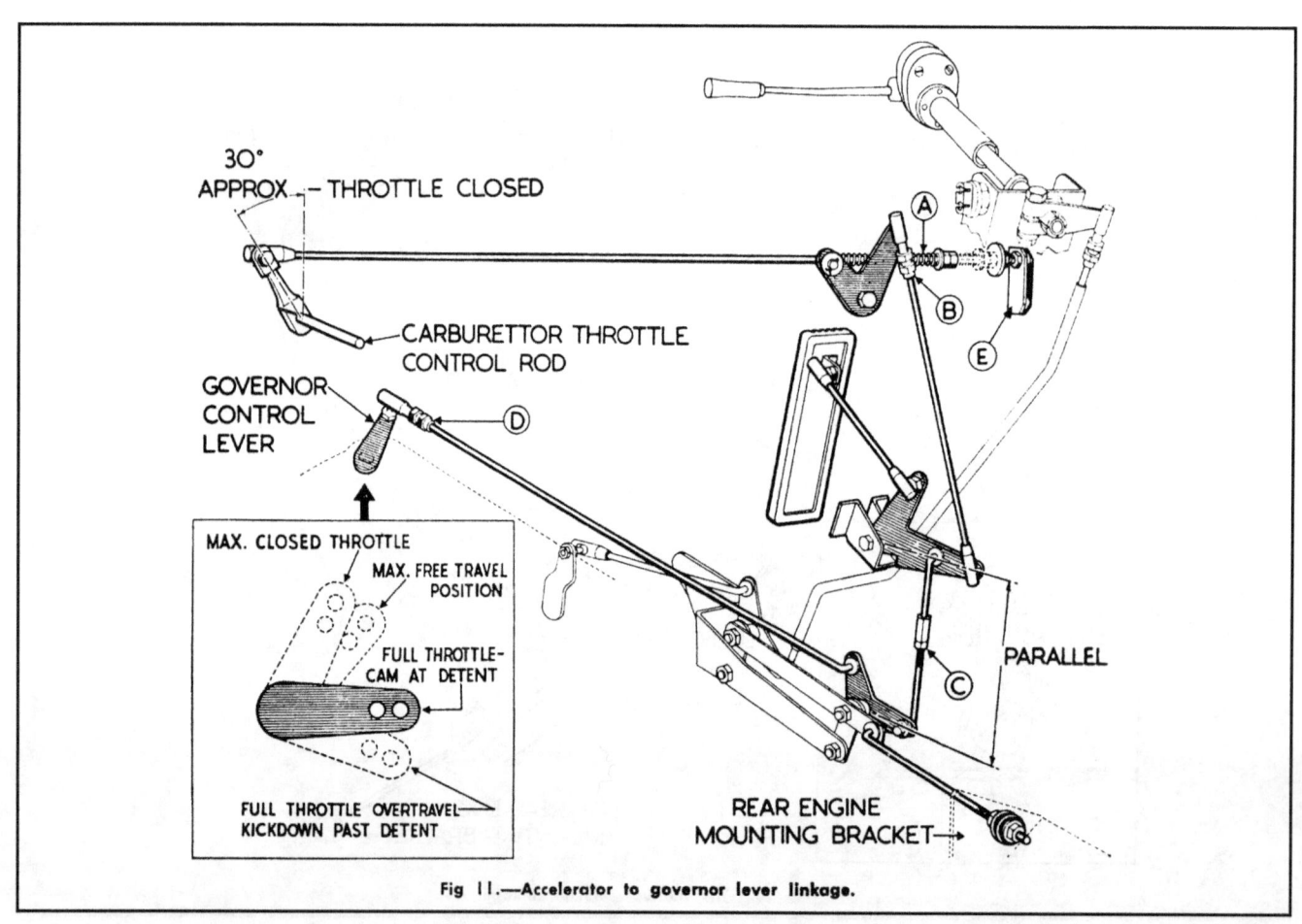

Fig 11.—Accelerator to governor lever linkage.

With the control rod to the governor lever disconnected:

Depress accelerator pedal to the full throttle position at the carburettors. (Do NOT depress pedal sufficiently hard to overcome "kickdown" overtravel spring (A, Fig 11) at rear of left hand camshaft cover).

Turn the governor lever to the full throttle position, that is, the position where solid resistance is felt before overcoming the cam detent (see inset Fig 11).

With the accelerator pedal and governor lever in these positions, adjust the length of the governor lever control rod at the adjustable joint (D, Fig 11) until ball pin will slip easily into the **inner** hole of the governor lever.

Check "kickdown" operation on road test.

"Anti-Creep" Throttle Switch Adjustment

The "anti-creep" throttle switch is attached to a bracket situated between the two carburettors (see Fig 8) and its operation is to close the electrical circuit of the "anti-creep" system which acts when the throttles are closed and the car is brought to rest by application of the brakes, providing the ignition switch is ON. When the accelerator is depressed for the car to move away, the throttle switch opens the electrical circuit and releases the "anti-creep" action.

Slacken the locknut (B) securing the "anti-creep" throttle switch to its bracket, and screw switch downwards so that the plunger in the centre of the switch (C) is not in contact with the operating lever (D).

Ensure that the throttle adjusting screws are on their stops and check the idling speed of the engine, which should be 500 rpm. If it is necessary to adjust the idling speed, rotate the two throttle adjusting screws by exactly equal amounts.

Adjust the position of the switch in the bracket so that the plunger in the centre of the switch is FULLY DEPRESSED by the operating lever with the carburettor throttles in the normal idling position. Tighten the locknut.

Check the operation and release of "anti-creep" action after bringing the car to a standstill by application of the brakes.

Brake Band Adjustment

To check or adjust any of the three bands use the following procedure:

Remove the setscrew and copper gasket from the pressure take-off hole in the servo mechanism **opposite** the adjustment screw of the band to be adjusted.

Carefully screw the Band Adjusting Tool J 4285 (A, Fig 12) into the pressure take-off hole, noting that the indicator plug (B) in the handle of the tool moves outwards as the tool is screwed into the adjustment hole. If the band is properly adjusted, the indicator plug will be flush with the end of the tool handle when the tool shoulder rests against the transmission case (see Fig 12). If, in screwing the tool into position, the indicator plug becomes flush with the end of the tool before the tool shoulder is against the transmission case, the band adjustment is too tight. As soon as it becomes apparent that the band is too tight, loosen the locknut and the adjusting screw on the opposite side of

Fig 12.—Band adjusting tool in position for forward band adjustment.
A. Band adjusting tool. B. Indicator plug.

the transmission and back off two turns before the tool (A) is screwed fully into position. **This is a necessary precaution since, if the tool is screwed against a tight band to the extent that the indicator plug is forced beyond the end of the tool handle, the tool may be damaged.**

If, with the band adjusting tool fully in place, the indicator plug is not flush with the end of the tool, band adjustment is required. To perform the adjustment loosen the locknut on the band adjustment screw and turn the screw in until the indicator plug in the tool handle is flush with the end of the handle.

Tighten the band adjusting screw locknut securely, making sure the adjusting screw does not turn.

Fig 13.—Band adjustment screws, and pressure take-off points for converter and reverse servo.

A. Converter pressure take-off.
B. Reverse servo take-off.
C. Low band adjustment screw.
D. Forward band adjustment screw.

115

Remove the band adjustment tool and instal the setscrew using a new copper gasket. Do not use any type of sealing compound when installing setscrews in the transmission. Tighten to 28 to 33 ft/lb torque.

Starter Cut-Out and Reverse Light Switches—Adjustment

The starter cut-out switch and the reverse light switch are attached to a bracket situated at the bottom of the manual selector control shaft (see Fig 15). Both switches are operated by a cam (C) which is secured to the manual selector control shaft.

The starter cut-out switch (A, Fig 15) serves to close the starer motor operating circuit only when the manual selector lever is in the P or N (Park or Neutral) position, this ensures that the engine cannot be started when the transmission is in any one of the driving ranges.

The reverse light switch (B, Fig 15) serves to close the reversing light circuit when the manual selector lever is in the R (Reverse) position and the ignition switch is ON.

Cars up to Chassis Number 736217 BW are fitted with a cam assembly which is secured to the selector shaft by the fulcrum lever clamp bolt situated at the bottom of the shaft (see Fig 15). The adjustment of the cam is as follows:

Place the manual selector lever in the D position.

Hold the fulcrum lever in position to avoid altering the manual selector linkage adjustment and slacken the clamp bolt.

While still holding the fulcrum lever, turn the cam until the lobe is just in contact with, but not depressing, the plunger of the starter cut-out switch (A). Tighten the fulcrum lever clamp bolt.

Fig 15.—Neutral starting switch.

A. Starter cut-out switch. B. Reverse light switch. C. Operating cam.

Check the operation of the two switches. With the ignition switched on, the starter circuit should be operative when the manual selector lever is in the N position but not when the lever is in the D position; the reverse lamp should be illuminated when the lever is in the R position but not when the lever is in the L position.

NOTE: When checking for non-operation of the starter circuit in the D range apply the hand brake firmly and depress the foot brake pedal; do not have the engine running when checking the reverse light operation.

Check the Manual Selector Linkage Adjustment, as described in section 1:14. If any adjustment is made to the linkage, recheck the operation of the starter cut-out and reverse light switches.

NOTE: A small range of adjustment for the individual switches is provided by having enlarged holes in the mounting bracket. To adjust, slacken the securing nut, move switch to desired position and tighten nut.

Cars after Chassis Number 736217 BW are fitted with a cam assembly which is secured to the selector shaft by a clamp bolt situated above the cam; this type of cam assembly is independent of the fulcrum lever. The adjustment of the cam is as follows:

Place the manual selector lever in the D position.

Slacken the clamp bolt securing the cam assembly to the selector shaft. Turn the cam until the lobe is just in contact with, but not depressing, the plunger of the starter cut-out switch. Tighten the cam assembly clamp bolt.

Check the operation of the two switches. With the ignition switched on, the starter circuit should be operative when the manual selector lever is in the N position

Fig 14.—Low and forward servo pressure take-off points and reverse band adjustment screw.

A. Forward servo pressure take-off.
B. Low servo pressure take-off.
C. Reverse band adjustment screw.

116

Fig 16.—Parking brake pawl adjustment.
A. Parking brake actuating rod. B. Locknut.

but not when the lever is in the D position; the reverse lamp should be illuminated when the lever is in the R position but not when the lever is in the L position.

NOTE: When checking for non-operation of the starter circuit in the D range apply the hand brake firmly and depress the foot brake pedal; do not have the engine running when checking the reverse light operation.

Check the Manual Selector Linkage Adjustment as described earlier.

Parking Brake Pawl — Adjustment

Remove the control rod from the selector valve lever and shift the lever to the N (Neutral) position (see Fig 10).

Raise the rear wheels and turn the propeller shaft, and at the same time move the selector valve lever toward the P (Park) position. If in correct adjustment, a slight ratcheting of the parking pawl on the parking brake gear should be felt as the lever is moved out of the Neutral position.

If any adjustment is necessary, remove the transmission oil pan. Loosen the locknut (B, Fig 16) on the parking brake actuating rod (A). Then, using a screwdriver, turn the rod as required to obtain the correct adjustment. Turning the rod anti-clockwise will move the pawl away from the gear, while turning it clockwise will move the pawl toward the gear.

Tighten the locknut to 3 to 4 ft/lb torque.

Instal a new oil pan gasket. Instal the oil pan and tighten the oil pan screws to 10 to 13 ft/lb torque.

Connect the control rod to the selector valve lever.

1:15 REMOVAL AND INSTALLATION

The transmission unit can be removed from the car leaving the torque converter and housing in position.

Removal:

Drain the oil from the transmission and the torque converter as described in section 1:13 of the "Maintenance" section under "Drain and Refill Transmission".

Disconnect the rear propeller shaft from the rear axle companion flange. Disconnect the front propeller shaft from the transmission companion flange. Remove the coil spring from between the centre bearing plate and mounting bracket. Remove the nuts from the studs supporting the two rubber insulators in the centre bearing plate. Slide the front and rear propeller shafts rearward.

Disconnect the control rod from the selector lever on the left-hand side of the transmission (B, Fig 29).

Disconnect the control rod from the governor control lever at the left-hand rear of the transmission casing (A, Fig 29).

Remove the two lower nuts securing the transmission casing to the converter housing, situated inside the housing.

Place the transmission lift under the transmission casing, and set to take weight of transmission unit.

Remove the two upper nuts securing the transmission casing to the converter housing. These nuts can be removed from below.

Remove the transmission by sliding assembly rearwards until the mainshaft is clear of the converter. Remove the oil transfer tube from the end of the mainshaft. If the oil transfer tube is not withdrawn with the mainshaft it will be necessary to remove the tube from the centre of the converter with a pair of long-nosed pliers.

Installation:

Using Spline Alignment Fixture (Tool No J 4283) position the splines on the transmission shafts as follows:

(a) Loosen the fixture thumb-screw and instal the fixture over the splines, inserting it into the

Fig 17.—Spline alignment fixture in position on transmission shafts.
A. Spline aligning fixture. C. Positioning pin.
B. Thumb-screw. D. Studs.

Fig 18.—The mainshaft oil transfer tube.
A. Oil transfer tube.

transmission as far as possible, ensuring that the positioning arm sector points towards one of the lower transmission casing studs.

(b) Move the positioning arm and universal joint companion flange until the positioning pin slips over one of the lower transmission casing studs.

(c) Tighten the thumb-screw to lock the positioning arm in place (see Fig 17).

(d) Remove the fixture carefully to prevent moving the splines out of alignment. **Instal the mainshaft oil transfer tube** (see Fig 18).

Instal the Alignment Fixture in the torque converter to position the internal splines as follows:

(a) Enter the alignment fixture into the torque converter until the splines are engaged on the fixture.

(b) Rotate the torque converter assembly and the spline alignment fixture until the positioning pin slips easily into the stud hole in the converter housing corresponding to the transmission casing stud on which the alignment of the fixture was set (see Fig 19).

(c) Remove the fixture carefully to prevent alteration of the alignment.

Raise the transmission assembly to the correct height and angle and carefully slide forward into the torque converter, ensuring that the transmission universal joint companion flange is not rotated. Secure the transmission casing to the converter housing with the four washers and nuts.

Connect the two wires to the anti-creep pressure switch.

Instal the speedometer pinion and cable and secure with the retaining clip.

Instal the control rod to the selector lever.

Instal the control rod to the inner hole of the governor control lever.

Instal the front and rear propeller shafts.

Fill the transmission assembly with oil as described in the "Maintenance" section under "Drain and Refill Transmission."

1:16 TORQUE CONVERTER

To remove the torque converter it is first necessary to remove the transmission unit as described in the previous section.

NOTE: See also 2:59

Removal:

Remove the starter motor from the right-hand side of the engine, noting the earth strap attached to the top bolt.

Remove the twin exhaust pipe by disconnecting the pipe at the manifold flanges and the intermediate pipe flange.

Disconnect the anti-roll bar from the two mountings attached to the chassis frame.

Disconnect the rear end of the compensator rod from the shackle supporting the transmission linkage fulcrum levers (see Fig 10). If it is required to slacken the rubber grommets at the rear engine mounting, unscrew the nut at onse side of the bracket only. Do NOT alter the length of the compensator rod; this rod is set so that the nut securing the rear fulcrum lever is in the centre of the large hole in the tie-plate, to allow compensation of the linkage for the movement of the engine on its mountings. Support the rear of the engine and remove the rear engine mounting brackets.

Remove the cover plate attached to the front face of the converter housing.

Slide the front seat rearward, lift out the centre carpet and detach the transmission cowl by removing the setscrews.

Lower the engine slightly, remove the bolts and nuts securing the converter housing to the engine crankcase, and remove housing.

By rotating the converter, remove the six self-locking nuts and washers securing the converter to the engine drive plate and withdraw converter assembly.

Installation:

The alignment mark O on the converter must be aligned with the mark O on the engine drive plate.

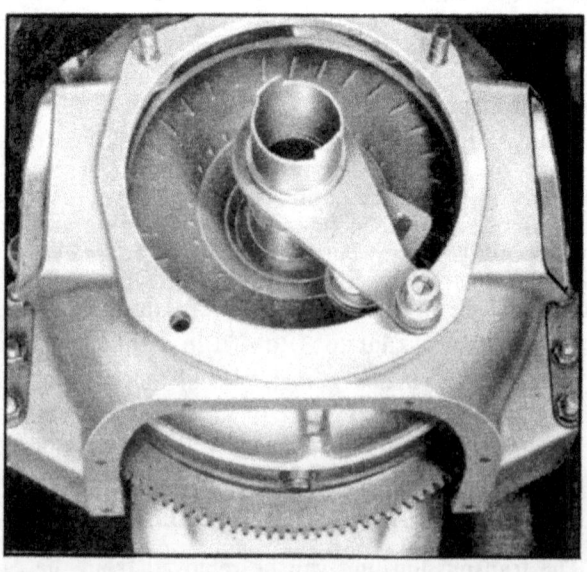

Fig 19.—Spline alignment fixture in position on the converter.

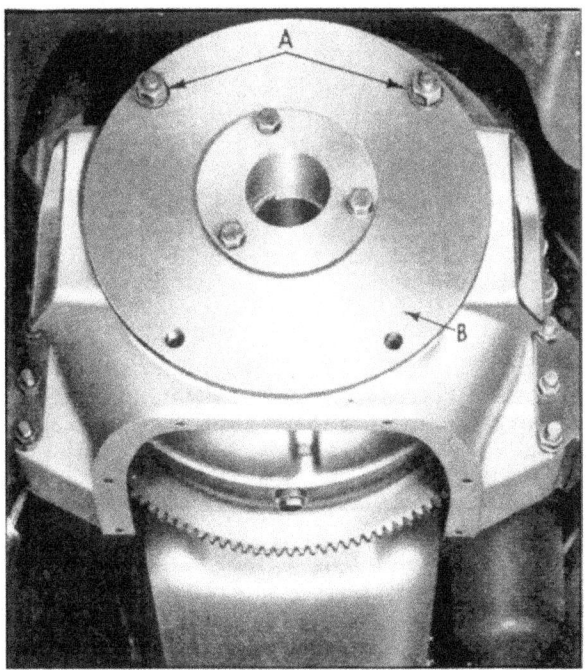

Fig 20.—The converter alignment flange in position.

A. Transmission securing nuts.   B. Alignment flange.

Instal the torque converter to the engine drive plate and **loosely** instal the washers and nuts.

Clean the mating faces of the engine crankcase and converter housing, instal the housing, noting that it is located by dowels. Instal the upper converter housing to crankcase bolts. Raise the engine, attach the rear engine mounting brackets and instal the remaining bolts.

Instal the starter motor, ensuring that the earth strap is fitted to the top bolt.

Position the Converter Alignment Flange (Tool No J4286) into the bore of the converter housing and over the pump drive fingers on the torque converter and instal the two top transmission casing securing nuts to hold the Alignment Flange in position (see Fig 20). Rotate the torque converter through two complete revolutions to centre the torque converter.

Tighten the nuts securing the converter to the engine drive plate. Remove Alignment Flange.

Refit the cover plate to the front face of the converter housing.

1:17 ANTI-CREEP PRESSURE SWITCH

This switch is screwed into the rear pump at the rear of the transmission case and serves to prevent operation of the anti-creep system while the car is moving forward.

Removal:

Disconnect the two wires from the switch.
Unscrew the switch from the rear pump.

Installation:

Screw the switch into the rear pump.
Connect the two wires to the switch.
Check the operation.

1:18 ANTI-CREEP SOLENOID VALVE

The anti-creep solenoid valve is attached to the chassis frame and serves to hold pressure on the rear brakes after the brakes have been applied to stop the car with the accelerator fully released.

Removal:

With the ignition switch in the off position, disconnect the two wires at the connectors.

Unscrew the two male union nuts securing the hydraulic pipes to the solenoid valve end nuts.

Remove the two bolts securing the solenoid valve to the chassis frame and remove the solenoid valve.

Installation:

Attach the solenoid valve to the chassis frame with the two securing bolts.

Connect the hydraulic pipes to the solenoid valve. Bleed the brake system.

Connect the wires to the solenoid valve connectors.

Check operation. With the rear wheels stationary, ignition switch on, and the accelerator fully released, depress the brake pedal firmly and release. Rear wheel brakes should now be set, preventing the rear wheels from turning. The rear wheel brakes should release when the ignition key is turned off or the accelerator is depressed.

1:19 OIL PAN AND SCREEN

Removal:

Drain the fluid from the transmission unit only.
Remove the setscrews which secure the oil pan to the transmission case and remove the pan.
Remove the screen retainer clip which permits removal of the gauze screen.

Inspection:

Clean the screen thoroughly and inspect for damage.
Inspect the oil pan flange for distortion.

Installation:

Place the oil screen in the shroud and instal the screen retainer clip making sure that it is snapped securely into place.

Coat the face of the transmission case with petroleum jelly and position a new gasket on the case.

Place the oil pan in position on the gasket, ensuring that pan does not interfere with pressure take-off plugs, and instal the retaining screws.

Tighten the setscrews to 10-13 ft lb torque.

Follow the recommended procedure outlined in the "Maintenance" section and fill the transmission with Type A automatic transmission fluid to the correct level.

1:20 OIL SCREEN SHROUD

Removal:

Remove the oil pan and oil screen.
Remove the three shroud-to-valve block set screws (A, Fig 47) which permits the removal of the reinforcing plate (C) and shroud (B).
Remove the oil screen shroud gasket.

Inspection:

Clean the shroud thoroughly and inspect for damage or distortion.

Installation:

Position a new oil screen shroud gasket on the valve block, ensuring that oil openings are aligned.

Place the shroud on the gasket and the shroud reinforcing plate on the shroud.

Align the holes of the shroud reinforcing plate, shroud, gasket, and valve block and instal the retaining setscrews. Tighten the screws to 6-8 ft lb torque.

Instal the oil screen retainer.

Instal the oil pan as outlined under Oil Pan and Oil Screen-Inspection and Installation.

1:21 TESTING

Testing the Car

NOTE: See Transmission Operation Chart 1:11

The following checks and tests will enable the operating condition of the Automatic Transmission to be determined. Any condition of improper operation shown by the checks can be found, with its possible causes, under "Diagnosis". It is necessary, when testing or making a diagnosis, that the transmission fluid be at operating temperature and the proper level as described under "Maintenance".

CAUTION — When testing, with the selector lever in one of the driving positions and the rear wheels held stationary, all the energy delivered to the torque converter by the engine is changed to heat; therefore, the engine must not be operated at high speed for more than 10 seconds at a time or for a total time greater than one minute in any half hour period.

1:22 SERVICE FLOOR CHECKS

1. **Fluid Level:** Check transmission fluid level and replenish if necessary (see "Maintenance").

2. **Engine Idling Speed:** Check idling speed and if necessary adjust to 500 rpm. (Before making any adjustment to the idling speed, slacken the locknut retaining the anti-creep throttle switch (see Fig 8) and screw switch downwards out of operation. After setting the engine idling speed, readjust the anti-creep throttle switch as described in Service Adjustments).

3. **Starter Cut-Out Switch:** Operate the starter switch while the hand control selector lever is in each of its positions. The starter should operate only while the selector lever is in P or N position.

4. **Hand Control Linkages:** Set the hand brake firmly, start the engine, then shift the selector lever to D position. So that the sound of the engine will be clearly noticeable, operate the engine at a speed slightly greater than idle speed. Slowly move the hand control selector lever from D position to N position, noticing the change in engine speed. The shift to neutral will be accompanied by a sudden increase in engine speed and should take place just before the selector lever reaches the N position detent. Next, shift the selector lever to L position. Then slowly move the selector lever to R position. An increase in engine speed, indicating the shift out of low, should occur when the selector lever has moved approximately two-thirds of the distance from L position to R position. Then, when the selector lever is moved slightly closer to the R position detent, the shift into reverse should take place, accompanied by a decrease in engine speed.

1:23 STALL SPEED TESTS

The stall speed is the maximum speed at which the engine can drive the torque converter impeller while the turbine is held stationary. Because the stall speed is dependent on engine characteristics as well as torque converter characteristics, it will vary with the condition of the engine as well as with the condition of the Automatic Transmission. Hence, it is necessary to determine the condition of the engine in order to correctly interpret a low stall speed.

Because an engine's performance at higher altitudes differs from its performance at lower altitudes, the stall speeds given below cannot be considered representative of stall speeds in regions of high altitudes. In such regions, representative stall speeds can be determined by testing several cars known to be normal.

With the engine in good condition and operating at sea level, the normal stall speed is 2,000 rpm.

Set the hand brake. Start the engine, then shift the hand control selector lever to D position. Apply the foot brake so that the car will not move. Operate the engine at full throttle and note the engine revolution counter reading. Repeat this procedure with the selector lever in the L position and also in the R position.

CAUTION. — Do not operate the engine at high speed, while the selector lever is in one of the driving positions and the rear wheels held stationary, for more than 10 seconds at a time or for a total time greater than one minute in any half hour period.

A stall speed of approximately 1400-1500 rpm, if the engine is normal, is caused by slippage of the torque converter stator free wheel unit.

A stall speed higher than normal is caused by slippage in the transmission; the specific unit that is slipping will be indicated in the "Diagnosis" section under the abnormal condition involved.

1:24 GOVERNOR SHIFT SPEEDS

(Up to transmission No J2426)

	Intermediate to Direct	Direct to Intermediate
Light throttle upshift	18 mph	—
Full throttle upshift	55 mph	—
Kickdown upshift	68 mph	—
Closed throttle downshift	—	12 mph
Limit of kickdown downshift	—	60 mph

NOTE: See also 2:51

1:25 OPERATION CHECKS

NOTE: See also 2:51

1. **Multiple Disc Clutch:** With hand control selector lever in L position, depress the accelerator to full throttle position and, when the car speed reaches approximately 15 mph, shift the selector lever to D position. A definite upshift should be felt.

2. **Engine Braking:** While driving the car at approximately 30 mph with the hand control selector lever in D position, release the accelerator pedal and shift selector lever from D position to L position. This should result in a rapid deceleration of the car and an increase in engine speed.

3. **Shift Speeds:** Make the shift speed checks with the hand control selector lever in D position.

(a) Light throttle upshift — from a standstill, accelerate the car gradually and note the speed at which the shift from intermediate drive to direct drive occurs.

(b) Closed throttle downshift — While operating the car in direct drive, release the accelerator pedal and allow the car to decelerate gradually. Note the speed at which the shift from direct drive to intermediate drive occurs.

(c) Full throttle upshift — From a standstill, depress and hold the accelerator pedal in full throttle position (not in kickdown position). Note the speed at which the transmission shifts from intermediate drive to direct drive as the car accelerates.

(d) Kickdown downshift — While driving the car at approximately 40 mph in direct drive, depress and hold the accelerator pedal in kickdown position. The transmission should shift immediately into intermediate drive range.

4. **Direct Drive Clutch:** While driving the car at approximately 25 mph with the hand control selector lever in D position, release the accelerator pedal and bring the car to a quick stop. As the speed of the car decreases, the transmission should shift smoothly from direct drive to intermediate drive and the car should stop smoothly without any signs of shuddering.

5. **Rear Pump, Parking and Reverse Interlocks:** While driving the car at approximately 30 mph shift the hand control selector lever to P and R positions, and return to D position. At this speed, while the selector lever is in P or R position, the car should roll freely and the transmission should seem to be in neutral.

6. **"Rocking":** With the car standing still, slowly move the hand control selector lever from L position to R position and back to L position several times while pressing lightly on the accelerator pedal. As the shifts are made, the car should rock backward and forward.

7. **Hill-holding:** While driving the car up a moderate (approximately 1 in 10) gradient with the hand control selector lever in D position, release the accelerator pedal and allow the car to stop on the grade without applying the brakes. As long as the engine is running and the selector lever is in D position, the car should not roll backward. However, on steeper gradients, if a heavily loaded car should roll backward it does not necessarily indicate improper operation of the Automatic Transmission.

8. **Parking Pawl:** While the car is standing still on a gradient, shift the hand control selector lever to P position. The parking pawl should prevent the car from moving.

1:26 ANTI-CREEP SYSTEM

1. While driving the car at approximately 10 mph with the hand control selector lever in D position, quickly apply and immediately release the brakes. Do not touch the accelerator pedal. The anti-creep pressure switch should open the anti-creep circuit so that the car rolls freely with no evidence of brake drag after the brake pedal is released.

2. While driving the car on level ground, release the accelerator pedal and apply the brakes, bringing the car to a complete stop. The car should not creep forward until the accelerator pedal is depressed.

3. While the car is standing still on level ground with the engine idling, the hand control selector lever in one of the driving positions, and the anti-creep system preventing the car from creeping, touch the accelerator pedal lightly and then release it. This should release the anti-creep slowly from a standstill.

Following all the above check and test procedures completely will disclose any condition of improper operation that might exist. The condition can then be found in the "Diagnosis" section and causes listed under the condition will indicate the repairs or adjustments necessary.

1:27 PRESSURE TESTS

A pressure test point is provided for testing each of the hydraulic units of the Automatic Transmission. The following procedures should be used when pressure tests are indicated in the "Diagnosis" section.

Front Pump:

1. With the engine stopped, remove the Allen-headed pipe plug at the transmission oil pan front flange and instal the pressure gauge fitting (see Fig 21). For convenience, place the gauge on the floor of the driver's compartment and allow the gauge line to pass through the oil level inspection hole to the transmission pressure take-off point.

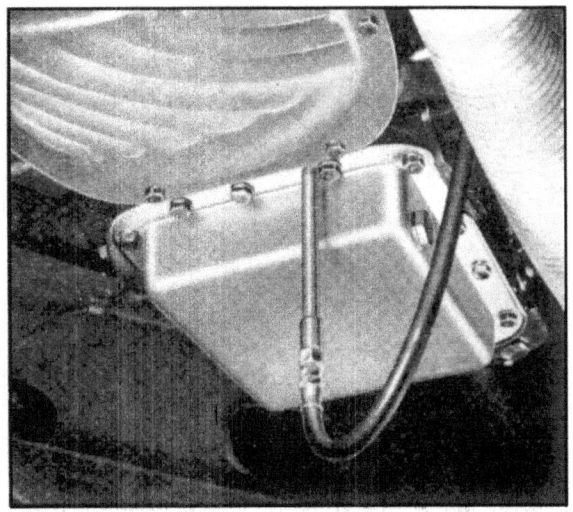

Fig 21.—Front pump pressure take-off.

2. With the hand control selector lever in the P or N position, start the engine and bring engine speed to 1,000 rpm. At this engine speed, the gauge should show a minimum of 60 lb per sq inch pressure.

3. Stop the engine. Remove the test equipment. Reinstall the Allen-headed pipe plug. Do not use any type of sealing compound when installing this or any other pipe plug in the transmission. Tighten to 15-18 ft lb torque.

Forward Brake Servo:

1. With the engine stopped, remove the setscrew and copper washer from the forward servo cover and install the pressure gauge fitting at this point (see Fig 22). For convenience, place the gauge on the floor of the driver's compartment and allow the gauge line to pass through the oil level inspection hole to the pressure take-off point.

2. With the engine running, apply the hand brake and footbrake firmly to prevent movement of the car and move the hand control selector lever to the D position. Gradually increase engine speed to 1000 rpm. At this speed, the gauge should show a minimum of 60 lb per sq inch pressure.

To prevent overheating of the transmission, the engine should not be run at speeds greater than idling speed with the selector lever in the D, L or R position and with the rear wheels stationary **for more than 30 seconds.**

Fig 23.—Reverse servo pressure take-off.

3. Before starting the engine, apply the hand brake and foot brake firmly to prevent movement of the car. Start the engine and increase engine speed to 1000 rpm. At this speed, the gauge should show a minimum of 160 lb per sq inch pressure.

To prevent overheating of the transmission, the engine should not be run at speeds greater than idling speed with the selector lever in the D, L or R position and with the rear wheels stationary **for more than 30 seconds.**

4. Stop the engine and remove the test equipment. Reinstall the setscrew in the brake cylinder, using a new copper gasket. Do not use any type of sealing compound when installing this or any other setscrew or gasket in the transmission. Tighten the setscrew to 28-33 ft/lb torque.

Low Brake Servo:

1. With the engine stopped, remove the setscrew and copper gasket from the low brake cylinder and

Fig 22.—Forward servo pressure take-off.

3. Stop the engine and remove the test equipment. Reinstall the setscrew in the forward servo cover, using a new copper gasket. Do not use any type of sealing compound when installing this or any other setscrew or gasket in the transmission. Tighten the setscrew to 28-33 ft/lb torque.

Reverse Brake Servo:

1. With the engine stopped, move the hand control selector lever to the R position.

2. Remove the setscrew and copper washer from the reverse brake cylinder and install the pressure gauge fitting at this point (see Fig 23). For convenience, place the gauge on the floor of the driver's compartment and allow the gauge line to pass through the oil level inspection hole to the transmission pressure take-off point.

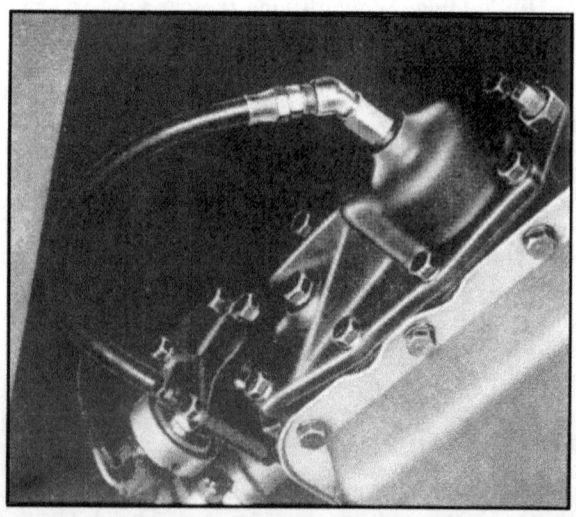

Fig 24.—Low servo pressure take-off.

instal the pressure gauge fitting at this point (see Fig 24). For convenience, place the gauge on the floor of the driver's compartment and allow the gauge line to pass through the oil level inspection hole to the transmission pressure take-off point.

2. With the engine running and the hand brake and the foot brake firmly applied to prevent movement of the car, place the hand control selector lever in the L position. Increase engine speed to 1000 rpm. At this speed, the gauge should show a minimum of 60 lb per sq inch pressure.

To prevent overheating of the transmission the engine should not be run at speeds greater than idling speed with the selector lever in the D, L or R position and with the rear wheels stationary **for more than 30 seconds.**

3. Stop the engine and remove the test equipment. Reinstall the setscrew in the low brake cylinder, using a new copper gasket. Do not use any type of sealing compound when installing this or any other setscrew or gasket in the transmission. Tighten the setscrew to 28-33 ft/lb torque.

Multiple Disc Clutch

1. With the engine stopped, remove the pipe plug from the transmission extension case and instal the pressure gauge fitting (F Fig 29). For convenience, place the gauge on the floor of the driver's compartment and allow the gauge line to pass through the oil level inspection hole to the transmission pressure take-off point.

2. With the engine running and the hand brake and foot brake applied firmly to prevent movement of the car, place the hand control selector lever in the D position. Increase engine speed to 1000 rpm. At this speed, the pressure gauge should show a minimum of 60 lb per sq inch pressure.

To prevent overheating of the transmission, the engine should not be run at speeds greater than idling speed with the hand control selector lever in the D, L or R position and with the rear wheels stationary **for more than 30 seconds.**

3. Stop the engine, remove the test equipment, and reinstall the pipe plug. Do not use any type of sealing compound when installing this or any other pipe plug in the transmission. Tighten the pipe plug to 15-18 ft/lb torque.

Torque Converter:

1. Remove the pipe plug at the torque converter pressure take-off point and instal the pressure gauge fitting (see Fig 25). For convenience, place the gauge on the floor of the driver's compartment and allow the gauge line to pass through the oil level inspection hole to the transmission pressure take-off point.

2. With the hand control selector lever in the N position and the engine running at approximately 1000 rpm, the pressure reading should be 25-35 lb per sq inch.

3. With the rear wheels jacked up and free to rotate, the hand control selector lever in the D position, and the engine running at 1,500 rpm, the pressure should be 25-35 lb per sq inch.

4. Stop the engine, remove the test equipment and reinstall the pipe plug. Do not use any type of sealing compound when installing this or any other pipe plug in the transmission. Tighten the pipe plug to 6-7 ft/lb torque.

Direct Drive Clutch:

1. With the engine stopped, remove the Allen-headed pipe plug from the transmission oil pan rear flange and instal the pressure gauge fitting at this point (G Fig 29). For convenience, place the gauge on the floor of the driver's compartment and allow the gauge line to pass through the oil level inspection hole to the pressure take-off point.

2. With the rear wheels of the car raised off the ground and free to rotate, and with the engine running at idling speed, move the hand control selector lever to the D position. The pressure gauge should show 0 lb per sq inch pressure at the direct drive clutch.

3. Increase engine speed to 1,500 rpm. At approximately 1,200 rpm the transmission should shift to direct drive. This will be indicated by a rapid pressure rise in the direct drive clutch. While in direct drive, the pressure gauge should show a minimum of 60 lb per sq inch pressure.

Fig 25.—Converter pressure take-off.

4. Check the direct drive clutch pressure during deceleration. When the speedometer indicates approximately 10-12 miles per hour, the pressure should drop to zero (0).

5. Remove the test equipment and replace the Allen-headed pipe plug. Do not use any type of sealing compound when installing this or any other pipe plug in the transmission. Tighten the pipe plug 15-18 ft/lb torque.

Rear Pump:

1. With the engine stopped, remove the anti-creep cables from the anti-creep pressure switch and remove the switch from the rear oil pump. Instal the pressure gauge fitting in the rear pump (C Fig 29). For conveni-

ence, place the gauge on the floor of the driver's compartment and allow the gauge line to pass through the oil level inspection hole to the transmission pressure take-off point.

2. With the engine running and the rear wheels held stationary, the pressure gauge should show a reading of zero (0) lb per sq inch pressure.

3. With the engine running at idling speed and the rear wheels raised from the floor and free to rotate, shift the hand control selector lever to the D position. Rear pump pressure should build up as indicated by a steady increase in pressure reading on the pressure gauge. At 20 mph on the speedometer, the rear pump pressure should be a minimum of 60 lb per sq inch.

4. Remove the test equipment and reinstall the anti-creep pressure switch in the rear pump. Do not use any type of sealing compound when making this installation. Connect the anti-creep cables to the anti-creep pressure switch.

1:28 FAULT-FINDING CHART

1. **Rear wheel brakes drag when starting from a standstill. (See Fig 26).**

Symptom	Test and Effect
(a) Remove ignition auxiliary fuse	Check if wheels are free.
(b) If wheels are not free	Check for possible mechanical fault.
(c) If wheels are free	Replace fuse, apply brakes and disconnect the wire at the throttle switch. If brakes release, replace switch.
(d) If brakes still do not release	Disconnect pressure switch-to-solenoid valve wire from connector at solenoid valve. If brakes release, this wire is earthed. Repair or replace wire.
(e) If brakes still do not release	Solenoid coil in solenoid valve assembly is earthed. Replace solenoid valve assembly.

2. **Anti-creep system does not operate.**

Symptom	Test and Effect
(1) Idling speed	Check and ensure idling speed is correct and throttle returning to its stop.
(2) Electrical test:	
(a) Circuit continuity	Disconnect cable from throttle switch. Using ammeter, check circuit for continuity by connecting through meter to earth. All tests with ignition on and wheels stationary.
(b) Amperage shown on meter in test (a)	Renew throttle switch.
(c) No amperage on meter in test (a)	Check ignition fuse. If blown, locate fault in ignition auxiliary circuit and repair.
(d) Fuse not blown in test (c)	Using voltmeter, test switch side of fuse for continuity.
(e) No current in test (d)	Check ignition switch terminal for supply. Cable colour, brown and blue.
(f) Supply correct in test (e)	Check ignition switch. Renew if faulty.
(g) Ignition switch correct in test (f)	Replace fuse feed cable. Colour white.
(h) Current supply present in test (d)	Using voltmeter, test voltage at cable connector. Situated under body, right-hand front door.
(i) Current voltage correct in test (h)	Check voltage at solenoid. Cable colour green.

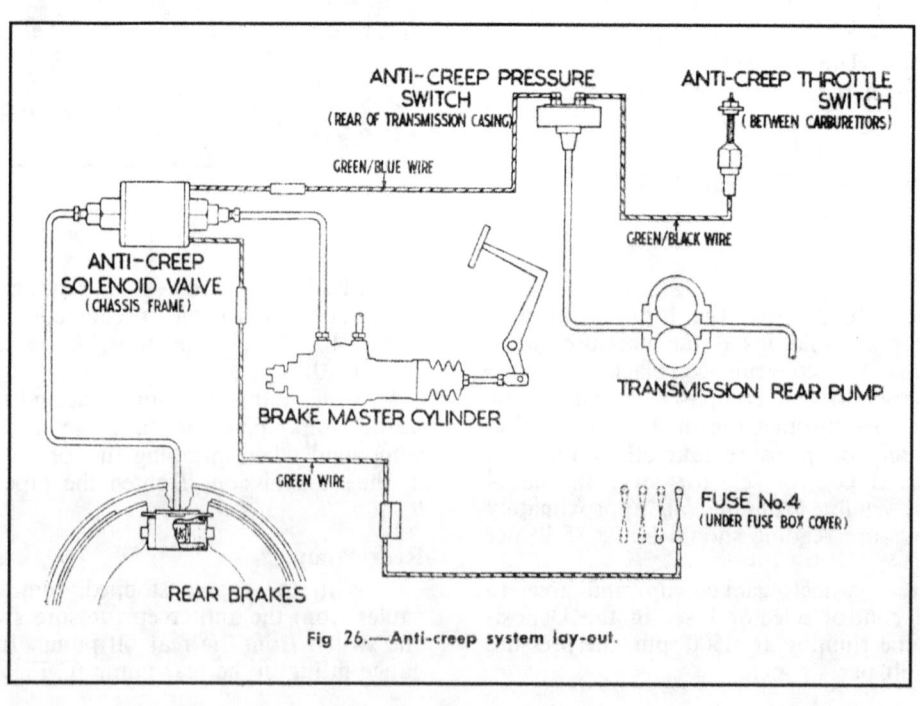

Fig 26.—Anti-creep system lay-out.

2. Anti-creep system does not operate.—(Continued.)

Symptom	Test and Effect
(j) No current voltage in test (h)	Renew cable from fuse. Colour green.
(k) No current at solenoid in test (j)	Renew cable from body junction. Colour green.
(l) Current correct at solenoid in test (j)	Disconnect cable, colour green and blue from solenoid unit. Earth solenoid terminal. Solenoid should operate.
(m) Solenoid does not operate in test (l)	Replace solenoid unit.
(n) Solenoid operates in test (l)	Replace cable on solenoid terminal and remove cable, green and blue, from pressure switch. Earth cable terminal to frame.
(o) Solenoid does not operate in test (n)	Renew
(p) Solenoid operates in test (n)	Replace cable at pressure switch terminal. Connect cable green and black to cable green and blue. Solenoid should operate.
(q) Solenoid operates in test (p)	Renew pressure switch.
(r) Solenoid does not operate in test (p)	Renew cable green and black, pressure switch to throttle switch.

3. Starter solenoid will not operate with selector lever in any position. (See Fig 27).

Symptom	Test and Effect
(a) Place selector lever in P or N position, switch on ignition	Check for battery current at battery terminal of solenoid switch.
(b) If no current is evident in test (a)	Check for dead battery. If battery is correct, check battery-solenoid cable, and battery earth cable for bad connections or damaged cable.
(c) If current is present in test (a)	Connect small terminal and battery terminal of solenoid switch. Solenoid should operate and engage starter.
(d) If starter does not operate in test (c)	Disconnect cable from starter motor and connect in series with voltmeter and test lamp. Test again. If current present, fault is in starter motor. Repair or replace.
(e) If current is not present in test (d)	Replace solenoid switch.
(f) If starter operates in test (c)	Connect cables to cut-out switch together. Starter should operate.
(g) If starter does not operate in test (f)	Check current to cut-out switch by pressing panel button and using a voltmeter in series with cable, colour white and red.
(h) If starter operates in test (f)	Check cut-out switch cam operation. If working correctly replace cut-out switch.
(i) If current is present in test (g)	Check cut-out-solenoid cable. Replace if faulty.
(j) If current is not present in test (g)	Check cut-out-junction box cable (fuse box cover). Replace if faulty.
(k) If cable is correct in test (j)	Check panel switch operation. If faulty, replace.
(l) If switch correct in test (k)	Replace switch — junction box cable.

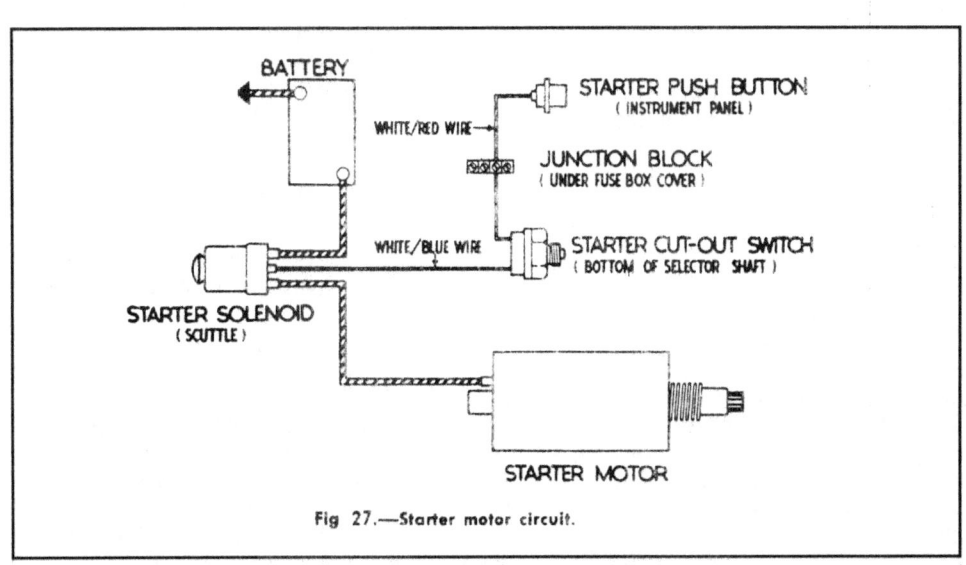

Fig 27.—Starter motor circuit.

1:29 DIAGNOSIS

The following contains a list of the abnormal conditions of operation that may be encountered with the Automatic Transmission. These conditions are arranged in groups, each group representing a general type of abnormal operation.

Group A includes all slipping conditions.
Group B includes dragging or sticking conditions and conditions resulting in poor performance.
Group C includes conditions of excessively noisy operation.
Group D includes conditions involving abnormal external oil leakage.
Group E includes the conditions caused by improper operation of the anti-creep system and the starter cut-out switch circuit.

When diagnosing the reason for abnormal operation it is first necessary to determine the exact operating conditions of the Automatic Transmission by following the procedure given in the "Testing" section under "Testing the Car". The "Operation Checks" described in the "Testing" section will enable the specific abnormal condition to be isolated; under the particular condition in this section a list of the possible causes will be found. The description of the causes indicate the rectification procedure to follow.

It should be borne in mind that the hydraulic system is common to all operating conditions and must be functioning if the other units are to operate properly. Usually, failure of the hydraulic system will make the transmission completely inoperative. However, it is possible for a slight malfunctioning of this system to result in early failure of one of the other units; hence a check of front pump pressure is recommended whenever trouble is encountered.

NOTE: See Part 2 Section 2:52 for supplementary information for first speed start transmission.

1:30 GROUP A

Automatic Transmission is inoperative or has excessive slippage accompanied by engine race.

The conditions in this group are characterised by failure of the Automatic Transmission to operate, or to operate only with excessive slippage. Conditions A.II-A.V, in most cases, are caused by a failure of one of the driving units to hold. Conditions A.VI-A.VIII usually are caused by failure of one of the hydraulic control units to operate properly.

A. I. Slipping excessively, or not operative, in all ranges except direct drive.
Causes
1. Low oil level (see Group D).
2. Incorrect manual selector linkage adjustment (see the "Service Adjustments" section).
3. Low front pump pressure:
   (a) Sticking front or rear pump relief valve.
   (b) Leakage caused by incorrect installation of the valve block assembly.
   (c) Damaged front pump drive fingers.
   (d) Excessive wear of front pump.
   (e) Internal oil leakage in transmission case oil passages.

A. II. Slipping excessively, or not operative, in low and intermediate drive.
Causes
1. Forward band slipping:
   (a) Incorrect adjustment.
   (b) Damaged or excessively worn lining.
   (c) Low pressure at forward servo.
2. Forward free wheel unit slipping.

A. III. Slipping excessively, or not operative, in reverse.
Causes
1. Reverse band slipping:
   (a) Incorrect band adjustment.
   (b) Damaged or excessively worn lining.
   (c) Low pressure at reverse servo.
2. Reverse free wheel until slipping.

NOTE.—In this case, the transmission will slip in reverse and also will lose its hill holding characteristic.

A. IV. Ineffective engine braking for deceleration in low.
Causes
1. Low band slipping:
   (a) Incorrect adjustment.
   (b) Damaged or excessively worn lining.
   (c) Low pressure at low servo.

A. V. Excessive slipping during acceleration in intermediate drive and loss of the hill holding characteristic. *(See also section A. V. in 2:52)*
Causes
1. Multiple disc clutch slipping:
   (a) Damaged or excessively worn disc facings.
   (b) Leakage in oil passages to the multiple disc clutch.

A. VI. Fails to shift to direct drive, or slips after direct drive clutch is engaged.
Causes
1. Improper governor valve operation:
   (a) Damaged governor.
   (b) Governor sticking on the governor shaft.
   (c) Governor valve sticking (closed).
2. High converter pressure preventing engagement of the direct drive clutch:
   (a) Sticking converter valve.
   (b) Leaking direct drive clutch piston seals.
   (c) Mainshaft valve assembly loose and twisted out of correct position.
3. Leakage in the direct drive clutch passage.
4. Blocked oil passage in collector ring.
5. Improper direct drive clutch operation:
   (a) Sticking or distorted direct drive clutch piston.
   (b) Clutch wear.
   (c) Broken oil seal rings on main shaft or front ring gear shaft.

A. VII. Engine cannot be cranked by pushing car, also reverse and park interlocks inoperative.
Causes
1. Rear pump pressure low:
   (a) Damaged or excessively worn rear pump parts.
   (b) Damaged rear pump drive gear.
   (c) Sheared rear pump drive gear pin.
   (d) Valve block assembly incorrectly installed.
   (e) Leaking valve block assembly gaskets.
   (f) Porous valve block castings.

(g) Leaking extension case gaskets.
(h) Porous extension case castings.

A. VIII. Car rolls free while selector lever is in P position.
Causes
1. Parking pawl does not engage:
   (a) Incorrect adjustment of the manual selector linkage.
   (b) Incorrect adjustment of the parking pawl linkage.
   (c) Extension case misaligned on the transmission case.
   (d) Parking pawl interlock piston stuck in the locked position.
   (e) Parking pawl or linkage binding.
   (f) Parking pawl or linkage broken.
2. Parking pawl slips after engagement:
   (a) Incorrect adjustment of the parking pawl linkage.
   (b) Sprung or damaged linkage, or excessive play in linkage.

1:31 GROUP B
Poor performance, engine labors and Automatic Transmission overheats.

The conditions in this group are characterised by poor performance in one or more of the driving ranges. Conditions B.I-B.V are usually caused by failure of one of the hydraulic control units to function. Conditions B.VI-B.XI are usually caused by failure of one of the driving units to release.

B. I. The engine labors or stalls when the selector lever is shifted to D.
Causes
1. Incorrect adjustment of accelerator-to-governor lever linkage.
2. Improper governor valve operation.
   (a) Governor binding.
   (b) Governor sticking on the governor shaft.
   (c) Governor valve sticking open due to:
      (1) Governor control detent piston sticking or installed backwards.
      (2) Governor control plunger and linkage binding.
      (3) Blocked governor valve drain passage.
3. Damaged main shaft oil seal ring or front planetary set ring gear oil rings.

B. II. The engine shudders or stalls when the car is stopped while the selector lever is in D.
Causes
1. Incorrect adjustment of accelerator-to-governor lever linkage.
2. Improper governor valve operation:
   (a) Damaged governor.
   (b) Governor sticking on the governor shaft.
   (c) Governor valve sticking open.
      (1) Governor control detent piston sticking or installed backwards.
      (2) Governor control plunger and linkage binding.
      (3) Blocked governor valve drain passage.
      (4) Damaged shaft oil seal rings or front ring gear oil seal rings.
      (5) Main shaft valve assembly out of position.

B. III. The transmission will not downshift at kickdown, or the kickdown shift speed range is incorrect.
Causes
1. Incorrect adjustment of accelerator-to-governor lever linkage.
2. Interference between the ball joint nut at the governor control lever and the extension case.
3. Improper governor valve operation:
   (a) Damaged governor.
   (b) Governor sticking on governor shaft.
   (c) Governor valve sticking open due to:
      (1) Governor control detent piston sticking or installed backwards.
      (2) Governor control plunger and linkage binding.
      (3) Blocked governor valve drain passage.
      (4) Detent plate stop screw out of adjustment.
4. High oil level.

B. IV. Transmission shifts into reverse immediately when selector lever is shifted to R at speeds greater than 5 mph.
Causes
1. Rear pump inoperative.
2. Reverse interlock valve inoperative.
   (a) Blocked reverse interlock valve oil passage.
   (b) Interlock valve sticking.

B. V. Parking pawl engages immediately when selector lever is shifted to P at speeds greater than 10 mph.
Causes
1. Rear pump inoperative.
2. Parking pawl piston inoperative.
   (a) Oil passage to parking pawl interlock piston blocked.
   (b) Parking pawl interlock piston sticking.

B. VI. Normal reverse operation—poor performance with engine laboring and transmission overheating, in forward ranges—car tends to creep rearward in neutral when anti-creep is released.
Causes
1. Reverse band dragging:
   (a) Incorrect band adjustment.
   (b) Leaking valve block assembly gaskets.
   (c) Porous castings in valve block assembly.
   (d) Reverse brake piston sticking.
   (e) Reverse band damaged or distorted.

B. VII. Normal low range operation—poor performance, with engine laboring and transmission overheating, in other ranges.
Causes
1. Low band dragging:
   (a) Incorrect band adjustment.
   (b) Leaking valve block assembly gaskets.
   (c) Porous castings in valve block assembly.
   (d) Low brake piston sticking.
   (e) Low band damaged or distorted.
   (f) Leaks between low and forward brake cylinders in low brake cylinder.
   (g) Leaks between low and forward brake cylinders in transmission case.

B. VIII. Normal forward operation—poor performance, with engine laboring, in reverse—car tends to creep forward in neutral when anti-creep is released.

Causes
1. Forward band dragging:
   (a) Incorrect band adjustment.
   (b) Leaking valve block assembly gaskets.
   (c) Porous castings in valve block assembly.
   (d) Forward brake piston sticking.
   (e) Forward band damaged or distorted.

B. IX. Normal operation in drive range—poor performance, with engine laboring, and transmission overheating, in other ranges.

Causes
1. Multiple disc clutch dragging:
   (a) Leaking valve block assembly gaskets.
   (b) Porous castings in valve block assembly.
   (c) Multiple disc clutch piston sticking.
   (d) Improper operation of the main shaft assembly.
   (e) Broken or damaged multiple disc clutch release springs.

B. X. Normal operation in direct drive—poor performance, with engine laboring, in other ranges.

Causes
1. Torque converter stator free wheel unit slipping.

B. XI. Normal operation at low speeds—poor performance, with transmission overheating, in direct drive.

Causes
1. Torque converter stator free wheel unit sticking.

1:32 GROUP C

Excessively noisy operation

C. I. Automatic Transmission excessively noisy when selector lever is in drive, low or reverse and car is standing still.

Causes
1. Low fluid level (see Group D).
2. Fluid intake screen clogged.
3. Damaged front pump drive fingers.
4. Damaged or excessively worn front pump parts.
5. Air leaks in the front pump intake passages in the transmission case or the front pump and collector ring assembly.
6. Improper valve action.

C. II. Automatic Transmission excessively noisy when car is moving forward.

Causes
1. Damaged or excessively worn rear pump parts.
2. Damaged or excessively worn rear pump drive gear.
3. Damaged or excessively worn speedometer drive gear or pinion.
4. Damaged or worn rear planetary gears. If only in low, front planetary gears defective.

1:33 GROUP D

Abnormal external fluid leakage

D. I. Fluid leak between the transmission and the torque converter.

Causes
1. Front pump oil seal damaged by front pump drive fingers.
2. Leaking collector ring gasket.
3. Leaking front pump-and-collector ring assembly.
4. Leaking torque converter.

D. II. Fluid leak at brake cylinders.

Causes
1. Damaged gaskets.
2. Uneven or warped gasket surfaces.

D. III. Fluid leak at extension case.

Causes
1. Damaged gaskets.
2. Uneven or warped gasket surfaces.
3. Improperly seated governor control shaft bushing.
4. Leaking governor control shaft detent plate stop screw.
5. Damaged parking pawl pivot pin O-ring seal.

D. IV. Fluid leak at selector control shaft.

Causes
1. Damaged selector control shaft O-ring seal.
2. Bore for selector shaft worn.

D. V. Fluid leak at transmission oil pan.

Causes
1. Damaged gasket.
2. Uneven or warped gasket surfaces.
3. Interferences between oil pan and pressure plugs.

1:34 GROUP E

E. I. Rear wheel brakes drag after brakes are applied and released while car is moving—brakes release when accelerator pedal is depressed.

Causes
1. Anti-creep pressure switch inoperative.
2. Rear pump pressure low.

E. II. Rear wheel brakes drag at all times—braking system normal.

Causes
1. Anti-creep solenoid valve sticking.
2. Anti-creep throttle switch and anti-creep pressure switch sticking.

E. III. Rear wheel brakes drag when starting from a standstill—braking system normal.

Causes
1. Anti-creep throttle switch earthed or sticking closed.
2. Anti-creep solenoid valve-to-anti-creep pressure switch wire earthed.
3. Anti-creep solenoid valve earthed or sticking.

E. IV. Car "creeps" (anti-creep system inoperative).

Causes
1. Carburettor throttles sticking slightly open.
2. Anti-creep throttle switch incorrectly adjusted.
3. Anti-creep throttle switch sticking open.
4. Anti-creep system fuse "blown".
5. Open circuit or an earth between anti-creep system fuse and the ignition switch.
6. Open circuit or an earth between the anti-creep solenoid valve and the fuse.

7. Open circuit or an earth in the anti-creep solenoid valve.
8. Open circuit between the anti-creep solenoid valve and the anti-creep pressure switch.
9. Anti-creep pressure switch sticking open.
10. Open circuit between the anti-creep pressure switch and the anti-creep throttle switch.
11. Check valves or gaskets allowing front pump pressure in rear pump line.

E. V. Starter solenoid inoperative with selector lever in any position.

Causes

1. Discharged battery.
2. Battery-to-starter solenoid cable damaged or not making good contacts.
3. Open circuit in the starter solenoid.
4. Inoperative starter motor.
5. Open circuit in the starter solenoid-to-starter cut-out switch.
6. Open circuit in the starter cut-out switch.
7. Open circuit in the starter cut-out switch-to-instrument panel push button.
8. Open circuit in the instrument panel push button switch.

E. VI. Starter solenoid operates with selector lever in low, reverse or drive position.

Causes

1. Maladjustment of the starter cut-out switch.

1:35 DISMANTLING AND REASSEMBLING

Extension Case Assembly

NOTE: See also 2:53

The extension case assembly is mounted on the rear of the transmission case and consists primarily of the governor assembly, parking pawl and toggle assembly, the rear oil pump, speedometer drive gear and the direct drive control mechanism. (See Fig 28.)

The centrifugal type governor controls the shift from intermediate to direct drive and from direct drive to intermediate. The governor operates the governor valve which regulates the flow of oil to the direct drive clutch. To accomplish the upshift, the governor valve allows oil pressure to apply the direct drive clutch, then on the down-shift the governor valve cuts off the oil pressure which permits the direct drive clutch to release. The direct drive control mechanism operates to prevent downshift under heavy acceleration short of kickdown.

The parking brake pawl and toggle assembly is operated by the selector lever. When applied, the dog of the parking brake pawl engages the teeth of the parking brake gear and prevents the rear wheels from turning in either direction.

The rear oil pump is of the external gear type. It supplies all of the oil pressure to operate the Automatic Transmission at higher car speeds and to operate the Automatic Transmission when pushing the car to start the engine.

Fig 28.—Extension case assembly.

A. Rear pump.
B. Toggle arm shaft.
C. Governor control lever.
D. Speedometer gear housing.
E. Governor assembly.
F. Governor control plunger.
G. Governor fork and valve.
H. Governor control rocker arm.
I. Direct drive pawl.

1:36 EXTENSION CASE

Removal:

NOTE: See also 2:53

Remove the four bolts and disconnect the front propeller shaft universal joint from the companion flange at the rear of the transmission.

Disconnect the control rod from selector valve lever (B, Fig 29) by removing the securing nut. Shift the lever to the Park position (fully forward position) to stop the mainshaft from turning when removing the universal joint companion flange nut.

Remove the flange nut and washers. Mark a spline of the mainshaft and the corresponding groove of the flange to facilitate reassembly. With a suitable extractor withdraw the flange from the mainshaft. Shift the selector lever out of the Park position.

Disconnect the control rod from the governor lever (A, Fig 29) by removing the securing nut.

Disconnect the speedometer cable by removing the retaining screw and clip and withdrawing end of cable from speedometer gear housing.

Disconnect the two wires from the anti-creep pressure switch.

Place an oil drain pan under the extension case. Remove the six setscrews. Slide the case rearward taking care not to drop the gears or spacers that may slide off the mainshaft during removal. Care should also be taken not to allow the mainshaft to move rearward, with possible dislocation of the thrust washers in the mainshaft assembly.

Before installing the extension case assembly, ensure that:

The ball check jet valve, situated below the aperture for the rear bearing, is free and seating properly.

NOTE: This ball check valve will not be present in some extension cases.

Both end brackets (B, Fig 30) of the governor assembly operate freely on the governer shaft.

The direct drive pawl unlocks the governor valve to allow the shift from direct drive to intermediate on deceleration. To do this, withdraw governor fork (G, Fig 28) and position the pawl (I, Fig 28) so that it locks the governor. Then, using a spring scale on the governor control lever (C, Fig 28) check the amount of pull required to release the governor valve. If more than 9 ounces pull is required, it is evident that a bind exists. Examine the direct drive pawl (1) rocker arm (H) and retaining plate, and governor fork (G) for burrs or damage. Check to make sure that the governor valve or governor control plunger assembly (F) is not sticking. If a bind exists in the governor control plunger assembly (F) or the governor valve, the extension case must be replaced.

The extension case and oil passages are clean.

The end play of the governor fork (A, Fig 30) in the groove of the governor end bracket (B) is not more than .030". If more than .030" clearance exists, replace the governor assembly.

Installation:

If the extension case assembly is to be replaced, remove the parking brake interlock piston and spring (A, Fig 31) from the case being replaced and install them in the new case. Insert the spring in the bore and slip the stem of the piston into the spring and push the piston into the bore of the case. Check the fit of the piston in the bore to ensure that it moves freely in the bore. Also, remove the accelerator control detent spring (B, Fig 31) and detent (A, Fig 32).

Fig 29.—Extension case assembly fitted.

A. Governor control lever.
B. Selector valve lever.
C. Anti-creep pressure switch.
D. Rear pump.
E. Governor adjusting screw.
F. Multiple disc clutch pressure take-off.
G. Direct drive clutch pressure take-off.

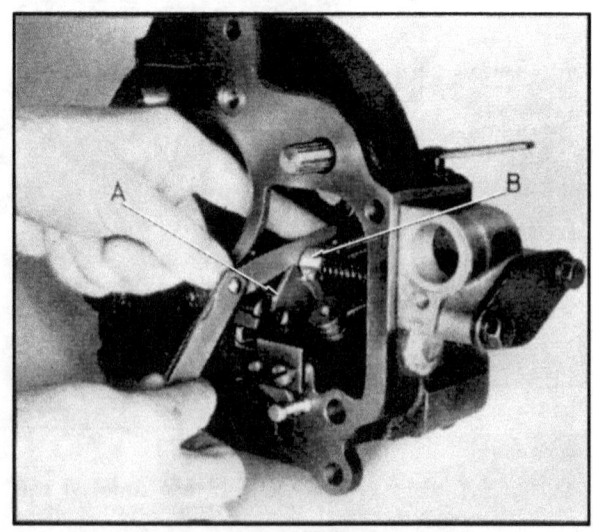

Fig 30.—Governor fork end play adjustment.
A. Governor fork.   B. Governor end bracket.

Instal in the new case with the tapered end first and place the spring in the bore on the top of the detent.

After ensuring that the parking brake interlock piston and spring and the accelerator detent and spring are assembled correctly in the case, apply a film of petroleum jelly to the machined face of the transmission case and place a new gasket in position on the case (see Fig 33). Ensure that all holes in the gasket are properly aligned with the holes in the case.

Shift the selector valve lever on the transmission to the Low position by pulling lever as far rearward as possible and then moving it one detent forward. Placing the selector valve lever in the Low position will turn the parking brake toggle arm shaft sleeve (A, Fig 34) so that the wide spline (B) is to the left and in an approximately horizontal position.

Make sure that the governor drive gear spacer, parking brake gear, governor drive gear, and universal joint flange spacer are installed in the correct order on the shaft. The chamfered side of the parking brake gear must be to the rear.

Lubricate all moving parts with Type A automatic transmission fluid.

Turn the toggle arm splined shaft (A, Fig 35) so that its wide spline (B) is to the left. Ensure that the governor direct drive pawl (I, Fig 28) is properly positioned as shown in Fig 28.

Lift the extension case into position on the shaft. Engage the splines of the toggle arm shaft with the toggle arm shaft sleeve splines. It may be necessary to move the selector valve lever slightly to facilitate the engagement. Push the case forward against the transmission main case. Instal the setscrews and tighten finger-tight only so that the companion flange, when installed, will centralise the oil seal and case assembly.

Push the selector valve lever on the transmission all the way forward into the Park position.

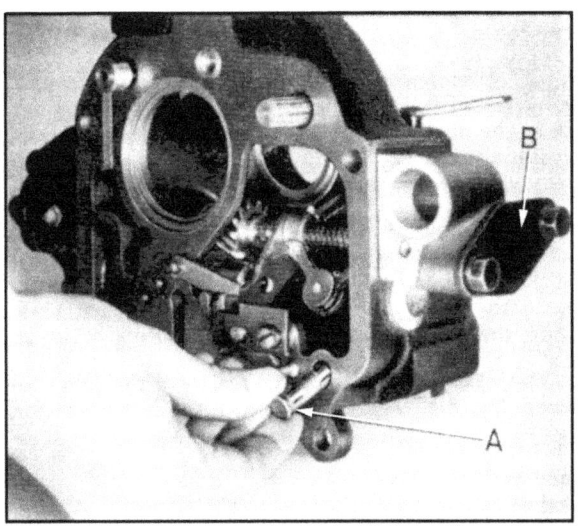

Fig 32.—Accelerator control detent removal.

A. Accelerator control detent.
B. Speedometer drive gear housing cover.

Align the punch marks of the transmission universal joint flange and the main shaft and instal the flange. Instal the tongued washer, lockwasher, and nut, and tighten to 60 to 80 ft/lb torque.

Tighten the extension case-to-transmission case setscrews to 28 to 33 ft/lb torque.

Connect the front propeller shaft universal joint to the companion flange at the rear of the transmission.

Check the operation of the parking brake pawl and toggle assembly as outlined under Parking Brake and Toggle Assembly—Adjustment.

Connect the electrical cables to the anti-creep pressure switch.

Fig 31.—Parking brake interlock piston removal.

A. Parking brake interlock piston and spring.
B. Accelerator control detent spring.

Fig 33.—Fluid passage holes in rear of main casing.

A. Multiple disc clutch passage.
B. Direct drive passage.
C. Valve body to governor passage.
D. Multiple disc clutch passage.
E. Rear pump pressure passage.
F. Rear pump intake passage.

Instal new gasket in speedometer gear housing, assemble the speedometer pinion in the cable, insert the end of the cable in the speedometer gear housing, and instal the retaining screw.

Check the Accelerator-to-Governor Lever Linkage and Manual Selector Linkage adjustments as described in "Service Adjustments".

Connect the control rod to the selector valve lever.

Connect the control rod to the governor lever.

Following the recommended procedure outlined in "Maintenance", fill the transmission with Type A automatic transmission fluid to the correct level.

1:37 GOVERNOR ASSEMBLY

Removal:

Remove the extension case.

Remove the two speedometer gear housing cover screws, cover (B, Fig 32) and gasket. These screws secure the speedometer gear housing to the extension case.

The extension case may be equipped with a one-piece speedometer drive gear and governor shaft assembly or the speedometer drive gear and governor shaft may be separate pieces with the gear splined to the shaft.

If equipped with the one-piece assembly, the assembly must be removed to permit removal of the speedometer gear housing. Pull the gear housing away from the extension case and withdraw the governor shaft and gear assembly from the governor assembly. Then remove the shaft and gear assembly from the speedometer gear housing.

If equipped with separate gear and shaft, slip the gear off the shaft and remove the speedometer gear housing. Then remove the shaft from the governor assembly.

Disengage the governor end bracket (A, Fig 36) from the governor fork. Slide the governor bearing (B) out of the governor adjusting yoke shoes (C) and remove

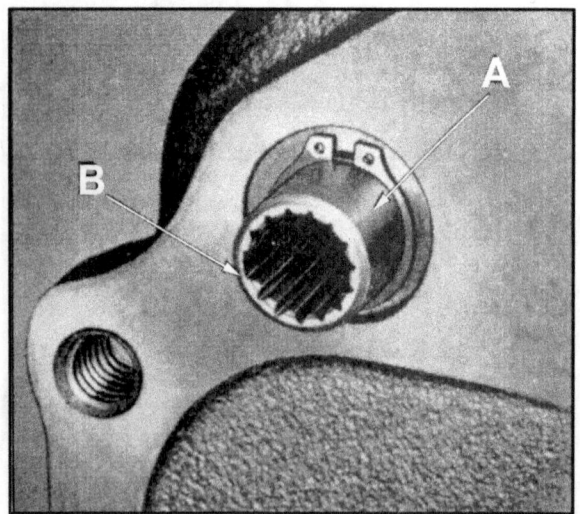

Fig 34.—Parking brake toggle arm shaft sleeve.
A. Toggle arm shaft sleeve.
B. Wide spline.

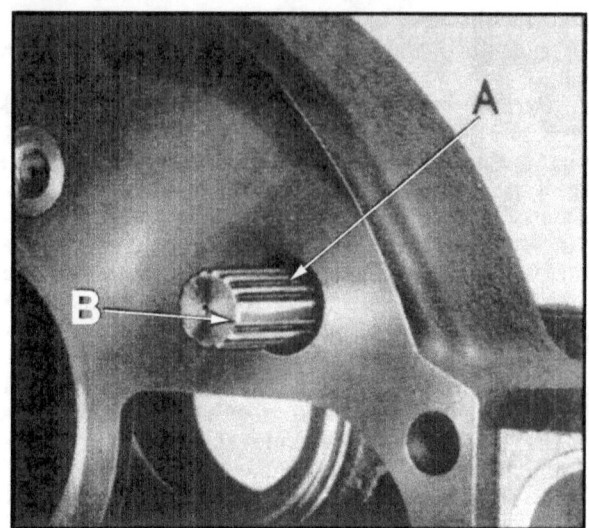

Fig 35.—Toggle arm shaft.
A. Shaft.   B. Wide spline.

the governor from the case. Then remove the adjusting yoke shoes.

Remove the spring from the governor.

Inspect the governor shaft and make sure it is free of burrs and that the splines are not scored.

Burrs on the governor shaft can be caused by the governor spring not seating properly in the governor end brackets.

Make sure the governor valve (B, Fig 37) operates freely within the valve sleeve.

Make sure the hydraulic detent piston (A, Fig 37) is in place. If it is the stepped type detent, the stepped end should be inserted in the cylinder first and the long plain end out.

Check the length of the governor spring to make sure the correct spring is used.

Insert one end of the governor spring in the governor; compress the spring and instal the other end.

Instal the governor adjusting yoke shoes.

Align the slots of the shoes and slide the governor bearing into position in the shoes. Then engage the groove of the governor end bracket with the governor fork.

Apply a light film of petroleum jelly to machined surface on the side of the extension case and place a new speedometer gear housing gasket in position on the case.

If equipped with a one-piece shaft, insert the governor shaft and speedometer drive gear assembly in the gear housing. Align the shaft and governor end bracket and insert the shaft in the governor. With the shaft through the governor assembly, hold the governor end bracket in place on the governor fork and engage the shaft in the splines of the rear pump gear. It may be necessary to shift the end of the governor slightly to gain alignment of the shaft with the rear pump gear.

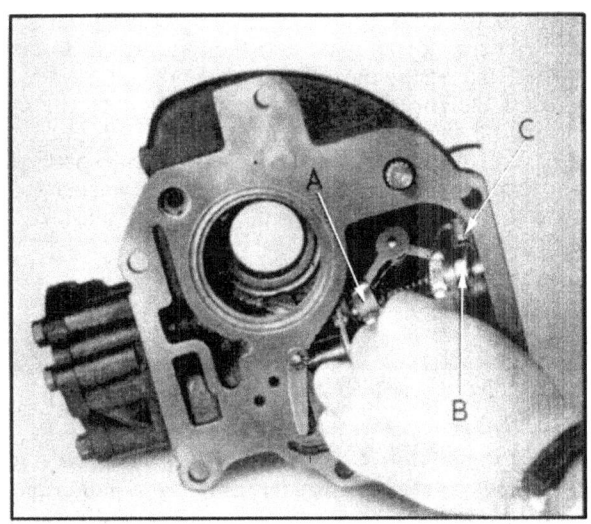

Fig 36.—Dismantling the governor.
A. Governor end bracket.
B. Governor bearing.
C. Yoke shoe.

If equipped with a two-piece assembly, insert the shaft in the governor end brackets and insert shaft into the rear oil pump gear. Instal the speedometer drive gear and housing.

Align the mounting holes of the gear housing with holes in the case. Position a new housing cover gasket and cover on the housing, making certain that gasket and cover are properly aligned with housing. The centre opening in the gasket is offset and improper installation will result in damage to the gasket. Instal the retaining screws. Tighten the screws to 10 to 13 ft/lb torque.

If installing a new governor, check the clearance between the governor end brackets when the governor valve is in its fully open position and the governor control lever is in its fully forward position. The clearance must be at least .005". If the clearance is less than .005", remove the acorn nut located on the rear of the extension case, loosen the lock nut (E, Fig 29), and turn the screw in (clockwise) until the minimum clearance is obtained.

If after road testing the car it is found that kickdown upshift is too high, turn the screw in (clockwise) a little at a time until the proper kickdown upshift speed is obtained. (See Governor Shift Speeds chart.)

Inspect and instal the extension case on the transmission.

Governor Shaft and Speedometer Drive Gear Assembly Removal and Installation:

Follow the procedure outlined under Governor Assembly.

Governor Adjusting Yoke Shoes Removal and Installation:

Follow the procedure outlined under Governor Assembly.

Governor Spring
(Note: See also 2:53)
Removal and Installation:

The governor spring is the one situated between the end brackets of the governor. Care should be taken to make certain the correct spring is used. The spring is identified by its free length, the spring should be $2\frac{1}{4}$" long.

Under no circumstances cut or stretch a spring to obtain the desired length.

For removal and installation of the governor spring, follow the procedure outlined under Governor Assembly.

Governor Return Spring
Removal:

Remove the extension case.

Using long nosed pliers, unhook the end of the governor return spring (A, Fig 38) from the governor

Fig 37.—Assembling the governor valve.
A. Hydraulic detent piston.
B. Governor valve.

Fig 38.—The governor adjusting yoke.
A. Governor return spring. B. Adjusting yoke.

adjusting yoke (B) and the other end of the spring from the anchor pin.

Installation:

Slip the end of the governor return spring over the anchor pin.

Hook the other end of the spring on the governor adjusting yoke.

Inspect and instal the governor extension case.

Governor Control Shaft and Lever
Removal:

Remove the governor assembly.

Unhook the governor return spring from governor adjusting yoke.

Hold the shaft in position, loosen the allen headed grub screw (see Fig 38) and withdraw the shaft from the assembly. Remove the governor adjusting yoke.

To remove the accelerator detent plate and plunger assembly, swing the plate and link toward the governor return spring anchor pin, push the plunger into the case, and remove the assembly.

Installation:

Insert the plunger in the hole in case from inside the case, slipping the rocker arm out of the way to allow the plunger to come through the case.

Ensure that the key is properly installed in the governor control shaft and insert the end of the shaft in the case. Hold the governor adjusting yoke in position and slip the shaft into the yoke. Align the key in the shaft with the keyway in the plate and insert the shaft in the plate.

Make sure the shaft is fully seated in the plate and tighten the grub screw securely.

Hook the governor return spring to the governor adjusting yoke.

Instal the governor assembly.

Governor Adjusting Yoke
Removal and Installation:

Follow the procedure outlined under Governor Control Shaft and Lever.

Governor Control Direct Drive Mechanism
Removal:

To remove the pawl (I, Fig 28) remove the cotter pin and flat washer and slip the pawl off the pivot pin.

Remove the rocker arm hairpin spring by slipping the end out of the hole in the rocker arm and then removing the other end from the hole in the case.

To remove the rocker arm (H), remove the retaining plate screw, retainer plate and spacing washer. Then, remove the rocker arm and flat washer from the pivot pin.

To remove the plunger, follow the procedure outlined under Governor Control Shaft and Lever — Removal.

Installation:

To instal the plunger, follow the procedure outlined under Governor Control Shaft and Lever — Installation.

Place the flat washer on the rocker arm pivot pin and place the rocker arm on the pin. Place the retainer plate on the rocker arm over the pin, slip the spacer washer between the plate and the case, align the spacer washer and instal the retaining screw.

Instal the rocker arm spring, making sure the upper end of the spring is in the hole of the rocker arm.

Ensure that there is a flat washer on the pawl pivot pin, then slip the pawl and another flat washer on the pin and instal the cotter pin. The pawl must be free to drop of its own weight.

Hydraulic Detent Piston
Removal:

Remove the governor assembly.

Move the governor valve out of the sleeve and remove the detent piston (A, Fig 37).

NOTE: If the detent piston is stuck in the bore, position the governor fork (G, Fig 28) so that it contacts the stop on the retainer plate. Cover the valve body-to-governor passage (C, Fig 33) and the multiple disc clutch passage (A) with the fingers. Then using compressed air, blow into the direct drive passage (B). This will force the piston out of the bore against the fork of the governor valve.

Installation:

There are two types of pistons used; the stepped type and the straight type.

It is very important that the stepped piston is installed correctly, that is, with the stepped end first and the long plain portion towards the governor fork.

Apply Type A automatic transmission fluid to the governor valve.

Carefully insert the valve in the sleeve and place the end of the fork in position in the notch of the direct drive rocker arm retaining plate.

Instal the governor assembly as outlined under Governor Assembly.

Governor Valve
Removal:

Remove the governor assembly.

Turn the governor fork so the end of the fork is out of the notch of the direct drive rocker arm retaining plate and slide the valve out of the sleeve.

Installation:

Ensure that the hydraulic detent piston is in place and properly installed as described in Governor Assembly.

Apply Type A automatic transmission fluid to the governor valve.

Carefully insert the valve in the sleeve and place the end of the fork in position in the notch of the direct drive rocker arm retaining plate.

Instal the governor assembly.

Parking Brake and Governor Drive Gears
Removal:

Remove the extension case.

Slide the universal joint flange spacer, governor drive gear, and parking brake gear off the shaft.

Installation:

Slip the parking brake gear on the shaft. The chamfered side of the gear must be to the rear of the transmission.

Instal the governor drive gear on the shaft.

Instal the universal joint flange spacer on the shaft.

Inspect and instal the extension case.

Parking Brake Pawl-and-Toggle Assembly
Removal:

Remove the extension case.

Using a small drift, loosen the pivot pin and toggle shaft by tapping the pin and shaft forward. Remove the pawl-and-toggle assembly (A, Fig 39) from the case.

On some transmissions the pivot pin hole and toggle shaft hole do not extend through the case, and, therefore, the pivot pin and toggle shaft cannot be removed with a drift. The end of the pivot pin is internally threaded (see Fig 39). To remove this pin, instal a screw in the pin and use a pair of pliers to pull the pin out of the case. The toggle shaft (C, Fig 39) can also be removed by means of a pair of pliers.

NOTE: On some extension cases, a steel or fibre spacer is used on the toggle shaft at the back of the toggle lever. Do not interchange washers; use only the same type washer when reassembling.

Lift the O-ring seal out of the groove of the pivot pin and the toggle shaft and remove the seals.

Remove the O-rings from the pivot pin and toggle shaft if so equipped. If the pivot pin and toggle shaft holes extend through the case, O-rings are used to prevent fluid leakage. If these holes are not open to the outside of the case, O-rings are not needed.

Installation:

If O-rings are used, apply Type A automatic transmission fluid to the new O-ring seals and instal them on the pivot pin and toggle shaft.

Position the pawl-and-toggle assembly (A, Fig 39) in the case with the dog of the pawl pointing downward.

Align the pivot pin hole of the pawl with the hole in the case and instal the pivot pin. (B, Fig 39).

Swing the end of the pawl-and-toggle assembly into position in the case, align the wide splines of the toggle shaft and the toggle lever, and instal the toggle shaft (C, Fig 39). If equipped with a spacer washer between the pawl-and-toggle assembly and the rear of the case, ensure that this washer is installed and positioned correctly. If necessary, to replace the washer, use only the same type of washer as used originally. Do not interchange the steel and fibre washers.

Inspect and instal the extension case.

Accelerator Detent and Spring
Removal and Installation:

Follow the procedure as outlined under Extension Case.

Parking Brake Interlock Piston and Spring
Removal and Installation:

Follow the procedure as outlined under Extension Case.

Extension Case Rear Oil Seal
Removal:

Remove the extension case.

Using a suitable brass drift, drive the oil seal rearward out of the extension case, being careful not to damage the rear pump drive gear or the bore of the extension case.

Installation:

Coat the outer surface of the seal with a suitable gasket sealer.

Using an arbor press, start the seal into the case ensuring that the seal is not cocked but enters the bore squarely. Press the seal in until it is flush with the case.

Inspect and instal the extension case.

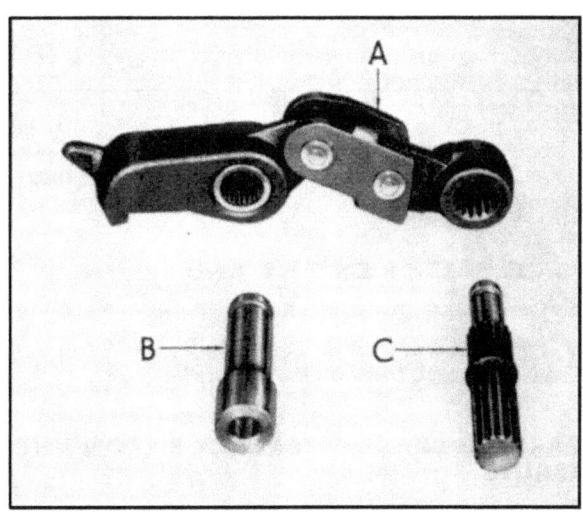

Fig 39.—The parking pawl and toggle assembly.
A. Pawl and toggle assembly.
B. Pivot pin.
C. Toggle shaft.

Fig 40.—Rear oil pump gasket.
A. Governor drain hole.   B. Gasket.

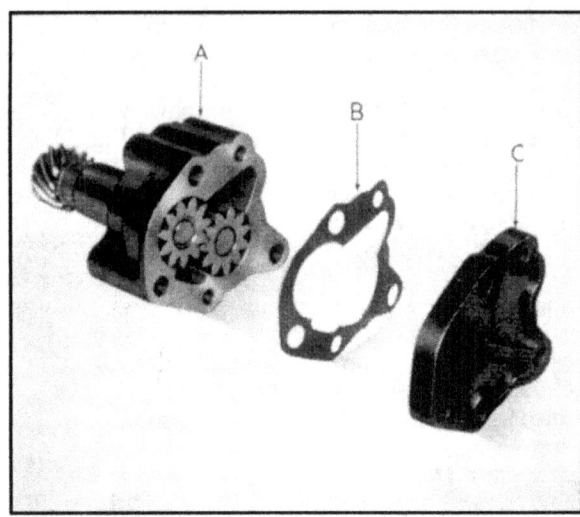

Fig 41.—Rear oil pump.
A. Body and gears.   B. Cover gasket.
C. Cover.

1:38 REAR OIL PUMP

Removal:

The rear oil pump may be removed without removing the extension case from the transmission if the extension case is equipped with a one-piece governor shaft and speedometer drive gear assembly. If equipped with a two-piece assembly, the case must be removed before removing the oil pump. To distinguish between the one- and two-piece assemblies, remove the speedometer gear housing cover (B, Fig 32) and check the position of the shaft. If the shaft is flush with the outer end of the gear when the gear is held in the operating position in the housing, it is a two-piece assembly. If the shaft is approximately $\frac{1}{2}''$ to $\frac{3}{4}''$ short of being flush, it is a one-piece assembly, instal the gear housing cover.

Disconnect the cables from the anti-creep pressure switch (C, Fig 29) and unscrew the switch from the pump.

Remove the three screws and slip the pump out of the case. If the two-piece speedometer drive gear and shaft assembly is used, hold the shaft to prevent removing it with the pump.

Ensure that the anti-creep pressure switch passage in the pump body is not obstructed.

Check to make sure that the governor drain hole (A, Fig 40) is open.

Check for worn or damaged gears, pump cover and pump body.

Installation:

Apply a film of petroleum jelly to the machined face of the extension case and position a new gasket (B, Fig 40) in place on the case. Ensure that the gasket does not obstruct the governor drain hole (A).

Insert the end of the pump through the opening in the case. Then keeping the face of the pump parallel to the face of the case, push the pump into the case and engage the splines of the pump gear and governor shaft. It may be necessary to turn the pump slightly to engage the splines.

If equipped with a two-piece speedometer drive gear and shaft assembly, hold the shaft to prevent moving the governor assembly and yoke out of position.

Instal the pump retaining screws and tighten to 15 to 18 ft/lb torque.

Instal the anti-creep switch and connect the cables.

Rear Oil Pump Cover Gasket
Replacement:

If a leak occurs between the pump body and cover, the cover may be removed and the gasket replaced. Removal of the two setscrews permits removal of the cover. The gasket is available in three thicknesses which can be identified by the colour.

.002" gasket — red .... Part No J20-761
.003" gasket — green or
 transparent ...... Part No J20-761/A
.005" gasket — blue .... Part No J20-761/B

Always use a gasket of the same thickness as the gasket to be replaced. While the cover is off for gasket replacement, inspect the cover for scoring or wear.

1:39 FRONT PUMP AND COLLECTOR RING ASSEMBLY

Removal:

Remove the transmission from the car.

Place the Ring Gear Retaining Clip J 4668-3 (A, Fig 43) on the main shaft and secure it in place with a rubber band (B). This clip prevents movement of the ring gear and eliminates the possibility of dislocating the thrust washers in the gear train.

Remove the setscrews securing the pump housing.

Tap the front pump housing loose from the transmission case and slide the assembly forward off the main shaft.

Remove the front ring gear front thrust washer (F, Fig 44) from the rear face of the front pump-and-collector ring assembly.

Thoroughly clean the assembly, making sure that the flange is clean and the oil passages are not obstructed.

Remove the five setscrews at the rear of the collector ring and remove the front pump.

Fig 42.—Front pump and collector ring.

Fig 43.—Ring gear retaining clip in position on mainshaft.

A. Retaining clip J4668-3.
B. Rubber band.

Lift the gears (see Fig 42) out of the housing.

Check for evidence of wear or damage to the gears, casting, or O-rings.

After making sure that the interior of the pump is clean, place the gears in position. The side of the gear having the drive lugs must be to the outside. Lubricate the gears with Type A automatic transmission fluid.

Clean the collector ring face. Align the front pump with the collector ring and instal the retaining screws.

Installation:

Check the end play of the assembly to determine the thickness of the front ring gear thrust washer that is required to obtain correct end play. Make certain that the companion flange is tight before checking the end play. Instal the gauge J-4668 (A, Fig 45) over the main shaft and ring gear shaft and fit it into the transmission case. Turn the hub of the gauge so that the indicator is over the start step. Then rotate the hub anti-clockwise while pushing the hub inward, keeping a steady pressure on the hub. The step over which the indicator is stopped by the next higher step, represents the thickness of the thrust washer to be used. The thrust washer thickness in thousandths is stamped on the face of the ring opposite the step.

Thickness	Part No	Fig reference
.052" — .054"	J20-388	F, Fig 44
.061" — .063"	J20-388A	
.072" — .074"	J20-388B	
.082" — .084"	J20-388C	

Apply a film of petroleum jelly to the collector ring flange and position a new gasket on the flange. Make sure that the gasket is flat and all holes of the gasket are properly aligned with the oil passages, indicated in Fig 44.

Coat the hub of the collector ring with petroleum jelly and place the front ring gear front thrust washer

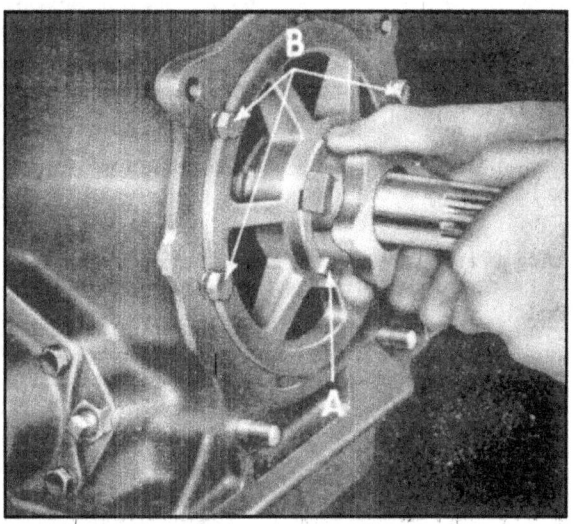

Fig 45.—Mainshaft end play gauge in position.

A. End play gauge.   B. Retaining screws.

on the rear face of the assembly, fully engaging the tongues of the washer in the slots. The steel face of the washer must be against the hub of the assembly.

Fill the pump with new oil through the elongated hole of the collector ring flange. (E, Fig 44).

Check the three seal rings to ensure that they are not broken or damaged, replace the rings as outlined under the Oil Seal Rings — Removal and Installation. Then, coat the rings with petroleum jelly and centre the rings in the grooves to prevent damage to the rings.

To ensure proper alignment and prevent shifting of the gasket when installing the assembly, instal a starting stud 1¼" long in the top hole of the case.

Hold the pump so that the elongated oil inlet hole and the round oil outlet hole in the flange are at the

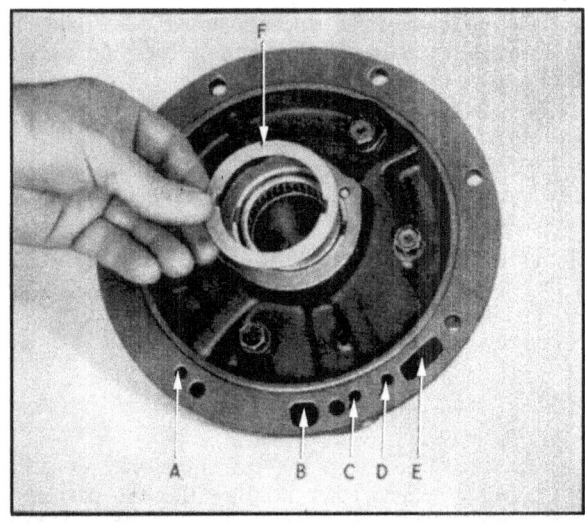

Fig 44.—Front ring gear front thrust washer.

A. Converter pressure passage.
B. Front pump pressure passage.
C. Direct drive passage.
D. Intermediate passage.
E. Front pump intake passage.
F. Front ring gear front thrust washer.

bottom and check to see that all oil passages are properly indexed with the corresponding passages in the case. Then slip the assembly on the main shaft. Using the starting stud, position the assembly on the case and instal the retaining setscrews. Tighten all screws to 15-18 ft/lb torque.

Remove the ring gear retaining clip from the main shaft. Ensure that the main shaft assembly turns freely in both directions while holding the ring gear shaft.

Instal the transmission in the car.

Front Pump Oil Seal
Removal:

Remove the front pump-and-collector ring assembly from the transmission.

Remove the five setscrews from the rear of the collector ring and remove the front pump.

Lift the gears out of the housing.

Then using a drift, drive the oil seal out of the housing, taking care not to damage the pump bush.

Clean the oil seal bore of the pump thoroughly to remove all of the old sealer.

Apply a sealer compound to the oil seal and using an arbor press, instal the oil seal in the housing. When pressing the seal into the housing maintain a clearance of .030" between the rear face of the seal retainer and the body casting to allow for the passage of oil. The lip of the seal should face towards the pump bush.

After making sure that the interior of the pump is clean, place the inner gear in position. The side of the gear having the drive lugs must be to the outside. Lubricate the gears with Type A automatic transmission fluid.

Clean the collector ring face. Align the front pump with the collector ring, instal the retaining screws, and tighten to specified torque.

Instal the assembly as outlined under Front Pump-and-Collector Ring Assembly.

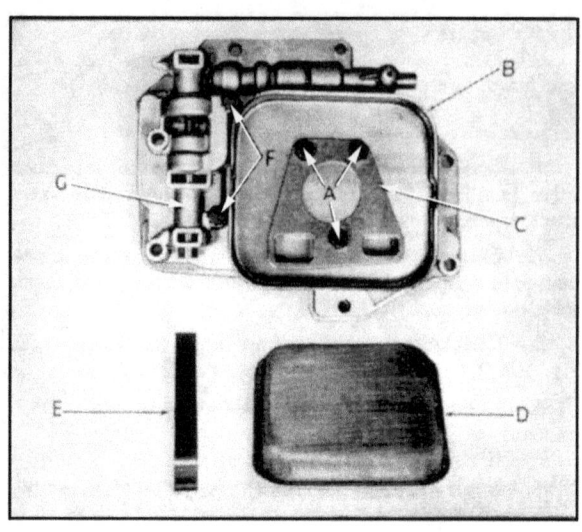

Fig 47.—Valve block, oil screen and shroud.

A. Shroud retaining screws.
B. Shroud.
C. Shroud reinforcing plate.
D. Oil screen.
E. Screen retainer.
F. Retaining screws.
G. Relief valve body.

Oil Seal Rings
Removal:

Remove the front pump-and-collector ring assembly.

To remove the ring, hold one half of the ring tightly in the ring groove; then press against the lower part of the other half which will cause the end of the ring to lift and separate the ends of the ring.

Then spread the ring just enough to permit removal from the groove and remove it from the shaft.

Installation:

Spread the ring just enough to permit slipping it over the shaft and instal it in the groove.

Hold one half of the ring tightly in the ring groove and press against the lower part of the other half which will lift one end of the ring above the other end. Then slide the finger toward the end of the ring and lock the ends of the ring together.

Inspect and instal the front pump-and-collector ring assembly.

1:40 VALVE BLOCK ASSEMBLY

The valve block assembly is mounted on the bottom of the transmission case and accommodates —
The **front and rear pump relief valves.**
The **converter valve.**
The **reverse interlock valve.**

NOTE: See also 2:58

Removal:

Drain the fluid from the transmission unit only.

Remove the setscrews holding the oil pan to the transmission case and remove the oil pan and gasket.

Remove the seven setscrews and remove the valve block assembly.

Remove the valve block base plate rear gasket.

Care must be taken to see that the selector valve is not moved out of its normal operating range.

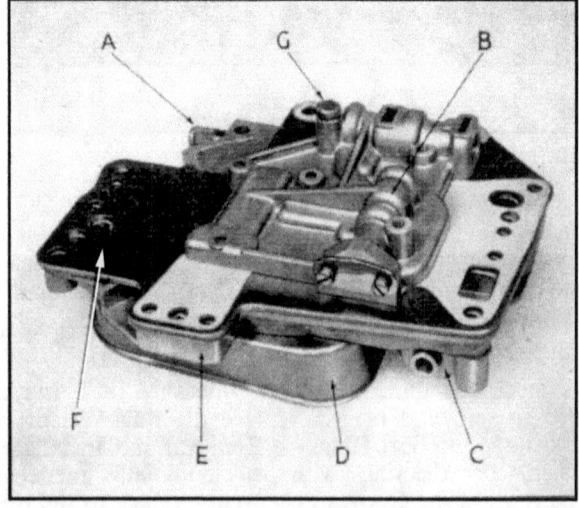

Fig 46.—Valve block assembly.

A. Selector valve.
B. Converter valve body.
C. Front and rear pump relief valve body.
D. Oil screen shroud.
E. Valve block manifold.
F. Valve block base plate.
G. Converter valve body screw.

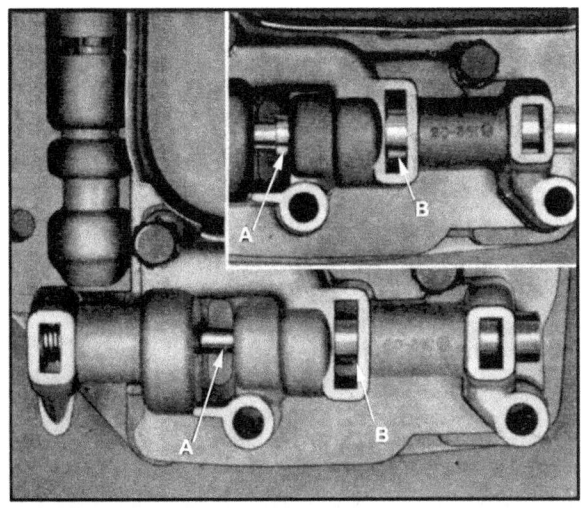

Fig 48.—Pump relief valves.
A. Rear pump relief valve.   B. Front pump relief valve.

Dismantling:

Remove the two setscrews (F, Fig 47) holding the relief valve body (G) to the valve block assembly and remove relief valve body and gasket. Remove the rear pump relief valve intake passage screen. Inspect the front pump relief valve (B, Fig 48) and rear pump relief valve (A) to ensure that neither valve is stuck open. The inset in Fig 48 shows both valves in the open position.

Remove the oil screen retainer (E, Fig 47) and screen (D). Remove the three shroud-to-block setscrews (A) which permit the removal of the shroud reinforcing plate (C) and shroud (B). Then remove the oil screen shroud gasket.

Turn the valve block assembly over and remove the set screw (G, Fig 46) holding the converter valve body (B) to the valve block. Then very carefully lift the converter valve body from the base plate and remove the converter ball check (B, Fig 53) and rear pump ball check (A) from the base plate (D). Then remove the converter control valve body gasket (C) from the base plate.

Separate the base plate from the valve block manifold and remove the valve manifold plate gasket and front pump ball check.

Check the position of the reverse interlock valve (see Fig 49). Inset shows the valve stuck open.

Ensure that the passages in the valve block manifold (see Fig 50) have no obstructions and check for signs of porosity.

Check the front pump ball check seat (B, Fig 51), it must be tight in the manifold.

Clean the rear pump relief valve intake screen.

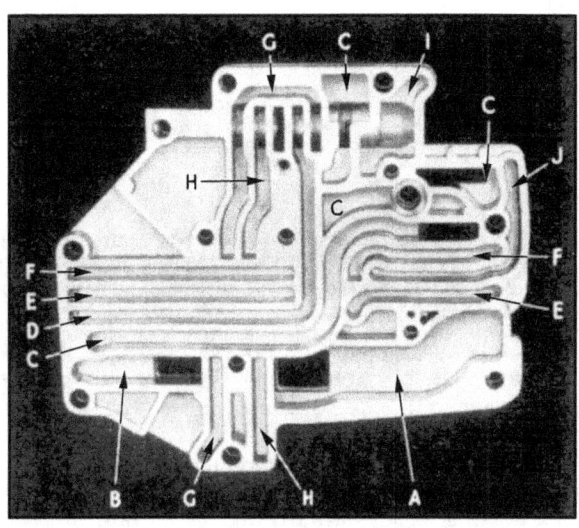

Fig 50.—Valve block manifold.

A. Front pump relief passage.
B. Rear pump relief passage.
C. Rear pump pressure passage.
D. Governor valve passage.
E. Multiple disc clutch passage.
F. Direct drive clutch passage.
G. Forward servo passage.
H. Low servo passage.
I. Reverse servo passage.
J. Converter pressure passage.

Reassembling:

Ensure that all parts of the valve block assembly have been thoroughly cleaned. Every precaution must be taken to keep parts clean during reassembly. Apply Type A automatic transmission fluid to the gaskets during the installation to keep the gaskets in place. The gaskets must be free of wrinkles.

Instal the front pump ball check in the valve manifold (see Fig 51). Place the manifold plate gasket (A, Fig 52) in position, ensuring that all holes are aligned. Then carefully place the base plate over the gasket.

Place the converter control valve body gasket in position on the base plate (see Fig 53). Place the converter ball check (B) and rear pump ball check (A) in the correct holes as shown in Fig 53. Then carefully place the converter control valve body over the ball check and position the body on the base plate. Install the setscrew (G, Fig 46). The valve is also held to the block by the shroud retaining setscrews and

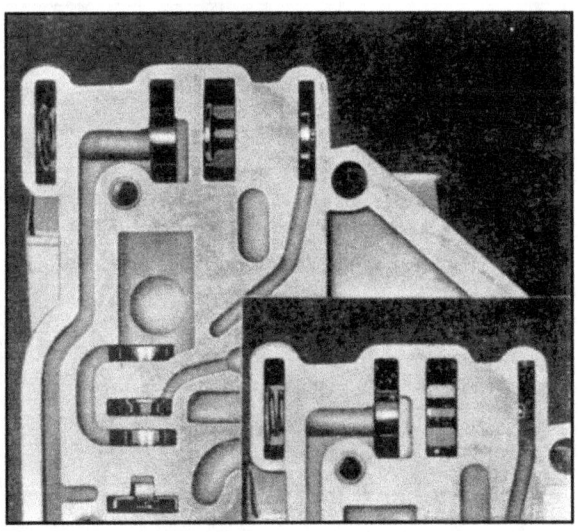

Fig 49.—Reverse interlock valve.

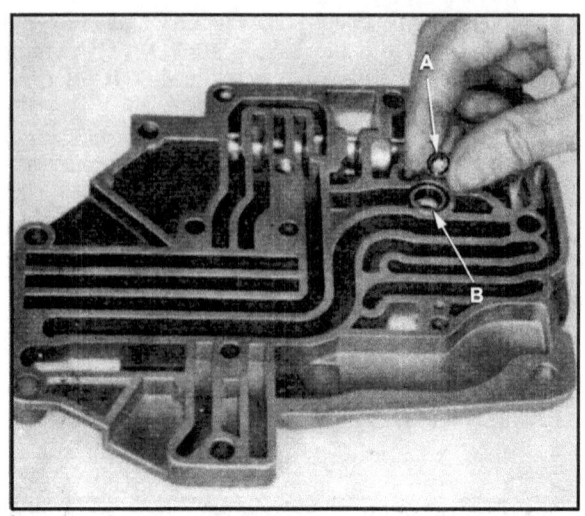

Fig 51.—Front pump ball check valve.
A. Ball check. B. Ball check seat.

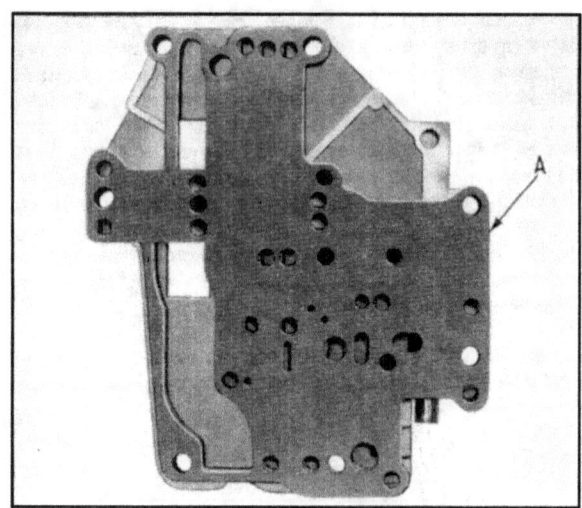

Fig 52.—A. Manifold plate gasket.

the relief valve body setscrews; therefore, do not fully tighten this screw as it may be necessary later to shift the converter valve body slightly to secure alignment when installing the other parts of the assembly.

Turn the assembly over and place the relief valve body gasket in position. Insert the rear pump relief valve screen in the passage and flush with or below the surface of the body. Place the relief valve body on the gasket and align the mounting holes. Instal the two setscrews (F, Fig 47) and shift the body as far as possible in an outward and downward direction with the valve block positioned as illustrated in Fig 47. Tighten the setscrews finger tight.

Place the oil screen shroud gasket on the valve block, making sure all openings are aligned. Instal the shroud (B, Fig 47) and shroud reinforcing plate (C) and instal the retaining setscrews (A) finger tight.

After making certain that all parts are properly positioned by inserting two long screws in front holes of valve body, tighten all the setscrews to 6 to 8 ft/lb torque.

Installation:

Apply a coat of petroleum jelly to a new valve block base plate rear gasket, place the gasket on the base plate, and align the holes of the gasket with the holes in the base plate.

Place the valve block assembly in position against the transmission case flange. Guide the inner selector valve lever into the slot of the selector valve, making sure that gaskets are properly aligned with the holes in the housing flange and valve block.

Instal the retaining setscrews and tighten finger tight.

Disconnect the control rod from the selector valve lever and move the lever through its full travel to make certain that a bind does not exist between the inner selector lever and selector valve. If there is a bind, loosen the valve block assembly setscrews and re-position the assembly to relieve the bind. Then tighten the setscrews to 10 to 13 ft/lb torque. Connect the control rod to the selector valve lever.

Instal the oil screen and retainer, making sure the retainer is not sprung and will hold the screen securely in the shroud.

Apply petroleum jelly to a new oil pan gasket and position the gasket on the transmission case flange.

Instal the oil pan and tighten the setscrews to 10 to 13 ft/lb torque.

Following the recommended procedure described in the "Maintenance" section, fill the transmission with Type A automatic transmission fluid.

1:41 MAIN SHAFT ASSEMBLY

The main shaft assembly (see Fig 54) is supported at the rear by a ball bearing and at the front by needle bearings in the front pump. The assembly consists primarily of the transmission main shaft, the two

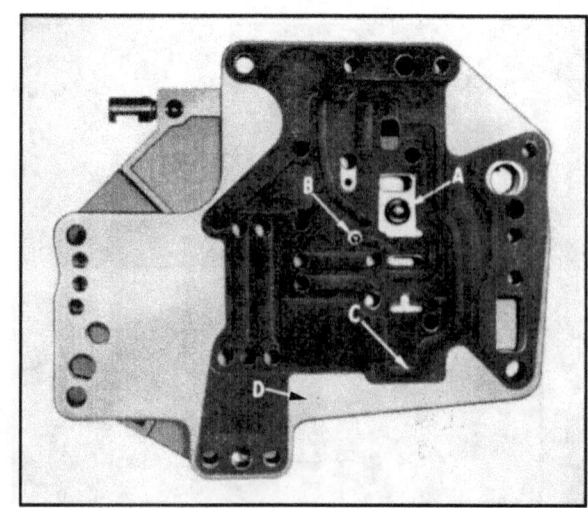

Fig 53.—Manifold base plate.
A. Rear pump ball check.   C. Converter valve body gasket.
B. Converter ball check.   D. Manifold base plate.

Fig 54.—Mainshaft assembly.

planetary gear sets, the three brake drums, the multiple disc clutch.

NOTE: See also 2:58 (Mainshaft Assembly)

Removal:

Remove the transmission.
Remove the front pump-and-collector ring assembly.
Remove the extension case.
Remove the universal joint flange spacer, governor drive gear, parking brake gear and governor drive gear spacer from the main shaft.
Then remove the main shaft rear bearing lock ring.
Turn the transmission assembly over and remove the oil pan and valve block assembly.
Make sure that the Ring Gear Retaining Clip J 4668-3 (see Fig 43) is securely in place on the shaft. Then tap the rear end of the main shaft forward with a soft hammer while slightly shaking the forward end of the shaft until the bearing passes through the case bore. Make sure that the main shaft bearing does not move on the main shaft to avoid displacing the thrust washers within the assembly. Pull the assembly forward, being careful not to disengage the ends of the bands from the struts or dislodge the bands from the guide at the top of the transmission case. Any cocking of the bands will hinder removal of the assembly. Remove the assembly from the front of the case.
Check the drums for scoring.
Inspect the case to make sure that the band guide strap and retaining rivets are tight.
Inspect the bands for wear or damage.

Installation:

If a new main shaft assembly is to be installed, do not remove the shipping clamps until after the assembly is installed in the case.
Support the main shaft assembly with one hand under the low drum, insert the assembly in the transmission case, thread it through the brake bands, and seat the bearing in the bore of the rear face of the case. Make sure the brake bands and anchor struts have not been moved out of position.
Instal the rear bearing lock ring; then push the assembly forward until the lock ring is seated against the rear face of the case.
Inspect and instal the valve block assembly and oil pan as outlined under Valve Block Assembly.

Turn the transmission over to rest on the oil pan.
If a new assembly was installed, remove the rear shipping clamp.
Inspect and instal extension case.
If a new main shaft assembly was installed, remove the front shipping clamp from the shaft of the new assembly and instal the Ring Gear Retaining Clip J4668-3. Install the front and rear shipping clamps on the old assembly.
With a new main shaft assembly, it will be necessary to check the end play of the assembly and determine the thickness of the front ring gear front thrust washer required to obtain the correct end play. End Play Gauge J4668 is used for this purpose.
Make certain that the companion flange is installed and the flange nut is tightened to the correct torque before checking the end play. Move the main shaft assembly rearward as far as possible. Instal the gauge J4668 (A, Fig 45) over the main shaft and ring gear shaft and fit it into the transmission case. Use three of the front pump retaining screws (B) to hold the gauge securely against the face of the case. Turn the hub of the gauge so that the indicator is over the start step. Then rotate the hub anti-clockwise while pushing

Fig 55.—Mainshaft assembly endplay thrust washer in position.
A. Thrust washer. B. Oil seal rings.

the hub inward, keeping a steady pressure on the hub. The step over which the indicator is stopped by the next higher step represents the thickness of the thrust washer to be used. The thrust washer thickness in thousandths is stamped on the face of the ring opposite the step.

Thickness	Part No.	Fig Reference
.052" — .054"	J20-388	
.061" — .063"	J20-388A	F, Fig 44
.072" — .074"	J20-388B	
.082" — .084"	J20-388C	

NOTE: If the indicator stops over either the high no-go step or the low no-go step, the assembly cannot be used in that particular transmission case. This might be due to high or low tolerances built up in the main shaft assembly and corresponding high or low tolerances of the transmission case, although the chances of this happening are very remote. If the indicator stops over the high no-go step, there is a possibility that while handling the assembly, the ring gear may have moved forward and the ring gear thrust washer may have dropped out of position or other internal parts of the assembly may be dislocated.

To ensure that the ring gear has not moved forward, measure the distance from the end of the ring gear shaft to the end of the main shaft. This should not be less than $1\tfrac{3}{16}"$. If the measurement is less than $1\tfrac{3}{16}"$, slip the ring gear off the shaft and reposition the thrust washer over the gear teeth, applying petroleum jelly to the washer to hold it in place. Ensure that the steel face of the washer is toward the rear of the transmission. Then coat the seal rings with petroleum jelly and reinstall the ring gear.

After obtaining the correct size thrust washer, instal it on the hub of the front pump-and-collector ring assembly so that the steel face of the washer is against the hub of the assembly. Inspect and instal the assembly.

Dismantling:

Slide the front ring gear (A, Fig 56) forward, disengage it from the front planetary carrier pinions, and remove it from the shaft.

It is not necessary to remove the ring gear oil seal rings unless they are to be replaced. If only one of the rings is damaged, all three rings must be replaced. To remove the oil seal ring, first turn the ring so that the split is at the top. Then hold the ring tight in the groove at one side and press against the lower part of the ring at the other side. This will cause the end of the ring to lift and separate the ends of the ring. Spread the ring just enough to permit removal from the groove and remove it from the shaft. The three rings are removed in the same manner.

The needle bearings and bushing of the front ring gear are not serviced separately but are available only as part of the ring gear assembly.

Remove the front ring gear thrust washer (C, Fig 56) from the front planetary carrier.

Fig 56.—Removing the front ring gear.

A. Ring Gear.   B. Front planetary set.   C. Thrust washer.

Remove the reverse drum-and-front planetary carrier assembly by sliding it forward off the main shaft (see Fig 57).

Remove the front sun gear thrust washer from the hub of the front planetary carrier. The thrust washer may stick within the front sun gear.

NOTE: See also 2:53 (Front sungear thrust washer)

If necessary to remove the planetary carrier from the reverse drum, first remove the snap ring by inserting a small screwdriver in the slot provided, lifting the end of the ring out of the groove and, then, pulling the ring completely out of the groove. Using an arbor press, press the carrier out of the drum.

The planetary carrier and pinions are not serviced separately, they are available only as an assembly.

Using Bearing Puller Plate, with Adaptor Rings J1298-B and Universal Puller HM-925, remove the rear bearing.

Remove the rear bearing spacer (D, Fig 59).

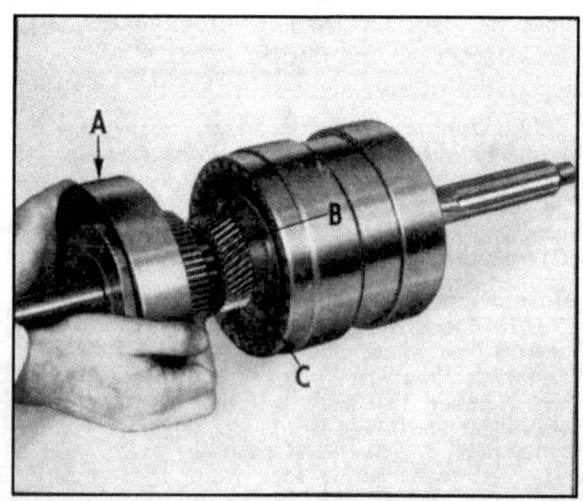

Fig 57.—Removing the reverse drum and front planetary assembly.

A. Reverse drum and front planetary carrier.   B. Front sun gear.   C. Multiple disc clutch.

Slip the forward brake drum assembly rearward and remove the drum assembly from the shaft.

Using a small screwdriver, remove the forward free wheel unit spacer snap ring (see Fig 58) and remove the spacer (A) from the drum. Remove the spacer dowel (B). Remove the free wheel unit snap ring and remove the forward wheel unit (C) from the drum.

NOTE: If, on transmissions with serial numbers J0001 to J0233 inclusive, it is required to replace either the forward free wheel unit Part Number J20-389A or the forward free wheel unit and brake drum assembly Part Number J20-394A, a complete forward free wheel unit and brake drum assembly Part Number J20394 and a spacer Part Number J20-375 must be fitted.

NOTE: See also 2:53 (Refer to the appropriate item heading within that section).

The forward brake drum bushing is not serviced separately but is available only as a part of the forward drum assembly.

Remove the rear sun gear thrust washer retainer (C, Fig 59) and thrust washer (B) from the sun gear (A).

Move the low brake drum plate snap ring so that the end of the ring is above one of the slots of the plate. Using a small screwdriver, lift the end of the ring and remove it from the groove. Then, pick the two dowels (E, Fig 59) out of the slots of the plate. Remove the plate assembly and the rear sun gear as an assembly (see Fig 60).

Slip the rear sun gear out of the reverse free wheel unit. Remove the free wheel unit snap ring and lift the free wheel unit out of the plate (see Fig 67).

The rear sun gear bushings are not serviced separately but are available only as part of the rear sun gear.

The low brake drum plate bushing is not serviced separately but is part of the low brake drum plate assembly.

Pull the main shaft rearward and remove the main shaft and rear planetary carrier as an assembly from the low brake drum assembly.

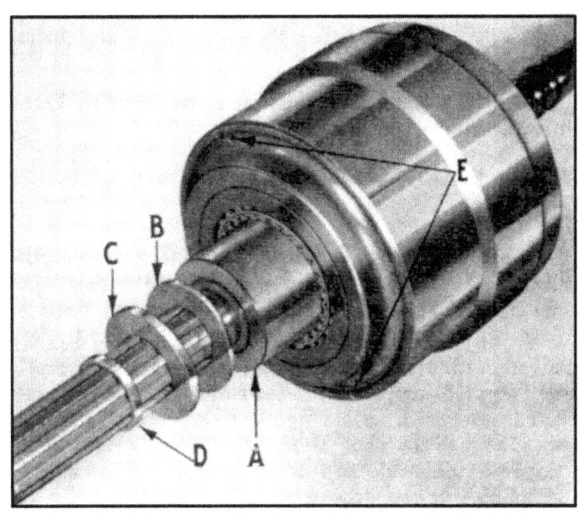

Fig 59.—Rear sun gear thrust washer.

A. Rear sun gear.
B. Thrust washer.
C. Thrust washer retainer.
D. Rear bearing spacer.
E. Dowels.

Remove the rear ring gear thrust washer (A, Fig 61).

Remove the rear planetary carrier oil seal ring retainer snap ring (B, Fig 61). The rear planetary carrier is not pressed on the splines of the main shaft but is held in position by the planetary carrier oil seal ring retainer and snap ring. Place the assembly in an arbor press and press the shaft out of the seal retainer and carrier. Remove the seal retainer (C), rear planetary carrier (D), and the carrier thrust washer (A, Fig 62) from the main shaft.

NOTE: The rear planetary carrier (D, Fig 61) is manufactured as either a Casting or a Forging which are slightly different in design. The cast type carrier has a counterbore (C, Fig 62), machined adjacent to the splined hole, into which fits a distance washer (B). The forged type carrier has no counterbore and the distance washer (B) is, therefore, not fitted. The thrust washer (A) is fitted to both types of carrier.

The oil seal rings of the main shaft and the planetary carrier oil seal ring are of the same type as used on the front ring gear. If necessary to remove the rings for replacement, remove in the same manner as outlined for the front ring gear seals. The rings of the main shaft must be replaced as a set.

The rear planetary carrier and pinions are not serviced separately, they are available as an assembly.

Slide the rear ring gear out of the low brake drum. With a sharp pointed tool, pick the inner O-ring seal out of the retainer and remove it from inside the bore of the ring gear. Pick the outer O-ring seal (B, Fig 63) out of the groove and slip it off the hub of the ring gear. If necessary remove the oil seal ring (C) or front planetary carrier snap ring (A) using snap ring pliers.

The ring gear bushings are not serviced separately but are available only as part of the ring gear assembly.

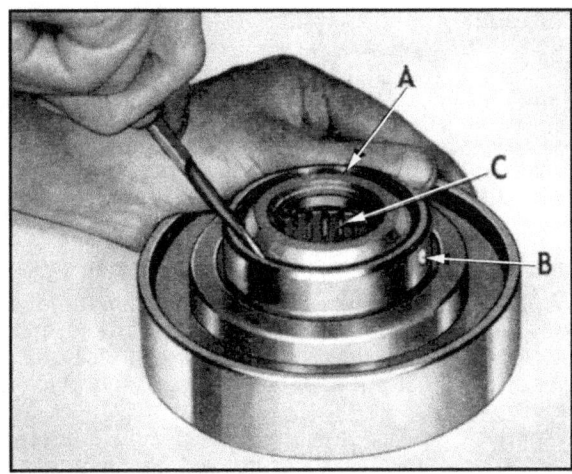

Fig 58.—Removing the forward free wheel unit spacer snap ring.

A. Spacer.   B. Spacer dowel.   C. Forward free wheel unit.

143

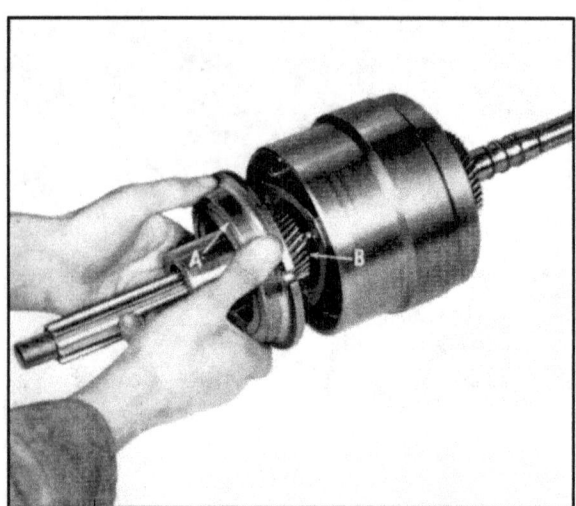

Fig 60.—Removing the low brake drum plate and rear sun gear.
A. Plate assembly.   B. Rear sun gear.

Place the low brake drum assembly in an arbor press and place three wood blocks, on the multiple disc clutch retractor spring retainer to form a bridge. Apply sufficient pressure to the retainer to relieve the pressure of the retainer against the snap ring. Using a small screwdriver, remove the snap ring. Then slowly release the arbor press to gradually relieve the retractor spring pressure. Remove the retractor spring retainer (H, Fig 64) and the retractor spring (G). Lift the clutch friction disc plates (E), discs (F) and retractor spring plate (D) out of the drum.

To facilitate the removal of the clutch position, insert $\frac{3}{16}$" diameter rods in the grooves as shown in Fig 65. The rods will permit the piston seal to slip past the circular grooves inside the drum. Lift the piston out of the drum. An alternative method can be used to remove the clutch piston. Using a .015" feeler stock 15" long and 2" wide, place the feeler stock around the inside of the drum. Lift the piston slightly, then making sure that feeler stock is at the bottom of the bore and completely surrounding the piston, remove the piston from the drum. To remove the piston inner seal (B, Fig 64) squeeze the seal to one side, pick it out of the groove, then pull the seal completely out of the groove and remove it from the drum.

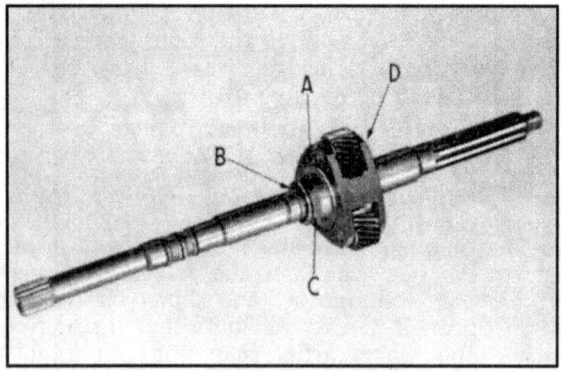

Fig 61.—Rear planetary carrier.
A. Rear ring gear thrust washer.   C. Oil seal ring retainer.
B. Snap ring.   D. Rear planetary carrier.

The bushing of the low brake drum is not serviced separately but it is available only as part of the low brake drum assembly.

Inspection:

Inspect all carriers, pinion ring gear and sun gear teeth for wear or damage. If any part of the gear set (planetary carrier, and pinions ring gear and sun gear) is damaged, the entire gear set must be replaced. The planetary carrier, ring gear and sun gear are available only in matched sets.

Inspect all bushing and mating surfaces for wear or scoring.

Inspect oil seal rings for wear or damage.

Inspect the thrust washers for wear or scoring.

Inspect the free wheel unit sprags for wear.

Inspect the lining of the multiple disc clutch friction discs.

Check the multiple disc clutch friction disc plates for dishing. Place the plate on a flat surface and, using a feeler gauge, check the clearance at the inner diameter of the plate. If the dish is more than .010", the plate must be replaced.

NOTE: See also 2:58 (Multiple disc clutch plates)

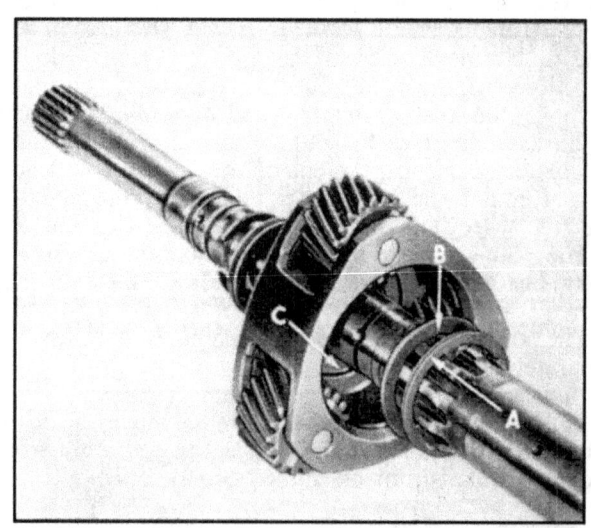

Fig 62.—Rear planetary carrier (cast type).
A. Thrust washer.   B. Washer (cast type carrier).   C. Counterbore.

Inspect the brake drums for scoring.

Make sure that the check valve in the multiple disc clutch cylinder is free.

Reassembling:

Apply Type A automatic transmission fluid to a new clutch piston inner seal. Hold the seal so that the lip of the seal is toward the drum. Stretch the seal just enough to slip it over the sun gear and place it in the groove.

Apply Type A automatic transmission fluid to the inside of the low brake drum and the multiple disc clutch piston ring. Instal ring in ring groove of the clutch piston. Place the $\frac{3}{16}$" rods in the grooves of the drum as during the piston removal. Compress the clutch piston ring and slip the piston into the drum. If the alterna-

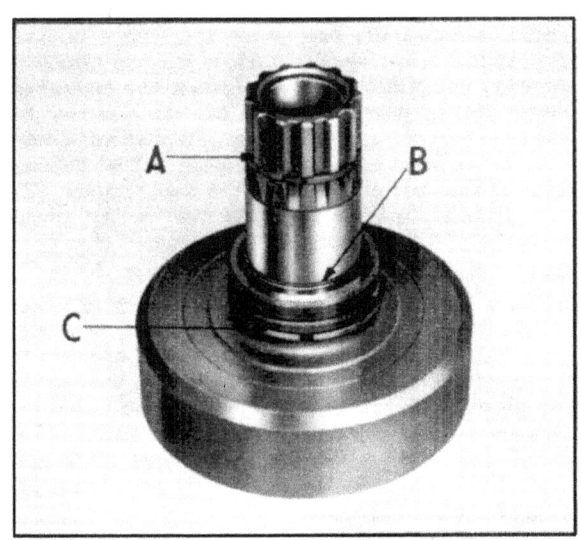

Fig 63.—Rear ring gear.

A. Front planetary carrier snap ring.
B. Outer "O" ring.
C. Oil seal ring.

tive method was used to remove the piston, place the feeler stock around the inside of the drum. Then compress the ring by slipping the piston within the sleeve formed by the feeler stock. Make sure the feeler stock is at the bottom of the bore and push the piston down into position.

Slip the multiple disc clutch retractor spring plate into the drum with the spring recesses up. Then, apply Type A automatic transmission fluid to the clutch friction plates and discs. Starting with the friction plate, place the plates and discs alternatively in the drum. Since the lugs are not evenly spaced, make sure that the lugs of the plates are in the same grooves with the master lugs of the retractor spring plate. The friction plates are dished and may be installed with the dish either to the front or rear, but all plates must have the dish in the same direction. Centre the discs around the sun gear and align the teeth of the discs.

Place the twelve springs in the grooves as indicated in Fig 66. Place the retractor spring retainer over the springs. Then, using an arbor press and the wood blocks as during the dismantling, compress the springs so that the retainer is just below the snap ring groove in the drum. Install the snap ring, making sure it is fully seated in the groove. Remove the assembly from the press.

Apply Type A automatic transmission fluid to the rear ring gear inner and outer O-ring seals and instal the seals. Do not stretch the outer seal any more than is necessary to slip the seal over the ring gear shaft. If the ring gear oil seal ring and the front planetary carrier snap ring have been removed, use a pair of snap ring pliers and instal the parts on the ring gear shaft.

Apply a coat of petroleum jelly to the oil seal ring and the outer O-ring seal and instal the rear ring gear in the low brake drum.

Place a rear planetary carrier thrust washer on the main shaft with the steel face of the washer to the front of the shaft and engage the washer with the splines of the shaft. Slip the rear planetary carrier on the front end of the main shaft, engage the splines and seat the carrier against the shoulder on the splines. Instal the planetary carrier oil seal ring in the retainer and slip the retainer on the main shaft. Place the assembly in an arbor press and press the shaft into the seal container.

Care must be taken to press on the inner portion of the retainer to prevent damage to the ring lands and binding of the ring. Ensure the ring is free in the groove. Instal the retainer snap ring.

Place the rear ring gear thrust washer over the shaft and on to the rear planetary carrier with the steel

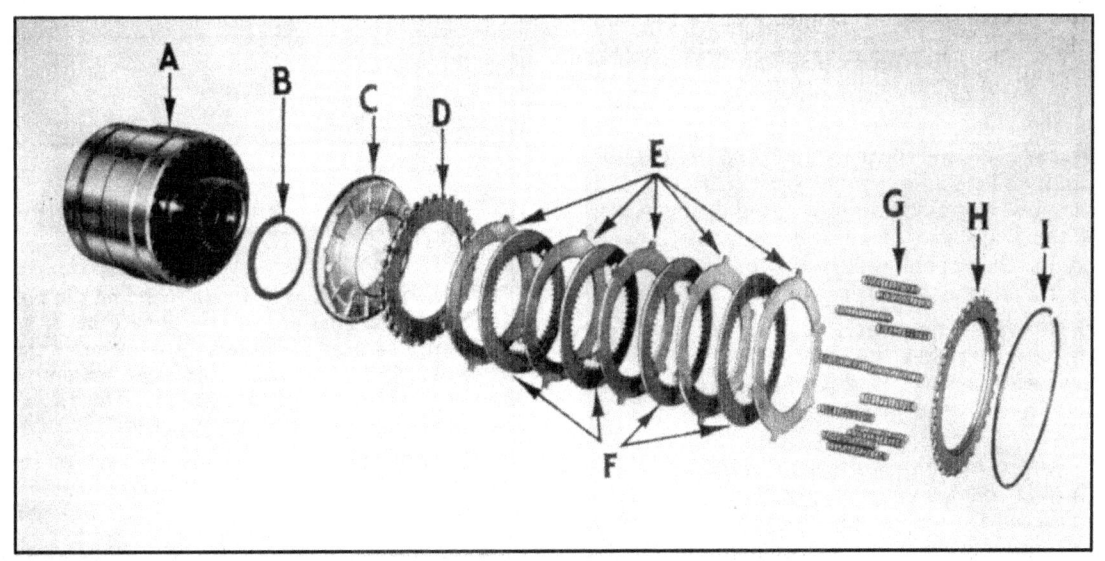

Fig 64.—Multiple disc clutch—exploded view.

A. Low brake drum.
B. Piston inner seal.
C. Clutch piston.
D. Retractor spring plate.
E. Friction disc plates.
F. Friction discs.
G. Retractor springs.
H. Retractor spring retainer.
I. Snap ring.

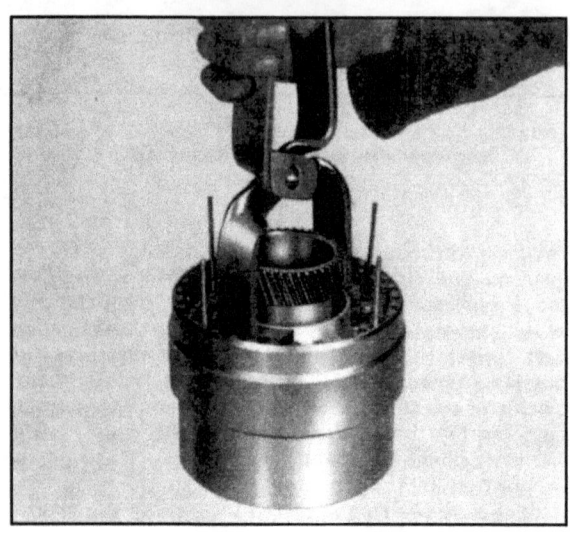

Fig 65.—Removing the clutch piston.

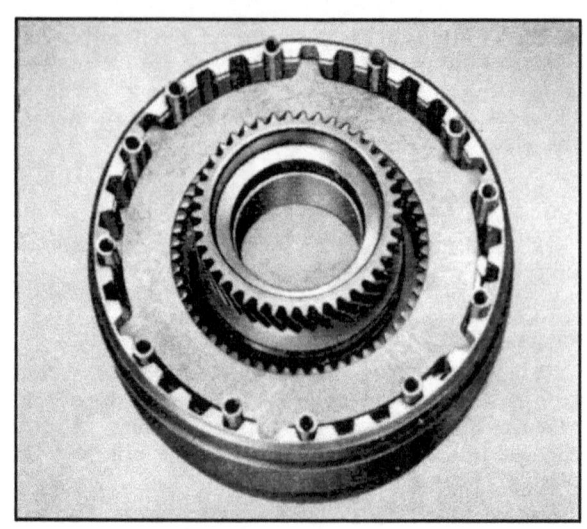

Fig 66.—Retractor springs in correct locations.

face of the washer against the carrier. Apply a light coat of petroleum jelly to the washer to hold it in place.

Instal the main shaft-and-rear carrier assembly in the rear ring gear and low brake drum assembly.

Instal the reverse free wheel unit in the low brake drum plate (see Fig 67) **ensuring that the side of the free wheel cage marked with arrows is upwards.** Then, instal the unit snap ring in the groove.

NOTE: See also 2:53 (Free wheel units)

Lubricate the rear sun gear bushings and the outside of the rear sun gear with Type A automatic transmission fluid and instal the sun gear on the shaft.

Place the low brake drum plate assembly over the end of the sun gear with the flat side of the plate toward the drum. Tilt the assembly slightly and slip the free wheel sprags down over the edge of the sun gear on one side. Then, with a small screwdriver, move each sprag outward slipping it over the edge of the gear and at the same time holding the free wheel unit against the sun gear. After all of the sprags are outside the edge of the gear, rotate the unit anti-clockwise and slide the assembly down on the sun gear. Seat the low brake drum plate in the drum. Align the slots of the plate and drum and place the dowels in position in the openings. Instal the snap ring making sure the ring is seated securely in the groove.

Place the forward free wheel unit in the forward brake drum, **ensuring that the side of the free wheel cage marked with arrows is downward.** Then instal the unit snap ring in the groove.

NOTE: If, on transmissions with serial numbers J0001 to J0233 inclusive, it is required to replace either the forward free wheel unit Part Number J20-389A or the forward free wheel unit and brake drum assembly Part Number J20-394A, a complete forward free wheel unit and brake drum assembly Part Number J20-394 and a spacer Part Number J20-375 must be fitted.

Place the forward brake drum assembly over the rear sun gear. Tilt the assembly slightly and slip the free wheel sprags down over the edge of the sun gear at one side. Then, with a small screwdriver, move each sprag outward slipping it over the edge of the gear and at the same time holding the free wheel unit against the sun gear. After all of the sprags are outside the edge of the gear, rotate the unit clockwise and slide the assembly down on the sun gear.

Slip the rear sun gear thrust washer on the shaft with the bronze face of the washer towards the sun gear and place it on the rear face of the gear. Instal the washer retainer.

Insert the free wheel unit spacer dowel (B, Fig 58) in the hub of the forward brake drum and position the spacer (A) within the drum. Then instal the spacer snap ring securely in the groove of the hub.

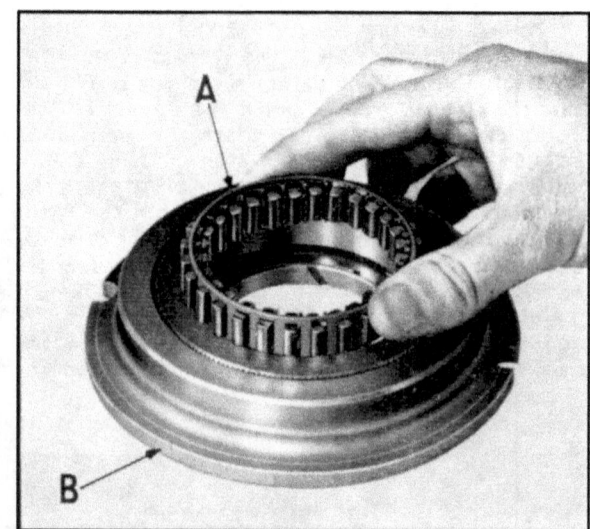

Fig 67.—Installing the reverse free wheel unit in the low brake drum plate.
A. Free wheel unit. B. Low brake drum plate.

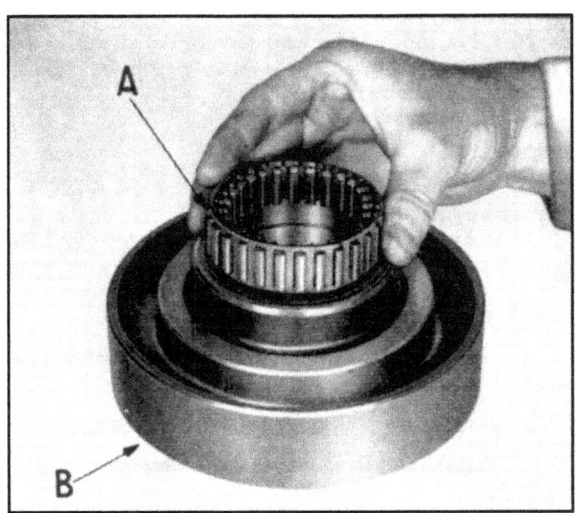

Fig 68.—Installing the forward free wheel unit in the forward brake drum.

A. Free wheel unit. B. Forward brake drum.

Instal the rear bearing spacer on the main shaft. Slip the bearing on to the shaft and by means of a piece of tubing instal the bearing.

Align the splines of the front planetary carrier and reverse brake drum and, using an arbor press, press the carrier into the drum. Instal the snap ring, being careful not to distort the ring.

Coat the front sun gear thrust washer with petroleum jelly and instal the washer within the front planetary carrier hub with the tangs in the slots and with the steel face against the hub.

Instal the reverse drum-and-front planetary carrier assembly. After engaging the carrier splines with the rear ring gear splines, it may be necessary to turn the assembly to engage the clutch friction disc teeth. Do not force the assembly into position as this may result in damage to the disc teeth.

Apply petroleum jelly to the front ring gear rear thrust washer and place it in position on the rear ring gear shaft splines with the steel face of the washer against the front planetary carrier.

If the front ring gear or main shaft oil seal rings have been removed, instal the new rings. Spread the ring just enough to permit slipping it over the shaft and instal it in the groove. Hold the ring tight in the groove at one side and press against the lower part of the ring at the other side. This will cause the end of the ring to lift. Then slide the finger toward the end of the ring and lock the ends of the ring together.

Coat the main shaft oil seal rings with petroleum jelly and instal the front ring gear.

Main Shaft Oil Transfer Tube

Removal:

Remove the transmission.

Slip the oil transfer tube out of the end of the main shaft. (See Fig 18.) If the tube does not come out with the transmission, use long nose pliers or snap ring pliers and remove it from the torque converter assembly.

Installation:

Slip the oil transfer tube into the end of the main shaft (see Fig 18).

Instal the transmission.

1:42 BRAKE BANDS

Removal:

Remove the transmission.

Remove the main shaft assembly.

Remove the brake anchor side strut (B, Fig 70) from the forward brake band (C) by pulling the band shoe away from the adjustment screw (A), disengaging the pin from the notch in the strut, and then removing the strut from the end of the adjustment screw. Disengage the other end of the band from the piston strut (D), lift the band out of the band guide, and move the band to the rear of the transmission case.

Disengage the low brake band in the same manner as the forward band and move it also to the rear of the case.

Back off the reverse band shoe from the piston strut, turn the band 90 degrees, spread it slightly, and slip the end of the band out of the case over the flange as shown in Fig 71. Then roll the top of the band forward out of the case. Care should be taken not to distort the band during the removal.

Remove the low and the forward bands in the same manner as the reverse band.

Ensure that the interior of the transmission case is clean.

Inspect the band linings for wear and the bands and shoes for damage.

Inspect the band guide strap and retaining rivets to make sure the guide is tight in the case and all rivets are tight.

Fig 69.—Brake band locations.

A. Forward brake band. B. Low brake band.
C. Reverse brake band.

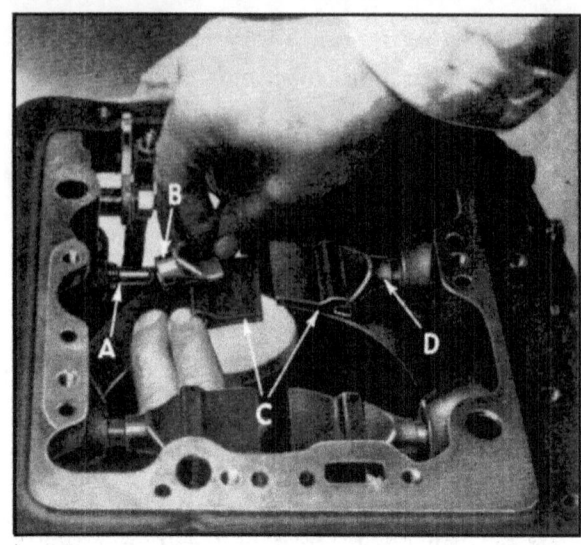

Fig 70.—Removing and fitting the brake bands.

A. Adjustment screw.
B. Anchor side strut.
C. Forward brake band.
D. Piston strut.

Fig 71.—Removing the brake bands from the transmission casing.

Installation:

The low and the forward bands are lighter than the reverse band and are interchangeable. **Do not under any circumstances interchange the reverse band with the low or forward bands.** Select one of the lighter bands. Slip one end of the band over the flange as during the band removal. Roll the top of the band into the case. Then turn the band so that the end of the band which has the offset pin is toward the low and forward piston side of the case. Then move the band to the rear of the case.

Instal the other band in the same manner as the first band and move it also to the rear of the case.

Instal the reverse band in the same manner as the other two bands except that the band is turned so that the end of the band which has the offset pin is toward the reverse piston strut.

All three bands are placed into position as follows: Set the band into the band guide strap at the top of the case. Engage the band on the piston side with the piston strut, making sure the pin is in the notch of the strut. Pull the shoes of the band together, without disengaging the piston strut, and slip the anchor side strut on the end of the adjustment screw. Then release the band and allow the shoe to engage the anchor side strut.

Ensure that the pins of all the band shoes properly engage the notches of their respective struts and that the bands are properly positioned in the guide strap.

Inspect and instal the main shaft assembly as outlined under Main Shaft Assembly.

Adjust the bands as outlined in "Service Adjustments." Instal the transmission.

Brake Anchor Side Strut

Removal:

Drain the oil from the transmission unit only.

Remove the oil pan setscrews and remove the oil pan and gasket.

Remove the valve block assembly.

All three brake anchor side struts are removed in the same manner. Loosen the band adjustment screw lock nut. Hold the shoes of the band together, being careful not to disengage the band from the piston strut, and back off the adjustment screw until the strut can be slipped off the screw and past the brake band shoe.

Installation:

All three brake anchor side struts are installed in the same manner. Hold the ends of the band together and slip the strut over the end of the adjustment screw. Screw in the adjustment and make sure that all struts are properly seated in the ends of the bands.

Adjust the brake bands as outlined in the "Service Adjustments".

Inspect and instal the valve block assembly as outlined under Valve Block Assembly.

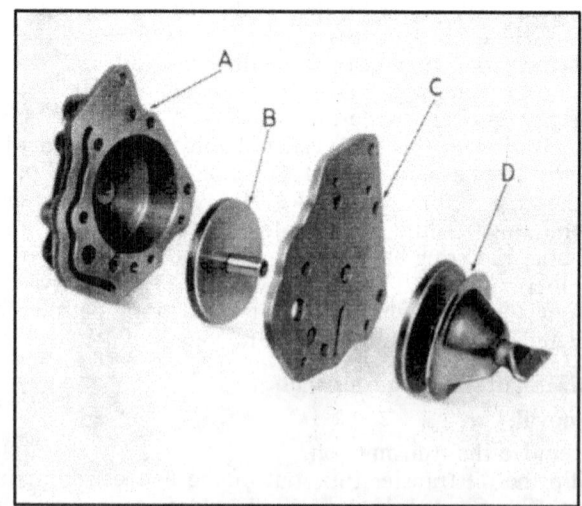

Fig 72.—Exploded view of the reverse servo unit.

A. Servo cylinder and gasket.
B. Outer piston.
C. Cylinder plate.
D. Inner piston.

Instal a new oil pan gasket, and instal the oil pan and retaining screws. Tighten the setscrews to 10 to 13 ft/lb torque.

Follow the recommended procedure outlined in "Maintenance" and fill the transmission with Type A automatic transmission fluid to the correct level.

1:43 REVERSE SERVO UNIT

The reverse servo unit is located on the left side of the transmission case and consists primarily of two pistons (see Fig 72). The pistons, actuated by oil pressure, control the operation of the reverse brake band. Two pistons are used to acquire smooth engagement of the brake band; the inner piston actuated by unrestricted oil pressure and the outer piston receiving oil pressure regulated by the reverse shuttle valve.

Reverse Brake Cylinder
Removal:

Remove the transmission.

While holding the low band adjustment screw, loosen and remove the adjustment screw lock nut (B, Fig 73). Remove the six retaining setscrews.

Remove the reverse brake cylinder and plate as an assembly from the case, being careful not to damage the threads of the low band adjustment screw. Remove the cylinder inner gasket (A, Fig 73) from the transmission case.

NOTE: Care should be taken to prevent the inner brake piston from coming out of the bore of the case. If it does, the oil pan and valve block must be removed and the inner piston reinstalled as outlined under Reverse Brake Inner Piston.

Dismantling:

Separate the reverse brake cylinder plate from the cylinder, lift the plate off the piston rod, and remove it from the cylinder. Remove the reverse brake cylinder outer gasket from the plate.

Fig 73.—Reverse servo inner gasket in position.

A. Gasket.   B. Low band adjustment screw.

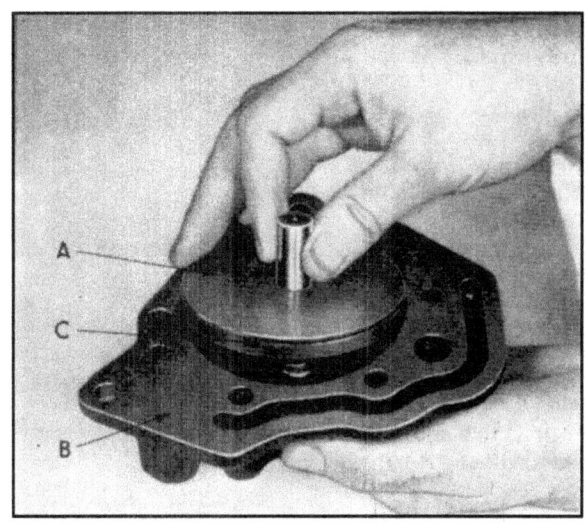

Fig 74.—Installing the outer piston in the reverse cylinder.

A. Outer piston.   B. Reverse brake cylinder.   C. Piston seal.

Grasp the reverse brake outer piston rod and pull the piston out of the cylinder.

Use a pointed tool or stiff piece of wire and pick the O-ring seal out of the groove in the plate. Discard the seal.

Clean all the parts thoroughly.

Check the gasket surface of the cylinder for warpage.

Make sure the cylinder plate is not warped.

Check the bore of the cylinder for pits or scoring.

Reassembling:

Lubricate a new piston seal with Type A automatic transmission fluid. Slip the edge of the seal into the groove of the piston at one point, making sure the lip of the seal is toward the outer face of the piston away from the piston rod. Then work progressively around the piston and seat the seal in the groove. Avoid stretching the seal any more than is necessary to instal it on the piston.

Lubricate a new O-ring seal with Type A automatic transmission fluid. Then instal the seal in the groove of the cylinder plate.

Holding the piston (A, Fig 74) at an angle, insert it in the cylinder (B), being careful not to damage the lip of the seal. After all of the piston is below the bottom edge of the cylinder, straighten the piston and push it into the cylinder.

Apply a thin coat of petroleum jelly to the machined surface of the reverse cylinder and place a new outer gasket on the cylinder (B), making sure that the holes of the gasket and cylinder are aligned.

Carefully slip the cylinder plate (C, Fig 72) over the rod of the outer piston (B) and position the plate on the cylinder.

Installation:

Apply a thin coat of petroleum jelly to the transmission case and place a new cylinder inner gasket (A, Fig 73) in position on the case.

Slip the reverse cylinder assembly over the low band adjustment screw (B). Position it on the case, and instal the retaining screws. Tighten the three 5/16" x 2¼" setscrews to 15 to 18 ft/lb torque and the remaining screws to 10 to 13 ft/lb torque.

Instal the low band adjustment screw lock nut.

Check the adjustment of the band and adjust, if necessary.

Recheck the tightening torque of the reverse cylinder retaining screws.

Instal the transmission unit.

Reverse Brake Cylinder Plate
Removal and Installation:

Follow the entire procedure outlined under reverse Brake Cylinder-Removal, and Installation.

Reverse Brake Outer Piston
Removal and Installation:

Follow the entire procedure outlined under Reverse Brake Cylinder — Removal and Installation.

Reverse Brake Inner Piston Assembly
Removal:

Remove the reverse brake cylinder assembly.

Remove the valve block assembly.

To remove the inner piston assembly from the transmission, first place the thumb against the piston spring retainer and the fingers on top of the piston. Then, with the thumb, push the assembly outward, disengaging the strut from the brake band shoe and remove the piston assembly from the case.

Mark the outer face of the inner piston to identify its location.

Lift the piston seal out of the groove of the piston. Then bring it over the top of the piston and pull it the rest of the way out of the groove. Discard the seal.

Dismantling:

Compress the piston spring by pushing the spring retainer toward the piston, and then remove the strut retaining pin and remove the strut from the piston rod. Slip the spring retainer and spring off the piston rod.

Some piston assemblies have the strut pressed on to the piston rod. This type should not be dismantled.

Clean the piston assembly thoroughly.

Check the bore of the case for pits or scoring.

If the piston assembly is not dismantled, check the spring to make sure it is not broken and make sure that the strut retaining pin is tight.

Reassembling:

Place the piston spring and spring retainer on the piston rod. Compress the spring, slip the strut over the end of the piston rod, align the holes of the strut and rod, and instal the strut retaining pin.

Installation:

Lubricate a new piston seal with Type A automatic transmission fluid. Slip the edge of the seal into the groove of the piston at one point, making sure the lip of the seal is toward the outer face of the piston away from the piston rod. Then work progressively around the piston and seat the seal in the groove. Avoid stretching the seal any more than is necessary to instal it on the piston.

Hold the piston assembly so that the offset notch of the strut is to the rear and insert the assembly in the bore of the case. Align the notch in the strut with the pin in the brake band shoe. Push the assembly into the bore, being careful not to turn the seal over or damage the lip of the seal.

Instal the reverse brake cylinder and valve block assembly.

Instal a new oil pan gasket and instal the oil pan and setscrews. Tighten the screws to 10 to 13 ft/lb torque.

Instal the transmission.

Reverse Shuttle Valve Assembly
NOTE: See also 2:48
Removal:

Place a clean pan under the reverse brake cylinder to catch the fluid as the shuttle valve assembly is removed. Unscrew the three setscrews indicated by the arrows in Fig 75 and remove the reverse shuttle valve assembly from the reverse brake cylinder.

Remove the shuttle valve assembly gasket from the reverse brake cylinder.

Inspect the shuttle valve (see Fig 76) and make sure that it is not stuck open. Inset of Fig 76 shows the valve in the open position.

Installation:

Apply a thin coat of petroleum jelly to the reverse brake cylinder and position a new shuttle valve gasket on the cylinder.

Place the shuttle valve assembly on the cylinder and instal the retaining screws. Tighten the 5/16" setscrew to 10 to 13 ft/lb torque and the two ¼" setscrews to 6 to 8 ft/lb torque.

Refill the transmission.

Fig 75.—Reverse shuttle valve location.

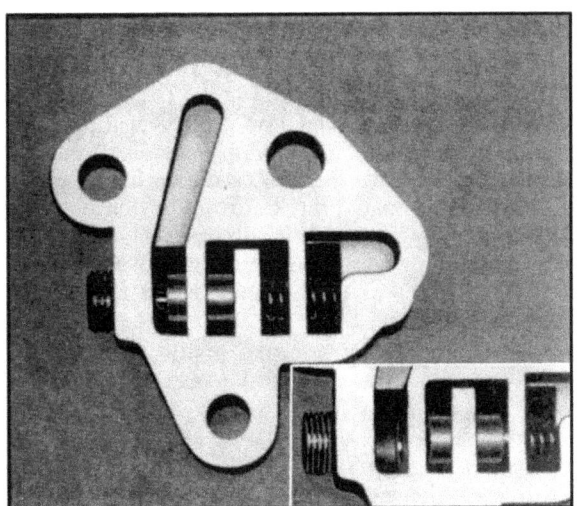

Fig 76.—The reverse shuttle valve.

1:44 LOW AND FORWARD SERVO UNITS

The low and forward servo units are located on the right side of the transmission case and control the operation of the low and forward brake bands.

NOTE: See also 2:53

Low Brake Cylinder
Removal:

Remove the dirt from the right side of the transmission.

While holding the reverse band adjustment screw, loosen and remove the lock nut (A, Fig 6).

Remove the low brake cylinder setscrews indicated by arrows in Fig 6.

Remove the low brake cylinder and plate from the case, being careful not to damage the threads of the reverse band adjustment screw. Remove the cylinder inner gasket from the transmission case.

NOTE: Care should be taken to allow the forward brake piston or the low inner brake piston to come out of the case. If either piston comes out, the oil pan and valve block must be removed.

Dismantling:

Separate the low brake cylinder plate from the cylinder, lift the plate off the piston rod, and remove the plate from the cylinder. Remove the low brake cylinder outer gasket from the plate.

Grasp the low brake outer piston rod and pull the piston out of the cylinder.

Use a pointed tool or stiff piece of wire and pick the O-ring seal out of the groove in the plate. Discard the seal.

Lift the piston seal out of the groove of the piston. Then bring it over the top of the piston and pull it the rest of the way out of the groove. Discard the seal.

Clean the parts thoroughly.

Check the gasket surface of the cylinder for warpage.

Make sure that the cylinder plate is not warped.

Check the bore of the cylinder for pits or scoring.

Reassembling:

Lubricate a new piston seal with Type A automatic transmission fluid. Slip the edge of the seal into the groove of the piston at one point, making sure the lip of the seal is toward the outer face of the piston. Then work progressively around the piston and seat the seal in the groove. Avoid stretching the seal any more than is necessary to instal it on the piston.

Lubricate a new O-ring seal with Type A automatic transmission fluid. Then instal the seal in the groove.

Holding the piston (B, Fig 78) at an angle, insert it in the cylinder, being careful not to damage the lip of the seal. After all of the piston is below the edge of the bore, straighten the piston and push it into the cylinder.

Apply a thin coat of petroleum jelly to the machined surface of the low cylinder and place a new outer

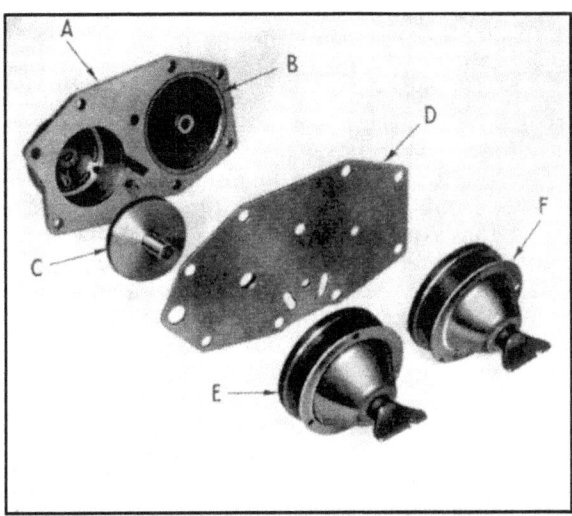

Fig 77.—Low and forward servo units.

A. Brake cylinder.
B. Outer gasket.
C. Low outer piston.
D. Cylinder plate.
E. Low inner piston.
F. Forward piston.

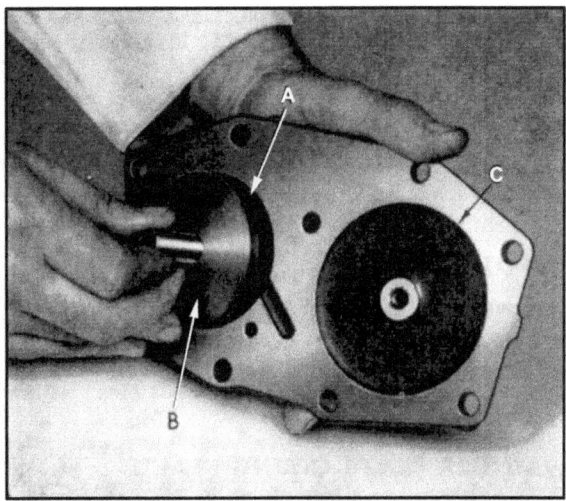

Fig 78.—Installing the outer piston.

A. Piston seal.   B. Low outer piston.
C. Low and forward brake cylinder.

gasket (B, Fig 77) in position on the cylinder making sure that the holes of the gasket and cylinder are aligned.

Lubricate the O-ring of the plate with Type A automatic transmission fluid. Then carefully slip the cylinder plate (D) over the rod of the outer piston (C) and position the plate on the cylinder.

Installation:

Apply a thin coat of petroleum jelly to the transmission case and place a new brake cylinder inner gasket in position on the case, making certain that the holes of the gasket and the case are aligned.

Slip the low brake cylinder assembly over the reverse band adjustment screw, position it on the case, and instal the retaining screws. Tighten the setscrews to 15 to 18 ft/lbs torque.

Instal the reverse band adjustment screw lock nut. (A, Fig 6.)

Adjust the bands as outlined in the "Service Adjustments" section.

Recheck the tightening torque of the cylinder retaining screws.

Low Brake Cylinder Plate
Removal and Installation:

Follow the entire procedure outlined under Low Brake Cylinder.

Low Brake Outer Piston
Removal and Installation:

Follow the entire procedure outlined under Low Brake Cylinder.

Low and Forward Brake Pistons
Removal:

Drain the fluid from the transmission unit only.
Remove the oil pan setscrews and remove the oil pan and gasket.
Remove the valve block.

Remove the low brake cylinder.
Mark the outer face of the pistons to identify their location.

To remove the inner low brake piston from the transmission, place the thumb against the piston spring retainer (A, Fig 79) and the fingers over the top of the piston to prevent dropping the assembly as it is removed. Then, with the thumb, push the assembly outward, disengaging the strut (B) from the brake band shoe (C) and remove the piston assembly from the case.

Remove the forward brake piston assembly in the same manner as the low brake piston assembly.

The seals are removed from both pistons in the same manner. Lift the seal out of the groove of the piston. Then bring it over the top of the piston and pull the seal the rest of the way out of the groove.

Discard the seals.

Dismantling:

Compress the piston spring by pushing the spring retainer toward the piston and remove the strut retaining pin and remove the strut from the piston rod. Slip the spring retainer and spring off the piston rod.

Some piston assemblies have the strut pressed on to the piston rod. This type should not be dismantled.

Clean the piston thoroughly.
Check the spring to make sure it is not broken.
Make sure that the strut retaining pin is tight.
Check the bores of the case for pits or scoring.

Reassembly:

Place the piston spring and spring retainer on the piston rod. Compress the spring, slip the strut over the end of the piston rod, align the holes of the strut and rod, instal the strut retaining pin.

Installation:

The installation procedure of the seals is the same for both pistons. Lubricate a new piston seal with Type A automatic transmission fluid. Slip the edge of the seal into the groove of the piston at one point, making sure that the lip of the seal is toward the outerface of the piston away from the rod. Then work progressively around the piston and seat the seal in the groove. Avoid stretching the seal any more than is necessary to instal it on the piston.

Both pistons are installed in the same manner. Hold the piston assembly so that the offset notch of the strut is to the front and insert the assembly in the bore of the case. Align the notch in the strut with the pin in the brake band shoe. Push the assembly into the bore, being careful not to turn the seal over or damage the lip of the seal.

Ensure that all brake band struts are properly engaged with the brake band shoes.

Inspect and instal the low brake cylinder.
Inspect and instal the valve block assembly.
Use a new oil pan gasket and instal the oil pan. Tighten the setscrews to 10 to 13 ft/lb torque.

Follow the recommended procedure outlined in "Maintenance", fill the transmission with Type A automatic transmission fluid to the correct level.

Fig 79.—Removing the inner low brake piston.
A. Piston spring retainer.   B. Piston strut.
C. Low brake band shoe.

Piston Seal
Removal and Installation:
Refer to the removal and installation procedure of the piston involved.

Cylinder Plate O-Ring Seal
Removal and Installation:
Refer to the removal and installation procedure of the cylinder plate involved.

1:45 MISCELLANEOUS

Selector Control Shaft and Lever
Removal:
Drain the fluid from the transmission unit only.
Remove the oil pan setscrews and remove the oil pan and gasket.
Disconnect the control rod from the selector valve lever (E, Fig 80).
Remove the nut (A), washers (B), which secure the selector control shaft inner lever (C) to the selector shaft (D).
Pull the shaft assembly outward and slip the selector control shaft inner lever off the shaft, then pull the shaft assembly out of the case.
Remove the cork packing from the transmission case.
Remove the O-ring seal from the groove in the selector shaft and then remove the flat washer from the shaft.
Clean the lever shaft and transmission bore.
Check the shaft and bore for roughness.
Ensure that the lever is tight on the shaft.

Installation:
With a screwdriver, blunt the leading edge of the selector shaft bore at the base of the packing gasket counterbore to prevent scuffing the O-ring seal during installation. Thoroughly clean the selector shaft bore and lubricate the bore with type A automatic transmission fluid.
Place a new cork packing in the counterbore.
Instal the flat washer on the selector control shaft. Lubricate the shaft and new O-ring seal with Type A automatic transmission fluid and instal the seal in the groove of the selector control shaft.
With a twisting motion, instal the selector control shaft into the transmission case. Turn the selector control shaft outer lever so that it points toward the top of the transmission. Align the flats of the selector shaft and selector control shaft inner lever and instal the lever on the shaft. Ensure that the inner lever (C, Fig 80) is in the slot of the selector valve (F) as shown in Fig 80.
Instal the washers (B), and nut (A) and tighten the nut securely.
Manually check for proper operation of the shaft and selector valve.
Connect the control rod to the selector valve lever.
Use a new oil pan gasket and instal the oil pan. Tighten the setscrews to 10 to 13 ft/lb torque.
Following the recommended procedure outlined in "Maintenance", fill the transmission with Type A automatic transmission fluid to the correct level.
Check, and adjust if necessary, the manual selector linkage and the accelerator to governor lever linkage.

Selector Control Shaft O-Ring Seal
NOTE: See also 2:53
Removal and Installation:
Follow the procedure outlined under Selector Control Shaft and Lever.

Selector Control Shaft Cork Packing
Removal and Installation:
Follow the procedure outlined under Selector Control Shaft and Lever.

Parking Brake Actuating Rod Assembly
Removal:
Before the parking brake actuating rod assembly can be removed from the case, the main shaft assembly must be removed as outlined under Main Shaft Assembly — Removal.
Remove the snap ring from the toggle shaft sleeve (A, Fig 34).
Remove the nut, washer and flat washer which hold the selector control shaft inner lever to the selector shaft. (See Fig 80.)
Disengage the forward band from the struts and move it forward. Remove the inner lever from the selector shaft, slip the toggle shaft sleeve out of the case, and thread the assembly out of the case.

Installation:
Insert the toggle shaft sleeve in case, align the flats of the selector shaft and the inner lever and instal the inner lever on the shaft. Make certain that the lever is in the slot of the selector valve.

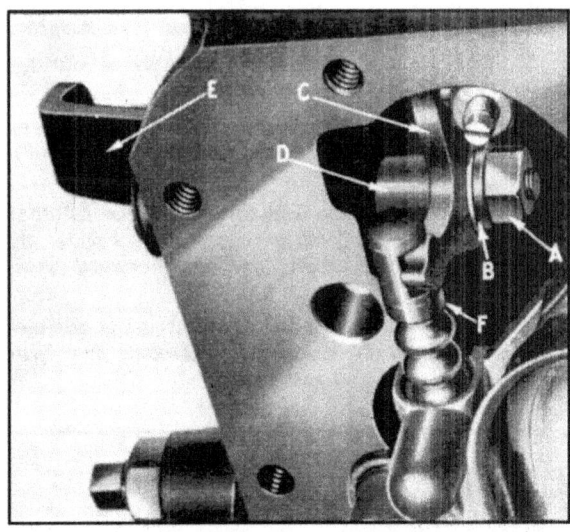

Fig 80.—Selector control shaft and lever.

A. Nut.
B. Washer.
C. Inner lever.
D. Selector shaft.
E. Selector valve lever.
F. Selector valve.

Instal the flat washer, lock washer, and nut on the shaft and tighten the nut securely.

Instal the snap ring on the toggle shaft sleeve.

Instal the forward brake band in position in the struts and the band guide.

Instal the main shaft assembly as outlined under Main Shaft Assembly — Installation.

Check the adjustment of the parking brake pawl and adjust if necessary as outlined under Parking Brake Pawl — Adjustment in the "Service Adjustments".

Transmission Case

Removal:

Remove the transmission.
   Remove the governor extension case.
   Remove the front pump-and-collector ring assembly.
   Remove the oil pan and valve block assembly.
   Remove the main shaft assembly.
   Remove the reverse brake cylinder and reverse brake inner piston.
   Remove the low and forward brake cylinder. Remove the low and forward pistons. Follow the procedure outlined under Low and Forward Servo Units.
   Remove the brake bands and struts as outlined under Brake Band — Removal. Remove the band adjustment screws and lock nuts.

Clean all parts removed from the old transmission case and thoroughly inspect the parts as outlined in the Inspection section of the part involved.

Clean the new transmission case thoroughly and make sure that all oil passages are open (see Fig 81). Check the operation of the parking brake actuating rod and toggle arm lever assembly to ensure it operates freely.

Installation:

Instal the band adjustment screws. Instal the brake bands and struts.

Instal the low and forward pistons. Instal the low and forward brake cylinder. Follow the procedure outlined under Low and Forward Servo Unit.

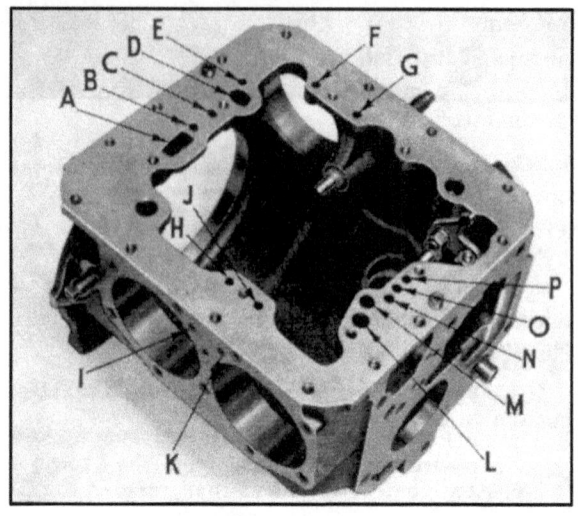

Fig 81.—Transmission case oil passages.
A. Front pump intake.
B. Multiple disc clutch.
C. Direct drive.
D. Front pump pressure.
E. Converter pressure.
F. Reverse pressure.
G. Pressure dome.
H. Low band servo.
I. Low band servo.
J. Forward band servo.
K. Forward band servo.
L. Rear pump intake.
M. Rear pump pressure.
N. Governor feed.
O. Multiple disc clutch.
P. Direct drive.

Instal the reverse brake piston and reverse brake cylinder.

Instal the main shaft assembly.

Instal the valve block assembly and oil pan.

Instal the extension case.

Instal the front pump-and-collector ring assembly.

Make the complete band adjustment, following the procedure outlined in "Service Adjustments".

Instal the transmission assembly.

Following the recommended procedure outlined in "Maintenance", fill the transmission with Type A automatic transmission fluid to the correct level.

Check, and adjust if necessary, the accelerator-to-governor lever linkage and the manual selector linkage.

NOTES

NOTES

INDEX – AUTOMATIC GEARBOX – PART 2

SECTION	PAGE	
		PART 2 - MODIFICATIONS TO THE AUTOMATIC GEARBOX
046	157	Elimination of Direct Drive Pawl (MK VII from Chassis 736871)
047-052	157-159	First Speed Start (FSS) Transmission (From Transmission J2426)
053	160	Servicing the FSS Transmission (Dismantling & Reassembly)
054-057	162-168	New Hydraulic System (NHS)(From Transmission J3001)
058	168	Servicing the NHS Transmission (Dismantling & Reassembly)
059	172	Modified Torque Converter Mounting (MK VII from Engine N3482 and XK140 from Engine G6615)
060	172	Split Parking Brake Rod (From Transmission 5011)
061	173	Intermediate Speed Hold (From introduction of MK VII & XK150)
062	175	Reverse Light & Starter Cut Out Switch Adjustment (All XK150)
063	176	Modification to Relay Valve (MK VII from Engine NA1938, XK150 from Engine V3208 & from introduction of MK IX)
064	176	Fault Diagnosis Chart (Faults, Causes & Remedies)
065	179	Service Tools
066	180	Torque Settings

AUTOMATIC GEARBOX - SERVICE
PART 2

This section is applicable to the later Mark 7, Mark 8, Mark 9 and XK models as it covers the changes and modifications that were subsequently made to the Borg Warner automatic gearbox. It is intended to be used in conjunction with PART 1, as the changes are cross referenced in the text such that the information contained in both PART 1 and PART 2 (when combined) cover the relevant service and repair information for all Mark and XK series of Jaguars that were equipped with automatic gearboxes.

2:46 ELIMINATION OF DIRECT DRIVE PAWL
(Effective from Mark VII Model, Chassis No 736871.)

With effect from the above chassis number the direct drive pawl is not fitted to the extension case assembly.

This modification has the effect of:—

(A) Allowing a downshift from direct drive to intermediate gear to be made at speeds below approximately 45 mph under conditions of heavy acceleration short of "kickdown". At speeds between 45 mph and 60 mph it is still necessary to depress the accelerator beyond normal travel to effect a "kickdown" change into intermediate gear.

(B) Automatically down-shifting from direct drive to intermediate gear when hill climbing on full throttle if the car speed drops below 45 mph.

The elimination of the direct drive pawl affects the Driving Instructions as follows:—

Additional Power and Acceleration
Refer to 1:12

(A) Below 45 mph depress the accelerator pedal to the full throttle position to effect a change into the intermediate range; the drive will continue in the intermediate range until the release of the accelerator or approximately 55 mph is reached.

(B) Between 45 mph and 60 mph depress the accelerator pedal all the way to the floorboard to effect a "kickdown" change into intermediate range; the drive will continue in intermediate range until release of the accelerator or approximately 68 mph is reached.

NOTE: Transmission units on and after serial number J2426 (introduction of First Speed Start Transmission) are fitted with a Second Speed Drive Pawl (A, Fig 82) which prevents an automatic change from intermediate to low at speeds above 3 mph.

This pawl is similar in appearance to the direct drive pawl but must on no account be removed from the extension case.

2:47 FIRST SPEED START TRANSMISSION
(Effective from Transmission J2426.)

With effect from the above transmission number the transmission unit is of a modified type. Externally, this type of transmission can be identified by

(a) A double piston fitted at the forward servo cylinder.
(b) No shuttle valve fitted to the reverse servo cylinder (see Fig 75).

The main difference in operation of the automatic transmission is the incorporation of first speed (low gear) start in the D (Drive) position with an automatic change between low and intermediate gear at 10-35 mph. The upshift between intermediate and direct drive remains the same, that is, between 18-55 mph.

The normal "kickdown" downshift is still available between direct drive and intermediate gear but no "kickdown" downshift is possible between the intermediate and low gears.

The manually selected L (Low) gear is still available as an emergency engine power range as the transmission will not normally change down from intermediate to low until approximately 3 mph.

Automatic changes between the gears will take place as follows, depending on the position of the accelerator pedal:—

Upshifts	m.p.h.
Low to intermediate, light throttle	10
Low to intermediate, full throttle	35
Intermediate to direct, light throttle	18
Intermediate to direct, full throttle	55

Downshifts	
Direct to intermediate, closed throttle	12
Intermediate to low, closed throttle	3

NOTE: The hydraulic system for automatic low in D range varies from that for selected low (L position) in the following respect:—

Automatic Low (D position). The forward band only is applied.
Selected Low (L position). The low and forward bands are applied.

This feature applies only up to the introduction of the new hydraulic system, that is, up to transmission serial number J3000.

2:48 GENERAL DESCRIPTION

(Refer to 1:1)

The first speed start transmission retains all the features of the Second speed start transmission except for "Hill Holding Characteristic".

Paragraph 5 (See 1:3)
The extension case assembly is similar to that used on the previous type of transmission unit, but in place of the direct drive control assembly a second speed drive mechanism is incorporated.

Paragraph 6 (See 1:3)
The governor valve, in addition to controlling the direct drive clutch, also controls the operation of the multiple disc clutch when the control lever is in the D position.

Paragraph 8 (See 1:3)
The reverse shuttle valve is not fitted, but an orifice in the reverse servo plate provides smooth engagement of the reverse band.

2:49 OPERATION

(Refer to 1:4)

The operation of the first speed start transmission is the same as for the Second speed start transmission described in Part I, except for the D (Drive range).

D or Drive. This position provides three automatic forward drive ranges:— low, intermediate and direct.

L or Low. It is not necessary to select this position to secure rapid acceleration from a standstill; this feature is incorporated in the D range.

D or Drive Position
Low.

With the selector lever in the D position, the pressure from the front pump is regulated by the front pump relief valve and directed by the selector valve to the forward band servo and to the governor valve in the extension case.

The pressure at the forward band servo applies the forward band, locking the forward drive drum to the transmission case. The sun gear of the rear planetary set is prevented from turning opposite the engine rotation by the action of the forward drive free wheel unit.

Power flow is from the engine, through the converter to the ring gear of the front planetary set. The front ring gear acting on the planet carrier pinions tries to turn the sun gear of the front planetary set opposite to engine rotation. The front sun gear is attached to the low drum and low drum plate. This assembly tries to rotate opposite to engine rotation, but is prevented from rotating by the reverse free wheel unit in the low drum plate which locks up on the sun gear of the rear planetary set. The rear sun gear is prevented from turning opposite engine rotation by the free wheel unit through the application of the forward band.

The locking of the low drum to the rear sun gear, by the reverse free wheel unit, performs the same function, in forward motion, as obtained by application of the low band on previous type units. The gear reductions and operations of the front and rear planetary sets are the same as in previous type units in the L position. The is no effective engine braking in the D range since the lock-up of the low drum is through the reverse free wheel unit which will free wheel when the torque is reversed. Effective engine braking is available by placing the selector lever in the L position as on the previous model.

As the car speed increases, the governor moves the governor valve outward sufficiently to permit oil pressure to apply the multiple disc clutch. This locks together the planet carrier and sun gear of the front planetary set and eliminates any gear reduction in the front planetary set while operating in intermediate drive. This type of transmission operates in intermediate drive and direct drive in the same manner as on the previous model.

When the governor valve moved outward sufficiently to permit application of the multiple disc clutch, it also permitted the second speed drive pawl to drop down at the back of the governor valve fork. This pawl prevents the governor valve from moving back to automatic low drive position, under heavy acceleration or kickdown, preventing the shut off of pressure to the multiple disc clutch. Otherwise the transmission would downshift from direct drive to automatic low drive on heavy acceleration or kickdown instead of from direct drive to intermediate drive.

When the accelerator is completely released, the rocker arm will move the second speed drive pawl up and out of the lock-out position. The governor valve may then move back to automatic low position, shifting the transmission to low drive, which in turn shuts off the pressure to the multiple disc clutch. This occurs at approximately 3 mph.

Hill Holding Characteristic

This feature does not apply to the first speed start type of transmission.

The chart following shows the units that are in operation for any given selector lever position.

2:50 DRIVING INSTRUCTIONS

(Refer to 1:12)

The variations in the driving instructions for cars fitted with the first speed start transmission are as follows:—

D (Drive) provides the normal forward driving range and includes automatic shifting between all low, intermediate and direct drive ranges. Virtually all forward driving, accelerating and stopping can be done

DRIVING UNITS

	Park	Neutral	DRIVE Low	DRIVE Intermediate	DRIVE Direct	Low	Reverse
Forward Band and Servo	—	—	Applied	Applied	Applied	Applied	—
Multiple Disc Clutch	—	—	—	Applied	Applied	—	—
Low Band and Servo	—	—	—	—	—	Applied	—
Reverse Band and Servo	—	—	—	—	—	—	Applied
Direct Drive Clutch	—	—	—	—	Applied	—	—
Forward Drum Free Wheel Unit	—	—	Locked	Locked	Free	Locked	‡Locked
Low Drum (Reverse) Free Wheel Unit	—	—	Locked	Free	*Locked	†Free	Locked
Parking Pawl	Locked	—	—	—	—	—	—

*Forward drum being driven in reverse — band not applied.
†Will lock up should low band slip.
‡Free wheels on coast and locked on drive.

with the lever in the D position. Once the engine is started and the lever is moved to D it can be left in this position for all normal driving. When accelerating, the transmission shifts automatically from low to intermediate between 10 and 35 mph and from intermediate to direct between 18 and 55 mph depending in the position of the accelerator pedal. On deceleration, it will shift automatically from direct drive to intermediate at approximately 12 mph and from intermediate to low at approximately 3 mph.

Roll-Back (See Roll-Back 1:12)
This feature does not apply.

2:51 TESTING

(Refer to 1:21 through 1:28)

Governor Shift Speeds

Upshifts   m.p.h.

Low to intermediate, light throttle	10
Low to intermediate, full throttle	35
Intermediate to direct, light throttle	18
Intermediate to direct, full throttle	55
Intermediate to direct, after "kickdown"	68

Downshifts

Direct to intermediate, closed throttle	12
Intermediate to low, closed throttle	3
Direct to intermediate, "kickdown"	Up to 60

Driving Units
Operation Checks

Shift Speeds

(a) Light throttle upshifts.—From a standstill, with the selector lever in the D position, accelerate the car gradually and note the speed at which the upshift from automatic low drive to intermediate drive, and from intermediate drive to direct drive occurs.

(b) Closed throttle downshifts.—While operating the car in direct drive, release the accelerator and allow the car to accelerate gradually. Note the speed at which the downshift from direct drive to intermediate drive and from intermediate drive to low drive occurs.

(c) Full throttle upshift.—From a standstill, depress and hold the accelerator pedal in the wide-open throttle position (not in kickdown position). Note the speed at which the upshift from low drive to intermediate drive and from intermediate drive to direct drive occurs.

(d) Kickdown downshift and upshift.—While driving the car at approximately 50 mph depress and hold the accelerator pedal in the kickdown position. The transmission should shift immediately from direct drive to intermediate drive. As the car speed continues to increase, note the speed at which the upshift to direct drive occurs.

Hill Holding

This characteristic does not apply to first speed start transmission.

2:52 DIAGNOSIS

(Refer to 1:29 through 1:34)

Condition A.V

The hill holding characteristic referred to does not apply.

Condition D.1V

The following causes apply:—
1. Damaged selector control shaft rubber lip seal.
2. Damaged selector control shaft.

In addition to the conditions listed in Group A the following condition applies:—

Slipping excessively or not operative in automatic low (selector lever in D position) or in reverse.

1. Reverse free wheel unit slipping.
2. Low brake drum plate dowels not in place.

2:53 DISMANTLING AND REASSEMBLING

Extension Case Assembly
(Refer to 1:35 and 1:36)

Paragraph 2

The governor controls the upshifts and downshifts between automatic low drive, intermediate drive, and direct drive while operating in the D position. To accomplish these upshifts, the governor valve moves outward as the car speed increases, allowing oil pressure to apply the multiple disc clutch, providing the shift from automatic low to intermediate drive. As the car speed continues to increase, the governor valve permits oil pressure to also apply the direct drive clutch providing direct drive. As the car speed decreases, the governor valve first shuts off the pressure to the direct drive clutch causing the transmission to downshift to intermediate drive. Then as the car speed continues to decrease, and with the accelerator completely released, the governor valve shuts off the pressure to the multiple disc clutch permitting the transmission to downshift to automatic low drive. During heavy acceleration, under approximately 45 mph or "kickdown" under approximately 60 mph, the governor will cause the transmission to downshift from direct drive to intermediate drive. It cannot downshift to automatic low drive under these conditions since the second speed drive pawl will stop the governor valve before it moves in far enough to shut off the pressure to the multiple disc clutch.

Extension Case

The removal, inspection, dismantling and installation instructions are the same as described in Part I. The procedure for removing the governor control second speed drive mechanism (A, Fig 82) is as given on page 220 for the "Governor Control Direct Drive Mechanism".

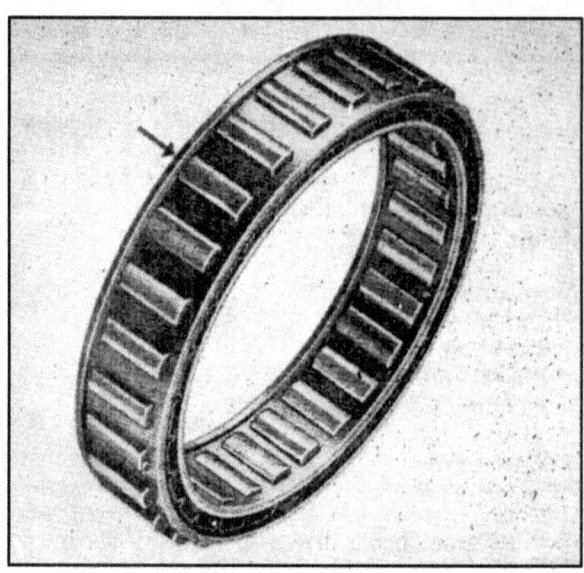

Fig 83.—The free wheel units must be installed so that the lip edge is towards the rear of the transmission unit.

Governor Spring
(Refer to 1:37)

A longer governor spring (B, Fig 82) is used. The free length of the spring is 2 5/8"; the spring used in transmission units prior to serial number J2426 is 2¼" long.

Mainshaft Assembly

The mainshaft has been redesigned to provide the automatic low start in D range.

Free Wheel Units
(Refer to 1:41)

The free wheel units (Fig 83) are of double-caged construction. The inner and outer cages are separate pieces and the sprags are held in position between the cages by a ribbon type spring. The length of the reverse wheel unit has been increased but remains the shorter of the two units.

Care should be taken when removing the forward free wheel unit snap ring to prevent the screwdriver from slipping down between the cages and the spring and damaging the parts. A snap ring is not used to retain the reverse free wheel unit in the low drum plate. It is held in position by the hub of the forward drive drum.

To instal the reverse free wheel unit, first place a heavy rubber band around the unit. Make sure all of the sprags are positioned in the slots of the cages. Then slip the unit into the low drum plate. Slip the rear sun gear into the unit by rotating the gear. Instal the forward free wheel unit in the same manner.

The units must be installed so that the lip or rolled edge of the unit is toward the rear of the transmission.

Fig 82.—Governor—first speed start transmission.
A. Second speed drive pawl.
B. Governor spring.

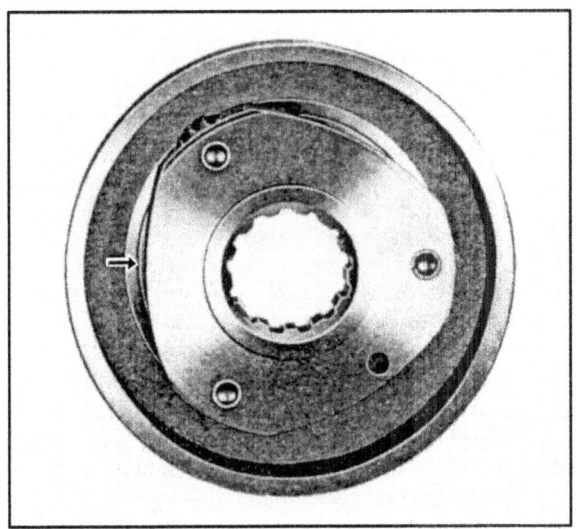

Fig 84.—Showing the undercut in the reverse drum to provide clearance for the pinion pins of the planetary carrier.

Forward Brake Drum and Rear Sun Gear
(Refer to 1:41)

Because of the longer reverse free wheel unit, the hub and bushing of the forward drum have been shortened. To obtain proper registry of the oil lubrication hole in the rear sun gear with the shorter bushing, it was necessary to relocate the hole.

The diameter of the free wheel unit race in the forward brake drum was decreased to permit proper clearance with the double cage free wheel unit. The diameter of the bronze spacer was also decreased.

Planetary Carriers
(Refer to 1:41)

The material and method of fabrication of planet carrier assemblies required a change in the reverse drum. The pinion pins have rolled or swaged ends. The ends are not flush with the carrier; therefore an undercut (indicated by the arrow in Fig 84) was necessary in the inner face of the reverse brake drum to provide clearance for the pin ends.

Front Sun Gear Thrust Washer
(Refer to 1:41)

The thrust washer does not have a locking tang. The inner edge is relieved at three places to provide lubrication for the front planetary set. The three projections serve as centring lugs.

When re-installing the thrust washer, make sure that the steel face is placed against the carrier, thereby putting the bronze face against the thrust surface of the front sun gear.

Multiple Disc Clutch
(Refer to 1:41)

The clutch friction discs have a different friction material. Friction discs used in the previous type of transmission unit must not be used in this transmission. (Refer to the Spare Parts Catalogue for the Jaguar Automatic Transmission. Publication No J.19.)

Reverse Servo Unit
(Refer to 1:43)

The reverse shuttle valve has been eliminated from the reverse brake cylinder. An orifice (indicated by the arrow in Fig 85) in the reverse brake cylinder plate retards the action of the outer piston, to provide smooth engagement of the reverse band. The action is similar to that obtained by the shuttle.

Low and Forward Servo Units
(Refer to 1:44)

The forward drive band is applied by two servo pistons.

The forward brake outer cylinder, cylinder plate and piston are serviced in a similar manner to the low brake cylinder.

Selector Control Shaft Seal
(Refer to 1:45)

The O-ring seal and the cork packing are replaced by a lip type rubber seal.

Removal

Follow the procedure outlined under "Selector Control Shaft and Lever — Removal".

Installation

Apply a light film of suitable gasket sealer to the outer surface of the new seal.

Using a suitable flat surface driver, force the seal into the counterbore of the case. Make sure the seal is not cocked but enters the bore squarely.

Instal the selector control shaft as outlined under "Selector Control Shaft and Lever — Installation".

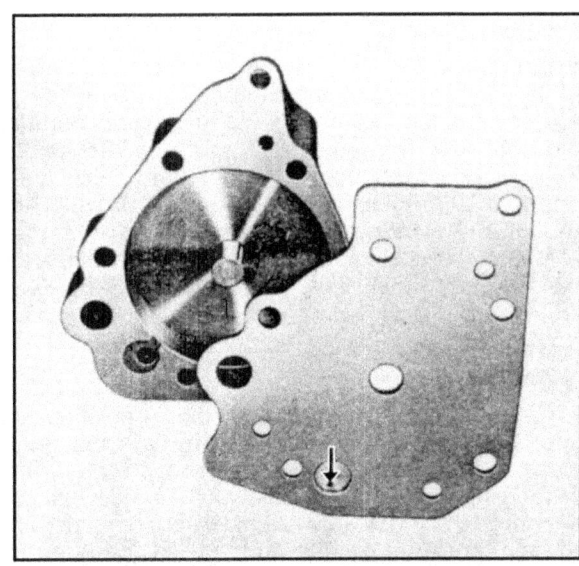

Fig 85.—Reverse brake cylinder and plate.

2:54 NEW HYDRAULIC SYSTEM

Effective from Transmission No J3001

With effect from the above transmission number a new hydraulic system is incorporated in the transmission.

All transmission units with this new hydraulic system are of the first speed start type (three-way upshift) and vary from the previous system in the following respects:—

1. The brake bands are applied initially by a line pressure of 20 lb per sq in which is then increased to 80 lb per sq in directing the pressure to an accumulator and then back to the main relief valve.
2. The converter pressure in first and reverse is increased to between 60 and 65 lb per sq in. This pressure is reduced to 30 lb per sq in in the valve block at the time the shift is made into intermediate.
   This is accomplished by directing multiple disc clutch oil pressure to the back of the converter shuttle valve, this brings into operation a restricting orifice in this passage. Reverse oil pressure is also directed to the back of the converter shuttle valve to reduce the 200 lb per sq in pressure in reverse to 60 lb per sq in for the converter.
3. Both the low and forward bands are applied for Automatic Low in the D Drive position.

P (Park) Position

With the selector lever in the P (Park) position, the selector valve does not admit oil pressure to the bands or clutches; however, with the engine running, the oil pressure from the front pump is directed to the converter valve to maintain a pressure of 20 lb/sq in maximum, and to provide lubrication for the transmission of internal parts. Oil pressure is also directed to the selector valve, where it is blocked from further flow.

N (Neutral) Position

With the selector lever in the N (Neutral) position, the selector valve does not admit oil pressure to the bands or clutches; however, with the engine running, the oil pressure from the front pump is directed to the converter shuttle valve to maintain a converter pressure of 20 lb/sq in maximum and to provide lubrication for the transmission internal parts. Oil pressure is also directed to the selector valve, where it is blocked from further flow, the same as in P (Park) position.

D (Drive) Position
Low (First Gear)

With the selector lever in the D (Drive) position, the selector valve allows oil pressure from the front pump to flow through passages to the forward servo cylinder, applying the forward band and also around the relay valve to the low servo cylinder, applying the low band. Oil pressure is also directed to the governor valve to the accumulator piston, compressing the accumulator piston against its spring thus allowing the pressure to flow to the top of the main relief valve piston. The movement of the main relief piston against the main relief valve spring increases the pressure against the main relief valve thus causing a corresponding increase in line pressure to 80 lb/sq in. This increased line pressure will then result in increasing the pressure in both the forward and low servos to 80 lb/sq in.

The increase in line pressure will also result in an increase in converter pressure to 60 lb/sq in. The pressure differential between line pressure and converter pressure being controlled by the orifice in the converter shuttle valve bushing.

Power flow is from the engine to the converter to the front planetary ring gear, and through the planet pinion gears to the planet carrier. The front sun gear is held stationary by the low band and the rear sun gear is held stationary through the action of the forward drive freewheel and the locked forward drive drum and band. Since the front planet carrier is splined to the ring gear of the rear planetary set, the power flow continues through the rear unit planet pinions to the rear planet carrier which is splined to the output shaft. The product of the ratios of the two planetary sets is 2.308 to 1. This ratio multiplied by the conversion ratio of the converter at stall gives a maximum overall ratio of approximately 5 to 1. As the car speed increases in low gear, and as the turbine speed and pump speed become substantially equal, the torque multiplication of the converter diminishes, the stator reaction member free wheels, and the converter becomes a hydraulic fluid coupling, transmitting engine torque to the transmission.

Intermediate (Second gear)

With the selector lever in D position, a further increase in speed will cause a corresponding increase in governor speed, sufficient to move the governor valve and allow oil pressure at 80 lb/sq in to flow to the relay valve piston, moving this piston and the relay valve to close off the passage supplying oil pressure to the Low servo and allowing the Low servo to drain thus releasing the Low band. From this same passage, oil pressure is allowed to flow to the converter shuttle valve piston, moving this piston and the converter shuttle valve. The movement of the converter shuttle valve causes the oil flowing to the converter to pass through a restricting orifice in the valve thus reducing converter pressure from 60 lb/sq in to 30 lb/sq in. At the same time, pressure from the governor valve has also flowed to the piston of the multiple disc clutch, locking this clutch and causing a shift into intermediate. Oil pressure from the pump and the main relief valve continues to be directed by the selector valve to the forward band servo mechanism at 80 lb/sq in and through the converter shuttle valve bushing to the converter at 30 lb/sq in.

Power flow is from the engine to the torque converter to the ring gear of the front planetary set. Since the front planetary set revolves at unity through the action of the multiple disc clutch and the reverse free wheel which is now unlocked, the power is transmitted with no torque multiplication from the front planetary carrier to the ring gear of the rear planetary set, as these units are directly connected together. Therefore, the rear planetary set transmits the power to the mainshaft at a torque ratio of approximately 1.4 to 1. The ratio of the rear planet multiplied by the ratio of the converter gives a maximum ratio of approximately 3.1 to 1 at stall. As the car speed increases and the turbine speed and impeller speed become the same the converter becomes a normal fluid coupling.

Direct

In direct drive the forward band and multiple disc clutch remain applied as in second speed, and oil continues to be directed through the converter shuttle valve to the converter at 30 lb/sq in. A further increase in speed will cause the governor to position the governor valve to allow oil pressure to flow to the piston of the direct drive clutch causing a shift into direct drive. At the time the governor valve moves to allow oil pressure into the direct drive clutch passage, oil pressure also flows to the hydraulic detent piston. The pressure against this piston is transmitted to the governor valve and fork assembly, effectively positioning the governor valve to allow unrestricted flow of oil pressure to the direct drive clutch. This prevents a condition where vehicle speed and throttle pressure would allow the governor to float and produce a "hunting" condition between intermediate and direct. Furthermore, at this vehicle speed, the oil pressure output of the rear pump becomes sufficient to supply the needs of the transmission hydraulic system. At this time the action of the main relief valve is such that it not only regulates the rear pump pressure but also returns the output of the front pump directly to the oil pan. Oil pressure from the rear pump is also directed to the reverse interlock valve, opening this valve and thus preventing any build up of pressure in the reverse servo if the shift lever should be moved to the reverse position during forward motion of the vehicle at these speeds. Oil pressure from the rear pump is also directed to the Parking interlock piston, moving this piston to prevent engagement of the parking pawl during forward motion of the vehicle at these speeds.

Power flow with the direct drive clutch engaged is from the engine through the direct drive clutch to the output shaft, by-passing the two planetary gear sets, through the free wheel units, and the torque converter unit. This provides a positive drive from the engine to the rear axle, and in this range there is no torque multiplication.

L (Low) Position

With the selector lever in the L (Low) position the selector valve directs oil pressure at 20 lb/sq in to the forward servo cylinder applying the forward band and also to the relay valve and through it to the low servo cylinder to apply the low band. This pressure is also directed to the accumulator piston, opening a passage to the top of the main relief valve piston. Movement of this piston increases the main relief valve spring pressure to increase line pressure to 80 lb/sq in. Oil pressure is also directed to the converter shuttle valve bushing where a restricting orifice reduces the line pressure to 60 lb/sq in going into the converter. Oil pressure is also directed to the top of the relay valve forcing this valve to the open position if a manual shift is made from D intermediate or direct to the L (Low) position.

In this L position, the selector valve also cuts off oil pressure to the governor valve and thus prevents application of the multiple disc clutch and direct drive clutch regardless of vehicle speed in the low range. If sufficient vehicle speed is attained, the rear pump will supply the requirements of the transmission hydraulic system and through the action of the main relief valve return the output of the front pump to the oil pan.

With the bands applied, the low band holds the sun gear of the front planetary set stationary while the forward drive band holds the sun gear of the rear planetary set stationary through the medium of the rear free-wheeling unit. In a simple planetary set a forward drive ratio is obtained through the planet carrier when the input is through the ring gear and the sun gear is held stationary. Engine braking is provided through application of the low band. Power flow in low is from the engine torque converter, to the ring gear of the front planetary set. The power then goes from the planet carrier of the front planetary set to the ring gear of the rear planetary and from the planet carrier of this set to the mainshaft. The product of the ratios through the front planetary set and the rear planetary set is approximately 2.3 to 1, which combined with the torque multiplication through the converter, gives a maximum torque ratio in low of approximately 5 to 1 through the automatic transmission.

R (Reverse) Position

With the selector lever in the R (Reverse) position, the selector valve directs oil pressure from the front pump and main relief valve to the reverse interlock valve. As no rear pump pressure is available in reverse, the reverse interlock valve allows oil pressure to flow to the reverse servo mechanism, applying the reverse band. Connecting passages also direct oil pressure to the accumulator piston and through to the top of the main relief valve outer piston and also to main relief valve inner piston. The application of oil pressure to both the outer and inner pistons of the main relief valve increases line pressure from 20 lb/sq in to 200 lb/sq in. Oil pressure is also directed to the area between the reverse shuttle valve piston and the reverse shuttle valve, thus moving the reverse shuttle valve into the converter supply passage, where by means of a small diameter orifice, the 200 lb/sq in line pressure is reduced to 60 lb/sq in entering the converter. In reverse gear, oil pressure for the hydraulic system is supplied by the front pump as the rear pump is being operated in reverse rotation and therefore supplies no pressure.

Power flow is from the engine to the torque converter to the front ring gear, and as the front planet carrier is being held stationary by the reverse band the front planet pinions cause a reverse rotation to the front unit sun gear.

This reverse rotation is transmitted to the rear sun gear through the front free wheel unit, which does not free-wheel in this reverse direction. Since the ring gear of the rear unit is splined to the front carrier it is also held stationary by the reverse band, rotation of the rear sun gear causes the rear planetary pinions to revolve around this stationary ring gear, and rotate the rear planet carrier and output shaft in the reverse direction. The product of the gear ratios supplied by the planetary sets is a reverse ratio of 2.009 to 1. The combination of this gear reduction and the torque multiplication through the torque converter provides a maximum reverse ratio of approximately 4.34 to 1 through the automatic transmission in reverse.

2:55 TESTING

(Refer to 1:21)

The following details supersede those given in the "Testing" section of the Automatic Transmission Service Manual for transmission units with the new hydraulic system.

Pressure Tests

A pressure test point is provided for testing each of the hydraulic units of the transmission. The following procedures should be used when pressure tests are indicated in the "DIAGNOSIS" section.

For convenience of making these pressure tests, position the gauge in a convenient place in the driver's compartment and allow the gauge line to go through the floor oil filter aperture to the transmission pressure take-off point.

Front Pump

1. With the engine stopped remove the Allen head pipe plug at the transmission sump front flange, and instal the pressure gauge and fitting (see Fig 21, in Part I).
2. With the selector lever in the N position start the engine and increase the speed to 1000 rpm. At this engine speed the gauge should read 20-30 lb/sq in.
3. With the engine running and rear wheels locked and the selector lever in D or L position, the pressure gauge should show a minimum reading of 70 lb/sq in at 1000 rpm.
4. Stop the engine, remove the test equipment, refit the Allen head pipe plug. Do NOT use any type of sealing compound when installing this or any other pipe plug in the transmission. Tighten the plug with a torque spanner to 15-18 lb/ft.

Forward Band Servo

1. With the engine stopped, remove the cap screw and copper washer from the forward band servo cylinder. Instal the proper pressure gauge fitting at this point (see Fig 22 in Part I).
2. With the engine running apply the hand and foot brakes firmly to prevent the car moving forward, and move the selector lever to the D position. Gradually increase engine speed to 1000 rpm. At this speed the gauge should show a minimum reading of 70 lb/sq in.

WARNING: To prevent overheating of the transmission the engine should not be run at speeds greater than idling with the selector lever in the D, L or R positions and with the rear wheels held stationary, for more than 30 seconds.

3. Stop the engine and remove the test equipment. Refit the cap screw in the forward band servo cover, using a new copper washer. Do not use any type of sealing compound when fitting this or any other cap screw or gasket in the automatic transmission. Tighten the cap screw with a torque spanner to 28-33 lb/ft.

Low Band Servo

1. With the engine stopped remove the cap screw and copper washer from the low servo cylinder and instal the proper pressure gauge fitting at this point (see Fig 24 in Part I).
2. With the engine running apply the hand and foot brakes firmly to prevent forward movement of the car. Place the selector lever in the L position and increase the engine speed to 1000 rpm. At this speed the gauge should show a minimum reading of 70 lb/sq in.
3. With the lever in the D position the gauge pressure should result as in 2.

WARNING: To prevent overheating of the transmission the engine should not be run at speeds greater than idling with the selector lever in the D, L or R positions, and with the rear wheels stationary, for more than 30 seconds.

4. Stop the engine and remove the test equipment. Refit the cap screw in the low servo cylinder.

Reverse Band Servo

1. With the engine stopped, remove the cap screw and copper washer from the reverse band servo cylinder, and instal the pressure gauge fitting at this point (see Fig 23 in Part I.)
2. With the engine running apply the hand and foot brakes firmly to prevent movement of the car and move the selector lever to the R position. Gradually increase engine speed to 1000 rpm. At this speed the gauge should show a minimum reading of 180 lb/sq in.

WARNING: To prevent overheating of the transmission the engine should not be run at speeds greater than idling with the selector lever in the D, L or R positions, and with the rear wheels stationary, for more than 30 seconds.

3. Stop the engine and remove the test equipment. Refit the cap screw in the servo cylinder using a new copper washer. Tighten the screw with a torque spanner to 28-33 lb/ft.

Multiple Disc Clutch

1. With the engine stopped remove the ⅛" pipe plug from the transmission extension case, and instal the pressure gauge fitting (See F Fig 29 in Part I).

2. Jack up the rear wheels of the car, and in the D position bring the rear wheel speed up to 15 mph at light throttle. At this speed the pressure gauge should show a minimum of 70 lb/sq in.

3. Stop the engine, remove the test equipment and refit the ⅛" pipe plug, tightening it with a torque spanner to 15-18 lb/ft.

Torque Converter

1. Remove the ⅛" pipe plug at the torque converter pressure take-off point (see Fig 25 in Part I).

2. With the selector lever in the N position and the engine running at approximately 1000 rpm the pressure reading should be 15-20 lb/sq in.

3. With the rear wheels locked and selector lever in the D, L or R positions the converter pressure reading should be 50-60 lb/sq in at 1000 rpm.

WARNING: To prevent overheating of the transmission the engine should not be run at speeds greater than idling with the selector lever in the D, L or R positions and with the rear wheels held stationary, for more than 30 seconds.

4. With the rear wheels jacked up and free to rotate, the selector lever in the D position and the engine running at 1500 rpm the pressure should be 20-30 lb/sq in.

5. Stop the engine, remove the test equipment, and refit the ⅛" plug, tightening the plug with a torque spanner to 6-7 lb/ft.

Direct Drive Clutch

1. With the engine stopped, remove the Allen head pipe plug from the transmission sump rear flange and instal the pressure gauge fitting at this point (G Fig 29 in Part I).

2. With the rear wheels of the car raised off the floor and free to rotate, and the engine running at idling speed, move the selector lever to the D position. The pressure gauge should show a zero reading at the direct drive clutch.

3. Slowly increase engine speed to 1500 rpm. At approximately 1200 rpm the transmission should change to direct drive. This will be indicated by a rapid pressure rise in the direct drive clutch, and whilst in direct drive the pressure gauge should show a minimum reading of 70 lb/sq in.

4. Check the direct drive clutch pressure during deceleration. When the speedometer indicates approximately 10 to 12 mph the pressure should drop to zero.

5. Remove the test equipment and replace the Allen pipe head plug, tightening the plug to 15-18 lb/ft.

Rear Pump

1. With the engine stopped, remove the anti-creep pressure switch from the rear oil pump. Instal the pressure gauge fitting in the rear pump orifice (C, Fig 29 in Part I).

2. With the engine running and the rear wheels held stationary the pressure gauge should show a zero reading.

3. With the engine idling and the rear wheels raised from the floor and free to rotate, move the selector lever to the D position. Rear pump pressure should build up as shown by a steady increase in pressure reading. At 20 mph on the speedometer the rear pump pressure should read 70 lb/sq in. Pressure will be recorded if the rear wheels turn, even though the manual selector lever is in the N position.

4. Remove the test equipment and re-instal the plug in the rear pump.

2:56 DIAGNOSIS
(Refer to 1:29)

The following details supersede those given in the "Diagnosis" section of the Automatic Transmission Service Manual for transmission units with the new hydraulic system.

1. **Transmission inoperative or has excessive slippage and engine race in low range, drive first and**

   (a) **Manual Control Linkage Disconnected or Improperly Adjusted.**

   (b) **Low Oil Supply.** Fill to proper level.

   (c) **Converter Valve Sticking.** Check converter pressure, and if pressure is zero or fluctuating between zero and 30 lb/sq in, depending upon engine speed, it will be necessary to dismantle the valve block and clean thoroughly, freeing all valves.

   (d) **Low Front Pump Pressure,** due to:—

     i Main relief valve, accumulator piston or main relief piston stuck open. Check front pressure in D or L position, and if this pressure is less than 70 lb/sq in at 1000 engine rpm with the transmission at normal operating temperature remove valve block, thoroughly clean and free all valves.

     ii Leakage in the valve block assembly.

     iii Front pump worn excessively. A pressure check in neutral will determine this, if valves in valve block are functioning normally.

     iv Damaged front pump tangs on torque converter impeller.

     v Rear pump check valve out of position or check valve seat damaged.

     vi Oil leak in passage from front pump to valve block.

     vii Valve block to front pump passage blocked.

     viii Damaged or missing front pump O ring.

   (e) **Stator Free Wheel Assembly Damaged or Worn Excessively.**

   (f) **Broken Fins in the Converter (Noisy).**

   (g) **Check all Band Adjustments and Servo Pressures.**

2. **Transmission inoperative or has excessive slippage and engine race in low range, drive first and drive second.**

   (a) **Forward Band Slipping,** due to:—

     i Incorrect adjustment.

     ii Lining worn excessively or band damaged.

     iii Forward drive servo piston sticking.

     iv Low pressure at forward drive servo unit because of blocked passage.

   (b) **Forward Drive Free Wheel not Holding.**

3. **Transmission inoperative or has excessive slippage and engine race in reverse.**

(a) **Reverse Band Slipping,** due to:—

    i Incorrect band adjustment.

    ii Low reverse servo pressure— check pressure. This pressure should not be less than 180 lb/sq in (14.06 kg/cm²) at 1000 rpm with transmission at normal operating temperature with selector lever in reverse position. If pressure is low dismantle the reverse servo and check for leaks caused by torn seal, blown gasket, or piston out of place. If the servo is all right dismantle the valve block and check for leaks or sticking main relief valve; reverse interlock valve may be stuck in a position to drain the reverse servo, front pump check valve may be leaking or out of place, allowing front pump pressure to open the reverse interlock valve and drain the reverse servo.

    iii Excessive wear of the front pump.

    iv Blow hole in transmission case inter-connecting passage to rear servo.

(b) **Damaged Reverse Free Wheel Unit.**

4. **Normal operation drive and low ranges when accelerating and in reverse, but ineffective braking after changing down into low (deceleration).**

(a) **Low Band Slipping,** due to:—

    i Incorrect low band adjustment.

    ii Low band damaged, or excessively worn lining.

    iii Low pressure (low servo). This pressure should not be less than 70 lb/sq in at 1000 rpm with transmission at normal operating temperature, selector lever in low position. If pressure is low dismantle low servo and valve block to check for leaks.

    iv Low servo piston sticking.

5. **Transmission fails to change to direct drive or slips after direct drive clutch is engaged; selector lever in D range.**

(a) **Accelerator Linkage Improperly Adjusted.**

(b) **Selector Lever Linkage Improperly Adjusted.**

(c) **High Oil Level.**

(d) **Faulty Governor Operation,** due to:—

    i Damaged governor, nicked governor shaft or nick on governor valve

    ii Governor sticking on the governor shaft.

    iii Governor valve sticking.

(e) **High Converter Pressure Preventing Direct Drive Clutch Engagement.**

    i Check direct drive clutch pressure. If this is correct, check converter pressure. If converter pressure is high move selector lever to N position. If converter pressure is still high, the converter valve is stuck in the open position; free converter valve in block assembly.

    ii If direct drive pressure comes up to normal and then the pressure drops slowly and converter pressure increases, it indicates an oil leak past the direct drive clutch piston seals or leaking transfer tube O ring seal—replace converter.

    iii If direct drive pressure comes up quickly and stabilises, and converter pressure increases to approximately the same pressure, it indicates that the mainshaft lubrication assembly is loose and twisted out of position in the mainshaft—replace mainshaft.

(f) **Improper Direct Drive Clutch Operation,** due to:

    i Sticking or distorted direct drive clutch piston.

    ii Clutch wear.

    iii Broken oil rings either on mainshaft or front ring gear shaft.

(g) **Direct Drive Clutch Hub Sticking on Mainshaft Splines.**

(h) **Blocked Direct Drive Oil Passage in Front Oil Pump Collector Ring.**

(i) **Check the Mainshaft Oil Transfer Tube and the Flywheel inside the Converter for Wear at Tube Contact Point.**

6. **Engine cannot be turned over by pushing car. Also reverse interlock does not operate.**

(a) **Rear Pump Pressure Low,** due to:—

    i Relief valve stuck open.

    ii Worn or damaged rear pump.

    iii Worn or damaged rear pump drive gear.

    iv Rear pump drive gear pin sheared.

    v Incorrectly assembled valve block.

    vi Valve block gaskets leaking.

    vii Porous valve blockcastings.

    viii Extension case gaskets leaking.

    ix Porous extension case castings.

    x Blocked rear pump passage to valve block.

7. **Transmission operates normally in low and reverse, but engine labors or slows when lever is placed in the D position.**

(a) **Improper Governor Operation.**

    i Check direct drive clutch oil pressure.

    ii Governor valve stuck in the open position allowing oil to go to the direct drive clutch (governor hydraulic detent piston sticking).

    iii Governor binding or sticking on governor shaft.

    iv Blocked governor valve drain passage.

    v Governor valve sleeve out of position in extension case.

(b) **Oil Leak from the Converter Pressure Passage to the Direct Drive Clutch. (Damaged Mainshaft Oil Rings or Front Planetary Ring Gear Oil Rings.)**

    i Mainshaft oil ring broken.

    ii Front ring gear oil ring broken.

iii Check distance of front ring gear from end of mainshaft to ensure correct position, dimensions should be 1-3/16".
iv Check collector ring passages for porosity.
v If after performing the above operations the condition still exists replace the converter.

8. **Transmission operates normally when starting in drive, low and reverse, but shudders or stalls when coming to a stop in drive range.**
   (a) **Accelerator Pedal to Governor Lever Linkage Improperly Adjusted.**
   (b) **Improper Governor Valve Operation,** due to:—
      i Damaged governor.
      ii Governor sticking on the governor shaft.
      iii Governor valve sticking open.
      iv Governor hydraluic detent piston sticking.
   (c) **Damaged Mainshaft Oil Rings or Damaged Front Ring Gear Oil Rings.**
   (d) **No Groove on End of Mainshaft Oil Transfer Tube.**
   (e) **Sticking Direct Drive Clutch Plate—Check Mainshaft Splines for Burrs or Damage.**
   (f) **Governor Valve Drain** not open — **Remove Rear Pump to Check.**
   (g) **If Operations A-F do not Correct the complaint replace the Converter Assembly.**

9. **Transmission operates normally in all ranges, but will not change down at "kick-down" between speeds of 18 and 55 mph.**
   (a) **Accelerator Linkage Improperly Adjusted.**
   (b) **Improper Governor Valve Operation,** due to:—
      i Damaged governor.
      ii Governor assembly sticking on governor shaft splines — free governor on splines throughout its full travel.
      iii Governor hydraulic detent piston sticking.
      iv Blocked governor valve drain passage.
      v Governor control cam stop screw incorrectly adjusted.
   (c) **High Oil Level.**

10. **Transmission operates normally in low range, direct reverse, but slips excessively in drive range above 12 mph and continues to drive in first.**
    (a) **Multiple Disc Clutch Slipping (Low Oil Pressure),** due to:—
       i Broken oil rings on front or rear ring gear units or on mainshaft.
       ii O ring seal on rear unit ring gear defective.
       iii Multiple disc clutch piston seal leaking.
       iv Make sure that holes in the mainshaft are indexed with holes in inner oil transfer tube and lubrication valve.
       v Multiple clutch piston sticking.
       vi Damaged or excessively worn disc facings.

   (b) **Governor Sticking,** due to:—
      i Nicks or burrs on governor spline shaft.
      ii Nicks or burrs on governor valve.

11. **Transmission shudders on acceleration or deceleration when in direct, but this condition disappears when in second, low, reverse, or neutral.**
    (a) **Transmission Forward Free Wheel Spacer is Seizing on Rear Sun Gear.**
       i Check for proper clearance and replace spacer if necessary.
    (b) **Transmission Forward Brake Drum Bushing is Seizing on Rear Sun Gear.**
       i Check for proper clearance. If clearance is insufficient, replace with new forward brake drum assembly.
    (c) **Check all Bushings for Proper Clearance.**

12. **When selector lever is moved to R (reverse) transmission shifts into reverse immediately at speeds above 5 mph.**
    (a) **Rear Oil Pump Inoperative.**
       i Check oil pump pressure.
    (b) **Reverse Interlock Valve Inoperative.**
       i Interlock valve sticking.
       ii Blocked reverse interlock valve oil passage.

13. **Normal reverse operation—transmission overheats, poor engine performance and engine laboring in forward ranges.**
    (a) **Reverse Band Drag.**
       i Check reverse band oil pressure.
       ii Leaking valve block assembly gasket.
       iii Valve block casting porous.
       iv Check reverse band adjustment.
       v Reverse servo piston sticking.
       vi Reverse band damaged or distorted

14. **Normal low range operation — transmission overheating with poor engine performance, and engine laboring in other ranges.**
    (a) **Low Band Drag.**
       i Check low band pressure.
       ii Leaking valve block assembly gaskets.
       iii Valve block casting porous.
       iv Incorrect band adjustment.
       v Low servo piston sticking.
       vi Low band damaged or distorted.
       vii Leaks between low and forward servo cylinders (outer).
       viii Leaks between low and forward servo cylinders in transmission case (inner).
       ix Low band relay valve sticking.

15. **Normal low and forward operation—poor engine performance with engine laboring in reverse.**
    (a) **Forward Band Drag.**
    (b) **Low Band Drag.**
       i Incorrect band adjustment.
       ii Check forward and low band pressure.
       iii Leaking valve block gasket.
       iv Porous valve block casting.

v Forward or low band servo piston sticking.
vi Forward or low band damaged or distorted.
vii Low band relay valve sticking.

16. **Normal operation in drive range above 12 mph —poor performance transmission overheating, engine laboring, in other ranges.**
    (a) **Multiple Disc Clutch Dragging.**
        i Check multiple disc clutch pressure.
        ii Leaking valve block gaskets.
        iii Porous valve block casting.
        iv Multiple disc clutch piston sticking.
        v Broken or damaged multiple disc clutch retractor springs.

17. **Normal operation in direct drive—poor performance, with engine laboring in other ranges, low stall speed.**
    (a) **Stator Reaction Hub broken in Front Pump and Collector Ring Assembly — Replace Front Pump and Collector Ring Assembly.**
    (b) **Torque Converter Stator Free Wheel Unit Slipping—Replace Converter.**

18. **Normal operation at low speeds—poor performance with transmission overheating in direct drive —stall speed normal. Free engine speed low.**
    (a) **Torque Converter Stator Free Wheel Unit Sticking—Replace Converter.**

19. **Car operates in all ranges, but has low stall speed, loss of performance and low top speed in direct and excessive transmission heating.**
    (a) **Converter Stator Free Wheel Assembled Incorrectly or Damaged.**
        i Replace converter.

20. **Transmission operates normally in all speed ranges, but whining noise is noticed when car is moving and noise increases with car speed. Noise cannot be heard when car is stationary and selector lever is in drive position.**
    (a) **Usually Indicates Noisy Rear Pump.**
        i Replace rear pump assembly if noise is excessive. Do not confuse rear pump noise with rear axle or tyre noise. Check pump operation with rear wheels raised. Rear pump noise can be distinguished from axle noise as no variation will be noticed between drive, change-over and overrun conditions.
    (b) **Check Oil Level.**
    (c) **Check Oil Intake Filter.**
        i If clogged, clean or replace.
    (d) **Check Rear Pump Cover Gaskets for Leaks.**

21. **Transmission has buzzing noise at any speed with selector lever in any position.**
    (a) **Check Linkage Adjustments.**
    (b) **Transmission Oil Level Low.**
    (c) **Transmission Oil Pump Filter Clogged with Lint or Dirt.**
    (d) **Front Oil Pump Sucking Air.**
        i Check pump gaskets.
        ii Check for porosity in pump castings.

22. **Transmission operates normally in all speed ranges, but a whining noise is present at all times and increases with engine speed when car is stationary and selector lever is in the drive position.**
    (a) **Usually indicates Noisy Front Pump.**
    (b) **Check Oil Level.**
    (c) **Check Oil Intake Filter.**
        i May be clogged with lint or dirt.

2:57 NORMAL EXTERNAL OIL LEAKS

23. **Oil leak between the transmission and the torque converter.**
    (a) **Front Pump Oil Seal Damaged.**
    (b) **Leaking Collector Ring Gasket.**
    (c) **Leaking Front Pump and Collector Ring Assembly.**
    (d) **Leaking Torque Converter.**
    (e) **Front Seal Assembly Contacting Pump Bushing.**

24. **Oil leak on servo cylinders.**
    (a) Damaged Gaskets.
    (b) Uneven or Warped Gasket Surfaces.
    (c) Blow Holes in Castings.

25. **Oil Leak at Extension Case.**
    (a) Damaged Gaskets.
    (b) Uneven or Warped Gasket Surfaces.
    (c) Blow Holes in Castings.
    (d) Improperly Seated Governor Control Shaft Bushing.
    (e) Leak at Governor Control Cam Stop Screw.

26. **Oil leak at selector control shaft.**
    (a) Bore out of round or Diameter of Bore too large.
    (b) Damaged Selector Shaft Oil Seal.

27. **Oil leak at transmission oil pan.**
    (a) Damaged Gasket.
    (b) Uneven or Warped Gasket Surfaces.

2:58 DISMANTLING AND REASSEMBLING
(Refer to 1:40)

Valve Block Assembly

The valve block assembly is mounted on the bottom of the transmission case, and, through a series of valves and passages within the assembly, controls and directs the flow of oil in the transmission.

The following are included in the valve block assembly:—

The selector valve which controls the oil flow from the oil pumps to the servo units, to the accumulator valve, and through the governor valve, to the multiple disc clutch, direct drive clutch and relay valve.

A main relief valve which regulates the pressure of the front and rear oil pumps.

A converter shuttle valve which regulates and supplies oil to the torque converter.

A reverse interlock valve which prevents application of the reverse band when the car is moving forward.

An accumulator valve which allows the bands to be initially supplied with low pressure followed immediately with high pressure.

A relay valve which controls application and release of the low band.

Removal

1. Drain the fluid from the transmission only.
2. Remove the sump and gasket.
3. Slacken the filter retainer screw, turn the retainer and remove the filter assembly.
4. Remove the seven 5/16" bolts holding the valve block assembly to the transmission case and remove the valve block.

Care should be taken to see that the selector valve is not moved out of its normal operating range.

Dismantling

Remove the eight ¼" bolts and washers from the top of the valve block and, by lifting directly upwards, remove the relief valve body (A), Fig. 86.

Remove the rear and front pump ball check valves (B) and (C) from their seats located in the base plate.

Remove the base plate to transmission case gasket (D).

Remove the base plate and the base plate manifold plate gasket.

Remove the converter and relay valve housing (A), Fig. 87, and gasket (B) from the manifold plate.

Selector valve. Turn the selector valve so that the milled slot is away from the selector valve detent ball and spring housing. Push the selector valve into the manifold, past the detent ball and spring. The ball is under spring pressure and in view of this, cup the hand over the opening to catch the ball as

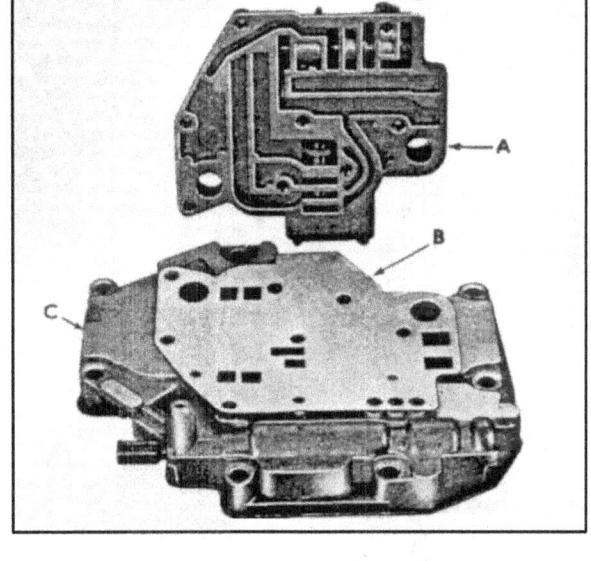

Fig 87.—Removing the converter and relay valve housing from the manifold plate.

A. Converter and relay valve housing.
B. Gasket.
C. Manifold plate.

the valve is pushed into the manifold, then remove the spring. The selector valve can then be removed from either end of the manifold plate.

NOTE: Some models are fitted with double detent springs and balls opposite each other. Great care must be exercised when removing the valve to ensure that the ball in the manifold plate housing does not move into the milled slot of the selector valve.

Reverse interlock valve. Using the spring compressor of Valve Spring Unloader, compress the reverse interlock valve spring. Then position the spring retainer tool between the spring and spring retainer. Remove the spring compressor and slip the spring retainer out of the body.

Instal the spring compressor again to permit removal of the retainer tool, then remove the compressor and remove the reverse interlock spring and piston.

Accumulator valve. Using valve spring unloader in the manner outlined for removal of the reverse interlock valve spring retainer, remove the accumulator valve spring retainer (C), spring (D) and valve (E), Fig. 88.

Main relief valve. Remove the main relief valve outer piston plug retainer (A) and plug (F).

Remove the main relief valve outer piston (G).

Remove the main relief valve inner piston (H) and the main relief valve spring (I).

Remove the main relief valve stop (B) and the main relief valve (J).

Converter shuttle valve. Remove the converter shuttle valve sleeve retainer (J), Fig. 89, and remove the sleeve (I).

Remove the converter shuttle reverse valve (H) and the converter shuttle direct valve (G).

Relay valve. Remove the two screws and washers (A), cover (B) and gasket (C) from the converter and relay valve body.

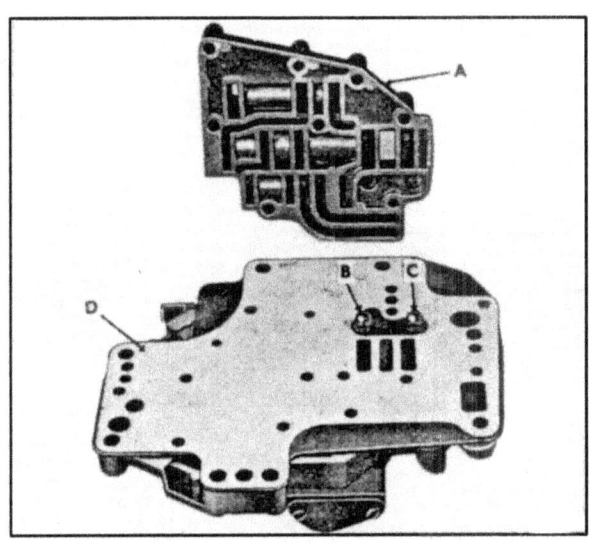

Fig 86.—Removing the relief valve body from the valve block (new hydraulic system).

A. Relief valve body.
B. Rear pump ball check valve.
C. Front pump ball check valve.
D. Gasket.

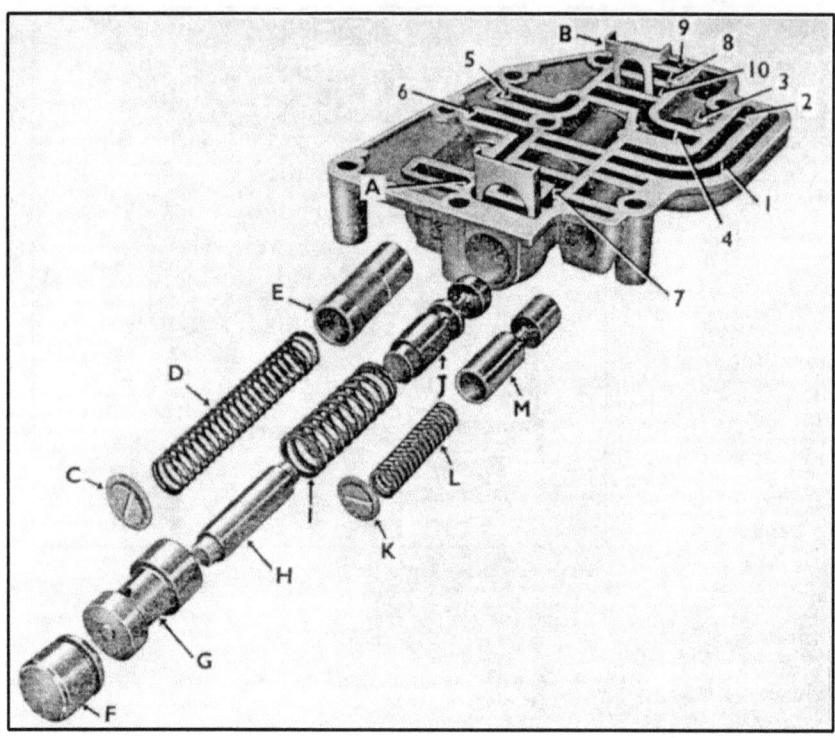

A. Main relief valve outer piston plug retainer.
B. Main relief valve stop.
C. Accumulator valve spring retainer.
D. Accumulator valve spring.
E. Accumulator valve.
F. Main relief valve outer piston plug.
G. Main relief valve outer piston.
H. Main relief valve inner piston.
I. Main relief valve spring.
J. Main relief valve.
K. Reverse interlock valve spring retainer.
L. Reverse interlock valve spring.
M. Reverse interlock valve.

Passages

1. Reverse interlock to reverse servo.
2. Selector valve to reverse interlock.
3. Front and rear pump pressure.
4. Rear pump pressure.
5. Selector valve to accumulator valve.
6. Accumulator to main relief valve outer piston.
7. Reverse pressure to main relief valve piston.
8. Front pump pressure.
9. Front and rear pump pressure.
10. Main relief valve dump.

Fig 88.—Accumulator, main relief and reverse interlock valves and passages.

Remove the relay valve plunger (D)
Remove the relay valve (E) and relay valve spring (F).

Inspection

Inspect all valves and valve bores in their respective bodies for evidence of scratches or scoring and for free operation. Slight scratches may be polished out to provide free operation. If a valve or valve body bore is badly scored or scratched a new body assembly must be installed.

Make sure that the passages in the valve block manifold, Fig 90, have no obstructions, and check for signs of porosity.

The front and rear pump check valve seats must be examined, and must be tight in the base plate. Fig 86.

Reassembly

Make sure that all parts of the valve block assembly have been thoroughly cleaned. Every precaution must be taken to keep parts clean during reassembly. Apply

A. Cover screws.
B. Cover.
C. Gasket.
D. Relay valve plunger.
E. Relay valve.
F. Relay valve spring.
G. Converter shuttle direct valve.
H. Converter shuttle reverse valve.
I. Valve sleeve.
J. Sleeve retainer.

Passages

1. Converter pressure.
2. Front and rear pump pressure.
3. Reverse pressure.
4. Low servo dump.
5. Forward servo.
6. Low servo.
7. Multiple disc clutch to relay valve.
8. Direct drive.

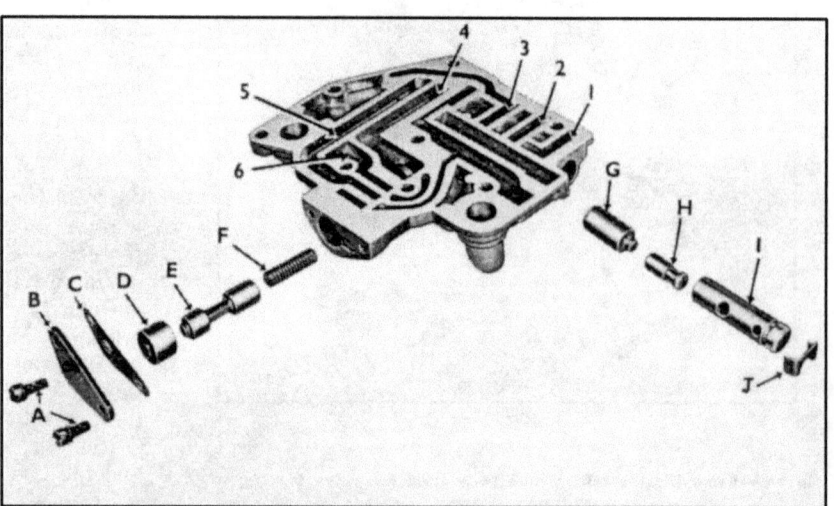

Fig 89.—Converter and relay valves.

Automatic Transmission Fluid to the gaskets during refitting to keep them in place. Gaskets must be free from wrinkles.

Relay valve. Instal the relay valve spring (F), Fig 89, in the bore of the relay valve (E), making sure the spring is in the counterbore of the body and fit the valve and spring towards the closed end of the bore. Fit the relay valve plunger (D) with the stop shoulder towards the cover. Using a new gasket, fit the cover plate screw and washers.

Converter shuttle valve. Fit the converter shuttle direct valve (G) into the valve body, so that the stop shoulder is towards the open end of the bore. Insert the converter shuttle reverse valve (H) into the converter shuttle sleeve (I) so that the annular face of the valve can seat against the converter shuttle seat. Fitting the valve in this manner will allow the small hole in the valve to be seen through the large hole of the sleeve. Insert the sleeve and valve assembly into the valve body with the open end of the sleeve towards the converter shuttle direct valve. Fit the converter valve retainer (J) in such a manner that the sleeve is positioned to expose both sleeve holes.

Accumulator valve. Fit the accumulator valve spring (D), Fig 88, in the bore of the accumulator valve (E) and fit the valve and spring as an assembly into its housing bore with the spring towards the open end of the bore. Using Valve Spring Unloader, compress the spring. Slip the retainer tool in position, withdraw the compressor and fit the retainer (C). Insert the spring compressor, remove the retainer tool and then remove the compressor, making sure that the retainer seats properly.

Reverse interlock valve. Instal reverse interlock valve spring (L) in the bore of the reverse interlock valve (M) and fit the valve and spring as an assembly into its housing bore with the spring towards the open end of the bore. Using Valve Spring Unloader in the same manner as outlined for the fitting of the accumulator valve retainer, instal the reverse interlock valve spring retainer (K).

Main relief valve. Instal the main relief valve (J) so that the lands of the valve are towards the closed end of its bore. With the valve in this closed position, fit the main relief valve stop (B). Fit the main relief valve spring (I). Insert the main relief valve inner piston (H) into the bore of the main relief valve outer piston (G). Instal the valves as an assembly into the body bore with the main relief valve piston towards the main relief valve and spring. Fit the main relief valve outer piston plug (F) and retainer (A).

Selector valve. Instal the selector valve in the valve block manifold with the milled slot at the detent housing. Make sure that the milled valve slot is turned away from the detent housing. Fit the spring and detent ball in the detent housing. Use a suitable drift, and force the ball down into the opening and hold the ball down with a small screwdriver inserted through the end of the bore, then carefully move the selector valve over the ball and, at the same time move the screwdriver off the ball. Move the valve

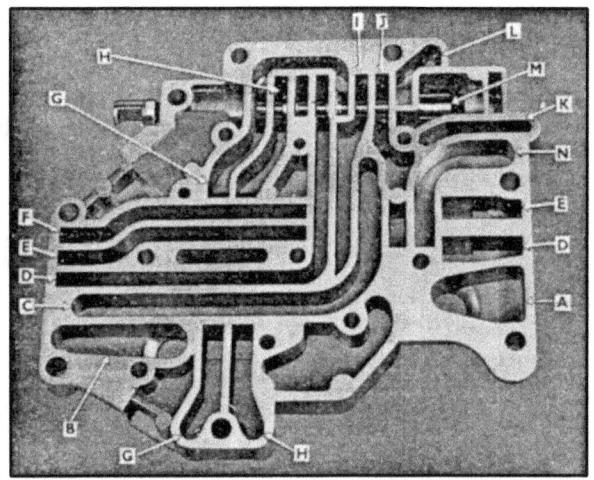

Fig 90.—Valve block manifold.

Passages

A. Front pump inlet.
B. Rear pump inlet.
C. Rear pump pressure.
D. Governor valve inlet.
E. Governor valve to multiple disc clutch.
F. Governor valve to direct drive clutch.
G. Selector valve to forward servo.
H. Selector valve to low servo.
I. Selector valve to accumulator valve.
J. Front and rear pump pressure.
K. Governor valve to converter.
L. Reverse interlock to reverse servo.
M. Selector valve to reverse interlock.
N. Front pump pressure.

down until the detent ball locks up in the groove in the valve.

Valve block main bodies and plates. Place the converter and relay valve body on a clean working table in its normal operating position. With a new gasket and using the large pump inlet holes as a guide, position the manifold plate on the converter and reverse valve body. Using a new gasket, fit the base plates. Fit front and rear check valves. Using a new gasket, instal the main relief housing. Fasten the assemblies with the eight ¼" bolts and washers. Tighten the bolts carefully to 6/8 lb/ft.

Refitting

Place the valve block in position against the inner selector control shaft lever into the slot of the selector valve. Make sure that the gasket is properly aligned with the holes in the housing and valve block.

Fit the seven retaining bolts and washers, finger tight only at present.

Disconnect the transmission rod from the selector lever and move the selector control shaft lever through its full travel to make sure that binding does not exist between the inner selector lever and selector valve. If binding does exist, reposition the assembly to relieve this, then tighten the bolts carefully to 10-13 lb/ft.

Check the adjustment of the parking pawl mechanism as outlined under Parking Pawl Adjustment section 1:14 of Part 1. Adjust if necessary.

Connect the transmission rod to the selector control shaft lever.

Pump inlet filter. With the deep portion of the filter towards the front, and using the inlet holes as guides, instal the filter assembly so that it seats securely over the pump inlet bosses located on the converter shuttle and relay valve housing. Fasten securely with the retaining clip, screw and washer.

Using a new gasket fit the sump (oil pan) and tighten the retaining screws to 10-13 lb/ft.

Following the recommended procedure outlined in the maintenance section, fill the transmission with automatic transmission fluid to the correct level.

Mainshaft Assembly (See 1:41)

Multiple Disc Clutch Friction Disc

The friction discs in the multiple disc clutch are thinner than used previously—.063" as against .098" To compensate for the decreased thickness of the friction discs a Spacer Plate is incorporated in the multiple disc assembly.

It is MOST IMPORTANT that friction discs of different thicknesses are not mixed within one multiple disc clutch assembly. Fit friction discs and spacer plate in accordance with details given in the Spare Parts Catalogue for the Jaguar Automatic Transmission, Publication J19.

Multiple Disc Clutch Plates

The clutch plates are dished .003" as against the .010" dishing of the plates used previously (see paragraph 7 of "Inspection" in 1:41 of Part 1).

2:59 TORQUE CONVERTER - MODIFIED MOUNTING

(Effective from Mark VII Model, Engine No N3482. XK140 Model, Engine No G6615)

(Refer to 1:16)

With effect from the above engine numbers the mounting of the torque converter to the crankshaft is modified as follows:—

(a) The six mounting studs on the torque converter are replaced by tapped holes and the converter is secured to the engine drive plate by setscrews and tab-washers instead of self-locking nuts.

(b) The engine drive plate is increased in size from 7½" to 11 1/16" dia.

(c) The starter pinion housing cut-away is increased to avoid any possibility of fouling the engine drive plate.

Interchangeability

Torque converter C10986 is interchangeable with converter C6843 provided that the modified mounting arrangement (that is, driveplate, setscrews and lockwashers) is used.

It is NOT necessary to fit a new starter C10980 as the existing starter can be modified by machining or filing a flat on the pinion housing as shown in Fig 91.

The existing reinforcing plate C6861 behind the engine drive plate is utilised with the new mounting arrangement.

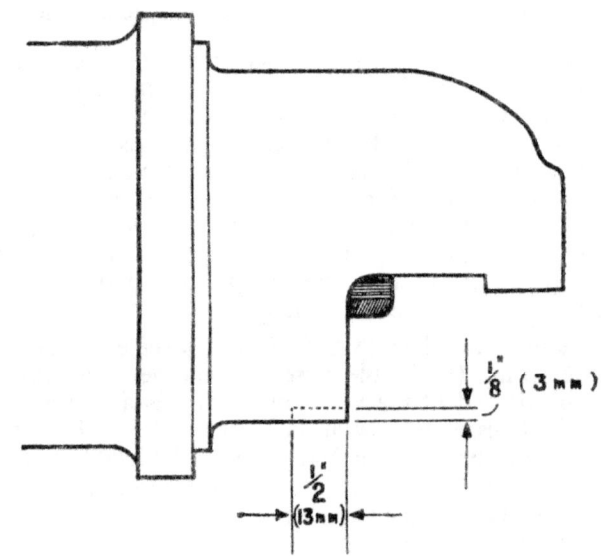

Fig 91.—Modification to starter pinion housing.

2:60 SPLIT PARKING BRAKE ROD

(Effective from Transmission No 5011)

With effect from the above transmission serial number a split type of parking brake rod is fitted.

This type of parking rod is spring-loaded between the two halves which allows the selector lever to be moved out of the P (Park) position without necessarily disengaging the pawl from the gear on the output shaft.

This allows a driving gear to be engaged so that the load on the pawl can be released if it has become firmly engaged owing to the car being parked on a steep gradient. (Refer to 1:12)

P (Park) Paragraph 2

When the car is stopped on a hill and the P (Park) position selected, the parking mechanism may become very firmly engaged due to the load on the pawl. To disengage the parking pawl under these conditions the following procedure should be adopted:—

To release transmission from P (Park) when facing UP HILL.

Start the engine.
Release the hand brake.
Select D and hold lever in this position (irrespective of the direction in which it is desired to move off).
Depress accelerator slowly until the car moves forward, indicating the release of the parking pawl.

The car is now "free" and can be driven away in the desired direction.

To release transmission from P (Park) when facing DOWN HILL.
Start the engine.
Release the hand brake.
Select R and hold lever in this position (irrespective of the direction in which it is desired to move off).

Depress accelerator slowly until the car moves backward, indicating the release of the parking pawl. The car is now "free" and can be driven away in the desired direction.

Parking Brake Actuating Rod
The "Removal and Installation" instructions for the split type of parking rod are as described in Part I.

2:61 INTERMEDIATE SPEED HOLD

(Applicable to Mark VIII and XK150 Models. Effective from commencement of production)

DESCRIPTION
The intermediate speed hold is an electrically-controlled mechanism which allows the driver:—
(a) To override the automatic upshift between intermediate (second) gear and direct drive.
(b) To effect a downshift from direct drive to intermediate (second) gear without depressing the accelerator pedal as for a "kickdown" change.

OPERATION
The operating mechanism consists of a solenoid (1, Fig 92) controlled by a manual switch mounted on the fascia. The solenoid plunger (3) is screwed into a ferrule (5) which in turn is screwed into a guide tube (6). The end of the governor valve (8) is threaded internally to take a connecting pin (7), the head of which is allowed limited free travel in the guide tube.

When the fascia switch is in the "Out" position the governor valve will operate normally and move inwards by virtue of the free travel of the connecting pin head in the guide tube.

Moving the fascia switch to the "In" position energises the solenoid, attracts the plunger which in turn withdraws the guide tube towards the solenoid.

If at the time the switch is moved to the "In" position the transmission is:

(a) **In Direct Drive,** the guide tube will contact the head of the connecting pin and draw the governor valve back to the intermediate position thus effecting a downshift. Independent of any increase in road speed the transmission will remain in the intermediate gear until such time as the switch is moved to the "Out" position, when the solenoid will become de-energised

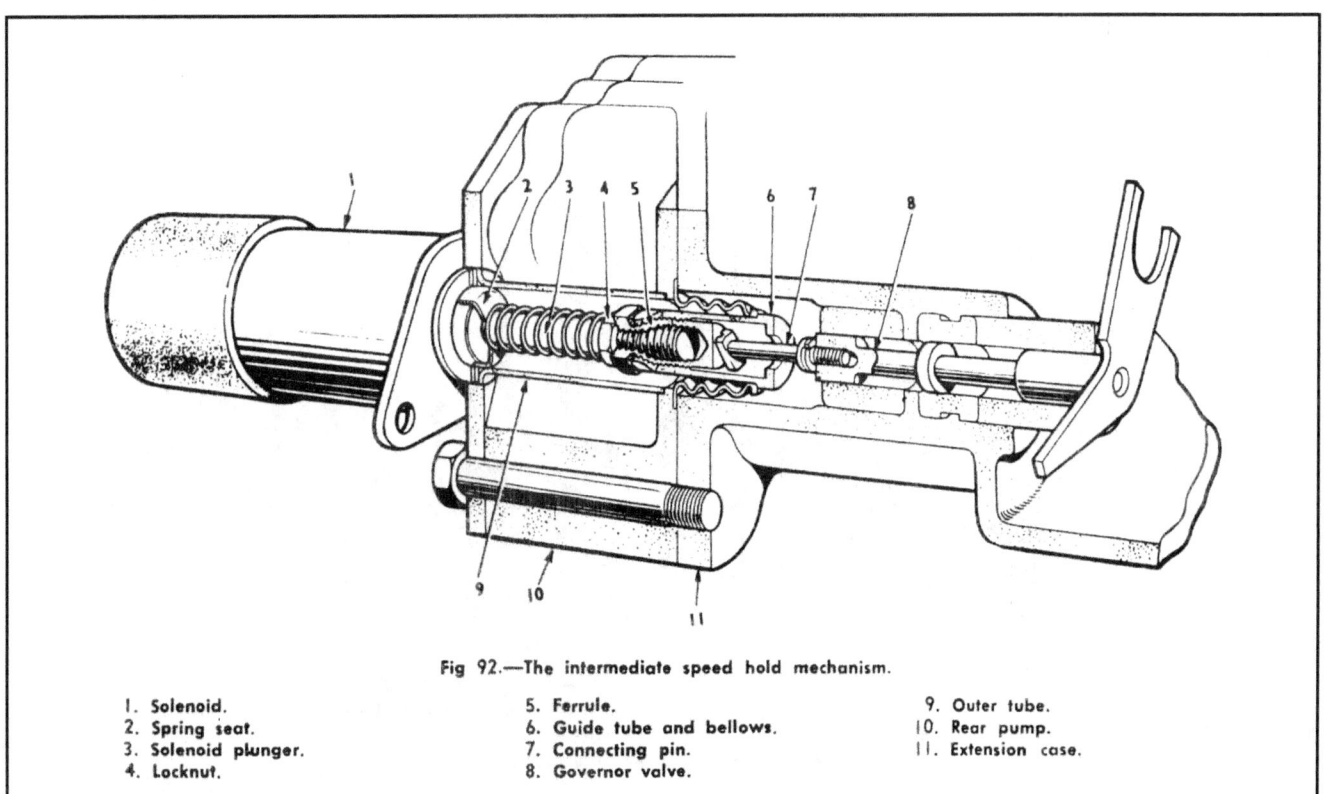

Fig 92.—The intermediate speed hold mechanism.

1. Solenoid.	5. Ferrule.	9. Outer tube.
2. Spring seat.	6. Guide tube and bellows.	10. Rear pump.
3. Solenoid plunger.	7. Connecting pin.	11. Extension case.
4. Locknut.	8. Governor valve.	

and the guide tube will move back through the action of the spring around the solenoid plunger. This will either cause an intermediate change into direct drive if the upshift speed has been obtained or will allow the change to take place when the normal upshift speed is reached.

(b) **In Low or Intermediate Gear,** the position of the guide tube will allow normal changes between these two gears but will restrain the governor valve from moving into the direct drive position regardless of any increase in governor speed.

DISMANTLING

Removal of Solenoid

Disconnect the solenoid wire from the feed wire at the snap connector.

Unscrew the three setscrews (two on some models) securing the solenoid (1, Fig 92) to the adaptor plate. Withdraw the solenoid, leaving the plunger in position.

Removal of Intermediate Speed Hold Mechanism

Remove the extension case from the transmission unit.

Remove the solenoid as described above. Remove the two washers and the outer tube (9).

Slacken the locknut (4) and screw the solenoid plunger (3) out of the ferrule (5).

Remove the rear pump from the extension case by unscrewing the three setscrews.

Unscrew the ferrule from the guide tube and unscrew the connecting pin (7) from the end of the governor valve.

Withdraw the guide tube and bellows assembly complete with the connecting pin.

To remove the connecting pin from the guide tube, tilt the pin until the head can be withdrawn through the hole in the end of the tube.

ASSEMBLING

Completely reassemble the intermediate speed hold mechanism pump and solenoid with the exception of the outer tube (9, Fig 92).

Adjust the position of the solenoid plunger (3) in the ferrule (5) so that with the solenoid energised as shown in Fig 92, and with the governor valve withdrawn inwards as far as possible by hand, there is a 3/16" to ¼" gap between the governor valve and the stop on the governor valve plate.

When correctly adjusted, tighten the locknut (4) and remove the solenoid. Refit the outer tube (9), the two rubber washers and the solenoid.

Refit the extension case to the transmission unit.

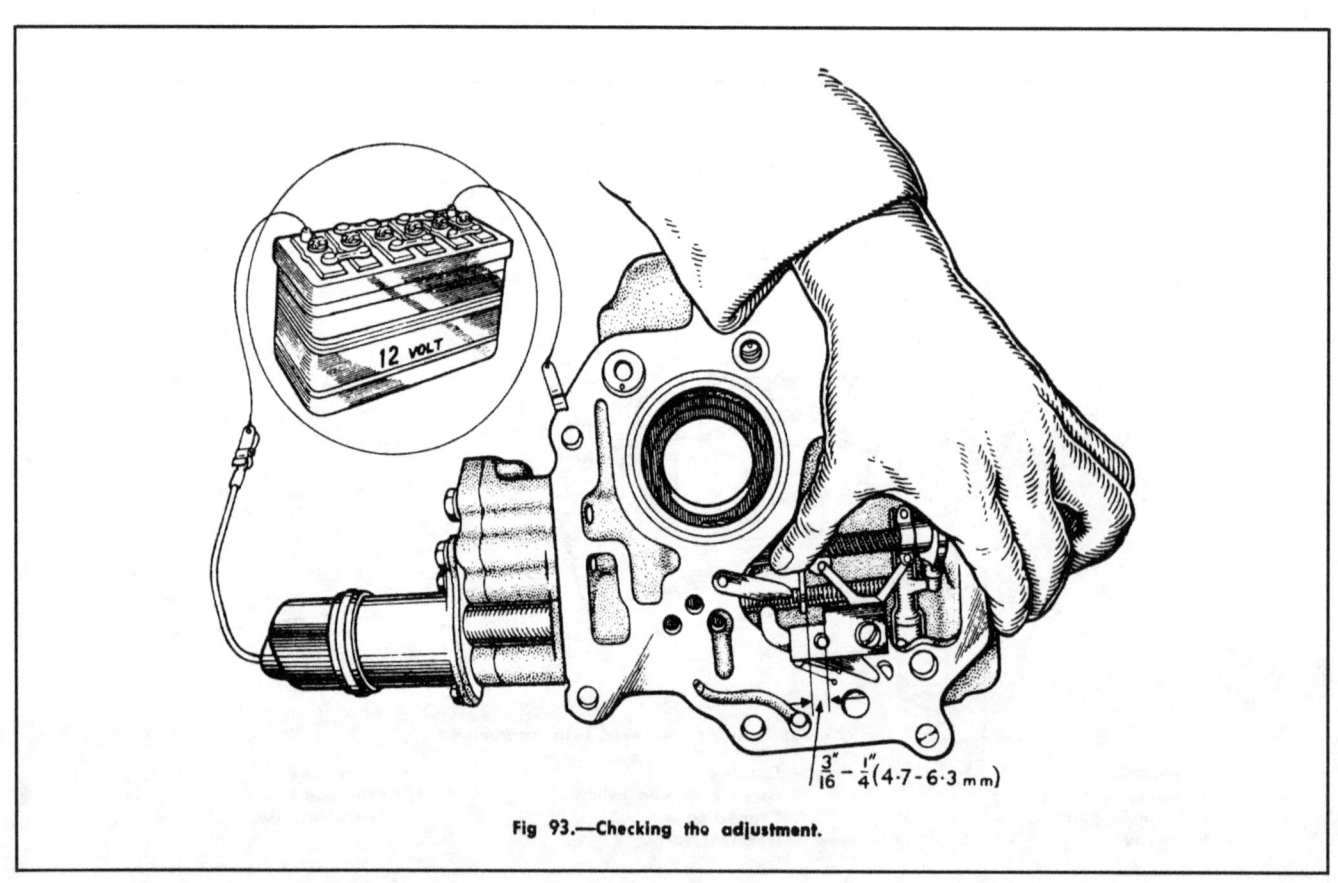

Fig 93.—Checking the adjustment.

2:62 ADJUSTMENT OF REVERSE LIGHT AND STARTER CUT-OUT SWITCH
(Applicable to XK150 Models)

On the above models the starter cutout-reverse light switch is situated behind the dash casing and is connected to the manual selector control linkage.

The purpose of the switch is to ensure that (a) the starter motor circuit is only operative when the manual selector lever is in the P (Park) or N (Neutral) so that the engine cannot be started when the transmission is in any one of the driving ranges; (b) the reverse light circuit is closed when the manual selector lever is in the R (Reverse) position and the ignition is switched on.

The method of adjustment for the switch is as follows:—

Remove the dash casing situated below the instrument panel.

Raise the boot lid so that the reverse light can be seen through the rear window. Alternatively the ammeter can be watched for a slight discharge when the reverse light becomes illuminated.

Switch on the ignition. Place the selector lever in the R (Reverse) position so that the centre line of lever is in line with the letter R; move lever $\frac{1}{8}''$ to $\frac{1}{4}''$ towards the L position.

Slacken the locking bolt nut which secures the switch bracket to the mounting bracket. Move the switch along the elongated hole so that the reverse light is extinguished. Slowly move the switch bracket until the reverse lamp lights up and tighten the nut.

Test the operation of the starter switch with the manual selector lever in the P, N and D positions. The starter should operate only when the lever is in the P or N position.

NOTE: When testing in the "D" position apply the footbrake firmly.

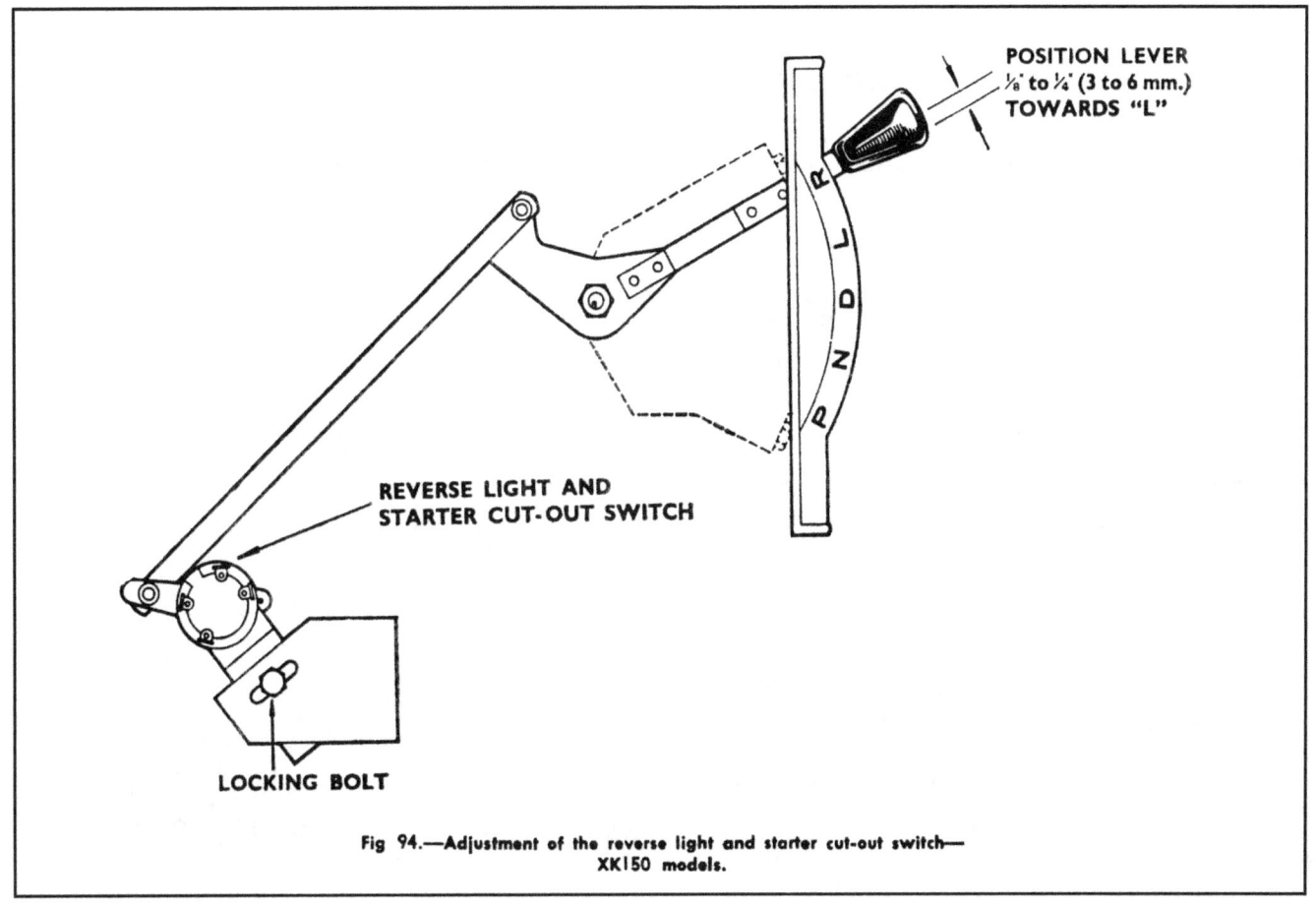

Fig 94.—Adjustment of the reverse light and starter cut-out switch—XK150 models.

2:63 MODIFICATION TO RELAY VALVE

Applicable to: Mark VIII Model. Effective from Engine No NA1938
XK150 Model. Effective from Engine No V3208
Mark IX Model. Commencement of production

With effect from the above engine numbers a modification is incorporated in the valve block to produce a smoother change between intermediate and low gear on closed throttle downshift.

The modification makes the relay valve inoperative and cuts off the hydraulic flow to the low band servo so that only the forward band is in operation for Automatic Low in the "D" position.

Initially the relay valve was rendered inoperative by dispensing with the valve spring (Item F, Fig 89) and inserting a slug (or double coil spring washer) between the relay valve plunger and the cover plate.

Later units incorporate a modified valve block which does not include a relay valve.

NOTE: For the selected low ("L") position both the forward and low bands are applied as described in 2:54.

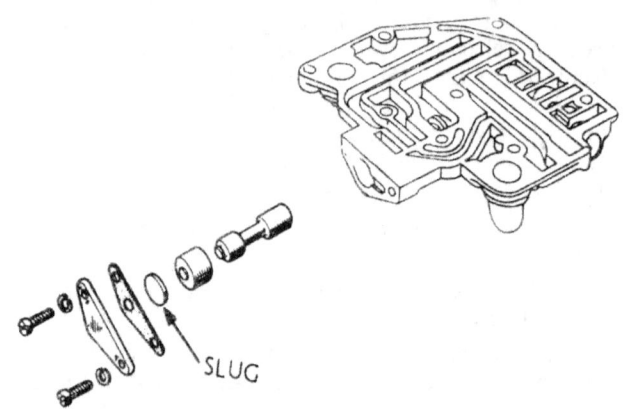

Fig 95.—Showing the modification which renders the relay valve inoperative.

2:64 SYSTEMATIC DIAGNOSIS AND RECTIFICATION CHART

(Not applicable to Second speed start transmission units)

Before any attempt is made at diagnosis, the fluid in the transmission must be of the correct specification. The fluid level also must be checked.

Selector and governor linkages must be correctly adjusted.

*A key to the Action numbers will be found at the end of this section.

Fault	Action *
Slip or Ineffective Drive	
Inoperative in D, L and R	1, 2, 3, 4, 5, 6, 7
Excessive slip on take-off in D, L and R	2, 3, 4, 5
Excessive slip on take-off in D only	2, 3, 4, 5, 8, 11, 12
Excessive slip on take-off in R only	2, 3, 4, 5, 10, 11, 12
Excessive slip on change from low to intermediate	2, 3, 13, 14, 15, 16, 12, 17, 18
Excessive slip on change from intermediate to direct drive	2, 3, 19, 14, 15, 16, 22, 21, 12, 20, 4, 17, 21

Fault	Action*
Drag or Engine Laboring	
Drag on down change from intermediate to low (HT models only)	13, 14, 18
Drag in R	7, 8, 9, 11
Drag in D and L	7, 10, 11
Drag in D, L and R	7
Engine stalls when selecting D or when coming to rest in D	19, 14, 22, 21
Judder on engagement of direct drive	21
Drag on change from low to intermediate (HT models only)	4
Poor hill-climbing, lack of acceleration in indirect ranges	7, 23
Judder while cruising in direct drive	7, 6

NOTE: *HT model indicates a transmission with an operative relay valve.*

Fault	Action*
Incorrect Operation	
Will not change up in D	13, 19, 20, 14, 32
Will not kick-down at speeds below 45 mph	24, 14
Over-sensitive on kick-down, "hunts" between direct and intermediate	24, 14
Starts in intermediate	24, 14, 13, 18
Will only move off in L	1, 6
Will only move off in R	1, 6
Selects reverse at speeds above 3-5 mph	25, 4
Parking pawl attempts to engage at speeds above 3-5 mph	25, 26, 31
Car cannot be push-started	1, 2, 25
Parking pawl will not engage	1, 26, 31
Ineffective engine braking on overrun in L	1, 9, 11
Excessive jerk when selecting D, L or R (Accumulator valve sticking)	7, 2, 8, 10, 4
Delay in taking up drive in D, L or R	2, 4, 7, 6
Poor acceleration and low maximum speed in direct drive, normal in indirect ranges (stall speed normal)	7, 21
Car creeps or drives in N	1, 8, 10, 21

Fault	Action*
Noisy Operation	
Rattling noise, more noticeable at idling speeds	1, 7, 24
Whine in direct drive at 30-40 mph (Do not confuse with axle or tyre noise)	28, 32
Whine at fast idling speed in all selector positions	29
Gear noise at low speed in indirect ranges	30
Knocking, scraping or grating noise in all selector positions	7, 27, 29, 6
Excessive swishing noise on take-off from rest	2, 24, 20, 23
Barking noise when selecting D, L or R	2, 4

* See Action Key below.

ACTION KEY

Where the "Action" line is divided, the following procedure should be adopted:— If the preceding pressure reading is incorrect, follow the upper line. If the pressure reading is correct, follow the lower line.

1. Check selector linkage.
2. Check fluid level.
3. Check front pump pressure.
4. Clean or overhaul valve block and clean filter.
5. Check front pump and drive tangs on converter hub.
6. Check freewheels and/or races.
7. Check external features (eg, engine performance, carburettor linkage, idling speed, brakes, anti-creep and halfshafts).
8. Check forward band adjustment, and/or condition of band and adjuster.
9. Check low band adjustment, and/or condition of band and adjuster.
10. Check reverse band adjustment, and/or condition of band and adjuster.
11. Check relevant servo pressure, and/or correct functioning of servo piston.
12. Check for blocked fluid passage, and/or damaged casting.
13. Check multi-disc clutch pressure.
14. Check action of governor, governor valve, hydraulic detent, and booster spring (if used).
15. Check oil rings, O-rings and oil seals in gear train.
16. Check gaskets on extension case, valve block and collector ring.
17. Check for tightness and correct position of lubrication valve and tube in mainshaft.
18. Check mechanical condition of multi-disc clutch pack, piston and retractor springs.
19. Check direct drive clutch pressure.
20. Check converter pressure.
21. Change torque converter and direct drive clutch assembly.
22. Check that transfer tube is correctly fitted, and has grooved front end.
23. Check stall speed. If low, change torque converter assembly.
24. Check governor linkage and second speed hold (if fitted).
25. Check rear pump pressure. If incorrect see 4 and 32.
26. Check action of parking pawl, interlock piston and spring.
27. Check for converter fouling bell-housing, gearbox, or adjacent parts.
28. Change rear pump assembly.
29. Inspect and if necessary replace front pump.
30. Inspect and if necessary replace gear train components.
31. Check adjustment of pawl actuating rod.
32. Check rear pump drive.

2:65 SERVICE TOOLS

Spline Alignment Fixture (Fig 96)
(Tool No J4283)

This fixture is necessary when installing the transmission unit, to align the splines of the transmission shafts with the mating splines in the torque converter. (See Part I, Figs 17 and 19.)

Converter Alignment Flange (Fig 97)
(Tool No J4286)

This flange is used to centralise the torque converter in its housing to ensure correct alignment with the transmission unit. (See Part I, Fig 20.)

Pressure Gauge and Adapters (Not Shown)
(Tool No J4270)

This pressure testing outfit is required for the checking of the hydraulic units incorporated in the transmission assembly. The adapters and flexible hose allow the gauge to be connected to convenient pressure take-off points in the transmission case.

Brake Band Adjusting Tool (Fig 98)
(Tool No J4285)

This tool is necessary for the accurate checking and setting of the brake bands incorporated in the transmission unit. (See Part I, Fig 12.)

Mainshaft End Play Gauge and Spline Locking Clip
(Tool No J4668) (Fig 99)

This gauge and spline clip are used to ascertain the thickness of thrust washer required to maintain the correct end-play of the mainshaft assembly. The thrust washer is supplied in four thicknesses and is fitted at the rear of the front pump assembly. (See Part I, Fig 45).

The Spline Locking Clip (J4668-3) is also used when removing and installing the front pump assembly to avoid misplacing the thrust washers within the mainshaft assembly. (See Part I, Fig 43.)

Mainshaft Rear Bearing Puller (Fig 100)
(Tool No HM925 and J1298-B)

The mainshaft rear bearing puller consists of a Universal Puller (HM925) and a puller Plate and Adapter Rings (J1298-B) which facilitate the withdrawal of the rear bearing from the mainshaft.

Adapter for Hoist (Not Shown)
(Tool No 31300)

The use of this adapter, in conjunction with a hoist, with greatly facilitate the removal and installation of the transmission unit.

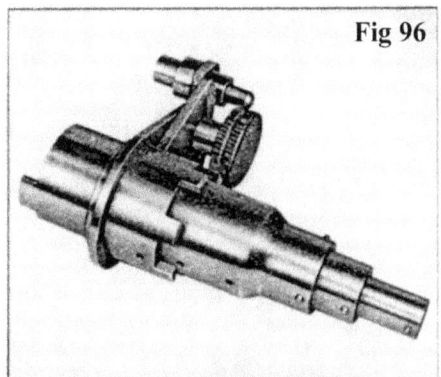
Fig 96

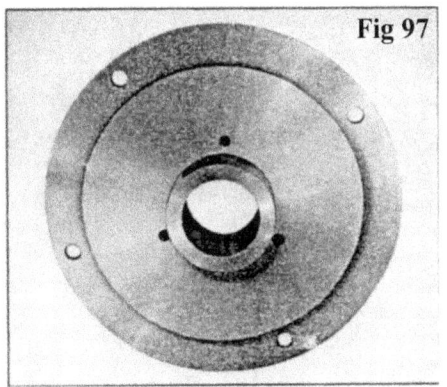
Fig 97

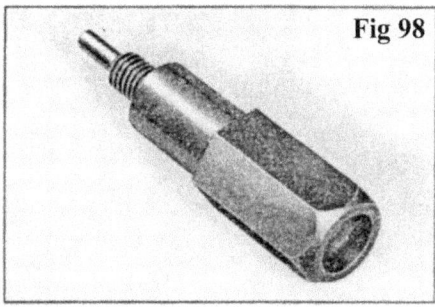
Fig 98

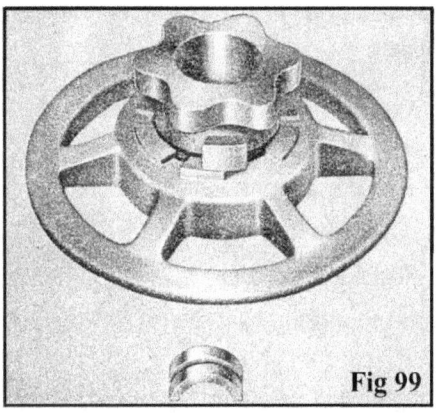
Fig 99

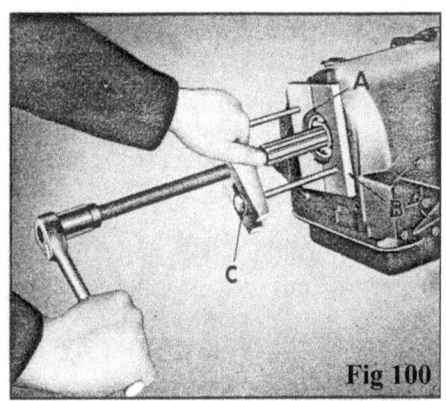
Fig 100

2:66 TORQUE SETTINGS

Part Name	Thread Size	Torque Required ft/lb
Band Adjusting Screw Nut	½-20	40-50
Brake Cylinder Screw (3 Adjusting and Gauge Ports)	⅜-16	28-33
Converter Control Valve Screw	No 10-24	3-4
Converter Valve Body to Manifold Screw	¼-20	6-8
Converter Housing Cover Screw	¼-20	6-8
Converter Drive Plate to Crankshaft Screw	7/16-20	66
Converter Drain Plug	⅜-24	15-20
Detent Cam to Shaft Setscrew	No 10-32	3-4
Extension Case to Transmission Case	⅜-16	28-33
Extension Case — Detent Cam Adjustment — Setscrew Nut	¼-20	14-17
Extension Case — Detent Cam Adjustment — Palnut	¼-20	3-4
Extension Case Pipe Plug	⅛ Pipe	8-10
Front Relief Valve Body to Manifold Screw	¼-20	6-8
Front Pump to Collector Ring Screw	¼-20	10-12
Front Pump to Collector Ring Screw	5/16-18	15-18
Front Pump and Collector Ring to Case Screw	5/16-18	15-18
Governor Stop to Extension Case Screw	¼-20	6-8
Governor Adjusting Shaft Bushing	9/16-18	25-30
Low Brake Cylinder to Case Screw	5/16-18	15-18
Lever to Selector Control Shaft Nut	5/16-24	6-8
Oil Pan to Transmission Case Screw	5/16-18	10-13
Pump Cover to Rear Pump Body Screw	¼-20	6-8
Parking Brake Actuating Rod Nut	¼-28	3-4
Reverse Cylinder to Case Screw	5/16-18	15-18
Reverse Cylinder to Case Screw (3″ long)	5/16-18	10-13
Rear Pump Pipe Plug	¼ Pipe	6-7
Reverse Brake Cylinder Pipe Plug	⅛ Pipe	8-10
Rear Pump Body to Extension Case	5/16-18	15-18
Speedometer Housing and Cover to Extension Case Screw	5/16-18	10-13
Shuttle Valve to Reverse Cylinder Screw	¼-20	8-9
Shuttle Valve and Reverse Cylinder to Case Screw	5/16-18	10-13
Shuttle Valve Assembly Pipe Plug	⅛ Pipe	6-7
Transmission Oil Pan Drain Plug	⅝-18	35-45
Transmission Case Pipe Plug	⅛ Pipe	8-10
Transmission to Converter Housing Stud Nut	7/16-20	23-28
Universal Joint Flange Nut	¾-16	60-80
Valve Block Assembly to Case Screw	5/16-18	10-13

NOTES

INDEX – PROPELLER SHAFT, REAR AXLE & SUSPENSION

SECTION	PAGE	
000	183	Basic Diagnostic Testing & Troubleshooting

PROPELLER SHAFT

001	183	Description
002	183	Maintenance
003	184	Removal & Disassembly
004	185	Reassembly

REAR AXLE

005	190	Description (Salisbury & E.N.V. Types)
006	190	Maintenance
007	190	Axle Shaft Removal
008	191	Axle Housing Removal
009	191	Reassembly

REAR SUSPENSION

010	192	Description
011	192	Maintenance
012	192	Spring Removal
013	192	Spring Reassembly
014	192	Dampers (Shock Absorbers)

GENERAL

015	193	Modifications by Engine Number & Model
016	193	Fault Diagnosis Chart

REAR AXLE
Basic Diagnostic Testing & Troubleshooting

A rear axle should not be disassembled until a thorough diagnosis is made of the trouble and symptoms observed during the operation of the car. The most common rear axle complaint is noise. Care must be taken to be sure that the noise is not caused by the engine, tires, transmission, wheel bearings, or some other part of the car.

Before road testing the car, make sure that sufficient lubricant is in the axle housing and inflate the tires to the correct pressure. Drive the car far enough to warm the lubricant to its normal operating temperature before making the tests.

Engine noise or exhaust noise can be detected by parking the car and running the engine at various speeds with the transmission in neutral. Use of a tachometer will assist in duplicating road speeds at which the noises occurred.

Tire noise can be detected by driving the car over various road surfaces. Tire noise is minimized on smooth asphalt or black-top roads. Switching tires can help to detect or eliminate tire noises.

Wheel bearing noise can sometimes be detected by jacking up each wheel in turn and feeling for roughness as the wheel is rotated. Wheel bearing noise is most obvious on a low-speed coast. Applying the brakes lightly while the car is moving will often reduce or eliminate the noise caused by a defective wheel bearing.

A car should be tested for axle and driveline noise by operating it under four driving conditions:
1. Drive: Higher than normal road-load power, where the speed gradually increases on level road acceleration.
2. Cruise: Constant speed operation at normal road speeds.
3. Float: Using only enough throttle to keep the car from driving the engine. Car will slow down (very little load on rear axle gears).
4. Coast: Throttle closed—engine is braking the car (load is on the coast side of the gear set).

Backlash or play in the running gear can be checked by driving the car on a smooth road at 25 mph (40 km./h.) and lightly pressing and releasing the accelerator pedal. Backlash is indicated by a slapping noise with each movement of the accelerator pedal.

Rear axle fault diagnosis chart

1. **Noise on acceleration**
   1a. Heavy heel contact on ring gear
2. **Noise on coast**
   2a. Heavy toe contact on ring gear
3. **Noise on both coast and acceleration**
   3a. Differential gears worn
   3b. Pinion and ring gears worn
   3c. Defective bearings
4. **Noise only when rounding a curve**
   4a. Damaged differential case gears
5. **Backlash**
   5a. Worn axle shaft splines
   5b. Loose axle shaft nut
   5c. Worn universal joints
   5d. Excessive play between pinion and ring gear
   5e. Worn differential bearings
   5f. Worn differential side gear thrust washers and/or case
6. **Vibration**
   6a. Worn universal joints
   6b. Universal spline not assembled according to matching arrows
   6c. Undercoating applied to drive shaft
   6d. Drive line center bearing out of alignment
   6e. Drive line angle incorrect

PROPELLER SHAFT, REAR AXLE & REAR SUSPENSION - SERVICE

1 Description

There are two types of propeller shaft fitted to the Jaguar cars covered by this manual both being of Hardy Spicer manufacture. The first type is a divided shaft in two parts and the second type is a single shaft which is similar to the rear portion of the first type. Because of this similarity only the divided type of propeller shaft is dealt with in this Chapter. It will be therefore necessary where the single shaft is fitted merely to ignore any reference to the first portion of the divided shaft.

The propeller shaft is attached at either end by flanged yokes connected to companion flanges at the gearbox mainshaft and rear axle pinion shaft by four bolts passing through the respective flange faces. The front shaft has a needle roller bearing universal joint at the front end and is supported by a deep grooved ballbearing at the rear end, the outer track of which is located in an oval housing attached to the chassis frame by flexible rubber bushes pinched by expansion bolts passing through them. The rear shaft is flange bolted to the first shaft (to the gearbox mainshaft for the single shaft) by four set bolts passing through the flange faces. Needle roller bearing universal joints are fitted to the front and rear of this shaft and a splined sliding joint is incorporated immediately behind the front universal joint.

A general arrangement of the divided and single propeller shafts is shown in **FIGS 1** and **2** respectively.

2 Maintenance

Routine maintenance consists of lubrication of the universal joints and the sliding spline each of which has a nipple for this purpose. The supporting centre bearing on the front propeller shaft is pre-lubricated and requires no attention except at overhauls when it should be packed with grease. Grease is not suitable as a lubricant for universal joint needle bearings, and gear oil as recommended should always be used. After high mileages check

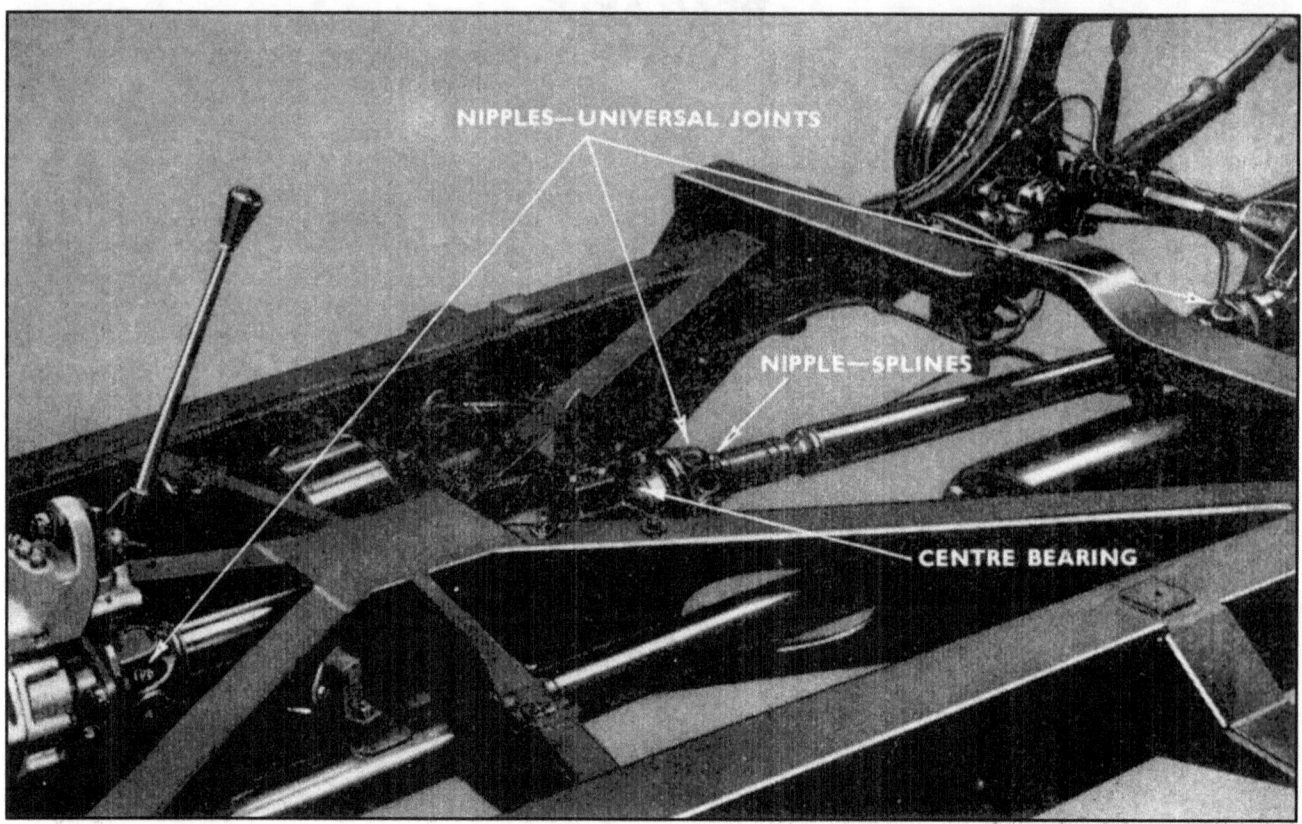

FIG 1 Divided propeller shaft

that the slotted nuts securing the flanged yokes to the gearbox mainshaft splines and rear axle pinion shaft splines are tight. Also check that the companion flange bolts are tight and that wear has not taken place in the universal joints. Wear on the thrust faces can be located by testing the lift in the joint either by hand or with a light bar. Wear in the needle roller bearings or the spline sliding joint is indicated if the shaft can be rotated relative to the flange yokes.

3 Removal

Jack-up the rear of the car to a height convienient for working on the propeller shaft, ensuring that chocks are placed in position under the front wheels.

From under the car on Mk VII models remove the hexagon adjustment nut from the handbrake mechanism and place the cable assembly clear of the propeller shafts to facilitate their removal.

Remove the splitpins and castellated nuts from the front companion flange (gearbox end). On XK 120 models it is first necessary to remove the gearlever knob then the carpet and gearbox cover to expose these nuts from above. On the Mk VII model they are accessible from below the car. In both cases the shaft will have to be rotated to gain access to the nuts so the gearlever must be placed in the neutral position. Mark the relative positions of the intermediate companion flanges joining the front and rear propeller shafts and the front companion flanges. This is to ensure that the shaft is replaced in its original position.

Remove the bolts from the joint companion flange and carefully ease the flanges apart. Remove the splitpins and castellated nuts from the intermediate companion flanges between the front and rear shafts. Ease the rear shaft flange away from the front shaft flange and support the weight of the rear shaft by securing to the chassis. Remove the two through bolts from the centre bearing housing oval flange and ease the housing clear of the chassis plates. Disengage and remove from its platforms the coil spring supporting the centre bearing.

Withdraw the front propeller shaft to the rear of the car.

Remove the splitpins and castellated nut from the rear companion flanges to the rear axle pinion after marking the respective position of the flanges. Remove the flange bolts whilst supporting the propeller shaft. Withdraw the shaft to the rear of the car.

Dismantling:

(a) Front propeller shaft and centre bearing:

The universal joint consists of a spider with four journals, each carrying a needle roller bearing assembly which is retained in the respective yoke ear by a circlip (see **FIG 4**).

Dealing with each bearing in turn remove the circlip. If any difficulty is experienced tap the bearing housing to release the tension on the circlip. Tap the yoke ear in the vicinity of the bearing with a copper or lead hammer until the bearing cage emerges. If the cage sticks, it is permissible to tap on the inner lip of the cap using a screwdriver or thin drift although extreme care must be taken to avoid damaging the cage. Pull the cage out vertically downwards to keep the needle rollers intact. Then remove the opposite bearing. The spider may then be removed from the yoke and the remaining bearings released.

The centre bearing consists of a deep grooved ballbearing 41 pressed into a housing which has an oval shaped bearer plate attached 44 (see **FIG 3**) and this assembly is mounted on the tail of the propeller shaft with a dust shield 42 between the housing and the shaft tubing. The bearing 41 is retained on the shaft by a flange coupling 37 which is bolted to the companion flange on the rear propeller shaft. This flange coupling is retained on the front propeller shaft by keyways in the coupling engaging with Woodruff keys 38 on the shaft and a castellated nut 39 with splitpin 40.

Remove the splitpin 40 and nut 39. Draw off the flanged coupling 37 and remove the Woodruff keys 38. Remove the outer dust cover 43. Drive the shaft through the bearing and housing. Press the bearing out of the housing. Scrap the dust covers 42 and 43.

(b) Rear propeller shaft:

Unscrew by hand the knurled dust cap 33 (see **FIG 4**) at the rear of the sliding joint. Observe the steel and cork washers 34/35 fitted behind the dust cap. Draw the splined sleeve yoke off the splines on the propeller shaft noting that arrows are stamped on the splined sleeve yoke and on the propeller shaft tube, when refitting, these arrows must be in line.

The universal joints at both ends of the rear propeller shaft are dismantled in the same manner as indicated for that on the front propeller shaft.

Inspection:

All parts should be washed in petrol and inspected. Any of them showing signs of pitting, corrosion, distortion or wear should be renewed.

Factory reconditioned propeller shafts are available on an exchange basis and it is recommended that advantage be taken of this scheme in preference to overhauling the original assembly. The spider and complete bearing assemblies of the universal joints are available in complete sets but if the eyes in the yoke are worn oval the bearing cages will no longer be the correct light drive fit in them so the yokes will require renewal. Since one yoke in each case is an integral part of the shaft it is preferable to fit a reconditioned shaft as oversize journals and bearings are not available.

If there are any signs of wear on the splines of the splined shaft or in the sleeve yoke a replacement shaft must be fitted.

If the centre bearing is worn it may be renewed but check the fit of the new bearing in its housing as this must be a press fit if it is not a new bearing housing will be required. The flange coupling must also be a good fit on the taper of the shaft and must be renewed it it is not. The bearing dust covers must be renewed every time the bearing is dismantled.

4 Reassembly

Reassembly is in general the reverse procedure of the dismantling process but the following points should be carefully carried out:

Before reassembling the universal joints remove the lubricating nipple and blow the oilways clear. Make sure the holes in the journals are thoroughly clean and free of grease. Also ensure that the lubricator boss is fitted away from the yoke

Assemble the needle rollers in the bearing races with

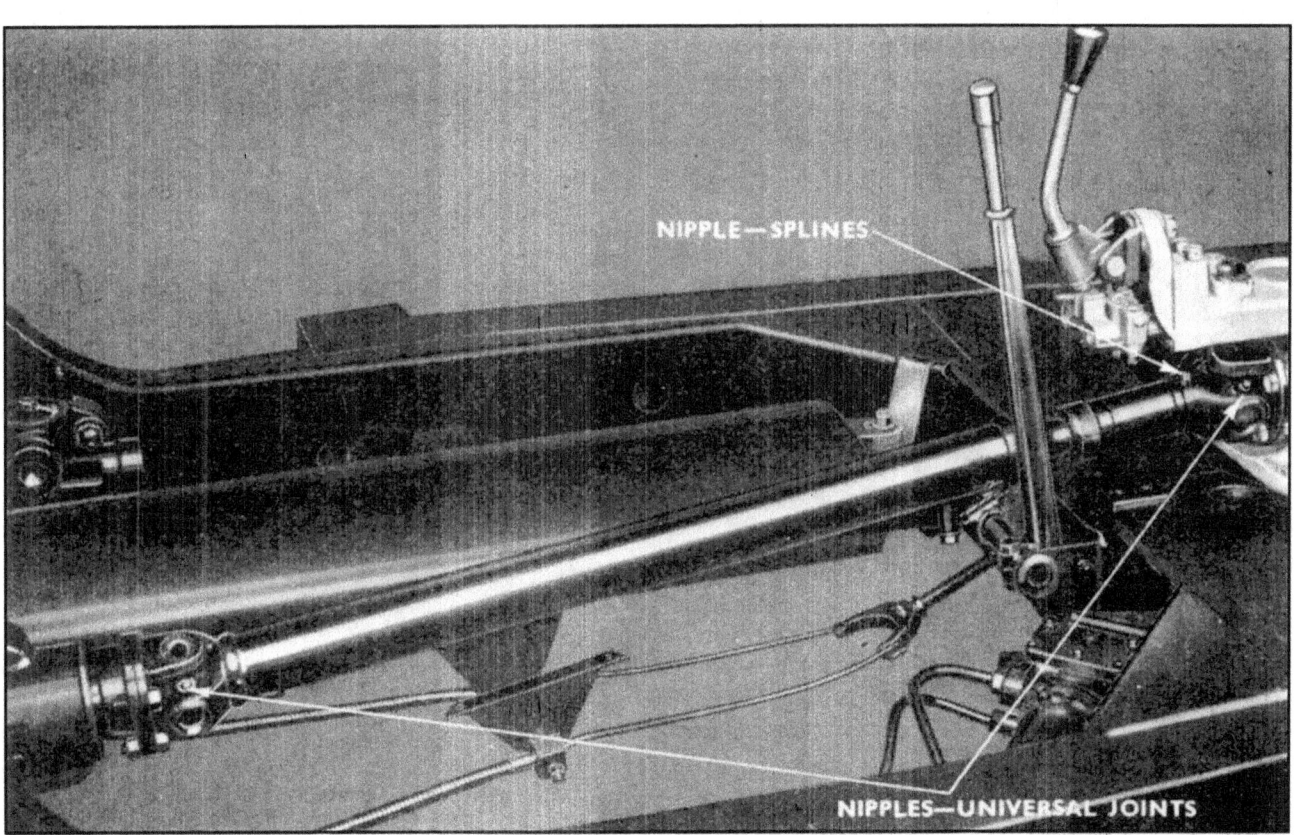

FIG 2 Single propeller shaft

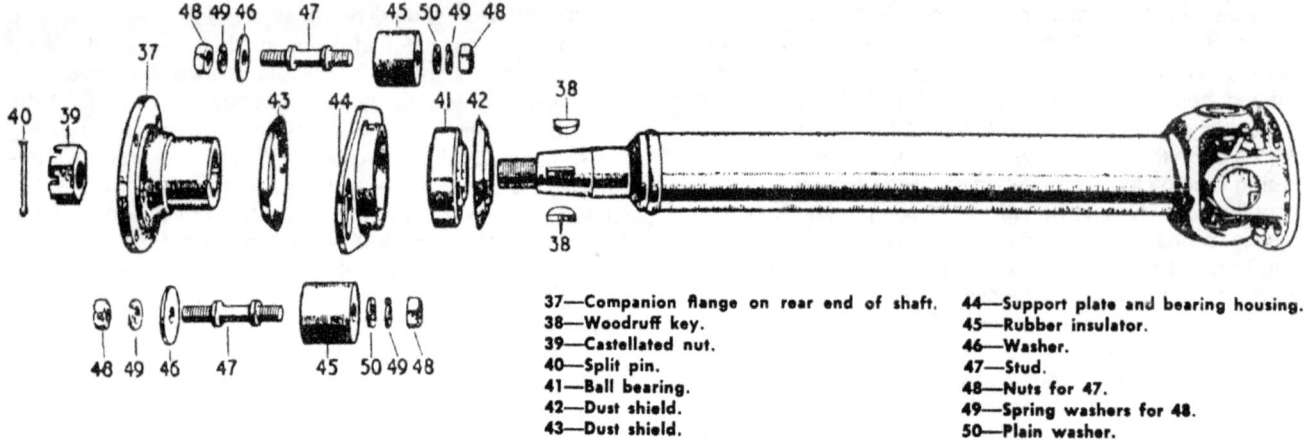

37—Companion flange on rear end of shaft.
38—Woodruff key.
39—Castellated nut.
40—Split pin.
41—Ball bearing.
42—Dust shield.
43—Dust shield.
44—Support plate and bearing housing.
45—Rubber insulator.
46—Washer.
47—Stud.
48—Nuts for 47.
49—Spring washers for 48.
50—Plain washer.

FIG 3   Front propeller shaft and centre bearing

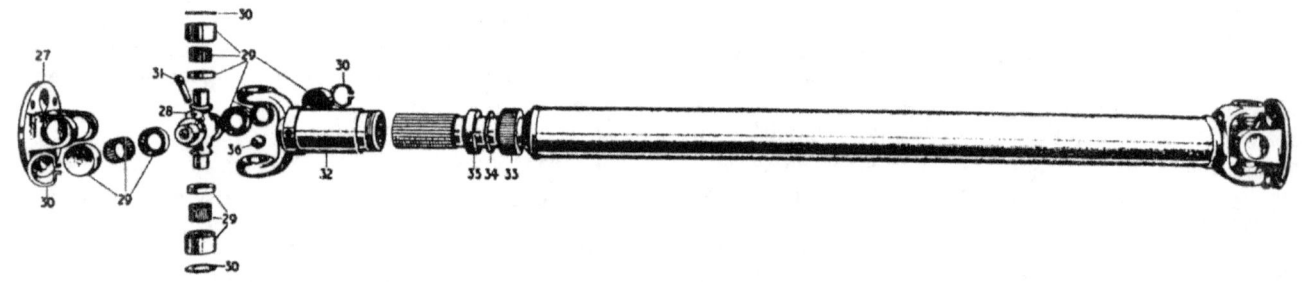

27—Flange yoke at each end of shaft.
28—Journal.
29—Needle bearing assembly.
30—Bearing retaining snap ring.
31—Grease nipple.
32—Splined sliding yoke.
33—Dust cap.
34—Steel washer.
35—Cork washer.
36—Grease nipple.

FIG 4   Rear or single propeller shaft

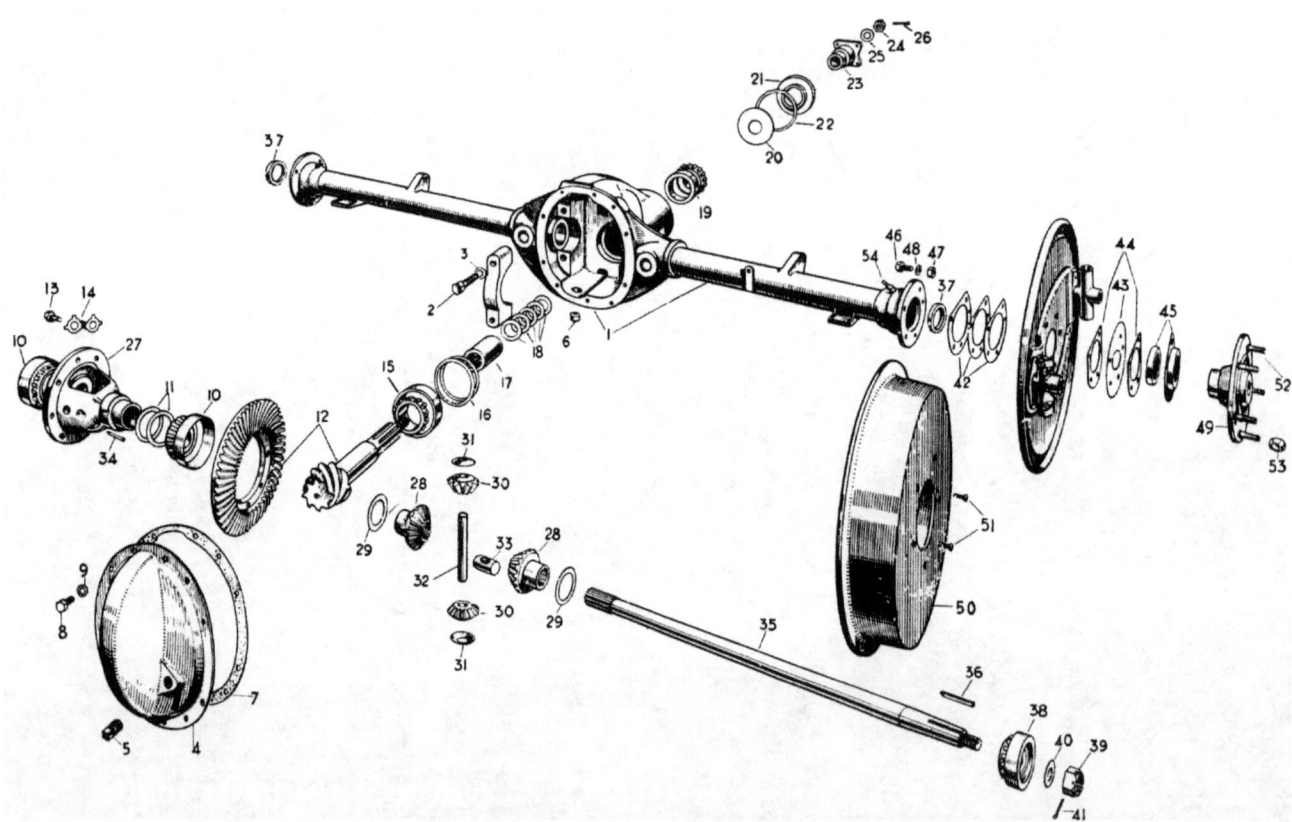

FIG 5   Salisbury axle (exploded view)

186

FIG 5 Salisbury axle (exploded view)

Carrier and Tube Assembly	1
Screw, Set, securing Differential Caps	2
Washer, Lock, on Set Screws	3
Cover for Carrier	4
Plug, Filler, on Cover	5
Plug, Drain, on Gear Carrier	6
Washer, Jointing, for Cover	7
Screw, Set, securing Cover to Carrier	8
Washer, locking Screws	9
Bearing, Roller, on Differential Case	10
Shim, adjusting Differential	11
Drive Gear and Pinion	12
Screw, Set, securing Ring Gear to Differential Case	13
Lock-Strap for Set Screws	14
Bearing, Roller, at rear end of Pinion	15
Shim, Adjusting, rear of Pinion	16
Spacer, between Front and Rear Bearings	17
Shim, Adjusting, front of Pinion	18
Bearing, Roller, at front end of Pinion	19
Slinger, Oil, on Pinion	20
Seal, Oil, Assembly, on Pinion	21
Gasket for Oil Seal	22
Flange, Companion, Assembly	23
Nut, securing Companion Flange Assembly to Pinion	24
Washer, between Nut and Companion Flange Assembly	25
Pin, Cotter, securing Nut	26
Case, Differential	27
Gear, Side, for Differential	28
Washer, Thrust, for Side Gears	29
Gear, Differential Pinion Mate	30
Washer, Thrust, for Pinion Mate Gears	31
Shaft for Pinion Mate Gears	32
Spacer, Axle Shaft, on Pinion Mate Gear Shaft	33
Pin, locking Pinion Mate Gear Shaft in Differential Case	34
Rear Axle Shaft	35
Key	36
Seal, Oil, in end of Axle Tubes	37
Bearing, Roller, for Hubs	38
Nut, Slotted, on Axle Shaft	39
Washer, under Nut	40
Cotter, securing Nut on Axle Shaft	41
Shim, adjusting Hub Bearing	42
Plate, retaining Hub Bearings	43
Washer, Jointing, at each side of Retainer Plate	44
Seal, Oil, Assembly	45
Screw, securing Rear Brake Assembly to Carrier Assembly	46
Nut on Screws	47
Washer, locking Nuts	48
Rear Axle Hub	49
Drum, Brake	50
Screw, Set, locating Brake Drum on Hubs	51
Stud, securing Brake Drum and Road Wheels to Hubs	52
Nut on Studs	53
Nipple, Grease, on Axle Tubes	54

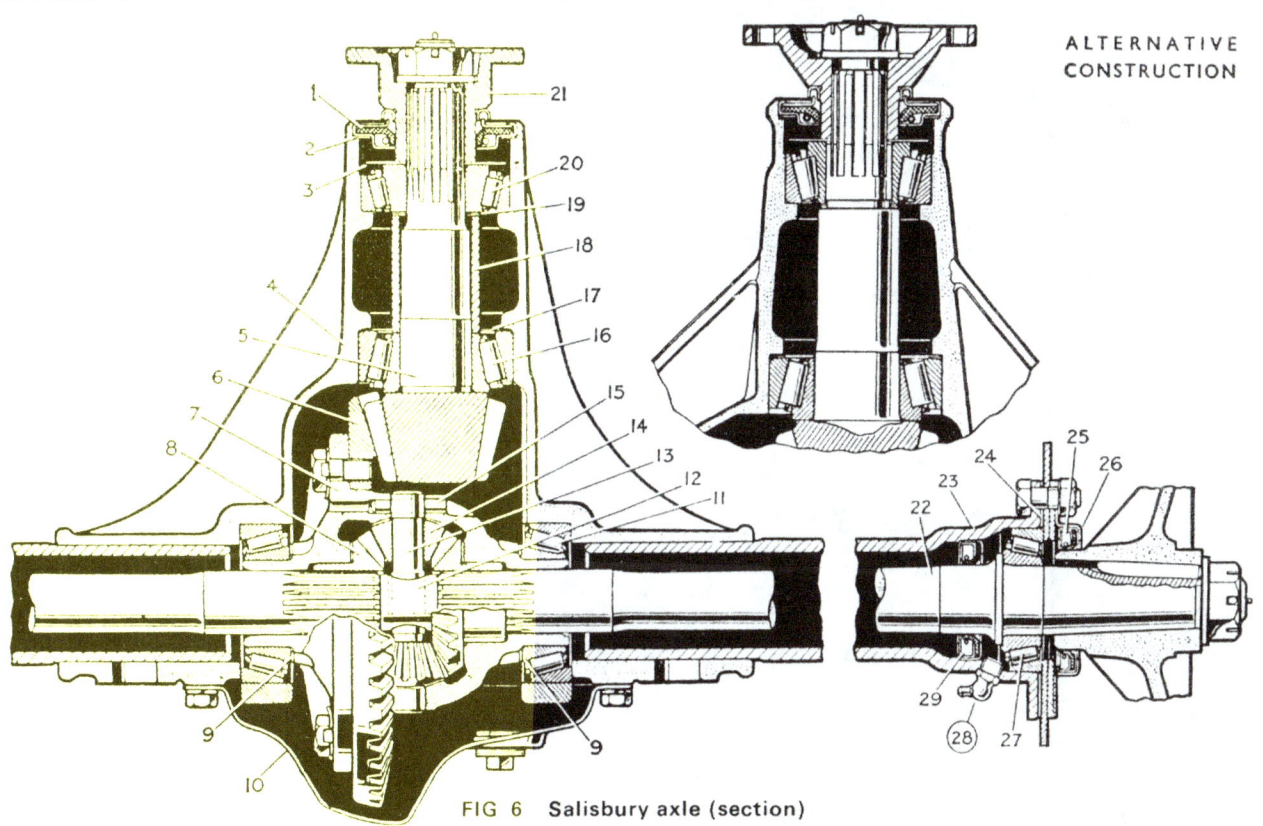

FIG 6 Salisbury axle (section)

1—Drive pinion oil seal.
2—Drive pinion oil seal gasket.
3—Drive pinion oil slinger.
4—Gear carrier.
5—Drive pinion.
6—Drive gear.
7—Differential case.
8—Differential side gear.
9—Carrier bearing shim.
10—Cover.
11—Carrier bearing.
12—Axle shaft spacer.
13—Pinion mate shaft.
14—Differential pinion.
15—Lock pin.
16—Drive pinion inner bearing.
17—Bearing shim (inner).
18—Bearing spacer.
19—Bearing shim (outer).
20—Drive pinion outer bearing.
21—Universal joint flange.
22—Axle shaft.
23—Axle tube.
24—Hub bearing shim.
25—Hub oil seal.
26—Oil seal container.
27—Hub bearing.
28—Grease nipple.
29—Axle shaft oil seal.

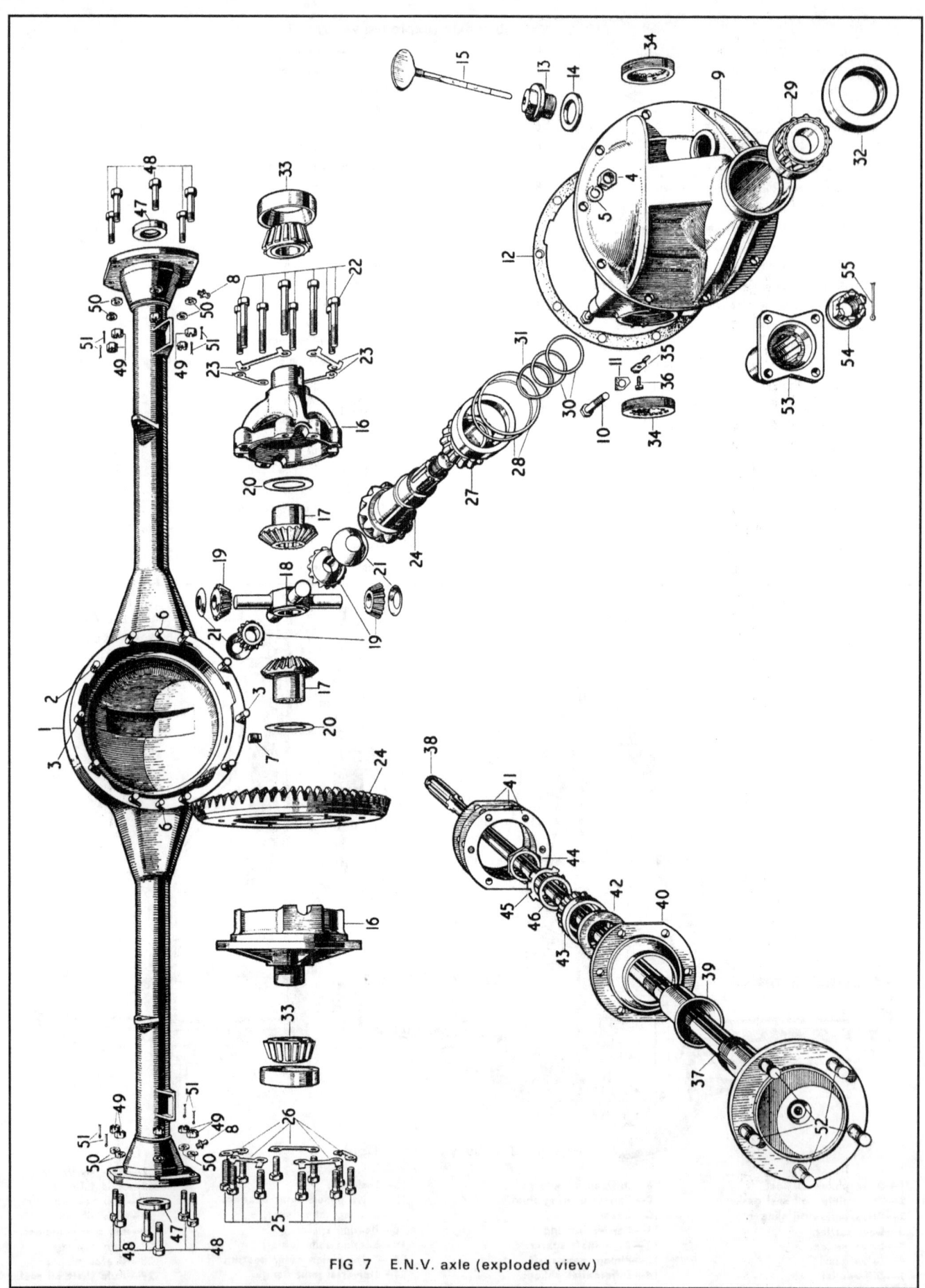

FIG 7   E.N.V. axle (exploded view)

FIG 7   E.N.V. axle (exploded view)

1	Axle Casing
2	Stud (Short) for the attachment of Pinion Housing
3	Stud (Long) for the attachment of Pinion Housing
4	Nut on Studs
5	Washer, Spring, under Nuts
6	Pin, Dowel, locating Pinion Housing on Casing
7	Plug, Oil Drain
8	Nipple, Grease, on outer end of Axle Casing
9	Pinion Housing (complete with Bearing Caps and Bolts)
10	Bolt, securing Bearing Caps
11	Plate, locking Bearing Cap Bolts
12	Washer, Jointing, between Pinion Housing and Axle Casings
13	Plug, Oil Filler
14	Washer, Jointing, for Oil Filler Plug
15	Dipstick
16	Case, Differential
17	Gear Side, for Differential
18	Piece, Star, for Differential Pinion Mate Gears
19	Gear, Differential Pinion Mate
20	Washer, Thrust, for Side Gears
21	Washer, Thrust, for Pinion Mate Gears
22	Bolt, securing Differential Case
23	Plate, locking Bolts
24	Crown Wheel and Pinion
25	Bolt, securing Crown-Wheel to Differential Case
26	Plate, locking Crown-Wheel Bolts
27	Bearing, Roller, Pinion Head
28	Shim, adjusting Pinion Head Bearing
29	Bearing, Roller, Pinion Shank
30	Shim, adjusting Pinion Shank Bearing
31	Piece, Distance, between Shank of Pinion and Shank Adjusting Shims
32	Seal, Oil, in end of Pinion Housing
33	Bearing, Roller, for Differential Box
34	Nut, adjusting Differential Box
35	Plate, locking Adjusting Nut
36	Screw, Set, securing Adjusting Nut Lock Plate to Bearing Cap
37	Rear Axle Shaft (combining Hub and Thrust Button)
38	Button, Thrust, on Inner End of Axle Shafts
39	Piece, Distance, on Shafts
40	Housing, for Hub Bearings
41	Shim, Adjusting, between Bearing Housing and Brake Anchor Plate
42	Seal, Oil, in Bearing Housings
43	Bearing, Roller, for Hubs
44	Nut, locking Hub Bearing on Axle Shaft
45	Washer, Tab, for Lock Nut
46	Washer, Tongued, between Tab Washer and Hub Bearing
47	Seal, Oil, for Axle Shaft
48	Bolt, securing Bearing Housing and Brake Anchor Plate to Axle Casing
49	Nut on Bolts
50	Washer, Spring, under Nuts
51	Pin, Split, through Nuts
52	Stud for Brake Drum and Road Wheels
53	Pinion Companion Flange
54	Nut, securing Companion Flange to Pinion
55	Pin, Split, through Nut

Vaseline, fill the cage with grease and tap it into position using a soft-nosed drift about $\frac{1}{32}$ inch smaller than the hole in the yoke. **It is essential that the bearing races should be a light drive fit in the yoke trunnions.**

When the bearing is in position fit the spring clip and complete the bearing on the opposite side in a similar manner. Then refit the other two bearings. If the spider appears to bind, tap the yoke lightly with a soft faced mallet after the spring clips have been fitted.

When assembling the splined sliding joint **it is essential that the lining up arrows stamped on the shaft and on the splined sleeve are in line** or damage will be caused by incorrect alignment of the yokes. Pack the centre bearing with good quality grease before assembly and ensure that new bearing dust covers are fitted.

Refitting the completed shaft is a reversal of the removal procedure but clean the flange faces and the registers first. Ensure that the flanges engage properly, lining up the marks made prior to dismantling, and tighten the securing bolts diagonally and evenly. The joint faces should bed down evenly all round.

When refitting the centre bearing assembly to the car check that the mounting rubbers are in good condition or renew as necessary.

REAR AXLE

5 Description

There are two types of rear axle fitted to the XK 120 model, these are the Salisbury and E.N.V. axles. All other models are fitted with the Salisbury type of rear axle. The axles are not interchangeable between models but it is possible to replace an E.N.V. type with a Salisbury type, or vice-versa (as a complete assembly) on the XK 120 model except for the brake backplates, hubs and handbrake cable assembly. On both types of axle there is very little the amateur mechanic can do to service the axle assemblies, due to the number of special tools and gauges required. It is therefore essential that a well equipped agent is used or an exchange axle acquired.

The Salisbury rear axle:

This axle assembly is of the semi-floating type with shim adjustment for all bearings and meshing of the hypoid drive gear and pinion matched assembly. The axle shafts are splined at the inner ends, which engage splines in the differential side gears, while the outer ends have tapers and keys to fit the rear wheel hubs. The hubs are supported by taper roller bearings pressed onto the axle shafts and located in the ends of the axle tubes. Outward thrust on either wheel is taken by the adjacent hub bearing, whilst inward thrust is transmitted through the axle shafts and slotted axle shaft spacer to the opposite bearing. Thus each hub bearing takes thrust in one direction only. A cover is fitted to the rear of the gear carrier housing which permits the inspection and flushing of the differential assembly without dismantling the assembly. The axle is shown in exploded and section form in **FIGS 5** and **6**.

The E.N.V. rear axle:

This rear axle is of the hypoid semi-floating type with shim adjustment of pinion shaft bearings but with adjusting nuts for the differential crownwheel. The axle shafts are splined at the inner ends to engage with splines in the differential side gears, the outer ends being integral with the hub, this assembly being attached to the flanges at either end of the axle casing by bolts passing through the bearing housings. The wheels are each supported on a taper roller bearing retained in a housing and the side-thrust from the wheels is transferable from one shaft to the other by a thrust button on the end of each axle shaft. The axle can either be partially dismantled for examination of the halfshafts and hub races fully dismantled which allows for removal of the differential without necessarily removing the axle casing from the chassis. The E.N.V. axle is shown in exploded form in **FIG 7**.

6 Maintenance

Maintenance on both types of rear axles consists only of correct lubrication. Periodically check the level of the oil in the rear axle by examining the dipstick provided on the E.N.V. type or the level plug fitted on the Salisbury type. Top up as necessary with the correct grade of lubricant i.e. to the high level on the dipstick or the level plug. Since hypoid oils of different brands may not mix satisfactorily, draining and refilling is preferable to topping up if the brand of oil in the axle is unknown.

The rear wheel bearings should be lubricated periodically with the recommended lubricant through the nipples provided. Care should be excercised when lubricating to prevent over-lubricating which may cause the lubricant to spread onto the brake linings. A bleed hole is provided on the axle casing to indicate when sufficient lubricant has been added.

7 Axle shaft removal

Jack-up the car at the rear and place blocks under the chassis frame. Slacken off all brake shoe adjustment by rotating the adjuster anti-clockwise after removal of the hub caps and road wheels. Release the handbrake. Remove the two setscrews locating each brake drum and ease the brake drums off. Continue the removal procedure for the appropriate type of axle fitted

E.N.V. type:

Remove the splitpins, slotted nuts and spring washers from the six bolts securing each bearing housing and brake backplate to the flange of the axle casing. Ease axle shafts away from the casing thus exposing the adjusting shims between the bearing housing and the backplate. Refit two bolts to secure the backplate in position and thus avoid damage to the brake hydraulic connections. Do not lose or transpose shims from side to side.

Slide out axle shaft. The bearing may be removed by bending back the locking tab of the tab washer and removing the securing nut. Remove and scrap the oil seal situated in the axle casing flange.

Salisbury type axle:

Remove the splitpin and slotted nut, and with a suitable extractor withdraw the hub from the axle shaft. At the rear of the backplate disconnect the metal hydraulic pipe from the wheel cylinder. Remove the clevis pin securing the handbrake cable to the operating lever which protrudes through the backplate. (A hole is provided in the handbrake cable bracket on the backplate to gain access to the clevis pin). Pull back the handbrake cable return spring and lever out the spring retainer from the top of the cable clevis and withdraw the cable.

Remove the five bolts and nuts securing the backplate to the end of the axle tube and withdraw the backplate. On the Mk VII model note the bearing retainer plate, two gaskets and oil seal at the front of the backplate and the shims fitted between the backplate and the flange of the axle tube. On the XK 120 models note the oil seal and gasket at the front of the backplate and the bearing retainer plate and shims fitted between the backplate and the axle tube flange. In either model do not lose or transpose these shims to the other side of the axle case as they determine the end float of the axles.

The axle shaft is now withdrawn with a special Salisbury extractor (tool No. S.E.102). Examine the rear hub bearing and if worn remove and renew. To remove the inner race of the bearing an extractor is required (Salisbury tool No. S.E.103). Inspect the oil seal and if found to be damaged withdraw and renew.

Refitting:

Refitting is the reverse of the removal procedure, but it is important to observe the following points; Wash the hub bearing in petrol and allow to dry before replacing to ensure that the end float of the axles may be determined accurately. On the Salisbury type axle ensure that the

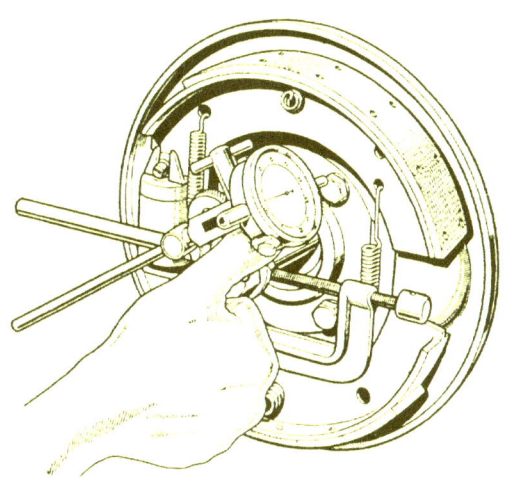

FIG 8   Checking axle end float

bearing outer race enters the bearing housing squarely, and if necessary renew the hub oil seal. Refit the shims, backplate, bearing retainer plate, gaskets and oil seal in the correct sequence as indicated in the removal procedure.

On the E.N.V. type axle fit new oil seals into their housings on the axle flange with the lip of the seal facing the centre of the axle.

Check the end float of both types of axle with a dial gauge as indicated in **FIG 8**. The end float for the Salisbury and E.N.V. axle shafts is .006 to .008 inch and .005 to .008 inch respectively. If the end float is incorrect add or subtract adjusting shims approximately the same amount on either side of the axle, until the end float is correct. This float is just perceptable by hand pressure in either direction. Adjusting shims are available for the Salisbury and E.N.V. type axles in the following sizes: .003, .005 .010, .030 inch and .002, .006, .010, .032 and .062 inch respectively.

The remaining operations are the reverse of the removal procedure.

On the Salisbury type axles as it was necessary to disconnect the brake hydraulic line the brakes must be bled as covered in **Chapter 10** after assembly has been completed.

Grease the hub bearings with the correct lubricant until grease appears at the bleed holes.

8 Axle housing removal

Remove the axle shafts as described in the preceeding section.

On cars fitted with the E.N.V. type axle disconnect the metal hydraulic pipe at the connection to each rear wheel cylinder and plug the end of the pipe to avoid loss of fluid. Remove the bolt securing the three way connection to the rear axle case and tie up the hydraulic pipe to the chassis frame. Disconnect the handbrake cable from the levers protruding through the backplate by removing the clevis pin and release the cable from its attachments to the rear axle case.

Remove the splitpins and castellated nuts securing the rear axle companion flange to the propeller shaft. Withdraw the bolts, ease the flanges apart and place the free end of the propeller shaft out of the way after marking the relative position of the flanges.

On the E.N.V. axle removal of the rear axle will be facilitated if the differential unit is withdrawn from the axle casing. To do this drain the rear axle and remove the ten nuts and spring washers securing the differential to the axle casing. Withdraw the differential unit carefully forward as it is quite heavy.

On cars fitted with the Salisbury axle drain the oil from the axle.

Remove the locknuts and securing nuts from the rear axle U-bolts then withdraw the bolts with their respective plates. Remove the two nuts and bolts each side securing the check straps (see **FIG 9**) to the chassis frame and withdraw the check straps. Disconnect the rear shock absorbers by removing the two nuts from each link arm and tapping the link arms out of the lugs on the axle casing and the shock absorber arms.

Remove the axle by sliding it to the right until the left-hand end of the casing is clear of the road spring and the exhaust tail pipe, lowering to the floor and withdrawing rearwards.

9 Reassembly

Reassembly is the reverse of the removal procedure with special attention to be made to the following points.

When the rear axle assembly has been attached to the rear springs it will be necessary to jack-up each spring to enable the shock absorber links and the check straps to be fitted. Check that the centre bolt of the spring seats in the dowel hole provided in the spring pad.

Check the end float of the axles as described previously in **Section 7** under 'Refitting'.

The brakes will be required to be bled and adjusted as described in **Chapter 10** of this manual.

REAR SUSPENSION

10 Description

The rear suspension (see **FIG 9**) consists of semi-eliptical spring controlled by hydraulic piston type dampers.

The springs are supported at either end in bonded rubber mountings the front one on a link arm and the rear on a shackle. The leaves of the springs are fitted with gaiters which serve to keep the springs clean and also to retain lubricant on the leaves.

The rear axle is attached to the springs by means of U-bolts and plates. To prevent excessive movement of the axle rubber buffers are fitted to check plates attached to the chassis adjacent to the rear axle.

11 Maintenance

Normal maintenance on the rear suspension consists of periodic lubrication of the road springs via the nipples provided on the gaiters and checking the fluid level in the shock absorbers.

The shock absorbers should be cleaned thoroughly before removing the filler cap as grit or dirt will damage the action of the shock absorber. The filler plug is fitted at the top of the shock absorber and the body should be completely filled with the correct fluid.

It is recommended that the rear suspension U-bolts, shackle and anchor bolts are tested for tightness at intervals of 10,000 miles and tightened as necessary.

12 Spring removal

Jack-up the rear of the car and lower onto stands placed beneath the chassis frame in front of the rear spring front anchorages. Remove the rear wing valance, hub caps and road wheels.

Lower the jack until the rear axle assembly is supported by the check straps. Remove the locknuts and securing nuts from the U-bolts and withdraw the U-bolts. Remove the nut securing the front anchor bolt and withdraw the bolt through the hole provided in the chassis.

Remove the securing nut from the spring shackle bolt and withdraw the bolt. Remove the spring by withdrawing to the rear of the car.

Dismantling:

Release the gaiter laces and remove the gaiters. Thoroughly clean the road springs and withdraw the bolts from the spring clips. Clamp the spring in a vice with the jaws of the vice engaging on the top and bottom leaves. Remove the nut from the centre bolt and release the vice slowly. Withdraw the leaves from the vice and press the bushes out of the spring eyes.

13 Spring reassembly

Clean each leaf spring and examine it for cracks or distortion. Check the centre bolt for wear or distortion and if faulty renew it. **It is essential that this is in good condition as it locates the spring in the clamp plate.**

Complete spring assemblies on both sides are required if any leaves are found defective or the springs have lost their curvature due to settling. These assemblies are available on an exchange basis.

Assemble the springs clean and well lubricated on the centre bolt and refit the bushes in the spring eyes.

Before replacing the shackle bolts, bushes and shackle they must be examined for wear and if necessary renewed.

When the spring has been replaced on the rear shackle and front anchor bolt it will be necessary to jack-up the spring into engagement with the rear axle to ease the fitting of the spring saddle U-bolts and nuts, taking care that the spring centre bolt is correctly located in the axle plate.

Before tightening the rear shackle nuts or front anchor bolt it is essential to have the weight of the car on the rear springs i.e. the car must be in the normal riding position. Failure to do this will result in premature failure of the steel and rubber bushes due to excessive load being applied to the rubber.

14 Dampers

The dampers fitted to Jaguar cars are the Girling double acting piston type as shown in the sections (see **FIGS 10** and **11**). Two adjusting screws are shown in the section, these however are set to extremely fine

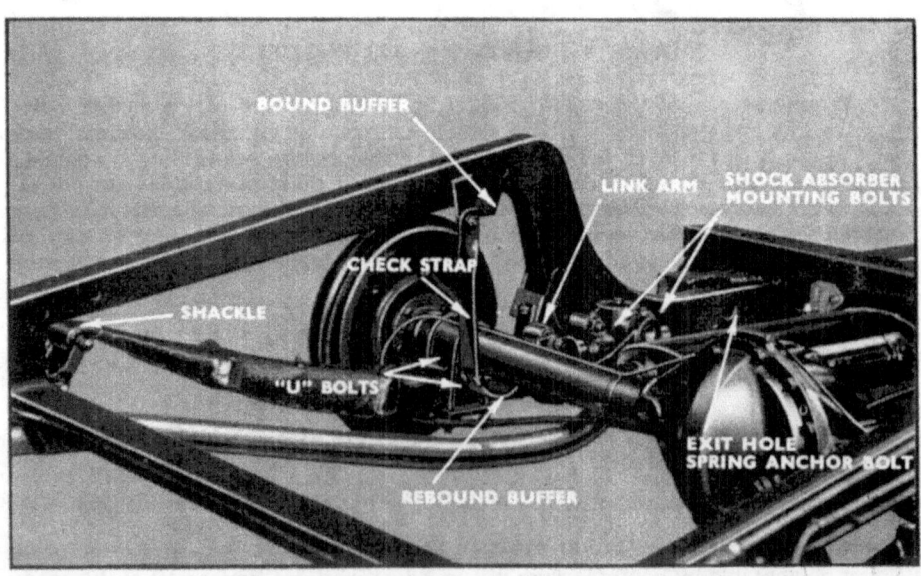

FIG 9 Rear suspension

limits by the manufacturers and no attempt should be made to alter them, as any adjustment will not improve the damper performance and may make the unit useless.

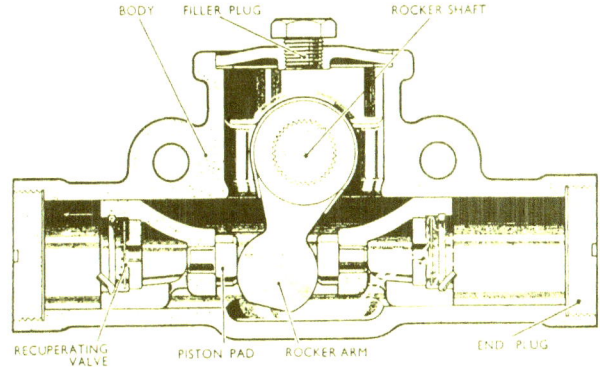

FIG 10　Damper (side elevation)

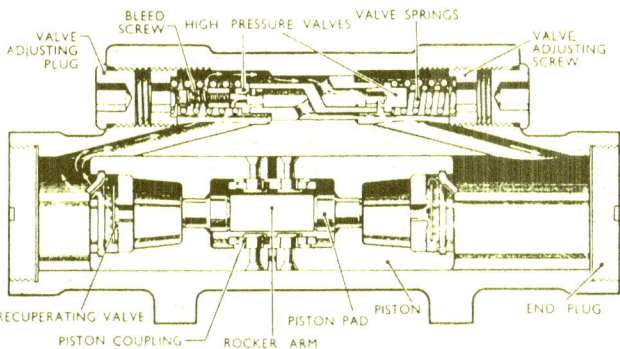

FIG 11　Damper (plan view)

Removal:

Jack-up the car to a convenient height for working on the shock absorber. Remove the nut and washer securing the link arm to the lug on the rear axle casing. Remove the two nuts, washers and bolts securing the damper to the chassis. Support the weight of the damper while tapping out the link arm on the axle casing. Lift the shock absorber clear of the car.

Testing:

Remove the damper from the car and bolt to a suitable plate using the fixing lugs. Clamp the plate in a vice to hold the unit, do not clamp the damper directly in the vice as it may be damaged.

Move the lever arm up and down throughout its complete stroke, when an even resistance should be felt. If the resistance is erratic and there is any free movement of the arm this indicates lack of fluid. Add fluid in the following manner: Thoroughly clean the top of the damper especially around the filler hole. Remove the filler plug and top up with the correct fluid at the same time work the lever arm through its full travel in both directions to expel any air trapped. **It is essential that absolute cleanliness is observed when topping up the dampers.**

If there is no improvement in the resistance to movement of the lever arm after topping up has been carried out the unit must be renewed. The unit must also be renewed if the lever arm is immoveable.

Refitting:

Refitting is the reverse of the removal procedure noting the following points. The damper link arm can be refitted in the wrong position so that it is imperative to check that the link arm passes downwards from the lug on the axle casing to the main damper arm **not upwards.** Ensure that the car is in the normal riding position before fully tightening any nuts to prevent excessive strain on the components.

GENERAL

15 Modifications

On Mk VIII models commencing at chassis numbers 760476 and 780462 for righthand and lefthand drive cars respectively along with all Mk IX, XK 140 and XK 150 models a different type of rear spring is fitted. This has either synthetic rubber or nylon interleaving between the springs and no lubrication gaiters are fitted. These springs are interchangeable with the old type on the Mk VIII model but should be changed in pairs.

On the models fitted with nylon interleaving it is recommended that the spring be bound with plastic tape to prevent the nylon working out from between the leaves.

16 Fault diagnosis

(a) Noisy axle

1 Insufficient or incorrect lubricant
2 Worn bearings
3 Worn gears

(b) Excessive backlash

1 Worn gears, bearings or bearing housings
2 Worn axle shaft splines
3 Worn universal joints
4 Loose or broken wheel studs

(c) Oil leakage

1 Defective seals in hub
2 Defective pinion shaft seal
3 Defective seals on universal joint spiders

(d) Vibration

1 Propeller shaft out of balance
2 Worn universal joint bearings
3 Wheels badly out of balance
4 Engine vibration see **Chapter 1**
5 Clutch see **Chapter 5**

(e) Rattles

1 Rubber bushes in damper links worn through
2 Dampers loose
3 U-bolts loose
4 Loose spring clips
5 Worn bushes in spring eyes and shackles
6 Broken spring leaves.

(f) Settling

1 Weak or broken spring leaves
2 Badly worn shackle pins and bushes
3 Loose spring anchorages

INDEX – FRONT SUSPENSION

SECTION	PAGE	
000	195	Basic Diagnostic Testing & Troubleshooting
001	195	Description
002	196	Maintenance
003	196	Torsion Bar Removal and reinstallation
004	197	Hub Removal
005	198	Suspension Disassembly
006	200	Suspension Reassembly
007	200	Anti-Roll Bar
008	200	Dampers (Shock Absorbers)
009	201	Suspension Geometry
010	201	Modifications by Engine Number & Model
011	201	Fault Diagnosis Chart

FRONT SUSPENSION
Basic Diagnostic Testing & Troubleshooting

Drive the car on a smooth road at about 30 mph (48 km./h.), and then take your hands off the steering wheel. The car should maintain a straight course. If the road is crowned, it may cause the car to wander toward the low side of the road and, therefore, it may be necessary to make this test evenly straddled over the center line. Choose a road with no traffic to make this test. On a windy day, the test should be duplicated by going back and forth over the same road. Uneven front-end angles will cause the car to wander to one side.

Hold your hand lightly on the steering wheel at about 30 mph (48 km./h.) to check whether any shocks are being transmitted back to the steering wheel. A constantly jiggling wheel indicates that the front wheels are out of balance. This constant movement is very tiring to a driver on long trips and is hard on every moving part of the front end.

Turn into a deserted side street at about 25 mph (40 km./h.), and then release the steering wheel; it should come back to a straight-ahead position without any assistance from the driver; otherwise, there is binding in the linkage, insufficient caster, or insufficient steering axis inclination.

To check for misalignment, inspect the front tires for uneven tread wear.

Front suspension fault diagnosis chart

1. **Excessive looseness**
   1a. Improper adjustment of the steering gear
   1b. Worn steering linkage
   1c. Loose wheel bearing adjustment on worm bearings
   1d. Worn ball joints
   1e. Loose steering gear mounting
2. **Hard steering**
   2a. Tight adjustment of the steering gear
   2b. Lubrication needed
   2c. Low tire pressure
   2d. Wheels out of alignment
   2e. Excessive caster
3. **Wanders**
   3a. Loose front wheel bearings
   3b. Loose steering linkage
   3c. Loose front end supports
   3d. Uneven tire pressure
   3e. Low pressure in both rear tires
   3f. Incorrect caster
   3g. Bent spindle arm
4. **Pulls to one side**
   4a. Uneven caster
   4b. Uneven camber
   4c. Uneven tire pressure
   4d. Frame out of alignment
   4e. Tire sizes not uniform
   4f. Bent spindle arm
5. **Shimmy, low speed**
   5a. Loose support arms
   5b. Loose linkage
   5c. Loose wheel bearings
   5d. Static unbalance of front wheels
   5e. Incorrect tire pressure
6. **Shimmy, high speed**
   6a. Dynamic unbalance of front wheels
   6b. Too much caster
7. **Squeals on turns**
   7a. Low tire pressure
   7b. Incorrect camber
   7c. Bent spindle arm
   7d. Frame out of alignment
8. **Excessive tire wear**
   8a. Improper toe-in
   8b. Improper turning radius
   8c. Underinflation
   8d. Overinflation
   8e. Grabbing
   8f. Excessive camber

FRONT SUSPENSION - SERVICE

1 Description

The front suspension fitted to the car consists of a torsion bar assembly controlled by telescopic, hydraulic dampers.

The torsion bars are positioned along the inner vertical faces of the chassis frame. Both ends of the torsion bar have raised splines which locate in a clamp bolt at the rear end and a splined muff at the front end (see **FIG 1**). The reaction lever is supported on a trunnion which is positioned by an adjusting barrel nut and bolt, the bolt being attached to the chassis frame. The splined muff at the front end is spigoted and bolted to the inner end of the lower wishbone lever.

The lower wishbone is mounted at its inner end to a bracket to the underside of the chassis frame. The outer end of the lower wishbone lever carries the ballpin which is the fulcrum and support of the wheel. Bolted to the outer extremity of the lower wishbone lever is a tie bar which runs forward to the front end of the lower wishbone lever bracket attached to the chassis frame. Also attached to the lower wishbone lever are the anti-roll bar and the lower end of the damper (shock absorber).

The anti-roll bar is attached to the lower wishbone lever on each side of the car and is supported in rubber bushes attached by brackets to the chassis. The upper end of the telescopic damper is connected to a mounting post.

The two upper wishbone levers together with their lever bracket form a triangle the base of which is formed by the upper wishbone bracket attached to the chassis. The apex of the triangle is formed by the junction of the two upper wishbone levers and the upper ball assembly.

The front hub is supported between the two ball assemblies upper and lower on which it pivots. Rubber bushes are fitted to all joints with the exception of the upper and lower ball joints.

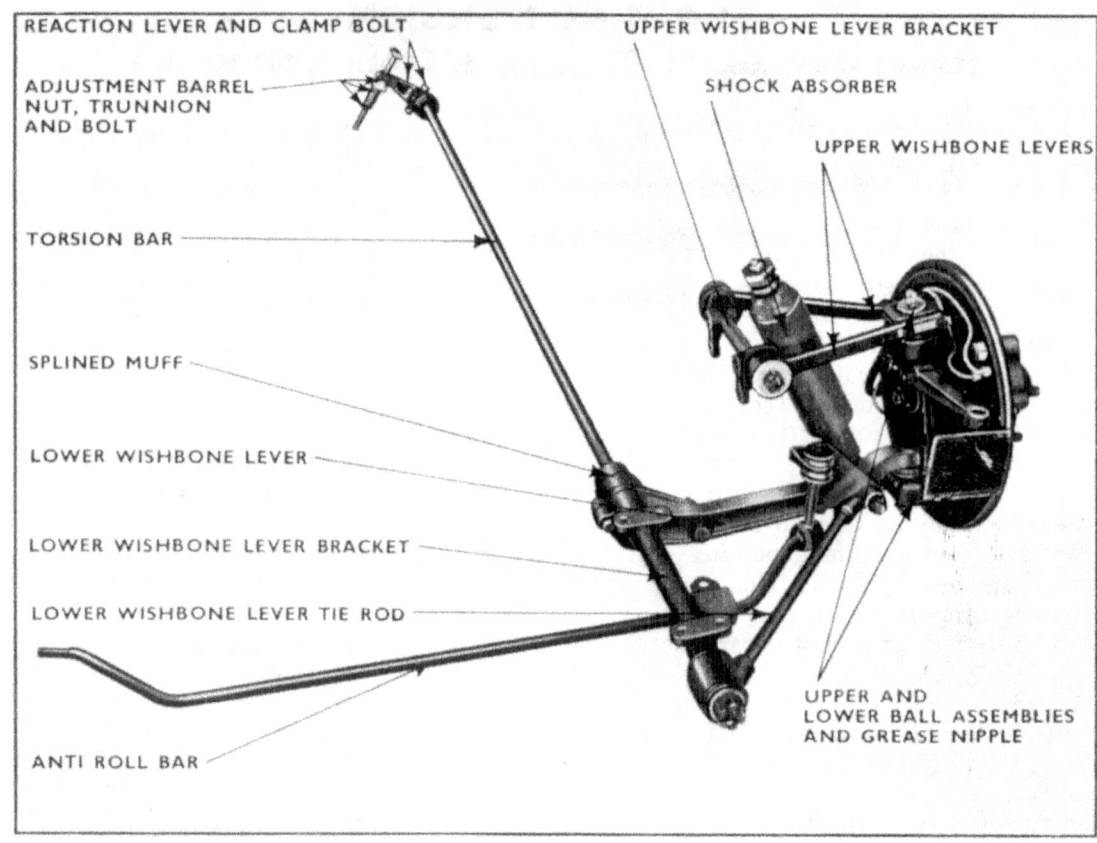

FIG 1 General arrangement of front suspension

2 Maintenance

Routine maintenance consists of lubrication to the upper and lower wishbone ball assemblies. The ball assemblies should be greased by means of the nipples provided, at intervals of 2500 miles. At intervals of 10,000 miles it is recommended that all suspension nuts and bolts are examined and tightened where necessary.

It is also advisable at this interval to check the rubber bushes for signs of deterioration and to check the torsion bar settings. The torsion bar setting is described in the following section.

3 Torsion bar removal and reassembly

Removal:

Place a support under the chassis frame. Jack-up under the lower wishbone lever and remove the road wheel. Leave the jack in position to relieve the load on the damper.

Disconnect the damper at the top mounting and draw the damper clear of its mounting post. Remove the splitpin and washer from the damper lower mounting and withdraw the damper. (If the original torsion bar is to be refitted it is only necessary to disconnect the upper damper mounting).

Remove the reaction lever locking bolt passing through the clevis crossmember into the lever (see **FIG 2**). Rotate the adjustment barrel nut in an anticlockwise direction until the nut is almost off the threads on the bolt. If the original torsion bar is to be refitted scribe a line at either end of the bar to indicate its position relative to the reaction lever and the splined muff.

Remove the setscrew with spring washer passing through the lower wishbone lever into the muff. Remove the splitpin, slotted nut, washer and bolt passing through the wishbone lever and the muff. Tap the muff off the wishbone rearwards along the splines on the torsion bar. Remove the muff coupling and torsion bar.

Reassembly:

The torsion bars are marked on the rear end face to indicate on which side of the car they are fitted as they are not interchangeable. The markings are O/S and N/S designating the offside and nearside respectively.

Enter the muff coupling shoulder to the rear, over the splines on the forward end of the bar aligning the marks made on removal.

If a new bar is to be fitted it will be necessary to engage the muff on the correct splines to enable adjustment at the barrel nut. To achieve this ensure that the adjustment barrel nut is just entered on the threads of the bolt and maintain a distance of $15\frac{5}{8}$ inch between the damper mountings. Simple distance pieces may be fabricated as shown in **FIGS 3** and **4**. This will correctly position the lower wishbone lever in relation to the torsion bar.

Enter the muff on the splines of the bar and the lower wishbone lever and secure in position with the setscrew, spring washer, bolt, washer, slotted nut and new splitpin.

Rotate the adjustment barrel clockwise until the locking setscrew hole in the reaction lever appears in the centre of

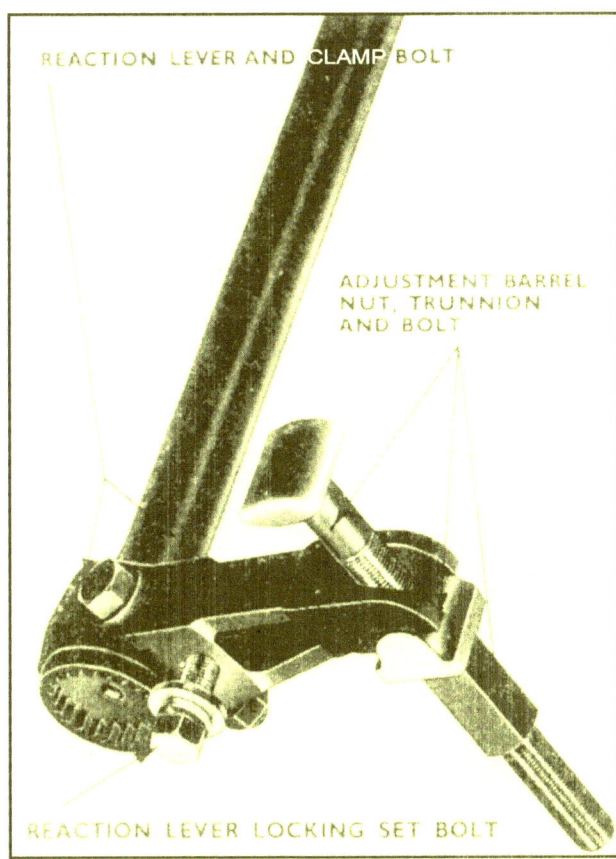

FIG 2 Torsion bar reaction lever

Bounce the front of the car on its suspension to ensure that it is free of all stickiness. Finally press down the front of the car and allow it to **rise slowly.**

If the suspension is correct a test piece of $8\frac{1}{2}$ inch should pass below the lever face of the chassis sidemember immediately adjacent to the point where the front end of the cruciform member meets the chassis sidemember on the Mk VII model. On the XK 120 model a test piece of $7\frac{1}{8}$ inch should just pass below the lower face of the most forward parallel section of the chassis frame.

If any adjustment is necessary it may be carried out at the reaction lever adjuster. Turning of the adjusting nut should only be carried out with the locking bolts released and the front of the car jacked up to reduce the load Clockwise rotation of the adjuster increases the torsion.

If there is not enough adjustment available on the reaction lever adjuster it will be necessary to slacken off the adjustment fully, slacken the reaction lever locking bolts, remove the two bolts from each of the splined muffs and turn the muff one spline in the correct direction on the torsion bar. Retighten the bolts on the muffs. Turning the muff clockwise viewed from the rear will increase the tension on the offside bar and reduce it on the nearside bar.

Screw up the adjustment nuts lower the car onto its wheels and recheck the suspension. Should correction be required on both sides it is recommended that adjustment should be carried out a little at a time until the required results are achieved.

Finally tighten the locking bolts.

the slot cut in the rear of the chassis crossmember. Fit the locking bolt but do not tighten until final adjustments have been made. Refit the damper and road wheel.

Adjustment:

It is assumed that the car is full of petrol oil and water if not weight must be added to compensate for any deficiency.

Place a 100 lb weight in front of each front seat in the XK 120 model. Check that the car is on completely level ground with the wheels in the straight-ahead position and ensure that the tyres are inflated to their correct pressures.

4 Hub removal

Jack-up the front of the car, remove the hub cap and road wheel. Remove the setscrews securing the brake drum and remove the brake drum. Prise off the dust cap 35 (see **FIG 5**), remove the splitpin 34 castellated nut 32 and washer 33. Withdraw the hub with outer bearing 31. Remove the inner bearing 29, coverplate 28 and felt grease retainer 27.

Thoroughly clean the hub and bearing to remove the old grease. Check the bearings for wear and replace as necessary. The bearings should not be replaced individually but in sets.

Refitting is the reverse of the removal procedure but before replacing the dust cap check the end float of the

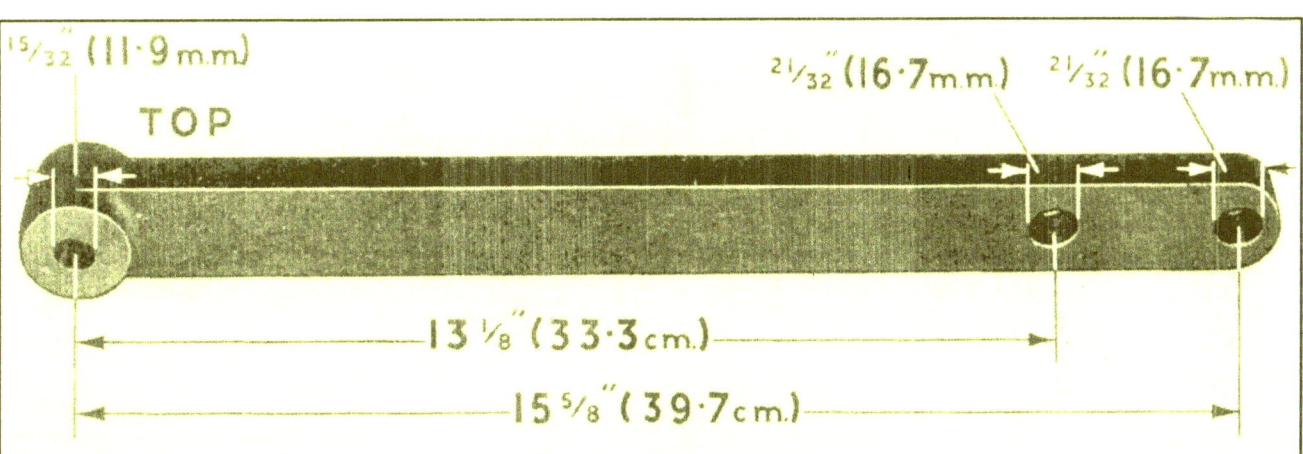

FIG 3 Distance piece Mk VII

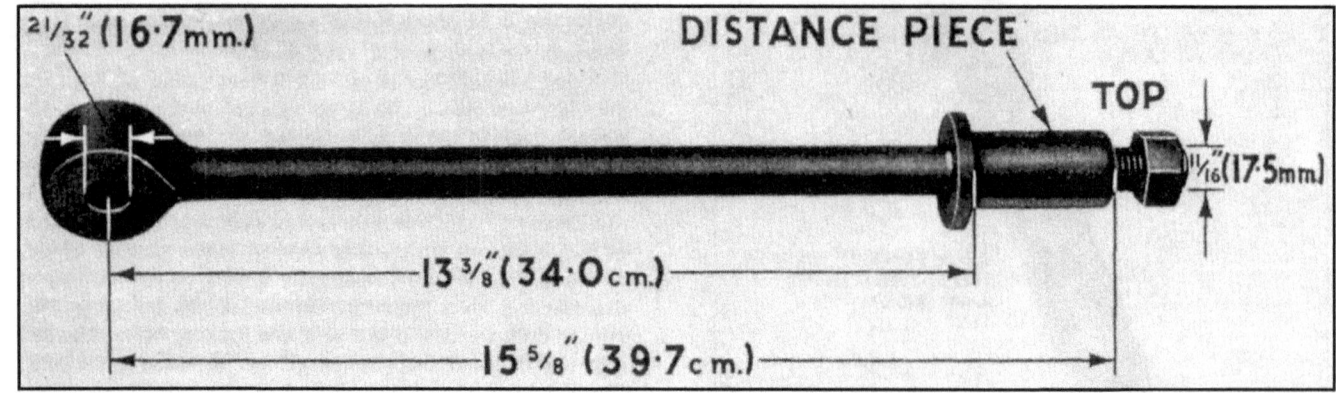

FIG 4 Distance piece XK 120

hub. This is carried out in the following manner. Tighten the castellated nut until there is no end float in the hub then loosen the nut one castellation and secure with a new splitpin. Recheck the end float with a dial gauge if available, this should be .005 inch. Regrease the hub until the excess exudes from the hole in the dust cap.

5 Dismantling the suspension

Upper wishbone lever assembly

Place a support under the chassis frame, jack-up under the lower wishbone lever and remove the road wheel. Leave the jack in position to support the torsion bar load.

Disconnect the shock absorber at the top mounting and withdraw clear of the top mounting post. Release the locking plates and remove the two nuts and bolts passing through the upper wishbone ball assembly and the two upper wishbone levers.

Observe the castor shims fitted between each face of the ball assembly and the respective wishbone lever (see **FIG 8**). **Do not lose or transpose these shims between sides or the castor angle will be altered.**

Remove the self-locking nuts from the two top bolts securing the wishbone bracket to the chassis frame mounting posts, noting the distance tube on the rear bolt. Remove the self-locking nuts from the two bottom bolts securing the wishbone bracket to the flange of the chassis frame mounting posts

Tie up the stub axle carrier to a convenient point on the chassis frame. Note the camber shims fitted betweeen the wishbone bracket and chassis frame. **These shims must be replaced in their original locations or the camber angle will be altered.** Lift out the wishbone levers complete with the mounting bracket.

Remove the brake drum and withdraw splitpins and castellated nuts securing the steering arm to the stub axle carrier. Withdraw the front bolt through the stub axle carrier and tilt the steering arm to clear the brake air scoop. Withdraw the steering arm to remove the splitpin and castellated nut from the upper ball assembly. Tap the shank of the ball assembly out of the taper in the stub axle carrier and remove the ball assembly. If difficulty is encountered in removing the ball assembly it may be necessary to heat the stub axle carrier around the ball assembly shank.

Remove the splitpin, castellated nut and washer from either end of the upper wishbone bracket and tap the levers off the ends of the bracket. Observe that each lever

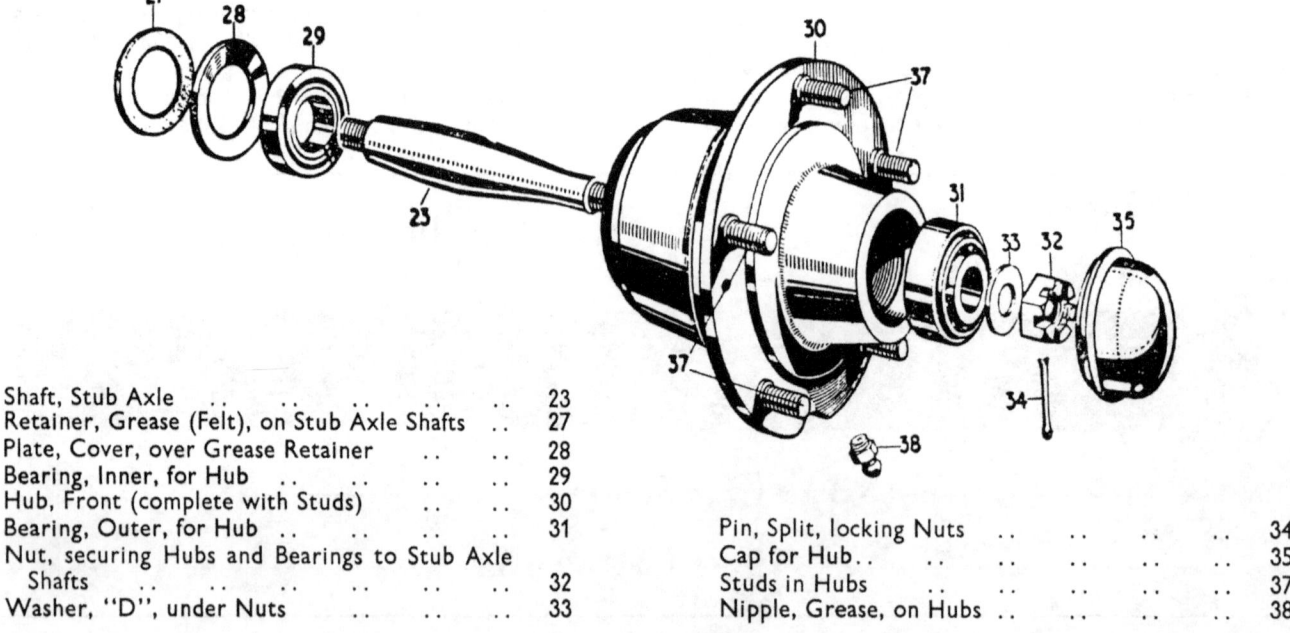

Shaft, Stub Axle	23
Retainer, Grease (Felt), on Stub Axle Shafts	27
Plate, Cover, over Grease Retainer	28
Bearing, Inner, for Hub	29
Hub, Front (complete with Studs)	30
Bearing, Outer, for Hub	31
Nut, securing Hubs and Bearings to Stub Axle Shafts	32
Washer, "D", under Nuts	33
Pin, Split, locking Nuts	34
Cap for Hub	35
Studs in Hubs	37
Nipple, Grease, on Hubs	38

FIG 5 Front hub

Lower wishbone assembly:

Place a support under the chassis frame. Jack-up the car under the lower wishbone lever and remove the road wheel. Leave the jack in position to relieve the load on the shock absorber. Remove the shock absorber by withdrawing the nuts on the top mounting and removing the splitpin and washer from the lower mounting. Lower the jack and place a support under the brake drum check that it is secure and put blocks under the rear wheels.

Release the tab washers locating the four setscrews which retain the ball socket cap and remove the setscrews and cap. Remove the .004 inch shims, spigot over ballpin and ballpin socket. Remove the splitpin and castellated nut from the shank of the ballpin and drive the ballpin downwards out of its taper in the lower wishbone lever. If the ballpin is difficult to remove apply heat to the area around the taper on the lower wishbone lever. The ballpin seal assembly will be left in position between the lower wishbone lever and the stub axle carrier.

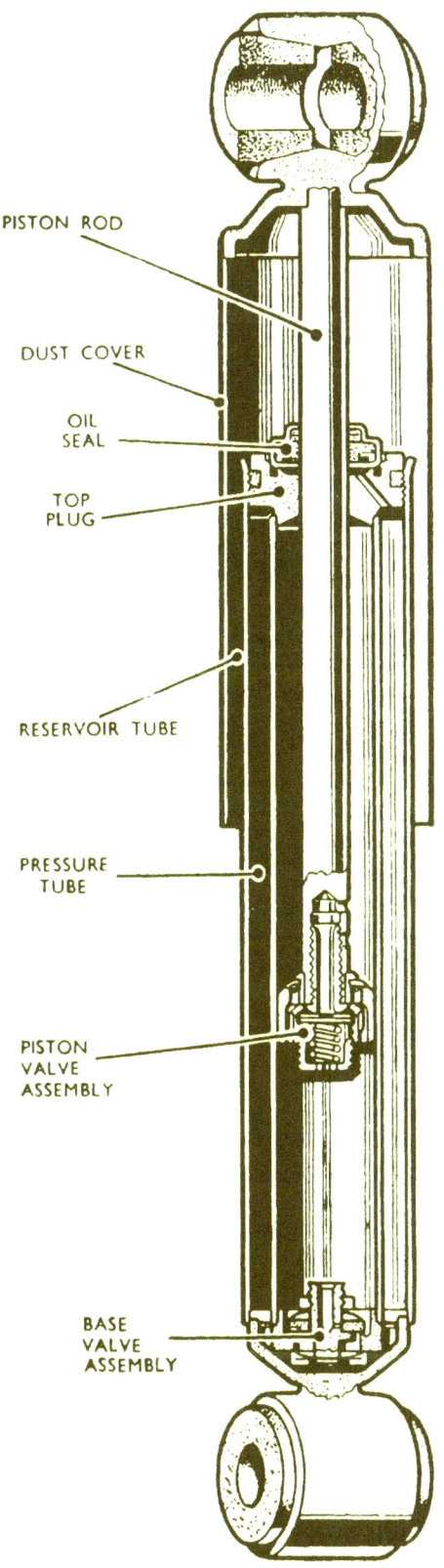

FIG 6   Girling damper

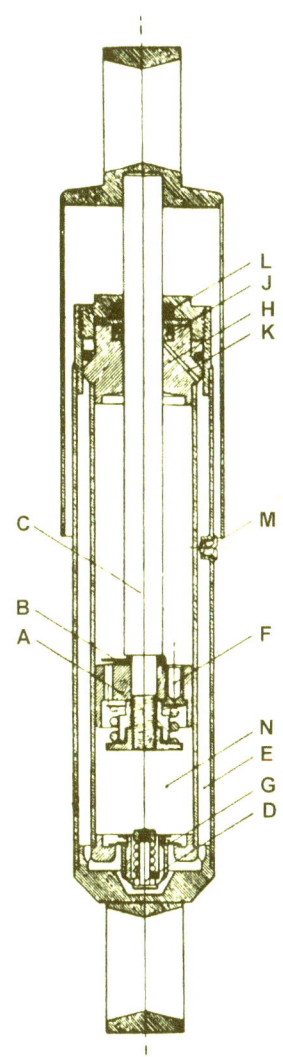

FIG 7   Newton damper

is mounted on two tapered rubber bushes.

Check the upper ball assembly for wear and replace the complete assembly if appreciable wear is found. Examine the tapered rubber bushes and renew if they show signs of wear or deterioation.

A Piston
B Valve
C Piston rod
D Spring-loaded valve
E Outer chamber
F Piston valve
G Valve
H Gland
J Seal
K Leak off port
L Outer seal
M Filler plug
N Working chamber

Remove the torsion bar as described in **Section 3**.

Remove the splitpin and castellated nut securing the anti-roll bar to the bracket on the extremity of the lower wishbone lever. Lift the wishbone lever up off the anti-roll bar, noting the position of the washer and rubber buffers. Remove the four self-locking nuts from the bolts securing the lower wishbone bracket to the bottom face of chassis sidemember. Lift out the lower wishbone assembly.

Remove the splitpin, castellated nut and washer securing the outer extremity of the lower wishbone lever tie rod to the lever. Remove the splitpin, castellated nut and washer from either end of the lower wishbone bracket and tap the tie rod and wishbone lever off the ends of the bracket.

Tap the pin which supports the lower end of the shock absorber and the tie rod from the outer extremity of the wishbone lever. Remove the nut and bolt securing the tie rod bracket to the wishbone lever and remove the bracket. Should it be necessary to remove the ball joint seal assembly the brake backplate must be removed. Remove the four screws retaining the seal carrier to the stud axle carrier and remove the seal assembly.

Examine the ballpin and socket for signs of wear and renew as necessary. It is recommended that if either needs renewing it is best to renew both.

Check the play in the ball and socket by replacing it in the stub axle carrier with the shims and tightening the socket cap screws. The ball should be free to move with a minimum amount of play. To adjust the ball play remove or add shims as necessary. The removal of a shim will reduce the amount of play at the socket and vice-versa.

Inspect the rubber bushes on which are mounted the lower wishbone lever and the tie rod, for signs of wear or deterioration. Renew as necessary.

6 Suspension reassembly

Reassembly is the reverse procedure of the dismantling process.

Ensure that the same number of castor and camber shims found on dismantling are refitted and in their original locations. If any doubt exists regarding these shims it is essential to check the castor and camber angles and reset them as necessary as described in **Section 9**.

When refitting the lower wishbone assembly do not tighten the torsion bar bolts until the torsion bar setting has been tested as described in **Section 3**.

It is essential that the car is in the normal riding position either before pre-loading is applied to any of the rubber bushes or before assemblies are finally locked up. If these precautions are not taken, excessive load will be applied with consequent damage and possible premature failure of the rubber bushes. **The rubber bushes should not in any circumstances be lubricated.**

Grease the ballpin joints with the correct lubricant.

7 Anti-roll bar

The anti-roll bar is connected to both lower wishbone levers and is supported by bushed brackets on the lower chassis member. To remove the anti-roll bar, remove the splitpin, castellated nut and washer from either extremity of the bar at the lower wishbone lever. Remove the two nuts and bolts securing the support brackets on the bottom face of each chassis member. Tap the anti-roll bar out of the brackets on the lower wishbone levers and draw clear from under the car.

Examine the rubber buffers for signs of wear or deterioration and renew as necessary.

Refitting is the reverse of the removal procedure. Check that the rubber buffers are correctly positioned and tighten the nuts with the car in the normal riding position. Do not lubricate the rubber buffers or bushes.

8 Dampers

Two types of damper are fitted to the Jaguar models covered by this manual, they are the Girling and the Newton and Bennett dampers. Both are of the telescopic type and it is recommended that both types are dismantled and reassembled by an authorized agent or that exchange units are obtained. The two dampers are shown in sections (see **FIGS 6** and **7**).

FIG 8 Castor and camber angle adjustment

Removal:

Place a support under the chassis frame. Jack-up the car under the lower wishbone lever and remove the road wheel. Leave the jack in position to relieve the load on the damper. Disconnect the damper by removing the hexagon nuts at the top mounting and the splitpin and washer from the lower mounting. Remove the damper from the top mounting post and withdraw from the car.

Testing:

Stand the unit upright with the bottom eye held in a vice and work the unit up and down through the full length of the stroke. Uniform resistance should be felt in each direction although the amount may differ with direction. A deficiency of fluid is indicated by a flat spot at either end of the stroke.

On the early type of Newton damper a filler screw is fitted M (see **FIG 7**). To top up this type of unit extend the unit fully and remove the filler screw. Lay the unit flat and fill with the correct grade of fluid. Stand the unit upright and allow excess fluid to drain off. Replace the filler screw and work the unit up and down until uniform resistance is felt. Re-check the fluid level by fully extending the unit the fluid level should just reach the filler hole in this condition.

The later Newton damper and the Girling damper have no filler plug and fluid replenishment necessitates dismantling.

Thoroughly clean the outside of the damper before dismantling as cleanliness is essential. The dismantling procedure will be described for the later Newton type the Girling type is similar.

Stand the unit upright with the bottom eye held in a vice. Extend the unit to expose the gland nut, which is unscrewed using a $\frac{3}{4}$ inch B.S.F. spanner. As the gland nut is of a zinc base alloy and therefore comparatively soft and easily damaged, use only the correct size spanner, or preferably a special key to register on the nut which is 1.2 inch across flats. When the gland is unscrewed a sharp upward pull on the piston rod will withdraw the complete inner assembly. Place the dismantled parts on a clean surface, wash out and if possible air blast the cylinder and dismantled parts before reassembly.

Insert the cylinder and foot valve assembly, making sure that it is correctly seated in the outer cylinders. Pour in 130 cc (300 cc for the Girling type) of the recommended fluid and insert the piston rod and gland assembly. Screw home the gland nut. Work the unit up and down through the full length of the stroke until uniform resistance is felt.

If after topping up, uneven or excessive resistance is felt the unit will require renewal

Refitting:

Refitting is the reverse of the removal procedure using a hand clamp to press the eye at the bottom of the damper over the rubber bush. It is essential that the car is in the normal riding position before preloading is applied to the lower mounting rubber bush.

9 Suspension geometry

Provision is made on all of the Jaguar models covered by this manual for adjustment of the suspension geometry.

The two angles which may be adjusted by the use of shims are the castor angle and the camber angle. The castor angle is that between a line drawn through the two ball joints and the vertical looking at the car from the side. The camber angle is that between the wheel and the vertical looking from the rear (or front) of the car.

Shims are provided at the upper wishbone members between the members and the ball joint for castor adjustment and between the upper wishbone bracket and and the chassis frame for camber adjustment (see **FIG 8**).

The measurement and setting of both angles requires specialist gauges and must be set accurately. This work is best left to a qualified agent. **Any attempt to adjust these angles without the proper measuring gauges may well have disastrous effects to the steering and tyre wear.**

10 Modifications

On Mk IX and XK 150 models the upper wishbone ball joint was increased in diameter to provide an increased angle of movement from the following chassis numbers.

	R.H. Drive	L.H. Drive
Mk IX	770220	790196
XK 150 Open 2 seater	820004	831698
XK 150 Fixed head coupé	824668	835882
XK 150 Drop head coupé	872325	837831

The new part number is C.14434 in both cases it is interchangeable with the type fitted to earlier models, but it will be also necessary to fit grease nipple C.9048, self-locking nut C.8737.5 and a plain washer C.791.

11 Fault diagnosis

(a) Wheel wobble

1 Worn hub bearings
2 Incorrectly adjusted or weak torsion bars
3 Uneven tyre wear
4 Worn suspension linkage
5 Loose wheel fixings

(b) 'Bottoming' of suspension

1 Check 2 in (a)
2 Rebound rubbers worn or missing
3 Faulty dampers

(c) Heavy steering

1 Check **Chapter 9**
2 Neglected lubrication of ball joints
3 Wrong suspension geometry

(d) Excessive tyre wear

1 Check 4 in (a); 3 in (b) and 2 in (c)
2 Check steering see **Chapter 9**

(e) Rattles

1 Check 2 in (a)
2 Lubrication neglected
3 Damper mounting loose
4 Anti-roll bar mountings loose, bushes worn
5 Check front brakes see **Chapter 10**

(f) Excessive 'rolling'

1 Check 2 in (a) and 3 in (b)
2 Anti-roll bar broken, mountings loose or bushes worn

INDEX – STEERING

SECTION	PAGE	
001	203	Description (General)
		RECIRCULATING BALL TYPE
002	203	Description
003	203	Maintenance
004	203	Removal
005	209	Disassembly
006	210	Reassembly
007	210	Refitting
008	211	Idle Lever Assembly Servicing
009	213	Steering Connections Servicing
		POWER ASSISTED STEERING
010	214	Description
011	214	Maintenance
012	214	Removal
013	214	Disassembly
014	216	Reassembly & Adjustments
015	216	Refitting
016	217	Pump Servicing
017	218	Bleeding the System
018	218	Fault Diagnosis Chart
		RACK AND PINION TYPE
019	218	Description
020	218	Maintenance
021	218	Removal
022	220	Disassembly
023	220	Reassembly
024	220	Refitting
025	220	Steering Column Servicing
026	223	Tracking & Alignment
027	223	Fault Diagnosis Chart – Applicable to all steering types

STEERING - SERVICE

1 Description (General)

There are three distinct types of steering unit fitted to the range of Jaguar cars covered by this manual. These are the recirculating ball, the power assisted recirculating ball and the rack and pinion types.

The first two types are fitted to XK 120, Mk VII, VIII and IX models, those fitted with the power assisted type have a prefix letter P to the chassis number.

The rack and pinion type is fitted only to the XK 140 and 150 models.

RECIRCULATING BALL TYPE

2 Description

The recirculating ball type unit is of high efficiency and the rocker shaft is transmitted through a sliding member running on a continuous train of ballbearings. The single start worm on the lower end of the inner column is supported at either end by crowded ball races, correctly adjusted by means of shims placed between the cover and the casing. The upper end of the column is locked in a composition bush which requires neither adjustment nor lubrication.

Formed on the sliding member is a conical abutment mating with similar faces on the rocker shaft and a bearing pin carrying a roller, runs in a slot in the coverplate. The rocker shaft is supported in bushes in the steering box and at its lower end has taper splines onto which the drop arm is secured by means of a castellated nut and splitpin.

Mk VII model

The drop arm (see **FIG 1**) is of a divided type and consists of a double-ended main arm which is pivoted and a free fit on a secondary arm. The secondary arm is splined to the rocker shaft and connected to the main arm by a rubber coupling. The main drop arm fulcrum is bushed and provided with a grease nipple. The front end of the drop arm is interconnected to a double-ended idle lever housed on the opposite chassis member by an adjustable track rod which passes through the front crossmember. The idle lever shaft is supported in two taper roller bearings in an aluminium housing which is packed with grease on assembly. No grease nipple is provided and the unit only requires replenishing with grease if it has been dismantled. The rear end of the drop arm and idle lever are interconnected to their respective steering arms with tie rods which are of a fixed length. The ends of the track rod and tie rods are connected by ball joints provided with grease nipples.

XK 120 model

The front end of the drop arm (see **FIG 2**) is interconnected to an idle lever on the opposite chassis member by an adjustable track rod, the ends of which have rubber bearings (early models were fitted with thread bearings and provided with grease nipples). Extensions of the track rod end are interconnected to their respective steering arms with tie rods which are of a fixed length. Early models were fitted with adjustable tie rods, but it is imperative that their lengths be maintained to within $\frac{1}{16}$ inch of 9 inch between ball centres.

On all models the steering swivels consist of two ball assemblies per side attached to the outer extremities of the upper and lower wishbone members and to the stub axle carriers. These ball assemblies form both the steering pivot and front suspension articulation.

Early Mk VII models and all XK 120 models are fitted with Ferobestos ball sockets for the lower steering swivels which do not require lubrication. A general arrangement of the steering is shown in **FIG 3**.

3 Maintenance

Accurate steering can be maintained only by regular lubrication. After overhauling and at the recommended mileage, when greasing the upper and lower ball joints as described in Chapter 8, also grease the nipples provided at the track rod and tie rods. On Mk VII models a nipple is also provided at the drop arm fulcrum. Every month or 2500 miles top up the steering box with the recommended lubricant through the filler plug provided. The filler plug has a plain hexagon head and should not be confused with the rocker shaft adjustment screw which is threaded externally. On the XK 120 model top up the steering idle lever housing with the recommended lubricant through the filler plug in the housing coverplate.

On no account should the steering idler be overlooked as lack of lubricant in this component may cause a serious breakdown due to additional load imposed on the steering gearbox. **Never use grease when topping up either of these boxes.**

Adjustment of the rocker shaft end float may be carried out without any dismantling or removal of the steering gearbox in the following manner. Jack-up the front of the car and remove the road wheel adjacent to the steering box. Turn the steering unit to the straight-ahead position. Check the end float in the rocker shaft N (see **FIG 4**) by applying a light bar under the nut attaching the drop arm to the rocker shaft. There should be no end float in the rocker shaft. If adjustment is required, retain the steering in the straight-ahead position and remove the preloading setscrew A and spring D. Clear off all dirt from the adjuster C then release the locknut B and screw down the adjuster by hand until it just touches the rocker shaft. Secure the adjuster C by tightening the locknut B. Replace and tighten the spring D and preloading setscrew A. It is important that the adjustment is carried out with the road wheels in the straight-ahead position since the conical faces on the rocker shaft are designed to give slightly more backlash towards the full lock positions. If the rocker shaft is adjusted without end play at the full lock positions it will be tight in the straight-ahead position. Test the steering from lock to lock to ensure that it is free.

Replace road wheel and remove jack.

The only other adjustment required under normal maintenance is that of tracking which is covered in **Section 9**.

4 Removal

Mk VII model:

The steering assembly on the Mk VII model consists of a separate steering box and inner column which are connected by a universal joint; couplings splined with the worm shaft and inner column being joined to a flange plate by rubber bushes.

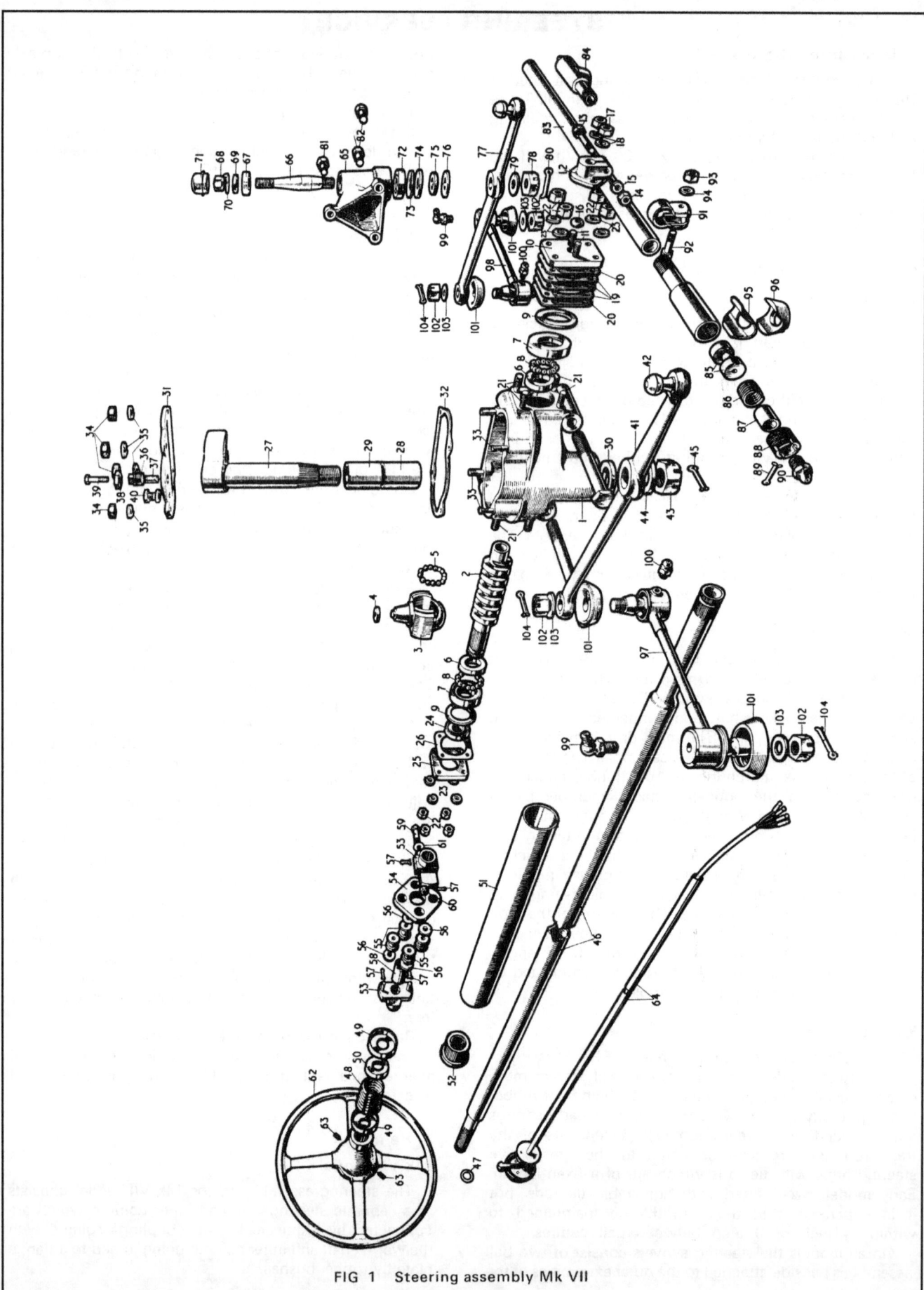

FIG 1 Steering assembly Mk VII

FIG 1   Steering assembly Mk VII

1	Steering Box
2	Worm
3	Main Nut (complete with Transfer Tube, Tube Retainer and Steel Balls) (supplied complete only)
4	Roller on Spigot of Main Nut
5	Ball (Steel) between Main Nut and Worm
6	Washer, Ball Race, at each end of Worm
7	Ball Race at each end of Steering Box
8	Ball (Steel) between Ball Race and Ball Race Washer
9	Washer, Packing, adjacent to Ball Races
10	Plate, End, at bottom of Steering Box
11	Stud in bottom End Plate
12	Bracket, Clip, on bottom End Plate
13	Bolt through Clip Bracket
14	Nut on Bolt
15	Washer, Spring, under Nut
16	Seal, Oil (Felt), between Clip Bracket and End Plate
17	Nut, securing Clip Bracket
18	Washer, Spring, under Nuts
19	Shim for bottom End Plate
20	Gasket for bottom End Plate
21	Stud, in Steering Box, for top and bottom End Plates
22	Nut on Studs
23	Washer, Spring, under Nuts
24	Seal, Oil, in Steering Box, for Worm
25	Plate, End, at top of Steering Box
26	Gasket for top End Plate
27	Rocker Shaft
28	Bush, in Trunnion of Steering Box
29	Bush for Rocker Shaft
30	Seal, Oil, at bottom of Trunnion, for Rocker Shaft
31	Plate, Cover, at top of Steering Box
32	Gasket, between Cover Plate and Steering Box
33	Stud, in Steering Box, for Cover Plate
34	Nut on Studs
35	Washer, Spring, under Nuts
36	Screw, in Cover Plate, adjusting Rocker Shaft
37	Spring, inside Adjusting Screw
38	Nut, locking Adjuster Screw
39	Bolt, tensioning Spring in Adjuster Screw
40	Plug, Filler, in Cover Plate
41	Drop Arm
42	Ball-Peg in Drop Arm
43	Nut, securing Drop Arm to Rocker Shaft
44	Washer, Plain, under Nut
45	Pin, Split, retaining Nut
46	Inner Column
47	Circlip at top of Inner Column
48	Cover, Dust, at top of Inner Column
49	Cup, Retaining, at top and bottom of Dust Cover
50	Cup, Retaining, at bottom of Dust Cover
51	Steering Outer Column
52	Upper Bearing Assembly
53	Coupling for Universal Joint
54	Flange for Universal Joint
55	Bush (Rubber) for Couplings
56	Washer, Plain, adjacent to Rubber Bushes
57	Pin, Split, retaining Washers and Bushes
58	Seal (Rubber) on Coupling
59	Bolt, Clinch, for Universal Joint
60	Nut on Bolts
61	Washer, Shakeproof, under Nuts
62	Steering Wheel (Telescopic)
63	Screw, Grub, in Hub of Steering Wheel
64	Steering Column Control
65	Housing for Idle Lever Shaft
66	Shaft, inside Housing, for Idle Lever
67	Bearing, Roller, at top of Shaft
68	Nut at top of Shaft
69	Washer "D" under Nut
70	Washer, Tab, locking Nut
71	Cap at top of Housing
72	Bearing, Roller, at bottom of Shaft
73	Cover, Dust, underneath bottom Bearing
74	Ring, Abutment, underneath bottom Bearing
75	Seal (Felt) around Abutment Ring
76	Washer, Plain, underneath Felt Seal
77	Lever, Idle
78	Nut, securing Idle Lever to Shaft
79	Washer, Plain, under Nut
80	Pin, Split, retaining Nut
81	Bolt, securing Idle Lever Assembly at top
82	Bolt, securing Idle Lever Assembly at sides
83	Tube only for Track Rod
84	End Assembly, right hand, for Track Rod
84	End Assembly, left hand, for Track Rod
85	Track Rod End Assembly
86	Socket for Ball Pins
87	Spring inside Track Rod Ends
88	Piece, Distance, inside Spring
89	Plug in Track Rod Ends
90	Pin, Split, retaining Plugs
91	Nipple, Grease
92	Clamp, securing Ends in Track Rod
93	Bolt through Clamps
94	Nut on Bolts
95	Washer, Plain, under Nuts
96	Plate, Oil Retaining, under Ball Pins
97	Seal, Oil (Rubber), under Track Rod Ends
98	Steering Tie Rod Assembly, Right Hand
99	Steering Tie Rod Assembly, Left Hand
100	Nipple, Grease, on outer end of Steering Tie Rods
101	Nipple, Grease, on inner end of Steering Tie Rods
102	Seal, Oil (Rubber), on ends of Steering Tie Rods
103	Nut, securing Levers to Tie Rods
104	Washer, Plain, under Nuts
	Pin, Split, retaining Nuts

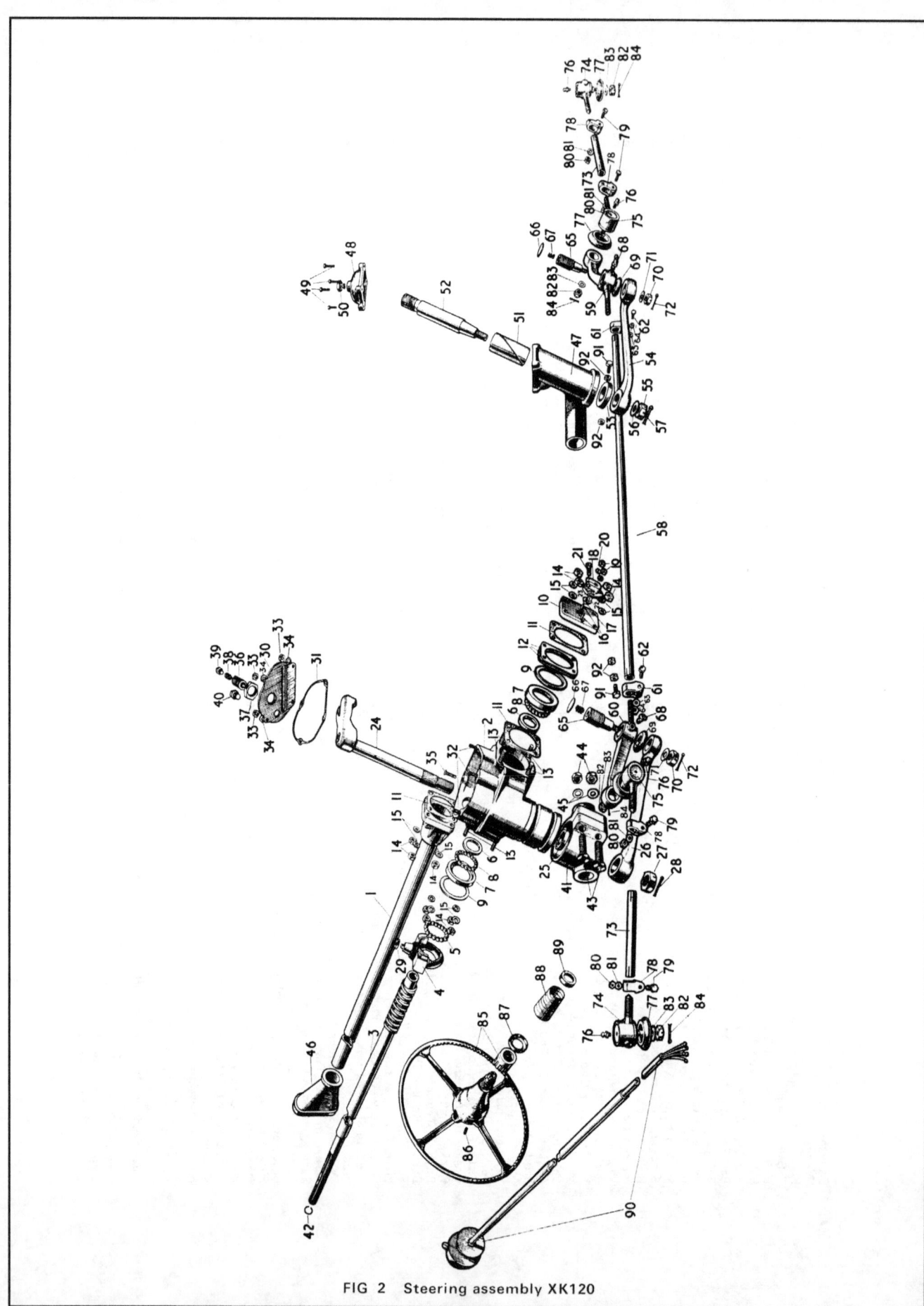

FIG 2 Steering assembly XK120

FIG 2 Steering assembly XK120

1	Column, Outer
2	Steering Box (complete with Trunnion Bush and Rocker Shaft Oil Seal Assembly)
3	Column, Inner
4	Main Nut (complete with Transfer Tube, Tube Retainer, Bolts, Tab Washers and Steel Balls) (supplied complete only)
5	Ball (Steel) between Main Nut and Worm on Inner Column
6	Washer, Ball Race, at each end of Inner Column Worm
7	Ball Race in each end of Steering Box
8	Ball (Steel) between Ball Race and Ball Race Washer
9	Washer, Packing, adjacent to Ball Races
10	Plate, End, at bottom of Steering Box
11	Gasket for Steering Box
12	Shim, between End Plate and Steering Box
13	Stud at each end of Steering Box
14	Nut, securing Outer Column and End Plate to Steering Box
15	Washer, Spring, under Nuts
16	Stud, in End Plate, for Clip Bracket
17	Seal, Oil (Felt), between End Plate and Clip Bracket
18	Bracket, Clip, on End Plate
19	Nut, securing Clip Bracket to End Plate
20	Washer, under Nuts
21	Bolt, through Clip Bracket
22	Nut on Bolt
23	Washer, Spring, under Nut
24	Rocker Shaft
25	Seal, Oil, for Rocker Shaft
26	Drop Arm
27	Nut, securing Drop Arm to Rocker Shaft
28	Pin, Split, securing Nut
29	Roller, on Spigot of Main Nut
30	Plate, Cover, at top of Steering Box
31	Gasket, between Cover Plate and Steering Box
32	Stud, in Steering Box, for Cover Plate
33	Nut, securing Cover Plate to Steering Box
34	Washer, Spring, under Nuts
35	Screw, securing Cover Plate to Steering Box
36	Screw, in Cover Plate, adjusting Rocker Shaft
37	Nut, locking Adjusting Screw in Cover Plate
38	Spring, inside Adjusting Screw
39	Bolt, in end of Adjusting Screw, retaining Spring
40	Plug, Filler, in Cover Plate
41	Bracket, Trunnion, securing Steering Unit at lower end
42	Circlip, on upper end of Inner Column, retaining Steering Wheel
43	Bolt, securing Trunnion Bracket to Chassis Frame
44	Nut on Bolts
45	Washer under Nuts
46	Grommet (Rubber) for Steering Unit
47	Housing for Screwed Shaft
48	Plate, Cover, on top of Housing
49	Screw, Shakeproof, securing Cover Plate
50	Plug, Oil Filler, in Cover Plate
51	Bush, in Housing
52	Shaft (Screwed) for Idle Lever
53	Seal (Rubber) in bottom of Housing
54	Lever, Idle
55	Nut, securing Idle Lever to Screwed Shaft
56	Washer under Nut
57	Pin, Split, locking Nut
58	Tube only for Track Rod
59	End, Track Rod (Left-Hand Thread) (complete with Screwed Pin Plate, Ref. 65, and Cover Plate, Ref. 66)
60	End, Track Rod (Right-Hand Thread) (complete with Screwed Pin Plate, Ref. 65, and Cover Plate, Ref. 66)
61	Clamp, securing Ends in Track Rod
62	Bolt through Clamps
63	Nut on Bolts
64	Washer, Spring, under Nuts
67	Spring, between Plates and Screwed Pins
68	Nipple, Grease, on Track Rod Ends
69	Seal (Rubber) between Levers and Track Rod Ends
70	Nut, securing Drop Arm and Idle Levers to Screwed Pins
71	Washer under Nuts
72	Pin, Split, locking Nuts
73	Tube only
74	Ball Joint Assembly, Left Hand
75	Ball Joint Assembly, Right Hand
76	Nipple, Grease, in Retaining Plates
77	Seal (Rubber) on Ball Joints
78	Clamp, securing Ball Joints in ends of Steering Connecting Tubes
79	Bolt through Clamps
80	Nut on Bolts
81	Washer, Spring, under Nuts
82	Nut, securing Track Rod Ends and Steering Arms to Ball Joints
83	Washer, under Nuts
84	Pin, Split, locking Nuts
85	Steering Wheel (Telescopic)
86	Screw, Grub, in Steering Wheel
87	Washer at top of Telescopic Dust Cover
88	Cover, Dust (Telescopic)
89	Washer at bottom of Telescopic Dust Cover
90	Steering Column Control
91	Bolt, Stop, for Steering Lock
92	Nut, locking Stop Bolts in position

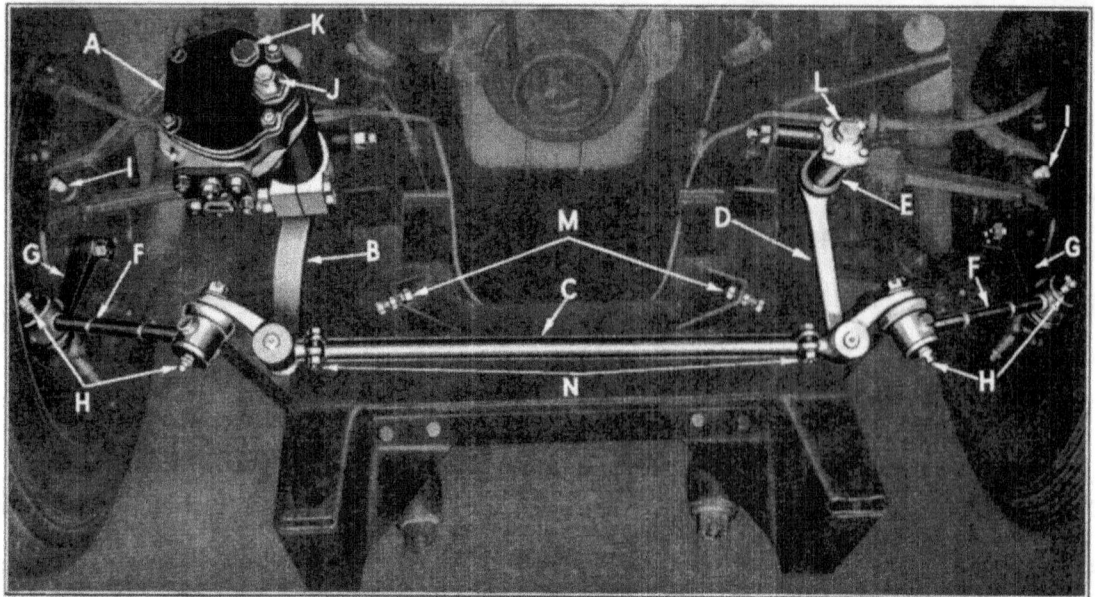

A. Steering Box.
B. Drop Arm.
C. Track Rod.
D. Idle Lever.
E. Idle Shaft Housing.
F. Tie Rods.
G. Steering Arms.
H. Nipples. Tie Rods.
I. Nipples. Upper Steering Swivels.
J. Rocker Shaft Adjuster.
K. Filler Plug. Steering Box.
L. Filler Plug. Idle Shaft Housing.
M. Steering Lock Stops.
N. Track Rod Clamps.

FIG 3 General arrangement of steering (XK120)

The following description covers the removal of both the inner and outer columns and the steering box. These items may be removed separately providing they are fully disconnected from one-another.

Jack-up the front of the car and remove the front road wheel on the steering column side. The steering box and universal joint are accessible from underneath the wing.

Disconnect the battery positive lead and set the road wheels in the straight-ahead position. Disconnect the four manette control wires from the junction box fitted to the wing valance on the steering column side. Slacken the clamp bolt of the stator tube bracket attached to the bottom end plate of the steering box. Unscrew the two grubscrews in the steering wheel hub and withdraw the manette control with a twisting motion. Plug the hole in the bottom end plate of the steering box to avoid loss of oil.

Remove the dash casing underneath the facia panel by unscrewing the drive screws. Remove the three bolts securing the flat transverse bracket underneath the outer column. Remove the pinch bolt from the clamp securing the outer column in the tube attached to the inside of the scuttle. Remove the drivers seat.

From underneath the wing remove the pinch bolt securing the upper coupling of the universal joint to the inner column. Remove the stator tube if not withdrawn with the manette control. Withdraw the inner and outer columns by pulling on the steering wheel.

Remove the splitpin and nut securing the steering tie rod inner ball joint to the rear end of the drop arm. Tap the ball joint out of its taper in the drop arm and place clear. Remove the splitpin from the end of the track rod and unscrew the end plug until the track rod end can be lifted from the ball on the front end of the drop arm.

Remove the two bolts and stud nut securing the steering box to the bracket on the chassis frame and remove the box.

XK 120 model:

Disconnect the battery positive lead. Set the road wheels in the straight-ahead position. On the super sports model disconnect the manette control wire from the horn relay box side. On the fixed head coupé model disconnect the four wires from the rubber snap connectors.

Unscrew the two grubscrews in the steering wheel hub and withdraw the manette control complete with the wiring harness. Rotate the steering wheel knurled adjustment ring until it is free. Remove the circlip at the top of the splined portion of the column. Draw off the steering wheel and remove the washers and telescopic dust cover.

From underneath the facia panel remove the drive screws securing the dash casing and withdraw the casing. Remove the outer clamp pinch bolt.

On righthand models only, detach the grommet between the outer column and the scuttle. Remove the three nuts securing the windscreen wiper motor to its bracket and place the motor clear. Remove the four bolts securing the windscreen wiper motor bracket to the scuttle and remove the bracket.

Jack-up the front of the car and remove the road wheel on the steering column side. From underneath the wing remove the wing valance plate by removing the securing bolts.

Remove the two bolts securing the brake fluid supply tank and tie it up adjacent to the engine. Tap back the washer securing the track rod end and remove the nut and

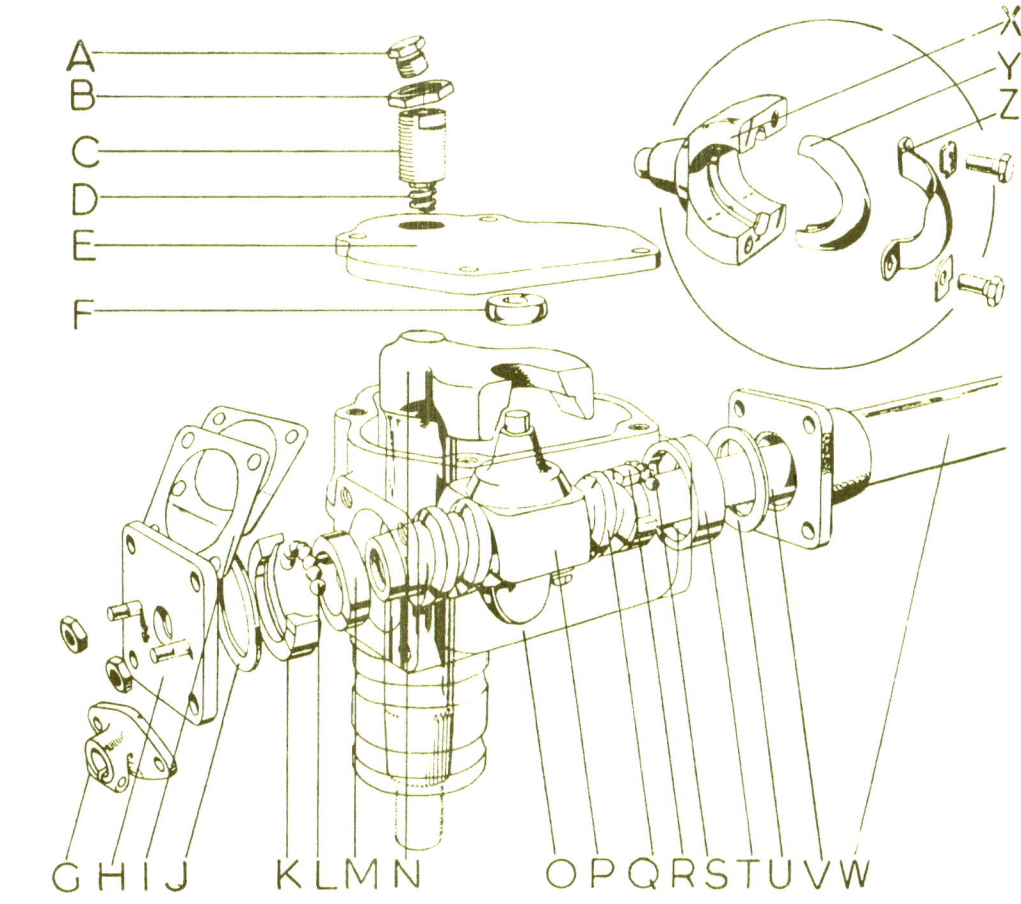

FIG 4 The steering box (XK120)

A.	Rocker Shaft Adjustment. Preload Set Screw.	N.	Rocker Shaft.
B.	Rocker Shaft Adjustment. Lock Nut.	O.	Steering Box.
C.	Rocker Shaft Adjustment. Adjuster.	P.	Nut.
D.	Rocker Shaft Adjustment. Preload Spring.	Q.	Worm.
E.	Cover Plate.	R.	Washer.
F.	Roller on Nut Spigot.	S.	Balls.
G.	Stator Tube Clip.	T.	Ball Race. Upper.
H.	End Plate.	U.	Packing Ring.
I.	Adjustment Shims. (Inner Column End Play.)	V.	Inner Column.
J.	Packing Ring.	W.	Outer Column.
K.	Ball Race. Lower.	X.	Nut with Ball Track.
L.	Balls.	Y.	Transfer Tube.
M.	Washer.	Z.	Clip retaining Transfer Tube.

pegged tab washer. Tap the track rod end out of its taper in the drop arm and place clear.

Remove the upper wishbone bracket front securing bolt which passes through the steering box trunnion. Lever the trunnion out of the upper wishbone bracket and manoeuvre the steering unit out from underneath the front wing.

5 Dismantling

Remove the three nuts and spring washers (see **FIG 4**) and one setscrew securing the coverplate to the steering box. Remove the coverplate E complete with the rocker shaft adjuster C and pre-loading spring D, observing the gasket fitted between the cover and gearbox. Withdraw the preloading setscrew A locknut B and adjuster C.

Remove the splitpin and nut securing the drop arm to the rocker shaft. Observe the line scribed on the drop arm and rocker shaft to facilitate correct reassembly. Using a suitable extractor draw the drop arm off the splines on the rocker shaft N. **Never try to hammer the drop arm off as the ball tracks may well be damaged by the hammering.** Observe the roller F on spigot of the main nut P which should now be removed. Remove and scrap the oil seal at the base of the rocker shaft lower bush.

XK 120:

Remove the four nuts and spring washers securing the outer column W to the steering box O and withdraw outer columns, observing the gasket between them. Withdraw the upper ball race T and packing washer U. Ensure that no balls are lost during this operation.

Mk VII:

Remove the pinch bolt securing the universal joint coupling to the worm shaft and withdraw the universal joint from splines. Remove the four nuts and washers securing the end plate H to the bottom of the steering box. Remove the end plate, observing the gasket and shims I. Remove the packing ring J and ball race K taking care not to lose any of the balls. Remove the four nuts and spring washers securing the end plate to the top of the steering box and remove the end plate. Remove the gasket oil seal, packing washer U, and withdraw the ball race T, taking care not to lose any of the balls. Unscrew the worm Q through the main nut P and withdraw from box.

On the XK 120 model remove two nuts and washers securing the stator tube bracket G to the end plate H. Withdraw the bracket complete with the stator tube. Remove four nuts with spring washers securing the end plate H to the steering box and remove the end plate, observing the shims I with gaskets either side. Remove the packing ring J and ball race K taking care not to lose any of the balls. Unscrew the inner column through the main nut and withdraw the column from the box. Lift out the nut P and remove the two setscrews and tab washers retaining the transfer tube to the main nut and remove the clip Z, tube Y and balls.

The steering box trunnion bracket may be removed by unscrewing the two nuts and withdrawing the bolts securing the split portion of the trunnion to the steering box.

On the Mk VII model remove the splitpin and nut securing the double-ended arm to the secondary arm and remove the bolt. Remove the two rubber bushes and plain washers. Lift off the double-ended arm from the secondary arm.

6 Reassembly

Thoroughly clean the steering gearbox inside and out and examine the rocker shaft housing bushes for wear renewing them if necessary. Examine all bearings for signs of wear especially the main nut and renew all components as necessary. Thoroughly clean the worm and examine for signs of wear this should only show after a considerable mileage.

On the XK 120 model fit the trunnion to the steering box and secure in position with the two bolts, washers and nuts. Do not fully tighten the nuts since the position of the trunnion on the steering box may have to be adjusted when the unit is fitted to the chassis.

Fit the balls in the nut assembly by packing it with grease, which will hold the balls in position and attach the transfer tube to the main nut with the clip, two studs and tab washers. Lock the setscrews with the tab washers and place the assembly in the steering box. Liberally grease the upper ball race to facilitate assembly of the balls; fit balls and outer race to the washer against the upper end of the worm. Enter the worm into the steering box and screw through the nut. When in position, fit the packing washer and new joint washer.

On the XK 120 model slide the outer column over the inner column and secure in position with the four nuts and spring washers.

Fit the oil seal and top end plate to the steering box and secure with four nuts and spring washers. In the case of the Mk VII model engage the universal joint coupling on the splines of the worm shaft so that the clamp bolt hole is in line with the annular groove around the shaft. Secure with the clamp bolt, shakeproof washer and nut.

Fit a new joint washer to the bottom face of the steering box and assemble the lower ball race and packing washer. Grease should be used to facilitate assembly of the balls. Fit the ball race and packing washer followed by the necessary number of shims to eliminate all end float of the inner column. Fit a new joint washer on the outside face of the shims, followed by the coverplate retaining this in position with the four nuts and spring washers. **It is essential that the inner column is not preloaded by the lack of shims otherwise indentation of the ball races may take place.**

On the XK 120 models refit the stator tube and bracket to the end plate so that the slot in the top end of the tube will be at the top centre position in the inner column. Secure the bracket with the two nuts and washers.

Fit a new rocker shaft oil seal at the bottom of the steering box. Ensure that the roller is in position on the spigot of the main nut. Insert the rocker shaft through the rocker shaft bushes and the oil seal already in position at the bottom of the steering box. Refit the coverplate with a new gasket and secure in position.

Refit the drop arm, ensuring that the locating line scribed on the boss matches the similar line on the end of the rocker shaft. Secure in position with the nut.

Check the main arm end float in the following manner. Disconnect the double-ended main arm from the short secondary arm by removing the damper bolt, washers and rubber buffers. With the rocker shaft nut fully tightened, test the double-ended drop arm for freedom of movement on the secondary arm by checking the end cleanace of the double-ended arm, which should be .002 to .006 inch. If this end float is found to be incorrect it may be adjusted by the insertion of shims between the nut flange and secondary (inner) arm after removal of the rocker shaft end nut. Shims are available for this purpose in the following thicknesses; .0025, .005 and .0075 inch. Finally check the alignment of the splitpin hole in the nut and rocker shaft with the nut fully tightened. If necessary, fit shims between the nut flange and the end faces of both secondary and main drop arms to effect alignment. These large shims should be fitted directly against the nut flange. The large shims for this purpose are available only in one thickness i.e. .010 inch.

Refit the splitpin to the rocker shaft and reconnect the secondary arm to the main arm.

Adjust the rocker shaft end float as described in **Section 3**.

7 Refitting

Mk VII model:

Refitting is the reverse of the removal instructions but attention should be given to the following points.

When refitting the inner and outer columns, pass the inner column through the aperture in the scuttle and engage the bottom splines in the splines of the universal joint coupling. Ensure that the annular groove is in line with the pinch bolt and fit pinch bolt. Before tightening the outer column and clamp bracket, position the upper face of the top bush 1 inch below the bottom of the inner column splines to ensure full travel of the telescopic steering wheel.

When refitting the steering wheel manette control, set the road wheels in the straight-ahead position. Fit the washers and telescopic dust cover and engage the steering wheel on the splines of the inner column so that one spoke is at the top centre position. Fit the circlip to the annular groove at the top of the inner column. Push the stator tube down the inner column until the bottom of the tube is flush with the end of the clip bracket attached to the bottom of the steering box. Temporarily tighten the clip bracket clamp bolt. Pass the manette control wires down through the stator tube and enter the keyed end of the manette into the slot of the stator tube. Slacken the clip bracket clamp bolt and centralize the trafficator hand control. Turn the manette control until the trafficator hand control is in the top centre position and tighten the clip bracket clamp bolt. Withdraw the manette control slightly and turn the cancelling ring until the split portion is also at the top centre position. Push the manette control fully home into the steering wheel hub and secure with the two grubscrews through the side of the hub.

Check that the trafficators cancel evenly on each side of the straight-ahead position.

XK 120 model:

As with the previous model refitting generally is the reverse procedure to that described for removal with special attention being given to the following points.

Ensure that the rubber grommet is fitted to the column before offering up the steering unit. Before tightening the steering unit mounting bolt, trunnion bolts and top clamp under the facia, ensure that the unit is not strained or distorted. It is advisable to tighten the top clamp bolt before tightening the steering nut mounting bolt and trunnion bolts. Refill the steering box with the correct grade of oil.

When refitting the track rod end to the drop arm it is important to carry out the following procedure: If the track rod end is of the rubber bearing type (see **FIG 5**) turn the drop arm to the straight-ahead position before entering the taper of the bearing bolt in the companion taper of the drop arm. If the track rod is of the thread bearing type (see **FIG 6**), turn the drop arm and road wheels to the full left lock position (applicable to both right and lefthanded steering). Rotate the thread bearing bolt clockwise as far as possible into its housing, overcoming the tension of the preload spring and then unscrew half a turn anticlockwise. Enter the taper of the bearing bolt in the companion taper of the drop arm and secure with the nut and a new pegged tab washer (splitpin and nut on early models).

On refitting the steering wheel and manette control the following points should be observed.

Set the road wheels to the straight-ahead position. Fit the telescopic dust cover and washers to the inner column and engage the steering wheel on the splines so that one spoke is at the top centre position. Fit the circlip to the annular groove at the top of the inner column.

On the fixed head coupé model pass the wiring harness down the centre of the inner column; centralize the trafficator hand control and ensure that the split portion of the cancelling ring is in line with this control. Enter the manette control tube in the inner column and feed the key of the manette control tube into the keyway of the stator tube; it may be necessary to rotate the manette control each way slightly to achieve this. Ensure that the trafficator hand control and split portion of the cancelling ring are in the top centre position and push the manette control fully home into the steering wheel hub. Secure with the two grubscrews through the side of the steering wheel hub. Check that the trafficators cancel evenly on each side of the straight-ahead position.

On the super sports model pass the horn wire down the centre of the inner column and enter the manette control tube into the steering wheel hub with the head of the 'Jaguar' on the horn push upright. Feed the key of the manette control tube into the keyway of the stator tube; it may be necessary to rotate the manette control each way slightly to achieve this. Push the manette control fully home into the steering hub and secure with the two grubscrews.

If when the manette control tube has been engaged with the stator tube, the the trafficator hand control (or the Jaguar) is not at the correct position it will be necessary to slacken the clamp bolt in the bracket attached to the bottom end plate of the steering box to enable the manette control to be turned to the correct position.

8 Idle lever assembly

Mk VII model:

Removal:

Jack-up the front of the car and remove the road wheel on the idle lever assembly side. Turn the steering to a position where the track rod end may be disconnected from the idle lever. Remove the splitpin from the end of the track rod and unscrew the end plug until the track rod can be lifted off the idle lever ball. Remove the splitpin from the nut securing the steering tie rod to the rear of the idle lever and remove the nut. Tap the ball joint out of its taper. Remove the three bolts securing the idle lever housing to the bracket and lift out the housing complete with lever.

Dismantling:

Remove the splitpin and nut securing the idle lever to the shaft. Withdraw the lever off the taper on the shaft and remove the plain washer, seal abutment ring and dust cover. Remove the domed cap on the top of the housing by levering under the flange. Tap back the tab washer and unscrew the nut. Remove the tab washer and the 'D' washer. Suitably support the idle lever housing and press the shaft through the inner race of the top or small bearing. Withdraw the shaft complete with large inner race.

Reassembly and refitting:

Examine all components for signs of wear and renew as necessary. Reassembly and refitting is the reverse process of the removal and dismantling procedures bearing the following points in mind. On reassembling do not tighten the nut at the top of the shaft until the taper in the idle lever has been fully tightened on the companion taper of the shaft. Finally tighten the nut sufficiently to preload the taper roller bearings slightly and

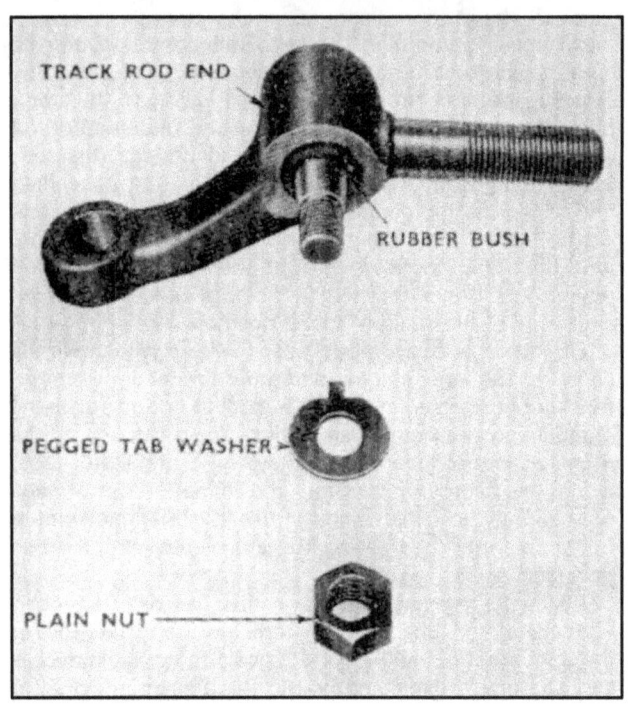

FIG 5 Track rod end rubber bearing type XK120

secure with a new tab washer. Pack the idle housing with the correct grade of grease.

When fitting the track rod end to the idle lever it is necessary to ensure that the ball is interposed between the two ball cups. The end plug should be screwed home to a position where the track rod can just be rotated by hand.

XK 120 model:

Removal:

Jack-up the front of the car and remove the road wheel wheel on the idle lever assembly side. Turn the steering to a position where the nut securing the track rod end to the idle lever may be removed. Tap back the tab washer and remove the nut and washer. Tap the track rod end out of the taper in the idle lever. Remove the upper wishbone front mounting bolt which passes through the idle lever housing and the smaller retaining bolt fitted underneath. Lift out the idle lever housing complete with idle lever.

Dismantling:

Tap back the tab washer and remove the nut and washer securing the idle lever to the shaft. Withdraw the idle lever from the lever shaft and unscrew the shaft anticlock-

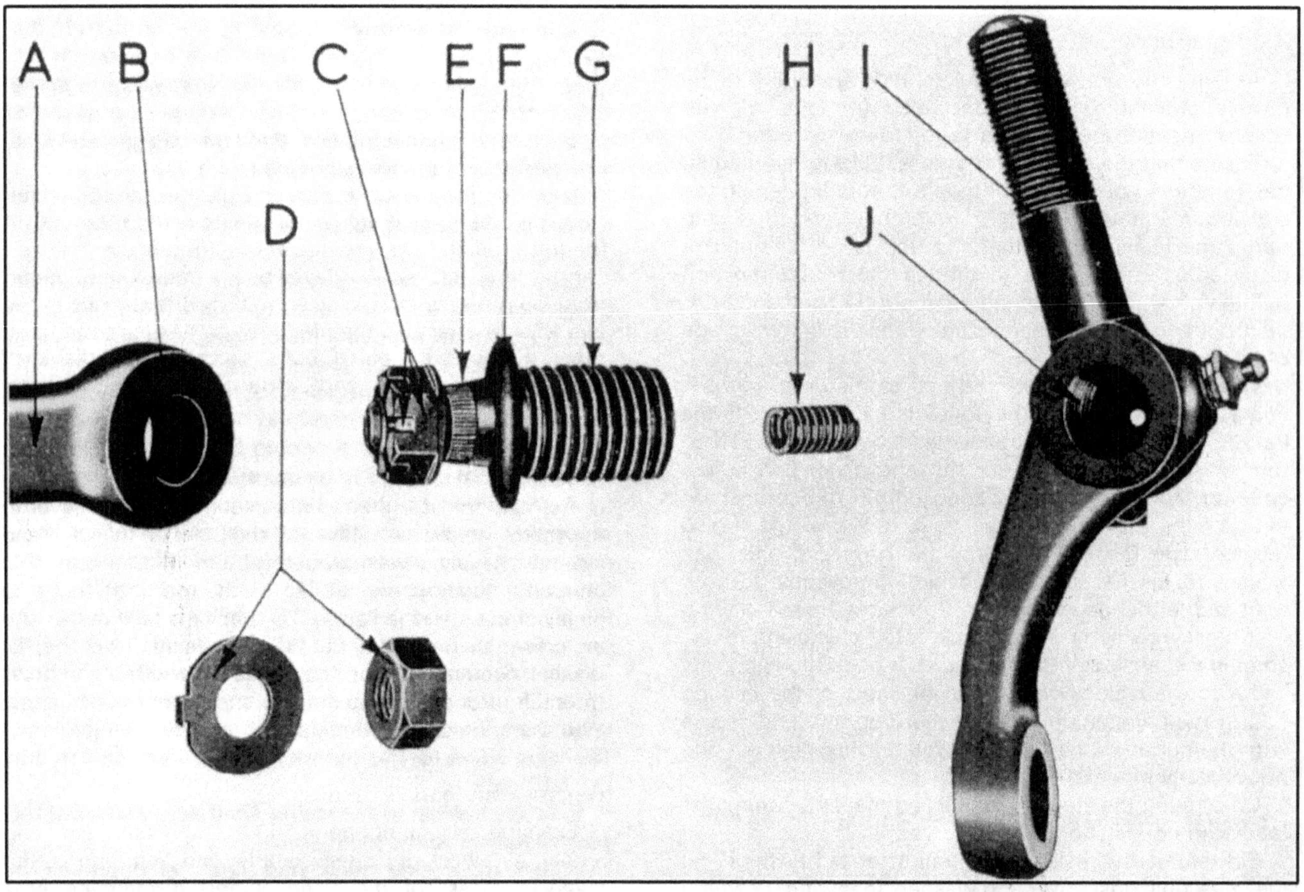

FIG 6 Track rod end early type XK120

A Steering drop arm (or steering idle lever)
B Taper hole
C Clotted nut, plain washer and splitpin
D Plain nut and pegged tab washer (alternative to 'C', later cars)
E Knurled and tapered shank
F Rubber seal
G Thread bearing bolt
H Preloading spring
I Track rod end
J Thread bearing housing

wise out of the housing. Remove the four screws securing cover to the top of the housing and remove the cover.

Reassembly:

Replace the top cover and secure with the four screws. Offer up the idler lever shaft into the housing rotate clockwise as far as it will go. Fit a new seal to the bottom of the shaft. Rotate the idle lever shaft anticlockwise half a turn and offer up the idle lever to the taper on the shaft, ensuring that the idle lever is in the full left lock position. Tap the idle lever on the taper and secure in position with a new pegged tab washer and nut.

Refitting:

Mount the idler lever housing at the front of the upper wishbone securing bracket on the chassis frame and secure with the two bolts and nuts.

On cars fitted with rubber bushed track rod ends set the idle lever in the straight-ahead position and tap the taper pin into the companion taper of the idle lever with a light blow from a soft metal hammer.

On early models having track rods fitted with thread bearings turn the idle lever to the full left lock position and rotate the track rod thread bolt in its housing as far as possible clockwise and then unscrew half a turn. Tap the track rod end taper into the companion taper of the idle lever.

Secure in position with a new pegged tab washer and nut. Remove hexagon plug situated on top of the idle lever housing and fill with the recommended lubricant.

9 Steering connections

The track rod consists of a hollow tube threaded internally at each end, into which are screwed the track rod ends, thus providing adjustment for the setting of the track. The tube is secured to the track rod ends by a clamp at each end.

To remove the track rod ends, jack-up the front of the car and remove the front road wheels. Moving the steering side to side as necessary to gain access to the track rod ends, remove the splitpins and slotted nuts on the XK 120 model securing the inner ball joint assemblies of the tie rods to the track rod ends and tap the ball joints out of the tapers. Tap back the tab washers and remove the plain nuts and washers retaining the track rod assembly to the steering drop arm and idler lever. Tap the track rod ends out of the drop arm and idle lever. Lift out the track rod assembly.

On the Mk VII model remove the splitpins from the end of the track rod and unscrew the end plug sufficiently to allow the track rod to be lifted off the ballpins on the drop arm and the idle lever. Note the rubber seal and seal retainer and renew if necessary.

To remove the track rod ends slacken the clamps at each end of the track rod tube. Unscrew the track rod ends from the tube noting that one end has a lefthand thread and the other a righthand thread.

The three different types of track rod end fitted to the car models are shown in **FIGS 5, 6** and **7**. The rubber bearing type (see **FIG 5**) cannot be dismantled and must be replaced as a unit. The other two types may be dismantled and examined for wear to the various components. These should be renewed as necessary.

Refitting is the reverse procedure to that described under removal, care being taken to check that the following points are adhered to. On refitting the track rod ends ensure that new rubber seals are fitted to the shanks of the thread bearing bolts or over the ballpins on the Mk VII model. Screw home the end plug on the Mk VII model track rod ends until the track rod may just be rotated by hand.

It is essential that the drop arm and idle lever are in the straight-ahead position before the taper bolts of the rubber bearing type track rod ends are engaged and located in position.

If the track rod assembly has been dismantled the steering track must be reset.

Steering track adjustment:

Track adjustment is best carried out by a service station which is equipped to make an accurate setting. However the owner may carry out a similar process as follows.

Check that the tyres are inflated to the correct pressures and the car is on level ground. Turn the wheels to the straight-ahead position. Measure the distance between the outer edges of the front wheel rims at the front and at wheel centre height. Mark the measuring points with chalk. Roll the car forward until the measuring marks are situated at the back of the wheels at centre height and repeat the measurement between them Compare the two measurements taken. The track is correct if the front measurement is between $\frac{1}{8}$ and $\frac{3}{16}$ inch less than the rear measurement. This difference in measurement being the correct toe-in figure.

If adjustment is required slacken the clamp bolts at either end of the track rod and rotate the rod in the required direction to produce the desired measurement. Tighten the clamp bolts and recheck the aforementioned measurements.

Steering tie rods:

The steering tie rods which connect the track rod ends to their respective steering arms are of a fixed type and non-adjustable for length. The ends of the tie rods are attached to the steering arms and track rod with normal ball joints which are of the non-adjustable type and cannot be dismantled.

Early XK 120 models were fitted with adjustable tie rods these rods must be kept within $\frac{1}{16}$ inch of 9 inches between ball centres.

To remove the tie rods remove the slotted nuts and splitpins securing the ball joints at either end of the rod to the steering arms and track rod respectively. Tap the ball joints out of their tapers and lift out the tie rods. The adjustable type of rod may be dismantled by removing the clamps at either end and unscrewing the ball joint. It is essential that on reassembly the track rod is adjusted to the correct length of 9 inch between ball centres. The ball joints should be replaced on both types if there are signs of wear.

Refitting is carried out in the following manner. Refit the tapers of the ball joint assemblies into the companion tapers of the steering arms and track rod; tap with a soft metal hammer and lock in this position with the slotted nuts and new splitpins. On the Mk VII model each tie rod must be fitted so that the ball end with the grease nipple

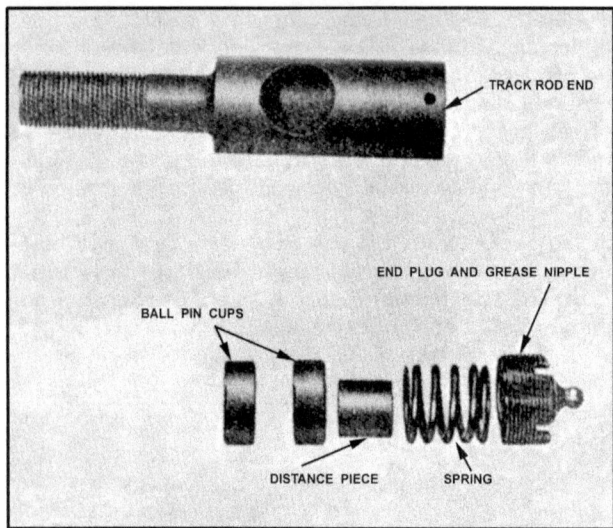

FIG 7 Track rod end Mk VII

in the top cap is at the steering arm end with the grease nipple on the other ball end facing forward. Check the steering track and reset if necessary.

POWER ASSISTED STEERING

10 Description

The power assisted steering consists of two main assemblies the pump and the steering unit. The eccentric rotor type pump driven off the rear of the generator shaft supplies oil from the reservoir, under pressure to the steering unit this oil is returned to the reservoir via the outlet at the top of the steering box. The interconnection between the pump, steering box and reservoir is by means of flexible hoses. A layout of the system is shown in **FIG 8**.

The pump supplies a continuous flow of oil through the system while the engine is running and the steering is in the straight-ahead position. Pressure is only created in the system when the steering column is rotated and is proportional to the effort applied to the steering wheel.

The steering box (see **FIG 9**) is of the re-circulating ball, worm and nut type in which hydraulic assistance is applied to a piston D forming part of the nut C. The piston works within a cast iron cylinder pressed into the steering box casing, hydraulic pressure being admitted to one side or other of the piston, depending on which direction the steering wheel is turned. Admission of oil to the appropriate pressure chamber is controlled by a selector valve K co-axially mounted within the hollow rear end of the worm-shaft G. The valve extends rearwards through the steering box top cover, and forms the input shaft to which the lower end of the steering column is directly connected. Rotary movement of the valve relative to the wormshaft open and closes ports in the wormshaft, and thus directs oil to the correct side of the piston.

When the steering wheel effort is at a minimum, centralization of the valve within the wormshaft is effected by the action of an interlock ball E which is loaded by a coil spring H located at the bottom of the valve.

The valve works between stops which prevent overloading and allow the steering to operate mechanically if the hydraulic system fails.

11 Maintenance

Maintenance on the steering linkage is similar to that described for the non-power assisted worm and nut steering. The only exception is on the drop arm which on the power assisted system has no grease nipple.

The oil level in the reservoir which supplies the steering box with oil must be checked regularly as if it falls below the low mark on the dipstick the power assistance to the steering will be effected.

To check the oil level clean around the filler cap of the reservoir then remove the cap which has the dipstick attached. Top up with the recommended grade of oil to the full mark on the dipstick and replace the reservoir cap. As with all hydraulic systems it is essential that absolute cleanliness is observed to prevent the ingress of foreign matter.

The reservoir filter should be removed and renewed at intervals of 20,000 miles. To remove the filter unscrew the reservoir cover retaining bolt and lift off the cover. The filter can then be lifted out from the bottom of the reservoir.

12 Removal

Jack-up the front of the car and remove the front road wheel on the steering column side. The steering box and rubber couplings will then be accessible from underneath the wing.

Remove the bolt securing the reservoir return hose banjo to the top end plate of the steering unit and drain the oil into a clean container. Undo the union securing the hose from the pump adaptor to the feed pipe on the lower end of the steering box.

Remove the pinch bolts from the jaw securing the lower steering column to the input shaft and from the jaw securing the lower column to the upper column. Withdraw the lower column up the splines of the upper column sufficiently to clear the steering unit.

Remove the splitpin and nut securing the steering tie rod inner ball joint to the rear end of the drop arm. Tap the ball joint out of its taper in the drop arm and place clear. Remove the splitpin from the end of the track rod and unscrew the end plug until the track rod end can be lifted from the ball on the front of the drop arm. Unscrew the three self-locking nuts securing the steering box to the chassis and withdraw the box.

13 Dismantling

Before dismantling the steering box thoroughly clean the outside of the box and arrange a clean portion on the bench for dismantling the box and laying out the components, as removed.

Extract the splitpin from the drop arm unit, unscrew the nut 46 (see **FIG 10**) and with a suitable extractor withdraw the drop arm 45 from the rocker shaft 34.

Remove the eight nuts securing the rocker shaft cover 41 to the steering box 1, and lift off the cover. Withdraw the rocker shaft from the steering box and extract the domed plunger 38 and the two coil springs 36 and 37. Collect the thrust washer 39 from the recess in the cover. Remove the eight nuts securing the top cover 23. Withdraw the complete wormshaft assembly by pulling the input shaft 15. Collect the ten loose ballbearings 7 that are left in the box.

Remove the four nuts securing the bottom cover 50 and withdraw the cover, eight springs 51 and the lower ball-

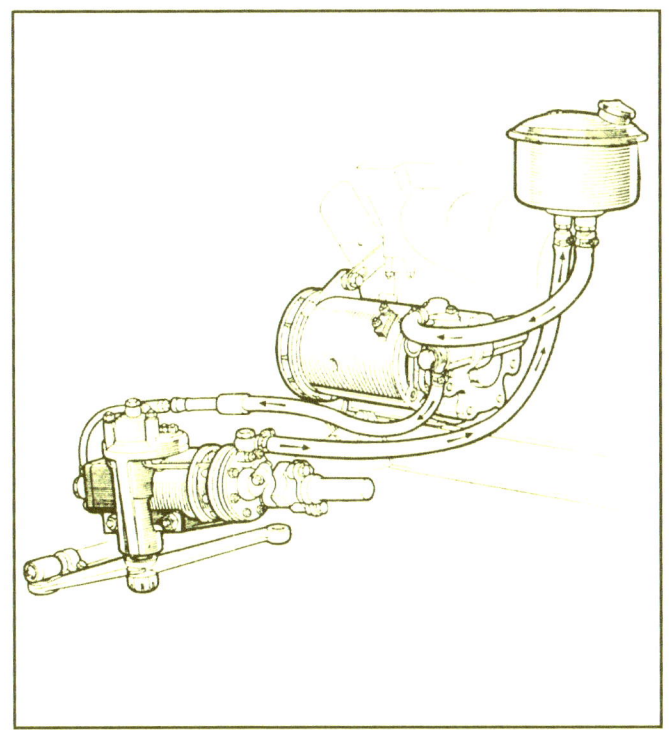

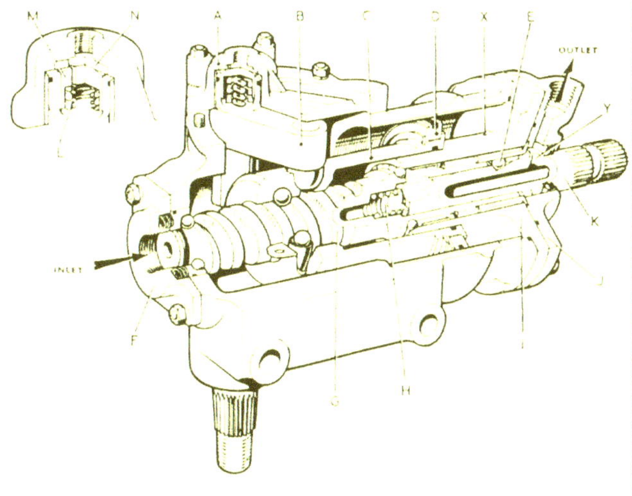

A—Rocker shaft cover plate.
B—Rocker shaft.
C—Main nut.
D—Piston.
E—Interlock ball.
F—Bottom end plate.
G—Worm shaft or inner column.
H—Valve spring and plunger.
I—Adjustable ball bearing.
J—Top end plate.
K—Selector valve.
L—Rocker shaft plunger springs.
M—Rocker shaft plunger.
N—Thrust pad.
X—Transfer hole.
Y—Outlet port.

FIG 8 Layout of power assisted steering

FIG 9 Steering box sectional view

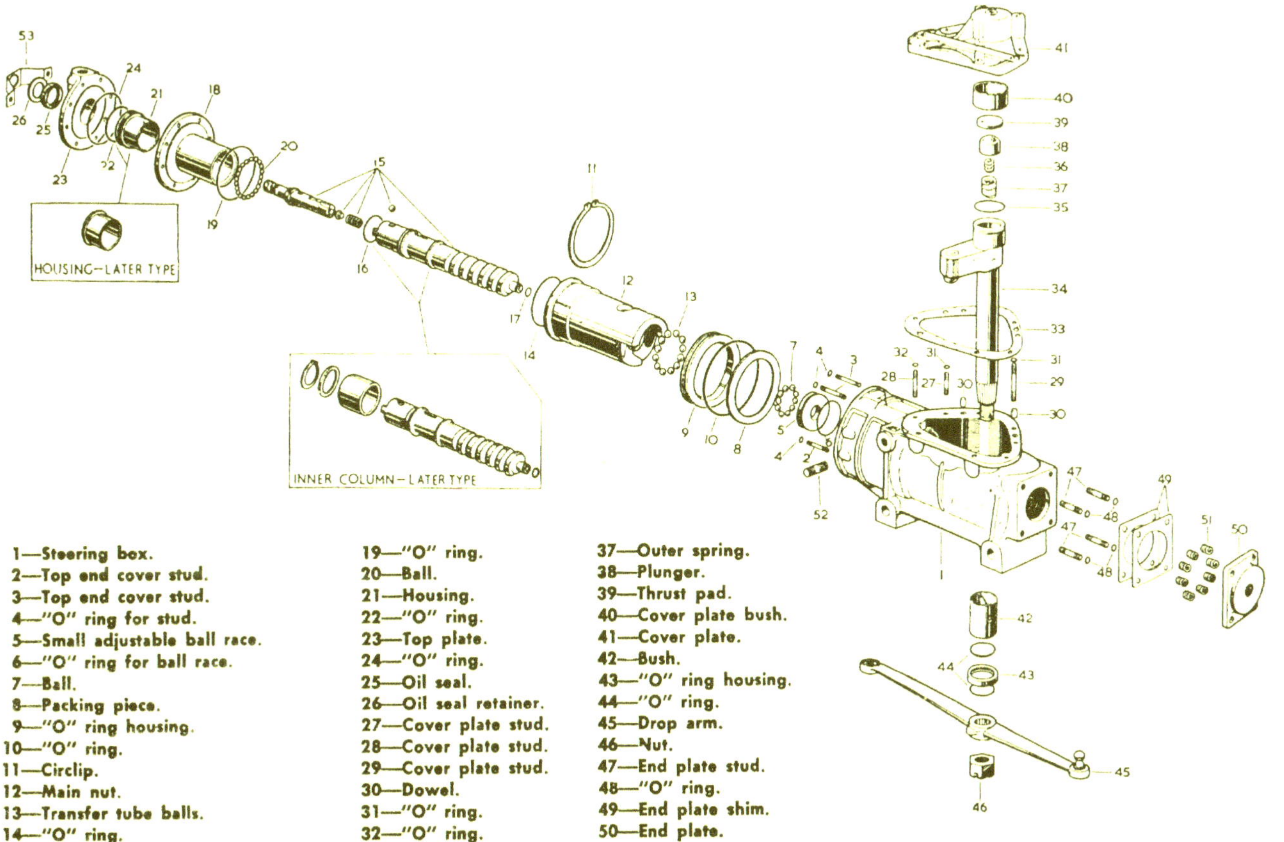

1—Steering box.
2—Top end cover stud.
3—Top end cover stud.
4—"O" ring for stud.
5—Small adjustable ball race.
6—"O" ring for ball race.
7—Ball.
8—Packing piece.
9—"O" ring housing.
10—"O" ring.
11—Circlip.
12—Main nut.
13—Transfer tube balls.
14—"O" ring.
15—Inner column and valve assembly.
16—Large "O" ring.
17—Small "O" ring.
18—Large adjustable ball race.
19—"O" ring.
20—Ball.
21—Housing.
22—"O" ring.
23—Top plate.
24—"O" ring.
25—Oil seal.
26—Oil seal retainer.
27—Cover plate stud.
28—Cover plate stud.
29—Cover plate stud.
30—Dowel.
31—"O" ring.
32—"O" ring.
33—Cover plate gasket.
34—Rocker shaft.
35—"O" ring.
36—Inner spring.
37—Outer spring.
38—Plunger.
39—Thrust pad.
40—Cover plate bush.
41—Cover plate.
42—Bush.
43—"O" ring housing.
44—"O" ring.
45—Drop arm.
46—Nut.
47—End plate stud.
48—"O" ring.
49—End plate shim.
50—End plate.
51—Spring.
52—Fixing stud.
53—Oil seal retaining plate.

FIG 10 Steering box exploded view

race 5. Withdraw the adjustable ballrace 18 from the main nut 12 and collect the twenty one loose balls of the upper ballrace 20.

Unscrew the main nut 12 from the worm shaft and collect the twelve recirculating balls 13. Withdraw the loose sleeve 21 from the adjustable ballrace. Hold the bottom of the wormshaft against a firm surface and press the input shaft 15 to release the interlocking ball between the wormshaft and valve. Withdraw the valve from the wormshaft and collect the valve spring and button.

14. Reassembly and adjustments

Clean all components thoroughly and examine them for signs of wear, renew as necessary. When reassembling the steering unit it is advisable owing to the high pressures existing in the system to renew all rubber 'O' rings, gaskets and sealing washers.

Pass the valve spring down the bore of the wormshaft with the button **uppermost. This is essential as if fitted the other way up the hydraulic flow will be cut off.** Insert the valve in the wormshaft so that the holes for the interlocking ball are in alignment. Hold the end of the wormshaft against a firm surface, press in the valve via the input shaft and fit the interlocking ball.

Assemble the twenty one $\frac{7}{32}$ inch balls to the upper ball bearing track on the wormshaft with grease and then slide the adjustable ballrace down the wormshaft to hold the balls in position. Assemble the twelve recirculating balls and retainer to the main nut with grease. Screw the wormshaft into the main nut until the nut is approximately half way along the wormshaft. Fit the ten $\frac{9}{32}$ inch balls to the bottom race and assemble the race, eight springs, shims and bottom cover to the steering box.

Coat the cylinder bore with the recommended grade of oil, and insert the assembly of the wormshaft and main nut into the steering box, with the transfer holes in the adjustable ballrace at approximately 45 deg to the rocker shaft cover. Take care not to disturb any of the ballbearings. Fit the loose sleeve into the bore of the adjustable ballrace.

Fit the top cover to the steering box taking care not to damage the oil seal on the serrations of the input shaft. A thin piece of paper wrapped around the serrations should obviate this but remember to remove all the paper after the top cover has been fitted. Secure the top cover with the eight nuts.

Fit the rocker shaft to the steering box, and insert the two coil springs and domed plunger into the rocker shaft bore. Locate the thrust washer in its recess in the rocker shaft cover with grease and fit the cover to the steering box with a new gasket and new rubber sealing rings.

Assemble the drop arm to the rocker shaft, noting the lines marked on these two components must be aligned. Refit the nut to secure the drop arm and lock with a new splitpin.

Fit the hose connection between the bottom cover and the rocker shaft cover with new copper washers either side of the banjo joints.

Wormshaft end float:

To check the end float of the wormshaft, all the components of the steering unit except the rocker shaft and top cover should be fitted to the steering box less their 'O' ring seals. As no top cover is fitted it will be necessary to temporarily secure the flange of the adjustable ballrace to the top of the steering box with two nuts.

Shims for the adjustment of end float are positioned between the bottom end cover and the steering box. Remove or add shims so that the wormshaft can be freely rotate without any perceptable end float. When this condition has been achieved remove one shim of .0025 inch to give the correct amount of preload.

Remove the components from the steering box replace the 'O' ring seals and then reassemble the steering box unit as previously described.

Rocker shaft end float:

As there is a certain amount of axial movement of the rocker shaft when the steering unit is turned from lock to lock it is essential that the end clearance is checked when it is in the highest position relative to the rocker shaft cover joint. This is when the centre of the rocker shaft ballpin is in alignment with the centre line of the wormshaft and the main nut (see **FIG 11**).

The end clearance of the rocker shaft is controlled by a thickness of thrust washer, interposed between the domed plunger and the rocker shaft cover. This thrust washer is available in four sizes: .154, .164, .174 and .184 inch.

To determine the size of thrust washer required the following procedure must be carried out:

1 Position the rocker shaft so that it is at its highest position shown in **FIG 11**. Fit the domed plunger less the two coil springs.
2 Take a measurement say A from the rocker shaft cover to the top of the domed plunger.
3 Take a measurement say B from the machined face on the rocker shaft cover to the bottom of the recess which houses the thrust washer.
4 Subtract dimension A from dimension B and to the difference figure add .020 inch. The additional figure is to allow for the thickness of the gasket and the minimum amount of clearance required. When this calculation has been carried out fit the thrust washer which is equal to this figure or the nearest smaller one i.e. if the resultant is .164 inch fit the thrust washer .164 inch thick. If the resultant figure after calculation is .183 inch fit a thrust washer .174 inch thick.

15 Refitting

Refitting is the reverse of the removal procedure but special attention should be given to the following points.

Before connecting the lower column jaw to the input shaft, set the road wheels in the straight-ahead position and turn the steering wheel so that the head of the 'Jaguar' is upright and two of the spokes are at the ten-to-two clock position. Check that the indicators cancel evenly on each side of the straight-ahead position. If not, an adjustment can be made by unclipping the switch cover, turning the steering wheel until the adjustment screws on the trigger are visible, slakening the screws and moving the trigger in the required direction. Should the adjustment screws be already hard up against the ends of the slots, then the adjustment will have to be made by a repositioning of the lower column jaw in relation to the input shaft of the steering box.

Check all hose connections for tightness and then bleed the system as described in **Section 17. Under no circumstances run the engine without the correct oil level in the reservoir or the pump may be damaged.**

16 The pump

The oil pump is of the eccentric rotor type and incorporates a combined flow and relief valve. The pump is attached to the rear of the generator and is driven from the generator by means of a rubber coupling.

Removal:

Disconnect the flexible hoses at the unions on the pump assembly and place the ends in a raised position to prevent drainage of the oil. Remove the nut and lock washers that secure the pump to the generator and remove the pump. If the flexible coupling assembly 24 (see **FIG 12**) comes away with the pump, withdraw it from the pump shaft 9.

Dismantling:

Thoroughly clean the exterior of the pump (see **FIG 12**) using care so that dirt does not enter either the inlet or outlet holes. Place the pump in a vice with soft jaws and remove the two setscrews 5 holding the intake adaptor 4. Remove the sealing ring 3. Unscrew and remove the five screws 18 securing the cover 13 to the pump body 1. Separate the body and cover.

Remove the sealing rings 6 and 7 from their grooves in the pump body. Remove the thrust washer 12 from the bearing hole in the cover. Release the circlip 11 and withdraw the rotor assembly 8 and drive pin 10 from the shaft 9. Ensure that the inner rotor is kept in the same relative position to the outer rotor **it must not be reversed**.

Withdraw the shaft 9 from the pump body. Drive the bearing seal 19 out of the pump body with a punch if it is

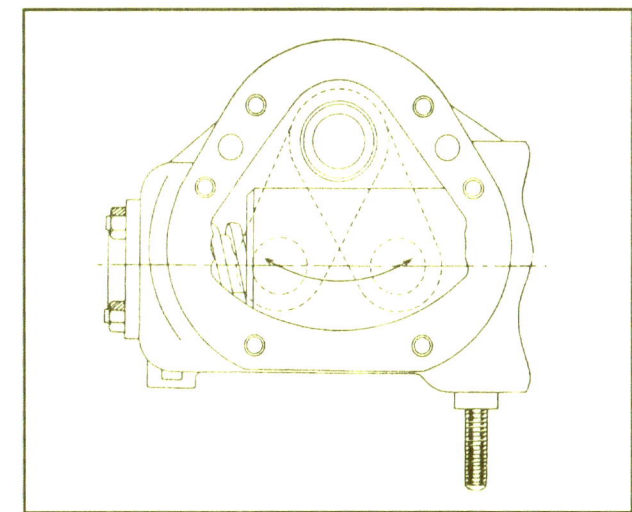

FIG 11   Highest positions of rocker arm

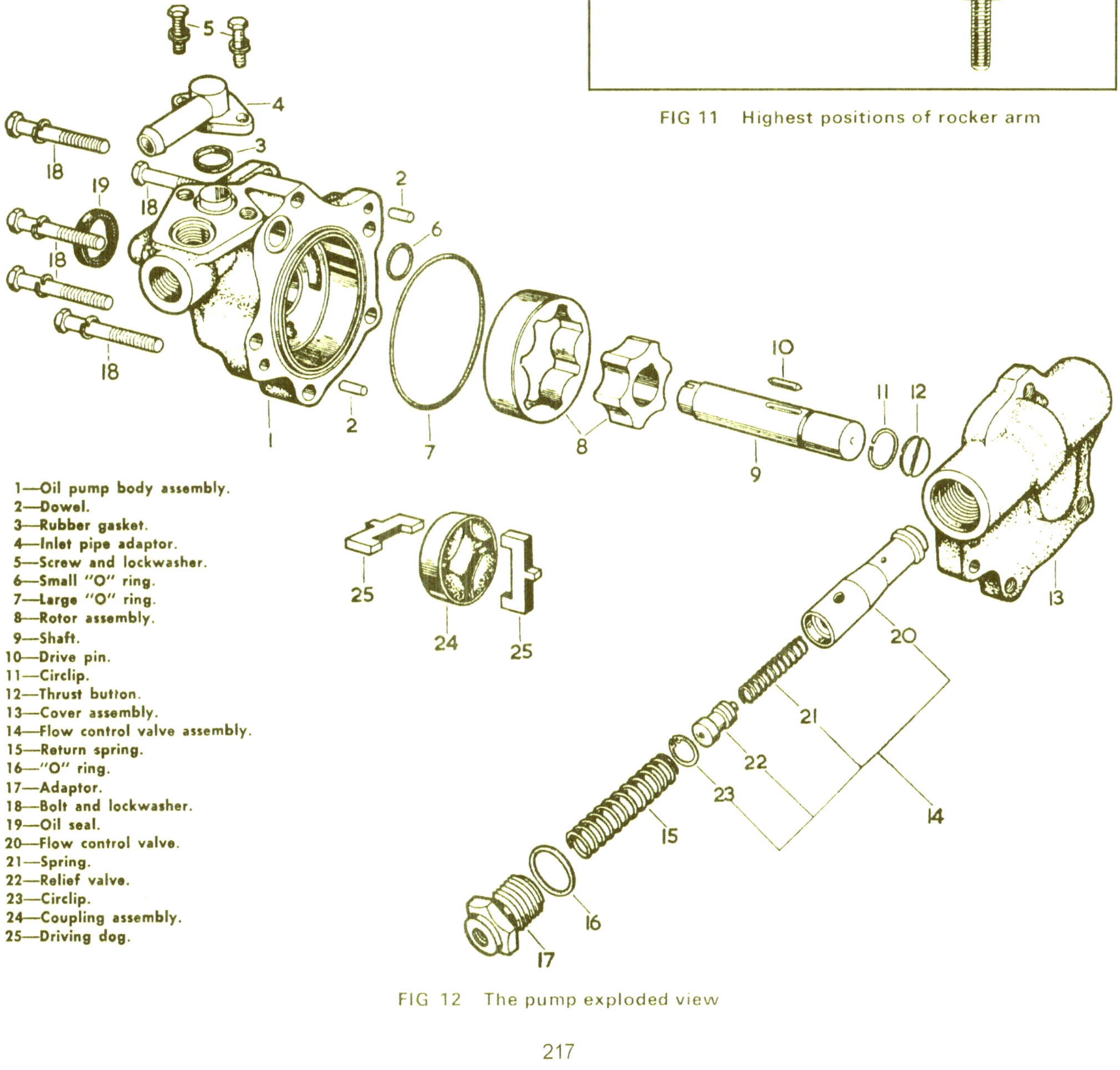

1—Oil pump body assembly.
2—Dowel.
3—Rubber gasket.
4—Inlet pipe adaptor.
5—Screw and lockwasher.
6—Small "O" ring.
7—Large "O" ring.
8—Rotor assembly.
9—Shaft.
10—Drive pin.
11—Circlip.
12—Thrust button.
13—Cover assembly.
14—Flow control valve assembly.
15—Return spring.
16—"O" ring.
17—Adaptor.
18—Bolt and lockwasher.
19—Oil seal.
20—Flow control valve.
21—Spring.
22—Relief valve.
23—Circlip.
24—Coupling assembly.
25—Driving dog.

FIG 12   The pump exploded view

worn or appears to be damaged. Remove the valve cap adaptor 17 and seal 16 from the pump cover. Withdraw the flow control valve spring 15 and flow control valve 20.

With a pair of circlip pliers remove the circlip 23 from the flow control valve. Withdraw the relief valve 22 and its spring 21 and place in a safe place to avoid damage to them.

Reassembly:

Wash all the components in a suitable solvent and dry thoroughly with non-fluffy cloth. Check the pump body end cover for signs of wear caused by the rotors. If there are signs of wear or scoring these components require renewal.

Grease the lip of a new seal 19 and place the seal in position with the lip towards the rotor. Press the seal into position using a piece of $1\frac{7}{32}$ inch diameter steel bar as a piloting tool. The seal should be pressed firmly home without squashing. Refit the shaft through the oil seal end rotating it gently to prevent damaging the oil seal.

Inspect the rotors for signs of wear or scoring and renew both if there are. If the parts appear satisfactory place them over the shaft in the pump body. Check the clearance between the rotors at all points with feeler gauges and if the clearance is found to exceed .006 inch renew the rotors. With a straightedge and feeler gauges check the end clearance of the rotors in the pump body; if this exceeds .0025 inch renew the pump body. With feeler gauges check the clearance between the driven rotor (larger) and bushing in the pump body. If this exceeds .008 inch it will be necessary to renew the pump body.

Refit the drive pin between the shaft and the drive rotor then replace the shaft circlip.

Carefully inspect the relief valve and ensure that it does not stick. All burrs should be carefully removed with a fine oil stone. Replace the valve spring in the flow control valve, install the relief valve in the control valve and secure both in position by means of the circlip. Install the flow control valve and spring in the pump cover and screw home the valve cap adaptor and seal.

Renew the 'O' ring seals in the pump body and refit the pump cover. Secure the body and cover with the five screws tightening them evenly to prevent distortion. **Check that the shaft rotates freely** there must be no binding.

Fit a new seal for the inlet pipe adaptor and replace the adaptor, secure with the two setscrews.

Refitting:

Place the flexible coupling assembly in the slot in the generator shaft. Line up the slot in the pump shaft with the driving tongue on the coupling and push pump into position on its mounting studs. Secure in position with nuts and lockwashers. Reconnect the flexible hoses to the pump. The system will then require bleeding as described in **Section 17**.

The pump must not be run with insufficient oil in the reservoir or with any of the flexible hoses disconnected or it may be seriously damaged.

17 Bleeding the system

The system will require bleeding when any part of the steering hydraulic system has been disconnected. The procedure is as follows:

Top up the reservoir to the full mark on the dipstick with the correct grade of oil. Start the engine and allow it to idle at the same time pour more oil into the reservoir until the level again reaches the full mark on the dipstick. Check all the hoses and their connections for signs of leaks. Increase the engine speed to approximately 1000 rev/min and turn the wheels fully in either direction five or six times. Drive the car for a test run and then recheck the oil level in the reservoir and examine the system for any signs of leakage.

18 Fault diagnosis

(a) High steering effort

1 Low oil level
2 Slipping (loose) fan belt
3 Pump valves stuck
4 Pump valves worn
5 Rotors worn or have excessive clearance
6 Oil leaks

(b) Noisy operation

1 Hoses rubbing against body or chassis
2 Air in system
3 Air leaks
4 Pump control valve stuck

RACK AND PINION TYPE

19 Description

The steering gear as fitted to the XK 140 and 150 models is of the high efficiency rack and pinion type in which motion is transmitted from the inner steering column through the pinion to the steering rack. Tie rods operating the steering arms are attached to each end of the steering rack by ball joints enclosed in rubber bellows.

The steering rack assembly is attached by rubber/steel bonded mountings to brackets on the front crossmember of the chassis frame between the front of the engine and the radiator. The lower steering column engages the end of the pinion shaft to which it is secured by a taper pin.

20 Maintenance

The maintenance on this type of steering consists only of regular lubrication via the nipples on the steering box and the tie rods.

When greasing the system do not over-lubricate or the rubber bellows will become distended. Check that the clips at the ends of the bellows are secure or dirt or water may enter and cause premature wear.

21 Removal

Before the steering housing can be removed the radiator and fixings must be withdrawn as follows.

Drain the water from the radiator by slackening off the drain tap underneath the front of the car. Slacken the top radiator hose clips and withdraw the hose. Loosen the bottom radiator hose clips and remove the bottom hose. Remove the two setscrews, nuts and shakeproof washers securing the lower half of the radiator cowl. Remove the set bolt and nut from either side of the upper radiator support bracket. Unscrew the two self-locking nuts underneath the radiator block and remove them together

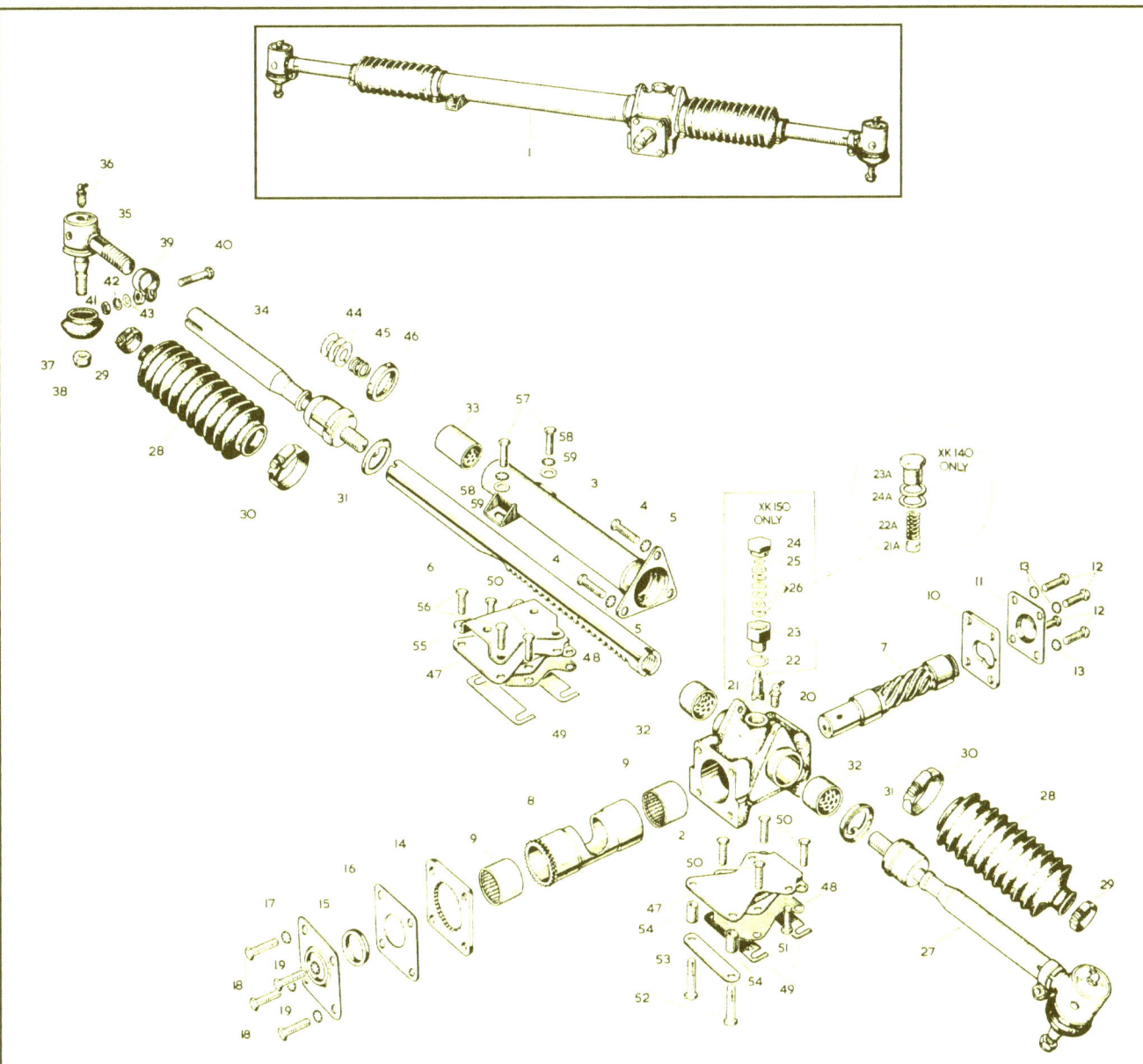

FIG 13 Rack and pinion steering

1. Steering assembly.
2. Pinion housing.
3. Rack tube
4. Setscrew.
5. Shakeproof washer.
6. Rack.
7. Pinion.
8. Eccentric sleeve.
9. Pinion bearing.
10. Locating plate.
11. Cover plate.
12. Setscrew.
13. Shakeproof washer.
14. Serrated flange.
15. Oil seal.
16. Retainer plate.
17. Retainer plate.
18. Setscrew.
19. Shakeproof washer.
20. Grease nipple.
21. Steering damper plunger.
22. Shim.
23. Screwed support.
24. Retainer cap.
25. Shim.
26. Belleville washer.
27. Tie rod assembly.
28. Rubber bellows.
29. Clip (small).
30. Clip (large)
31. Tab Washer.
32. Bush.
33. Rack tube bush.
34. Tie rod ball joint.
35. Ball joint.
36. Grease nipple.
37. Rubber seal.
38. Self locking nut.
39. Clamp.
40. Clamp bolt.
41. Nut.
42. Spring washer.
43. Plain washer.
44. Ball joint shim.
45. Spring.
46. Tab washer.
47. Rubber/steel mounting.
48. Shim.
49. Shim.
50. Setscrew.
51. Setscrew.
52. Bolt.
53. Bridge piece.
54. Sleeve.
55. Rack tube support.
56. Setscrew.
57. Setscrew.
58. Shakeproof washer.
59. Plain washer.

with the washers and rubber mounting washers. Carefully lift out the radiator turning the fan blade to avoid fouling the lower radiator hose stub pipe.

Chock the rear wheels and jack-up the front of the car with the jack positioned under the front chassis crossmember. Remove the self-locking nut from both steering tie rod ball joints and tap out the ball joint from the steering arms into which they are a taper fit, by tapping on the side face of the steering arms. Remove the nut and washer retaining the taper pin in the lower steering column. Tap out the taper pin. Remove both front road wheels. Unscrew and remove the four bolts retaining the steering housing mounting brackets to the chassis frame together with their shakeproof washers.

Note the position and number of shims under the mounting brackets to ensure that they are replaced correctly. Withdraw the steering unit through either wheel arch.

22 Dismantling

Release the clamp bolts (see **FIG 13**) and remove the ball joints 34 and 35. Loosen the clips securing the bellows 28 to the rack housing and tie rods and remove the bellows. Bend back the locking plate tabs 31 between the two tie rod ball assemblies 27, 34 and the rack 6. Remove the tie rods and ball housings complete. Bend back the locking tabs 46 on the ball housings, remove the housing locknuts, springs 45 and shims 44 noting the number of shims.

Remove the three bolts 4 and shakeproof washers 5 retaining the rack tube 3 and withdraw the tube. Remove the four bolts 18 and shakeproof washers 19 securing the pinion shaft retaining plate 16 and 17.

Withdraw the retaining plates together with the oil seal 15 and serrated flange 14. Remove the four bolts 12 and shakeproof washers 13 securing the coverplate 11. Withdraw the coverplate and locating plate 10. Remove the screwed cap 23a, shims 24a and plunger 21a from the pinion housing. Rotate the pinion 7 until it disengages with the lefthand end of the track (for lefthand drive cars the righthand end) and withdraw the pinion.

Slide the rack 6 out of its housing 3. Withdraw the eccentric sleeve 8 from the pinion housing 2.

23 Reassembly

Thoroughly clean, dry and examine all components of the assembly; parts showing signs of wear must be renewed. Particular attention should be paid to the condition of the bellows and outer ball joint seals. The two outer ball joint assemblies 34 and 35 (see **FIG 13**) cannot be dismantled and if worn should be replaced as complete units. Carefully examine the tie rod ball seats and renew as necessary.

Examine the bush 32 in the end of the rack tube for signs of wear and renew if worn. This bush is a press fit. It is also self-lubricating so that a new bush will require a good soaking in clean engine oil before fitting. As the bush is pre-finished it should not be reamed after fitting. Examine and replace if necessary the needle roller races 9 in the eccentric sleeve. Removal is accomplished by drifting out from the opposite ends.

Refit the eccentric sleeve to the pinion housing. Apply a generous coating of grease to the rack and insert it in the housing. Grease and reassemble the pinion, rotating it until the pinion meshes with the rack. Replace the locating plate and end plate and secure with the four setscrews and shakeproof washers.

Rack adjustment:

Locate the eccentric sleeve with the serrated plate and revolve in a clockwise direction until no backlash can be felt in the pinion. When the correct position has been found the serrated plate may not line up with the holes in the pinion housing. By turning the serrated plate over, it should be possible to obtain the required position without having to alter the setting to the eccentric sleeve. Replace the oil seal 15 (see **FIG 13**) and retainer plates and secure with the four setscrews and washers. Replace the rack tube and secure with the three setscrews and washers.

Pinion pre-load:

To obtain the correct pre-load, remove enough shims to make the turning of the pinion heavy, then insert a shim at a time until the pinion may be turned with the thumb and forefinger.

Reassemble the tie rod ball housings using new locking tab washers. Screw the tie rods into the ends of the rack and secure with new tab washers. Refit the bellows and secure firmly with their clips

Replace the steering arm ball joints and retaining clips, noting that the righthand ball joint has a lefthanded thread.

24 Refitting

Refitting is the reverse of the removal procedure but attention should be made to the following points.

If the car has covered a large mileage, it is advisable to fit new steering housing mounting rubbers 47 (see **FIG 13**).

The lower half of the fan cowl must be positioned before the radiator assembly can be replaced.

Check that the rubber mounting washers are in place on the radiator mounting studs before lowering the radiator onto them.

25 The steering column

Removal XK 140 see **FIG 14**: (XK 150 is similar)

Position the front wheels in the straight-ahead position. Detach the earth lead from the battery. Detach the horn push from the connector at the lower end of the outer steering column. Slacken off the nut retaining the cotterpin at the base of the outer steering column and tap the nut with a hide mallet to free the cotterpin. Slacken off the pinch bolt and remove the clamp bolt securing the outer steering column to the scuttle.

Withdraw the steering column assembly.

Dismantling:

Remove the four grubscrews 31 (see **FIG 14**) situated around the steering wheel boss, disconnect the horn cable and withdraw the horn button. Remove the large nut 37 and washer 38 retaining the steering wheel. Pull the steering wheel off the splines by exerting a sudden pressure under the wheel.

Collect the two halves of the split collet 36 and remove the cup 34, telescopic dustcover 32 rubber washer 35 and cup 33. Remove the circlip, spring cover and spring from the base of the outer steering column (10, 9 and 8).

Withdraw the inner column, remove the spring clip and stop button 13 to part the male column 12 from the inner column. Prise off the slip ring 14 by lifting up the prongs, and remove the two halves of the rotor 16 and 17 and withdraw the horn cable contact 19 through the centre of the column.

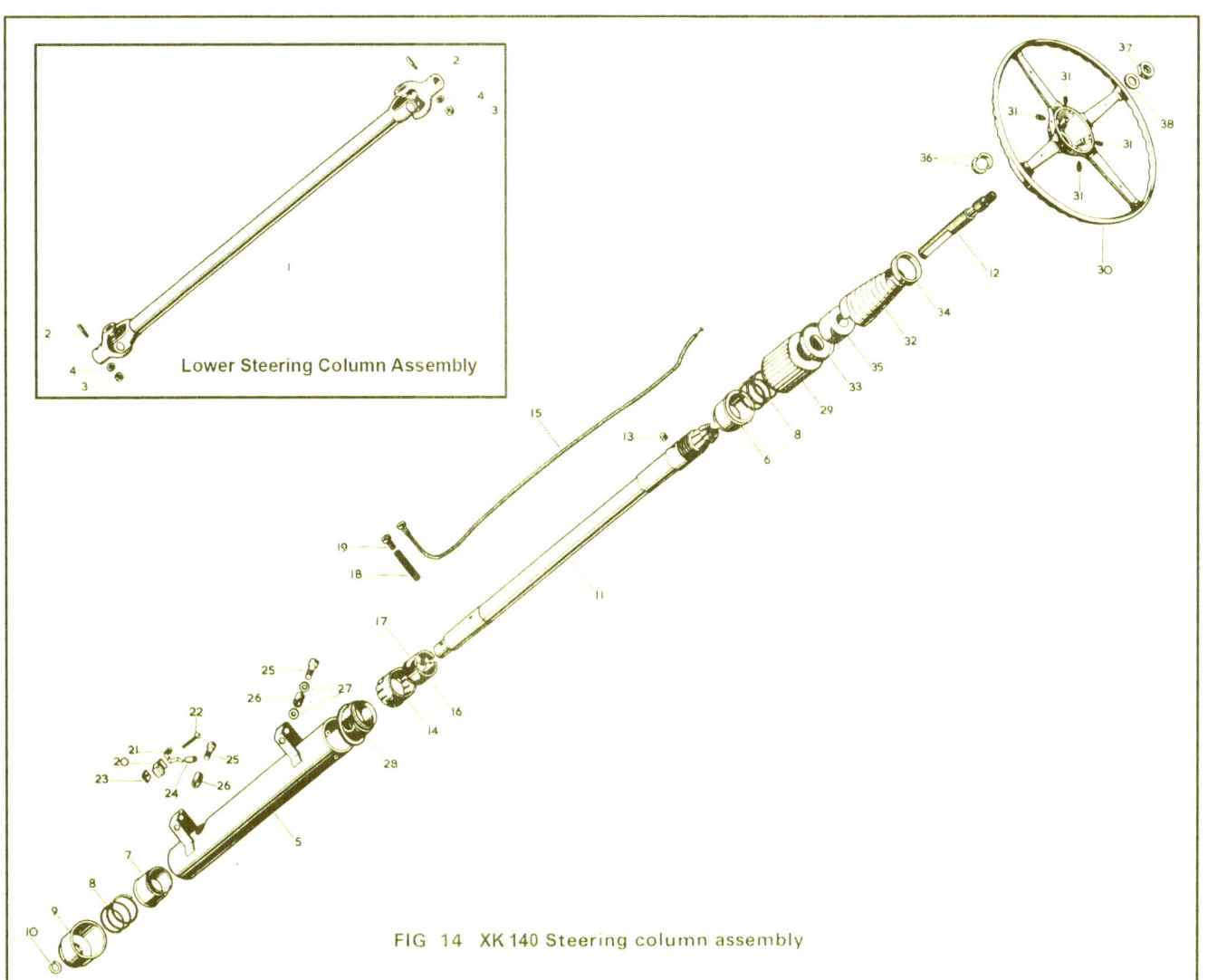

FIG 14 XK 140 Steering column assembly

1	Lower Steering Column Assembly	20	Holder
2	Taper pin	21	Contact
3	Nut	22	Bolt
4	Washer	23	Nut
5	Outer Tube	24	Rubber sleeve
6	Ball race	25	Bolt
7	Ball race	26	Spacer tube
8	Spring	27	Spacing washer
9	Cover	28	Grommet
10	Circlip	29	Locknut
11	Column	30	Steering Wheel
12	Male Column	31	Grub screw
13	Stop Button	32	Dust cover
14	Slip ring	33	Large cup
15	Cable Assembly	34	Small cup
16	Rotor (bottom half)	35	Distance washer
17	Rotor (top half)	36	Split collet
18	Spring	37	Nut
19	Contact	38	Washer

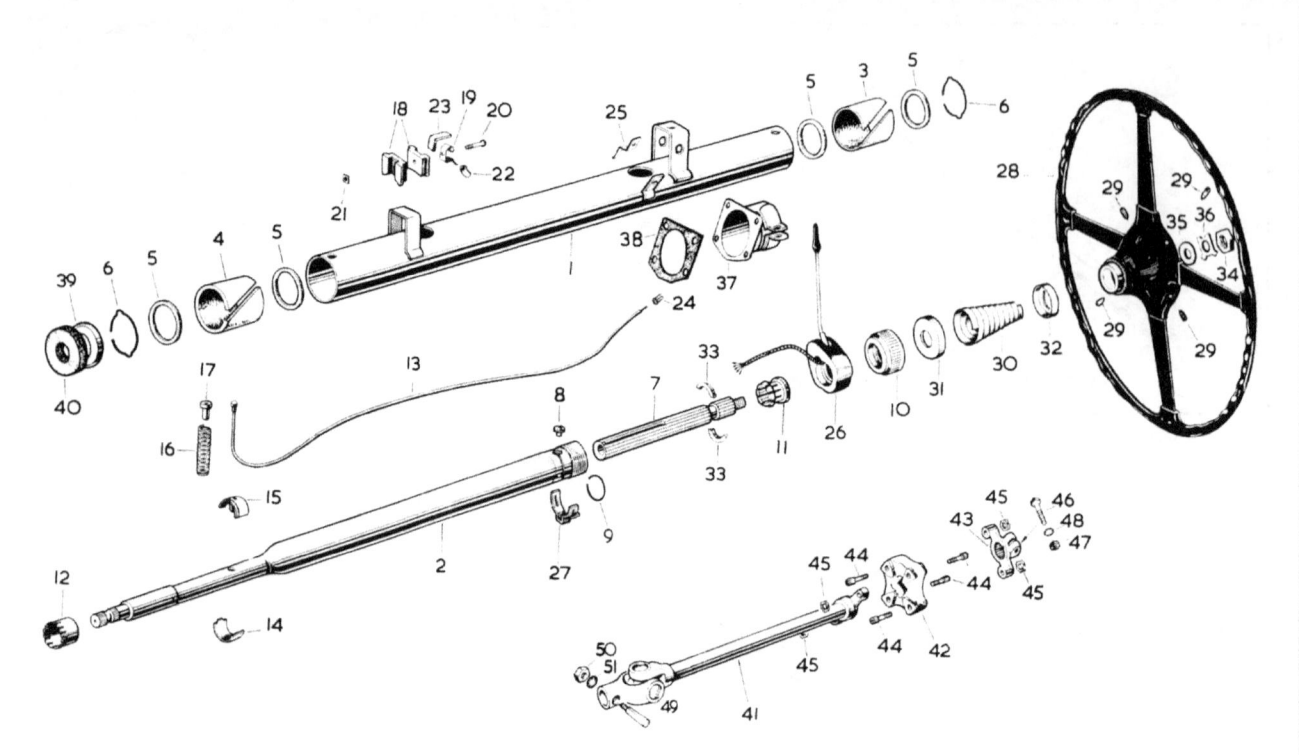

FIG 15 XK 150 Steering column assembly

1. Outer Tube.
2. Inner column.
3. Felt bush (Upper).
4. Felt bush (Lower).
5. Washer.
6. Spring Clip.
7. Male Inner column.
8. Stop button.
9. Spring Clip.
10. Locknut.
11. Split Collet.
12. Slip Ring.
13. Cable Assembly.
14. Rotor (bottom half).
15. Rotor (top half).
16. Spring.
17. Horn cable contact.
18. Contact holder.
19. Cable contact.
20. Bolt.
21. Nut.
22. Insulating sleeve.
23. Insulating strip.
24. Eyelet.
25. Horn earth contact.
26. Direction Indicator control.
27. Direction Indicator striker.
28. Steering wheel.
29. Grub screw.
30. Telescopic dust cover.
31. Cup (large).
32. Cup (small).
33. Split collett.
34. Nut.
35. Washer.
36. Tab Washer.
37. Steering column scuttle bracket.
38. Rubber seal.
39. End cap.
40. Rubber washer.
41. Lower steering column.
42. Lower steering column coupling.
43. Upper jaw for coupling.
44. Coupling cap screw.
45. Lockwasher.
46. Bolt.
47. Nut.
48. Shakeproof washer.
49. Taper pin.
50. Taper pin nut.
51. Shakeproof washer.

Reassembly:

Reassembly is the reverse of the dismantling procedure. Care should be taken when refitting the horn cable contact and rotors to ensure that the cable contact and spring do not touch the slip ring 14.

Refitting:

Refitting is the reverse of the removal procedure but care must be taken to ensure that the upper steering column and steering wheel are in a central position with the road wheels straight-ahead before engaging the splines (or lining up the taper pin holes in the lower steering column).

26 Tracking

Before checking or adjusting the alignment of the front wheels, the setting of the torsion bars must be checked and adjusted to a height of $11\frac{1}{4}$ inch.

With the car on a level surface with the correct tyre pressures place the front wheels in the straight-ahead position. Measure the distance between the outer edges of the front wheel rims at the front and at centre wheel height. Mark the measuring points with chalk then roll the car forward until the measuring marks are situated at the back of the wheels at centre height and remeasure between marks. Compare the two measurements taken the track is correct if the front measurement is equal to or $\frac{1}{8}$ inch less than the rear measurement.

If adjustment is required, slacken the clamp bolt at the end of each steering tie rod tube; also slacken off the outer bellow clips to avoid distorting the bellows. Turn the tie rods by equal amounts in the correct direction to obtain the right tracking.

Tighten the clamp bolts and recheck the tracking alignment. Finally tighten the bellow clips after ensuring that they are free from distortion.

Note:

The tracking alignment as described above is best carried out by a service station which has specialized equipment to obtain the high level of accuracy required.

27 Fault diagnosis (applicable to all steering types)

(a) **Wheel wobble**

1 Unbalanced wheels and tyres
2 Slack steering connections
3 Incorrect steering geometry
4 Excessive play in steering gear
5 Incorrectly adjusted torsion bars
6 Worn hub bearings

(b) **Wander**

1 Check 2, 3 and 4 in (a)
2 Front suspension and rear axle mounting points out of line
3 Uneven tyre pressures
4 Uneven tyre wear
5 Weak dampers

(c) **Heavy steering**

1 Check 3 in (a)
2 Very low tyre pressures
3 Neglected lubrication
4 Wheels out of track
5 Steering gear maladjusted
6 Steering columns bent or misaligned
7 Steering column bushes tight

(d) **Lost motion**

1 End play in steering column
2 Loose steering wheel, worn splines
3 Worn steering box and idier
4 Worn ball joints
5 Worn suspension system

NOTES

INDEX – BRAKES & BRAKING SYSTEM

SECTION	PAGE	
000	225	Basic Diagnostic Testing & Troubleshooting
		DRUM BRAKES
001	226	Description
002	226	Maintenance & Adjustment
003	227	Master Cylinder Service (Girling & Lockheed)
004	232	Drum & Brake Shoe Service
005	234	Wheel Cylinders
006	234	Servo Unit Description & Inspection
007	236	Flexible Hoses
008	236	Bleeding the Hydraulic System
009	236	Handbrake Maintenance & Adjustment
		DISC BRAKES
010	237	Description
011	238	Maintenance & Adjustment
012	239	Master Cylinder Service
013	240	Disc & Brake Pad Service
014	242	Handbrake Maintenance & Adjustment
015	243	Bleeding the Hydraulic System
016	243	Servo Unit Construction & Operation
017	244	Fault Diagnosis Chart

BRAKING SYSTEM
Basic Diagnostic Testing & Troubleshooting

Perhaps the most common complaint about brakes is that the car cannot be brought to a satisfactory stop. As the lining wears, the brake pedal must be pushed down farther and farther in order to move the brake shoes into contact with the drums. Eventually, it reaches the floorboard, and an emergency application does not stop the car. When this happens, it is necessary to adjust the position of the brake shoes so that they are closer to the drums. This restores the pedal to its former position.

Generally, a soft pedal, or one that goes slowly to the floorboard under continued pressure, is caused by air trapped in the hydraulic lines or by a leak in the system. The system must be bled to get rid of the air. To repair the leak, the defective unit must be removed. However, it is considered good practice to overhaul the entire hydraulic system in the event of a leak in any one part, because all of the units are in the same condition; unless repaired at the same time, they too will soon leak.

Another frequent complaint has to do with noise. Actually, the squeals and squeaks that are heard are due to loose parts, which cause high-frequency vibration.

Drum brake fault diagnosis chart

TROUBLES & CAUSES

1. **Pedal goes to floorboard**
   1a. Brake shoes out of adjustment
   1b. Brake fluid level low
   1c. Leaking lines or cylinders
   1d. Air in brake lines
   1e. Defective master cylinder
2. **One brake drags**
   2a. Incorrect shoe adjustment
   2b. Clogged brake line
   2c. Sluggish wheel cylinder piston
   2d. Weak brake shoe return spring
   2e. Loose wheel bearing
   2f. Brake shoe binding on backing plate
   2g. Out-of-round drum
3. **All brakes drag**
   3a. Insufficient play in master cylinder push rod
   3b. Master cylinder relief port plugged
   3c. Lubricating oil in system instead of hydraulic fluid
   3d. Master cylinder piston sticking
4. **Car pulls to one side**
   4a. Brake fluid or grease on lining
   4b. Sluggish wheel cylinder piston
   4c. Weak retracting spring
   4d. Loose wheel bearing
   4e. Wrong brake lining
   4f. Drum out-of-round
5. **Soft pedal**
   5a. Air in system
   5b. Improper anchor adjustment
   5c. Improper linings
   5d. Thin drums
   5e. Warped brake shoes
6. **Hard pedal**
   6a. Wrong brake lining
   6b. Glazed brake lining
   6c. Mechanical resistance at pedal or shoes
7. **One or more wheels grab**
   7a. Grease or hydraulic fluid on lining
   7b. Loose wheel bearings
   7c. Loose front end supports
   7d. Loose backing plate
   7e. Distorted brake shoe
   7f. Improper brake lining
   7g. Primary and secondary shoes reversed
8. **Erratic braking action**
   8a. Loose brake support
   8b. Loose front end suspension parts
   8c. Grease or hydraulic fluid on lining
   8d. Binding of the shoes in the guides
   8e. Sticking hydraulic wheel cylinder piston
9. **Noisy brakes**
   9a. Loose backing plate
   9b. Loose wheel bearing adjustment
   9c. Loose front end supports
   9d. Warped brake shoes
   9e. Linings loose on shoes
   9f. Improperly installed brake shoes

Disc brakes

Disc brakes are generally mounted on the front wheels, and non-servo, drum-type brakes are mounted on the rear. On other installations, all four wheels have disc brakes. The brakes are frequently actuated by a power unit on the larger cars.

The usual hydraulic brake troubleshooting procedures apply with the following Troubleshooting Chart showing specific complaints:

Disc brake fault diagnosis chart

TROUBLES & CAUSES

1. **Brake pedal meets no resistance; brake pedal has soft or spongy feel**
   1a. Insufficient brake fluid in reservoir
   1b. Air in brake system
2. **Brake pedal can be depressed without braking effect, after bleeding**
   2a. Leaky brake lines
3. **Brake pedal can be depressed after extensive downhill driving (soft and spongy)**
   3a. Inferior or low boiling point fluid, with overheated brake system
   3b. Air in system
4. **Brakes heat up during driving and fail to release**
   4a. Compensating port in master brake cylinder blocked
   4b. Power unit push rod incorrectly adjusted so that master cylinder piston is not released.
   4c. Piston of wheel cylinder sticking
5. **Poor braking effect in spite of high pedal pressure**
   5a. Oil or grease on friction pads
   5b. Glazed friction pads

6. **Brakes pull to one side**
   6a. Brake fluid, oil, or grease on friction pads of one wheel
   6b. Excessive wear of one brake caliper friction pad
   6c. Calipers not parallel to brake disc
7. **Brakes chatter**
   7a. Excessive lateral runout of brake disc
   7b. Bad contact pattern of friction pads
   7c. Rough surface on brake disc
8. **Frequent replenishing of brake fluid in reservoir needed**
   8a. Brake line system leaks
   8b. Master cylinder leaks
   8c. Wheel cylinder leaks
9. **Leaky wheel cylinder**
   9a. Leaking piston seal
   9b. Cylinder walls scored or pitted
   9c. Rust formation on cylinder wall

BRAKING SYSTEM - SERVICE

DRUM BRAKES

1 Description

Hydraulic brakes are fitted to all cars covered by this manual. The Mk IX and XK 150 models are fitted with disc brakes.

The remaining models are fitted with the normal internal expanding shoe and drum type brakes, each unit being operated by hydraulic wheel cylinders.

When the brake pedal is depressed the master cylinder piston forces fluid along the pipelines into the various wheel cylinders (see **FIG 1**), the pistons of which are then actuated. These force the brake shoes against the drum to provide the required braking effort. On pedal release, strong springs across the shoes push the wheel cylinders back into their bores, thus forcing the fluid to return to the master cylinder. On some models a vacuum servo unit is fitted. This unit is interposed between the master cylinder and the wheel cylinder, and by applying the vacuum provided at the engine inlet manifold assists the braking effort applied at the brake pedal.

The handbrake, incorporating a thumb operated ratchet release in the handle, is located on the floor at the side of the drivers seat. This brake operates via a mechanical linkage on the rear wheels only.

Three types of drum brakes are fitted to Jaguar cars these are the Girling type, the early Lockheed and later Lockheed. All three have the same general arrangement but differ in detail on application of the brake shoe via the wheel cylinders. The Girling type is fitted to the Mk VII models and both types of Lockheed are fitted to XK 120 models. The most obvious difference between the two Lockheed models is that the later type has a tandem cylinder arrangement, i.e. two fluid reservoirs, as the front and rear wheels have independant hydraulic systems.

2 Maintenance and adjustment

The fluid level in the reservoir should never be allowed to fall below 1 inch from the top of the reservoir tank. If the fluid level falls too low air may enter the hydraulic system

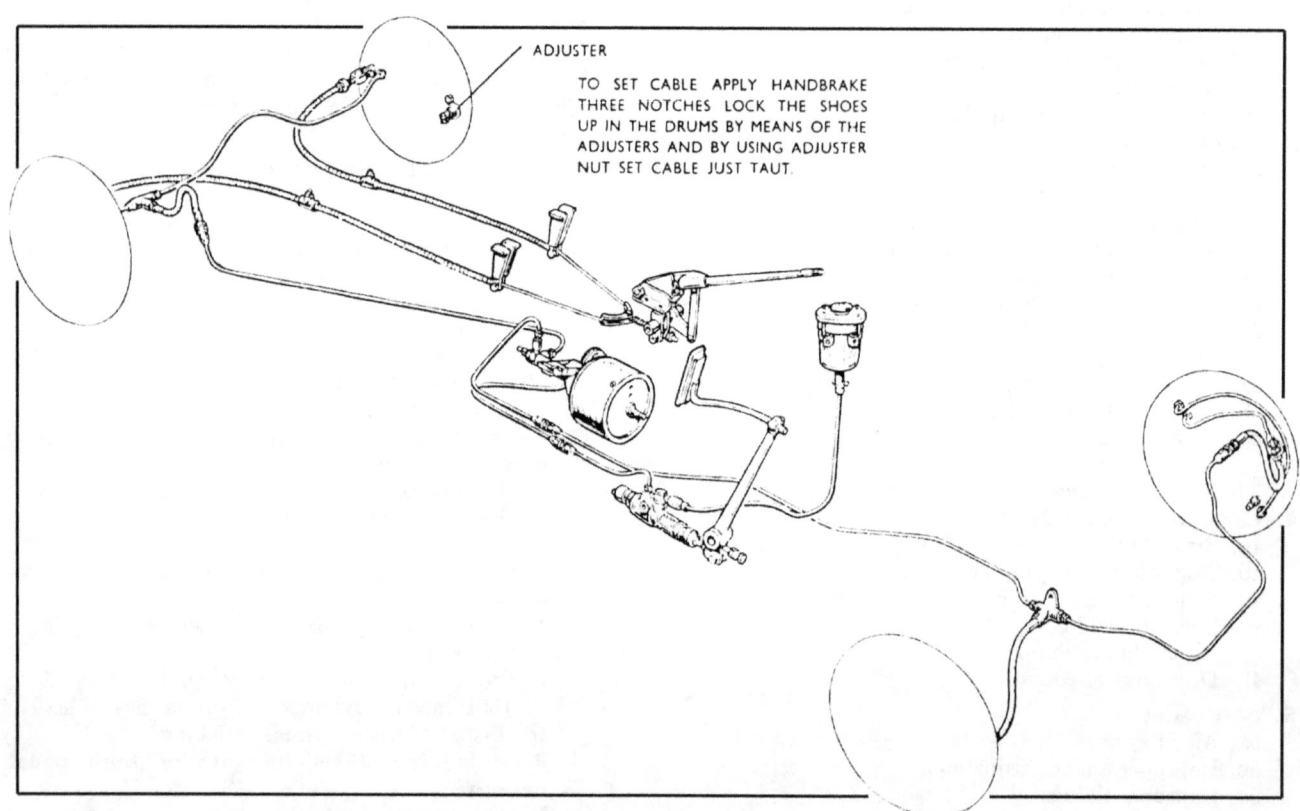

FIG 1 General brake layout

making it necessary to bleed it. Air is compressible and its presence in the system gives a spongy feeling to the brakes.

To top up the fluid reservoir, clean around the top of the reservoir tank and remove the filler cap. Top up the reservoir tank with the correct grade of brake fluid, as given in the Technical Data contained in the appendix to this manual. On models fitted with tandem tanks it is necessary to apply the procedure to both reservoirs.

Adjustment of the brakes is similar on all three types of systems fitted, where this is provided for. On the Girling and later Lockheed types the front brakes are self-adjusting and no provision is made for adjustment.

Jack-up the end of the car at which brake adjustment is required and place chocks under the wheels at the other end. On models fitted with Lockheed brakes remove the road wheels. The adjusting screws on this type of brake are accessible through a hole in the brake drum (see **FIG 2**) and are adjusted by means of a screwdriver.

To align the hole with the adjuster(s) turn the drum and shine a torch through the hole in the drum until the adjuster can be seen. On the Girling type brakes an external square adjusting screw is provided (see **FIG 3**).

The method of adjustment is to turn the adjusting screw until the brake shoes come into contact with the brake drum and then reverse the direction of adjustment until the drum is just free to rotate. On the Girling and early Lockheed types the adjusting screw is turned clockwise to expand the brake shoes on the later Lockheed type the direction is reversed.

When adjusting the front brakes on the models fitted with early Lockheed brakes the adjusting procedure must be carried out with both adjusting screws fitted to each front wheel

Having carried out the preceeding adjustment apply the brakes hard to centralize the brake shoes and recheck the adjustment. Repeat the adjustment on the other wheel(s). Check that the brake shoes are not binding or rubbing the brake drums or ineffective braking and rapid wear of the linings will occur.

The handbrake is automatically adjusted by the adjustment of the rear wheels on all models. However, excessive movement of the handbrake lever due to cable stretch may need to be taken up as described in **Section 9**.

The only other maintenance procedure required on the braking system is the regular lubrication of the mechanical linkage between the pedal and the master cylinder, and the handbrake linkage.

3 The master cylinder

The importance of absolute cleanliness when dealing with hydraulic parts such as the master cylinder cannot be over-stressed. Clean off road dirt and grease before removing the units from their mountings. Dismantle on a clean bench and do not handle internal parts with dirty or greasy hands. Never use petrol, paraffin, trichlorethylene or other similar cleaning agents to wash the unit or internal components since this will have a tendency to destroy rubber parts. Place components in a vessel containing clean brake fluid and, after soaking, wipe clean with a clean non-fluffy rag.

When all parts have been cleaned and are thoroughly dry, carry out an examination and scrap all rubber seals which show signs of deterioration. If doubt exists, comparison with new parts will indicate whether replace-

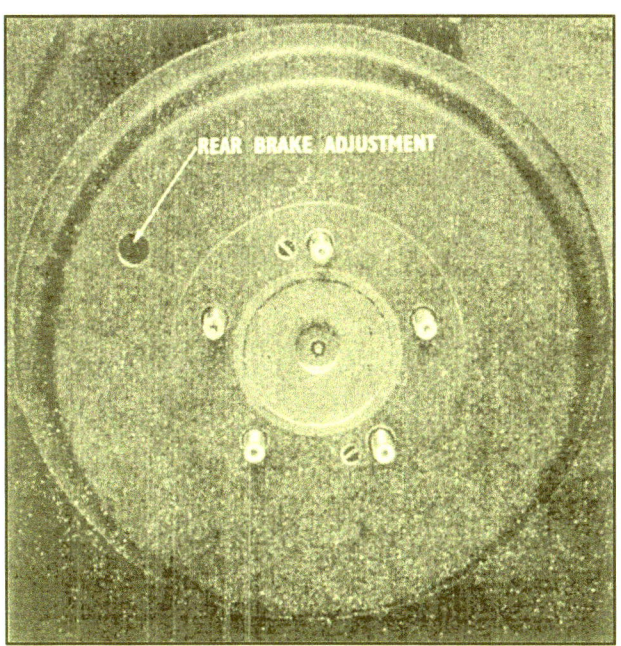

FIG 2 Rear brake adjustment (Lockheed type)

FIG 3 Rear brake adjustment (Girling)

ments are required. Never endeavour to clear out the internal bore of flexible hydraulic pipes by probing since this will undoubtedbly result in rupture of the pipe. Where the flexible hydraulic pipes are choked or perished fit replacements.

If the hydraulic system is found to be contaminated by oil, grease or the incorrect type of fluid it will be necessary

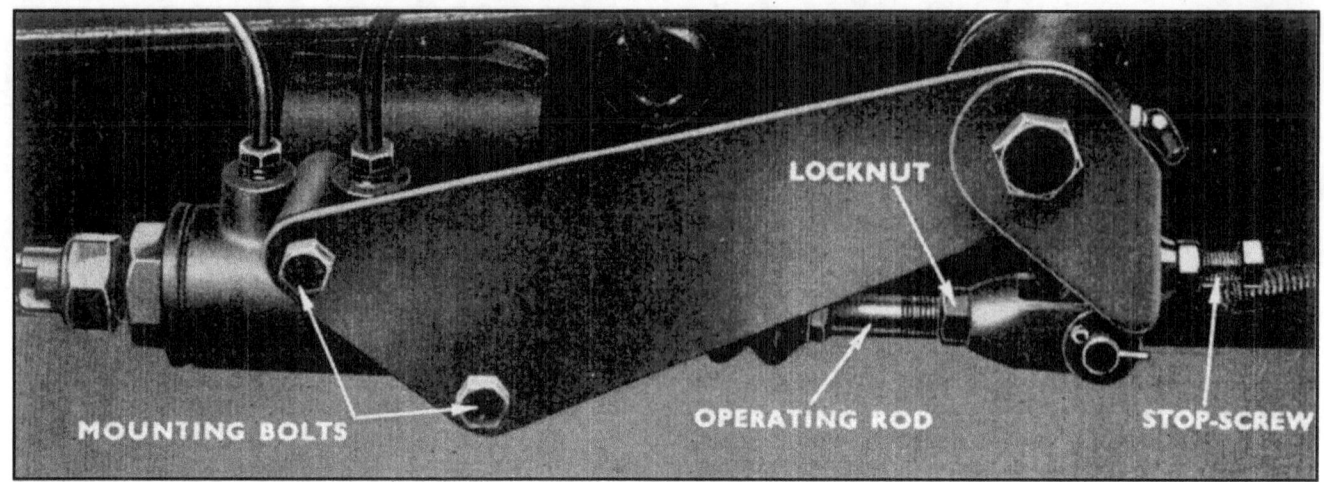

FIG 4 Master cylinder (Girling)

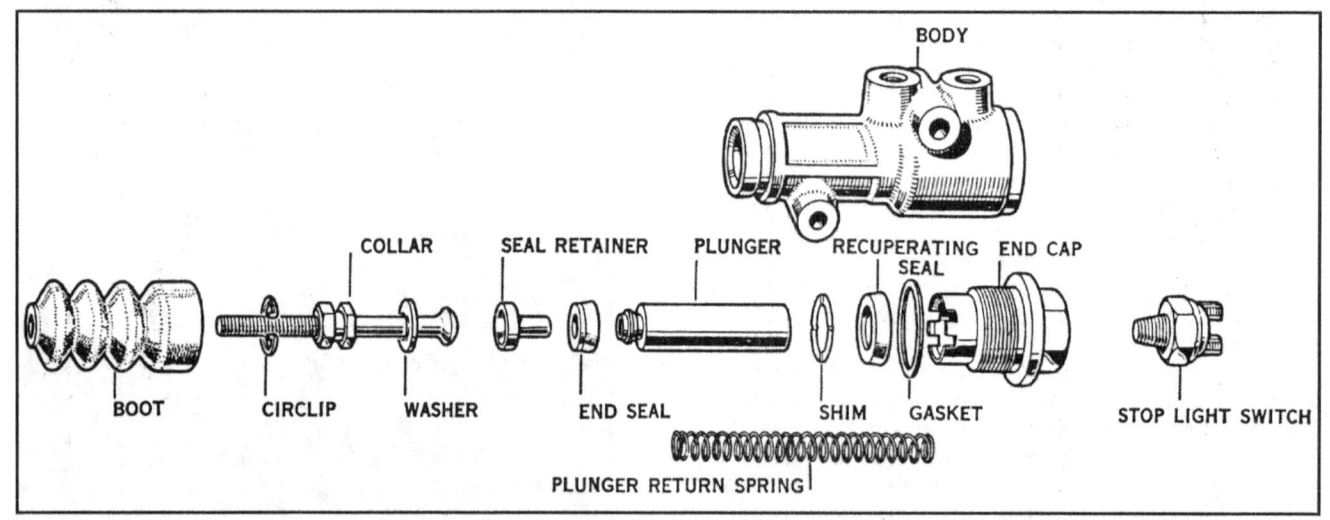

FIG 5 Master cylinder exploded view (Girling)

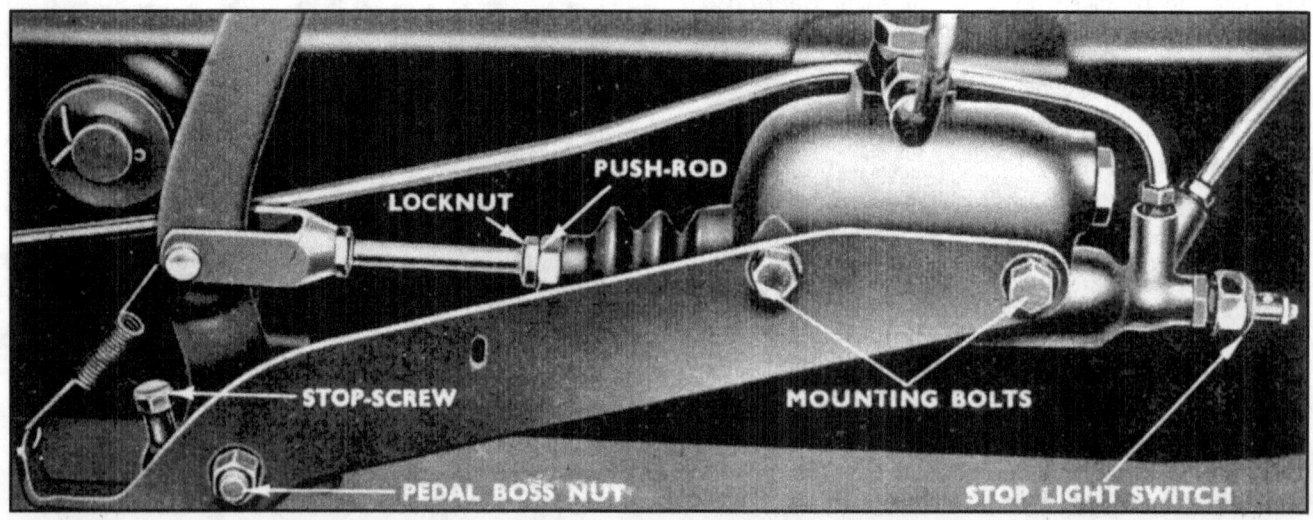

FIG 6 Master cylinder (Early Lockheed type)

228

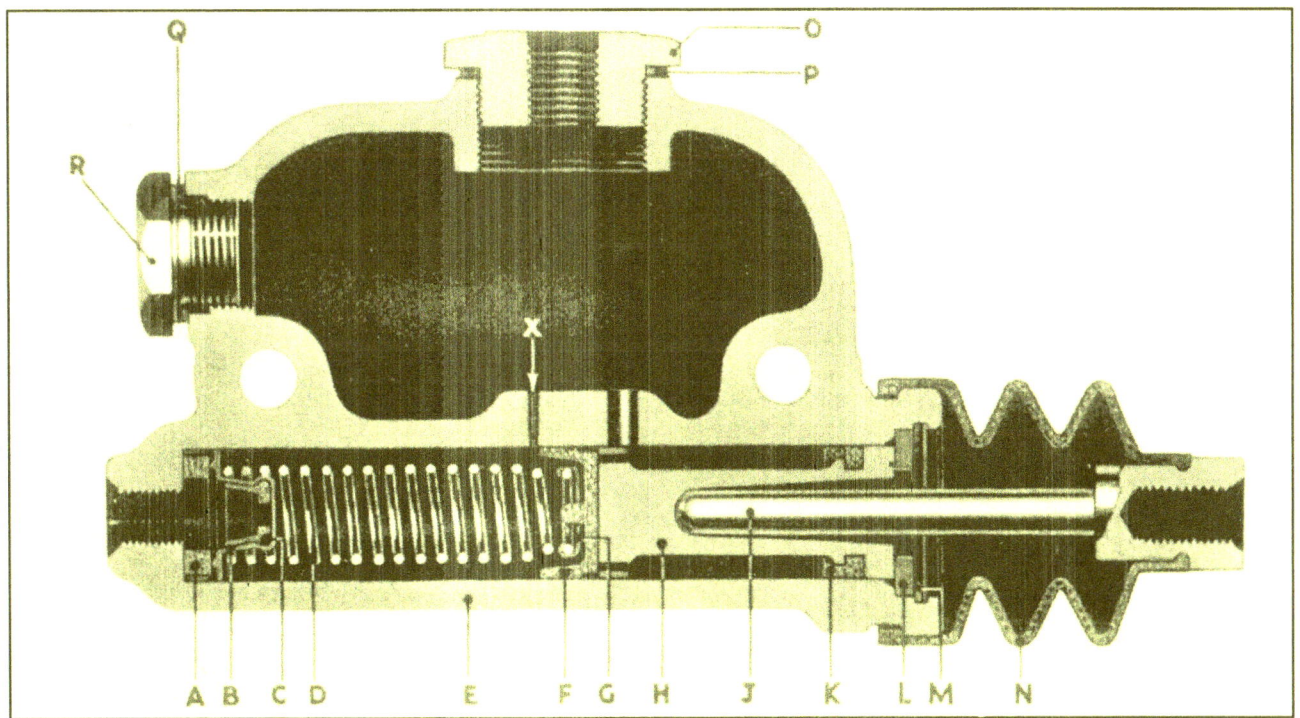

FIG 7 Master cylinder sectioned view (Early Lockheed type)

to drain off the system and flush it through thoroughly with clean fluid of the recommended grade. It will also be necessary if the system has been contaminated to replace all seals, hoses and gaskets.

Girling type brakes:

To remove the master cylinder proceed as follows: Disconnect the lower hose clip from the rubber hose beneath the reservoir and drain the reservoir into a clean container. Disconnect the operating rod from the footbrake pedal by removing the clevis pin and pedal return spring. From the rear of the master cylinder disconnect the two stoplight wires. Remove the two bolts securing the master cylinder to the mounting bracket (see FIG 4) and withdraw the cylinder.

Prepare a clean space upon which to work and lay the parts before dismantling.

Dismantling:

Unscrew the end cap and gasket (see FIG 5) and withdraw the plunger return spring, pull back the rubber boot and remove the circlip with pliers, then withdraw the pushrod. Push the plunger out from the pressure end and detach the seal retainer and end seal. Remove the recuperating seal and shim from the body.

Carefully examine all parts and renew any that appear worn or damaged. It is especially important to renew any seals which appear distorted or lack resilience.

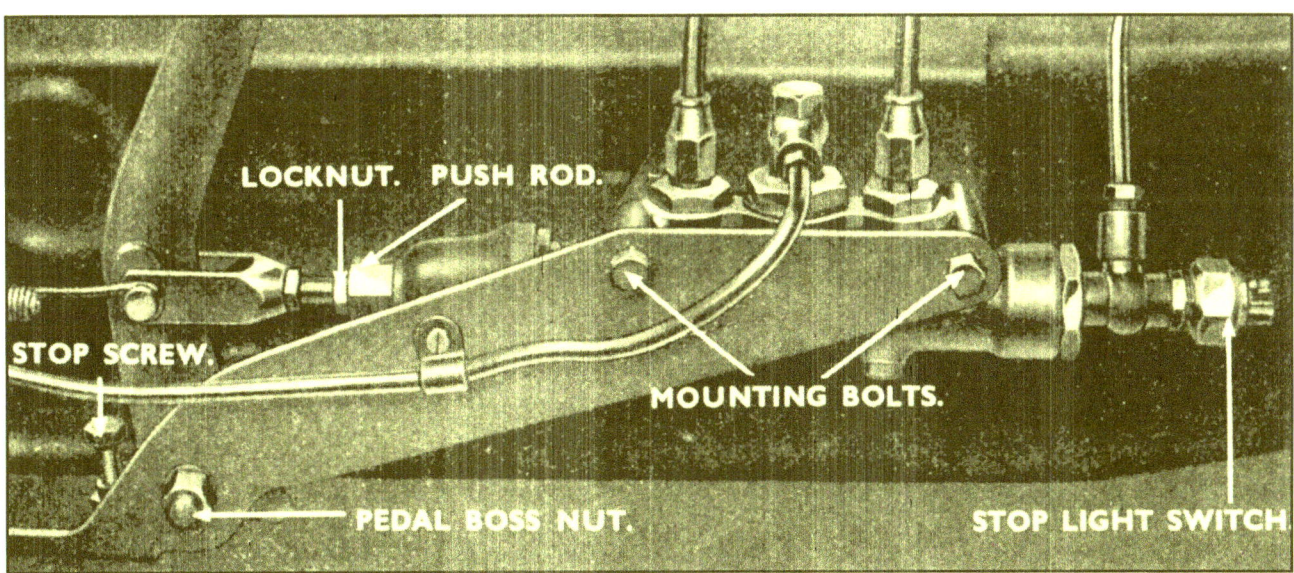

FIG 8 Master cylinder (Late Lockheed type)

229

Reassembly:

Thoroughly clean all parts with clean Girling brake fluid which must not be used again. The rubber seals and the plunger should be smeared with clean fluid immediately before assembly. Insert the steel shim into the pressure end of the cylinder against the shoulder formed inside. Replace the recuperating seal with the back of the seal towards the shim. Fit the end seal to the plunger with the lip of the seal first, facing away from the concave end of the seal retainer, which fits next. Insert the plunger open end first into the cylinder from the pushrod end, easing the end seal carefully into the bore.

Insert the pushrod assembly, round end first into the bore and replace the washer and circlip. Pack the boot with Girling rubber grease No. 3 Red and fit it over the pushrod with the small end seating in the collar. Insert the plunger return spring in the other end. Replace the end cap and gasket, and tighten them firmly, taking care not to damage the stoplight switch.

Refitting the master cylinder is the reverse of the removal procedure. Check the brake pedal free travel as described for the Lockheed type system.

Early Lockheed type:

Removal:

Jack-up the car and remove the road wheel nearest to the master cylinder. Disconnect the supply pipe union from the banjo connection on top of the master cylinder and drain the contents of the supply tank into a clean container. At the front of the master cylinder (see **FIG 6**) unscrew the two pipe unions from their banjo connections and disconnect the two wires from the stoplight switch. Remove the pedal stem from the footbrake pedal by unscrewing the retaining bolt and nut. Unscrew the two bolts passing through the master cylinder and the nut at the footbrake pedal boss. Withdraw the master cylinder and footbrake pedal complete.

Dismantling:

Remove the rubber boot N (see **FIG 7**), push the piston H down the bore of the cylinder to release the pressure on the piston stop L, remove the circlip M and the piston stop. Withdraw the piston, rubber cup F, return spring D, valve body B complete with the rubber cup C and the rubber washer A. Remove the secondary cup K by stretching it over the end flange of the piston, using only finger pressure to prevent damage. Some later models are fitted with a piston washer between the piston and main cup this washer should be fitted with the concave side towards the main cup.

Reassembly:

Dip all parts in clean brake fluid and assemble them wet. Fit the secondary cup K on the piston H, so that the lip of the cup faces the piston head, and gently work the cup round the groove with the fingers to ensure that it is properly seated. Place the rubber washer A in position in the bottom of the cylinder bore. Fit the rubber cup C in the metal body B and assemble the body on the larger end of the return spring D.

Assemble the retainer G on the smaller end of the return spring and insert the assembly into the cylinder so that the valve body is in contact with the rubber washer. Insert the main cup F into the cylinder, lip foremost, taking care not to damage or turn back the lip of the cup. Press the piston H into the cylinder, taking care again not to damage or turn back the lip of the secondary cup K. Insert the piston stop L and fit the circlip M, ensuring that it beds evenly in the groove. Refit the rubber boot N.

Fill the cylinder with clean Lockheed brake fluid and test the master cylinder by pushing the piston inwards and allowing it to return unassisted. After a few applications, fluid should flow from the outlet connection in the cylinder body.

Refitting is the reverse of the removal procedure. It will be necessary to bleed the system as described in **Section 8** and check the brake pedal free travel as described for the later type Lockheed brakes.

Later Lockheed type:

Removal:

Jack-up the car and remove the road wheel nearest to the master cylinder. Disconnect the supply pipe unions from the tilting valve assemblies on top of the master cylinder and drain the contents of the supply tank into a clean container. At the front of the master cylinder unscrew the pipe union from the banjo connection and disconnect the two wires from the stoplight switch.

At the top of the master cylinder unscrew the pipe unions from their connections. Remove the two bolts passing through the master cylinder (see **FIG 8**) and slacken the nut at the footbrake pedal boss. Ease the rubber boot from the pedal pushrod and withdraw the master cylinder.

Dismantling:

Remove the boot 2 (see **FIG 9**) and pushrod 1 from the rear end of the master cylinder body. Insert a suitable rod and push both the pistons forward to the end of their travel and remove both the front inlet 24 and rear inlet adapter (tilting valve) assemblies 22. Release the pistons and remove the outlet adapter 30 from the centre position on top of the master cylinder. Remove the retaining circlip 3 and stop washer 4 from the rear end of the cylinder. Remove the outlet adapter 18 from the front end of the cylinder and withdraw the primary and secondary piston 6/10 and attendant parts.

Reassembly:

Carefully check all parts for cleanliness and lubricate by immersion in hydraulic brake fluid before assembly. Lubricate the bore of the master cylinder with hydraulic fluid before refitting any components.

Fit the taper seals 8 and 9 to the secondary piston 10 with the wider ends facing away from each other. Fit the taper seal 5 to the primary piston 6 with the wider end facing the longer portion of the piston. From the pushrod end of the cylinder insert the secondary piston, seals rearmost, taking care not to damage the lips of the seals. Push the piston down the bore of the cylinder, and observe the movement through the rear tilting valve hole. When the forward seal appears, depress the top edge of the seal with a blunt instrument i.e. a pencil to avoid damage to the seal. Push the piston to within 1 inch of the forward end and fit the stop screw 19 with its gasket 20 to the base of the master cylinder.

Fit one of the return springs 7 in the rear end of the secondary piston, and insert the primary piston, seal rearmost, into the bore of the cylinder taking care not to

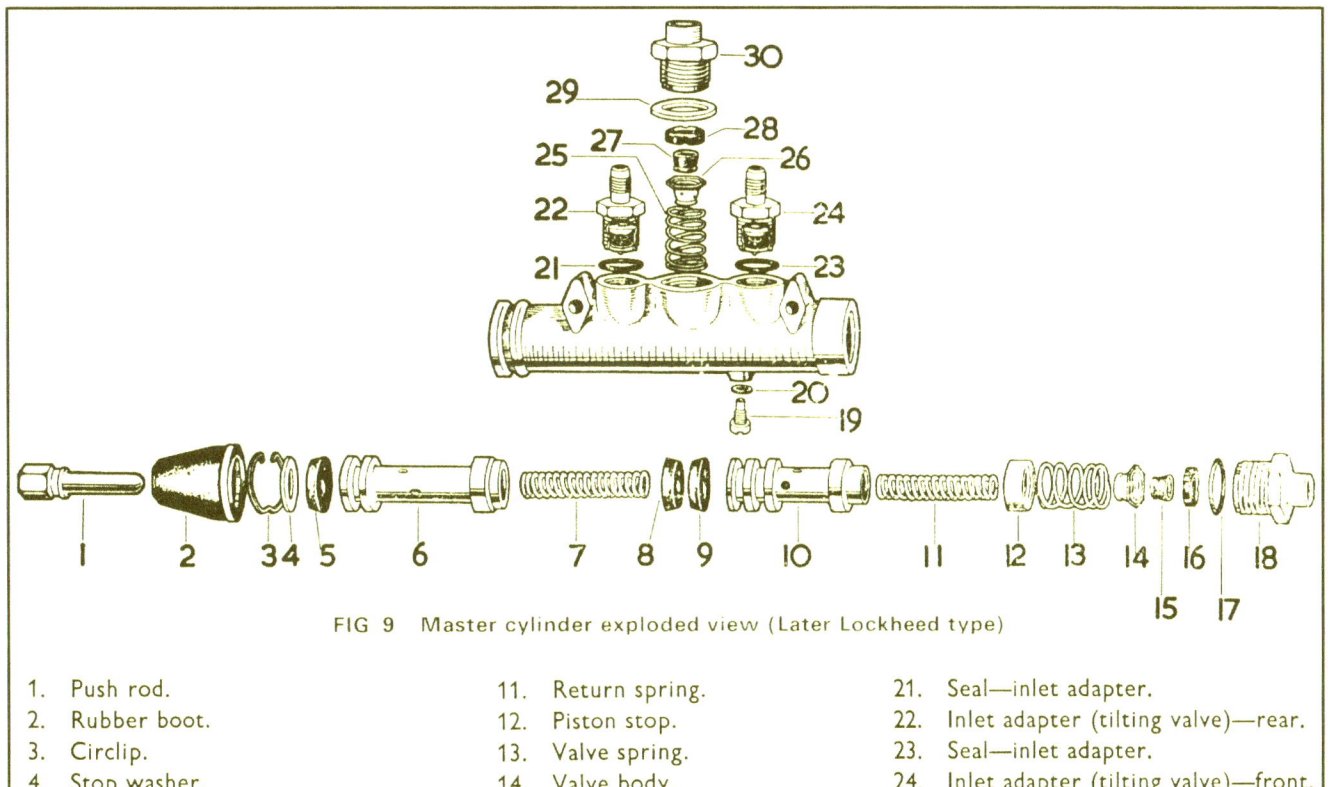

FIG 9 Master cylinder exploded view (Later Lockheed type)

1. Push rod.
2. Rubber boot.
3. Circlip.
4. Stop washer.
5. Seal—primary piston.
6. Primary piston.
7. Return spring.
8. Rear seal—secondary piston.
9. Front seal—secondary piston.
10. Secondary piston.
11. Return spring.
12. Piston stop.
13. Valve spring.
14. Valve body.
15. Valve cup.
16. Valve washer.
17. Seal—outlet adapter.
18. Outlet adapter.
19. Stop screw.
20. Gasket—stop screw.
21. Seal—inlet adapter.
22. Inlet adapter (tilting valve)—rear.
23. Seal—inlet adapter.
24. Inlet adapter (tilting valve)—front.
25. Valve spring.
26. Valve body.
27. Valve cup.
28. Valve washer.
29. Gasket—outlet adapter.
30. Outlet adapter.

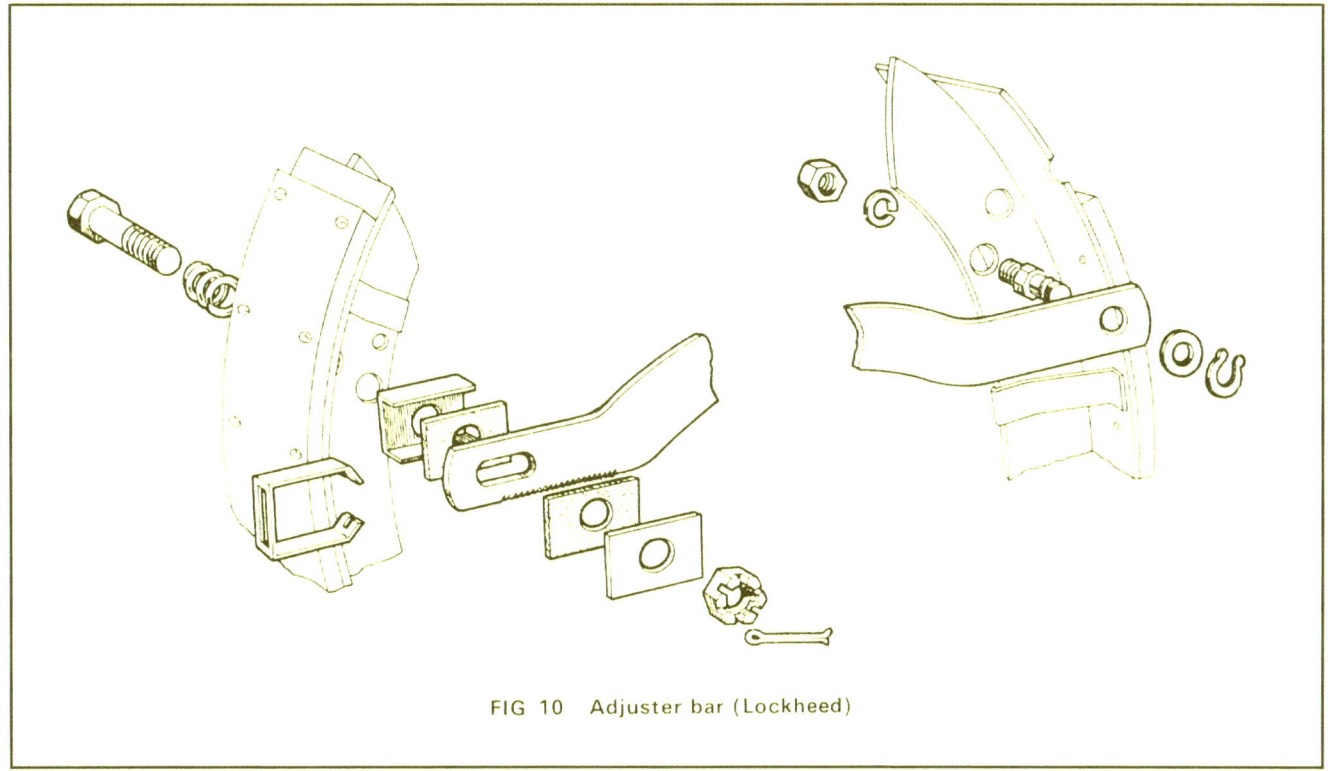

FIG 10 Adjuster bar (Lockheed)

damage the lip of the seal. Push the piston down the bore and fit the stop washer 4 and circlip 3.

Insert the remaining return spring 11 in the front end of the secondary piston, and fit the piston stop 12 and valve spring 13. Assemble the rubber valve washer 16 and valve assembly 14 and 15 to the front outlet adapter 18 and screw home into the end of the master cylinder.

Assemble the rubber valve washer 28, valve assembly 26 and 27 and valve spring 25 to the top outlet adapter 30 and screw home into the top of the master cylinder. Insert a suitable rod in the rear end of the cylinder and push both pistons fully forward in the cylinder. With the pistons held in this position screw home both of the tilting valve assemblies. Fit the rubber boot 2 and pushrod 1.

Refitting is the reverse of the removal procedure. It will be necessary to bleed the hydraulic system as described in **Section 8.**

Ensure that there is $\frac{1}{32}$ inch. clearance between the master cylinder and the pedal pushrod. If adjustment is required it may be carried out in the following manner. Check that the brake pedal is not being prevented from returning to the full off position. Ease the small end of the rubber boot towards the master cylinder until the end of the boot is off the enlarged diameter of the pushrod. Slacken the locknut adjacent to the pushrod hexagon and rotate the hexagon until a minimum clearance of $\frac{1}{32}$ inch is obtained, which entails a margin safety, $\frac{1}{4}$ to $\frac{3}{8}$ inch free travel at the pedal pad. This free movement can be felt if the pedal is depressed gently by hand.

Tighten the locknut and reposition the rubber boot.

4 Dismantling brakes

The brake shoe removal is similar in all models except for the front brakes of the later Lockheed type, these are dealt with separately.

Jack-up the car and remove the appropriate road wheel, chocking the remaining wheels and releasing the handbrake. Where adjustment is provided, slacken the adjuster screw as far as it will go to bring the brake shoes away from the drum. Unscrew the two setscrews securing the brake drum and withdraw the drum off the shoes.

Pull one of the brake shoes, against the spring tension, away from the back plate. On releasing the tension of the pull off springs the remaining brake shoe will fall away.

Front wheels later Lockheed type:

Jack-up the car and remove the road wheel and brake drum as described previously.

Remove the circlips (see **FIG 10**) and plain washers and detach the adjuster bars from the brake shoes. Collect the pad plates and the friction pads and disengage the ratchet springs from the adjuster bars carefully to avoid straining the springs.

Pull the toe of one brake shoe against the load of the pull-off spring and disengage the shoe from the slots in the wheel cylinder piston and the opposing wheel cylinder body, disconnect the pull-off spring from the brake shoe and the anchor pin. Repeat the procedure for the other brake shoes.

Having removed the brake shoes (all models) it is essential that the pistons in the wheel cylinders are held in position, by wire or elastic around the piston and cylinder. If this is not carried out and the brake pedal is depressed the pistons will be forced out of the cylinders and the hydraulic fluid drained from the system.

Brake linings:

Whenever examination shows that the brake shoe linings are unduly worn i.e. down to the securing rivet heads they must be renewed. If this is not carried out the brakes will become very inefficient and the brake drums will be damaged by the rivet heads. Scoring of the drum if light may be removed by a specialist who will machine the internal face of the drum. This work must be done to a very high degree of accuracy so that the drum remains concentric to the brake shoes. If the drum is badly scored it must be renewed since machining will enlarge the internal diameter of the drum sufficient to alter the braking geometry.

Renewal of brake linings is best carried out on an exchange basis with factory approved replacement shoes. This is because specialist facilities are needed to ensure that the new linings are concentric with the drums and are bedded down correctly on the brake shoe. If concentricity and bedding down are not achieved the brakes will not function correctly. When renewing linings it is essential to fit complete sets of shoes and check that the correct lining material has been used. If linings of different materials are mixed on refitting, the brakes will be out of balance due to the varying characteristics of the lining materials.

Do not attempt to clean oily linings, as nothing permanent can be done. It is therefore essential that care is taken to ensure that no grease or oil comes in contact with the linings.

Refitting of the brake shoes is the reverse of the removal process care being taken to observe the following. Lightly grease the pivot ends of the brake shoe before fitting and ensure that this grease does not come into contact with the linings when refitting. Check that the pull-off springs are in their correct location by referring to **FIGS 11, 12, 13, 14, 15** and **16,** which show the relative positions for all the various types of brake.

On models fitted with Girling type brakes it is necessary to adjust the brake shoe steady posts when replacement shoes are fitted or if there is evidence of uneven wear across the width of the lining.

The steady posts one for each shoe, are threaded in the brake plate and should contact the underside of the brake shoe web. The end of the steady post, accessible at the rear of the backplate, is provided with a screwdriver slot and locknut **FIGS 11** and **12.**

To adjust the steady post proceed as follows: At the rear of the brake backplate slacken the steady post locknut, and rotate the post anticlockwise with a screwdriver about four turns. Lock the shoes in the brake drum by applying the brakes firmly and rotate the post clockwise until the post bears against the shoe web. Without moving the post secure it in position with the locknut.

Repeat the procedure for the other brake shoe.

Refitting brake shoes later Lockheed type:

Pass the adjuster bar bolt (see **FIG 10**) with the coil spring under its head, through the appropriate hole in one of the brake shoes and temporarily secure by partially fitting a nut. Hook a pull-off to the shoe and attach the other larger hooked end of the spring to one of the anchor pins. Using the closed end of one of the wheel cylinders as an abutment for the heel of the shoe, and exercising extreme caution to avoid damaging the wheel cylinder boot, pull the toe of the shoe against the load of the pull-

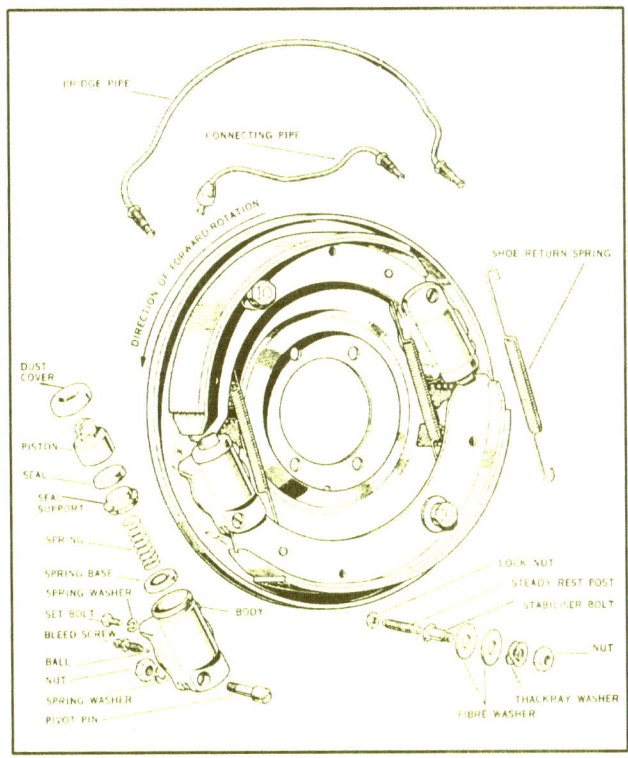

FIG 11 Front brake assembly (Girling)

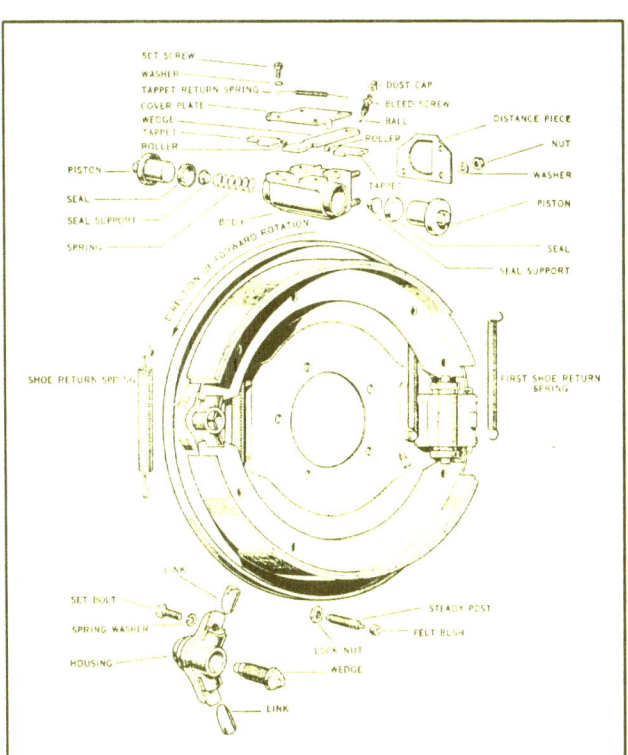

FIG 12 Rear brake assembly (Girling)

FIG 13 Front brake assembly (early Lockheed)

FIG 14 Rear brake assembly (early Lockheed)

off spring, and locate the toe within the slot in the piston. The heel can then be tapped into position in the slot of the opposing wheel cylinder. Repeat the procedure to attach the other brake shoe then centralize the shoes in relation to the backplates. Fit the ratchet springs to the adjuster bars, paying particular attention to ensure correct assembly. Remove the nuts, offer up one of the adjuster bars and an inner pad plate and friction pad to the brake shoes and adjust the ratchet spring until the clearance between the anchor pin and the appropriate hole in the adjuster bar is on the outside of the pin. Position a friction pad and outer pad plate on the outside of the adjuster bar. Repeat for the other adjuster bar. Both adjuster bars can now be attached to the brake shoes, using the nuts and the circlips, fitting the plain washers under the latter parts. The correct load on the bolts is obtained by securing the nuts up tight and then slackening back two flats or one third of a turn. The operation of the adjusters should now be checked by pulling the toe of each shoe so that the pin moves to the outer edge of its enlarged hole. When released it is essential that the shoe returns promptly and unassisted to its fully off position. Refit brake drum and road wheel.

5 Wheel cylinders

Removal:

The wheel cylinders on the front wheels are removed as follows. Remove the brake shoes as described in **Section 4**. Unscrew and remove the hydraulic connections to the cylinder. Plug the ends of the pipe to prevent loss of fluid.

Remove the nuts securing the wheel cylinder to the backplate and withdraw the wheel cylinder clear. On the back wheel cylinders it is first necessary to remove the clevis pin securing the handbrake cable to the operating lever, which protrudes through the backplate before following the same procedure as described for removal of the front wheel cylinders.

Dismantling:

Withdraw the piston and cover from the end of the wheel cylinder. On the rear wheel cylinders push out the handbrake lever pivot pin and remove the lever. Apply gentle air pressure to the union hole at the rear of the cylinder to blow out the rubber cup, cup filler and spring. Sections and exploded views of the various types of wheel cylinders are shown in **FIGS 11, 12, 15, 16, 17** and **18**.

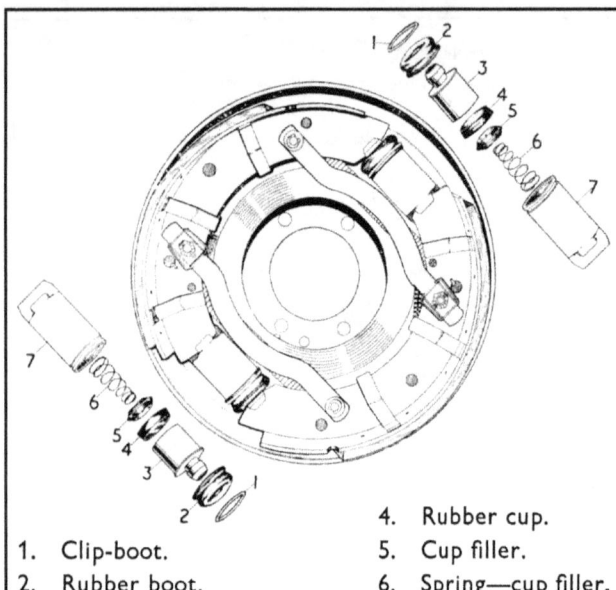

1. Clip-boot.
2. Rubber boot.
3. Piston.
4. Rubber cup.
5. Cup filler.
6. Spring—cup filler.
7. Wheel cylinder.

FIG 15 Front brake assembly (later Lockheed)

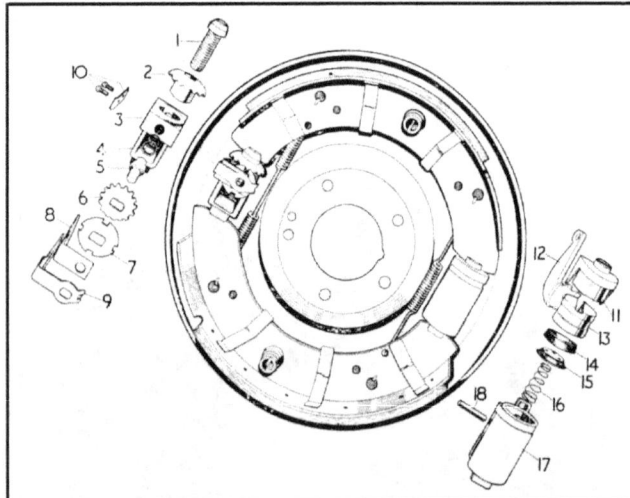

1. Adjustment screw.
2. Adjustment wheel.
3. Adjuster body.
4. Spring.
5. Adjustment stud.
6. Pinion.
7. Plate—pinion.
8. Bracket.
9. Clicker spring.
10. Locking plate and setscrews.
11. Piston and cover.
12. Lever—hand-brake operation.
13. Piston.
14. Rubber cup.
15. Cup filler.
16. Spring—cup filler.
17. Wheel cylinder.
18. Fulcrum pin.

FIG 16 Rear brake assembly (later Lockheed)

Reassembly:

Reassembly is the reverse of the dismantling procedure with the addition of the following points. Immerse the components in clean brake fluid prior to refitting and check that there are no signs of scoring or wear on the components, renew parts where necessary. Ensure that the rubber cup and seals are the correct way round i.e. with the lip or widest end facing into the cylinder and refit to the cylinder very carefully to avoid damage to the seals.

Refitting is the reverse of the removal procedure. It will be necessary to bleed the system as described in **Section 8**.

6 The servo unit

The Vac-Hydro brake servo is fitted to Jaguar models with Girling brake systems and assists brake operation by means of the vacuum created by the engine. The degree of assistance is progressive throughout the full travel of the brake pedal, and proportional to the effort applied by the driver, up to the maximum vacuum available in the induction manifold. The servo unit is designed to permit communication between the master cylinder and the

FIG 17 Front wheel cylinder (early Lockheed)

wheel cylinders to allow normal braking to be made when there is any loss of vacuum.

Before leaving the manufacturers works the servo units are correctly adjusted, tested and lubricated to withstand long periods of service without attention. It should therefore be unnecessary to interfere with the unit in any way unless a major overhaul is required or if brake trouble has been traced positively to the servo unit.

Removal:

The servo unit is situated between the cruciform and righthand side member of the chassis frame and is accessible from underneath.

Brush away road dirt in the immediate vicinity of the servo pipe connections, disconnect the two hydraulic

FIG 18 Rear wheel cylinder (early Lockheed)

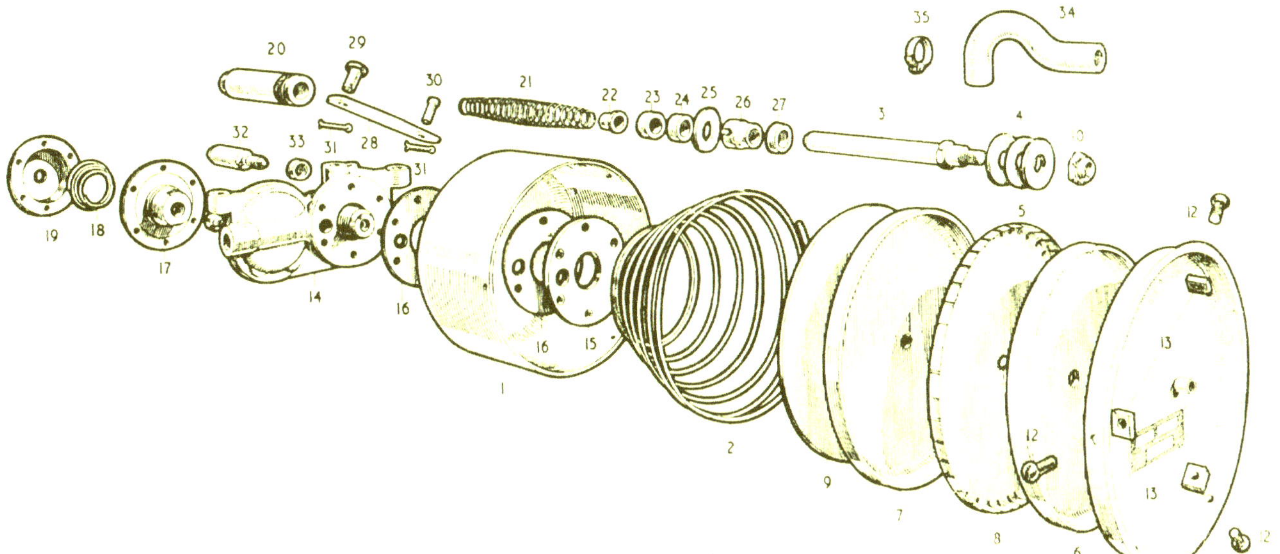

FIG 19 Servo unit exploded view

Cylinder for Brake Servo 1	Cover, Dome, for Valve Body 19
Spring, Return, for Piston 2	Body 20
Piston-Rod 3	Spring (Barrel), inside Hydraulic Cylinder 21
Washer (Steel) on Piston Rod 4	Spreader for Seal 22
Washer (Fibre) on Piston Rod 5	Seal 23
Back-Plate, supporting Expanding Ring 6	Plunger 24
Leather Seal, inside Cylinder 7	Washer (Copper), at top of Seal Retainer .. 25
Ring, expanding Leather Seal 8	Retainer for Seal, in Valve Body 26
End-Plate, retaining Expander Seal 9	Seal, in Valve Body 27
Nut, Self-Lock, at end of Piston Rod 10	Reaction Lever 28
End Cover for Cylinder 11	Pin, Clevis, for Reaction Lever Pivot 29
Screw, securing End Cover 12	Pin, Clevis, securing Reaction Lever to Diaphragm Valve Assembly 30
Nut, square, on Screws 13	Pin, Split, retaining Clevis Pins 31
Valve Body 14	Plunger 32
Plate, inside Cylinder, clamping Valve Body .. 15	Seal on Plunger 33
Gasket, between Valve Body and Cylinder, and Clamping Plate and Cylinder 16	Breather Hose for Brake Servo Unit 34
Diaphragm Valve Assembly inside Valve Body .. 17	Clip, securing Hose to Breather Pipe on Servo .. 35
Spring, Return (Conical) for Diaphragm Valve .. 18	

connections and the vacuum connection. While supporting the unit from below, remove the three nuts securing the servo unit to the top of the support member.

Immediately after removal, plug the connections on the servo to prevent the ingress of foreign matter.

It is of the utmost importance that extreme care should be exercised during the whole of the time the servo is being handled to prevent mineral fluids of any type from coming into contact with the rubber seals. Absolute cleanliness is most essential and the unit must never be immersed in a cleaning bath or degreasing plant. When assembling, smear all components with clean brake fluid.

Servicing:

Stand the unit (see **FIG 19**) with the hydraulic cylinder upright and allow the fluid to drain from the vacuum cylinder via the breather pipe, discard the fluid.

Check the valve lever for freedom of movement, cleanliness, etc, and re-lubricate the axis pins. This assembly has wide clearances this should not be confused with excessive wear. If it is considered necessary to remove the lever and pin, replace the pins correctly with the heads towards the fixing bosses of the servo.

Check that when the spherical head of the plunger under the lever is depressed a .020 inch feeler gauge will pass between the lever face and the head of the plunger. Check the splitpins for security.

Immediately prior to refitting, inject approximately one-eighth of a pint of the recommended grade of brake fluid into the vacuum cylinder via the breather pipe.

Refitting:

Refitting is the reverse of the removal procedure. The hydraulic system will require to be bled as described in **Section 8**.

7 Flexible hoses:

When removing flexible hoses (see **FIG 20**) it is essential that they are disconnected at the support bracket end first, otherwise rupture of the hose is likely to occur.

At the support bracket on the brake backplate, unscrew the union securing the metal pipe to the end of the flexible hose. Hold the hexagon of the flexible hose and sleeve situated underneath the support bracket, unscrew the locknut, and release the hose. Unscrew the hose at the other end allowing the hose to rotate.

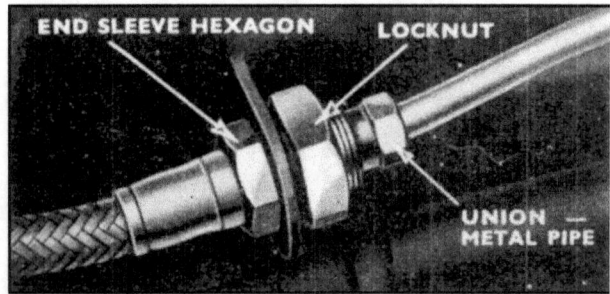

FIG 20 Flexible hose removal

Examine the hose for signs of deterioration such as perishing and renew as necessary. It will be necessary to renew the hose if it is badly choked, **do not attempt to clear the bore by probing.**

Refitting is the reverse of the removal procedure. When refitting the flexible hose at the support bracket end ensure that the hose does not twist, by holding the hexagon of the sleeve with a spanner whilst tightening the locknut.

After refitting the hose it will be necessary to bleed the system as described in **Section 8**.

8 Bleeding the system

This operation is not part of routine maintenance, but it must be carried out if any part of the hydraulic pipe lines have been disconnected, or if the fluid level in the reservoir rank has fallen so low that air has entered the system. The presence of air is generally indicated by a spongy feeling of the brake pedal and a loss of braking power. After complete dismantling, more than one supply tank full of fluid may be needed to refill the system. It is therefore necessary to have sufficient fluid available to keep the supply tank topped up throughout the process of bleeding. If the fluid in the supply tank drops at any time during the bleeding operations to such a low level that air can enter the system it will be necessary to make a fresh start. If a servo unit is fitted the system must not be bled with the engine running. Before starting work pump the brake pedal several times to destroy any vacuum in the servo reservoir. Bleeding is carried out as follows:

With every hydraulic connection secure and the supply tank topped up with the correct grade of hydraulic fluid, remove the rubber cap if fitted to the bleed screw on the wheel furthest from the master cylinder. Clean the bleed screw thoroughly. Fit a rubber or plastic tube over the bleed screw and immerse the free end of the tube below the level of some clean fluid in a clean glass jar.

Open the bleed screw one full turn with a suitable spanner. Then depress the brake pedal steadily, whilst an assistant stands by to tighten the bleed screw just before the pedal reaches the end of its stroke. Allow the brake pedal to return without assistance. Fluid and air bubbles will be seen coming out of the tube into the jar.

Continue this pumping action, pausing after each stroke to top up the fluid reservoir. When fluid without any air bubbles is seen to emerge from the tube, the bleed screw may then be tightened whilst the brake pedal is held firmly against the floorboards.

Repeat this operation on each wheel checking that the fluid level in the reservoir is maintained.

On models fitted with the later Lockheed type of brakes, there is a tandem master cylinder it is therefore necessary to apply the foregoing procedure to two wheels at a time, one front and one back wheel. In this case it is necessary to check that both compartments of the fluid reservoir chamber are topped up throughout the operation.

Fluid which has been bled off into the jar will will be dirty and aerated and should not be used to top up the system.

Having completed the foregoing procedure apply the brake hard several times and repeat the bleeding operation. This procedure is carried out with the engine running to release any small pockets of air trapped within the servo unit, where fitted.

9 The handbrake

Removal of cable:

At the handbrake lever end, remove the clevis pin securing the handbrake cable yoke to the adjusting rod

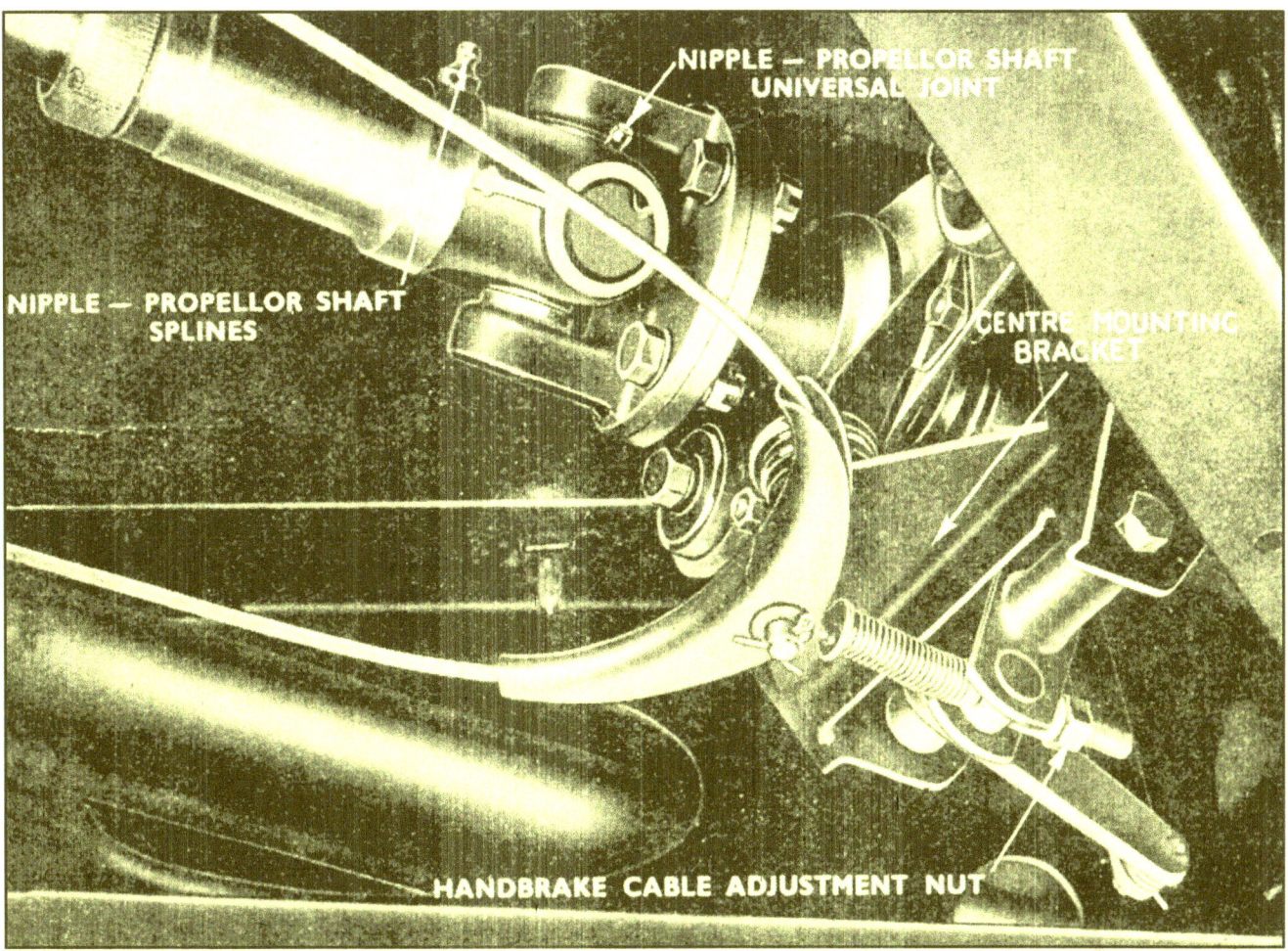

FIG 21 Handbrake cable adjuster

(see **FIG 21**). At the rear of the backplate remove the clevis pin securing the handbrake cable to the lever which protrudes through the backplate A hole is provided in the handbrake bracket on the backplate to provide access to the clevis pin.

Pull back the cable return spring, lever out the spring retainer from the top of the cable clevis and withdraw the handbrake cable. Detach the handbrake cable from the brackets and clips on the rear axle case and from the abutment bracket underneath the propeller shaft. The cable can now be removed.

Examine the cable for signs of deterioration and fraying, renew as necessary. Before fitting the handbrake cable liberally coat it with grease, this will provide a protective coating as well as lubrication.

Refitting is the reverse of the removal procedure. Check that the handbrake is correctly adjusted as described in the following section.

Adjustment:

Adjustment of the handbrake is automatically carried out when adjusting the rear brakes. It only becomes necessary to adjust the handbrake cable when excessive movement is required at the handbrake lever to apply the brakes or a new cable has been fitted. The handbrake cable should not be adjusted until normal brake adjustment as described in **Section 2** has been carried out on the rear wheels.

Jack-up the rear wheels and place chocks under the front wheels. Lock the rear brake shoes to the drum by means of the brake adjusters. Adjust the handbrake cable by means of the adjuster at the yoke (see **FIG 21**) to give two to three notches free movement at the handbrake lever. Slacken off the rear brake adjusters two clicks when the wheels should rotate freely.

Adjustment must on no account be made other than in in the manner described, as haphazard adjustment to the cable may preload the rear brake shoes, causing the brake shoes to bind. When the handbrake is released no tension should exist in the cable.

DISC BRAKES

10 Description

Disc brakes are fitted to the Mk IX and XK 150 models only and are fitted to all four wheels. Two types of Lockheed brake systems are fitted both are very similar in operation, the only major difference is in the caliper piston assemblies, where the later type is designed so that the brake pads may be changed quickly and easily.

The brake systems consist of a caliper which straddles a disc, the disc being an integral part of the wheel hub. Bolted to the caliper on either side of the disc are cylinder blocks, containing a piston connected to which there is a pad carrier and brake pad. Hydraulic pressure is applied to the cylinder blocks by means of a master cylinder

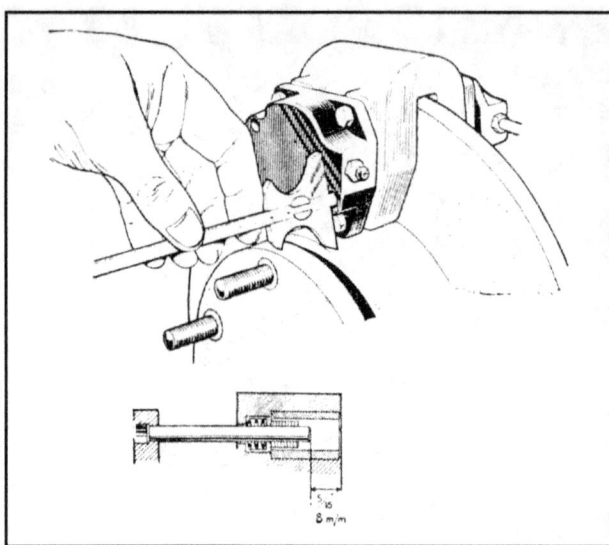

FIG 22 Measurement of pad wear

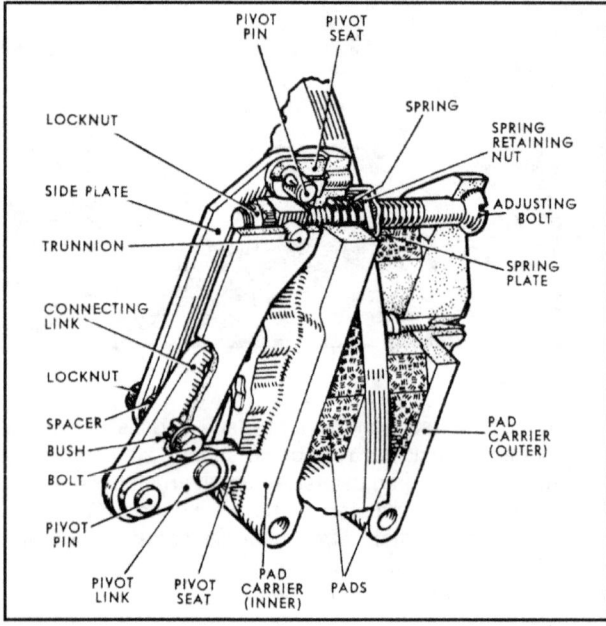

FIG 23 Handbrake caliper

connected to the brake pedal. This hydraulic pressure forces the pistons out of the cylinders to bring the friction pads in contact with the disc to provide the braking effort.

To assist the braking effort applied at the brake pedal there is a vacuum servo unit. This unit assists in producing hydraulic pressure by applying the vacuum pressure obtained within the engine inlet manifold.

The handbrake is fitted to the rear brake calipers and consists of an independent disc brake system mechanically operated by the handbrake lever.

11 Maintenance and adjustment

It is essential that the fluid level in the hydraulic fluid supply tank is not allowed to fall below 1 inch from the top of the tank or air may be allowed into the system. To top up the system clean around the top of the reservoir cap, unscrew the cap and then top up the reservoir with the correct grade of hydraulic fluid. If it is found that the fluid level requires frequent topping up examine the hydraulic system for signs of leakage.

Both the front and rear wheel brakes are so designed that no manual adjustment to compensate for brake friction pad wear is necessary, as this automatically takes place when the footbrake is applied. At intervals of approximately 5000 miles or if a loss of braking efficiency is noticed the brake friction pads (two per wheel) should be examined for wear.

On the early type of disc brakes this examination is carried out using a depth gauge to measure the distance between the face of the brake cylinder and the retractor pin as shown in **FIG 22**. If this distance is $\frac{5}{16}$ inch or more the pads will require renewal. On the later type the pad may be examined from the rear of the caliper and pad renewal is required when the pad thickness is down to $\frac{1}{4}$ inch or less.

When trying to measure the retractor pin depth on the early type brakes it may be found that a metal sleeve prevents access to the retractor pin hole. This sleeve may be removed and discarded as it is provided solely for the protection of the retractor pin during transportation after manufacture.

The handbrake requires adjustment when there is excessive travel on the handbrake lever. To adjust the handbrakes to compensate for friction pad wear carry out the following procedure. Jack-up the rear of the car and place chocks under the front wheels. Remove both rear wheels and release the handbrake.

Unscrew the adjuster bolt (see **FIG 23**) and insert a feeler gauge of .004 inch thickness between the handbrake pad and the wheel disc. Tighten the adjuster bolt until the pad just nips the feeler gauge. Withdraw the feeler gauge and check the disc for free rotation. Repeat this procedure for the remaining rear brake. Replace the road wheels and lower the car.

If there is still excessive movement on the handbrake lever it will be necessary to adjust the handbrake cables as described in **Section 14**.

The brake servo air cleaner should be cleaned at regular intervals in the following manner. Remove the air cleaner from the righthand wing valance and wash it in methylated spirits. After drying out re-lubricate the wire mesh with clean brake fluid.

The complete brake system is designed to require the minimum of attention and providing the hydraulic fluid is not allowed to fall below the recommended level no defects should normally occur. Fluid loss must be supplemented by periodic topping up the reservoir with fluid of the same specification of that in the system. If the recommended brand of fluid is not available and it is intended to use one of the alternative approved brands, the complete system must be drained before the substitution of one fluid for another.

The inclusion of air in the system will be indicated by sluggish response of the brakes and spongy action of the brake pedal. This condition may be due to air induction at a loose joint or at the reservoir in which the fluid level has been allowed to drop to low. These defects must be immediately remedied and the complete system bled. Similarly bleeding the system is equally essential following the servicing operation involving the disconnecting of part of the hydraulic system.

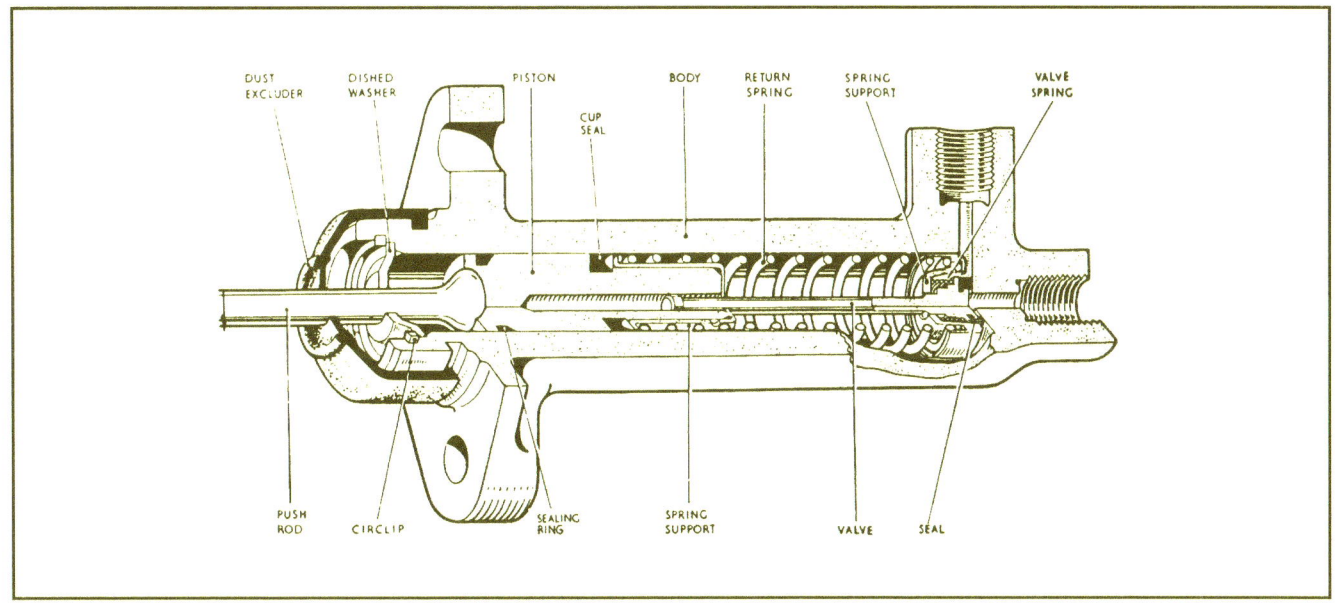

FIG 24 Master cylinder sectional view

12 The master cylinder

When dismantling any part of the hydraulic system the components should be thoroughly cleaned externally. Brake system fluid should be used for cleaning internal components and except where otherwise stated the use of petrol, paraffin or chemical grease solvents should be avoided as they may be detrimental to the rubber components.

Throughout the dismantling and assembly operations it is essential that the work bench be maintained in a clean condition and that the components are not handled with dirty or greasy hands. The precision parts hould be handled with extreme care and should be carefully placed away from tools or other equipment likely to cause damage. After cleaning all components should be dried with lint free rag.

When it is not the intention to renew the rubber components, they must be carefully examined for serviceability. There must be no evidence of defects such as perished, excessive swelling, cutting or twisting, and where doubt exists comparison with new parts may prove to be of some assistance in making an assessment of their condition. The flexible pipes must show no signs of deterioration or damage and the bores should be cleaned with a jet of compressed air. No attempt should be made to clear blockages by probing as this may result in internal damage which is not visible. Partially or totally blocked flexible pipes should always be renewed. When removing or refitting a flexible pipe (see **Section 7**) the end sleeve hexagon should be held with the appropriate spanner to prevent the pipe from twisting. A twisted pipe will prove detrimental to efficient brake operation.

Removal:

Disconnect the hydraulic pipe connections to the master cylinder and drain the fluid into a clean container. Remove the clevis pin securing the forked end of the pushrod to the brake pedal. Unscrew the bolts securing the master cylinder to the mounting bracket and withdraw the master cylinder.

Dismantling:

Ease the dust excluder (see **FIG 24**) clear of the head of the master cylinder. With a suitable pair of pliers remove the circlip, this will release the pushrod complete with dished washer. Withdraw the piston and remove the 'O' ring. Withdraw the valve assembly complete with springs and supports. Remove the valve sealing ring from the bush.

Reassembly:

Examine all the components for signs of wear and renew as necessary.

Lubricate the seals with brake fluid just prior to assembly. Fit the valve seal around the bush and fit the 'O' ring in the groove around the piston. Place the seal bush in position on the valve stem and insert the piston into the spring support, ensuring that the head of the valve engages the piston bore.

Slide the complete assembly into the cylinder body taking particular care to lubricate the bore with clean fluid and not damage or twist the 'O' ring.

Position the pushrod and depress the piston sufficiently to allow the dished washer to seat on the shoulder at the head of the cylinder. Fit the circlip and check that it fully engages in the groove. Fill the dust excluder with clean rubber grease and reset it around the head of the master cylinder.

Refitting is the reverse of the removal procedure. After refitting it is necessary to check that the correct amount of free travel is obtained at the master cylinder pushrod. This free movement is provided by clearance between the enlarged head of the pushrod, the piston and dished washer. No adjustment of this clearance is allowed for so that if the free movement is not obtained the unit should be checked for correct assembly. This clearance is necessary or pressure may build up within the system causing the brakes to drag or remain on. The normal clearance provided gives approximately $\frac{1}{4}$ inch free movement at the brake pedal and this can be felt if the brake pedal is depressed gently by hand.

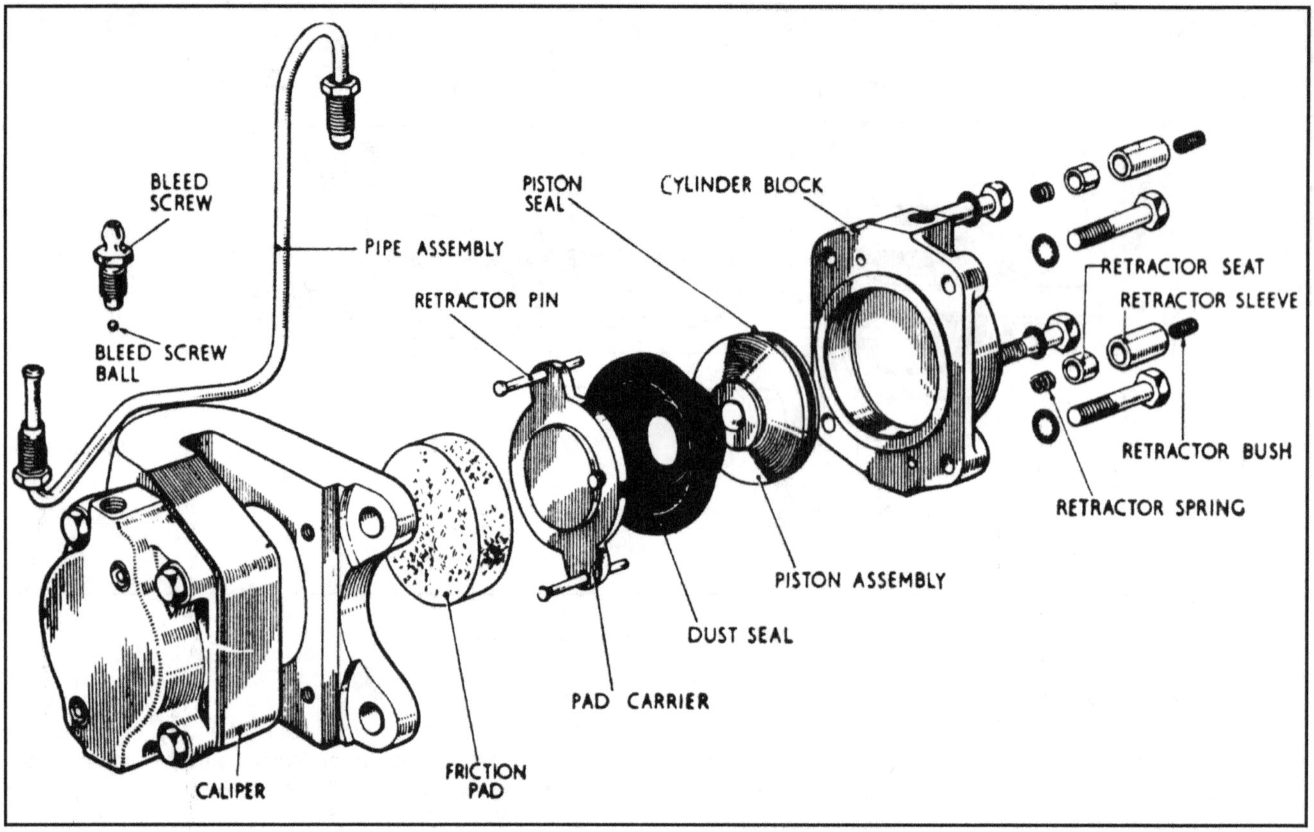

FIG 25 Front caliper exploded view (early type)

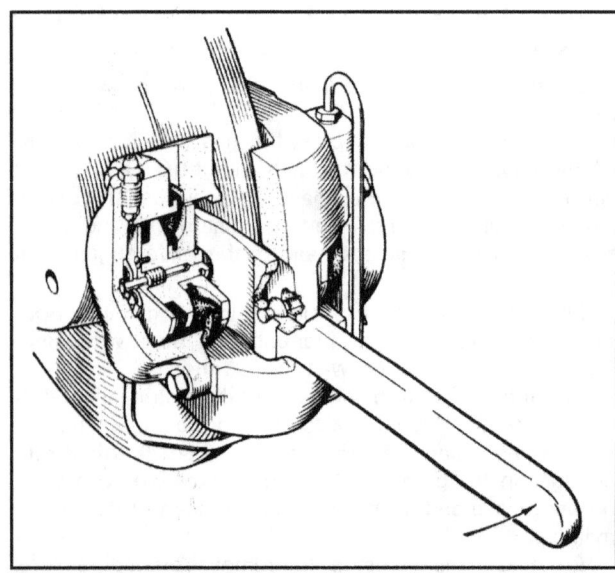

FIG 26 Piston resetting

13 Dismantling the brakes

Early type Lockheed brakes:

Jack-up the car at the appropriate wheel and remove the road wheel. Disconnect the hydraulic pipe unions, remove the pipe assembly (see **FIG 25**) and plug the open end of the supply pipe to avoid loss of hydraulic fluid. Unscrew the four securing bolts on each cylinder block and remove the cylinder blocks complete with piston and pad assemblies.

If the dismantling has been carried out to renew the brake pads only it will be necessary to hold the pistons in the cylinder block to do this, press the carrier plate and cylinder block firmly together to press the piston back into the cylinder and reset the retractor pins. To reset the retractor pins, press the pin heads into their recesses in the carrier plate and, holding them in this position, ensure that the retractor bushes are pressed well home into their housings on the outer face of the cylinder block.

Renewal of the brake pads is then achieved in the following manner:

Carefully prise the pad from the carrier plate using a sharp knife, and clean away any traces of cement from the face of the carrier plate. During this operation be careful not to twist the carrier plate relative to the block, as this may distort the retractor pins. Trichlorethylene may be used sparingly to clean the carrier plate but extreme care should be taken to see that this fluid does not come into contact with any rubber components.

Lightly smear the annular face of the carrier plate with Dunlop General purpose cement, do not smear the raised centre portion. Press the pad firmly onto the plate, ensuring the correct location of the alignment screw, and remove all traces of excess cement which may be squeezed out.

If further dismantling is not required to be carried out the components may be reassembled in the reverse manner to which they were removed and then the system bled. Further dismantling will require the removal of the retractor pins using a $\frac{3}{32}$ inch diameter punch. This process should be carried out carefully by lightly tapping the punch with a hammer. Remove the carrier plate and temporarily return the pins to their housings.

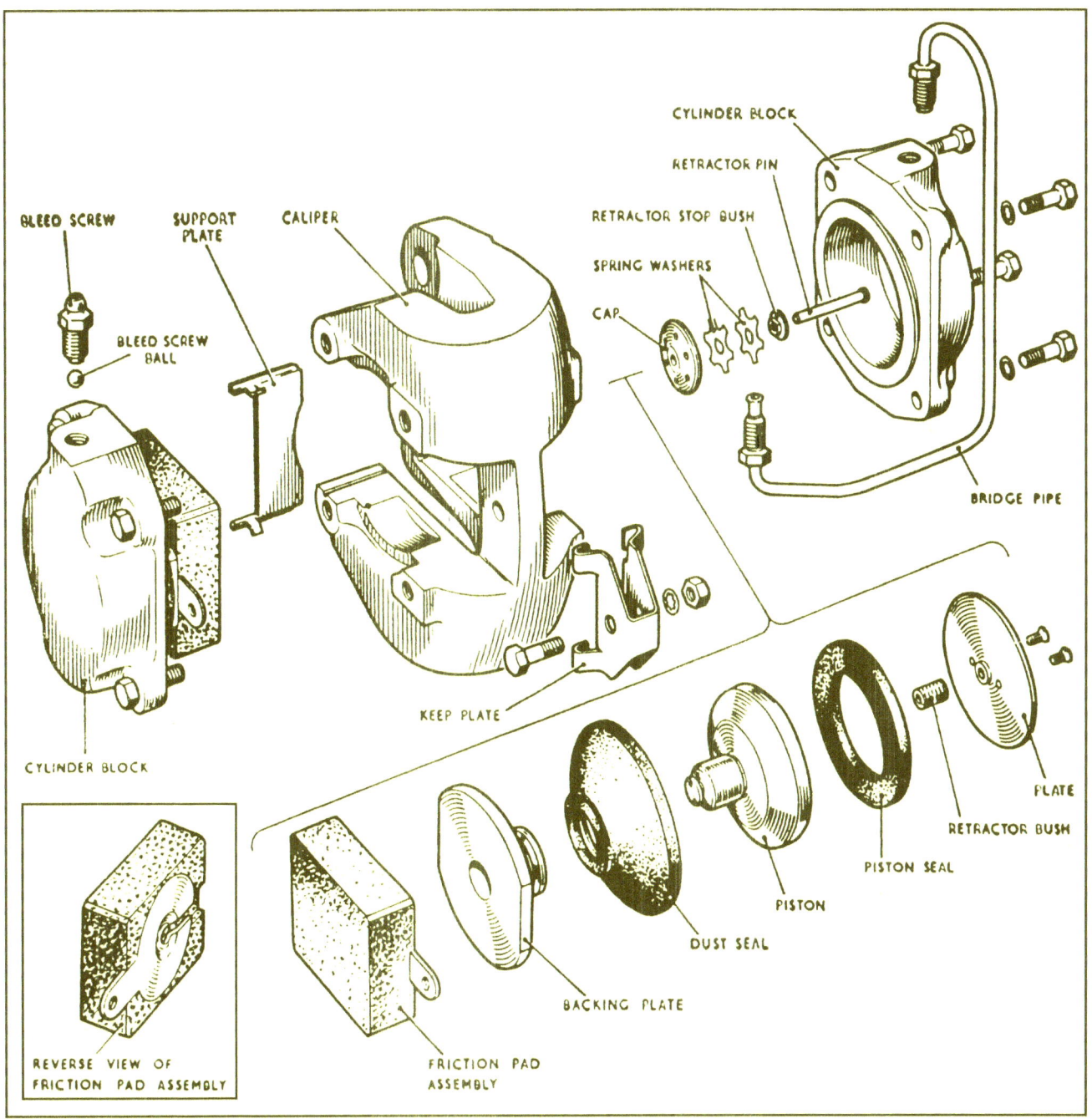

FIG 27 Front caliper exploded view (later type)

Disengage the dust seal from the cylinder block and withdraw the piston assembly. Carefully prise off the piston seal retainer washer which is a press fit on the inner face of the piston and then remove the piston seal. Remove the dust seal from the ball joint plug.

Reassembly:

Examine the components carefully and renew if any show signs of wear or deterioration. It is recommended that if a new piston seal is fitted a new dustcover should also be fitted. Clean the cylinder bore and check it for signs of scoring.

Fit the dust seal in position under the shoulder of the ball joint, taking care to avoid harmful stretching and to ensure that the rubber lip is not trapped or twisted.

Lightly lubricate the piston seal with brake fluid and fit it to the piston. Press the retaining washer onto the piston and lightly peen it over at three points. Insert the piston into the cylinder and spring the outer rim of the dust seal into its housing.

Locate the carrier plate, refit the retractor pins and reset them as previously described.

The remaining reassembly is carried out in the reverse manner to that described for dismantling. Bleed the system as described in **Section 8**.

The later or quick change Lockheed type brakes:

Renewing the friction pads:

The friction pads fitted have been selected as a result of intensive development and it is therefore essential that only the correct materials are used when replacing.

Jack-up the car at the appropriate wheel and remove the road wheel. Remove the nut, washer and bolt securing the keep plate (see **FIG 27**) and withdraw the plate. With a suitable hooked implement engaged in the hole in the lug on the friction pad withdraw the defective pad assembly.

Thoroughly clean the backing plate, dust seal, and the surrounding area of the caliper. Half empty the hydraulic fluid reservoir as the following operation of pressing the pistons into the cylinder bores, may cause the reservoir to overflow and cause damage to the paintwork.

Insert the forked end of the piston resetting tool (No. 7840) into the space between the caliper bridge and one of the piston backing plates, with the fork astride the projecting piston spigot and its convex face bearing on the piston backing plate (see **FIG 26**). Locate the spigot end of the lever pin in the keep plate bolt hole in the caliper. Pivot the lever about the pin to force the piston to the base of its cylinder.

Withdraw the tool and insert the new friction pad assembly. Repeat this procedure for the opposite piston assembly. Refit the keep plate securing it in position with the nut, bolt and washer.

Repeat the foregoing procedure on the remaining three wheels as it is essential that brake pads are renewed in complete sets. Top up the fluid reservoir tank to the correct level.

Dismantling:

Remove the brake pads (see **FIG 27**) as described in the foregoing paragraphs. Disconnect the hydraulic pipe connections to the cylinder blocks, remove the bridge pipe and block the fluid supply pipe to prevent loss of fluid.

Remove the mounting bolts securing the cylinder blocks to the caliper and withdraw the cylinder blocks. Thoroughly clean the blocks externally before proceeding with further dismantling.

Disengage the dust seal from the groove around the cylinder block face. Connect the cylinder block to a source of fluid supply and apply pressure to eject the piston. The supply pipe from the master cylinder may be used for this purpose if an alternative supply is not available. Remove the screws securing the plate to the piston, lift off the plate and piston seal, withdraw the retractor bush from within the piston bore. Carefully cut away and discard the dust seal.

Support the backing plate on a bush of sufficient bore diameter to just accommodate the piston. With a suitable tubular distance piece placed against the end of the piston spigot and located around the shouldered head, press out this piston from the backing plate. Care must be taken during this operation to avoid damaging the piston.

Reassembly:

Engage the collar of a new dust seal with the lip on the backing plate, avoiding harmful stretching. Locate the backing plate on the piston spigot and with the piston suitably supported, press the backing plate fully home.

Insert the retractor bush into the bore of the piston. Lightly lubricate the piston seal with brake fluid and fit it to the piston face. Attach and secure the plate with the screws and peen the screws over to lock them.

Check that the piston and cylinder bore are thoroughly clean and show no signs of damage. Locate the piston assembly on the end of the retractor pin and with the aid of a hand press, slowly apply an even pressure to the backing plate to press the assembly into the cylinder bore. During this operation ensure the piston assembly is in correct alignment in relation to the cylinder bore, and that the piston seal does not become twisted or trapped as it enters. Engage the outer rim of the dust seal in the groove around the cylinder block face and ensure that the two support plates are in position.

Reassemble the cylinder blocks to the caliper. Fit the bridge pipes in their correct positions i.e. with the hairpin bend furthest away from the road wheel. Reconnect the supply pipe and refit the brake pads as described under friction pad renewal. Bleed the hydraulic system as described in **Section 15**.

14 The handbrake

Relining:

Unscrew and remove the adjuster bolt and locknut and swing the pad carriers away from the disc (see **FIG 28**). Remove the splitpin securing the side plates pivot pin and withdraw the pivot pin.

Remove the rivets from both carriers and prise off the worn linings. Place new linings in position and secure them with new rivets.

Place the side plates against the inner carrier as shown in **FIG 28**. Hold the locknut firmly against the outer face of the trunnion and screw in the adjuster bolt until three or four threads engage the locknut. Align the holes in the side plates and pivot seat, fit the pivot pin and secure it with the splitpin. Reset the pad clearance as described in **Section 11**.

Cable adjustment:

The handbrake cable will only require adjustment if the handbrake lever travel is excessive with the correct clearance at the handbrake linings. Adjustment is carried out as follows:

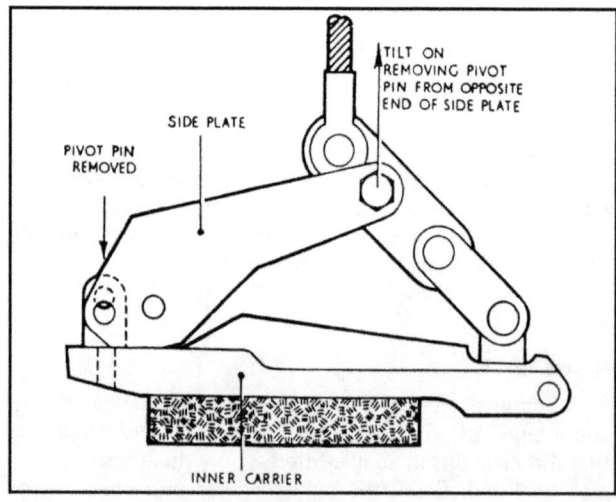

FIG 28 Handbrake relining

Jack-up the rear of the car and place chocks under the front wheels. Remove the rear road wheels and release the handbrake.

Screw in the adjuster bolt at the handbrake caliper on each rear wheel disc until the pads are in hard contact with the disc. Remove the clevis pin securing the fork end to the operating link at the front end of the main cable. Slacken the locknut and adjust the position of the fork end so that with the clevis pin refitted there is no slack in the main cable and the two cross-cables. It is however important to ensure that the cables are not under tension.

Refit the clevis pin and reset the handbrake pad clearance with a .004 inch thick feeler gauge. Refit the rear wheels and lower the car.

15 Bleeding the system

Bleeding the system on the models fitted with disc brakes is exactly the same as that described for models with drum brakes in **Section 8**.

16 The servo unit:

Description:

The vacuum servo is a unit which provides the driver with a degree of assistance when applying the brakes, and is installed in the line between the master cylinder and the brake assemblies; power for its operation is supplied by atmospheric pressure and by vacuum from the engine inlet manifold. The unit consists mainly of a booster piston, a slave cylinder and a control valve.

Operation:

When the servo is at rest (see **FIG 29**) the valve piston D and the diaphragm A are in the normal position; valve B is open and valve C is closed, the valves being maintained in position by a tapered spring.

A pipe connection communicates the slave cylinder L with the engine inlet manifold so that, when the engine is running, vacuum is present within chambers P and Q. Additionally, whatever degree of vacuum exists within chamber P will also be present in chamber N, via the opening in the centre of the diaphragm A, and to chamber R via the pipe.

Upon depressing the brake pedal, fluid is displaced from the master cylinder to the wheel cylinders, via the slave cylinder, and passes through the holes in the slave piston H, cup J, spring guide K and the adaptor M.

Meanwhile the fluid pressure developed by the master cylinder is also felt upon the rear face of the valve piston D which is displaced against the load of the diaphragm spring; this movement deflects the diaphragm A until it bears against the valve B, and the seal thus formed isolates the suction source from chambers N and R. Continued movement of the piston opens the air valve C permitting air to enter chamber N and to pass to chamber R via the external pipe.

This reduction in the degree of vacuum causes the vacuum piston to move forward, at the same time transmitting the movement to the pushrod E, allowing it to move nearer to the cup J and seal off the hole in its centre, thus creating a locked line of fluid to the brakes; con-

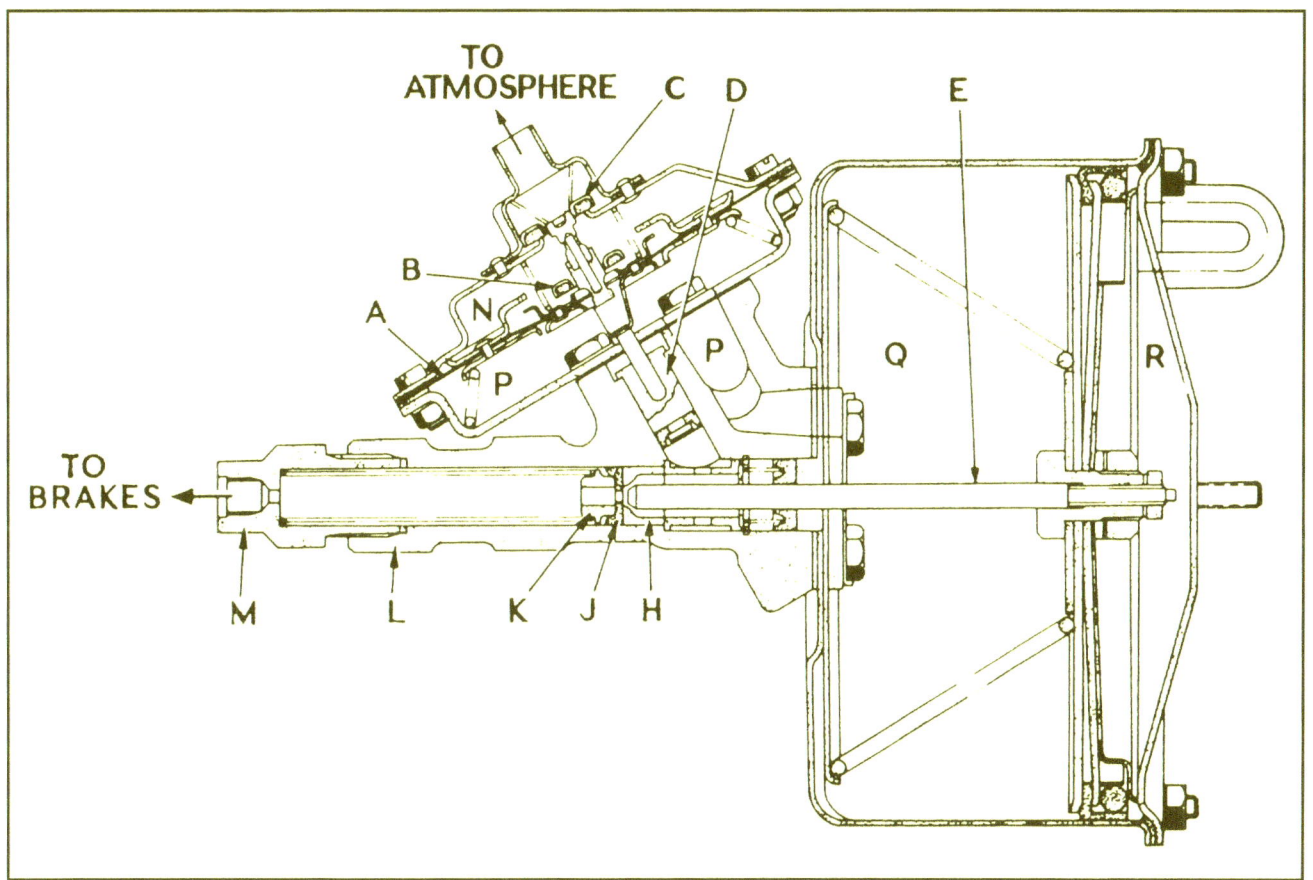

FIG 29 Servo unit sectional view

tinued movement of the piston increases the pressure in the slave cylinder and the brake line, thereby assisting the driver in applying the brakes. The reduction of vacuum is also present within chamber N, resulting in the creation of a pressure difference across the diaphragm in operation to the force applied by the master cylinder pressure to the piston D; when these opposing forces balance, the rearward deflection of the diaphragm allows the outer valve to close on its seat and prevent further entry of air.

Greater effort upon the brake pedal increases the thrust upon the piston D which re-opens the outer valve and allows a greater amount of effort to be performed by the vacuum piston when opposing forces on the diaphragm are once more in balance the air valve will again close onto its seal.

It is apparent therefore that the diaphragm acts as a proportioning device ensuring that the performance of the servo is substantially progressive. When the brake pedal is released, pressure is removed from the valve piston D allowing the diaphragm to return to its original position, and reconnect chambers N and R to the manifold. The spring is then able to return the piston to the off position, causing the pushrod E to move away from the cup in the slave cylinder and so permit the fluid to return from the brakes to the master cylinder.

17 Fault diagnosis

(a) 'Spongy' pedal

1 Leak in the hydraulic system
2 Worn master cylinder
3 Leaking wheel cylinders
4 Air in the system
5 Gaps between shoes and linings

(b) Excessive pedal movement

1 Check 1 and 4 in (a)
2 Excessive lining wear
3 Very low fluid level in supply tank
4 To much free movement of pedal

(c) Brakes grab or pull to one side

1 Brake backplates loose
2 Scored, cracked or distorted drum or disc
3 High spots in drum, disc not running true
4 Unbalanced shoe adjustment
5 Wet or oily linings or pads
6 Worn or loose rear spring fixings
7 Front suspension or rear anchorages loose
8 Worn steering connections
9 Mixed linings (pads) of different grades
10 Uneven tyre pressures
11 Broken shoe return springs, bent retractor pins
12 Seized handbrake cable

NOTES

NOTES

INDEX – ELECTRICAL SYSTEM

SECTION	PAGE	
001	247	Description
002	247	Battery
003	247	Generator Testing
004	248	Generator Removal & Disassembly
005	248	Generator Servicing
006	249	Starter Testing
007	249	Starter Examination
008	249	Starter Servicing
009	250	Control Box Description (Regulator & Cut-Out)
010	250	Control Box Settings & Adjustments
011	252	Fuses
012	252	Headlamps Settings & Adjustments
013	252	Trafficators & Flasher Units
014	253	Horn Adjustment
015	254	Windscreen Wipers & Wiper Motor Servicing
016	254	Fault Diagnosis Chart

ELECTRICAL SYSTEM - SERVICE

1 Description

All cars covered by this manual have 12 volt electrical systems in which the positive battery terminal is earthed. There is a regulator in the control box which gives output control of the charging circuit to prevent damage to the battery by overcharging.

The headlamps use the double filament dipping system, the bulb holder in the lamps is in a preset position so that focusing is not required.

There are wiring diagrams in the Technical Data section to enable those with some electrical experience to trace and correct wiring faults.

Serious mechanical and electrical defects in the generator and starter motor are best cured by fitting new units on an exchange basis, but instructions for their adjustment by a reasonably competent engineer have been included in this chapter. To carry out adjustments to the electrical control gear demands the use of precise measuring instruments. Unreliable instruments will make accurate adjustment impossible.

2 Battery

This is a 12 volt lead/acid type using dilute sulphuric acid as an electrolyte. The life of the battery is a hard one and it will be considerably shortened by the lack of regular maintenance. An obvious sign of trouble is corrosion of terminals and surrounding parts. This causes an increase in electrical resistance and leakage. Clean off corrosion by washing with dilute ammonia, then dry the parts and smear the terminal posts with petroleum jelly. Use anti-sulphuric paint on adjacent metal parts such as the battery bolts, the strap and the tray. The top of the battery must always be dry and clean, as dampness encourages the spread of corrosion and provides a path for electrical leakage.

The electrolyte:

The level of the electrolyte must be maintained just above the top of the perforated plate covering the separators. **Never add acid, top up with distilled water only.** The condition of the battery can be checked by measuring the specific gravity of the electrolyte in each cell with a hydrometer.

The specific gravity of a fully charged battery is 1.280 to 1.300 if a figure below this is obtained the battery requires charging. All six cells should read approximately the same. If one cell differs radically from the rest it may be due to an internal fault or possibly there has been spillage or leakage of the electrolyte. If it has been spilled add more with the same specific gravity. This can be made by adding sulphuric acid to distilled water. It is dangerous to add water to acid as the acid is liable to spit.

If the battery is in a low state of charge, take the car for a long daylight run or connect it to a 5 amp charger until it gases freely, taking out the vent plugs and keeping it away from naked lights when it is gassing.

If the battery is unused for long periods, give it a freshening charge every month. **Never leave it in a discharged condition.**

3 Generator testing

The generator is a specially finished shunt-wound two pole two brush machine, arranged to work in conjunction with a compensated voltage control regulator unit. A fan draws cooling air through the generator, inlet and outlet holes being provided in the end brackets of the unit. Ballbearings are fitted at each end of the armature shaft as shown in **FIG 1**.

Checking generator output:

1. Inspect the drive belt and adjust if necessary as described in **Chapter 4**.
2. Check that the generator and control box are correctly connected. The generator terminal D must be connected to control box terminal D and generator terminal F to control box terminal F.
3. Switch off all lights and accessories, disconnect the cables from the generator terminals D and F and connect the terminals with a short length of wire.
4. Start the engine and set it to run at normal idling speed, with the negative lead of a good quality moving coil voltmeter connected to one generator terminal the other lead being connected to a good earth.
5. Gradually increase the engine speed, when the voltmeter reading should rise rapidly without fluctuation. Do not allow the voltmeter reading to reach 20 volts and do not race the engine in an attempt to increase

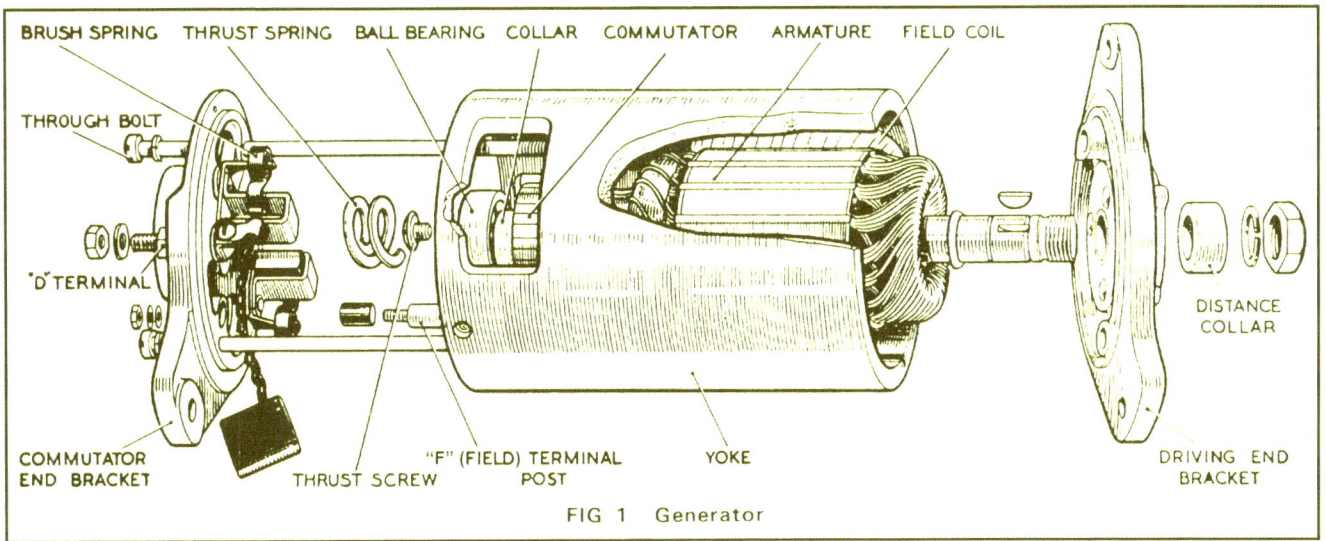

FIG 1 Generator

the voltage. A fast idling speed of 1000 rev/min should be sufficient.

6 If there is no reading check the brush gear.
7 If the reading is only $\frac{1}{2}$ to 1 volt the field winding may be faulty.
8 If the reading is approximately 6 volts the armature winding may be faulty. Excessive sparking of the commutator during this test also indicates a defective armature or brushes.
9 If a radio suppression capacitor is fitted between the output terminal and earth, disconnect the capacitor and retest the generator. If a reading is now given on the voltmeter, the capacitor is defective and must be renewed.

4 Generator removal and dismantling

Disconnect the battery positive lead. Remove the connections from the generator, noting the yellow wire is connected to terminal D. Loosen the two mounting bolts and the adjuster screw and push the generator towards the engine to release the fan belt tension. Remove the mounting bolts and the adjuster screw and lift out the generator, disengaging the fan belt.

Remove the spindle nut and withdraw the driving pulley. Remove the brush cover band, and whilst holding back the brush springs carefully withdraw the brushes. Remove the nut spring washer and flat washer from the field terminal on the commutator end bracket (see **FIG 1**). Unscrew and withdraw the two through bolts; the commutator end bracket can now be withdrawn from the generator yoke. Lift out the driving end bracket together with the armature. The driving end bracket may be separated from the armature by a hand press. This is however only necessary if the bearing requires renewal or a new armature is to be fitted.

5 Generator servicing

Brushes:

Refit the brushes in the commutator end bracket. Check that the brushes move freely in their holders by holding back the brush springs and pulling gently on the flexible connectors. If a brush is inclined to stick remove it from its holder and clean its sides with a petrol moistened cloth. Be careful to replace the brushes in their original positions in order to retain the correct rubbing contact with the commutator. Brushes which have worn so that they will not bed properly on the commutator must be renewed.

Test the brush spring pressures using a spring balance held radially to the commutator. The tension of the springs when new is 36 to 44 oz, it is permissible for this value to fall to 30 oz before renewal is necessary.

Commutator:

A commutator in good condition will be smooth and free from pits or burned spots. Burnt commutator segments are a sign of broken armature wires. Short circuited windings cause darkening of the overheated coils and badly burned commutator segments. To clean the commutator use a petrol moistened cloth. If this is ineffective, carefully polish with a strip of fine glasspaper while rotating the armature. **Do not file and do not use emery paper** as grains of emery may become embedded in the copper segments.

To remedy a badly worn commutator, mount the armature with or without the drive end bracket in a lathe, rotate at high speed and take a light cut with a very sharp tool. Do not remove more metal than is necessary. After skimming, undercut the insulation between the segments to a depth of $\frac{1}{32}$ inch. with a hacksaw blade ground down to the thickness of the insulation, making sure that the blade is kept straight and upright all the time.

Field coils:

These are tested in the following manner:

Connect a 12 volt battery between the field terminal F and the generator yoke putting a good quality moving coil ammeter in series. The armature reading should be approximately 2 amps. If the reading is much more it shows that the field coil insulation has broken down; no reading indicates a break in the wiring of the coils. In either case the field coils require renewal.

Armature:

This can only be thoroughly tested with suitable equipment not normally available to the average owner. It can be tested however by substitution. **No attempt should be made to machine an armature core or to true a distorted armature shaft.** A defective armature must be renewed.

Bearings:

Bearings which are worn to such an extent that they will allow side movement of the armature shaft must be renewed.

The ballbearing at the driving end is renewed as follows:

Knock out the rivets which secure the bearing retainer plate to the end bracket and remove the plate. Press the bearing out of the end bracket and remove the corrugated washer, felt washer and oil retaining washer. Before fitting the replacement bearing see that it is clean and pack it with high melting point grease.

Place the oil retaining washer, felt washer and corrugated washer in the bearing housing in the end bracket, locate the bearing in the housing and press it home by means of a hand press. Fit the bearing retainer plate, insert new rivets from the inside of the end bracket and open the rivets by means of a punch to secure the plate rigidly in position.

The ballbearing at the commutator end is secured to the armature shaft by a thrust screw, and can be withdrawn with an extractor after the screw has been removed. See that the new bearing is packed with high melting point grease, force it home against the shoulder on the armature shaft and insert and tighten the thrust screw.

Reassembly:

Reassembly is the reverse procedure of dismantling, however it is essential not to fit the brushes until the generator is reassembled or they may well be damaged. Having refitted the brushes check that the springs are pressing properly on them

6 Starter testing

The electric starting motor is a four-pole four brush machine having an extended shaft which carries the engine starter drive. The starter motor is shown in **FIG 2** and the two types of drive gear the R.E. and Eclipse are shown in **FIGS 3** and **4** respectively.

If the starter lacks power or fails to turn the engine, first check to see if the engine can be turned over by hand. If not, the cause of the stiffness in the engine must be located and remedied after referring to **Chapter 1**. Next make sure that the battery is well charged.

Switch on the lights and operate the starter control. If the lights go dim but there is no sound from the starter it may be jammed. To free a jammed starter, remove the cap from the end of the armature shaft and turn the end of the shaft with a suitable spanner. If the lamps retain their full brilliance when the starter control is operated, check the switches and their connections for continuity. If the starter refuses to turn it must be removed for examination.

7 Starter examination

Removal:

Disconnect the cable from the positive terminal on the battery and the cable from the terminal on the starter. Unscrew the two setbolts securing the starter to the flywheel housing.

Replacement is the reverse of this procedure, but after the starter has been refitted the securing bolts should be slackened slightly, the starter operated for a few turns and then finally tightened. Do not omit to refit the earth strap to the top securing bolt.

Examination:

Remove the cover band (see **FIG 2**) and test the freedom of the brushes in their holders. Clean them in the manner described for the generator brushes and renew those that are badly worn or where the flexible leads have been exposed. Clean the commutator with a petrol moistened cloth. Hold the starter body in a vice and test it by connecting heavy gauge cables to a 12 volt battery. One cable must be connected to the starter terminal the other held against the body or end bracket. Under these light load conditions the starter should run at very high speed. If it does not it requires dismantling.

8 Starter servicing

Remove the brushes from their holders. Unscrew the terminal nuts from the terminal post (see **FIG 2**). Screw the two through bolts from the commutator end bracket and remove the end bracket from the yoke. Remove the driving end bracket complete with armature and drive from the starter motor yoke. If it is necessary to remove the armature from the driving end bracket it can be done by means of a press after the drive has been dismantled.

Brushes:

Test the brush springs with a spring balance the correct tension is between 30 and 40 oz. If the tension is low fit new springs.

Two of the brushes are connected to terminal eyelets attached to the brush boxes on the commutator end bracket and two are connected to the field coils.

The flexible connectors must be removed by unsoldering and the connectors of the new brushes secured in their place by soldering. The brushes are pre-formed so that bedding to the commutator is unnecessary.

Commutator:

The commutator is reconditioned in the same way as that used for the generator commutator. **The insulation between the commutator segments must not be undercut.**

Field coils:

Test the field coils for continuity by connecting a 12 volt battery with a 12 volt bulb in series between those points of the field coils at which the brushes are connected. Failure of the lamp to light indicates an open circuit. If the

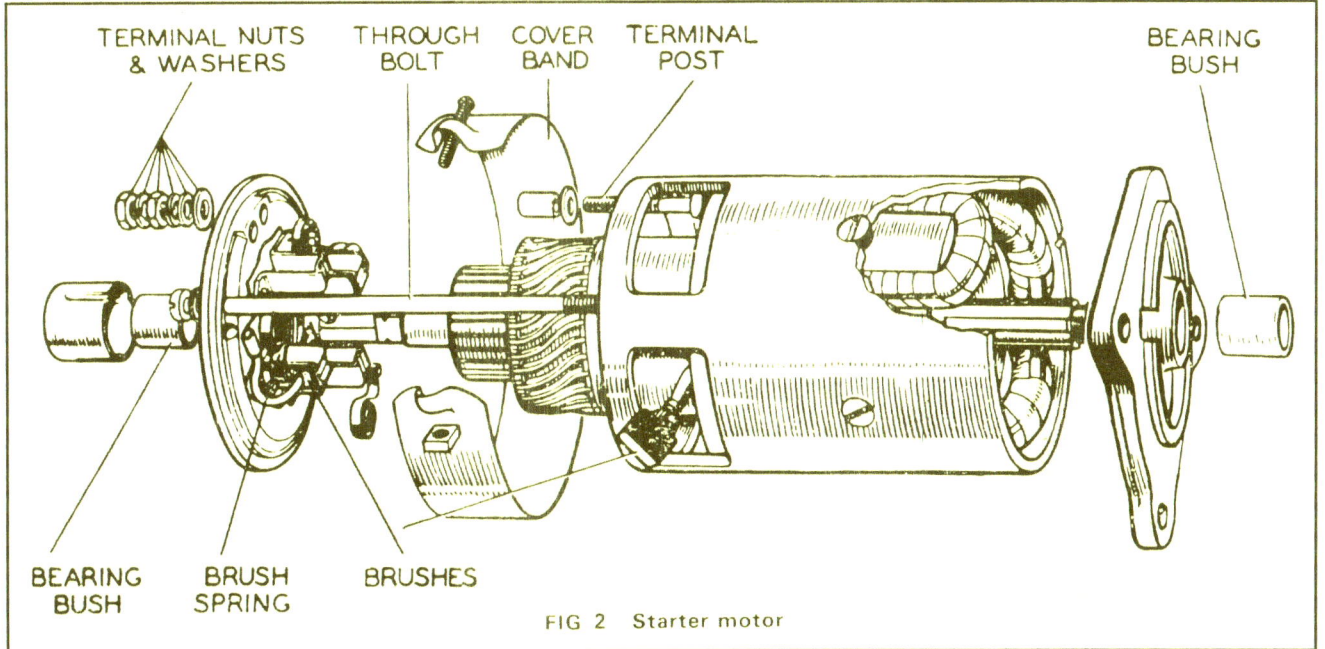

FIG 2 Starter motor

bulb lights it is still possible that there is a leakage path to earth in the coils. Check this by removing one lead and holding it against a clean part of the yoke. If the bulb lights then there is a connection to earth and the coils will require replacement with new ones.

Armature:

Examination of the armature may reveal the cause of failure, for example, conductors lifted from the commutator are due to the starter motor being engaged while the engine is running and thus causing the armature to be rotated at excessive speed. A damaged armature must in all cases be renewed—**no attempt should be made to machine the armature core or to true a distorted shaft.**

Bearings:

These are of porous bronze and renewing them is best left to a service agent because they must not be reamed after fitting.

Starter drive:
R.E. type:

Remove the retaining pin A (see **FIG 3**) from the centre sleeve B, and then slide the drive back along the shaft and remove the key C. Withdraw the drive unit from the shaft.

Remove the retaining ring D from the inside end of the pinion and barrel assembly E and then withdraw the pinion and barrel assembly and washers F.

Unscrew the locating nut G, this is held in position on the sleeve B by caulking and on reassembly will thus require a new sleeve. Remove the washer H, restraining spring J, control nut K and withdraw the screwed sleeve L. Remove the centre coupling plate M, friction washer N and rubber unit assembly O. Finally remove cushioning spring P and transmission plate Q.

Reassembly is the reverse of the preceeding operation.

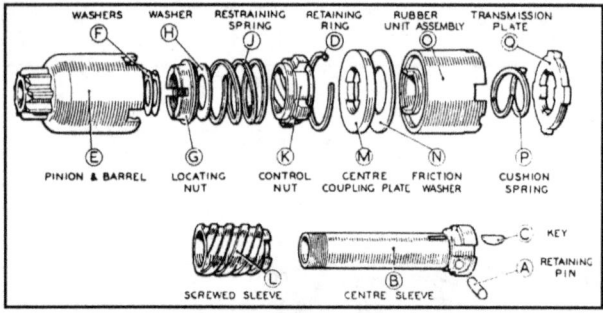

FIG 3 'R.E.' starter drive

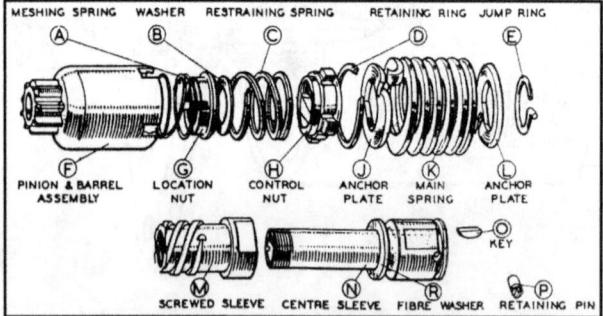

FIG 4 'Eclipse' starter drive

Eclipse type:

Press in the anchor plate L (see **FIG 4**) and main spring K and pull out the retaining pin P and then slide the drive back along the shaft and remove the key O. Withdraw the drive unit from the shaft.

Remove the retaining ring D from inside the end of the pinion and barrel assembly F and slide off the pinion and barrel assembly and meshing spring A. Unscrew the location nut G; this is held in position by caulking and thus on refitting a new sleeve N will be required.

Remove the washer B, restraining spring C, control nut H and withdraw the screwed sleeve M. Remove the anchor plate J, main spring K and fibre washer R. The anchor plate L can be removed from the centre sleeve assembly N by withdrawing the jump ring E.

Reassembly is the reverse of the dismantling procedure.

Both types of drive should be washed in petrol and allowed to dry. **Never lubricate the drive unit** as this will cause it to pick up dirt and it may sieze.

9 The control box—description

The control box (see **FIG 5**) contains the regulator and the cut-out. The regulator controls the generator output in accordance with the load on the battery and its state of charge.

The cut-out is an automatic switch for connecting or disconnecting the battery and the generator. This disconnection is necessary because the battery would otherwise discharge through the generator if it was stationary or running slowly.

10 The control box—settings
Regulator adjustment:

The regulator is carefully set during manufacture and should not require adjustment. However if the battery does not keep in a charged condition or becomes constantly overcharged, indicated by rapid evaporation of electrolyte, it may be advisable to check the settings. It is important before altering the regulator settings to check that the battery is not faulty or that the drive belt to the generator is not slipping.

Electrical setting:

The electrical setting can be checked without removing the cover from the control box. Withdraw the cables from the terminals marked A and A1 at the control box and join the wires together Connect the negative lead of a good quality 0-20-volt moving coil voltmeter to the D terminal on the generator and connect the other lead from the meter to a good chassis earth. Slowly increase the speed of the engine until the voltmeter needle flicks and then steadies; this should occur between the limits given in the Technical Data for the appropriate ambient temperature. If the voltage reading falls outside these limits adjust the regulator as follows:

Shut off the engine and remove the control box cover. Release the locknut holding the adjusting screw (see **FIG 5**) and turn the adjusting screw clockwise to raise the setting or anticlockwise to reduce it. Repeat the above until the correct setting is obtained. Do not run the engine above half throttle or false readings may be obtained. Remake the original wiring connections.

Mechanical setting—Refer to FIG 6.

1 Slacken the two armature fixing screws F and insert a .018-in feeler gauge between the back of the armature A and the regulator frame E.
2 Press the armature back against the frame and down on to the bobbin core D. Keep the gauge in position and lock screws F. Remove the feeler gauge.
3 Check the gap between the armature and the bobbin core. It should be within .012 to .020 in. If outside these limits add or remove shims C from behind the fixed contact.
4 Remove the gauge and press down the armature. The gap between the contacts should lie between .006 and .017 in.

Cut-out adjustment:

Electrical setting:

If the regulator setting is within the correct limits, but the battery is still not receiving current the cut-out may be out of adjustment. Remove the cable from the terminal marked A on the control box (ensuring the bared end does not come into contact with the chassis). Remove the voltmeter lead from the D terminal of the unit and connect it to terminal A. Run the engine as before at a fairly low speed; the cut-out should operate, when a voltmeter reading should be given of the same value for the regulator test. If there is no reading the cut-out setting may be badly out of adjustment. To check the voltage at which the cut-out operates, remove the control box cover, and reconnect the voltmeter to terminal D. Start the engine and slowly increase its speed until the cut-out contacts are seen to close, this should occur at 12.7 to 13.3 volts. If it does not, slacken the locknut on the cut-out adjusting screw and turn the screw clockwise to raise the voltage or anticlockwise to lower it. Repeat the test and continue to adjust until the correct reading is obtained. Tighten the locknut and remove the voltmeter.

Mechanical setting:

If for any reason the cut-out armature has to be removed from the frame, care must be taken to obtain the correct gap settings on reassembly. The correct settings can be obtained as follows:

Slacken the two armature fixing screws (see **FIG 7**) and also the two screws securing the fixed contact. Insert a .008 inch gauge between the back of the armature and the cut-out frame and a .011 to .015 inch gauge between the core face and the armature. A .005 inch brass shim is fitted to the underside of the armature and the gap must be measured between the core face and the underside of this shim.

Press the armature down and back against the two gauges and tighten the armature fixing screws. With the gauges still in position, set the gap between the armature and the stop plate to .030 to .034 inch.

Remove the gauges and tighten the screws securing the fixed contact. Insert a .025 inch gauge between the core face and the armature. Press the armature down to the gauge. The gap between the contacts should now measure .002 to .006 inch. Adjust the gap, if necessary, by adding or removing shims beneath the fixed contact plate.

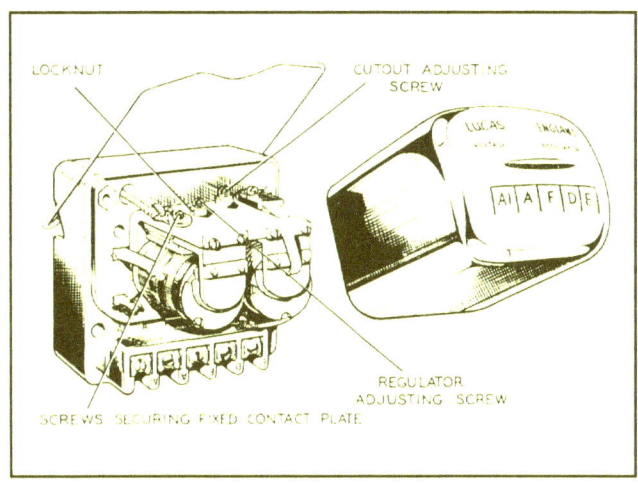

FIG 5 Control box

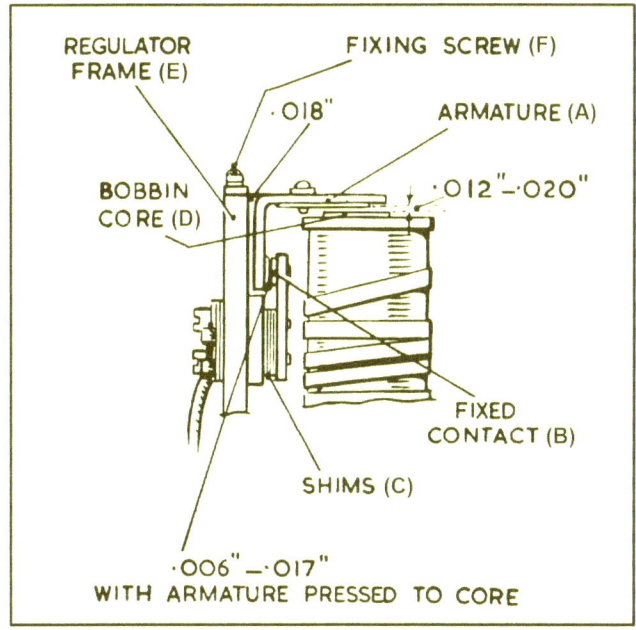

FIG 6 Regulator mechanical setting

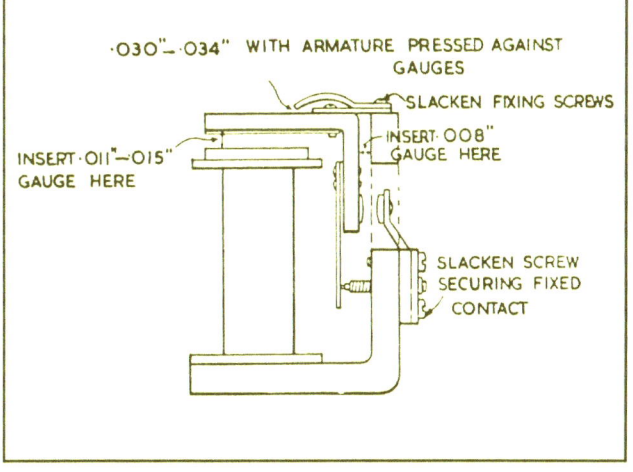

FIG 7 Cut-out mechanical setting

Fuse 1	Side and tail lights
Fuse 2	Headlamps and headlamp warning light
Fuse 3	Panel, interior lights and cigar lighter
Fuse 4	Carburetter, petrol gauge, windscreen wipers, air conditioner motor, stoplamps, horn relay, reverse lights flasher units.

FIG 8 Fuses Mk VII

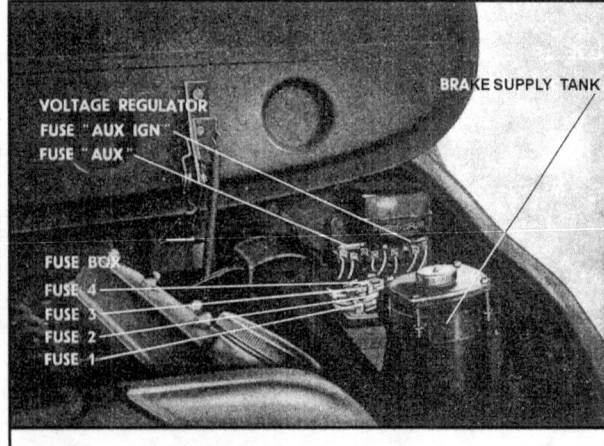

'Aux'	Interior lights
'Aux Ign'	Brake lights, petrol gauge, windscreen wipers, petrol warning light, flasher lights and flasher unit, horn relay, air conditioner motor.
Fuse 1	Cigar lighter
Fuse 2	Side, tail and reverse lights
Fuse 3	Headlamp dipper
Fuse 4	Headlamps and headlamp warning lamp.

FIG 9 Fuses XK 120

If the cut-out contacts appear burnt or dirty, place a strip of fine glasspaper between the contacts, then, with the contacts closed by hand, draw the paper through. This should be done two or three times with the rough side to each contact. **Do not use emery or a carborundum stone for cut-out contacts.**

11 Fuses

Should any component in the electrical system fail it is possible that the fuse protecting that circuit has blown. If a replacement of the correct capacity also blows this indicates a fault in the circuit and a careful examination should therefore be carried out to ascertain the fault. The fuses are located on the engine side of the scuttle and serve the various circuits as follows: (referring to **FIGS 8** and **9**).

12 Headlamps

Pre-focused headlamps require no adjustment when a new bulb is fitted provided the lamp is already correctly set. To replace the bulb proceed as follows:

Remove the front rim by unscrewing the securing screw (see **FIG 10**) and lifting off rim. Slacken the four screws which secure the flange of the light unit and turn the unit in an anticlockwise direction to detach the flange from the securing screws, when the light unit can be lifted out of the lamp body. Twist the back shell in an anticlockwise direction and pull it off (see **FIG 11**). The bulb can then be removed. Refitting is the reverse of the foregoing procedure.

Beam setting:

Accurate beam setting is best left to a service station but adjustment may be made by the owner if desired. The adjusting screws for the headlamp both horizontal and vertical are exposed on removal of the front rim. Screwing in any of the screws will adjust the beam towards that screw.

The fog lamps are similar to the headlamps except that the adjustment screws are also the securing screws. This means that the screws should not be turned to remove the lamp or the beam setting will be affected. The lamp is removed by pushing in against the springs on the screws and twisting.

13 Trafficators and flasher units

Trafficators:

In normal service the trafficators require very little maintenance apart from lubrication. To lubricate the trafficator arm apply **one drop** of thin machine oil to the catch pin as indicated in **FIG 12**.

Bulb replacement is effected by removing the screw at the end of the arm and sliding off the arm cover. When replacing the arm cover, slide it along the arm until the side plates engage with the slots below the pivot bearing.

Flasher unit:

These cannot be dismantled for subsequent reassembly. In the event of failure, first check the bulbs and the fuse. If in order the appropriate wiring diagram in the Technical Data may be referred to and the flasher circuit connections checked over.

Then switch on the ignition and check that the positive, B terminal is at 12 volts. Finally connect together terminals B and L at the flasher unit and operate the direction indicator switch if the lamps now work the unit is defective and must be renewed.

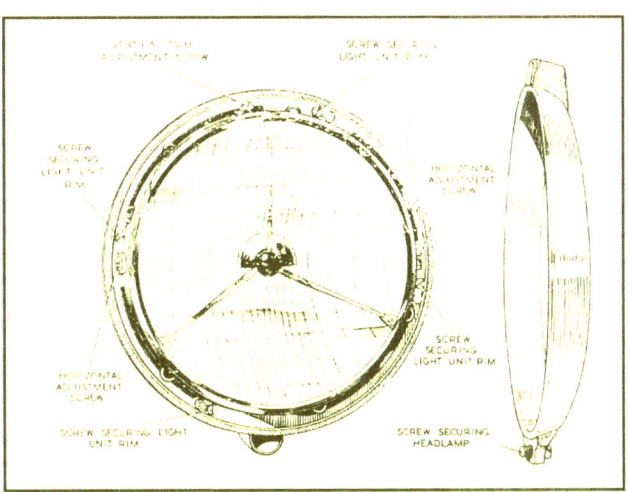

FIG 10 Headlamp beam adjustment

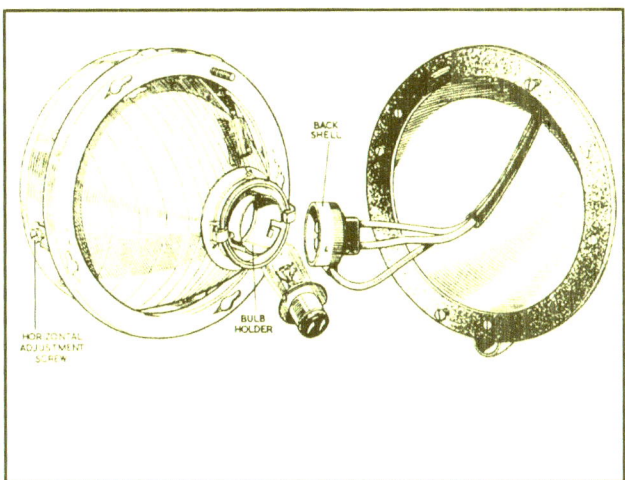

FIG 11 Headlamp bulb replacement

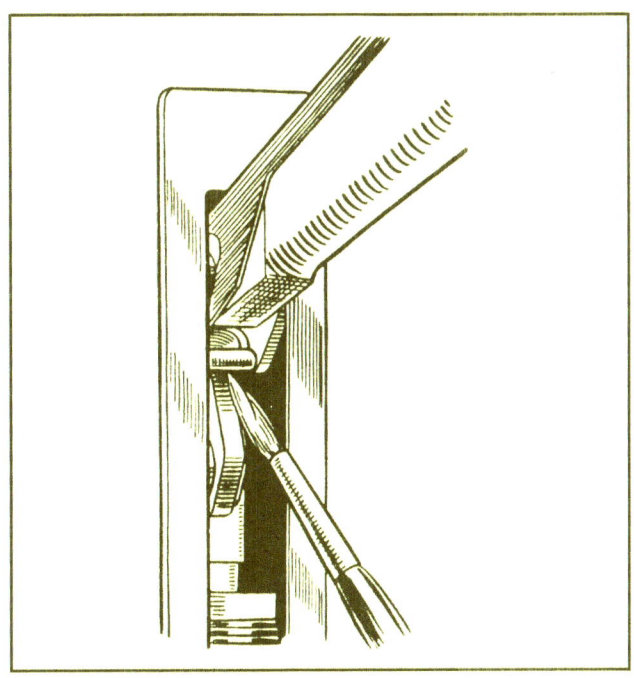

FIG 12 Trafficator lubrication

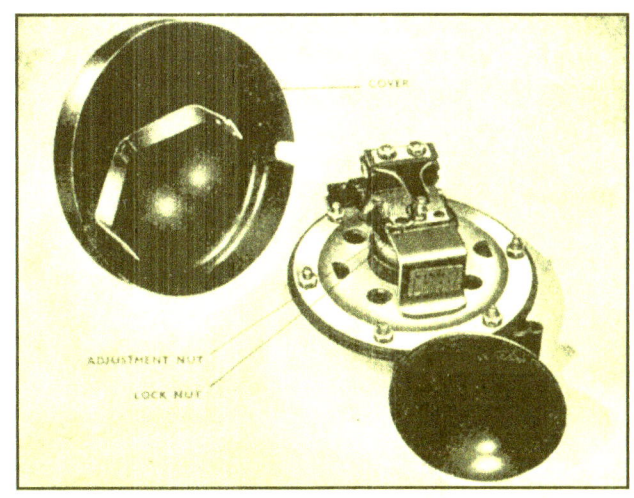

FIG 13 Horn

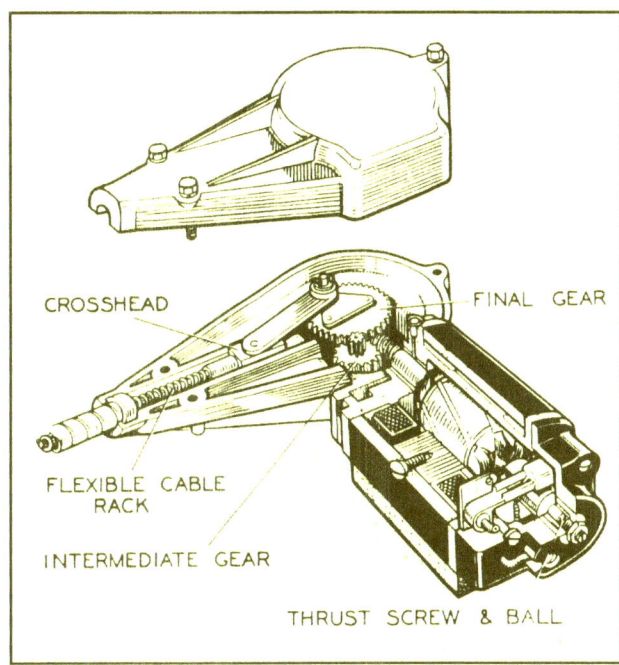

FIG 14 Windscreen wiper motor single speed

14 Horn

If one of the horns fails or falters it does not follow that the horn has broken down. First check the wiring connections and the securing bolts as both may affect the horn performance. If no faults can be found the horn may require adjustment. Adjustment does not alter the pitch or the note but merely takes up the wear of moving parts. When adjusting one of the horns disconnect the other horn and short out the fuse to prevent it blowing. Remove the horn from its supporting bracket by releasing the two securing bolts. Remove the centre screw from the domed cover and lift off the cover. Remove the two wiring connections and lift the horn clear. To adjust slacken the locknut on the fixed contact (see **FIG 13**) and rotate the adjusting nut until the contacts are just separated. Then turn the adjusting nut half a turn in the opposite direction and secure it in this position by tightening the locknut. Replace the horn in position and test it. If it still fails to operate it will require renewal.

15 Windscreen wipers

Apart from the renewal of perished wiper blades the windscreen wipers require no periodic maintenance. To ensure their efficient operation, however the windscreen must be kept clean. Oil and tar spots should be removed with methylated spirits. **Do not use wax or silicon based polishes on the windscreen.**

Servicing:

If the wiper fails to operate, or operates unsatisfactorily, switch on the wiper and note the current being supplied to the motor, either on the panel ammeter or preferably on a 0-20-amp moving coil ammeter connected in the wiper circuit. Then proceed as follows:

1 Wiper takes no current:

Examine the fuse protecting the wiper. If it has blown, examine the wiring of the motor circuit, and that of all other circuits protected by the fuse, for evidence of chafed leads or shortcircuits. Replace any leads that are found faulty.

2 Wiper takes abnormally low current:

First ensure that the battery is not discharged. If the current is that normally taken by the field coils only (see Technical Data), a fault in the armature or brush gear must be suspected.

Remove the screws securing the commutator end cover (see **FIG 14**) and lift off cover. Clean the commutator with a cloth moistened with petrol, and carefully remove any carbon dust from between the commutator segments. Check that the brushes bear firmly on the commutator. If they are loose, and do not make contact, the tension spring must be removed. If they are stiff they should be freed by working them backwards and forwards by hand.

3 Wiper takes abnormally high current:

The normal current is given in the Technical Data. If the ammeter reading is in excess of this the commutator, armature or bearings may be at fault. Check that the armature can rotate freely. Remove the commutator cover and clean the commutator paying particular attention to any pieces of carbon that may be short circuiting adjacent segments.

Remove the brush gear and withdraw the two screws securing the fibre plate. Pull the plate carefully away from the motor body and examine the two leads to the field coils for signs of short circuiting. If there are signs of this failure unsolder the leads, slip a new piece of sleeving over the leads and reconnect them.

If the performance of the motor is still unsatisfactory, the fault may be due to the armature which can only be checked by substitution. Renew if necessary. Excess current consumption may also be caused by friction in the driving cable caused by sharp bends in the cable, check that there are no sharp bends and if necessary add suitable packing under the motor mounting bolts to straighten the run of the cables.

4 Motor operates but does not drive the arms:

Examine the wiper arms making sure that they are firmly secured to their spindles. Remove the cover of the gearbox and examine the gearbox. Rotation of the armature should cause a push-pull motion of the cable rack. If it does not and components are found to be faulty the gearbox will require renewal.

Self-parking adjustment:

On models fitted with a two-speed wiper motor the mechanism incorporates a self-parking adjustment. This adjustment is to ensure that in the parked position. the wiper blades come to rest along the windscreen lower edge. The adjusting screw is adjacent to the cable outlet on the motor gearbox. To raise the parked position. the adjuster should be tuned clockwise and to lower turned anticlockwise.

16 Fault diagnosis

(a) Battery discharged

1 Terminals dirty or loose
2 Lighting circuit shorted
3 Generator not charging
4 Regulator or cut-out not working properly
5 Battery faulty

(b) Insufficient charging current

1 Loose or corroded battery terminals
2 Generator driving belt slipping

(c) Battery will not hold charge

1 Low electrolyte level
2 Battery plates suphated
3 Electrolyte leakage from battery
4 Plate separators ineffective

(d) Battery overcharged

1 Voltage regulator needs adjusting

(e) Generator output low or nil

1 Belt broken or slipping
2 Regulator unit out of adjustment
3 Worn bearings, loose pole pieces
4 Commutator worn burnt or shorted
5 Armature shaft bent or worn
6 Insulation proud between commutator segments
7 Brush sticking, springs weak or broken
8 Field coil wire shorted, broken or burned

(f) Starter motor lacks power or will not operate

1 Battery discharged, loose cable connections
2 Starter pinion jammed in mesh with flywheel gear
3 Starter switch or solenoid faulty
4 Brushes worn or sticking, leads detached or shorting
5 Commutator dirty or worn
6 Starter shaft bent
7 Engine abnormally stiff

(g) Starter motor runs but does not turn engine

1 Pinion sticking on sleeve
2 Broken teeth on pinion or flywheel gears

(h) Noisy starter pinion when engine is running

1 Restraining spring weak or broken

(j) Starter motor inoperative
1 Check 1 and 4 in (f)
2 Armature or field coils faulty

(k) Starter motor rough or noisy
1 Mounting bolts loose
2 Damaged pinion or flywheel gear teeth
3 Main pinion spring broken

(l) Lamps inoperative or erratic
1 Battery low, bulbs burned out
2 Faulty earth of lamps or battery
3 Wiring switch faulty, loose or broken wiring connections

(m) Wiper motor sluggish, taking high current
1 Faulty armature
2 Bearings out of alignment
3 Commutator dirty of short circuited
4 Wheelbox spindle binding, cable rack tight in housing housing

(n) Wiper motor operates but does not drive arms
1 Wheelbox gear and spindle worn
2 Cable rack faulty
3 Gearbox components worn

(o) Fuel gauge does not register
1 No battery supply to gauge
2 Gauge casing not earthed
3 Cable between gauge and tank unit earthed

(p) Fuel gauge registers 'Full'
1 Cable between gauge and tank unit broken or disconnected

NOTES

INDEX – BODYWORK, AIR CONDITIONING & HEATER

SECTION	PAGE	
001	257	Body Damage & Repair
002	257	Door Trim Panels Removal & Replacement
003	257	Door Locks Removal
004	258	Door Locks Maintenance, Lubrication & Adjustment
005	258	Door Glass Removal & Replacement
006	259	Window Winders Removal & Replacement
007	260	Sliding (Sun) Roof, Maintenance, Removal & Replacement
008	261	Facia (Instrument) Panel, Removal & Replacement
009	262	Air Conditioning & Heater

BODYWORK - SERVICE

1 Body finishing

It is almost inevitable that the bodywork of the older car will suffer from some superficial damage at least. In remedying this a perfect finish can only be obtained by exercising initial care in removing all traces of rust, levelling up and rubbing down. It is most important that rust traces are removed thoroughly or the work carried out will have to be repeated due to the very rapid spread of rust which will occur. Spray painting is the best method of matching new paintwork with old, but it is a good idea to leave large areas to the expert. The same thing applies to the repair of severe damage to sheet metalwork, where the specialist technique of panel-beating is not usually within the powers of the amateur. It is tempting to knock out small dents with a hammer, but too much beating may result in stretching the metal causing it to pop in and out. It is a far better plan to fill such dents.

If a filler such as primer surfacer or paste stopper is used it is essential to remove any wax polish from the original finish by the use of a solvent such as white spirit. When the filler has dried, rub it down with 400 grade 'wet or dry' paper until the surface is smooth and flush with the surrounding area. Apply the retouching paint by spray, keeping it wet in the centre and light and dry around the edges. After a few hours of drying time, use a cutting compound to remove the dry spray and finish with liquid polish. Colour matching old and new paint is extremely difficult so it is preferable to spray a complete wing rather than a small patch.

2 Door trim panels

Removal:

Remove the door capping by unscrewing the four screws (see **FIG 1**). Prise up the felt strip which is tacked to the door facia capping. Unscrew the four screws at the top of the door facia capping and remove the capping by lifting it upwards, to disengage the spring clips from their holes in the door panel.

From underneath the arm rest unscrew the two drive screws and remove the rest by lifting it upwards. Remove the door lock safety catch by unscrewing the centre screw. Remove the securing screw from the bottom of the door handle and remove the handle. Detach the door lock trigger and handle clip by removing the securing screws.

Push back the sleeve in the centre of the window winder escutcheon, drive out the securing pin and remove the handle and escutcheon.

On the front doors remove the tool compartment push-button escutcheon by rotating it anticlockwise.

Carefully pull back the trim from the top of the door panel and remove the trim casing by prising outwards to release the spring clips from their holes in the edge of the door panel.

On the XK 120 models the door trim casing is secured in position by screws and hence these must be removed before attempting to release the trim casing.

Refitting is the reverse of the removal procedure.

3 Door locks — removal

Mk VII

Remove the door trim casing as described in the preceeding section. Remove the setscrew 9 (see **FIG 2**) securing the outer door frame pillar. Wind the window up fully to allow movement of the door glass frame. Remove the four screws securing the lock in position on the door edge. Remove the two screws securing the inside handle remote control and the two screws securing the door lock catch (not fitted to drivers door). On the door edge turn the toggle catch to the fully down position, withdraw the lock to the inside of the door and remove the lock assembly through the aperture in the door panel.

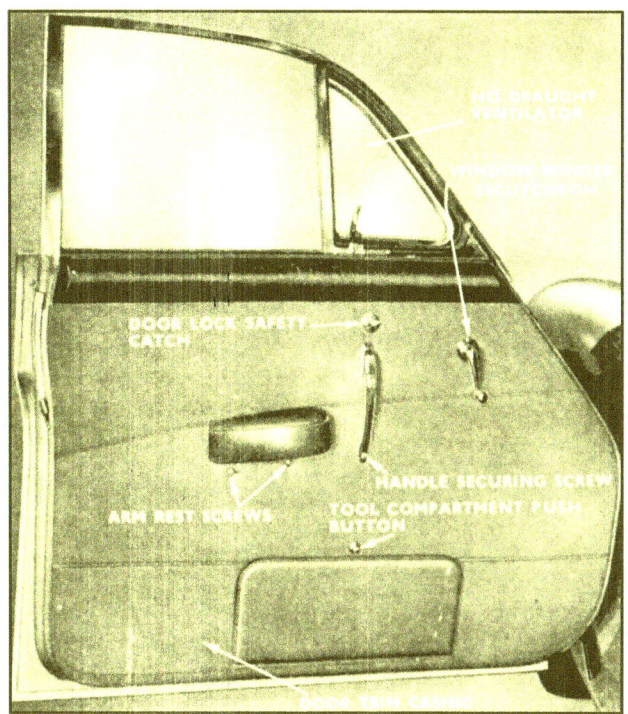

FIG 1   Door trim removal

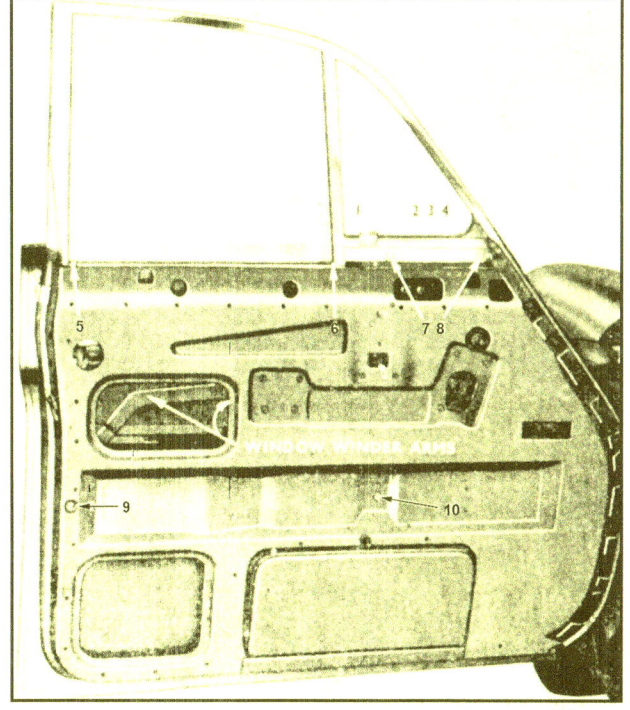

FIG 2   Front door glass removal Mk VII

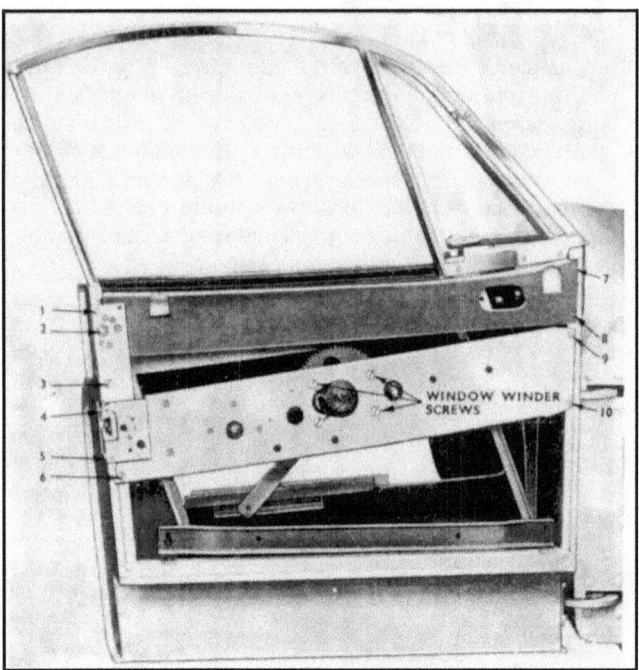

FIG 3 Front door glass removal XK 120

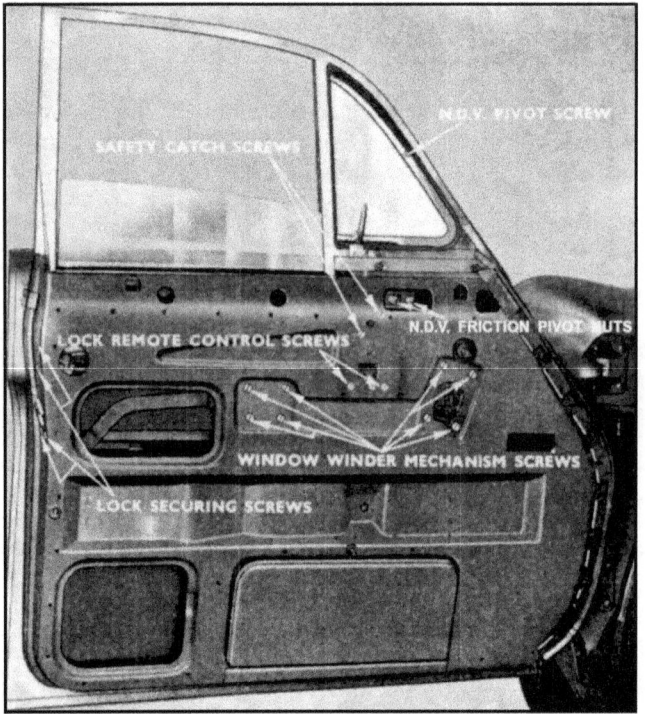

FIG 4 Window winder removal front Mk VII

XK 120 Super sports:

Remove the door trim casing as previously described. Remove the door pocket by unscrewing the two screws at each side and lifting it outwards. Operate the door lock safety catch until the splitpin securing the link from the lock to the safety catch is visible through the hole at the top rear of the door. Remove the splitpin and disconnect the link arm noting the flat and belleville washer. Remove the five countersunk screws and nuts securing the door lock to the door panel and withdraw the lock from inside. To remove the door lock safety catch and link, unscrew the two countersunk screws securing the catch to the door panel and withdraw the catch through the hole in the door panel.

XK 120 Fixed head coupé:

Remove the door trim casing as previously described. Remove the door lock supporting plates (see **FIG 3**) by removing the ten screws securing them, complete with the window winder mechanism withdrawing the window winder arm from its slide channel. Lower the glass to the bottom of the frame. The door lock is now accessible on the inside of the door lock support plates and can be dismantled as necessary.

In all cases refitting is the reverse of the removal procedure.

4 Door locks — maintenance

Lubrication:

At the recommended mileage lubricate the door hinges, boot lid hinges and locks, and the door locking mechanism with an oil can filled with S.A.E. 30 lubricating oil. Check that all body screws, nuts and bolts are secure and tighten as necessary.

Adjustment:

Adjustment of the door striker plate should only be necessary when the striker itself has been renewed. However if the nose of the striker plate is badly worn, a new striker plate must be fitted and carefully positioned by a process of trial and error which can be proved by checking the door closing action and the position of the door when closed. Slacken off the striker securing screws just enough to allow the striker to be tapped into a slightly different position and retighten the screws. When the striker is correctly positioned the door will close easily without apparent lift or drop.

If the striker plate is adjusted to its full limit and the positioning is not correct the door may be adjusted positionally by the addition or subtraction of shims between the door hinge and the hinge panel. Shims may be placed under the striker plate if it is necessary to bring the plate closer to the door.

5 Renewing glass

Front Mk VII model:

Remove the door trim casing as described in **Section 2**.

Slacken the two no draught ventilator friction pivot nuts (see **FIG 4**) accessible through the aperture in the door panel. Remove the screw securing the no draught ventilator frame to the pivot. Then remove the ventilator by lifting upwards to withdraw the spindle at the bottom of the frame from the friction pivot clamping plates.

Remove the ten screws (see **FIG 2**) securing the glass frame to the door. Note that the two centre screws 2 and 3 in the ventilator surround rubber channel secure the ventilator friction pivot brackets, which should be held during the removal of the screws and nuts, and withdrawn through the aperture in the door panel.

Wind the window fully down and lift the glass frame upwards and tilt towards the inside edge of the door so that the brackets at the bottom of the frame clear the aperture at the top of the door. Wind the window up until the outer window arm is visible through the door aperture (see **FIG 2**). Slide the window inwards and disengage the window arm from the guide channel. Wind the window up fully, disengage the inner winder arm from the guide channel and withdraw the glass. Note the position of all washers and packing pieces on removing so that they may be refitted in their correct positions.

Rear Mk VII model:

Remove the door trim casing as described in **Section 2** (see **FIG 5**). Remove the following: the eight screws securing the glass frame to the door panel, the ventilator rubber surround screws 1 and 2, the securing screws of the ventilator 3 and 4, the securing screws 5 and 6, the screw and nut 7 with its packing pieces and screw 8 which is accessible through the hole in the edge of the door panel.

Pull the glass frame and glass bodily outwards to clear the door aperture and withdraw the frame upwards. Wind the window up fully, disengage the window arm from the guide channel and remove the glass.

The no draught ventilator is removed by unscrewing the screw and nut securing the operating arm to the slide plate on the glass frame, opening the ventilator fully and removing the four screws at its hinge.

XK 120 model:

Remove the door trim casing as previously described. Remove the door lock support plates by removing the ten screws indicated in **FIG 3** and withdrawing the winder arm from the slide channel. Lower the glass to the bottom of the frame.

Turn back the outer end of the door glass felt and remove the screw 1 (see **FIG 6**) securing the chromium plate frame to the door panel. Remove the five remaining screws indicated in **FIG 6**. Hold the door glass in at the bottom of the frame and remove as an assembly by lifting upwards.

The no draught ventilator may be removed in the following manner:

Open the ventilator fully and remove the screw and nut securing the operating arm to the slide plate on the glass frame. Pull back the rubber at the bottom end of the channel and remove the screw securing the pivot block to the channel. Gently tap the pivot block out of the channel and release the ventilator from its top pivot.

In all cases the refitting procedure is the reverse of that described for removal.

6 Window winders

On the Mk VII model remove the glass and frame as described in the preceeding section on the XK 120 model remove the door trim casing as described in **Section 2**.

Remove the window winder securing screws as indicated in **FIGS 3, 4** and **5**, and then withdraw the window winder mechanism through the door aperture. Failure of the window winder mechanism occurs only after considerable useage and is normally due to wear on the operating gear teeth. The mechanism should in this case be renewed as a complete unit.

Refitting is the reverse of the removal procedure.

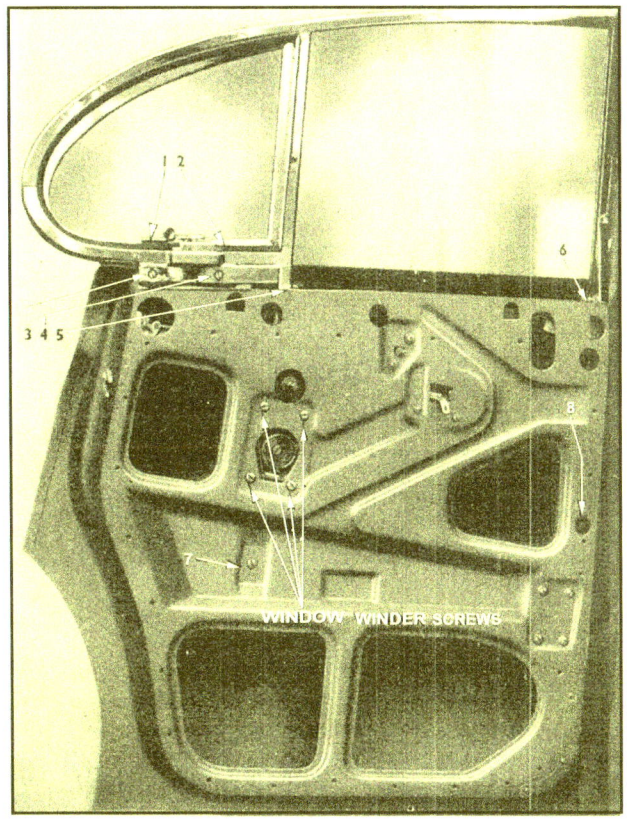

FIG 5 Window winder removal rear Mk VII

FIG 6 Ventilator removal XK 120

FIG 7 Sliding roof

Cleaning is best carried out by using compressed air, if this is not readily available then it is possible to use a thin cane or a flexible cable. The front outlet holes for the sliding roof are accessible with the roof open, but to gain access to the rear outlet holes it will be necessary to remove the sliding roof.

Removal:

Open the sliding roof approximately 4 inch; do not open any further than this amount or the top of the roof panel may be scratched on removal. Remove the two side polished wood capings by unscrewing the securing screws and withdrawing downwards. Remove the screw securing each slide bracket (see **FIG 7**) and press the brackets outwards to clear the channel slide rails. Raise the front edge of the roof panel and withdraw the panel forwards.

Refitting:

Enter the locking bar into the slot at the rear edge of the sliding roof and push it back until the panel will enter the aperture. Replace the slide brackets in position and centralize them with a pointed instrument pulling the brackets fully inwards to ensure correct location of the securing screws. Refit the two slide bracket retaining screws, centralize the sliding roof panel and tighten the screws. Refit the polished wood cappings.

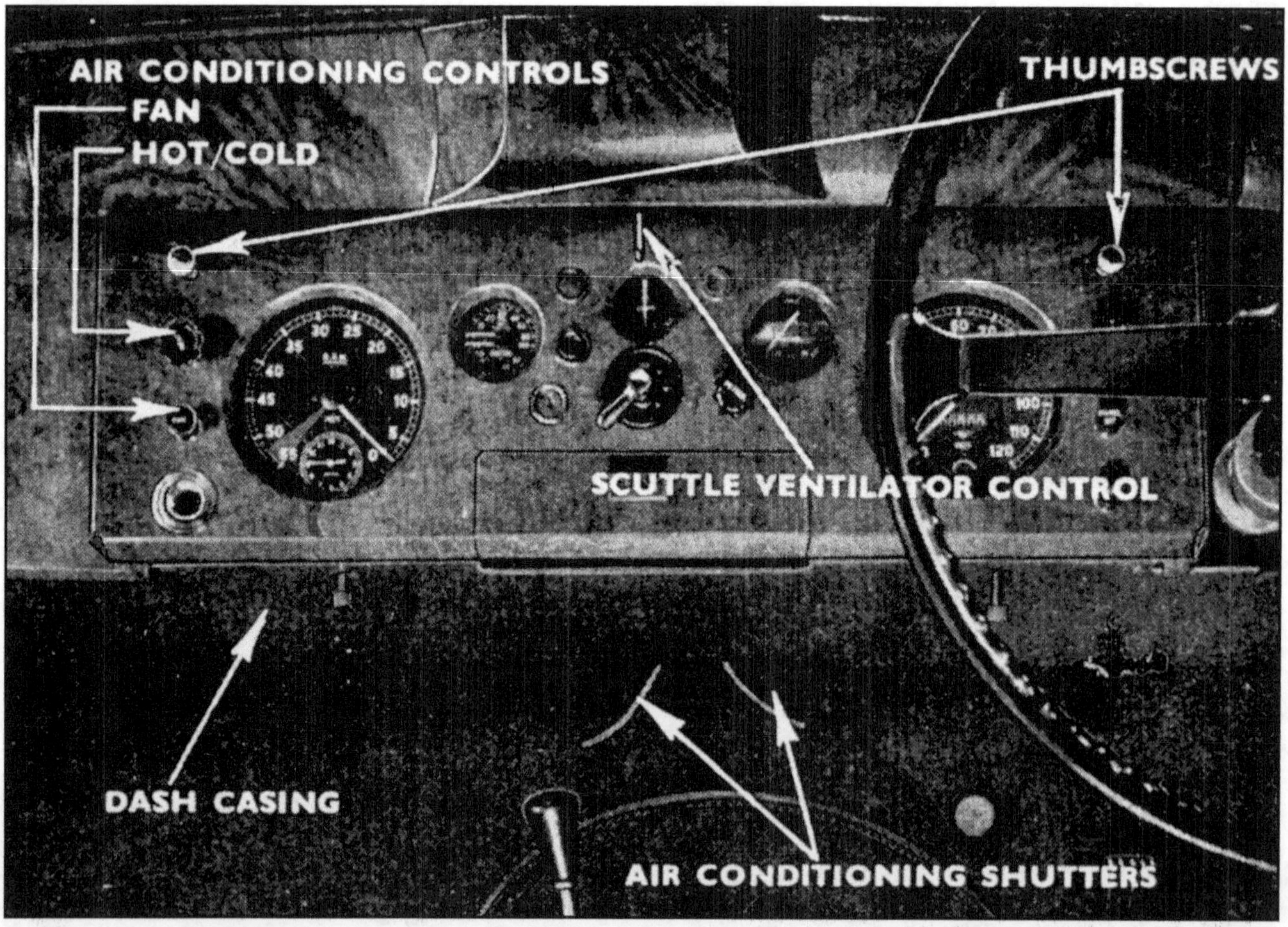

7 Sliding roof

Maintenance:

It is advisable to clear out the sliding roof drain tubes situated in each corner periodically or if it is suspected that the tubes are blocked.

FIG 8 Facia Mk VII

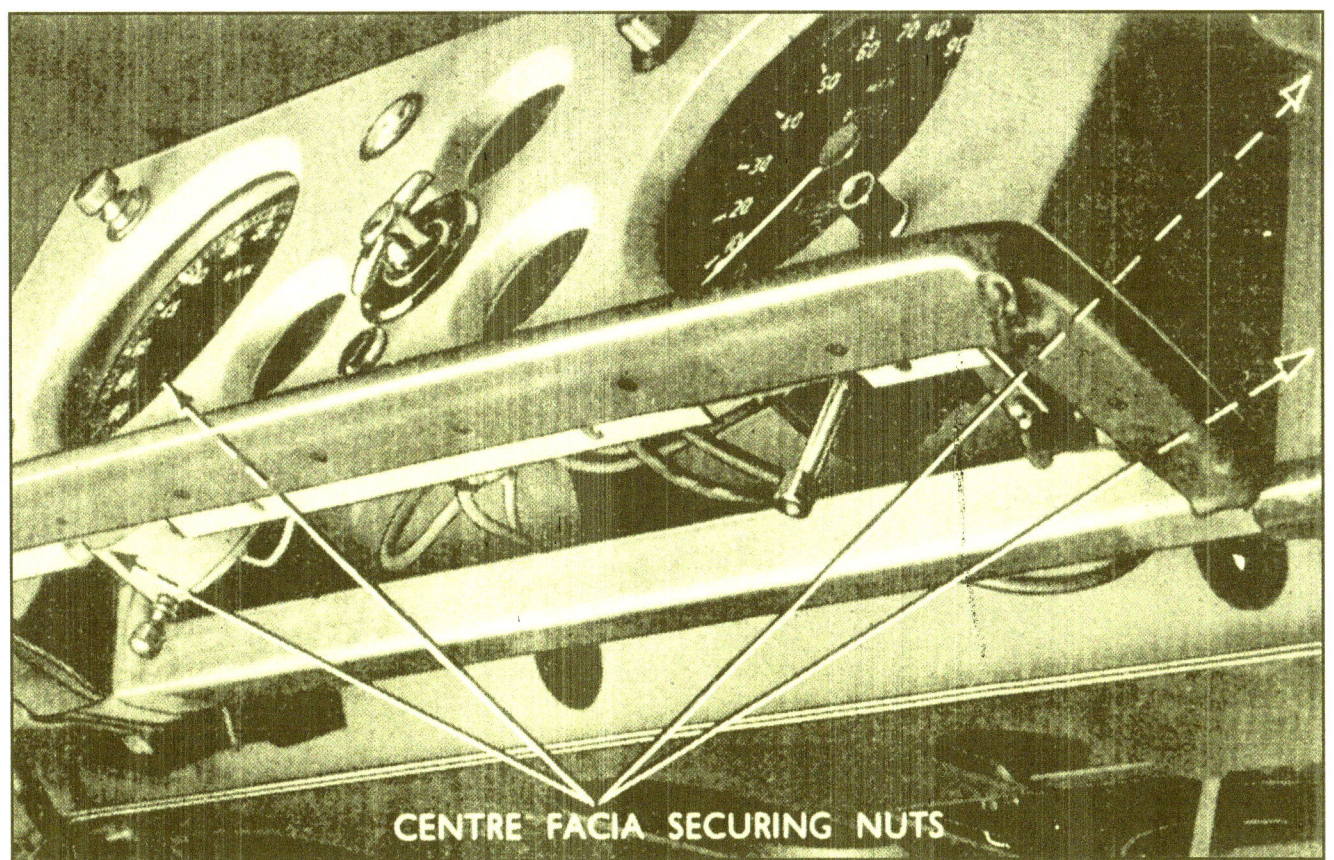

FIG 9 Facia XK 120

8 Removing facia panel

Disconnect the battery positive lead. Remove the two drive screws securing the dash casing to the centre facia panel. Remove the seven control knobs all of which are retained by a spring loaded pin registering in a hole in the knob. Remove the cigar lighter and the ignition key. Unscrew and remove the bolt on either side, securing the lower edge of the facia to the support brackets. Unscrew the two thumb screws situated at the top corners of the facia panel (see **FIG 8**), withdraw the glove drawer slightly and remove the facia panel.

XK 120 Super sports model:

Remove the trim casing from above the facia by removing the thirteen drive screws. Disconnect the battery positive lead and remove the two nuts or setscrews from each side of the instrument panel securing the panel to the facia structure (see **FIG 9**) then disconnect the speedometer and revolution counter cables at the rear of the instruments by unscrewing the knurled securing nuts. Disconnect the oil pressure and water temperature gauges from the rear of the facia by removing the retaining plates. Disconnect all electrical wires from the instruments marking them so that they may be reconnected in their correct locations.

Set the road wheels in the straight-ahead position. Disconnect the manette control wire from the horn relay box fitted to the wing valance on the steering column side. Unscrew the two grubscrews in the steering wheel hub and withdraw the manette control complete with the wiring harness. Rotate the steering wheel knurled adjusting ring until it is free and remove the circlip at the top of the splined portion of the steering column. Draw off the steering wheel and remove the washers and telescopic dust cover.

Remove the grab rail from the passengers side by unscrewing the two nuts at the rear of the facia. If a heater is fitted disconnect the fan switch. Unscrew the four screws securing the facia to the dash and remove the facia.

Refitting is the reverse of the removal procedure but attention should be paid to the following instructions when refitting the steering wheel and manette control. Set the road wheels to the straight-ahead position. Fit the telescopic dust cover and washers to the inner column and engage the steering wheel on the splines so that one spoke is at the top centre position. Fit the circlip to the annular groove in the top of the column. Pass the horn wire down the centre of the inner column and enter the manette control tube into the keyway of the stator tube rotating it slightly in either direction. Push the manette control fully home into the steering wheel hub and secure with two grubscrews inserted through the side of the steering wheel hub.

If when the manette control tube has been engaged with the stator tube, the head of the Jaguar on the horn push is not upright, it may be repositioned by slackening the clamp bolt in the bracket attached to the bottom end plate of the steering box.

On the other XK 120 models it is not necessary to remove the instrument connections or the steering wheel to remove the facia panel which is secured in the same manner as the super sports model.

FIG 10 Temperature control tap XK 120

9 Air conditioning equipment

Description:

The air conditioning equipment consists of a centrifugal fan and a heater unit. The fan draws air from outside the car and passes it over the heater unit into the interior of the car. The heater unit is a small radiator which is connected into the engine cooling water system, the rate of water flow through the unit being controlled by a temperature valve. This valve is directly operated in the engine compartment on the XK 120 models (see **FIG 10**) or remotely on the facia panel as on the Mk VII model (see **FIG 8**).

Operation:

By utilizing a suitable combination of the settings a flow of cold or heated air can be obtained to deal with any of the varying climatic conditions liable to be met. Examples of suggested settings are given as a guide as follows:

Unit not in use	Close scuttle ventilator Switch the fan to 'Off' Close the gallery shutters Turn the temperature control to 'Cold'
Demisting with cold air	Open scuttle ventilator Switch the fan to 'On' Close the gallery shutters Turn the temperature control to 'Cold'
Cold air conditioning and demisting	Open scuttle ventilator Switch the fan to 'On' Open the gallery shutters Turn the temperature control to 'Cold'
Demisting with hot air	Open scuttle ventilator Switch fan to 'On' Close the gallery shutters Turn the termperature control to 'Hot'
Warm air conditioning and demisting	Open scuttle ventilator Switch fan to 'On' Open the gallery shutters Turn the temperature control to 'Hot'

No scuttle ventilator is fitted to the XK 120 models so that reference for this in the control settings should be ignored for these models.

FIG 11 Heater and fan unit

Heater unit removal:

Mk VII:

Drain the cooling system with the car standing on level ground by opening the radiator drain tap situated at the top lefthand side of the radiator block, and the engine drain tap situated at the lefthand rear of the cylinder block. If the cooling system contains antifreeze the mixture should be collected in clean containers. Turn the temperature control knob to the 'Hot' position or the water in the heater unit will be isolated from the engine system and will not drain out.

From underneath the facia panel remove the dash casing by unscrewing the drive screws. Disconnect the two demister hoses from the heater stub pipes, which protrude through the scuttle, by slackening the securing clips.

Remove the rubber elbow of the inlet and outlet pipes from the temperature control tap and the front face of the heater casing (see **FIG 11**) respectively. Remove the four bolts securing the brackets at the rear of the heater casing to the scuttle. At the hose between the fan unit and the heater casing, slacken the clip securing the hose to the heater casing and withdraw the heater unit.

Refitting is the reverse of the removal procedure but ensure that the 'T' shaped end of the water tap control rod is engaged with the slot in the water tap connection when offering up the heater unit to the scuttle.

Heater unit removal:

XK 120:

Drain the cooling system as described for the Mk VII model.

From underneath the facia panel remove the dash casing by unscrewing the drive screws. Remove the three nuts and one setscrew from the top of the heater box at the rear of the engine compartment. At the top of the heater box slacken the bottom clip of the hose connecting the water tap unit. Slacken the lower clip of the rubber elbow connecting the outlet pipe to the heater unit (see **FIG 11**).

From inside the car lower the heater unit; disconnect the electrical wires and demister hoses, if fitted, and remove the heater, taking care not to spill any water retained in the heater unit.

Refitting is the reverse of the removal procedure.

NOTES

INDEX - APPENDIX

PAGE

265   GENERAL DATA

266   TECHNICAL SPECIFICATIONS

278   TUNING DATA

283   LUBRICATION & ROUTINE MAINTENANCE

WIRING DIAGRAMS

Page	Diagram No.	Description	Drive	Signal Type
286	W79600	3 ½ LITRE MK. VII 1951-1952 Chassis Nos. 710001-711801	RHD	(Trafficators)
287	W79602	3 ½ LITRE MK. VII 1952-1953 Chassis Nos. 711802-716016	RHD	(Trafficators)
288	W35250-1	3 ½ LITRE MK. VII 1953-1954 Chassis Nos. 716017-722754	RHD	(Trafficators)
289	W79601-1	3 ½ LITRE MK. VII 1951-1952 Chassis Nos. 710001-711801	RHD	(Turn Signals)
290	W79603	3 ½ LITRE MK. VII 1952-1953 Chassis Nos. 711802-716016	RHD	(Turn Signals)
291	W35251	3 ½ LITRE MK. VII 1953-1954 Chassis Nos. 716017 Onwards	RHD	(Turn Signals)
292	W79620	3 ½ LITRE MK. VII 1951-1952 Chassis Nos. 730001-732208	LHD	(Trafficators)
293	W79621-1	3 ½ LITRE MK. VII 1951-1952 Chassis Nos. 730000 Onwards	LHD	(Turn Signals)
294	W79622	3 ½ LITRE MK. VII 1952-1953 Chassis Nos. 732209-736521	LHD	(Trafficators)
295	W79623	3 ½ LITRE MK. VII 1952-1953 Chassis Nos. 732209-736521	LHD	(Turn Signals)
296	W35260-1	3 ½ LITRE MK. VII 1953-1954 Chassis Nos. 736522-738183	LHD	(Trafficators)
297	W35261-1	3 ½ LITRE MK. VII 1953-1954 Chassis Nos. 736522-738183	LHD	(Turn Signals)
298	W94601	XK120 1950-1954 - RHD		
299	W94641	XK120 1950-1954 - LHD		
300	W94602	XK120 1952-1954 Fixed Head Coupe RHD & LHD		
301	W835251	MK. VIII 1957 RHD & LHD (September 1957 publication date)		
302	W835251B	MK. VIII 1957-1958 RHD & LHD (June 1958 publication date)		
303	J86-793	XK140 1955 RHD & LHD		
304	W05494081	MK.IX 1958-1960 RHD & LHD (March 1959 publication date)		
305	J86-795	XK150 1957 RHD & LHD		
306	W54945600	XK150 1959 RHD & LHD (January 1960 publication date)		

GENERAL DATA

Models	Mk VII	Mk VIII	Mk IX	XK 120	XK 140	XK 150
Year of manufacture	1951-57	1957-59	1958-61	1949-54	1954-57	1957-61
Track:						
Front	4 ft. 8 in.	4 ft. 8½ in.	4 ft. 8 in.	4 ft. 3 in.	4 ft. 3 in.	4 ft. 3⅝ in.
Rear	4 ft. 9½ in.	4 ft. 10 in.	4 ft. 10 in.	4 ft. 2 in.	4 ft. 3½ in.	4 ft. 3⅝ in.
Wheelbase	10 ft.	10 ft.	10 ft.	8 ft. 6 in.	8 ft. 6 in.	8 ft. 6 in.
Turning circle	36 ft.	36 ft.	36 ft.	31 ft.	33 ft.	33 ft.
Ground clearance	7½ in.	7½ in.	7½ in.	7⅛ in.	7⅛ in.	7⅛ in.
Height	5 ft. 3 in.	5 ft. 3 in.	5 ft. 3 in.	Sports 4 ft. 4½ in. Coupé 4 ft. 5 in.	D.H. Coupé 4 ft. 5½ in. F.H. Coupé 4 ft. 7 in.	D.H. Coupé 4 ft. 7 in. F.H. Coupé 4 ft. 7 in.
Width	6 ft. 1 in.	6 ft. 1 in.	6 ft. 1 in.	5 ft. 2 in.	5 ft. 4½ in.	5 ft. 4½ in.
Length (overall)	16 ft. 4½ in.	16 ft. 4½ in.	16 ft. 4½ in.	14 ft. 5½ in.	14 ft. 8 in.	14 ft. 9 in.
Weight (dry)	33 cwt.	34 cwt.	34 cwt.	25 cwt (approx)	25½ cwt. (approx)	26 cwt. (approx)

CAPACITIES

	Mk VII	Mk VIII	Mk IX	XK 120	XK 140	XK 150
Engine (sump)	21 pints	19 pints	19 pints	21 pints	22 pints	13 pints
Engine (total)	24 pints	22 pints	22 pints	24 pints	25 pints	15 pints
Gearbox	2½ pints	2½ pints	2½ pints	2½ pints	2½ pints	2½ pints
Gearbox (with overdrive)	4 pints	4 pints	4 pints		4 pints	4 pints
Automatic transmission	15 pints	15 pints	15 pints		15 pints	15 pints
Rear axle	3½ pints	3½ pints	3½ pints	3½ pints	3½ pints	3½ pints
Cooling system	22 pints	22 pints	22 pints	25½ pints	25 pints	23 pints
Fuel tank	L.H. 8 gals. R.H. 9 gals.	L.H. 8 gals. R.H. 9 gals.	L.H. 8 gals. R.H. 9 gals.	15 gals.	14 gals.	14 gals.

RECOMMENDED LUBRICANTS

Engine:	
Summer	S.A.E. 30
Winter	S.A.E. 20
Tropical (above 90°F.)	S.A.E. 40
Carburetter piston dampers	S.A.E. 30
Gearbox	S.A.E. 30
Automatic transmission	Automatic transmission fluid type 'A' (AQ.ATF)
Rear axle	S.A.E. 90 E.P.
Steering gear	S.A.E. 140 E.P.
Power steering	Automatic transmission fluid type 'A' (AQ.ATF)
Wheel bearings	W.B. grease
Universal joints	S.A.E. 140 E.P.

TYRE PRESSURES

	Front	Rear
Mk VII:		
Normal driving	23 p.s.i.	25 p.s.i.
For high speed driving	25 p.s.i.	27 p.s.i.
Mk VIII and Mk IX:		
Normal driving	23 p.s.i.	25 p.s.i.
For high speed driving	29 p.s.i.	31 p.s.i.

TECHNICAL SPECIFICATIONS
ENGINE

Type	XK—3½ litre—Twin O.H.C.	3.8 litre Twin O.H.C.
Bore	3.2677	3.425
Stroke	4.1732	4.1732
Number of cylinders	6	6
Firing order	1–5–3–6–2–4	1–5–3–6–2–4
Nominal H.P.	25.6	28.15
Capacity	210 cu inch (3442 cc).	230.6 cu inch (3781 cc).
Compression ratio	7:1 or 8:1	7:1 or 8:1 or 9:1
B.H.P.	8:1 C.R.: 160 at 5200 rev/min	8:1 C.R.: 220 at 5500 rev/min
	7:1 C.R.: 150 at 5200 rev/min	7:1 C.R.: 190 at 5500 rev/min
		9:1 C.R.: 250 at 5500 rev/min
Maximum torque	195 lb ft at 2500 rev/min	213 lb ft at 4000 rev/min

CYLINDER BLOCK

Material	Chromium iron
Cylinder bores—Nominal	83 mm. (3.2677 inch)
Maximum rebore size	+.030 inch (.76 mm.)
Bore size for fitting liners	3.392 in. to 3.391 in. (86.16 to 86.13 mm)
Outside diameter of liner	3.3945 in. to 3.3955 in. (86.22 to 86.25 mm)
Interference fit	.0025 in. to 0045 in. (.06 to .11 mm)
Overall length in liner (when fitted)	6 31/32 in. (17.7 cm)
Outside diameter of lead-in	3.390 in. to 3.391 in. (86.1 to 86.13 mm)
Size of bore honed after assembly into block—	
Nominal	83 mm (3.2677 in.)
Main line bore for main bearings	2.9165 in. +.0005 in. —.0000 in.
	(74.08 +.013 mm —.000 mm)

CYLINDER HEAD

Material	Aluminium alloy
Interference fit of inserts	.0023 to .0037
Valve seats:	
Angle—Inlet	30 deg.
Exhaust	45 deg.
Width—Inlet	3/32 nominal
Exhaust	5/32 nominal
Port size:	
Inlet	1 3/8 inch
Exhaust	1 1/4 inch

CRANKSHAFT

Thrust taken at	Centre bearing thrust washers
Number of journals	7
Main bearing journal diameter	2.7495 to 2.75
Undersize for regrinding	—.020, —.030, —.040
Minimum regrind diameter	—.040
End float	.004 to .006
Thrust washers available	.091 to .093 and .095 to .097
Crankpin:	
Diameter	2.086 +.0006 —.000
Length	1 3/16 +.0007 —.0002
Undersize for regrinding	—.020, —.030, —.040
Minimum regrind diameter	—.040
Method of sealing oil:	
Front end of shaft	Wick type seal
Rear end of shaft	Split seal assembly

MAIN BEARINGS

Type	White metal steel-backed or lead/bronze shells
Number of main bearings	7
Clearance on crankshaft (diameter)	.0015 to .003
Undersizes	—.020, —.030, —.040
Length:	
Front, centre and rear	1½ inch ±.005
Intermediate	1 inch ±.005

CONNECTING RODS

Length between centres	7.75
Small end lubrication	Pressure
Small end bearings:	
Type	Steel backed phosphor/bronze bush
Bore size	.875 to .8752
Bore for bush	1.000 ±.0005
Big end bearings:	
Type	White metal steel-backed or lead bronze shell
Diameter (outer)	2.233 to 2.2335
Diametrical clearance	.001 to .0025
End float on crankpin	.006 to .0087
Big end:	
Bore size (forging)	2.233 to 2.2335
Width (forging)	1.1875 —.006 —.008

GUDEGEON PINS

Type	Fully floating 'Aerolite' or 'Brico'
Method of securing	Circlips in piston
Diameter	'Aerolite' .87485 to .8751
	'Brico' .0875 to .8752
Fit in piston	'Aerolite', tap fit at 68°F.
	'Brico', palm push fit at 68°F.

PISTONS

Type	'Brico' semi-split oval skirt, or 'Aerolite' solid oval skirt
Removal	From above
Standard size:	
Grade F	3.2673 to 3.2676
G	3.2677 to 3.2680
H	3.2681 to 3.2684
J	3.2685 to 3.2688
K	3.2689 to 3.2692
Oversizes available	+.005, +.010, +.015, +.020, +.030
Skirt clearance (bottom of skirt 90 deg to gudgeon hole)	'Brico' .0015 to .0021
	'Aerolite' .001 to .0016
Gudgeon pin bore	'Brico' .875 ±.0001
	'Aerolite' .875 +.0003 +.0005
Maximum weight variation between any two pistons	3.5 grams

PISTON RINGS

Number of compression	2
Number of oil control	1 slotted scraper

Width:
- Compression ... .0777 to .0787
- Oil control ... .155 to .156

Thickness:
- Compression ... .124 to .130
- Oil control ... .119 to .127

Side clearance in groove:
- Compression ... .001 to .003
- Oil control ... .001 to .003

Gap fitted:
- Compression ... .015 to .020
- Oil control ... .011 to .016

INLET & EXHAUST VALVES

	Inlet	Exhaust
Material	Silicon chrome steel	Austenitic steel
Head diameter	1.750 ±.005	1.4375 ±.005
Stem diameter	.3125 —.0025 —.0035	.3125 —.0025 —.0035
Length	4.125, +.000 —.010	4.0156 ±.005
Valve lift	.3125	.3125
Seat angle	30 deg	45 deg
Valve timing:	**Mk VII**	**XK 120**
Inlet opens	10 deg B.T.D.C.	15 deg B.T.D.C.
Inlet closes	50 deg A.B.D.C.	57 deg A.B.D.C.
Exhaust opens	57 deg B.B.D.C.	57 deg B.B.D.C.
Exhaust closes	15 deg A.T.D.C.	15 deg A.T.D.C.
Tappet clearance (cold)		
Inlet	.004	.006
Exhaust	.006	.008

VALVE SEAT INSERTS

Material ... Cast iron (centrifugally cast)

Inside diameter:
- Inlet ... 1.375 ±.001
- Exhaust ... 1.250 ±.001

Interference fit in head ... .0023 to .0037

Seat angle:
- Inlet ... 30 deg
- Exhaust ... 45 deg

VALVE GUIDES

Material ... Cast iron
Inside diameter ... .3125 ±.0005

Length:
- Inlet ... 1.8125
- Exhaust ... 2.3125

Interference fit in head ... .0005 to .0022
Fitted height above head ... .3125

VALVE SPRINGS

	Inner	Outer
Type	Dual	
Free length	1.515	1.775
Fitted length:		
Valve closed	$1\frac{7}{32}$	$1\frac{5}{16}$
Valve open	$\frac{29}{32}$	1 inch
Fitted load:		
Valve closed	20 +1.5 lb −.000 lb	36 +1.5 lb −.000 lb
Valve open	42 lb	60 lb
Number of free coils	6	5
Wire diameter	.104	.128

TAPPETS, TAPPET GUIDES & ADJUSTING SHIMS

Tappet:
  Material ... Chilled cast iron
  Outside diameter ... 1.375 −.0015 −.00075
  Diametrical clearance ... .0005 to .0022
Tappet guide:
  Material ... Cast iron
  Inside diameter ... 1.355 to 1.357
Interference fit in head ... .0023 to .0037
Adjusting shim thickness ... .085 to .103 in .001 steps, etched 'A' to 'S'

CAMSHAFT

Type ... Twin—overhead
Method of taking thrust ... Front end
Bearing type ... White metal/steel backed shells
Bearing journals:
  Number ... 4 per shaft
  Type ... White metal/steel backed shells
  Diameter ... 1.0 −.001 −.0005
  Length:
    Front ... 1.500 inch
    Others ... 1.3125
    Diametrical clearance ... .0005 to .002
Permissible end float ... .0045 to .008

TIMING CHAIN & SPROCKETS

Type ... Duplex flat back
Pitch ... $\frac{3}{8}$ inch
Number of pitches ... 100 Top chain
                      82 Bottom chain
Sprocket teeth:
  Crankshaft ... 21
  Intermediate—outer ... 28
  Intermediate—inner ... 20
  Camshaft ... 30
  Idler ... 21
Chain tensioning:
  Top chain ... Eccentric mounting of idler sprocket
  Bottom chain:
    Early ... Spring blade
    From engine No. G.4431 ... Reynolds hydraulic

LUBRICATION SYSTEM

Type	Forced feed
Type of pump	Early gear type
	Rotor type from engine No. G.1908
Type of pump drive	Skew gear from crankshaft
Normal pressure (hot)	40 to 50 p.s.i. at 2000 rev/min
Pump internal gears:	
Diametrical clearance	.0045 to .007
End float	.0015 to .0035
Oil pressure release valve springs:	
Free length	$2\frac{3}{32}$ inch
Fitted length	1.500
Wire diameter	.048
Number of free coils	14

TORQUE SETTINGS lbs ft

Cylinder head	54
Connecting rods	37
Main bearings	83
Flywheel securing	67
Camshaft bearing caps	15
Crownwheel securing (Salisbury)	40 to 50

IGNITION SYSTEM

Ignition coil

Type	B.12
Service No.	45012.A
Primary resistance	4.0 to 4.4 ohms
Slow-speed sparking gap	0.44 inch
High-speed test	3500 (distributor rev/min)
Test volts	12.5 maximum
Approximate running current 1000 rev/min	1.0 amps
Approximate stall current	2.9 amps

Distributor

Make	Lucas	
Type:	**Mk VII**	**XK 120**
Early engine 7:1 CR.	DVX6A.40249.B	
Later engine 7:1 CR.	DVX6A.40263.B	DVX6A, GC47.40198.B
8:1 CR. engines	DVX6A.40276.B	DVX6A, GC48.40199.B

Design data:

Open period	22 deg ±4 deg
Closed period	38 deg ±4 deg
Firing angles	0 deg, 60 deg, 120 deg, etc. ± 1 deg

Design Data:

Centrifugal advance data:

Service No.	Type	Control begins rev/min	Intermediate rev/min	degrees	Control ends rev/min	degrees
40198.B	GC.47	150 to 300	850	8 to 10½	1380	16 to 18
40199.B	GC.48	450 to 580	1050	6 to 8	1600	13 to 15
40249.B	GC.49	140 to 300	850	8 to 10½	1400	16 to 18
40263.B	GC.50	500 to 700	1250	9 to 12	1650	16 to 18
40276.B	GC.53	380 to 500	925	6½ to 8½	2025	18 to 20

Note: Rev/min and degrees given in the above table are distributor revolutions and degrees. Rotation clockwise

CARBURETTERS

Mk VIII, Mk IX and XK 150:
   Make ... Twin S.U.
   Type ... H.D.6
   Needle (standard 8:1 Compression ratio) ... T.L.

XK 150 'S':
   Make ... Triple S.U.
   Type ... H.D.8
   Needle ... U.E.

	Mk VII	XK 120
Make	Twin S.U.	Twin S.U.
Type	H.6	H.6
Needle size:		
Standard	S.M.	R.F.
Weak	S.K.	R.G.
Jet size	.100 inch	.100 inch
Starting carburetter needle	435/8	435/8

Fuel pumps:
   Mk VII ... Two S.U. type L.C.S. electric
   XK 120 ... Single S.U. type L.C.S. electric

COOLING SYSTEM

Radiator core type ... Film
Water pump type ... Centrifugal
              Drive ... Fan belt
Fan belt (angle of 'V') ... 32 deg

	Mk VII	Mk VIII	Mk IX	XK 120	XK 140	XK 150
Total capacity pints	22	22	22	$25\frac{1}{2}$	25	23

THERMOSTAT

	Mk VII	Mk IX	XK 120
Manufacture	British thermostat	Smiths	Smiths
Commences to open	70 to 75°C	70 to 75°C	60 to 63°C
Fully open	78°C	90°C	80°C
Valve lift	$\frac{3}{8}$ inch	$\frac{3}{8}$ inch	$\frac{3}{8}$ inch

CLUTCH

Make ... Borg and Beck
Model ... 10 A6.G
Outside diameter ... $9\frac{7}{8}$ inch
Type ... Dry single plate
Release bearing ... Graphite
Driven plate type ... Borglite

	Mk VII	XK 120
Thrust springs:		
Number	12	12
Colour	Cream	Yellow
Fitted load	125 lb	140 lb
Driven plate damper springs:		
Number	8	8
Colour	4 Light Grey and 4 Maroon and Light Green	Violet and Red

GEARBOX

Type:
- Early Mk VII and XK 120 .... S.H. or J.H. Series—4 speed and reverse
- Later Mk VII and XK 120 .... S.L. or J.L. Series—4 speed and reverse
- Early Mk VII and XK 120 .... Prefix S.H. or J.H. to gearbox number
- Later Mk VII and XK 120 .... Prefix S.L. or J.L. to gearbox number
- Location of gearbox number ...... Stamped on top rear lefthand side of casing and on rim of core plug aperture in top corner. Also on plate on scuttle under bonnet.

Synchromesh ...... 2nd, 3rd and top

Ratios:
- Top 1.0:1
- 3rd 1.367:1
- 2nd 1.982:1
- 1st 3.375:1
- Reverse 3.375:1

Gearbox ratios (J.S. series):
- Top 1:1
- 3rd 1.283:1
- 2nd 1.86:1
- 1st and reverse 3.378:1

Bearings:
- Clutch shaft—main ...... Hoffman 340 K (ball)
- Spigot ...... Porous bronze bush
- Main shaft—Spigot ...... Roller
- Intermediate ...... Hoffman RMS 12½ L (roller)
- Intermediate ...... Hoffman MS 12½ K (ball)
- Rear ...... Hoffman MS 12 (ball)
- 2nd Speed gear ...... Needle rollers
- 3rd Speed gear ...... Needle rollers

Countershaft—Front and rear ...... Needle rollers
Reverse gear ...... Phosphor bronze bush
Fit of reverse gear on shaft ...... .0014 to 0024
Countershaft end float ...... .002 to .004
Mainshaft end float ...... .002 to .006
Second gear end float on mainshaft ...... .002 to .004
Third gear end float on mainshaft ...... .002 to .004

LAYCOCK de NORMANVILLE OVERDRIVE UNIT

Ratio ...... 0.778:1 or 0.820:1

Serial No.	Model	Hydraulic pressure p.s.i.
28.1482	Jaguar XK 140	480 to 500
28.3034	Jaguar XK 150	540 to 560
28.1516	Jaguar XK 150	480 to 500
28.3020	Jaguar XK 150	480 to 500
28.1270	Jaguar Mk VII & VIII	480 to 500
28.3018	Jaguar Mk IX	540 to 560

PROPELLER SHAFT

Type:
- Mk VII ...... Hardy Spicer divided shaft with centre support bearing.
- XK 120 ...... Hardy Spicer single shaft.

Universal joint:
- Type ...... Needle roller
- Number: Mk VII 3
- XK 120 2

Centre support bearing (Mk VII):
- Type ...... Ballbearing
- Mounting ...... Flexible

REAR AXLE

Salisbury Axle:
Type ... Semi-floating with hypoid final drive
Installation:
   Mark VII ... Type 2HA
   XK 120 ... Type 2HA standard or type 4HA high rates.

Ratios:
   Type 2 HA (Mk VII) ... 4.27:1
   Type 2 HA (XK 120) ... 3.77:1
   Type 4 HA (XK 120) ... 3.21:1
Adjustment ... Shims
Axle shaft end float ... .006 to .008
Differential bearing pre-load ... .008 shim allowance
Pinion bearing pre-load ... 8 to 12 lb/in
Backlash ... Etched on drive gear (.004 minimum).

E.N.V. Axle:
Type ... Semi-floating with hypoid final drive
Installation ... Fitted to certain proportion of XK 120 cars.

Ratios:
   Standard ... 3.64:1
   High ... 3.27:1
   Alternative ... 3.92:1, 4.3:1 or 4.56:1
Adjustment:
   Pinion ... Shims
   Crownwheel ... Adjusting nuts
Axle shaft end float ... .005 to .008
Backlash ... .006

Mk VIII—Mk IX:
Ratios:
   Synchromesh or Automatic transmission ... 4.27:1
   Synchromesh with Overdrive ... 4.55:1

XK 140—XK 150:
Ratios:
   Synchromesh gearbox ... 3.54:1
   Synchromesh with overdrive ... 4.09:1
   Automatic transmission (XK 150) ... 3.54:1

FRONT SUSPENSION

Type ... Independent torsion bar
Torsion bar length ... 52 inch

	Mk VII	**XK 120**
Caster angle	0 deg ±¼ deg	3 deg positive (5 deg prior to chassis No. 660126 R.H.D. 670439 L.H.D.)
Camber angle	1 deg ±¼ deg positive	1¾ deg to 2 deg positive
Swivel inclination	8 deg	5 deg
Ground clearance	7½ inch	7⅛ inch
Shock absorbers	Girling	Newton

XK 140 and XK 150 models:
Caster angle ... 1½ deg to 2 deg positive
Camber angle ... ½ deg to 1 deg positive
Swivel inclination ... 5 deg
Wheel alignment (toe-in) ... Parallel to ⅛ inch toe-in

REAR SUSPENSION

	Mk VII	XK 120
Type	Semi-elliptic leaf springs	
Springs:		
Number of leaves	9	7
Free camber	6 inch	5½ inch
Laden camber. Spring flat	875 lb	585 lb
Spring eye diameter	1 inch −.016 / .026	1 inch −.016 / .026
Shock absorbers:		
Type	Girling Hydraulic piston PV.7	

STEERING GEAR

Steering unit:
  Type ... Burman recirculating ball
  Adjustments:
    Inner column end float ... Shims under plate
    Rocker shaft end float ... Adjusting screw and pre-load spring.

	Mk VII	XK 120
Steering wheel diameter	18 inch	17 inch
Caster angle	0 deg ±¼ deg	3 deg positive (5 deg prior to chassis No. 660126 R.H.D. 670439 L.H.D.)
Camber angle	1 deg ±¼ deg positive	1¾ deg to 2 deg positive
Swivel pin inclination	8 deg	5 deg
Wheel alignment	⅛ inch to 3/16 inch toe-in	⅛ inch to 3/16 inch toe-in
Turning circle	36 ft	31 ft

Steering unit (Mk VIII and Mk IX models):
  Make ... Burman
  Type ... Hydraulically assisted worm and re-circulating ball
  Ratio at centre of travel ... 20:1
  Number of turns lock to lock ... 3½
  Turning circle ... 36 ft
Oil pump:
  Make ... Hobourn-Eaton
  Type ... Eccentric rotor
  Location ... Rear end of generator
  Operating pressure ... 600 to 650 p.s.i.
Wheel alignment (toe-in) ... ⅛ to 3/16 toe-in

Steering unit (XK 140 and XK 150 models):
  Type ... Rack and pinion
  Adjustment:
    Mesh ... Eccentric sleeve
  Number of turns lock to lock ... 2¾
  Wheel alignment (toe-in) ... Parallel to ⅛ inch toe-in

BRAKES

Mk VII models
- Make ... Girling autostatic hydraulic
- Type ... Two leading shoe-front
- Drum diameter ... 12 inch
- Lining:
  - Material ... Mintex M.14 bonded
  - Total area ... 207 sq in
  - Length ... $11\frac{1}{2}$ inch
  - Width ... $2\frac{1}{4}$ inch
  - Thickness ... $\frac{1}{4}$ inch
- Master cylinder bore ... $\frac{3}{4}$ inch
- Wheel cylinder bore:
  - Front ... $1\frac{1}{4}$ inch
  - Rear ... $\frac{3}{4}$ inch
- Shoe adjustment:
  - Front ... Self-adjusting
  - Rear ... Screwed wedge

XK 120 models
- Make ... Lockheed hydraulic
- Type ... Two leading shoe—front
- Drum diameter ... 12 inch
- Lining:
  - Material ... Mintex M.14
  - Total area ... 207 sq in
  - Length ... $11\frac{1}{2}$ inch
  - Width ... $2\frac{1}{4}$ inch
  - Thickness ... $\frac{3}{16}$ inch
- Master cylinder bore ... 1 inch
- Wheel cylinder bore ... $1\frac{1}{8}$ inch
- Shoe adjustment:
  - Front ... Two micram adjusters
  - Rear ... Single micram adjuster

Mk IX and XK 150 models:
- Make ... Dunlop disc
- Type ... Vacuum assisted hydraulic
- Servo unit type ... Lockheed $6\frac{7}{8}$ inch
- Friction pad material:
  - Early Mk IX and XK 150 ... Ferodo DS.5
  - Later Mk IX ... Mintex M.33
- Introduction of quick change friction pads:
  - Mk IX models ... At commencement of production
  - Mk 150 models: **Commencing Chassis Nos.**
    - Open 2-Seater ... 82004 R.H.D.   831712 L.H.D.
    - Drop head coupé ... 827236 R.H.D.   837836 L.H.D.
    - Fixed head coupé ... 824669 R.H.D.   835886 L.H.D.

BORG WARNER AUTOMATIC TRANSMISSION

General data

Maximum torque ratio of converter		2.15:1
Low gear reduction		2.308:1
Intermediate gear reduction		1.435:1
Direct drive—no converter		1:1
Reverse gear reduction		2.009:1
Rear axle ratio		4.27:1
Lubricant		Automatic transmission fluid type 'A' (AQ.ATF)
Capacity		15 Imp. pints

Governor shift speeds early type

	Intermediate to Direct	Direct to Intermediate
Light throttle upshift	18 mph	—
Full throttle upshift	55 mph	—
Kickdown upshift	68 mph	—
Closed throttle downshift	—	12 mph
Limit or kickdown downshift	—	60 mph

Governor shift speeds later or, first speed start type

Upshifts
	mph
Low to intermediate, light throttle	10
Low to intermediate, full throttle	35
Intermediate to direct, light throttle	18
Intermediate to direct, full throttle	55
Intermediate to direct, after 'kickdown'	68

Downshifts
Direct to intermediate, closed throttle	12
Intermediate to low closed throttle	3
Direct to intermediate, 'kickdown'	Up to 60

ELECTRICAL EQUIPMENT

Battery:
- Make and type—Mk VII ... Lucas 12 volt G.T.W.11.A
- XK 120 (Home): ... Lucas 6 volt S.T.X.W.11.E (2 off)
- XK 120 (Export): ... Lucas 6 volt S.T.Z.W.11.E (2 off)
- Number of plates in each cell ... 11
- Ampere-hour capacity:
  - At 10 hour rate ... 63
  - At 20-hour rate ... 72
- Volume of electrolyte required to half fill one cell ... ½ pint
- Initial charging current (amps) ... 4½
- Normal recharge current (amps) ... 7

Specific gravity of electrolyte (corrected to 60°F):
- Home trade and climates normally below 80°F. (27°C.)
  - Filling ... 1.350
  - Fully charged ... 1.280 to 1.300
- Sub-tropical climates 80° to 100°F. (27° to 38°C.)
  - Filling ... 1.320
  - Fully charged ... 1.250 to 1.270
- Tropical climates over 100°F. (38°C.)
  - Filling ... 1.300
  - Fully charged ... 1.220 to 1.240
- Maximum permissible electrolyte temperature during charge:
  - Climates normally below 80°F. 27°C.) ... 100°F. (38°C.)
  - Climates between 80° to 100°F. (27° to 38°C.) ... 110°F. (43°C.)
  - Climates frequently above 100°F. 38°C.) ... 120°F. (49°C.)

CONTROL BOX - REGULATOR

Make	Lucas
Type:	
Mk VII, XK 120 and XK 140	RB.106.1 or RB.106.2
Mk VIII, IX and XK 150	RB.310

CONTROL BOX - REGULATOR SETTINGS

Cut-out:
- Cut-in voltage ... 12.7 to 13.3 volts
- Drop-off voltage ... 9 to 10 volts
- Reverse current ... 3 to 5 amps

Regulator settings on open circuit:

Temperature:	Voltage:	Setting:
10°C. (50°F.) cold climate	16.1 to 16.7 volts	14.6 to 15.2 volts
20°C. (68°F.) normal temperature	15.8 to 16.4 volts	14.4 to 15.0 volts
30°C. (86°F.) hot climate	15.6 to 16.2 volts	14.2 to 14.8 volts
40°C. (104°F.) very hot	15.3 to 15.9 volts	14.0 to 14.6 volts

GENERATOR

Nominal voltage	12
Cutting-in speed (rev/min)	900 to 1050
At generator volts	13
Maximum output (amps:	
Mk VII, XK 120 and XK 140	20
Mk VII, IX and XK 150	25
At rev/min:	
Mk VII, XK 120 and XK 140	1500 to 1700
Mk VII, IX and XK 150	4000
At generator volts	13.5
On resistance load (ohms)*	0.67
Field resistance (ohms)	6

*Resistance load must be capable of carrying 20 amperes without overheating.

STARTER MOTOR

Nominal voltage	12
Lock torque (lb ft)	22
Current (amps)	430 to 450
Voltage	7.4 to 7.8
Torque at 1000 rev/min (lb ft)	8.3
Current (amps)	200 to 220
Voltage	9.8 to 10.2

WINDSCREEN WIPERS

	Model CR.4	Model CRT.14
Normal current consumption (motor cold and driving both blades on wet screen)	1.75 to 3 amps	2 to 3.25 amps
Stall current (motor cold)	5.5 to 6.5 amps	7.8 to 8.5 amps
Armature resistance (between adjacent commutator segments)	.85 to 1.05 ohms	.8 to 1 ohms
Field coil resistance	15 to 16 ohms	8.4 to 9 ohms
Field current (approximate)	.8 amps	1.4 amps

TUNING DATA

The following tables are a summary of the recommended carburetter needles, distributor and sparking plugs for various Jaguar engines; standard production conditions are printed in bold type. The Lucas service number is stamped on the distributor body.

MK 7 1951-1954

Compression ratio	Type of cylinder head	Cam lift	Carburetters	Carburetter needles With std. air cleaner	Carburetter needles With AC disc air cleaner	Distributor Lucas service number	Distributor Contact breaker gap (inch)	Static ignition timing	Champion sparking plug type Touring	Champion sparking plug type Racing
Prior to Engine No. B.2917	**Standard**	**5/16 in.**	**Standard 1¾ in. bore**	**S.M. SK**	—	**40263.A** or 40263.B	**.010-.012** .014-.016	**5°BTDC** 5°BTDC	**L10S**	**L11S**
After Engine No. B.2917	Standard	5/16 in.	Standard 1¾ in. bore	S.R. C.I.W.	—	40263.A or 40263.B	.010-.012 .014-.016	5°BTDC 5°BTDC	L10S	L11S
7:1	Standard	3/8 in.	Large type 2 in. bore	—	V.R. Weaker V.E.	40263.B	.014-.016	5°BTDC	L10S	L11S
	'C' type	3/8 in.	Large type	—	V.R. Weaker	40445.A	.014-.016	5°BTDC	L10S	L11S
Prior to Engine No. B.2917	Standard	5/16 in.	Standard 1¾ in. bore	S.M. SK	—	40276.A or 40276.B	.010-.012 .014-.016	5°BTDC 5°BTDC	N8B	NA8
After Engine No. B.2917	Standard	5/16 in.	1¾ in. bore	S.R. Weaker C.I.W.	—	40372.A	.014-.016	3°BTDC	N8B	NA8
	Standard	3/8 in.	Large type 2 in. bore	—	V.R. Weaker V.E.	40372.A	.014-.016	3°BTDC	N8B	N8A
8:1	'C' type	3/8 in.	**Standard 1¾ in. bore**	R.G.	—	40249.B	.014-.016	TDC	NA8	NA10
	'C' type	3/8 in.	Large type 2 in. bore	—	V.R. Weaker V.E.	40445.A	.014-.016	5°BTDC	NA8	NA10

				MK 7 1954-1956 TYPE 'M'						
				Carburetter needles			Distributor			Champion sparking plug type
Comp. ratio	Type of cylinder head	Cam lift	Exhaust system	With std. air cleaner	With AC disc air cleaner	Carbs.	Lucas service number	Contact breaker gap (inch)	Static ignition timing	Touring	Racing
7:1	Std.	⅜ in.	Std.	S.R. Weaker C.I.W.	—	Standard 1¾ in. bore	40435.A	.014-.016	5°BTDC	L10S	L11S
	'C' type	⅜ in.	Sports silencer and larger dia. tail-pipe	S.L.	—	Standard	40435.A	.014-.106	5°BTDC	L10S	L11S
8:1	Std.	⅜ in.	Std.	S.R. Weaker C.I.W.	—	Standard 1¾ in. bore	40372.A	.014-.016	TDC	N8B	NA8
	'C' type	⅜ in.	Sports silencer and larger dia. tail pipe	—	S.J.	Standard 1¾ in. bore	40436.A	.014-.016	6°BTDC	NA8	NA10
	'C' type	⅜ in.	Sports silencer and larger dia. tail pipe	—	V.R. Weaker V.E.	Large type 2 in. bore	40455.A	.014-.016	6°BTDC	NA8	NA10
9:1	'C' type	⅜ in.	Sports silencer and larger dia. tail pipe	—	V.R. Weaker V.E.	larger type 2 in. bore	40445.A	.014-.016	5°BTDC	NA8	NA10

MK 8

Compression ratio	Type of cylinder head	Cam lift	Exhaust system	Carburetters Type	Needles	Distributor Lucas service number	Contact breaker gap (inch)	Static ignition timing	Champion sparking plug type and gap Touring	Racing
7:1	'B' type (Light blue top)	3/8	Twin	SU HD.6 1¾" bore	T.L.	40578.A	.014–.016	4°BTDC	L7 (.25)	L5 (.25)
8:1	'B' type (Light blue top)	3/8	Twin	SU HD.6 1¾" bore	T.L.	40576.A	.014–.016	6°BTDC	N5 (.25)	N3 (.25)

MK 9

Compression ratio	Type of cylinder head	Cam lift	Exhaust system	Carburetters Type	Needles	Distributor Lucas service number	Contact breaker gap (inch)	Static ignition timing	Champion sparking plug type and gap Touring	Racing
7:1	'B' type (Dark blue top)	3/8	Twin	SU HD.6 1¾" bore	T.U.	40640.A	.014–.016	4°BTDC	L7 (.25)	L5 (.25)
8:1	'B' type (Dark blue top)	3/8	Twin	SU HD.6 1¾" bore	T.U.*	40640.A	.014–.016	4°BTDC	N5 (.25)	N3 (.25)
9:1	'B' type (Dark blue top)	3/8	Twin	SU HD.6 1¾" bore	T.U.*	40665.A	.014–.016	5°BTDC	N5 (.25)	N3 (.25)

*T.L. needles fitted to early cars

XK120

Compression ratio	Type of cylinder head	Cam lift	Carburetters	Carburetter needles With AC disc air cleaner	Carburetter needles With AC remote air cleaner	Distributor Lucas service number	Contact breaker gap (inch)	Static ignition timing	Champion sparking plug type Touring	Champion sparking plug type Racing
7:1	Standard	5/16 in. or 3/8 in.	Standard 1¾" bore	R.F. Weaker R.G.	W.O.2 Weaker W.O.3	40198.A or 40198.D or 40249.B	.010-.012 .014-.016 .014-.016	5°BTDC 5°BTDC 5°BTDC	L10S	L11S
	'C' type	3/8 in.	Larger type 2" bore	V.R. Weaker V.E.	—	40445.A	.014-.016	5°BTDC	L10S	L11S
8:1	Standard	5/16 in. or 3/8 in.	Standard 1¾" bore	R.F. Weaker R.G.	W.O.2 Weaker W.O.3	40199.A or 40199.D or 40199.E	.010-.012 .014-.016 .014-.016	5°BTDC 7°BTDC 7°BTDC	N8B	NA8
	'C' type	3/8 in.	Standard 1¾" bore	R.G.	D.G.	40249.B	.014-.016	TDC	NA8	NA10
	'C' type	3/8 in.	Standard 2" bore	V.R. Weaker V.E.	—	40445.A	.014-.016	5°BTDC	NA8	NA10
9:1	'C' type	3/8 in.	Standard 1¾" bore	R.C.	—	40328.A	.014-.016	TDC	NA8	NA10
	'C' type	3/8 in.	Standard 2" bore	V.R. Weaker V.E.	—	40293.A	.014-.016	3°BTDC	NA8	NA10

XK140

Compression ratio	Type of cylinder head	Cam lift	Carburetters	Carburetter needles With std. air cleaner	Carburetter needles With AC disc air cleaner	Distributor Lucas service number	Distributor Contact breaker gap (inch)	Static ignition timing	Champion sparking plug type and gap Touring	Champion sparking plug type and gap Racing
7:1	Std.	⅜ in.	Single or dual	S.J. Weaker L.B.A.	—	Standard 1¾" bore 40435.A	.014-.016	8°BTDC	L10S	L11S
7:1	'C' type	⅜ in.	Dual	S.R.	W.O.2	Standard 1¾" bore 40435.A	.014-.016	8°BTDC	L10S	L11S
8:1	Std.	⅜ in.	Single or dual	S.J. Weaker L.B.A.	—	Standard 1¾" bore 40436.A	.014-.016	10°BTDC	N8B	NA8
8:1	'C' type	⅜ in.	Dual	S.R.	W.O.2	Standard 1¾" bore 40199.E	.014-.016	10°BTDC	NA8	NA10
8:1	'C' type	⅜ in.	Dual	—	V.R. Weaker V.E.	Large type 2 in. bore 40293.A	.014-.016	5°BTDC	NA8	NA10
9:1	'C' type	⅜ in.	Dual	—	V.R. Weaker V.E.	Large type 2" bore 40445.A	.014-.016	5°BTDC	NA8	NA10

XK150 - 3.4 Litre engine

Compression ratio	Type of cylinder head	Cam lift	Exhaust system	Carburetters Type	Carburetters Needles	Distributor Lucas service number	Distributor Contact breaker gap (inch)	Static ignition timing	Champion sparking plug type and gap Touring	Champion sparking plug type and gap Racing
7:1	'B' type (Light blue top)	⅜ in.	Twin	SU HD.6 1¾" bore	T.L.	40578.A	.014-.016	4°BTDC	L7 (.25)	L5 (.25)
8:1	'B' type (Light blue top)	⅜ in.	Twin	SU HD.6 1¾" bore	T.L.	40576.A	.014-.016	6°BTDC	N5 (.25)	N3 (.25)
9:1	'B' type (Light blue top)	⅜ in.	Twin	SU HD.6 1¾" bore	T.L.	40617.A	.014-.016	5°BTDC	N5 (.25)	N3 (.25)

XK150 'S' - 3.4 Litre engine

Compression ratio	Type of cylinder head	Cam lift	Exhaust system	Carburetters Type	Carburetters Needles	Distributor Lucas service number	Distributor Contact breaker gap (inch)	Static ignition timing	Champion sparking plug type and gap Touring	Champion sparking plug type and gap Racing
8:1	Straight Port (Gold top)	⅜ in.	Twin	SU Triple HD.8 2" bore	U.E.	40670.A	.014-.016	9°BTDC	N5 (.25)	N3 (.25)
9:1	Straight Port (Gold top)	⅜ in.	Twin	SU Triple HD.8 2" bore	U.E.	40616.A	.014-.016	9°BTDC	N5 (.25)	N3 (.25)

LUBRICATION AND ROUTINE MAINTENANCE

Recommended Lubricants

Key to Chart	Component	SAE	Capacity
6	Engine: 　Summer 32°F to 90°F 　Winter below 32°F 　Tropical above 90°F	30 20 40	See "Capacities" in "General Data" Section
7	Gearbox Automatic Transmission	30 Automatic Transmission Fluid Type "A" (AQ-ATF)	2½ Pints 15 Pints
10	Rear Axle Steering Box (not power steering) Steering Rack Housing (XK models)	Hypoid 90 EP 140 140	3½ Pints
5	Power Steering Reservoir	Automatic Transmission Fluid Type "A" (AQ-ATF)	
	Steering Idler Lever Housing 　(Early XK120)	140	
15	Brake and Clutch Reservoirs	Hydraulic Brake Fluid SAE Spec. 70 RI	
	Carburettor Hydraulic Piston Damper Distributor and all oil can lubrication	30 30	
8-18-19	Universal Joint Needle Bearings	140	
19	Propeller Shaft Spline		
1-2-4-11-12 14-16-17	All Chassis Nipples	General purpose grease or high melting point grease	
	Water Pump (Mark VII and XK120) Fan Bearing	Water Pump Grease HT Grease	
3-9-13-20	Wheel Bearings	WB or HT Grease	
16	Clutch and Brake Pedals	General purpose grease	

Grease Nipple Location and Number

Component	Mark VII-VIII and IX	XK120	XK140-XK150
Steering:			
Track Rod	(2) one each joint		
Tie-rods	(4) two each rod	(4) two each rod	(2) one each rod
Front Wheel 　Bearings	(2) one each wheel	(2) one each wheel	(2) one each wheel
Wheel Swivels	(4) two R.H., two L.H.	(4) two R.H., two L.H.	(4) two R.H., two L.H.
Brake Pedal	(1) one nipple	(1) one nipple	(1) one nipple
Clutch Pedal	(1) one nipple	(1) one nipple R.H. drive (2) two nipples L.H. drive	(1) one nipple
Universal Joints	(3) one each joint	(2) one each joint	(2) one each joint
Propeller Shaft 　Spline	(1) at centre joint	(1) at front joint	(1) at front joint
Hand Brake 　Cable/s	Mark VII — one each rear cable Mark VIII-IX — one at front cable	(2) one each rear cable	(2) one each rear cable
Rear Wheel 　Bearings	(2) one each wheel	(2) one each wheel	(2) one each wheel
Rear Spring 　Gaiters	Mark VII only — (4) two each rear 　spring	(4) two each rear spring	
Fan Bearing	Mark VII only — (1) one nipple	(1) one nipple	
Water Pump 　Bearing	Mark VII only — (1) one nipple	(1) one nipple	

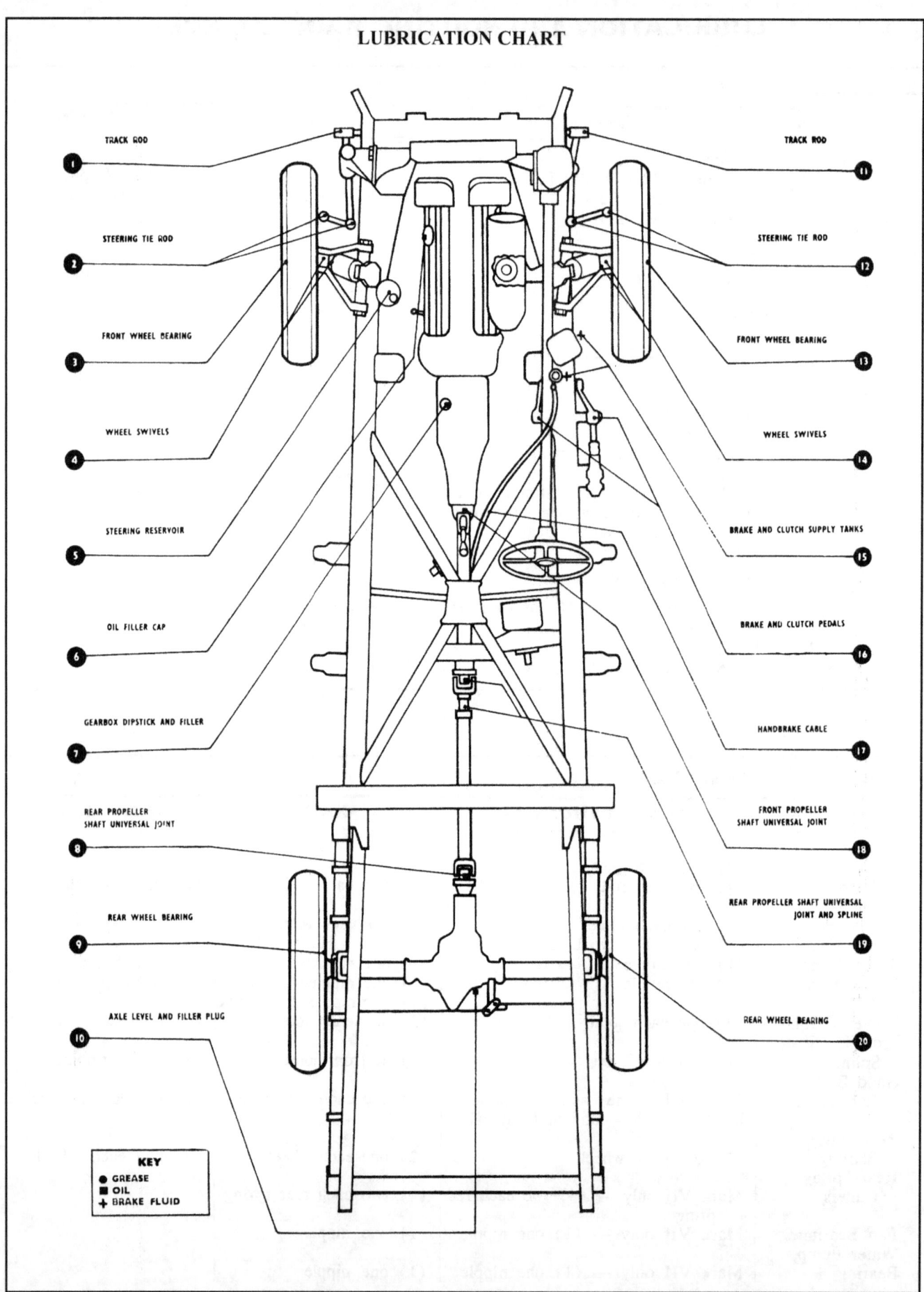

LUBRICATION AND ROUTINE MAINTENANCE CHART

Key to Chart	Operation
	Daily
	Check engine oil level
	Check radiator water level
	Weekly
	Check tyre pressures
	Check fluid level in brake and clutch master cylinder reservoirs
	Monthly
	Check battery electrolyte level and connections
	Every 1,250 miles
5	Check and top up power steering oil reservoir (if so equipped)
	Check and top up automatic transmission oil reservoir. (Automatic models)
	Every 2,500 miles
6	Drain engine sump and refill
	Clean oil filter element
7	Check gearbox oil level and top up if necessary. (See Note 1.)
10	Check rear axle oil level and top up if necessary
1 and 11	Lubricate steering track rod ball joints. (Marks VII-VIII-IX and early XK120)
	Lubricate steering housing. (XK models with rack and pinion steering)
	Top up steering box. (Models without power assisted steering)
	Top up idler lever housing. (Early XK120 models)
2 and 12	Lubricate steering tie-rod ball joints
4 and 14	Lubricate wheel swivels
16	Lubricate foot brake and clutch pedals. (Brake pedal only on XK120, R.H.D.)
8-18 and 19	Lubricate propeller shaft universal joints. (Marks VII-VIII and IX)
8 and 18	Lubricate propeller shaft universal joints. (XK120-140 and 150)
	Lubricate propeller shaft spline. (All models)
19	Lubricate handbrake cables. (See Note 2.)
17	Lubricate carburettor piston dampers
	Lubricate distributor and check contact points

Key to Chart	Operation
15	Check fluid level in brake and clutch supply tanks
	Check clutch pedal free travel and adjust if necessary
	Check carburettor slow running
	Check handbrake adjustment
	Clean air cleaner element. (Oil bath type)
	Lubricate fan and water pump bearings. (Mark VII and XK120 models)
	Every 5,000 miles
	Carry out 2,500 mile service above
	Clean adjust and test sparking plugs
	Clean carburettor filters
3 and 13	Lubricate front wheel bearings
9 and 20	Lubricate rear wheel bearings
	Check fan belt and adjust if necessary
	Renew oil filter element
	Clean air filter element (felt type)
	Examine brake friction pads for wear. (Disc brakes)
	Carry out oil can lubrication of (a) seat runners and adjusting mechanism, (b) handbrake ratchet, (c) door hinges and locks, (d) boot hinges and lock, (e) bonnet hinges and catches, (f) windscreen wiper arms (g) accelerator linkage
	Every 10,000 miles
	Carry out 2,500 and 5,000 mile services
7	Drain and refill gearbox (and overdrive if fitted. (See Note 3.)
	Clean overdrive oil pump filter (if overdrive fitted. (See Note 4.)
10	Drain and refill rear axle
	Clean petrol pump filters
	Check and top up rear shocker absorbers. (Lever-arm type)
	Check and adjust wheel bearings if necessary
	Check and tighten all chassis and body bolts, nuts and screws
	Every 15,000 miles
	Drain and refill automatic transmission unit
	Every 20,000 miles
	Change steering oil reservoir filter. (Power assisted steering only)

Note 1: On cars fitted with overdrive, checking the gearbox oil level will also check the level of the oil in the overdrive unit, as the oil is common to both units.

Note 2: On Mark VII and all XK models there are two handbrake cables at the rear of the mechanism with one grease nipple to each cable.

Note 3: If the car is fitted with an overdrive remove the drain plug at the base of the overdrive casing, in addition to the gearbox drain plug. After refilling the gearbox and overdrive with oil through the gearbox dipstick hole, recheck the oil after the car has been run as a certain amount of oil will be retained in the hydraulic system of the overdrive.

Note 4: The overdrive oil pump filter is accessible through the drain plug hole and is secured by a central screw; the filter should be removed for cleaning at the time of draining the oil.

OVERDRIVE UNIT — IMPORTANT

It is most essential that absolute cleanliness is exercised when refilling the gearbox and overdrive units with oil, as any foreign matter that enters may seriously affect the hydraulic operation of the overdrive.

The oil in the gearbox and overdrive units must always be kept to the correct level on the dipstick otherwise the operation of the overdrive will be affected.

AUTOMATIC TRANSMISSION UNIT

Detailed instructions, "Checking the Fluid Level" and "Draining and Refilling" the Automatic Transmission unit are given in the Automatic Transmission Section.

W79600 - MK 7 RHD 1951-1952

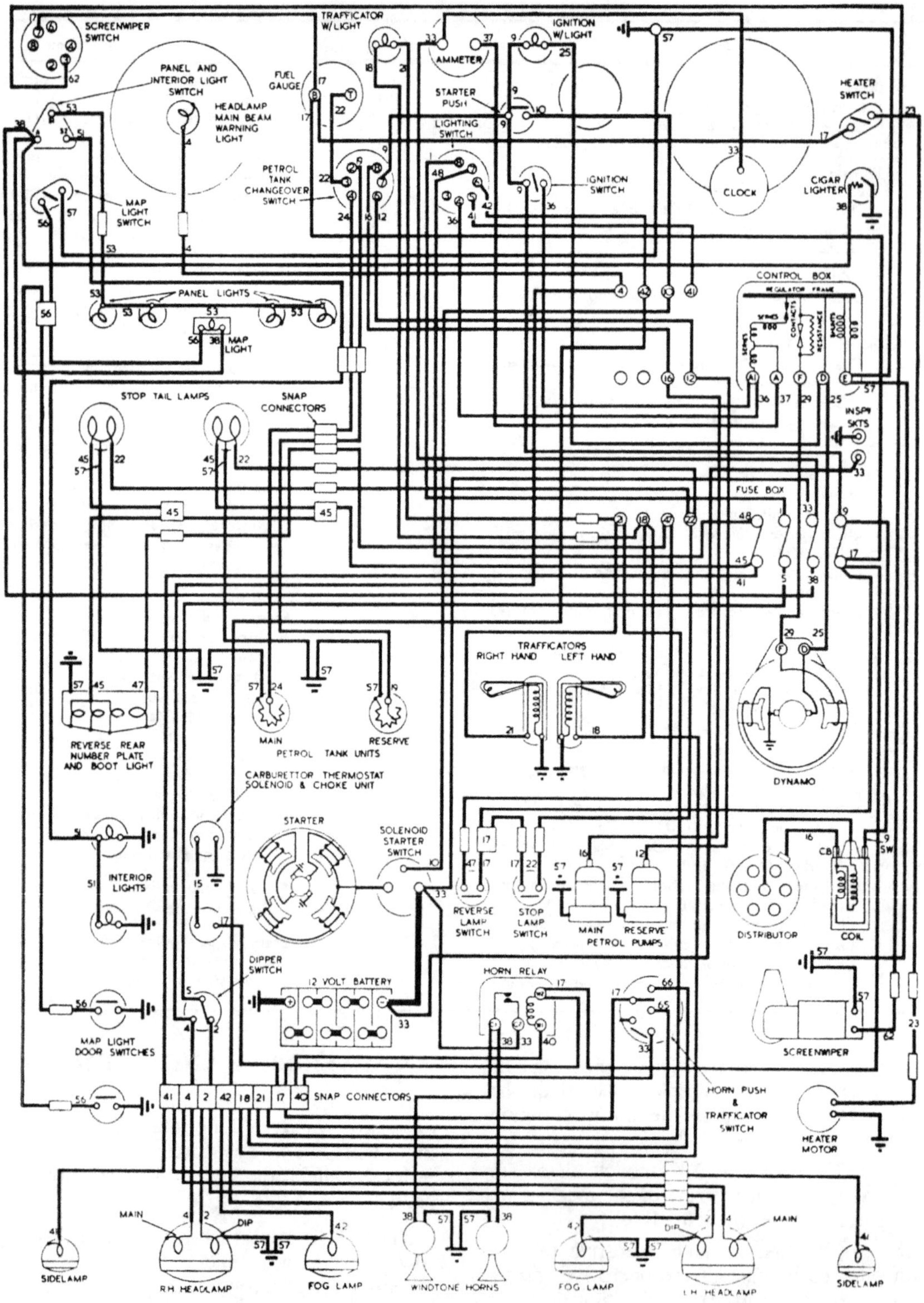

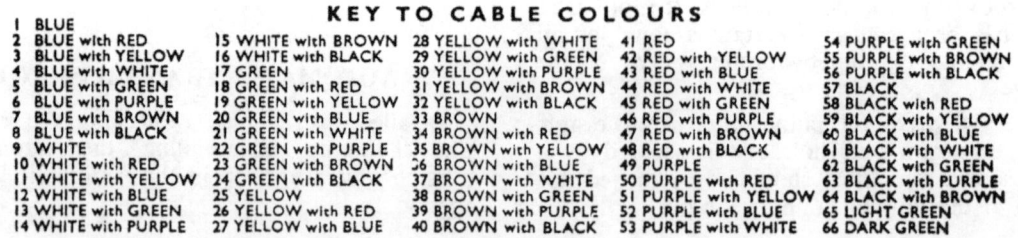

KEY TO CABLE COLOURS

1 BLUE		28 YELLOW with WHITE	41 RED	54 PURPLE with GREEN
2 BLUE with RED	15 WHITE with BROWN	29 YELLOW with GREEN	42 RED with YELLOW	55 PURPLE with BROWN
3 BLUE with YELLOW	16 WHITE with BLACK	30 YELLOW with PURPLE	43 RED with BLUE	56 PURPLE with BLACK
4 BLUE with WHITE	17 GREEN	31 YELLOW with BROWN	44 RED with WHITE	57 BLACK
5 BLUE with GREEN	18 GREEN with RED	32 YELLOW with BLACK	45 RED with GREEN	58 BLACK with RED
6 BLUE with PURPLE	19 GREEN with YELLOW	33 BROWN	46 RED with PURPLE	59 BLACK with YELLOW
7 BLUE with BROWN	20 GREEN with BLUE	34 BROWN with RED	47 RED with BROWN	60 BLACK with BLUE
8 BLUE with BLACK	21 GREEN with WHITE	35 BROWN with YELLOW	48 RED with BLACK	61 BLACK with WHITE
9 WHITE	22 GREEN with PURPLE	36 BROWN with BLUE	49 PURPLE	62 BLACK with GREEN
10 WHITE with RED	23 GREEN with BROWN	37 BROWN with WHITE	50 PURPLE with RED	63 BLACK with PURPLE
11 WHITE with YELLOW	24 GREEN with BLACK	38 BROWN with GREEN	51 PURPLE with YELLOW	64 BLACK with BROWN
12 WHITE with BLUE	25 YELLOW	39 BROWN with PURPLE	52 PURPLE with BLUE	65 LIGHT GREEN
13 WHITE with GREEN	26 YELLOW with RED	40 BROWN with BLACK	53 PURPLE with WHITE	66 DARK GREEN
14 WHITE with PURPLE	27 YELLOW with BLUE			

W79602 - MK 7 RHD 1952-1953

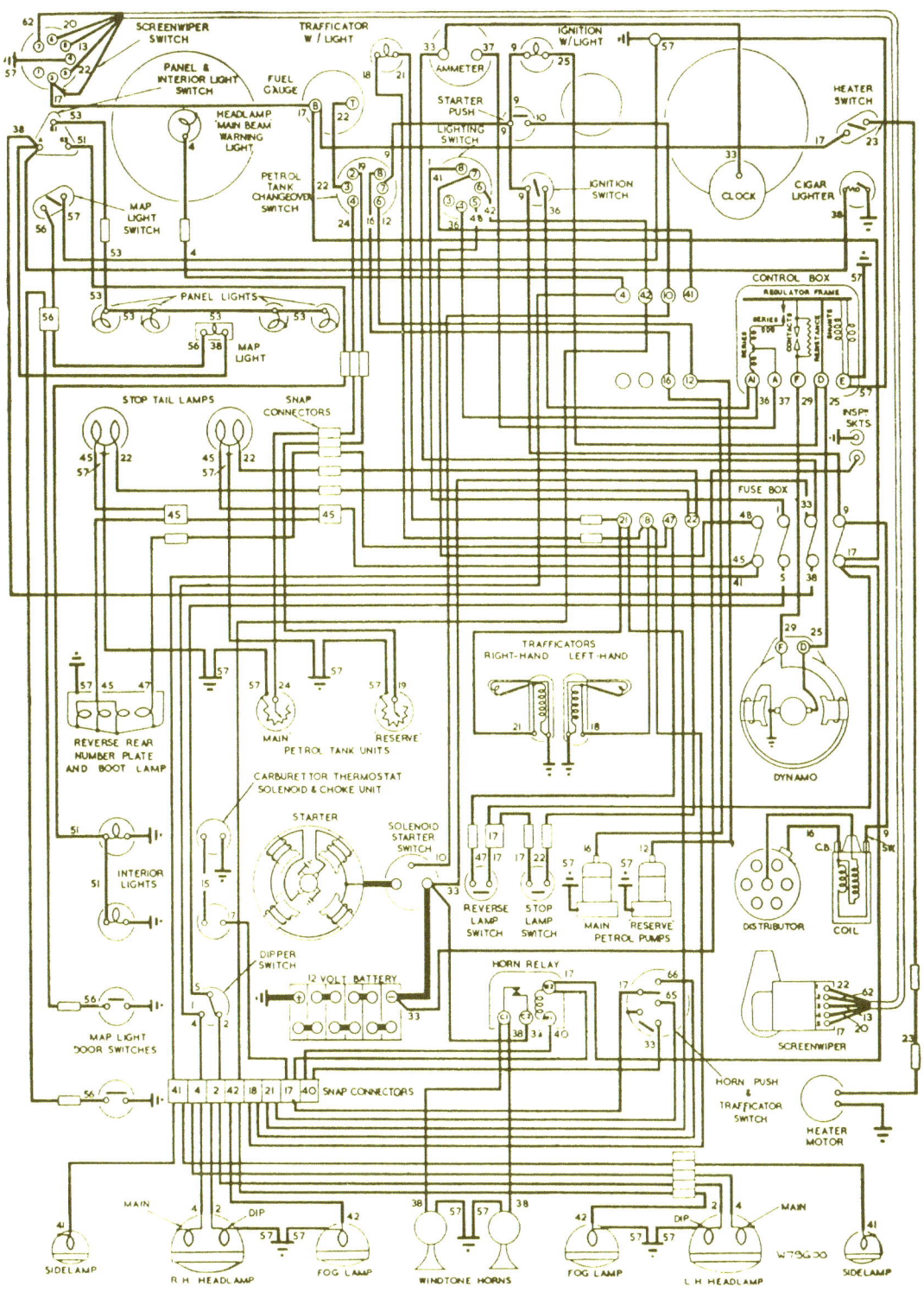

KEY TO CABLE COLOURS

1 BLUE	15 WHITE with BROWN	28 YELLOW with WHITE	41 RED	54 PURPLE with GREEN
2 BLUE with RED	16 WHITE with BLACK	29 YELLOW with GREEN	42 RED with YELLOW	55 PURPLE with BROWN
3 BLUE with YELLOW	17 GREEN	30 YELLOW with PURPLE	43 RED with BLUE	56 PURPLE with BLACK
4 BLUE with WHITE	18 GREEN with RED	31 YELLOW with BROWN	44 RED with WHITE	57 BLACK
5 BLUE with GREEN	19 GREEN with YELLOW	32 YELLOW with BLACK	45 RED with GREEN	58 BLACK with RED
6 BLUE with PURPLE	20 GREEN with BLUE	33 BROWN	46 RED with PURPLE	59 BLACK with YELLOW
7 BLUE with BROWN	21 GREEN with WHITE	34 BROWN with RED	47 RED with BROWN	60 BLACK with BLUE
8 BLUE with BLACK	22 GREEN with PURPLE	35 BROWN with YELLOW	48 RED with BLACK	61 BLACK with WHITE
9 WHITE	23 GREEN with BROWN	36 BROWN with BLUE	49 PURPLE	62 BLACK with GREEN
10 WHITE with RED	24 GREEN with BLACK	37 BROWN with WHITE	50 PURPLE with RED	63 BLACK with PURPLE
11 WHITE with YELLOW	25 YELLOW	38 BROWN with GREEN	51 PURPLE with YELLOW	64 BLACK with BROWN
12 WHITE with BLUE	26 YELLOW with RED	39 BROWN with PURPLE	52 PURPLE with BLUE	65 LIGHT GREEN
13 WHITE with GREEN	27 YELLOW with BLUE	40 BROWN with BLACK	53 PURPLE with WHITE	66 DARK GREEN
14 WHITE with PURPLE				

W35250-1 - MK 7 RHD 1953-1954

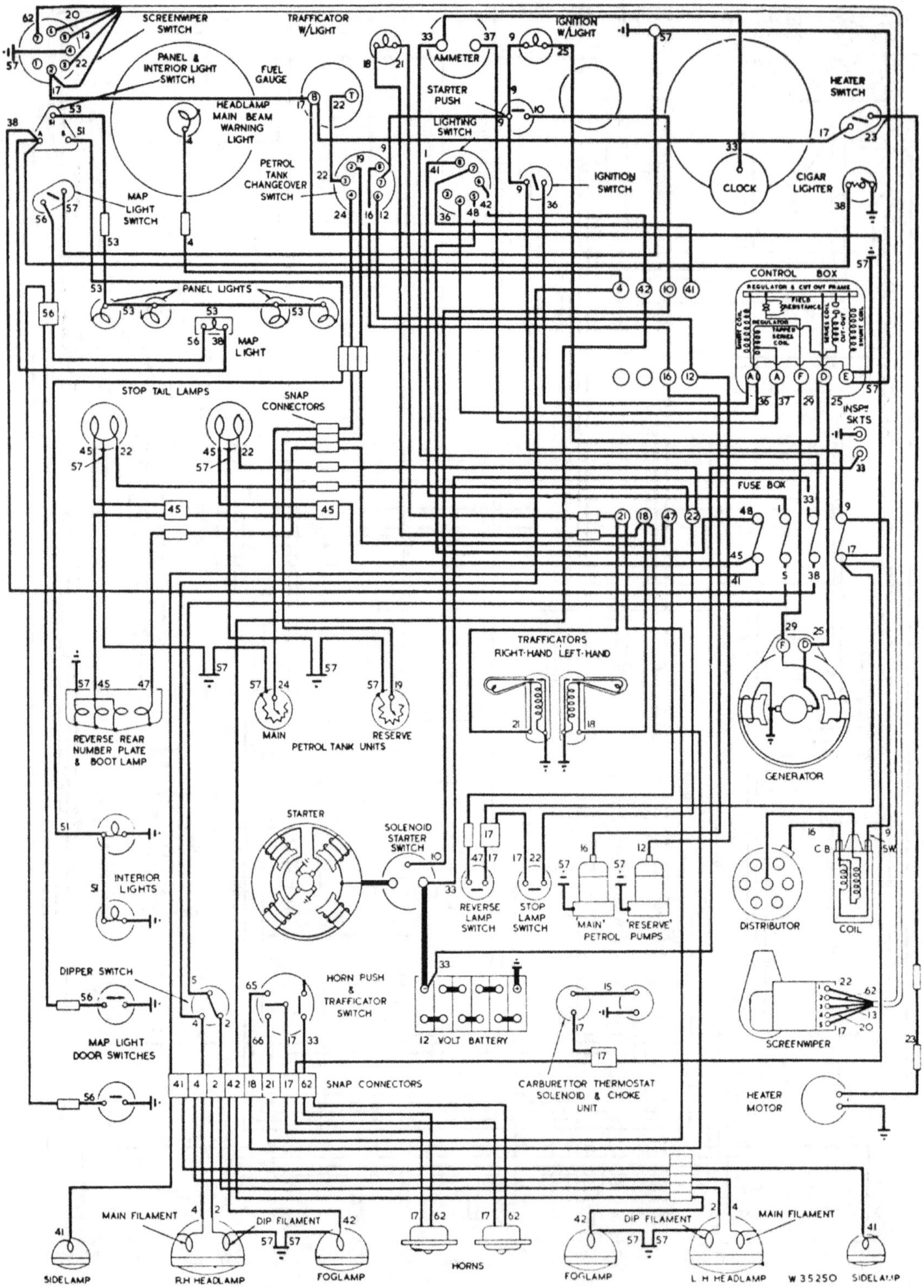

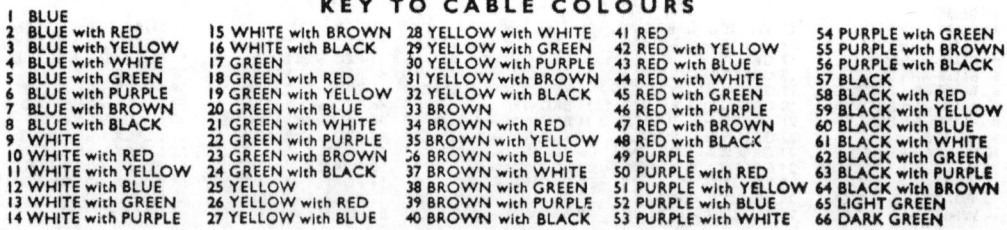

KEY TO CABLE COLOURS

1 BLUE			41 RED	54 PURPLE with GREEN
2 BLUE with RED	15 WHITE with BROWN	28 YELLOW with WHITE	42 RED with YELLOW	55 PURPLE with BROWN
3 BLUE with YELLOW	16 WHITE with BLACK	29 YELLOW with GREEN	43 RED with BLUE	56 PURPLE with BLACK
4 BLUE with WHITE	17 GREEN	30 YELLOW with PURPLE	44 RED with WHITE	57 BLACK
5 BLUE with GREEN	18 GREEN with RED	31 YELLOW with BROWN	45 RED with GREEN	58 BLACK with RED
6 BLUE with PURPLE	19 GREEN with YELLOW	32 YELLOW with BLACK	46 RED with PURPLE	59 BLACK with YELLOW
7 BLUE with BROWN	20 GREEN with BLUE	33 BROWN	47 RED with BROWN	60 BLACK with BLUE
8 BLUE with BLACK	21 GREEN with WHITE	34 BROWN with RED	48 RED with BLACK	61 BLACK with WHITE
9 WHITE	22 GREEN with PURPLE	35 BROWN with YELLOW	49 PURPLE	62 BLACK with GREEN
10 WHITE with RED	23 GREEN with BROWN	36 BROWN with BLUE	50 PURPLE with RED	63 BLACK with PURPLE
11 WHITE with YELLOW	24 GREEN with BLACK	37 BROWN with WHITE	51 PURPLE with YELLOW	64 BLACK with BROWN
12 WHITE with BLUE	25 YELLOW	38 BROWN with GREEN	52 PURPLE with BLUE	65 LIGHT GREEN
13 WHITE with GREEN	26 YELLOW with RED	39 BROWN with PURPLE	53 PURPLE with WHITE	66 DARK GREEN
14 WHITE with PURPLE	27 YELLOW with BLUE	40 BROWN with BLACK		

W79601-1 - MK 7 RHD 1951-1952 (Export)

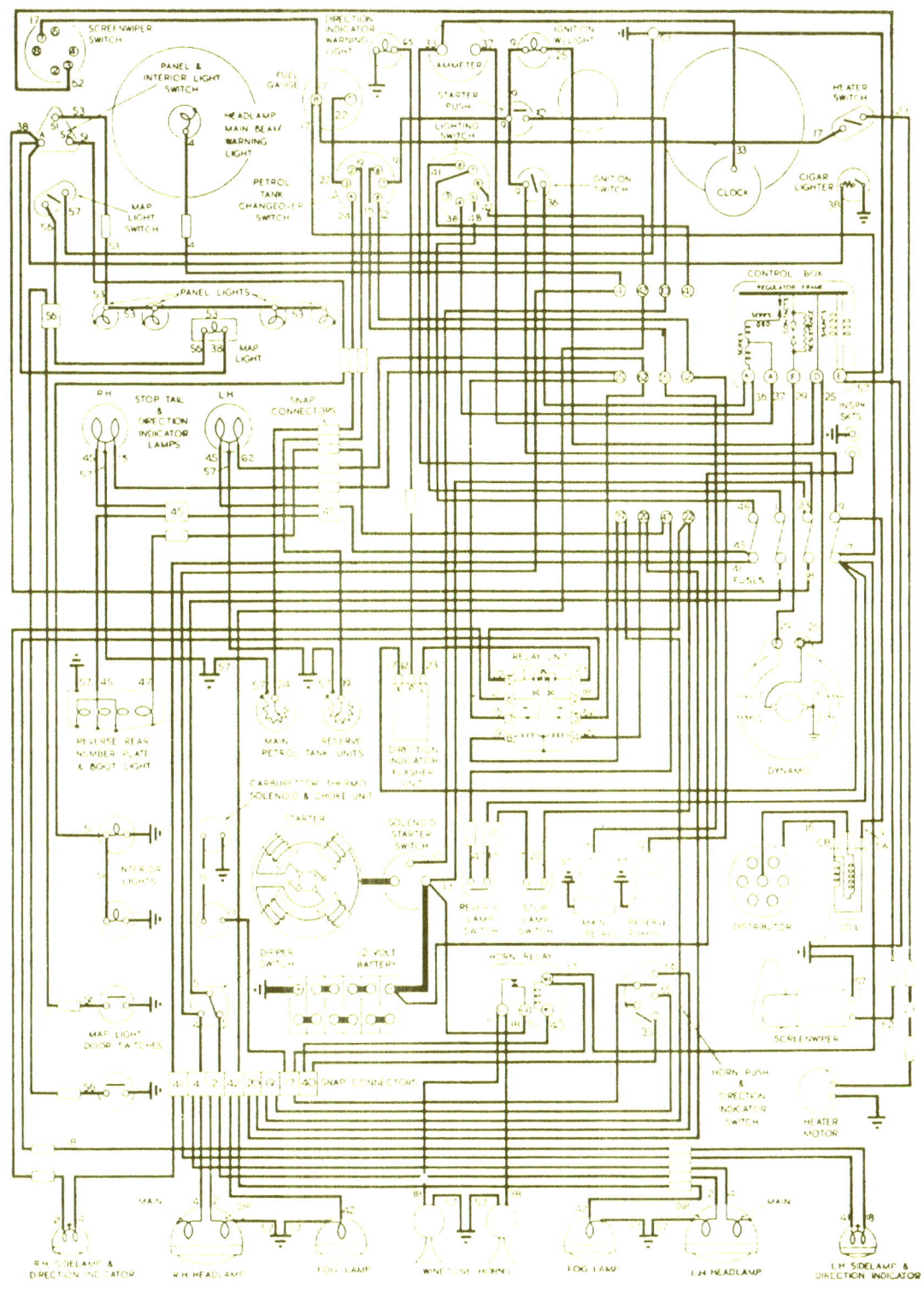

KEY TO CABLE COLOURS

1 BLUE	15 WHITE with BROWN	28 YELLOW with WHITE	41 RED	54 PURPLE with GREEN
2 BLUE with RED	16 WHITE with BLACK	29 YELLOW with GREEN	42 RED with YELLOW	55 PURPLE with BROWN
3 BLUE with YELLOW	17 GREEN	30 YELLOW with PURPLE	43 RED with BLUE	56 PURPLE with BLACK
4 BLUE with WHITE	18 GREEN with RED	31 YELLOW with BROWN	44 RED with WHITE	57 BLACK
5 BLUE with GREEN	19 GREEN with YELLOW	32 YELLOW with BLACK	45 RED with GREEN	58 BLACK with RED
6 BLUE with PURPLE	20 GREEN with BLUE	33 BROWN	46 RED with PURPLE	59 BLACK with YELLOW
7 BLUE with BROWN	21 GREEN with WHITE	34 BROWN with RED	47 RED with BROWN	60 BLACK with BLUE
8 BLUE with BLACK	22 GREEN with PURPLE	35 BROWN with YELLOW	48 RED with BLACK	61 BLACK with WHITE
9 WHITE	23 GREEN with BROWN	36 BROWN with BLUE	49 PURPLE	62 BLACK with GREEN
10 WHITE with RED	24 GREEN with BLACK	37 BROWN with WHITE	50 PURPLE with RED	63 BLACK with PURPLE
11 WHITE with YELLOW	25 YELLOW	38 BROWN with GREEN	51 PURPLE with YELLOW	64 BLACK with BROWN
12 WHITE with BLUE	26 YELLOW with RED	39 BROWN with PURPLE	52 PURPLE with BLUE	65 LIGHT GREEN
13 WHITE with GREEN	27 YELLOW with BLUE	40 BROWN with BLACK	53 PURPLE with WHITE	66 DARK GREEN
14 WHITE with PURPLE				

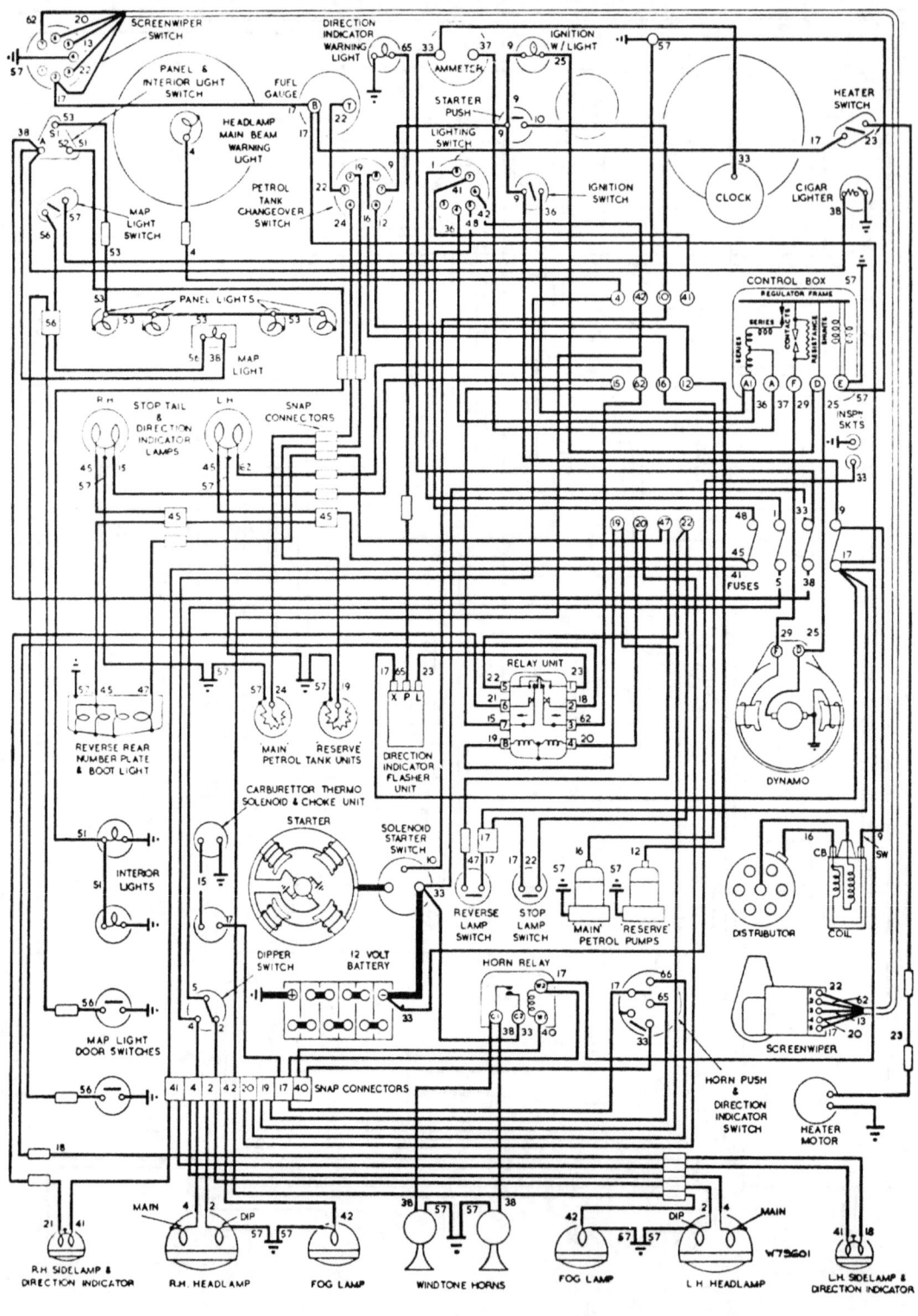

W79603 - MK 7 RHD 1952-1953 (Export)

KEY TO CABLE COLOURS

1 BLUE	15 WHITE with BROWN	28 YELLOW with WHITE	41 RED	54 PURPLE with GREEN
2 BLUE with RED	16 WHITE with BLACK	29 YELLOW with GREEN	42 RED with YELLOW	55 PURPLE with BROWN
3 BLUE with YELLOW	17 GREEN	30 YELLOW with PURPLE	43 RED with BLUE	56 PURPLE with BLACK
4 BLUE with WHITE	18 GREEN with RED	31 YELLOW with BROWN	44 RED with WHITE	57 BLACK
5 BLUE with GREEN	19 GREEN with YELLOW	32 YELLOW with BLACK	45 RED with GREEN	58 BLACK with RED
6 BLUE with PURPLE	20 GREEN with BLUE	33 BROWN	46 RED with PURPLE	59 BLACK with YELLOW
7 BLUE with BROWN	21 GREEN with WHITE	34 BROWN with RED	47 RED with BROWN	60 BLACK with BLUE
8 BLUE with BLACK	22 GREEN with PURPLE	35 BROWN with YELLOW	48 RED with BLACK	61 BLACK with WHITE
9 WHITE	23 GREEN with BROWN	36 BROWN with BLUE	49 PURPLE	62 BLACK with GREEN
10 WHITE with RED	24 GREEN with BLACK	37 BROWN with WHITE	50 PURPLE with RED	63 BLACK with PURPLE
11 WHITE with YELLOW	25 YELLOW	38 BROWN with GREEN	51 PURPLE with YELLOW	64 BLACK with BROWN
12 WHITE with BLUE	26 YELLOW with RED	39 BROWN with PURPLE	52 PURPLE with BLUE	65 LIGHT GREEN
13 WHITE with GREEN	27 YELLOW with BLUE	40 BROWN with BLACK	53 PURPLE with WHITE	66 DARK GREEN
14 WHITE with PURPLE				

W35251 - MK 7 RHD 1953-1954 (Export)

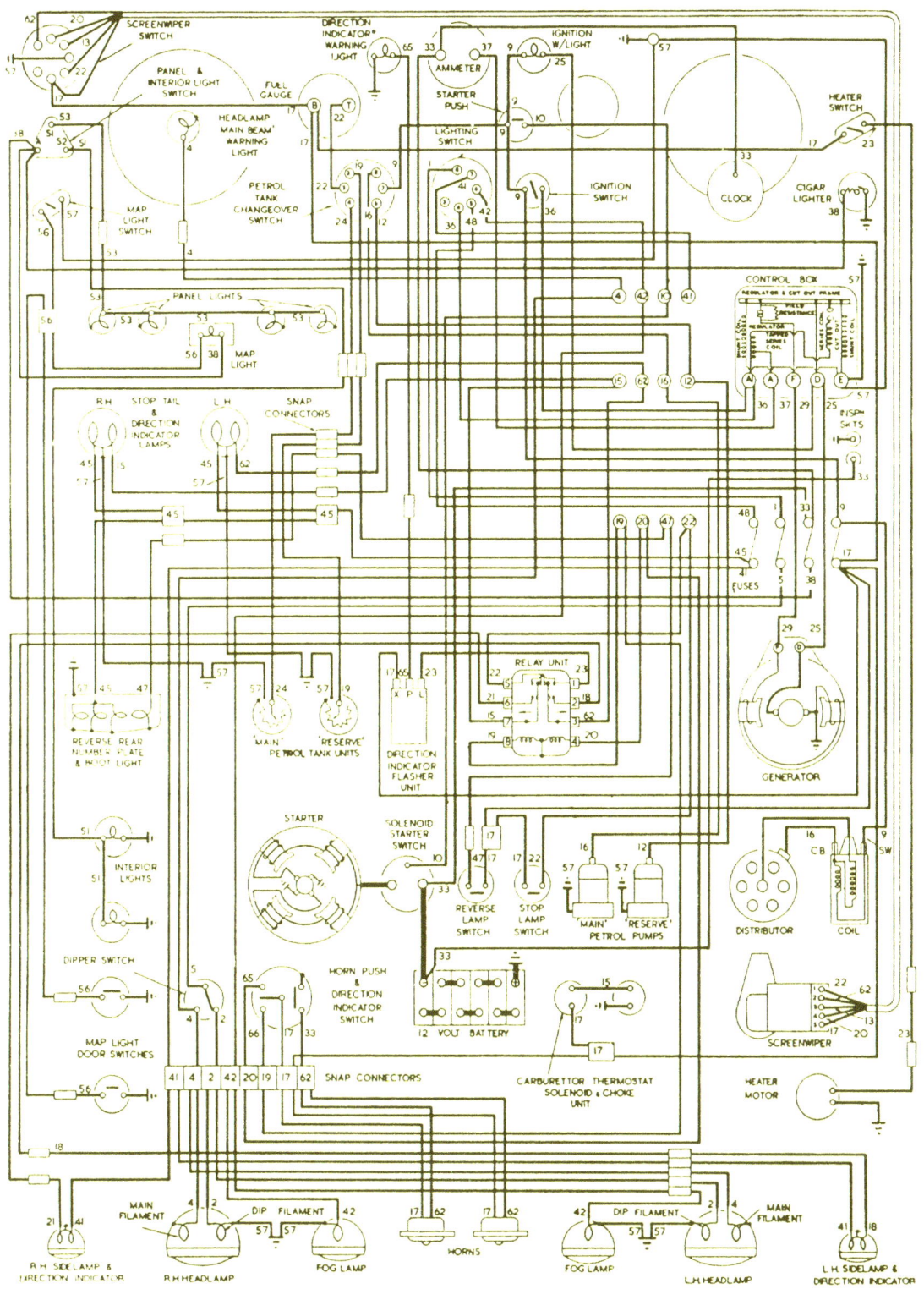

KEY TO CABLE COLOURS

1 BLUE	15 WHITE with BROWN	28 YELLOW with WHITE	41 RED	54 PURPLE with GREEN
2 BLUE with RED	16 WHITE with BLACK	29 YELLOW with GREEN	42 RED with YELLOW	55 PURPLE with BROWN
3 BLUE with YELLOW	17 GREEN	30 YELLOW with PURPLE	43 RED with BLUE	56 PURPLE with BLACK
4 BLUE with WHITE	18 GREEN with RED	31 YELLOW with BROWN	44 RED with WHITE	57 BLACK
5 BLUE with GREEN	19 GREEN with YELLOW	32 YELLOW with BLACK	45 RED with GREEN	58 BLACK with RED
6 BLUE with PURPLE	20 GREEN with BLUE	33 BROWN	46 RED with PURPLE	59 BLACK with YELLOW
7 BLUE with BROWN	21 GREEN with WHITE	34 BROWN with RED	47 RED with BROWN	60 BLACK with BLUE
8 BLUE with BLACK	22 GREEN with PURPLE	35 BROWN with YELLOW	48 RED with BLACK	61 BLACK with WHITE
9 WHITE	23 GREEN with BROWN	36 BROWN with BLUE	49 PURPLE	62 BLACK with GREEN
10 WHITE with RED	24 GREEN with BLACK	37 BROWN with WHITE	50 PURPLE with RED	63 BLACK with PURPLE
11 WHITE with YELLOW	25 YELLOW	38 BROWN with GREEN	51 PURPLE with YELLOW	64 BLACK with BROWN
12 WHITE with BLUE	26 YELLOW with RED	39 BROWN with PURPLE	52 PURPLE with BLUE	65 LIGHT GREEN
13 WHITE with GREEN	27 YELLOW with BLUE	40 BROWN with BLACK	53 PURPLE with WHITE	66 DARK GREEN
14 WHITE with PURPLE				

W79620 - MK 7 LHD 1951-1952 (Export)

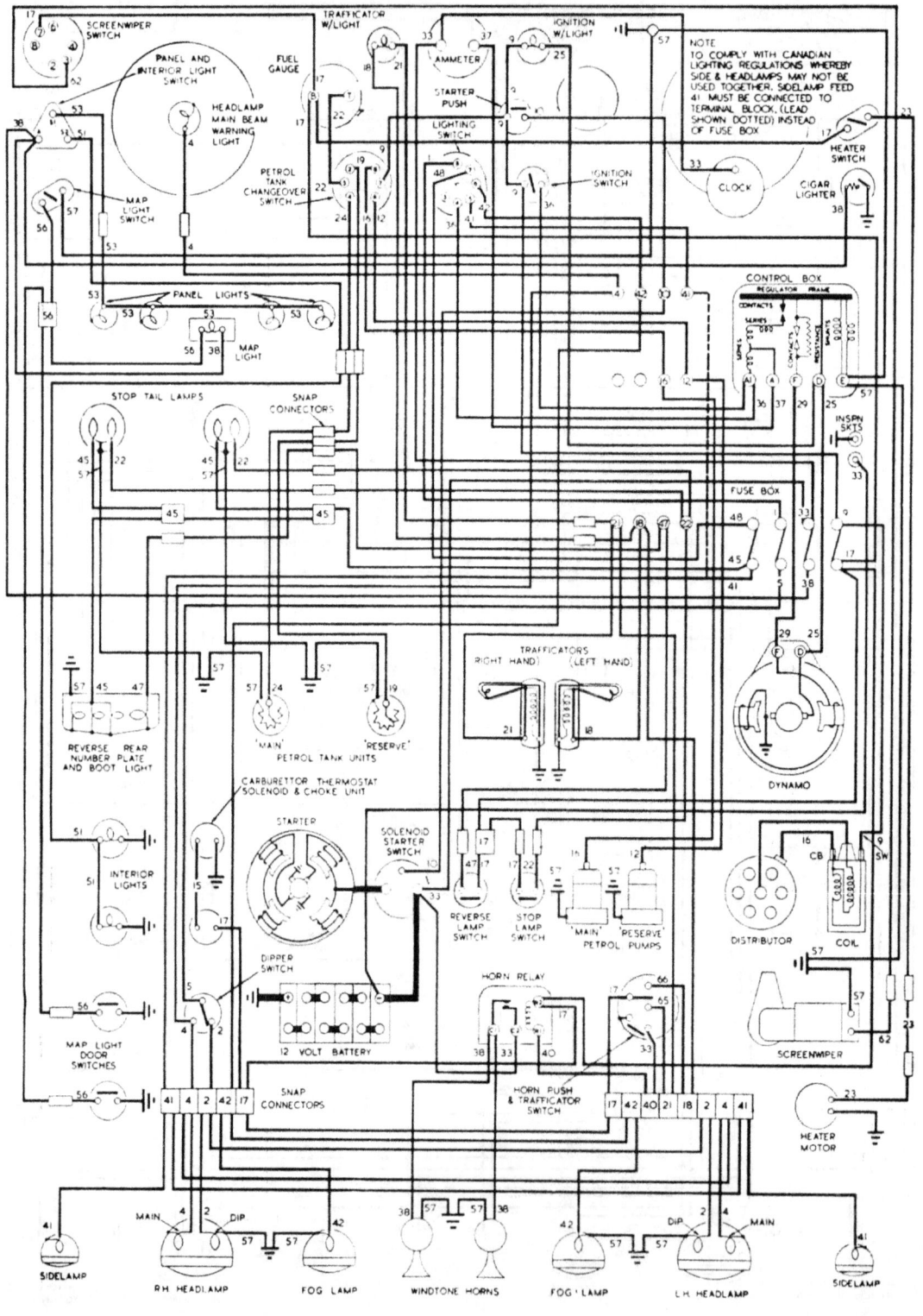

KEY TO CABLE COLOURS

1 BLUE	15 WHITE with BROWN	28 YELLOW with WHITE	41 RED	54 PURPLE with GREEN
2 BLUE with RED	16 WHITE with BLACK	29 YELLOW with GREEN	42 RED with YELLOW	55 PURPLE with BROWN
3 BLUE with YELLOW	17 GREEN	30 YELLOW with PURPLE	43 RED with BLUE	56 PURPLE with BLACK
4 BLUE with WHITE	18 GREEN with RED	31 YELLOW with WHITE	44 RED with WHITE	57 BLACK
5 BLUE with GREEN	19 GREEN with YELLOW	32 YELLOW with BLACK	45 RED with GREEN	58 BLACK with RED
6 BLUE with PURPLE	20 GREEN with BLUE	33 BROWN	46 RED with PURPLE	59 BLACK with YELLOW
7 BLUE with BROWN	21 GREEN with WHITE	34 BROWN with RED	47 RED with BROWN	60 BLACK with BLUE
8 BLUE with BLACK	22 GREEN with PURPLE	35 BROWN with YELLOW	48 RED with BLACK	61 BLACK with WHITE
9 WHITE	23 GREEN with BROWN	36 BROWN with BLUE	49 PURPLE	62 BLACK with GREEN
10 WHITE with RED	24 GREEN with BLACK	37 BROWN with WHITE	50 PURPLE with RED	63 BLACK with PURPLE
11 WHITE with YELLOW	25 YELLOW	38 BROWN with GREEN	51 PURPLE with YELLOW	64 BLACK with BROWN
12 WHITE with BLUE	26 YELLOW with RED	39 BROWN with PURPLE	52 PURPLE with BLUE	65 LIGHT GREEN
13 WHITE with GREEN	27 YELLOW with BLUE	40 BROWN with BLACK	53 PURPLE with WHITE	66 DARK GREEN
14 WHITE with PURPLE				

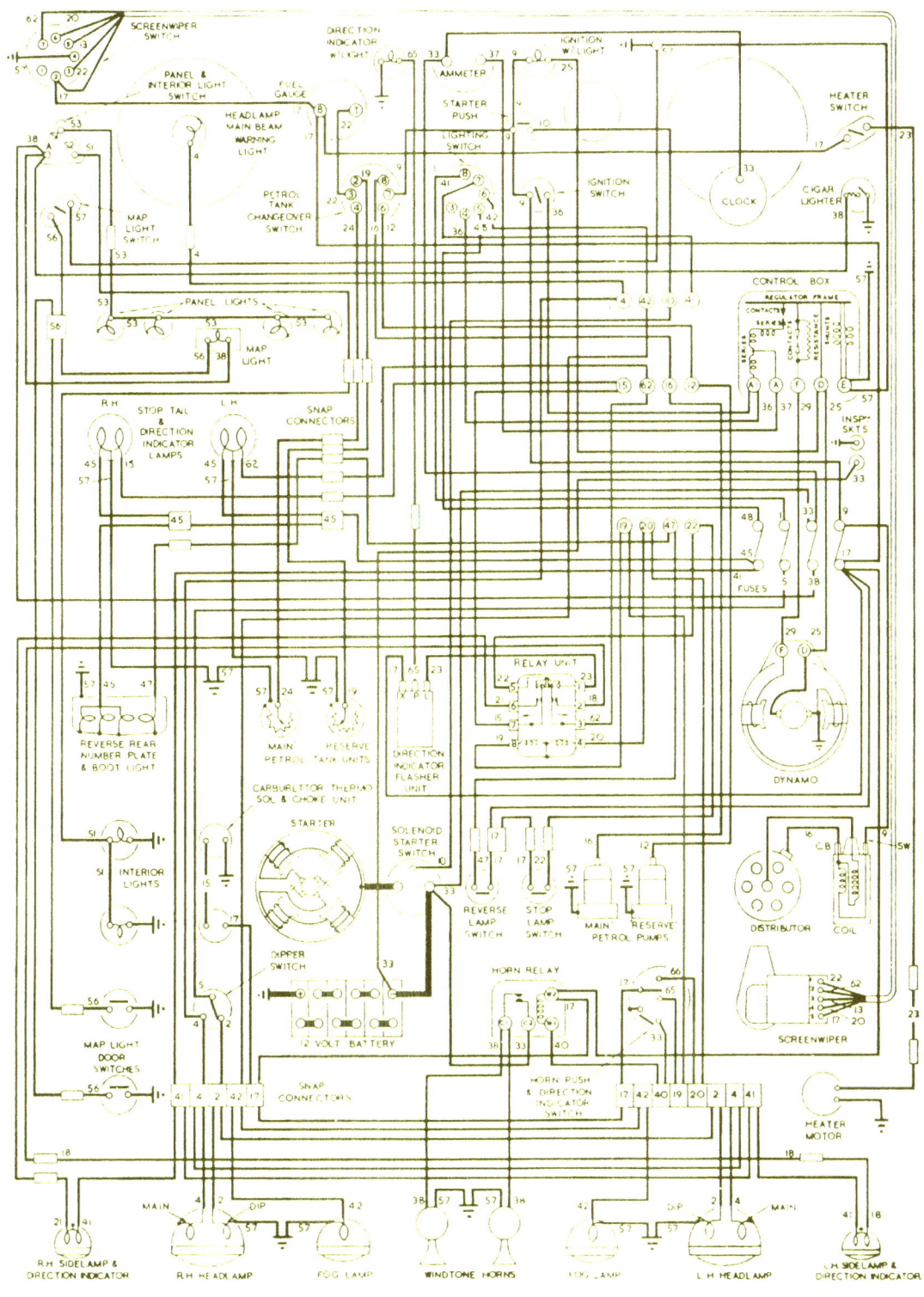

W79622 - MK 7 LHD 1952-1953 (Export)

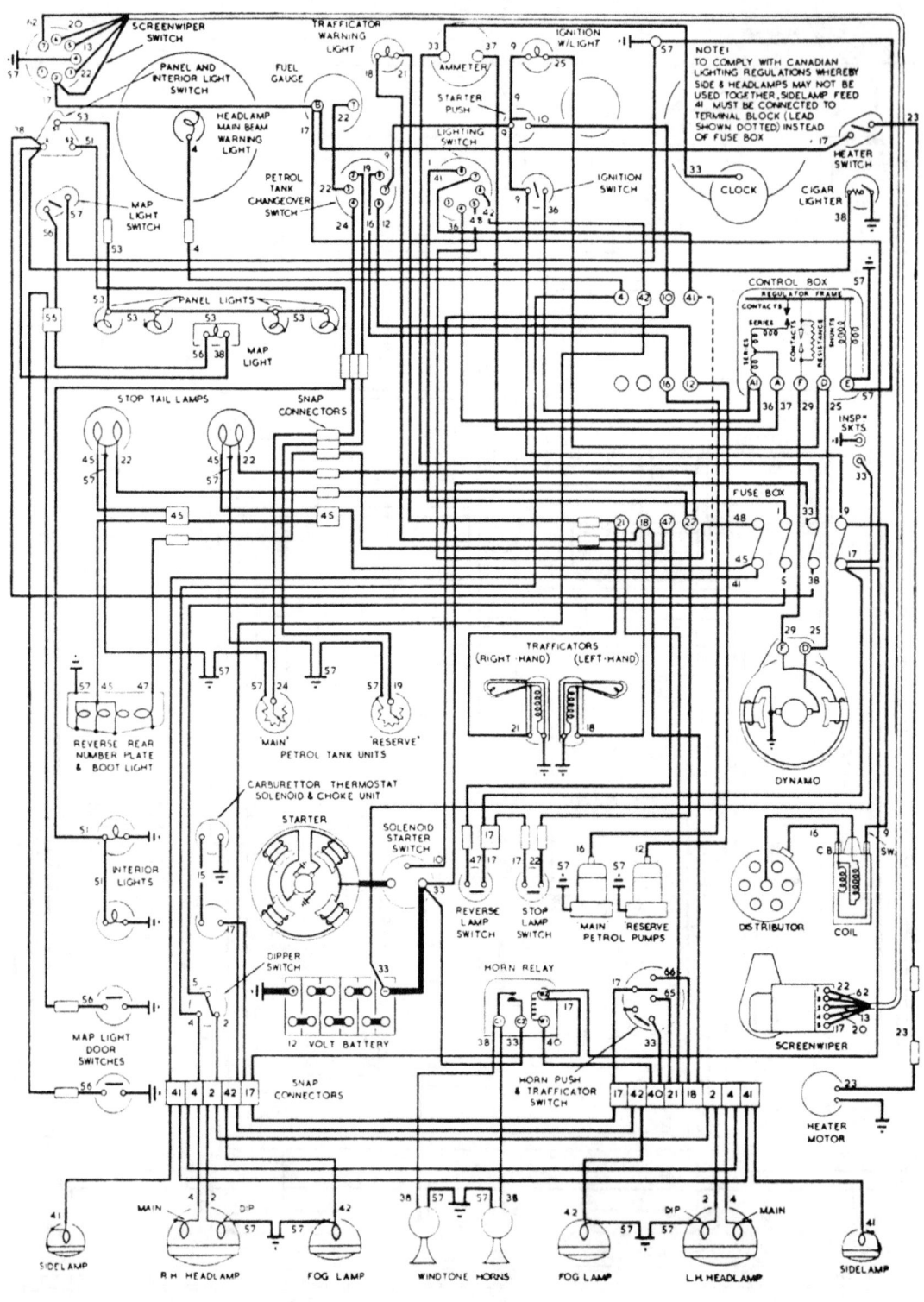

KEY TO CABLE COLOURS

1 BLUE	15 WHITE with BROWN	28 YELLOW with WHITE	41 RED	54 PURPLE with GREEN
2 BLUE with RED	16 WHITE with BLACK	29 YELLOW with GREEN	42 RED with YELLOW	55 PURPLE with BROWN
3 BLUE with YELLOW	17 GREEN	30 YELLOW with PURPLE	43 RED with BLUE	56 PURPLE with BLACK
4 BLUE with WHITE	18 GREEN with RED	31 YELLOW with BROWN	44 RED with WHITE	57 BLACK
5 BLUE with GREEN	19 GREEN with YELLOW	32 YELLOW with BLACK	45 RED with GREEN	58 BLACK with RED
6 BLUE with PURPLE	20 GREEN with BLUE	33 BROWN	46 RED with PURPLE	59 BLACK with YELLOW
7 BLUE with BROWN	21 GREEN with WHITE	34 BROWN with RED	47 RED with BROWN	60 BLACK with BLUE
8 BLUE with BLACK	22 GREEN with PURPLE	35 BROWN with YELLOW	48 RED with BLACK	61 BLACK with WHITE
9 WHITE	23 GREEN with BROWN	36 BROWN with BLUE	49 PURPLE	62 BLACK with GREEN
10 WHITE with RED	24 GREEN with BLACK	37 BROWN with WHITE	50 PURPLE with RED	63 BLACK with PURPLE
11 WHITE with YELLOW	25 YELLOW	38 BROWN with GREEN	51 PURPLE with YELLOW	64 BLACK with BROWN
12 WHITE with BLUE	26 YELLOW with RED	39 BROWN with PURPLE	52 PURPLE with BLUE	65 DARK GREEN
13 WHITE with GREEN	27 YELLOW with BLUE	40 BROWN with BLACK	53 PURPLE with WHITE	66 LIGHT GREEN
14 WHITE with PURPLE				

W79623 - MK 7 LHD 1952-1953 (Export)

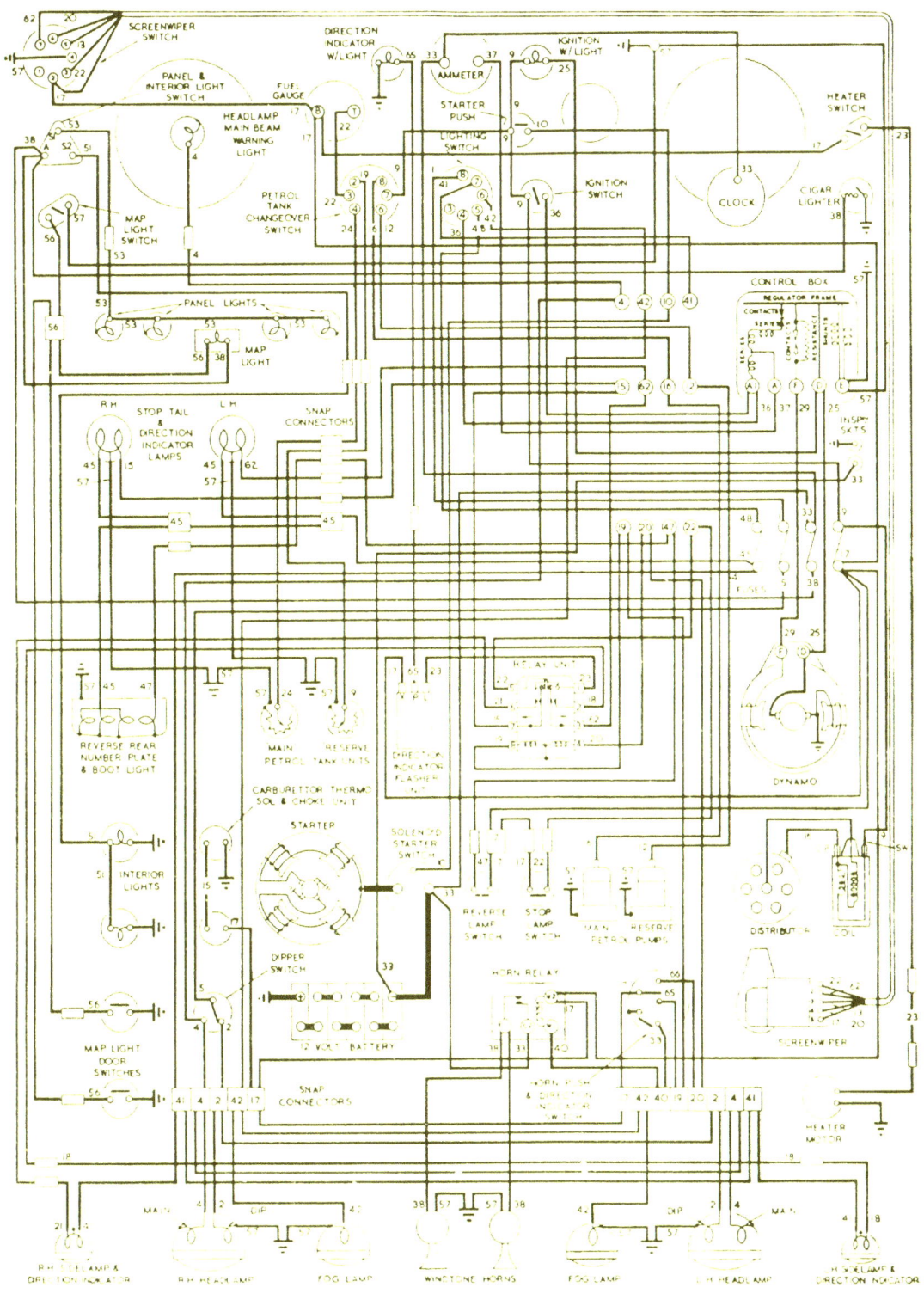

KEY TO CABLE COLOURS

1 BLUE	15 WHITE with BROWN	28 YELLOW with WHITE	41 RED	54 PURPLE with GREEN
2 BLUE with RED	16 WHITE with BLACK	29 YELLOW with GREEN	42 RED with YELLOW	55 PURPLE with BROWN
3 BLUE with YELLOW	17 GREEN	30 YELLOW with PURPLE	43 RED with BLUE	56 PURPLE with BLACK
4 BLUE with WHITE	18 GREEN with RED	31 YELLOW with BROWN	44 RED with WHITE	57 BLACK
5 BLUE with GREEN	19 GREEN with YELLOW	32 YELLOW with BLACK	45 RED with GREEN	58 BLACK with RED
6 BLUE with PURPLE	20 GREEN with BLUE	33 BROWN	46 RED with PURPLE	59 BLACK with YELLOW
7 BLUE with BROWN	21 GREEN with WHITE	34 BROWN with RED	47 RED with BROWN	60 BLACK with BLUE
8 BLUE with BLACK	22 GREEN with PURPLE	35 BROWN with YELLOW	48 RED with BLACK	61 BLACK with WHITE
9 WHITE	23 GREEN with BROWN	36 BROWN with BLUE	49 PURPLE	62 BLACK with GREEN
10 WHITE with RED	24 GREEN with BLACK	37 BROWN with WHITE	50 PURPLE with RED	63 BLACK with PURPLE
11 WHITE with YELLOW	25 YELLOW	38 BROWN with GREEN	51 PURPLE with YELLOW	64 BLACK with BROWN
12 WHITE with BLUE	26 YELLOW with RED	39 BROWN with PURPLE	52 PURPLE with BLUE	65 LIGHT GREEN
13 WHITE with GREEN	27 YELLOW with BLUE	40 BROWN with BLACK	53 PURPLE with WHITE	66 DARK GREEN
14 WHITE with PURPLE				

W35260-1 - MK 7 LHD 1953-1954 (Export)

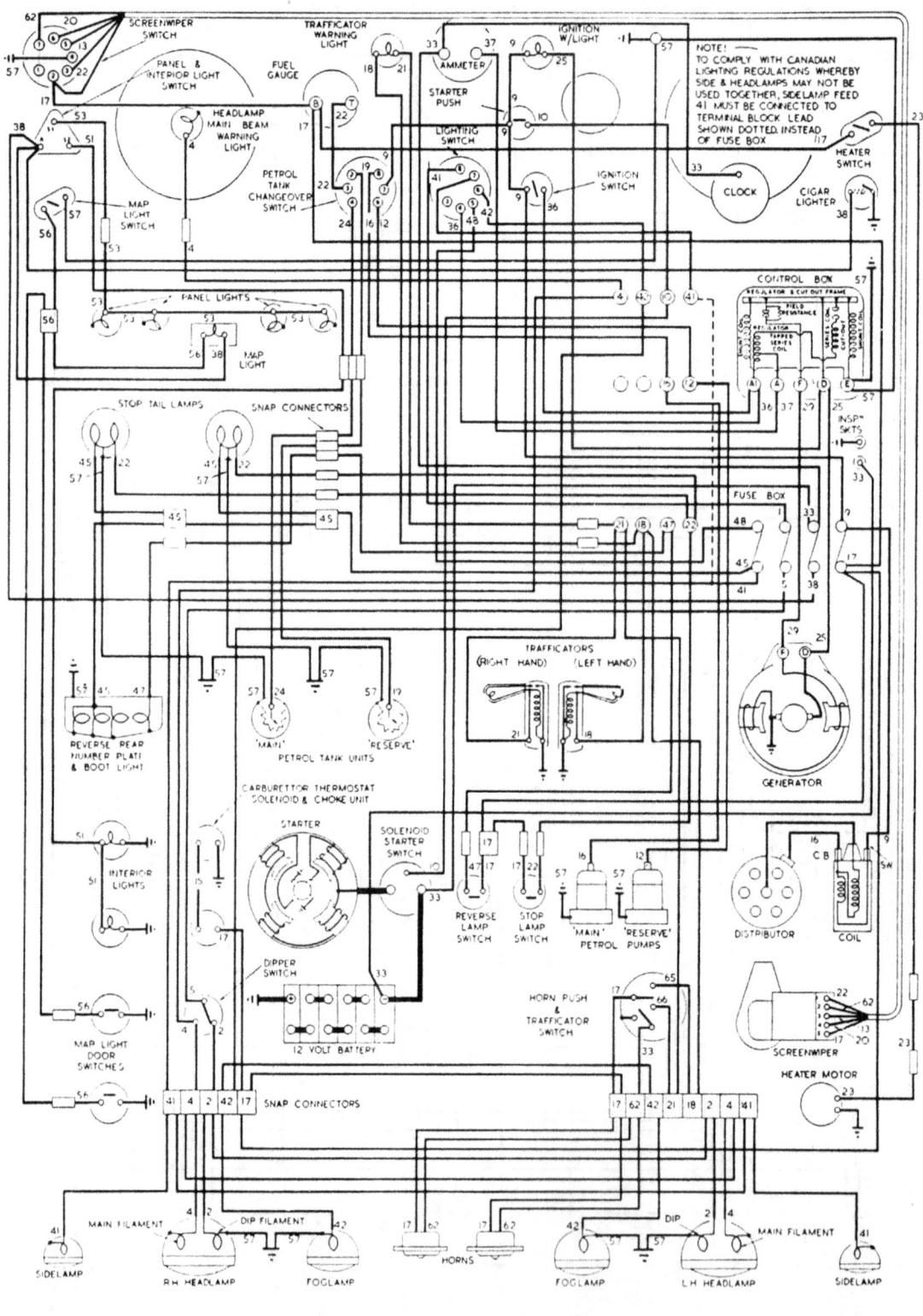

KEY TO CABLE COLOURS

1 BLUE		28 YELLOW with WHITE	41 RED	54 PURPLE with GREEN
2 BLUE with RED	15 WHITE with BROWN	29 YELLOW with GREEN	42 RED with YELLOW	55 PURPLE with BROWN
3 BLUE with YELLOW	16 WHITE with BLACK	30 YELLOW with PURPLE	43 RED with BLUE	56 PURPLE with BLACK
4 BLUE with WHITE	17 GREEN	31 YELLOW with BROWN	44 RED with WHITE	57 BLACK
5 BLUE with GREEN	18 GREEN with RED	32 YELLOW with BLACK	45 RED with GREEN	58 BLACK with RED
6 BLUE with PURPLE	19 GREEN with YELLOW	33 BROWN	46 RED with PURPLE	59 BLACK with YELLOW
7 BLUE with BROWN	20 GREEN with BLUE	34 BROWN with RED	47 RED with BROWN	60 BLACK with BLUE
8 BLUE with BLACK	21 GREEN with WHITE	35 BROWN with YELLOW	48 RED with BLACK	61 BLACK with WHITE
9 WHITE	22 GREEN with PURPLE	36 BROWN with BLUE	49 PURPLE	62 BLACK with GREEN
10 WHITE with RED	23 GREEN with BROWN	37 BROWN with WHITE	50 PURPLE with RED	63 BLACK with PURPLE
11 WHITE with YELLOW	24 GREEN with BLACK	38 BROWN with GREEN	51 PURPLE with YELLOW	64 BLACK with BROWN
12 WHITE with BLUE	25 YELLOW	39 BROWN with PURPLE	52 PURPLE with BLUE	65 DARK GREEN
13 WHITE with GREEN	26 YELLOW with RED	40 BROWN with BLACK	53 PURPLE with WHITE	66 LIGHT GREEN
14 WHITE with PURPLE	27 YELLOW with BLUE			

W35261-1 - MK 7 LHD 1953-1954 (Export)

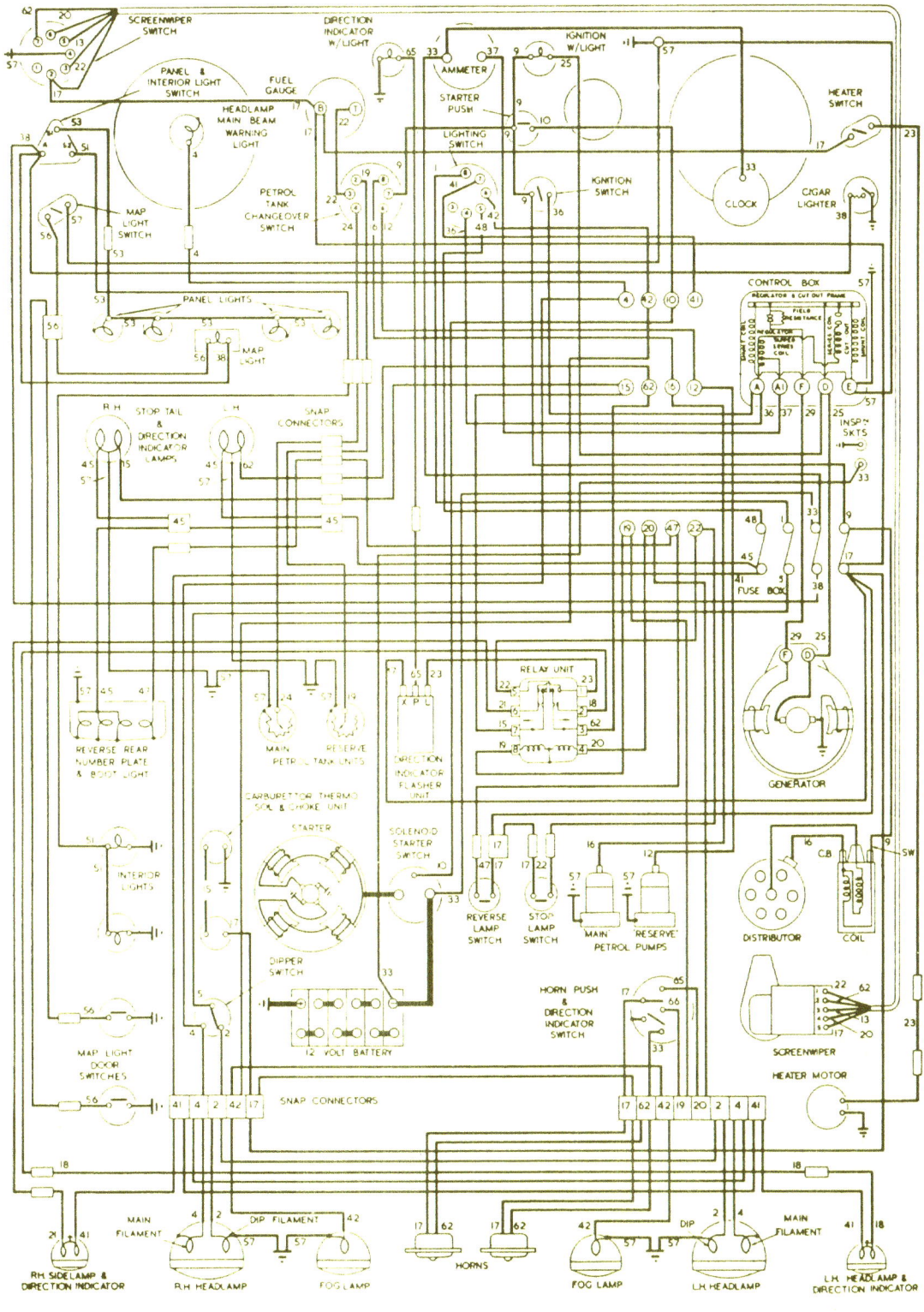

KEY TO CABLE COLOURS

1. BLUE
2. BLUE with RED
3. BLUE with YELLOW
4. BLUE with WHITE
5. BLUE with GREEN
6. BLUE with PURPLE
7. BLUE with BROWN
8. BLUE with BLACK
9. WHITE
10. WHITE with RED
11. WHITE with YELLOW
12. WHITE with BLUE
13. WHITE with GREEN
14. WHITE with PURPLE
15. WHITE with BROWN
16. WHITE with BLACK
17. GREEN
18. GREEN with RED
19. GREEN with YELLOW
20. GREEN with BLUE
21. GREEN with WHITE
22. GREEN with PURPLE
23. GREEN with BROWN
24. GREEN with BLACK
25. YELLOW
26. YELLOW with RED
27. YELLOW with BLUE
28. YELLOW with WHITE
29. YELLOW with GREEN
30. YELLOW with PURPLE
31. YELLOW with BROWN
32. YELLOW with BLACK
33. BROWN
34. BROWN with RED
35. BROWN with YELLOW
36. BROWN with BLUE
37. BROWN with WHITE
38. BROWN with GREEN
39. BROWN with PURPLE
40. BROWN with BLACK
41. RED
42. RED with YELLOW
43. RED with BLUE
44. RED with WHITE
45. RED with GREEN
46. RED with PURPLE
47. RED with BROWN
48. RED with BLACK
49. PURPLE
50. PURPLE with RED
51. PURPLE with YELLOW
52. PURPLE with BLUE
53. PURPLE with WHITE
54. PURPLE with GREEN
55. PURPLE with BROWN
56. PURPLE with BLACK
57. BLACK
58. BLACK with RED
59. BLACK with YELLOW
60. BLACK with BLUE
61. BLACK with WHITE
62. BLACK with GREEN
63. BLACK with PURPLE
64. BLACK with BROWN
65. LIGHT GREEN
66. DARK GREEN

W94601 - XK120 RHD

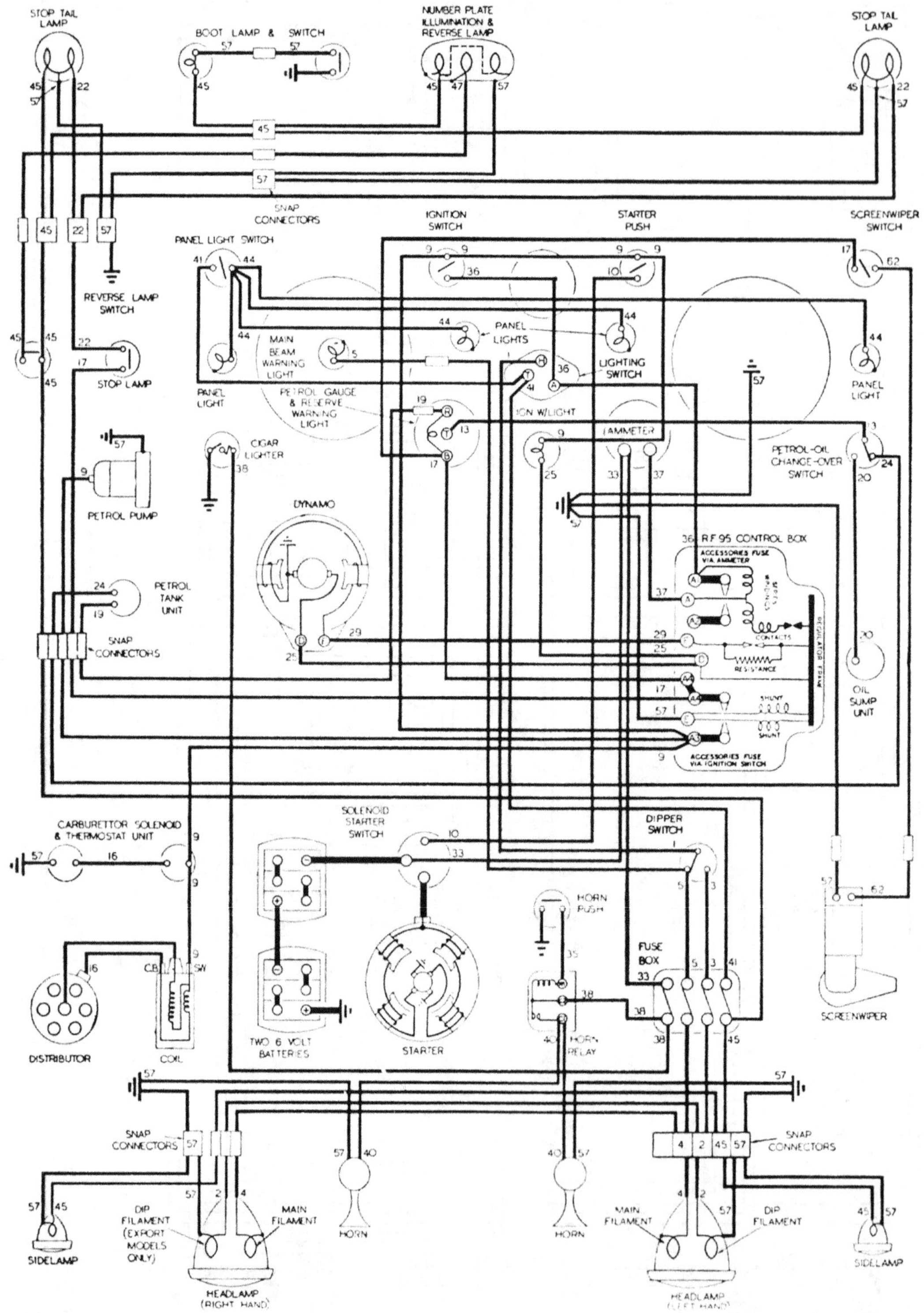

KEY TO CABLE COLOURS

1 BLUE	15 WHITE with BROWN	28 YELLOW with WHITE	41 RED	54 PURPLE with GREEN
2 BLUE with RED	16 WHITE with BLACK	29 YELLOW with GREEN	42 RED with YELLOW	55 PURPLE with BROWN
3 BLUE with YELLOW	17 GREEN	30 YELLOW with PURPLE	43 RED with BLUE	56 PURPLE with BLACK
4 BLUE with WHITE	18 GREEN with RED	31 YELLOW with BROWN	44 RED with WHITE	57 BLACK
5 BLUE with GREEN	19 GREEN with YELLOW	32 YELLOW with BLACK	45 RED with GREEN	58 BLACK with RED
6 BLUE with PURPLE	20 GREEN with BLUE	33 BROWN	46 RED with PURPLE	59 BLACK with YELLOW
7 BLUE with BROWN	21 GREEN with WHITE	34 BROWN with RED	47 RED with BROWN	60 BLACK with BLUE
8 BLUE with BLACK	22 GREEN with PURPLE	35 BROWN with YELLOW	48 RED with BLACK	61 BLACK with WHITE
9 WHITE	23 GREEN with BROWN	36 BROWN with BLUE	49 PURPLE	62 BLACK with GREEN
10 WHITE with RED	24 GREEN with BLACK	37 BROWN with WHITE	50 PURPLE with RED	63 BLACK with PURPLE
11 WHITE with YELLOW	25 YELLOW	38 BROWN with GREEN	51 PURPLE with YELLOW	64 BLACK with BROWN
12 WHITE with BLUE	26 YELLOW with RED	39 BROWN with PURPLE	52 PURPLE with BLUE	65 LIGHT GREEN
13 WHITE with GREEN	27 YELLOW with BLUE	40 BROWN with BLACK	53 PURPLE with WHITE	66 DARK GREEN
14 WHITE with PURPLE				

W94641 XK120 LHD

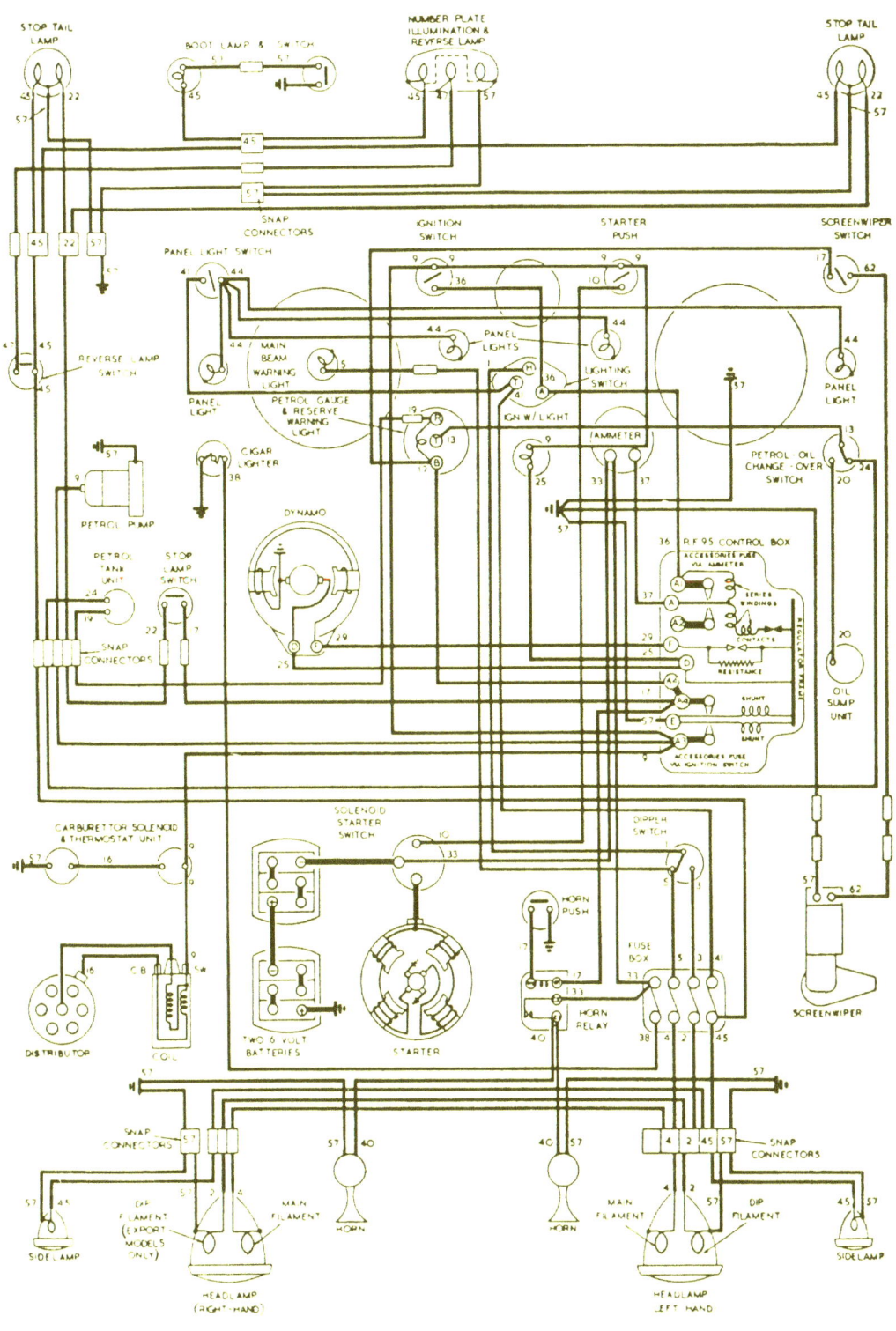

KEY TO CABLE COLOURS

#	Colour	#	Colour	#	Colour	#	Colour
1	BLUE	15	WHITE with BROWN	28	YELLOW with WHITE	41	RED	54	PURPLE with GREEN
2	BLUE with RED	16	WHITE with BLACK	29	YELLOW with GREEN	42	RED with YELLOW	55	PURPLE with BROWN
3	BLUE with YELLOW	17	GREEN	30	YELLOW with PURPLE	43	RED with BLUE	56	PURPLE with BLACK
4	BLUE with WHITE	18	GREEN with RED	31	YELLOW with BROWN	44	RED with WHITE	57	BLACK
5	BLUE with GREEN	19	GREEN with YELLOW	32	YELLOW with BLACK	45	RED with GREEN	58	BLACK with RED
6	BLUE with PURPLE	20	GREEN with BLUE	33	BROWN	46	RED with PURPLE	59	BLACK with YELLOW
7	BLUE with BROWN	21	GREEN with WHITE	34	BROWN with RED	47	RED with BROWN	60	BLACK with BLUE
8	BLUE with BLACK	22	GREEN with PURPLE	35	BROWN with YELLOW	48	RED with BLACK	61	BLACK with WHITE
9	WHITE	23	GREEN with BROWN	36	BROWN with BLUE	49	PURPLE	62	BLACK with GREEN
10	WHITE with RED	24	GREEN with BLACK	37	BROWN with WHITE	50	PURPLE with RED	63	BLACK with PURPLE
11	WHITE with YELLOW	25	YELLOW	38	BROWN with GREEN	51	PURPLE with YELLOW	64	BLACK with BROWN
12	WHITE with BLUE	26	YELLOW with RED	39	BROWN with PURPLE	52	PURPLE with BLUE	65	LIGHT GREEN
13	WHITE with GREEN	27	YELLOW with BLUE	40	BROWN with BLACK	53	PURPLE with WHITE	66	DARK GREEN
14	WHITE with PURPLE								

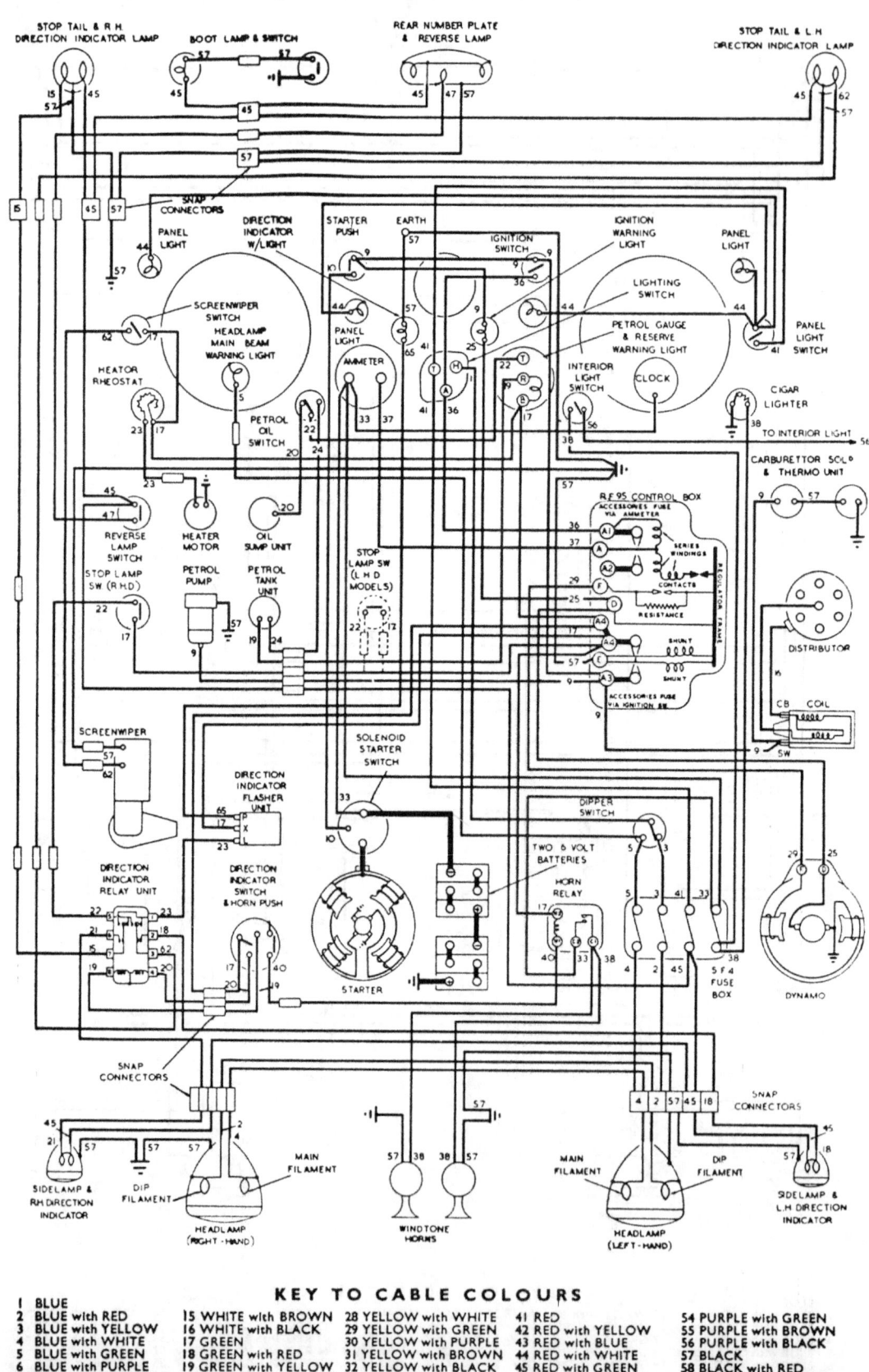

W835251 - MK 8 1957

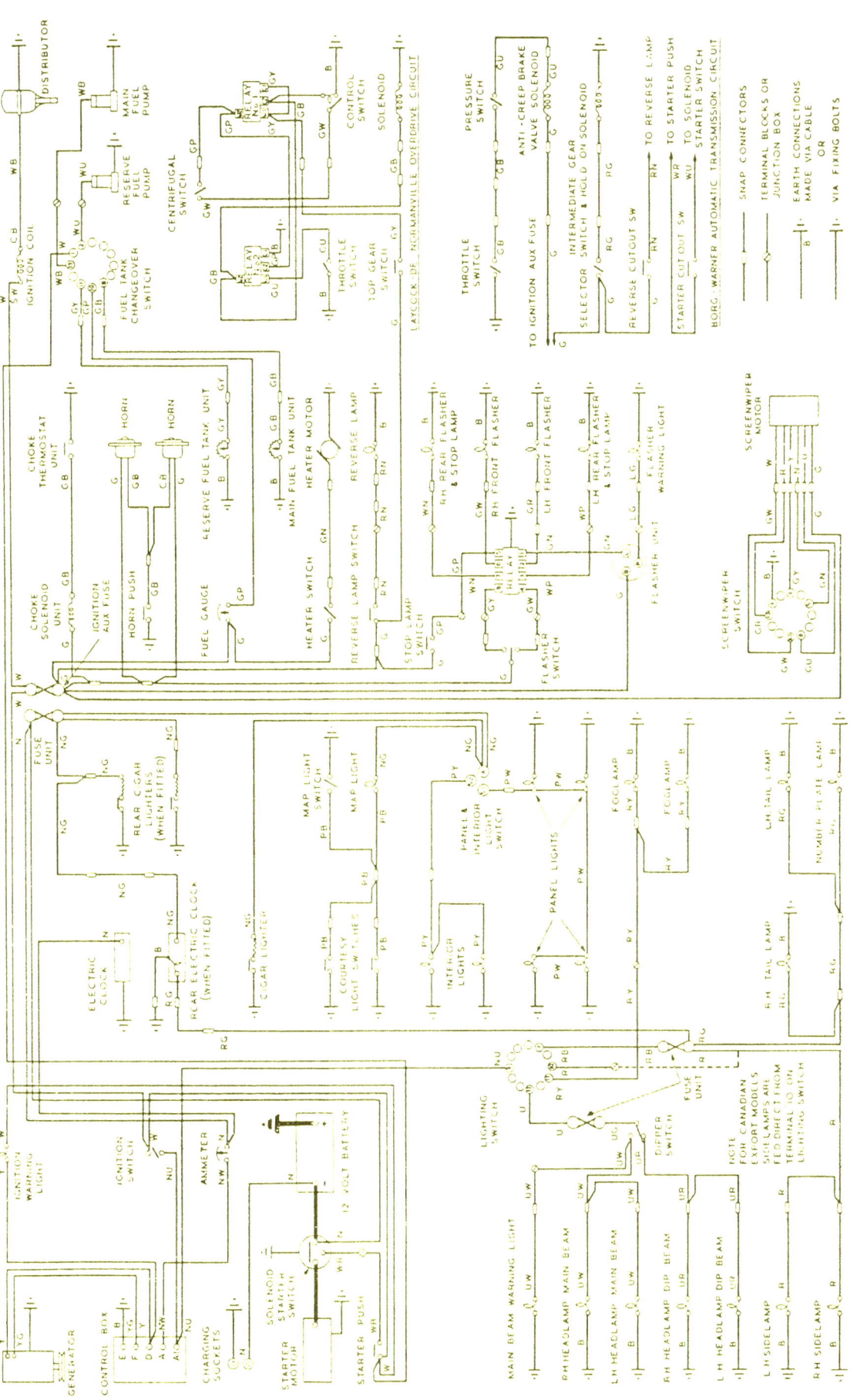

W835251B - MK 8 1957-1958

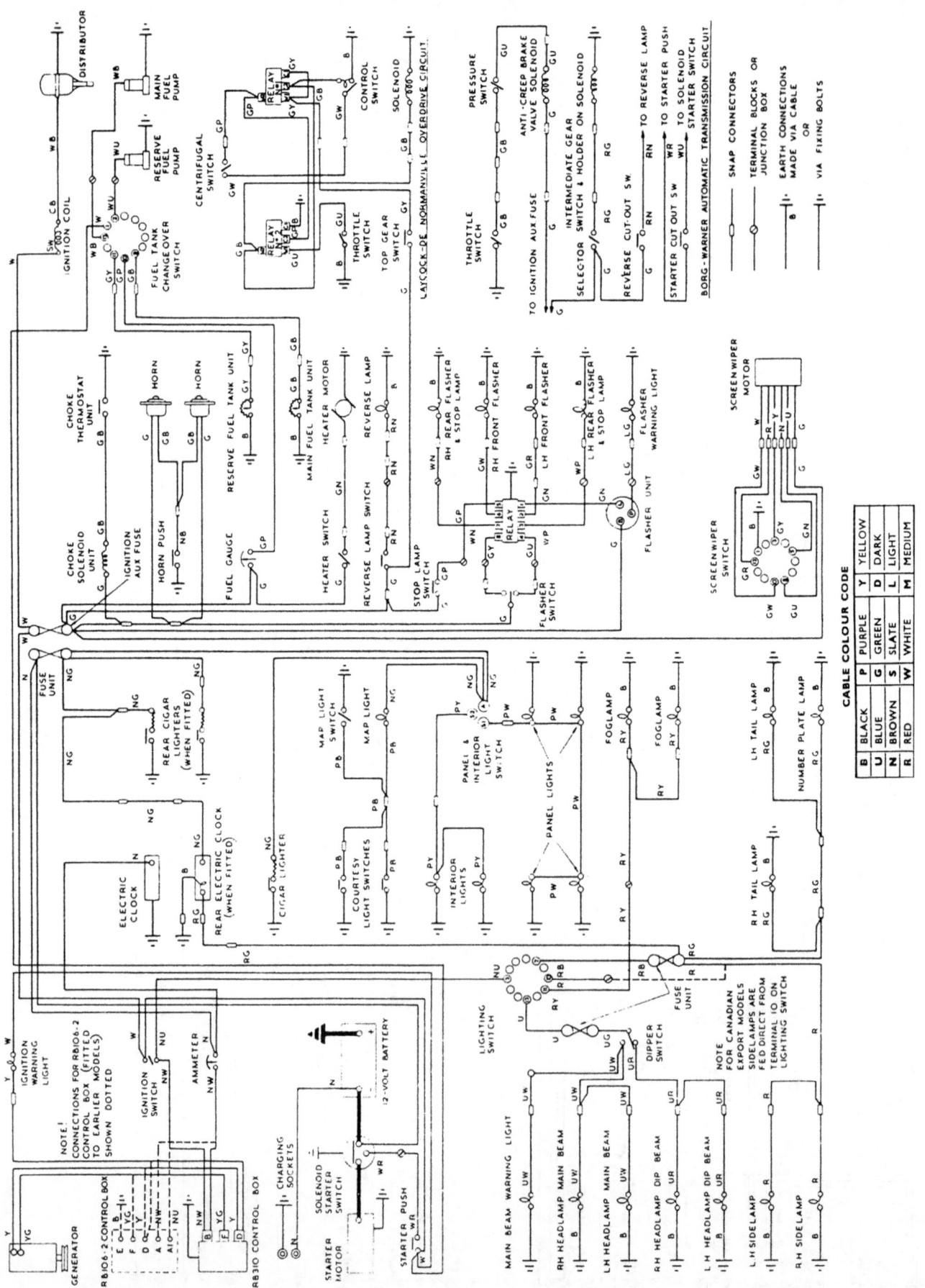

J86-793 - XK140 1955

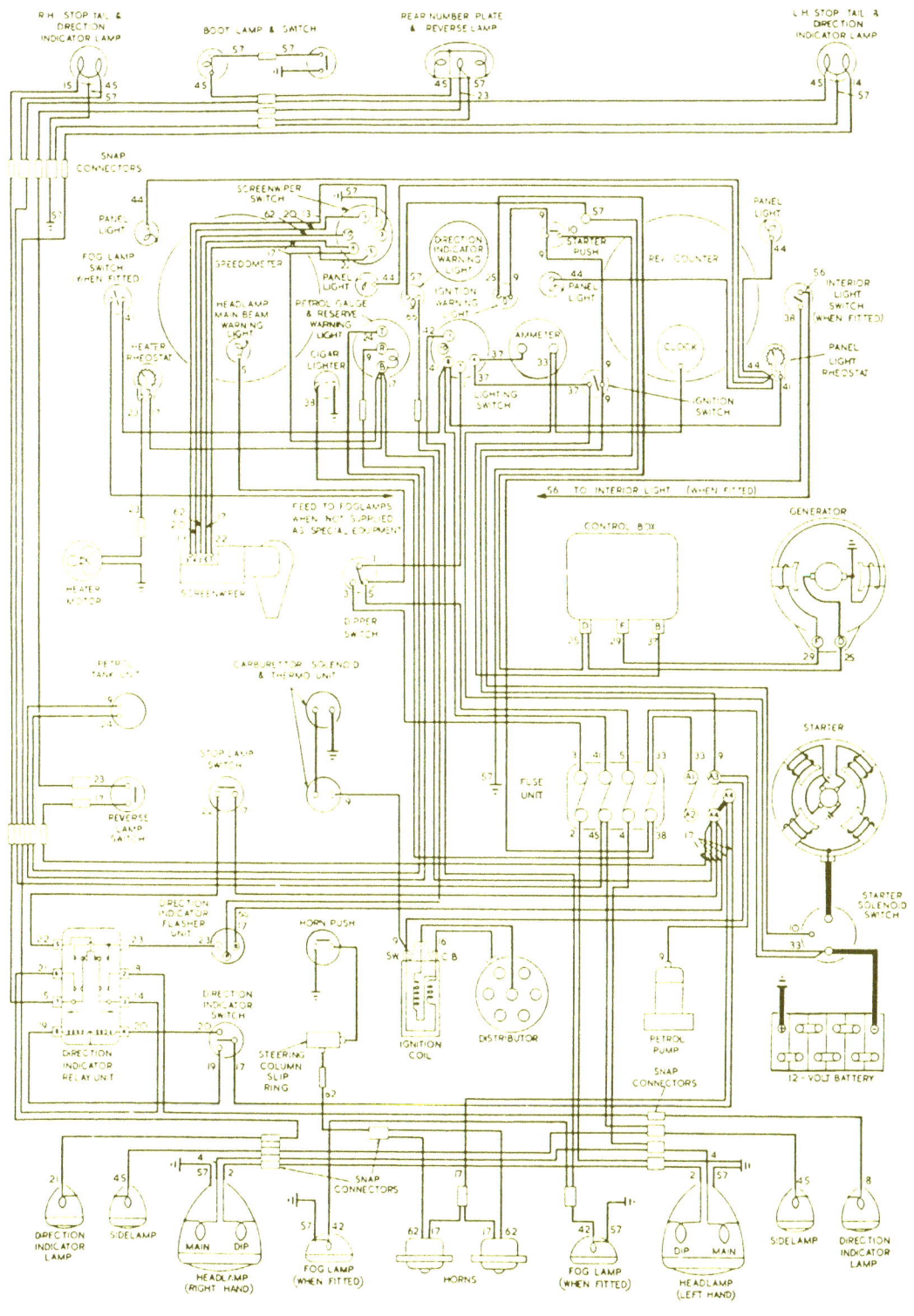

KEY TO CABLE COLOURS

1 BLUE	15 WHITE with BROWN	28 YELLOW with WHITE	41 RED	54 PURPLE with GREEN
2 BLUE with RED	16 WHITE with BLACK	29 YELLOW with GREEN	42 RED with YELLOW	55 PURPLE with BROWN
3 BLUE with YELLOW	17 GREEN	30 YELLOW with PURPLE	43 RED with BLUE	56 PURPLE with BLACK
4 BLUE with WHITE	18 GREEN with RED	31 YELLOW with BROWN	44 RED with WHITE	57 BLACK
5 BLUE with GREEN	19 GREEN with YELLOW	32 YELLOW with BLACK	45 RED with GREEN	58 BLACK with RED
6 BLUE with PURPLE	20 GREEN with BLUE	33 BROWN	46 RED with PURPLE	59 BLACK with YELLOW
7 BLUE with BROWN	21 GREEN with WHITE	34 BROWN with RED	47 RED with BROWN	60 BLACK with BLUE
8 BLUE with BLACK	22 GREEN with PURPLE	35 BROWN with YELLOW	48 RED with BLACK	61 BLACK with WHITE
9 WHITE	23 GREEN with BROWN	36 BROWN with BLUE	49 PURPLE	62 BLACK with GREEN
10 WHITE with RED	24 GREEN with BLACK	37 BROWN with WHITE	50 PURPLE with RED	63 BLACK with PURPLE
11 WHITE with YELLOW	25 YELLOW	38 BROWN with GREEN	51 PURPLE with YELLOW	64 BLACK with BROWN
12 WHITE with BLUE	26 YELLOW with RED	39 BROWN with PURPLE	52 PURPLE with BLUE	65 DARK GREEN
13 WHITE with GREEN	27 YELLOW with BLUE	40 BROWN with BLACK	53 PURPLE with WHITE	66 LIGHT GREEN
14 WHITE with PURPLE				

W05494081 - MK 9 1958-1960

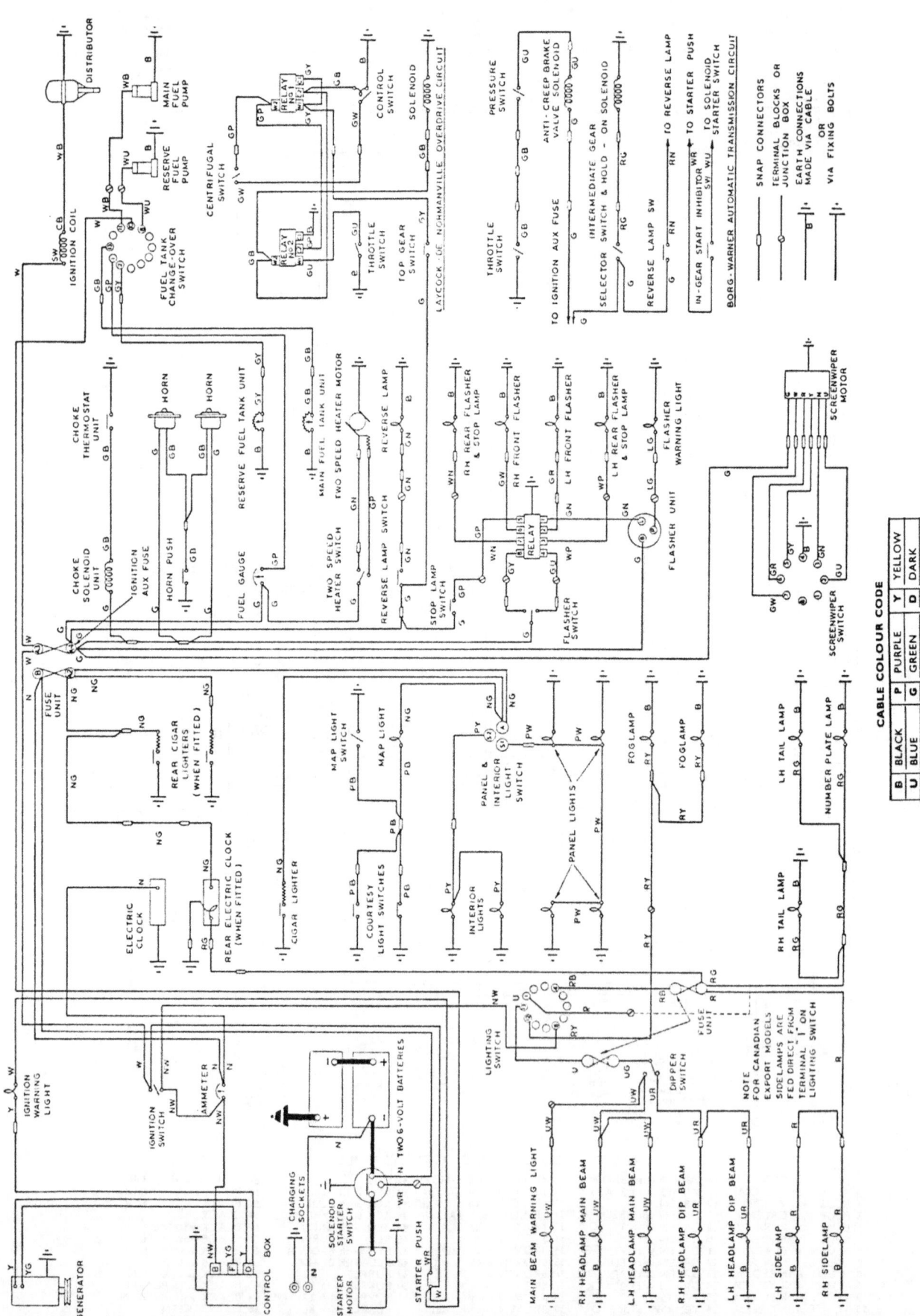

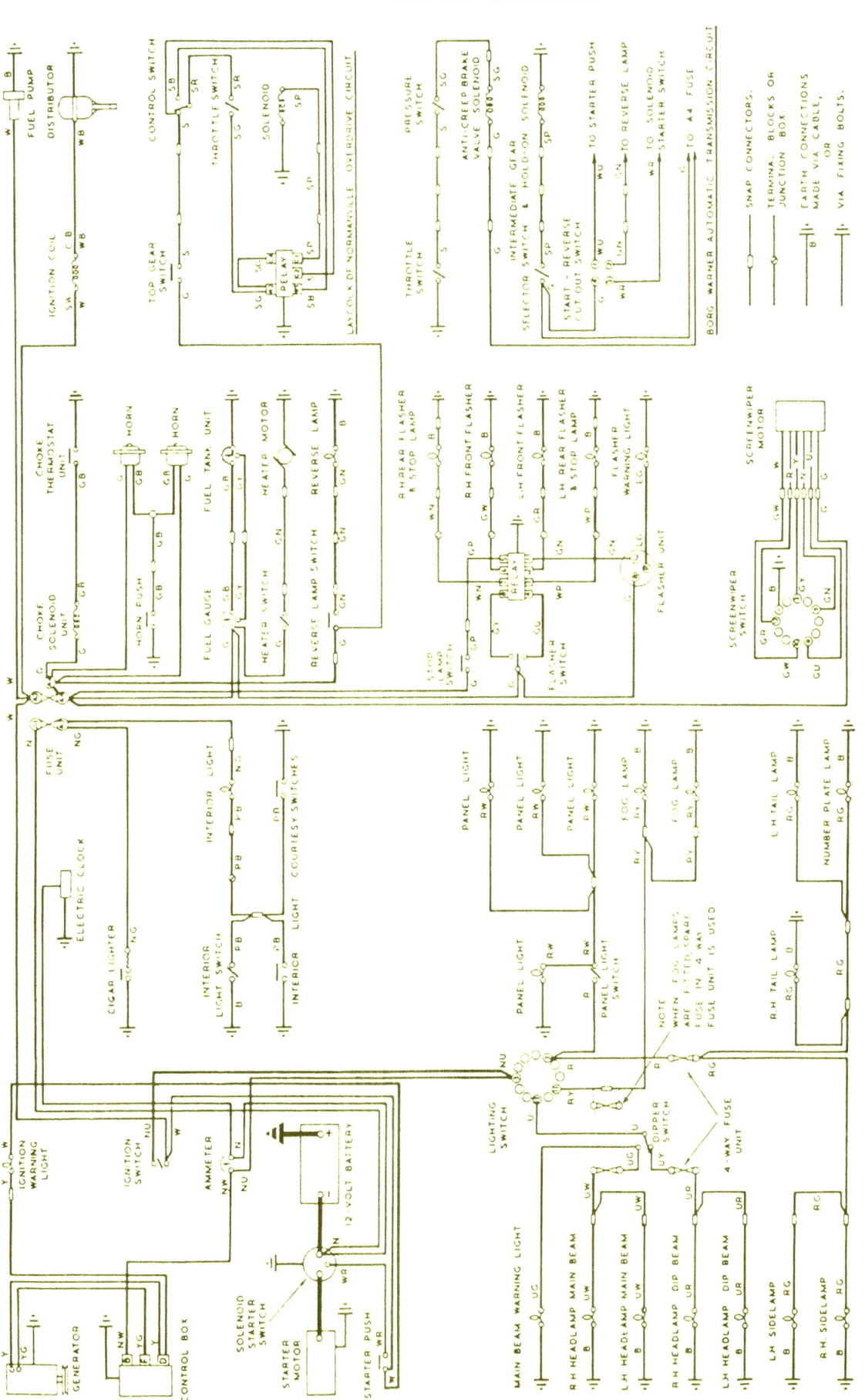

W54945600 - XK150 1959

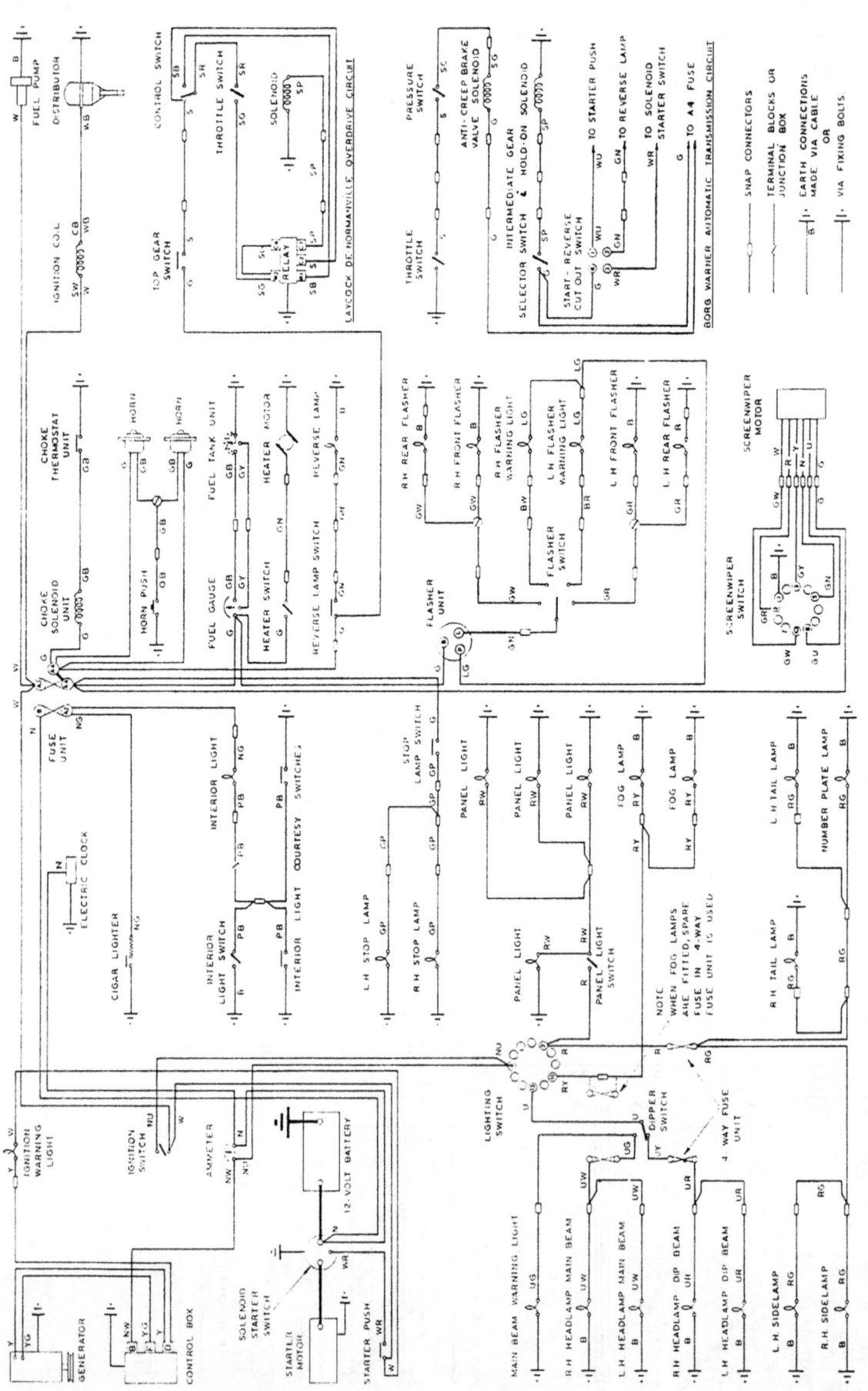

VELOCEPRESS MANUALS - MOTORCYCLE

1930'S BRITISH MOTORCYCLE CARBS & ELEC COMPONENTS (BOOK OF)
1930'S BRITISH MOTORCYCLE ENGINES (OVERHAUL & MAINTENANCE)
1930'S BRITISH MOTORCYCLE GEARBOXES & CLUTCHES (BOOK OF)
AJS 1932-1948 SINGLES & TWINS 250cc THRU 1000cc (BOOK OF)
AJS 1945-1960 SINGLES 350cc & 500cc MODELS 16 & 18 (BOOK OF)
AJS 1955-1965 SINGLES 350cc & 500cc (BOOK OF)
ARIEL 1932-1939 PREWAR MODELS (BOOK OF)
ARIEL 1933-1951 (WORKSHOP MANUAL)
ARIEL 1939-1960 4 STROKE SINGLES (BOOK OF)
ARIEL 1958-1964 LEADER & ARROW (BOOK OF)
BMW R26 R27 (1956-1967) FACTORY WORKSHOP MANUAL
BMW R50 R50S R60 R69S (1955-1969) FACTORY WORKSHOP MANUAL
BSA BANTAM ALL MODELS FROM 1948 ONWARDS (BOOK OF)
BSA SINGLES & V-TWINS UP TO 1927 (BOOK OF)
BSA SINGLES & V-TWINS UP TO 1935 (BOOK OF)
BSA SINGLES & V-TWINS 1936-1939 (BOOK OF)
BSA SINGLES & V-TWINS 1936-1952 (BOOK OF)
BSA OHV & SV SINGLES 250-600cc 1945-1954 (BOOK OF)
BSA OHV & SV SINGLES 250cc 1954-1970 (BOOK OF)
BSA OHV SINGLES 350 & 500cc 1955-1967 (BOOK OF)
BSA TWINS 1948-1962 (BOOK OF)
BSA TWINS 1962-1969 (SECOND BOOK OF)
DOUGLAS 1929-1939 PREWAR ALL MODELS (BOOK OF)
DOUGLAS 1948-1957 POSTWAR ALL MODELS FACTORY SHOP MANUAL
DUCATI 160cc, 250cc & 350cc OHC MODELS FACTORY SHOP MANUAL
HONDA 50 ALL MODELS UP TO 1970 INC MONKEY & TRAIL (BOOK OF)
HONDA 90 ALL MODELS UP TO 1966 (BOOK OF)
HONDA 125-150cc TWINS C/CS/CB/CA FACTORY WORKSHOP MANUAL
HONDA 250-305 TWINS C/CS/CB FACTORY WORKSHOP MANUAL
HONDA C100 SUPER CUB FACTORY WORKSHOP MANUAL
HONDA C110 SPORT CUB 1962-1969 FACTORY WORKSHOP MANUAL
HONDA TWINS & SINGLES 50cc THRU 305cc 1960-1966 (BOOK OF)
HONDA TWINS ALL MODELS 125cc THRU 450cc UP TO 1968 (BOOK OF)
J.A.P. ENGINES 1927-1952 & MOTORCYCLES 1934-1952 (BOOK OF)
LAMBRETTA 1947-1957 ALL 125 & 150cc MODELS (BOOK OF)
LAMBRETTA 1957-1970 LI & TV MODELS (SECOND BOOK OF)
MATCHLESS 1931-1939 ALL MODELS 250cc THRU 990cc (BOOK OF)
MATCHLESS 1945-1956 350 & 500cc SINGLES (BOOK OF)
MATCHLESS 1955-1966 350 & 500cc SINGLES (BOOK OF)
NEW IMPERIAL ALL SV & OHV FROM 1935 ONWARDS (BOOK OF)
NORTON 1932-1939 PREWAR MODELS (BOOK OF)
NORTON 1932-1947 (BOOK OF)
NORTON 1938-1956 (BOOK OF)
NORTON 1955-1963 MODELS 19, 50 & ES2 (BOOK OF)
NORTON 1955-1965 DOMINATOR TWINS (BOOK OF)
NORTON 1957-1970 TWINS FACTORY WORKSHOP MANUAL
NSU PRIMA 1956-1964 ALL MODELS (BOOK OF)
NSU QUICKLY 1953-1963 ALL MODELS (BOOK OF)
PANTHER 1932-1958 LIGHTWEIGHT MODELS 250 & 350cc (BOOK OF)
PANTHER 1938-1966 HEAVYWEIGHT MODELS 600 & 650cc (BOOK OF)
RALEIGH MOPEDS 1960-1969 (BOOK OF)
RALEIGH MOTORCYCLES 1919-1933 (BOOK OF)
ROYAL ENFIELD 1934-1946 SINGLES & V TWINS (BOOK OF)
ROYAL ENFIELD 1937-1953 SINGLES & V TWINS (BOOK OF)
ROYAL ENFIELD 1946-1962 SINGLES (BOOK OF)
ROYAL ENFIELD 1958-1966 250cc & 350cc SINGLES (SECOND BOOK OF)
ROYAL ENFIELD 736cc INTERCEPTOR FACTORY WORKSHOP MANUAL
RUDGE 1933-1939 (BOOK OF)
SUNBEAM 1928-1939 (BOOK OF)
SUNBEAM 1946-1957 S7 & S8 (BOOK OF)
SUZUKI 50cc & 80cc UP TO 1966 (BOOK OF)
SUZUKI T10 1963-1967 FACTORY WORKSHOP MANUAL
SUZUKI T20 & T200 1965-1969 FACTORY WORKSHOP MANUAL
TRIUMPH 1935-1939 PREWAR MODELS (BOOK OF)
TRIUMPH 1935-1949 (BOOK OF)
TRIUMPH 1937-1951 (WORKSHOP MANUAL)
TRIUMPH 1945-1955 FACTORY WORKSHOP MANUAL
TRIUMPH 1945-1958 TWINS (BOOK OF)
TRIUMPH 1956-1969 TWINS (BOOK OF)
VELOCETTE 1925-1970 ALL SINGLES & TWINS (BOOK OF)
VESPA 1951-1961 (BOOK OF)
VESPA 1955-1963 125 & 150cc & GS MODELS (SECOND BOOK OF)
VESPA 1955-1968 GS & SS (BOOK OF)
VESPA 1963-1972 90, 125 & 150cc (THIRD BOOK OF)
VILLIERS ENGINE UP TO 1959 INC. 3 WHEELERS (BOOK OF)
VILLIERS ENGINE UP TO 1969 (BOOK OF)
VINCENT 1935-1955 (WORKSHOP MANUAL)

www.VelocePress.com

VELOCEPRESS TECHNICAL BOOKS – MOTORCYCLE

CATALOG OF BRITISH MOTORCYCLES (1951 MODELS)
INDIAN PONYBIKE, BOY RACER & PAPOOSE ILL PARTS LIST & SALES LIT
MOTORCYCLE ENGINEERING (P.E. Irving)
SPEED AND HOW TO OBTAIN IT (Motor Cycle Magazine UK)
TUNING FOR SPEED (P.E. Irving)

VELOCEPRESS MANUALS - THREE WHEELER'S

BSA THREE WHEELER (BOOK OF)
VINTAGE MORGAN THREE WHEELER (BOOK OF)

VELOCEPRESS MANUALS - AUTOMOBILE

AUSTIN-HEALEY 6-CYLINDER WORKSHOP MANUAL
AUSTIN-HEALEY SPRITE & MG MIDGET WORKSHOP MANUAL 1958-1971
BMW 600 LIMOUSINE FACTORY WORKSHOP MANUAL
BMW 600 LIMOUSINE OWNERS HAND BOOK & SERVICE MANUAL
BMW 2000 & 2002 1966-1976 WORKSHOP MANUAL
BMW ISETTA FACTORY WORKSHOP MANUAL
CORVAIR 1960-1969 WORKSHOP MANUAL
CORVETTE V8 1955-1962 WORKSHOP MANUAL
JAGUAR E-TYPE 3.8 & 4.2 SERIES 1 & 2 WORKSHOP MANUAL
JAGUAR MK 7, 8, 9 & XK120, 140, 150 WORKSHOP MANUAL 1948-1961
METROPOLITAN FACTORY WORKSHOP MANUAL
MGA & MGB OWNERS HANDBOOK & WORKSHOP MANUAL
MG MIDGET TC, TD, TF & TF1500 WORKSHOP MANUAL
PORSCHE 356 1948-1965 WORKSHOP MANUAL
PORSCHE 912 WORKSHOP MANUAL
TRIUMPH TR2, TR3, TR4 1953-1965 WORKSHOP MANUAL
VOLKSWAGEN TRANSPORTER, TRUCKS & WAGONS 1950-1979 WSM
VOLVO 1944-1968 ALL MODELS WORKSHOP MANUAL

VELOCEPRESS TECHNICAL BOOKS - AUTOMOBILE

FERRARI 250/GT SERVICE AND MAINTENANCE
FERRARI GUIDE TO PERFORMANCE
FERRARI OWNER'S HANDBOOK
FERRARI TUNING TIPS & MAINTENANCE TECHNIQUES
HOW TO BUILD A FIBERGLASS CAR
HOW TO BUILD A RACING CAR
HOW TO RESTORE THE MODEL 'A' FORD
MASERATI OWNER'S HANDBOOK
OBERT'S FIAT GUIDE
PERFORMANCE TUNING THE SUNBEAM TIGER
SOUPING THE VOLKSWAGEN
SOLEX CARBURETORS (EMPHASIS ON UK & EU AUTOMOBILES)
SU CARBURETORS (EMPHASIS ON UK AUTOMOBILES)
WEBER CARBURETORS (EMPHASIS ON ALFA & FIAT)

VELOCEPRESS BOOKS & GUIDES - AUTOMOBILE

ABARTH BUYERS GUIDE
COMPLETE CATALOG OF JAPANESE MOTOR VEHICLES
FERRARI 308 SERIES BUYER'S AND OWNER'S GUIDE
FERRARI BERLINETTA LUSSO
FERRARI BROCHURES AND SALES LITERATURE 1946-1967
FERRARI BROCHURES AND SALES LITERATURE 1968-1989
FERRARI OPP, MAINTENANCE & SERVICE H/BOOKS 1948-1963
FERRARI SERIAL NUMBERS PART I - ODD NUMBERS TO 21399
FERRARI SERIAL NUMBERS PART II - EVEN NUMBERS TO 1050
FERRARI SPYDER CALIFORNIA
HENRY'S FABULOUS MODEL "A" FORD
MASERATI BROCHURES AND SALES LITERATURE

VELOCEPRESS BOOKS – RACING

CARRERA PANAMERICANA - MEXICAN ROAD RACE (BOOK OF)
DIALED IN - THE JAN OPPERMAN STORY
IF HEMINGWAY HAD WRITTEN A RACING NOVEL
LE MANS 24 (THE BOOK THAT THE FILM WAS BASED ON)
VEDA ORR'S NEW REVISED HOT ROD PICTORIAL

AUTOBOOKS WORKSHOP MANUALS & BROOKLANDS ROAD TEST PORTFOLIOS

FOR A COMPLETE LISTING OF THE AUTOBOOKS & BROOKLANDS TITLES THAT WE CURRENTLY HAVE AVAILABLE, PLEASE VISIT OUR WEBSITE.

Please check our website:

www.VelocePress.com

for a complete
up-to-date list of
available titles

www.ingramcontent.com/pod-product-compliance
Lightning Source LLC
Chambersburg PA
CBHW060245240426
43673CB00047B/1880